EYEWITNESS TO DISCOVERY

*First-Person Accounts of More Than Fifty of the
World's Greatest Archaeological Discoveries*

EYEWITNESS TO DISCOVERY

First-Person Accounts of More Than
Fifty of the World's Greatest
Archaeological Discoveries

Edited by

BRIAN M. FAGAN

OXFORD UNIVERSITY PRESS
New York   Oxford

Oxford University Press

Oxford   New York

Athens   Auckland   Bangkok   Bogotá   Buenos Aires   Calcutta
Cape Town   Chennai   Dar es Salaam   Delhi   Florence   Hong Kong   Istanbul
Karachi   Kuala Lumpur   Madrid   Melbourne   Mexico City   Mumbai
Nairobi   Paris   São Paulo   Singapore   Taipei   Tokyo   Toronto   Warsaw

and associated companies in

Berlin   Ibadan

Library of Congress Cataloging-in-Publication Data
Eyewitness to discovery : first-person accounts of more than
fifty of the world's greatest archaeological discoveries /
edited by Brian M. Fagan
p. cm. Includes bibliographical references and index.
ISBN 0-19-508141-2
ISBN 0-19-512651-3 (Pbk.)
1. Archaeology—History.
2. Excavations (Archaelology)—History.
3. Antiquities.
I. Fagan, Brian M.
CC100.E94 1996 930—dc20 96-23005

1 3 5 7 9 10 8 6 4 2

Printed in the United States of America
on acid-free paper

ACKNOWLEDGMENTS

My greatest debt is to Liza Ewell and Linda Morse of Oxford University Press; they commissioned this book and encouraged me during the long, and often frustrating, process of development and writing. I appreciate their guidance and never-waning enthusiasm. Julie Ruiz-Sierra was an invaluable colleague at an early stage in the research. Her long hours in various libraries yielded rich intellectual treasures. Chris Scarre gave crucial advice at an early stage in the project. Will McCormack and Molly Shapiro provided editorial assistance at every step along the way. Alan Gottlieb shouldered the laborious work of photographic research. I am grateful to the anonymous reviewers who made invaluable suggestions when the book was in outline. Their insights enabled me to cull much irrelevant and inappropriate material. Lastly, my thanks to the contributors to this volume, many long-dead, who not only made remarkable discoveries, but wrote about them in compelling prose. They have made archaeology immeasurably richer by their writings.

Santa Barbara, California   B.F
January 1996

CONTENTS

PART III: ARCHAEOLOGY BECOMES A SCIENCE

EYEWITNESS TO DISCOVERY

*First-Person Accounts of More Than Fifty of the
World's Greatest Archaeological Discoveries*

Introduction

Gold-laden pharaohs, grinning skeletons, long-forgotten civilizations mantled in swirling mists: the world of archaeology evokes adventure and romance. A hundred years ago, an archaeologist could still journey to remote lands and find a lost civilization in a month. Today, the world's ancient civilizations are familiar archaeological stamping grounds. Archaeology, once a lighthearted treasure hunt and little more than an adventure, is now a sophisticated, multidisciplinary science with strong roots in the social sciences and humanities. A century and a quarter after Heinrich Schliemann announced the discovery of Homeric Troy, archaeology still retains its aura of romance, its well-deserved reputation for startling discoveries wrested from clinging soil. Its reputation stems in part from the adventurous Victorians, in part, also, from the sheer fascination of digging up something hidden for thousands of years, once crafted and used by someone who lived long ago.

Archaeologists have come a long way from the pith-helmeted professors of cartoon fame. The great archaeologists of the mid-nineteenth century wrecked cities with their reckless digging. Austen Henry Layard dug tunnels through Assyrian Nineveh. Heinrich Schliemann employed engineers who had worked on the Suez Canal to advise him on earthmoving. Until the 1920s, archaeologists served but informal apprenticeships, working alongside experienced diggers and learning firsthand. The training was, at best, casual. In the early years of the twentieth century, British archaeologist Leonard Woolley of Ur fame cut his teeth on Hadrian's Wall in northern England, where he dug almost unsupervised. He then excavated Nubian cemeteries in the Sudan with American scholar Randall MacIver, again under minimal supervision, after which he was considered qualified to run a major British excavation into the Hittite city at Carchemish on the Euphrates. Woolley took his work seriously, but always treated the lighter side of archaeology as though it were part of a "Great Game." Before World War I, archaeology was still a rather casual pastime, with little discipline and few standards. Woolley even found time to engage in some informal espionage while digging at Carchemish. He spied on the German engineers building the nearby railroad to Baghdad.

Woolley and his contemporaries of the 1920s and 1930s made truly remarkable discoveries, often working alone or with only a few colleagues, while presiding over large teams of unskilled workers. The classic excavations in the Near East, undertaken between the two world wars, were often large-scale operations, moving more soil in a season than a modern dig would dissect in half a dozen. We use the word "dissect" deliberately, for modern archaeology is a world apart from Leonard Woolley's great excavations at Ur or Howard Carter's painstaking improvisation in Tutankhamun's tomb. Scientific excavation began in the late nineteenth century with the Germans at Olympia and with the redoubtable General Pitt-Rivers in England. But the disciplined methods pioneered by these scholars did not come into wide use until Mortimer Wheeler in England, and others elsewhere, applied near-military principles of organization to archaeological excavations of every kind. Excavations like Wheeler's classic digs at Roman Verulameum and on Maiden Castle in the 1930s trained dozens of younger archaeologists in proper digging methods and laid the foundations for the extraordinary standards maintained by many fieldworkers today. Late-twentieth-century archaeologists undergo formal training in survey techniques and excavation methods, work under close supervision on digs of many kinds, and acquire a detailed knowledge of computers, artifact analysis, food remains, and archaeological theory long before directing an excavation on their own. They learn from the beginning that the archaeological record is a finite resource, that even expert excavation destroys the archives of the past. Their discoveries often come not from spectacular excavations, but from the screens of computers or from finds like pollen grains, which are invisible to the naked eye.

This book is about archaeological discoveries and the men and women who made them. The theme of discovery is a constant thread through the complex history of archaeology itself. Whenever and wherever archaeologists have searched for the past, they have made discoveries, large and small, seemingly trivial or of the utmost importance. But many people believe that the nineteenth century was the classic era of archaeological discovery, that we shall never see discoveries like those of Layard at Nineveh and Schliemann at Troy again. They are wrong, for the pace of spectacular archaeological discovery has continued unabated throughout the twentieth century. And what discoveries! Arthur Evans dug into the Palace of Minos at Knossos just three years into the new century and found an entire civilization. After a seven-year search, Howard Carter and Lord Carnarvon unearthed Tutankhamun's tomb, arguably the greatest archaeological discovery of all time. Woolley at Ur; the Anglo-Saxon Sutton Hoo ship burial in eastern England; the grave of the Maya Lord Pacal at Palenque, Mexico; and, only a few years ago, the stupendous graves of the Lords of Sipán in Peru: the honor roll of spectacular finds continues to unfold as we write. The recent discovery of the tomb of the sons of Egyptian pharaoh Ramesses II in the Valley of the Kings may yield rich and undisturbed royal burial chambers in coming years. The twenty-first century promises extraordinary breakthroughs. The royal burial mound of Emperor Qin Shihuangdi, the first ruler of a unified China, promises astonishing riches. Siberia and much of southern Asia are still virtually unexplored. New prospecting technologies offer tantalizing possibilities. Satellites high in space map entire ancient road systems and locate lost cities on Central Asia's ancient Silk Road. A new generation of subsurface radar devices promises to allow scientists to examine a site without excavating a spadeful of dirt. We are moving from an era of constant excavation into one where "nonintrusive investigation" is the rule of the day. A Victorian digger would have plowed ahead regardless, destroying a priceless site willy-nilly, removing important finds as quickly as possible. Today, we know that the archaeological record, under siege from looters and industrial development, is a precious, nonrenewable resource. So discovery will come as much from high technology as from the trowel, and from investigations conducted in haste before sites are destroyed or buried by the relentless pace of modern development.

How do archaeologists make their discoveries? Chance accounts for many spectacular finds. Well-organized Peruvian grave robbers happened upon the undisturbed sepulchers of the Lords of Sipán. Bedouin shepherds looking for lost goats found the Dead Sea Scrolls. But a surprisingly large number results from the qualities and skills of archaeologists, which raises an interesting question. What qualities lead excavators to their discoveries? Patience and the ability to persist can bring rich rewards, as they did for Howard Carter in the Valley of the Kings. An eye for landscape, a sense for the patterns of ancient settlement, the ability to project oneself back into a long vanished world: these skills have helped archaeologists locate ancient Mayan ceremonial centers in dense rain forest and find long-abandoned Roman field systems. Common sense, keen powers of observation, and, above all, curiosity are essential attributes for any student of the past. There are now thousands of archaeologists working in every corner of the world, but surprisingly few of them are endowed with those unique qualities of curiosity that turn a prosaic excavator into a brilliant one. Curiosity led Arthur Evans from the minute inscriptions on Minoan seals in the Athens flea market to the Palace of Knossos and a long-forgotten early civilization. Curiosity impelled George Bass and his colleagues to alert local sponge divers to search for distinctive piles of eared copper ingots off Turkish coasts. The result was the discovery of a Bronze Age ship wrecked off Uluburun on the southern coast more than 3,300 years ago. Almost all the discoveries in these pages resulted from an archaeologist's curiosity.

Sheer persistence, endless patience, and technical skill are essentials. But there is another magical archaeological quality, which by no means all excavators possess—a conviction, nay a passion, that their instincts are correct, that a find will be made. I vividly remember Louis Leakey lecturing at Cambridge in 1958 and proclaiming that it was only a matter of time before an early human fossil would come from Olduvai Gorge in East Africa, where he had worked sporadically since 1951. Mary Leakey unearthed *Zinjanthropus boisei*, a robustly built ape-human 1.75 million years old, at Olduvai the very next year. The Leakeys would never have made this extraordinary discovery if they had not followed up on their instinct that human fossils would be found in Olduvai Gorge's ancient lake beds one day. And Louis Leakey had that hunch in 1931! An archaeologist's instinct is powerful, compelling, perhaps best described as an overwhelming sense that one knows where to find what one is searching for.

When tomb robber Giovanni Belzoni was searching for the entrance to the Pyramid of Khafra at Giza in 1817, he succeeded where others had failed because he used what he called his "pyramidical brains." In fact, he followed logic and a strong sense of instinct, relying on his experience to find the right spot. He duly penetrated the empty burial chamber, the first person to do so since medieval times. His name can be seen painted in soot on the chamber wall to this day. Instinct is when the past reaches out to you from the soil, a magical moment when you shut your eyes and an ancient city is repopulated—comes alive with people, voices, even smells. Just for a moment, you are transported back over the centuries and become a participant in the world you excavate. Your mind explores walls, temples, houses; senses where to dig; looks at the topography like its owners of centuries past. When combined with curiosity, logical reasoning, and common sense, instinct is the most powerful weapon in the archaeologist's armory.

Archaeological discovery unveils the past, brings us face to face with the triumphs and tragedies of those who have gone before. All of us, whether archaeologist or traveler in search of the past, make discoveries about ancient times for ourselves. There have been archaeological tourists for more than two thousand years. Roman tourists scratched graffiti on ancient Egyptian temples and crowded their way through the narrow passageways of the Pyramids of Giza. Wealthy European aristocrats enjoyed the Grand Tour through Mediterranean lands for centuries, collecting antiquities for their cabinets of curiosities. Victorian travelers invaded Egypt by the hundreds, earnest Baedekers in hand, wandering among the soaring columns of Karnak's Hypostyle Hall, imagining Egypt as it once was, and discovering the past for themselves without the noise and bustle of diesel buses and package tours. You could sit alone in the high seats of the Greek amphitheater at Epidauros on a spring morning and allow the evocative stanzas from Euripides to flow over you from the stage far below. In 1821, British traveler Sir Robert Ker Porter rode his horse up the great double flight of stairs at Persepolis, Iran, a place haunted by legend, by the ghosts of the past. A later traveler, Robert Byron, complained bitterly:

> In the old days you rode up the steps on to the platform. You made a camp there, where the columns and winged beasts kept their solitude beneath the stars, and not a sound or movement disturbed the empty moonlit plain. You were alone with the ancient world. . . . Today you step out of a motor, while a couple of lorries thunder by in a cloud of dust. You enter by leave of a porter, and are greeted by . . . a code of academic malice compiled from Chicago. These useful additions clarify the intelligence. You may persuade yourself, in spite of them, into a mood of romance. But the mood they invite is that of a critic at an exhibition. That is the penalty of greater knowledge.

We have sacrificed beauty for knowledge, for once it was like being drunk to see ruinous beauty under a full moon. This is what Jean François Champollion and his young friends experienced, as they deciphered the inscriptions at the Temple of Dendera for the first time by the light of a full moon. And it was similar emotions that caused Victorian traveler Amelia Edwards to compare the great columns at Karnak to the mighty trunks of a redwood forest. One of the fascinations of archaeological discovery is its many facets, its many opportunities. Here we celebrate archaeological discoveries made on surveys and in excavations, give a flavor of excavation and discovery as archaeologists have experienced it over more than a century. Only occasionally do we pause to evoke the past, to see it through the eyes of nonarchaeologists, who sometimes see things that we artifact-obsessed archaeologists miss.

This book was long in gestation, the selections the subject of prolonged debate and careful review. In the end, I decided to focus the book on major archaeological discoveries, rather than offer a more eclectic approach, and to group the writings into three sections. A chronological approach has the advantage that we can follow the development of archaeology from its stirring beginnings as a glorified treasure hunt into a sophisticated late-twentieth-century science. Part I covers the establishment of human antiquity in 1859, and the discovery of human origins and Stone Age societies. In Part II, we range widely over the world of archaeological discovery, from the heroic adventures of nineteenth-century excavators to the dramatic finds of recent years. The selections are grouped geographically rather than chronologically, on the assumption that most readers will browse their favorite areas rather than read the book from cover to cover. Part III uses a variety of writings to explore the transformation of archaeology from an amateur pastime into a sophisticated science, with, again, the emphasis on discovery and reconstruction, not necessarily hard data.

Discoveries are personal things, experiences unique to those who make them. As much as possible, I have tried to include writings in the first person, written by the actual discoverer. This was not always possible, in which case, I have turned to well-written accounts by authors acquainted with the site and discovery at firsthand. I am satisfied that the result is a well-balanced selection of writings, which convey the essence, the excitement of archaeological discovery. My only regret is that space restrictions forced me to omit so many important discoveries and much fine writing.

Eyewitness to Discovery is a celebration of what writer Rose Macaulay once called "the soaring of the imagination into the high empyrean where huge episodes are tangled with myths and dreams. It is the stunning impact of world history on its amazed heirs." These pages show just how powerful this impact can be.

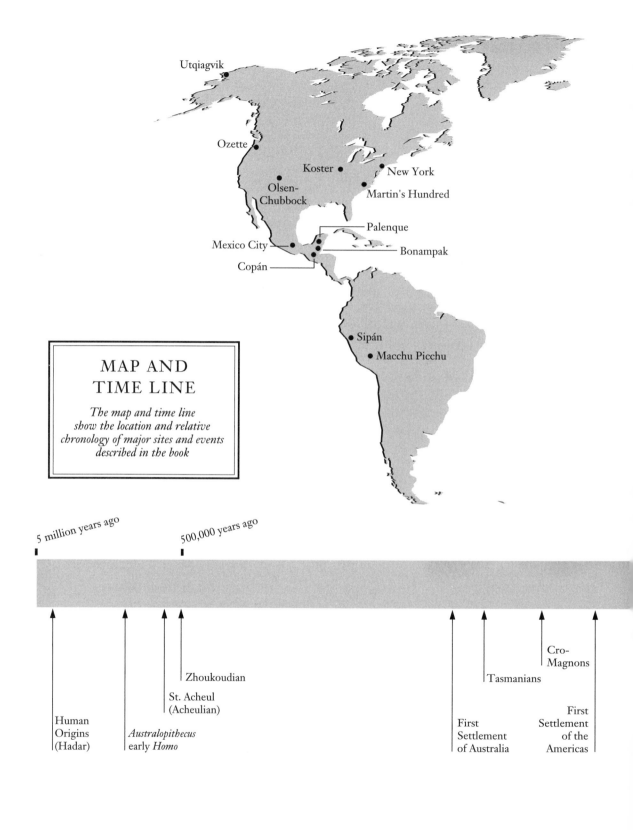

Utqiagvik

Ozette

Koster

New York

Olsen-
Chubbock

Martin's Hundred

Palenque

Mexico City

Bonampak

Copán

Sipán

Macchu Picchu

MAP AND
TIME LINE

*The map and time line
show the location and relative
chronology of major sites and events
described in the book*

5 million years ago

500,000 years ago

Zhoukoudian

St. Acheul
(Acheulian)

Cro-
Magnons

Tasmanians

Human
Origins
(Hadar)

Australopithecus
early *Homo*

First
Settlement
of Australia

First
Settlement
of the
Americas

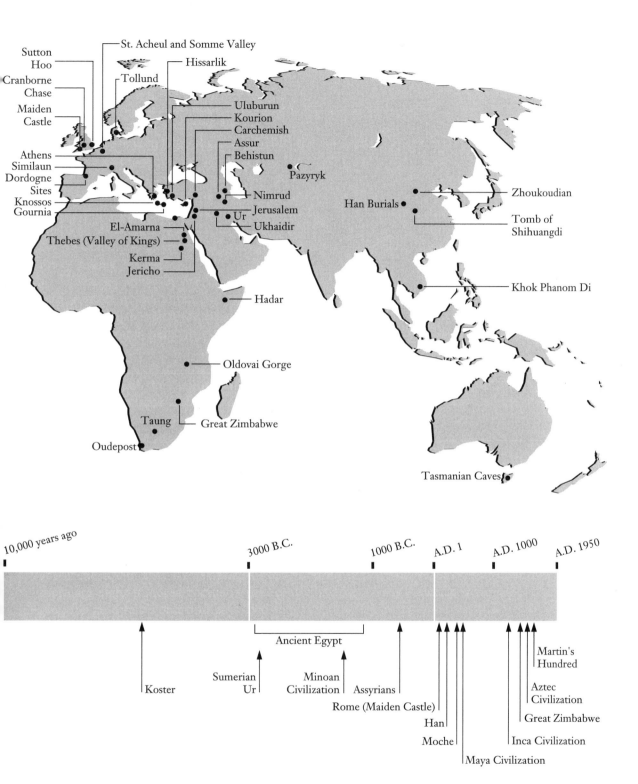

Sutton Hoo
St. Acheul and Somme Valley
Cranborne Chase
Hissarlik
Maiden Castle
Tollund
Uluburun
Kourion
Carchemish
Athens
Assur
Similaun
Behistun
Dordogne
Pazyryk
Sites
Zhoukoudian
Knossos
Nimrud
Han Burials
Gournia
Jerusalem
Tomb of Shihuangdi
El-Amarna
Ur
Thebes (Valley of Kings)
Ukhaidir
Kerma
Jericho
Khok Phanom Di
Hadar
Oldovai Gorge
Taung
Great Zimbabwe
Oudepost
Tasmanian Caves

10,000 years ago
3000 B.C.
1000 B.C.
A.D. 1
A.D. 1000
A.D. 1950

Ancient Egypt

Koster

Sumerian Ur

Minoan Civilization

Assyrians

Rome (Maiden Castle)

Han

Moche

Maya Civilization

Inca Civilization

Aztec Civilization

Great Zimbabwe

Martin's Hundred

PART I
THE DISCOVERY OF
HUMAN ORIGINS

A man who has once looked with the archaeological eye will never see quite normally. He will be wounded by what other men call trifles. It is possible to refine the sense of time until an old show in the bunch grass or a pile of nineteenth century beer bottles in an abandoned mining town tolls in one's head like a hall clock. This is the price one pays for learning to read time from surfaces other than an illuminated dial. It is the melancholy secret of the artifact, the humanly touched thing.

—Loren Eiseley, *The Night Country*, 1971

e live in a world of shadows, the shadows of those who came before us. Their images flicker on the canvas of history like the tracery of flames from a campfire in a large cavern. Our ancestors have bequeathed us a vast legacy of documents, fading memories, and material things—deserted temples, ruined cities, mere scatters of broken animal bones and abandoned tools. The human past beguiles, fascinates, and obsesses us. Discovering its often subtle reflections ranks among the most satisfying of passions. And no archaeological discoveries have aroused so much controversy and passion as those bearing on human origins and the antiquity of humankind.

EARLY PHILOSOPHICAL SPECULATIONS: EIGHTH CENTURY B.C. ONWARD

Since the beginnings of civilization, the learned and wise have been curious about the world of the past. In the eighth century B.C., the Greek writer Hesiod wrote about a glorious, heroic past of kings and warriors. The earliest age of history was one of gold, when people were at leisure. The last was an age of iron, when everyone worked hard and suffered great sorrow. During the sixth century B.C., King Nabonidus of Babylon searched for the temple of the goddess Ishtar at Agade near Babylon. His workers labored vainly for three years until a violent rainstorm exposed a gully through the mound and the foundations of an ancient shrine. The discovery "made the king's heart glad and caused his countenance to brighten," a contemporary tablet tells us. Nabonidus was merely exercising his royal curiosity, but was among the first to experience the thrill of archaeological discovery.

Hesiod and other Greek and Roman philosophers speculated about a remote past. In sharp contrast, medieval and Renaissance scholars in the Christian West assumed that the story of human origins was set down in the first chapter of Genesis. The Creation was a matter of faith and unquestioning belief. "Time we may comprehend," wrote Elizabethan philosopher Sir Thomas Browne. " 'Tis but five days older than ourselves." Scholarly clergy pored over the Scriptures, believing that they were the literal historical truth. In 1650, Archbishop James Ussher of Armagh used the genealogies in the Old Testament to date the creation to the year 4004 B.C. He encapsulated all of human history within a dogmatic six thousand years, "teeming with delighted existence," as an early nineteenth-century theologian put it. The Ussherian chronology dominated scholarly perspectives on the past for two centuries.

HERCULANEUM AND POMPEII: 1738 AND AFTER

While the devout grappled with biblical genealogies, people of wealth and leisure were traveling to Mediterranean lands on the Grand Tour, studying antiquities and collecting examples of classical art from dealers in Italy. By the eighteenth century, the Grand Tour became an essential part of the nobility's education. On returning from their travels, the gentlemen displayed their antiquarian treasures in cabinets of curiosities in their stately houses. Then, in 1738, came the first excavations into the dense volcanic ash at the foot of Mount Vesuvius. Engineer Cavaliere Rocco Gioacchino de Alcubierre used tools and gunpowder to tunnel through more than fifteen meters of lava. His men unearthed bronze statuary and, finally, the stairs of an amphitheater. An inscription announced that this was the "Theatrum Herculanense."

First Herculaneum, then Pompeii, came to light, entire Roman cities buried by a sudden and catastrophic eruption of Vesuvius in A.D. 79. The excavators' shovels unearthed public buildings and lavishly decorated private houses as well as the cavities in the soil left by the bodies of men, women, and children fleeing the ash, their bodies lying where they collapsed. With these rough-and-ready excavations, the eighteenth-century world experienced the first thrill of archaeological discovery. But the real hero of Herculaneum was J. J. Wincklemann, a cobbler's son from Germany who became librarian to Cardinal Albani and supervisor of all antiquities around Rome. Wincklemann was never allowed to dig himself and could study the finds only through a back door. But his *History of the Art of Antiquity*, written in the 1760s, helped put the study of the buried Roman cities and of classical art on a new, more systematic footing.

Alcubierre was not the first excavator, but it was his discoveries that fueled the flames of popular interest in the past. Those who first dug into Herculaneum and Pompeii were motivated both by curiosity and by a burning lust to acquire and own the past, a lust that is with us to this day. This was the passion that led British nobleman and diplomat Lord Elgin to remove the marbles from the Parthenon and other young men like the artist Charles Cockerell to strip ancient Greece of its masterpieces without apparent remorse.

"A Thick Fog": 1750–1850

Inevitably, to become an antiquary, to collect or study the past, was soon considered fashionable, the attribute of a well-rounded gentleman. But only the wealthiest noblemen could take the Grand Tour. Many humbler landowners indulged their antiquarian interests at home. They collected antiquities of every kind, most of them "so exceedingly old that no Bookes doe reach them." Some of the more ambitious early-nineteenth-century collectors dug into ancient earthworks and burial mounds, amassing enormous collections of prehistoric urns, weapons, and human remains. English wool merchant William Cunnington was so enthusiastic that he opened no fewer than 465 British burial mounds, sometimes several a day. In the evenings, the diggers would dine together, their finds littering the dining table. Archaeological discovery was still a matter of collecting and conviviality.

Only a few scientists puzzled over the meaning of the jumbled artifacts. "Everything that has come down to us from heathendom is wrapped in a thick fog," complained Danish antiquary Rasmus Nyerup, as he wrestled with the problem of classifying his small museum. Nyerup's collections became the nucleus of the National Museum of Denmark. His successor as curator was Christian Jurgensen Thomsen, a merchant's son with a passion for order. In 1809, he boldly arranged the museum's exhibits according to a three-age system, with a Stone Age, "when very little or nothing at all was known of metals"; a Bronze Age; and an Iron Age. Thomsen's three-age system was entirely theoretical, with no basis in actual archaeological discovery in the field, but some in the thinking of classical writers like Hesiod and Lucretius. One of his museum assistants, Jens Jacob Worsaae, had been excavating burial mounds since he was a young man. He set out to test the three-age system by stratigraphic observation. Worsaae dug burial sites where layers with no metal artifacts underlay levels with bronze tools, and still later ones where iron weapons were in use. By 1830, his observations had confirmed that the three-age system had chronological validity. Thomsen's classification is still used to subdivide prehistoric time in much of the world.

THE ANTIQUITY OF HUMANKIND: 1800–1859

Christian Jurgensen Thomsen provided a broad framework for the prehistoric past, at a time when a brave new world of archaeology was coming into being. By the time he set out his three-age system, stratigraphic geology was achieving wide acceptance, as engineers laid out the canal systems and railroads that carried the products of the Industrial Revolution. The new geology was based on the Law of Superposition, which stated that the earliest geological layers lay at the bottom of any accumulated sequence of strata, whence stratigraphy, the study of geological layers. In 1809, learned men and women were well aware that antiquities lay beneath the soil and that they represented a past considerably earlier than that of the Greeks and Romans. But who were these ancient peoples who apparently used stone and bronze before iron? How long ago had they lived, and what were their connections with known historic Europeans? Were they inhabitants of the present, six-thousand-year-old earth, or of some earlier globe destroyed by the last of the great floods? Prehistoric archaeology was born when archaeologists began grappling with these questions rather than merely digging up objects. Above all, they searched for human origins and for the first civilizations.

In 1800, the chronology of human origins was shackled by theological dogma, by James Ussher's calculations that the Creation had taken place on the evening of October 22, 4004 B.C. Even eminent scientists believed that God had created the world and its inhabitants in six days. They were reluctant to challenge established theological dogma, for heresy was no small matter in the early nineteenth century. So when an obscure Suffolk squire named John Frere reported to the Society of Antiquaries of London in 1797 that he had found humanly manufactured stone tools in the same levels as the bones of long-extinct animals like tropical hippopotamuses, his report was quietly ignored. But human artifacts and extinct animals soon came from sealed layers in Belgian and English caves, adding to a growing body of evidence for the contemporaneity of humans and long-vanished mammalian species. Furthermore, stratigraphic geologists could find no traces of the universal "deluges," which paleontologist Jacques Cuvier and others claimed to have wiped out entire populations of dinosaurs and other prehistoric animals. By the 1850s, many geologists had quietly come to believe that the world was considerably older than Genesis allowed. They argued that there was no theoretical reason why humans could not have lived on earth at the same time as long-extinct animals.

In 1859, biologist Charles Darwin published *On the Origin of Species*, his essay on the theory of evolution by natural selection. Here, at last, was a theoretical explanation for human biological change over long periods of time. A year before, Britain's Royal Society had commissioned excavations at Brixham Cave in southwestern England, where stone tools and extinct animal bones were said to lie sealed under a layer of stalagmite. The excavations had confirmed the report and turned experts' eyes to the Somme Valley across the English Channel, where Jacques Boucher de Perthes, an eccentric French customs officer turned antiquarian, had long argued that the stone axes and bones he found in deep river gravels had accumulated before "the Deluge," the biblical flood. For years, scientists and fellow antiquarians had laughed at Boucher de Perthes. Even Darwin thought that his findings were "rubbish." In 1859, geologist Joseph Prestwich and archaeologist John Evans (the father of Arthur Evans, the excavator of the Minoan civilization) visited Boucher de Perthes and themselves extracted axes and bones from the same ancient strata. These two pillars of the European scientific community returned to London and publicly announced their acceptance of a high antiquity for humankind. British archaeologist Glyn Daniel once called 1859 the *annus mirabilis*, the miracle year, of archaeology, for it was then that the study of human evolution and prehistory became legitimate endeavors.

But who were the human beings who had manufactured the simple handaxes from the Somme gravels? In 1856, quarry workers unearthed a primitive-looking human skull in a cave in Germany's Neander Valley. The Neanderthal skull had massive eyebrow ridges and a bun-shaped skull, quite unlike a modern human in appearance. At first, the experts dismissed the cranium as that of a pathological idiot. But in 1863, the great biologist Thomas Huxley, a ferocious champion of Darwin's theories, affirmed that the Neanderthal skull was indeed that of an archaic human, one of the possible ancestors of *Homo sapiens sapiens*. With the publication of Huxley's *Man's Place in Nature*, modern paleoanthropology, the study of human evolution and origins, was born. Huxley called human origins the "question of questions" for humankind. It still remains a major focus of archaeological discovery, as anthropologist vies with anthropologist in a never-ending quest for the earliest humans of all.

PITHECANTHROPUS AND CRO-MAGNONS: 1860–1900

The intense furor created by the establishment of human antiquity continued for years, as cartoonist and cleric alike lambasted the notion that humans were descended from apes. But while biologist Thomas Huxley battled the ecclesiastical establishment and the cartoonists sharpened their pencils, archaeologists began the long task of filling in the blank landscape of early prehistory. Boucher de Perthes's stone axes represented the earliest human occupation of Europe known in Victorian times. Between 1859 and 1900, amateur and professional archaeologists in Europe and North America searched diligently for early human fossils. The discovery of the Neanderthal skull in Germany in 1856 produced the first fossil evidence of archaic humans. Thomas Huxley himself established the anatomical relationships between the beetle-browed Neanderthal skull and humans' closest living relative, the chimpanzee. With the Neanderthal skull firmly established as a primitive human form, scientists searched diligently for the "missing link" between modern humans and apes. Dutch physician Eugene Dubois was so obsessed with the "missing link" that he wangled a posting as an army surgeon to Indonesia in 1890, convinced that he would find ancient human remains in the tropical rain forests of Southeast Asia. In one of the remarkable coincidences of science, he did indeed find the first specimens of *Pithecanthropus* (now *Homo erectus*) in Java, an archaic human with primitive-looking skull and modern, but robust limbs. But his fellow scientists laughed at his claims and discoveries. Dubois retired into seclusion until new discoveries in China during the 1920s vindicated his theories.

By the time Eugene Dubois went out to Java, European archaeologists had fleshed out the Stone Age, Bronze Age, Iron Age sequence validated stratigraphically by Jens Jacob Worsaae in the early nineteenth century. French lawyer Edouard Lartet and his English banker friend Henry Christy had excavated into the enormous rock shelters that lined the Vezère River near the small village of Les Eyzies in southwestern France. Lartet identified different levels of human occupation by their animal remains and artifacts, discovering a series of Ice Age foraging cultures that had flourished at a time when Europe was much colder than it is today. In 1868, Lartet's son Louis unearthed a group of modern-looking skeletons in the Cro-Magnon rock shelter just behind the new Les Eyzies railroad station. These, Lartet and Christy realized, were the people who had crafted the fine stone artifacts and delicate bone harpoons from their exca-vations, artisans capable of engraving animals and elaborate designs on their antler tools and weapons. The Cro-Magnons had lived during the Ice Age and were the successors of the Neanderthals.

Lartet, Christy, and their contemporaries considered the Cro-Magnons primitive cave people, adept at living in Ice Age landscapes, but less intelligent than modern humans. But the discovery of Ice Age art proved the stereotype wrong. When in 1879 the Marquis de Sautola's nine-year-old daughter came across the magnificent bison paintings in the caves at Altamira in northern Spain, scientists flatly refused to believe that the Cro-Magnons were capable of such brilliant artistry. Some accused Sautola of employing a modern artist to paint the bison. As so often happens, unexpected archaeological discoveries like the art of Altamira and the tomb of the Egyptian pharaoh Tutankhamun are so spectacular that they challenge established scholarly opinion. Ice Age art was finally validated only with the discovery of paintings inside the sealed La Mouthe cave near Les Eyzies in the early years of the twentieth century.

AUSTRALOPITHECUS AND HUMAN ORIGINS: 1924 ONWARD

The modern era of research into human origins began with Eugene Dubois's discovery of *Pithecanthropus* in Java in the 1890s, and with the highly controver-sial excavation of "Piltdown Man" in southern England in the early years of the twentieth century. For fifty years, the modern-looking Piltdown skull, with its apelike jaw, distorted all interpretations of early human evolution. By the time it was exposed as an ingenious forgery in 1953, a host of new discoveries had turned Piltdown into an evolutionary anomaly.

Dubois was vindicated by the exciting fossils unearthed from Zhoukoudian Cave, near Beijing, in the 1920s. The new finds bore a close resemblance to Dubois's archaic humans and were soon grouped under the general label *Homo erectus* (human who stands upright). As Chinese and European excavators la-bored at Zhoukoudian, anatomist Raymond Dart announced the finding of an apelike human at Taung in South Africa. Dart named his new fossil *Australopi-thecus africanus* (southern ape-human of Africa), a gracile, short-statured homi-nid, which he considered to be a direct ancestor of humans. A storm of contro-versy greeted Dart's announcement from scientists mesmerized with Piltdown. It was not until the 1950s that Dart was vindicated by the discrediting of Pilt-down and by a growing collection of australopithecine fossils. Then Louis and Mary Leakey unearthed *Australopithecus boisei* and *Homo habilis* at Olduvai Gorge in East Africa in 1959 and 1960, adding an entirely new chapter to early human evolution. The new potassium–argon dating method dated *Australopithecus boisei* to 1.75 million years ago, tripling the chronology of human origins overnight. Since 1959, the Leakey family, Don Johanson, Tim White, and other scientists have extended the ancestry of humans back to more than 4 million years ago, with their excavations in fossil-bearing beds on the shores of Lake Turkana in northern Kenya and in the Hadar region of Ethiopia.

Nearly 150 years after Jacques Boucher de Perthes's discoveries in the Somme Valley, we now know that Charles Darwin was right when he pointed to Africa as the cradle of humanity. But it is in the nature of archaeological discovery that the finds described in this volume, and many others, have posed more questions about early human evolution than they have answered. And therein lies the fascination of archaeology itself.

The Antiquity of Humankind

JACQUES BOUCHER DE PERTHES AND JOHN EVANS

Few controversies raged more furiously in the nineteenth century than the passionate debate between scientists and theologians over the age of humanity. Religious dogma taught that God had created the world in 4004 B.C., leaving only six thousand years for all of human existence. But antiquarians, biologists, and geologists were troubled by this short chronology, which flew in the face of an increasing body of field observations of geologic strata in which manufactured stone tools came from the same levels as the bones of long-extinct animals like the arctic mammoth and the saber-toothed tiger. Could it be, they wondered, that the antiquity of humankind extended back far into an uncharted past—tens of thousands, if not millions, of years ago? Confirmation of human antiquity was long in coming, but finally received validation in the year when Charles Darwin's On the Origin of Species *was published amid clamorous controversy. Two figures, an obscure customs officer and a respected scientist, played leading roles in this important scientific development.*

Jacques Boucher de Crèvecoeur de Perthes (1788–1868) worked as a minor customs official in the northern French town of Abbeville in the Somme Valley. His official duties were far from arduous, so Boucher de Perthes developed a passion for archaeology and the pleasures of the table. It is said, indeed, that many of his archaeological visitors went to Abbeville for the food rather than the science. Boucher de Perthes collected what he called "Celtic" artifacts, both crudely and finely made stone axes unearthed by the men dredging the channel of the Somme. These were finely polished axes, which we now know were made by Stone Age farmers. Boucher de Perthes himself was more interested in the cruder, flaked axes, which he dug out of the river gravels alongside the bones of tropical animals like elephants and hippopotamuses. He labeled these artifacts "Pre-Celtic," or "diluvial," considering them to date from the time of the Great Flood recorded in Genesis. When Boucher de Perthes exhibited his finds in Abbeville and Paris in 1838 and 1839, his fellow antiquarians and the scientific establishment merely laughed at him. The eccentric customs officer suffered not only from his controversial finds, but also from his long-windedness. He also published obvious natural stones, claiming that they were humanly manufactured, which did his arguments no good. His five-volume work De la création *(1838–1841) was considered nonsense. Fellow scien-*

tists would smile gently and tactfully move away when he would mention stone axes or "diluvium." Nevertheless, Boucher de Perthes continued to collect, finding the bones of extinct animals and stone tools in the same gravel layers at quarry after quarry along the Somme. He became convinced that the two were contemporary and that they dated to before the biblical flood, a conclusion that flew in the face of prevailing scientific thought. The title of his second book, Antiquités celtiques et antédiluviennes *(1847) revealed the author's new perspective. Again ridicule, but a handful of geologists went to Boucher de Perthes's gravel pits and were convinced of the validity of his finds.*

Antiquités celtiques appeared in a changing scientific atmosphere. Boucher de Perthes himself strained scientific credulity, but rumors of his stratified findings crossed the English Channel. The British scientific establishment was a small one in 1859, but it exercised enormous influence over scientific thinking and public opinion throughout much of Europe and in the United States. The biologists Charles Darwin and Thomas Huxley; Charles Lyell and Joseph Prestwich, both geologists with a long experience of observing stratigraphic layers; and John Evans, a well-known collector and archaeologist, were at the core of this small group of articulate and well-connected scientists. They had been instrumental in setting up a Royal Society committee to supervise excavations at Brixham Cave in southwestern England in 1858. The excavators found the bones of cave bears, mammoth, and reindeer, also stone tools, in a cave earth layer sealed by twenty centimeters of stalagmite. By itself, Brixham Cave seemed to offer convincing evidence of the contemporaneity of humans and extinct animals. As the committee discussed the cave, a number of British geologists visited Boucher de Perthes's Somme quarries, where the geologic strata were much earlier but still yielded humanly manufactured artifacts. At a time when Darwin's theory of evolution was being widely discussed, firsthand investigation by a highly qualified archaeological and geological team seemed appropriate.

In early summer 1859, John Evans and Joseph Prestwich crossed the Channel to examine Boucher de Perthes's sites and discoveries. John Evans (1823–1908) was a prosperous papermaker, with eclectic scientific interests. He collected prehistoric artifacts of all kinds and was a leading expert on ancient stone tools. Prestwich was an experienced field geologist who had studied stratigraphic profiles throughout Europe. Boucher de Perthes entertained his English colleagues royally. Evans himself dug out an ax from the very same gravel layer as the bones of an elephant. The two men returned home convinced that the Somme finds, like Brixham Cave, demonstrated once and for all that humans had lived on earth for far longer than was espoused by the Ussherian chronology. Their subsequent reports to the Royal Society and the Society of Antiquaries of London were models of scientific clarity and soon led to the widespread acceptance of the notion that human origins extended much farther back than the mere six thousand years calculated from the Scriptures.

The two accounts that follow offer a dramatic contrast: the rambling discourse of Jacques Boucher de Perthes, who is still trapped in traditional thinking, and the clear account by John Evans, a champion of a rapidly developing Victorian science. Evans, who believed, we are told, in "peace, prosperity, and papermaking," set the tone for the new science of archaeology.

Gentlemen,

Nearly a quarter of a century has gone by since I addressed you here on the antiquity of man and his probable contemporaneity with the giant mammals, which species, destroyed in the great diluvial catastrophe, have not reappeared on earth.

This theory which I submitted for your consideration was new: that man who prior to the flood lived among the giants who were his predecessors in creation was never given recognition by science.

Rejected by science, this theory was also rejected by opinion; one century before, this view, which accepted the human giants without question, did not want to believe in the giant animals, and in each elephant bone science saw the bone of a human.

Today science believes in the elephants but no longer believes in the giants. In this respect science is right, but its skepticism was too far afield when it denied that man had lived during the period which preceded the diluvian formation or the cataclysm which gave the terrestrial surface its present configuration. It is this lacuna in our history, this ignorance of ours of the first steps of man on earth, to which I draw your attention; it is on these primitive peoples, their customs, their habits, their monuments, or the vestiges they must have left, that I desire to shed some light.

Your advice has not failed me; I had used it amply when in our meetings of 1836 to 1840 I brought out this theory as a complement to my book *De la création*, adding that this fossil man or his artifacts should be found in the diluvium or the deposits called tertiary. If you did not follow all my ideas, you did not deny them either; you heard them, not with the intention of condemning them but with that of judging them; you agreed with the principle but you wished proof.

Alas! I had none to give you; I was still dealing with probabilities and theories. In a word, my science was nothing but an anticipation. But this anticipation of mine had become certitude; though I had not analyzed a single stratum, I believed my discovery to be fact.

I was quite young when this thought first engrossed me. In 1805, when I was in Marseilles at the home of M. Brack, brother-in-law of Georges Cuvier and a friend of my father, I went to see a rock shelter called the Grotte de Roland, in the vicinity. My main purpose was to look there for the bones about which I had often heard Cuvier speak. I collected several specimens. Were they fossils? I did not dare say.

Later, in 1810, I visited another rock shelter. . . . They claimed to have found there some human skeletons. It was possible, but we did not see any. We collected, as I did at Marseilles, animal bones, and I collected several stones which seemed to me to be worked. . . .

When in 1836 I spoke to you on worked stones of the diluvial age, stones which had yet to be discovered, I had formed a collection of these from rock shelters, tombs, peat bogs, and similar areas. While collecting these stones which evidently were no longer in their primitive deposits, the idea came to me that I should find out what could have been their origin or the composition of this deposit. The yellow coloring of a few was the first indication. Only on the exterior, this coloring was not that of the patina of the flint. I concluded that it must be due to the ferruginous nature of the soil with which it was originally in contact. A certain stratum of the soil of the diluvium fulfilled this condition; the shade was surely that of my axes. They had definitely lain there; but was this location the effect of a recent occurrence and of a secondary altering, or did it date from the formation of the layer? There was the question.

In the affirmative case, that is, if the ax had been in the layer since its origin, the problem was resolved: the man who had made the instrument had existed prior to the cataclysm which formed the layer. Here there is no further possible doubt since the diluvial deposits do not present, as do the peat bogs, an elastic and permeable mass; nor like the bone caves, an inconcealable cavern, open to all who come, and which from century to century served as a sanctuary and then as a tomb to so many diverse beings. . . .

In the diluvial formations . . . each period is clearly divided. The horizontally superimposed layers, these strata of different shades and materials, show us in capital letters the history of the past: the great convulsions of nature seem to be delineated there by the finger of God.

Though united in a single group today like the foundation of a wall, all these levels are not brothers; centuries may separate them, and the generations which saw the birth of one did not always see the formation of the next. But since the day when each bed was laid and solidified, it remained integrally the same; in being compressed, it neither lost nor gained anything. Nothing was introduced from above, nor was there any secondary infiltration: each stratum is exempt from the influence of that which followed it and that which preceded it; homogeneous and compact, its modification required an influence no less powerful than that which created it. As one now sees it, so it was on the day of its formation. If a landslide or some type of action altered its regularity, an oblique or perpendicular line, cutting the horizontal line, would tell you so.

Here, gentlemen, the proofs start. They will be unanswerable: this human work for which we search, this work about which I tell you, *it is there* and has been there since the day that it was brought there. No less immobile than the layer itself, it came with the layer; it was held there as was the layer; and because it contributed to the layer's formation, it existed before it.

These shellfish, this elephant, this ax or the person who made it, were, therefore, witnesses to the cataclysm that gave our country its present configuration. Perhaps the shell, the elephant, and the ax were already fossilized at this time; could they be the debris surviving from an earlier deluge, the souvenirs of another age? Who can put limits on the past? Is it not infinite, as is the future? Where, then, is the man who has seen the beginning of any one thing? Where is he who will see it end? Let us not bargain over the duration of ages; let us believe that the days of the creation, those days that began before our sun, were the days of God, the interminable days of the world. Let us remember, finally, that for this eternal God a thousand centuries are no more than one second, and that He put on earth causes and effects which these thousands of centuries have not made any less young than they were at the time that His hand created them.

But all these foundations of the earth, all these schistose, chalky, clayey, and sandy layers which cover its core, are not the result of a sudden cause—of a convulsion or of a deluge. If the power of one torrent could have lifted in a day these beds torn away from other beds, there are also forces that are the consequence of slow action and of successive deposits from still water which, accomplishing their work, made hills and built mountains, not with masses thrown on masses, but with grains of sand scattered on grains of sand. Now, if we agree that the layers at Menchecourt and others were raised by an imperceptible accumulation, by a succession of deposits and sediments, the antiquity of these bones and these axes which lie under several meters of slowly accumulated sand, covered by a layer of lime or of clay, then covered again by a bed of varied chalk and of broken stones, and the whole covered by a thick layer of vegetal soil—this antiquity, I say, will be much greater than that which the rapid formation of diluvial beds appears to be.

After having reminded you of the configuration of the terrain and the nature of the elements of which it was composed, I will repeat to you on which principles, in 1836 and 1837, I established the probability of the presence of man and his works, and the type of certitude that I had of finding them there. I based this certitude:

1st, upon the tradition of a race of men destroyed by the flood;

2nd, upon the geological proofs of this flood;

3rd, upon the existence in this era of mammals closely related to man and unable to live except within the same atmospheric conditions;

4th, on the proof, thereby acquired, that the earth was habitable for man;

5th, on the basis [that] in all the regions, islands, or continents where one found these large mammals, man lived or had lived, from which one might conclude that if the animals appeared on earth before the human species, man followed closely, and at the era of the flood was already sufficiently numerous to leave signs of his presence;

6th, and finally, that these human remains had been able to escape the notice of geologists and naturalists because the difference of structure which exists between the fossil types and their living analogues could have existed between antediluvian man and those of today so that one might have confused them with other mammals; that physical probabilities, present and past experience, geology as well as history, and finally universal belief come to the support of tradition; that evidently a race of men, prior to the last cataclysm that had changed the surface of the earth, had lived there at the same time and probably in the same area as the quadrupeds whose bones have been discovered.

You recognize the truth of this reasoning, but you ask of me, why were these terrains rather than others the burial place of primitive man or the repository of his artifacts?

I answer that the diluvial torrent, while sweeping the terrestrial surface, had done that which, daily, on a lesser scale, our rainstorms do when, collecting objects in the ground which are not solidly enough fixed by their weight or their appendages, they carry articles along and throw them in some sewer; or, when the rains do not find anything but flatlands, spread them there in more or less thick layers. Then, if you examine these layers, their analysis will indicate with certainty the areas which the flood had crossed; you will know if it had crossed a populated or desert country, a town or fields, a prairie or forest, a cultivated field or stony or arid ground; you will see also whether the area had been populated by men or by animals. In brief, in this residue of a storm you cannot only follow its course, but can describe occurrences along the way.

Without doubt, as the days pass, this analysis will become less easy; all the soluble bodies will have changed shape or will dissolve in the earthy mass, but the solid objects will still be there.

So does the torrent proceed, upsetting things, carrying off and piling up all that it seizes, forming enormous masses composed of objects belonging to every kingdom and works produced by every intelligence. There also the soft or perishable parts have disappeared; there is nothing left but that which survived the trial of time.

It is, therefore, within these ruins of the ancient world, in these deposits which have become their archives, that one must look for these traditions and, for want of medallions and inscriptions, to defend these rough stones which, in their imperfection, prove no less surely the existence of man than if he had made an entire Louvre.

Thus, strongly convinced of your approbation, I carried on my work. Circumstances favored me: immense works undertaken for the fortifications at Abbeville, the digging of a canal, the railroad tracks that were being built, revealed from 1830 to 1840 numerous strata of diluvium on top of which rests a part of our valley; the chalk which forms its base rises thirty-three meters above the sea level, an immense bench which from the basin of the Somme goes to rejoin that of Paris, and thus advances toward the center of France.

A vast field was therefore open to my studies. The number of days I passed bending over these terraces which had become for me the arena of science and my promised land! The thousands of flint chips, let us say the millions, that had not been revealed to my eyes. I did my work conscientiously; all that by color or by a special cleft were distinguished from others I collected; I examined all the facets, the least broken edge did not escape me; several times I believed I had found this painfully sought evidence: it may have been, but so meager! I found there an indication, but it was not proof.

Finally, this proof came: it was at the end of 1838 that I submitted to you my first diluvial axes. It was also about this time, or in the course of the year 1839, that I brought them to Paris and showed them to several members of the Institute, notably to my respected friend M. A. Brongniart, who was perhaps more interested in the fact that my discovery was only illusory since, with Cuvier, he had established as a principle that man, new on the earth, was not

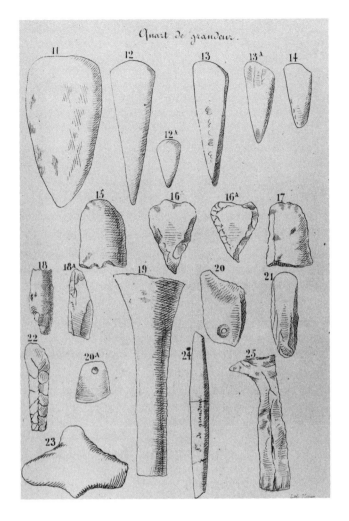

*Stone implements from Abbeville discovered by
Jacques Boucher de Perthes and illustrated in his
book* De la création *(1838–1841).*

contemporary with the great antediluvian pachyderms. However, M. Brongniart, far from discouraging me, strongly encouraged me to continue.

Meanwhile, I swear to you that he could not, sirs, see the hand of man in these rude efforts. I saw axes, and I saw correctly, but the working was vague and the angles blunt; their flattened forms differed from those of the polished axes, the only axes which were then known; finally, if the traces of working were revealed there, it was necessary to see them with eyes that believed. I had them, but I alone had them; my belief had little influence; I had not one disciple.

I needed other proofs, as well as more research, and to attain them I took some associates. I did not choose them from among the geologists. I would not have found any; at the least mention of axes and of diluvium I saw them smile.

It was, therefore, among the [quarry] workers that I looked for my helpers. I showed them my stones, and also drawings which represented that which they were supposed to have been before the diluvial abrasion.

In spite of this care, it took me several months to organize my students, but with patience, with rewards distributed opportunely, and above all with the discovery of several well-shaped bits that I found under their eyes in some layers, I tried to mold them as skillful as myself, and before the end of 1840 I was able to offer you, and to submit to the examination of the Institute, twenty flints in which the human hand was detectable.

M. Brongniart no longer doubted me; M. Dumas, his son-in-law, adopted his opinion. From this moment on I had proselytes. Their number was small in comparison with the opposition. My collection, which grew rapidly and which, from the start, I left open to the curious, attracted a few, but practical men disdained to come and see. Let us say, they were afraid; they feared to make themselves accomplices to that which they called a heresy, almost humbug; they did not question my good faith, but they doubted my good sense.

I hoped that the publication of my book on the antediluvian antiquities, which appeared first under the title of *De l'industrie primitive* would disperse these doubts; but on the contrary. Except yourselves, sirs, with whom I found constant support, nobody believed me. In 1837 the theory was accepted without too many difficulties; when, realizing this theory had become a fact that everyone could verify, no one wished to believe it any more, and they confronted me with an obstacle larger than objection, than criticism, than satire, than persecution: *disdain*. They no longer discussed the theory; they did not even bother to deny it; they forgot it.

Thus my theory slept peacefully until 1854. Then Doctor Rigollot, who, according to hearsay, had been for ten years my constant adversary, deciding to judge the question for himself, visited the exposures of Abbeville, and subsequently those of Saint-Acheul and of Amiens. His conversion was prompt; he saw that I was correct. Honest man that he was, he declared it loudly in a brochure that you all know.

Think of their finding flint axes and arrowheads at Abbeville in conjunction with bones of elephants and rhinoceroses forty feet below the surface in a bed of drift. In this bone cave in Devonshire, now being excavated by the Geological Society, they say they have found flint arrowheads among the bones, and the same is reported of a cave in Sicily. I can hardly believe it. It will make my ancient Britons quite modern if man is carried back in England to the days when elephants, rhinoceroses, hippopotamuses, and tigers were also inhabitants of the country. . . .

Easter Sunday. . . . Prestwich has altered his plans about Abbeville and seeing M. Boucher de Perthes's collections and investigating the gravel pits where the flint weapons are found in conjunction with the bones, and has got

*Sir John Evans, as seen in a
portrait from 1900.*

up a party of some of the best men in the Geological Society for the purpose. As it has been deferred till after Easter I could not resist accepting his invitation to join in. . . . I have accordingly arranged to go to Abbeville on *Tuesday* and return on Thursday to London. . . . I shall miss seeing the collection of M. Boucher de Perthes but be in time I hope for the gravel pit. . . .

May 1st 1859. I crossed from Folkestone to Boulogne and had as rough a passage as the strongest stomach could desire. . . . I had about an hour and a half in Boulogne and at nine took the train to Abbeville, where I found Prestwich waiting for me at the station, and very glad to see me, as of all the party he had asked to meet him there I was the only one who came. We went straight to bed and soon after seven the next morning M. Boucher de Perthes, the first discoverer of the stone axes we were in pursuit of, came to take us to some of the gravel pits from whence his collection had been derived. A. M. Marotte, the curator of the museum, accompanied us but we did not succeed in finding anything. We then adjourned to the house of M. de Perthes, which is a complete museum from top to bottom, full of paintings, old carvings, pottery, etc., and with a wonderful collection of flint axes and implements found among the beds of gravel and evidently deposited at the same time with them—in fact the remains of a race of men who existed at the same time when the deluge or whatever was the origin of these gravel beds took place. One of the most remarkable features of the case is that nearly all if not quite all of the animals whose bones are found in the same beds as the axes are extinct. There is the mammoth, the rhinoceros, the urus—a tiger, etc., etc. After the examination of his museum M. de Perthes gave us a most sumptuous *déjeuner à la fourchette* and we then set off for Amiens. Of course our object was if possible to ascertain that these axes had been actually deposited with the gravel, and not subsequently introduced; and we had received intelligence from Amiens that in one of the gravel pits an axe was to be seen in its original position, which made us set off at once. At Amiens we were met by the president of their Society of Antiquaries and the public librarian, MM. Dufour and Garnier, and with them a M. Pinsard, an architect. We proceeded to the pit, where sure enough the edge of an axe was visible in an entirely undisturbed bed of gravel and eleven feet from the surface. We had a photographer with us to take a view of it so as to corroborate our testimony and had only time to get that done and collect some twelve or fifteen axes from the workmen in the pit when we were forced to take the train again to Abbeville. The early part of Friday we spent in and about Abbeville and returned to London in the afternoon reaching home or rather the Euston Hotel about midnight. All together I enjoyed the trip very much, and am now only troubled to find time to write an account of our investigations for the Antiquaries, as Prestwich is going to do for the Royal Society.

Finding Beijing Man

J. Gunnar Andersson

Dutch physician Eugene Dubois's claims for the existence of primitive forms of humans in Southeast Asia were greeted with skepticism in the 1890s. They were overshadowed by the Piltdown skull from southern England, which was closer to home and more modern-looking. This was hardly surprising, since the find was an ingenious forgery. Dubois was not vindicated until the 1920s, when the Zhoukoudian Cave near Beijing in China yielded remarkably similar crania, with heavy brow ridges and retreating foreheads. The Zhoukoudian human fossils, classified as Sinanthropus *(Chinese human), lay in the same levels as crude stone tools, the bones of many game animals, and thick hearths. Dubois's* Pithecanthropus *and the Chinese* Sinanthropus *soon became* Homo erectus, *a general taxonomic label for archaic humans of 1 million years ago or more.* Homo erectus *has subsequently turned up in both tropical Africa and Europe, but the origins of and evolutionary relationships among African, European, and Asian fossils are a matter of continuing controversy. These once controversial humans are now known to have lived in Asia from at least 1.8 million years ago to somewhere within the past 150,000 years.*

Swedish explorer and fossil hunter J. Gunnar Andersson (1876–1960) spent long periods in China, where he became fascinated with stories of "dragons' bones," much valued for their magical and pharmaceutical uses. Dragons' teeth led him to Zhoukoudian (Chou K'ou Tien) Cave, a giant fissure in a limestone cliff filled with fossil animal bones. His account of the first investigation of the cave in 1921 advancing his conviction that human fossils lay in the deposits is an interesting byway of archaeological discovery. Subsequent excavations by Davidson Black and Chinese archaeologists produced a remarkable collection of Homo erectus *fossils, which were, unfortunately, mislaid during the chaotic early months of World War II. Over the past half century, many more* Homo erectus *fragments have come from Zhoukoudian and elsewhere in China, showing that this archaic human form evolved considerably over hundreds of thousands of years. The Zhoukoudian fossils have been dated to between 450,000 and 230,000 years ago.*

J. Gunnar Andersson describes his discoveries of Zhoukoudian in this selection from his reminiscences, Children of the Yellow Earth, *published in 1934. In his day, fossil hunting in remote lands was a constant adventure story.*

(French priest and paleontologist Teilhard de Chardin, mentioned in the extract, was a prominent student of the Chinese Stone Age and a sophisticated Catholic philosopher. He had a reputation as a practical joker. Some experts believe that he was involved in the Piltdown forgery.)

One day in February 1918 I met in Peking J. McGregor Gibb, professor of chemistry at the mission university which at that time bore the somewhat pretentious title of Peking University. He knew that I was interested in fossils and consequently he told me that he had just been out at Chou K'ou Tien, about 50 kilometres south-west of Peking, a place which I have already described on a couple of occasions during my story.

He had there heard of a place called "Chicken Bone Hill," Chi Ku Shan. It was so called because red clay had been found there full of the bones of birds. Professor Gibb had himself visited the place and had brought back to Peking various fragments of the bone-bearing clay. He was kind enough to show me these fragments. They consisted of the characteristic red clay which fills up the cavities in the limestone in many places in the district of Chou K'ou Tien, but the remarkable thing about this particular clay was that it was full of small bones, most of them hollow and evidently belonging to birds.

Gibb's description was so alluring that I visited the spot on the 22nd–23rd March in the same year.

Chou K'ou Tien's primary distinction is the numerous limestone quarries in the Ordovician limestone, and the bones are to be found in the middle of such an old quarry. The bone-bearing clay rises like a detached pillar from the bottom of the quarry. Its total height is 5:5 metres. It is clear that the clay at one time filled a cavity in the limestone and that the limestone burners had carefully preserved this mass of clay, which thus gradually changed its character from being a filling of a cavity to that of a detached pillar.

We may ask ourselves why the workmen so carefully avoided this clay deposit, of which they could easily have got rid. The explanation is perhaps to be found in a story told to us while we were there collecting bones:

"Once upon a time, more than a hundred years ago, there was a cave here in which lived foxes, which devoured all the chickens in the neighbourhood. In the course of time some of these foxes were transformed into evil spirits. One man tried to kill the foxes, but the evil spirits drove him mad."

It seems not improbable that the superstition associated with this bone deposit protected it from disturbance.

During our visit we only broke off a small portion of the middle of the pillar and found the bones of a couple of species of rodents, as well as of one smaller and one larger beast of prey, but especially numerous bones of birds.

We were much pleased with our discovery, which was the first of fossil bones. But the bones were small, and belonged, as it seemed, to common and possibly still surviving forms. It also seemed probable that the age of the deposit was not great. . . .

But when Dr. Zdansky came out to China in the early summer of 1921 in order to assist me in the excavation of the *Hipparion* deposits, we agreed that he should first of all journey to Chou K'ou Tien and excavate on Chicken Bone Hill in order to obtain some knowledge of conditions in Chinese country districts.

Just at that time there arrived in Peking the famous mammal palaeontologist, Dr. Walter Granger, from the American Museum of Natural History in New York, in order to take up his duties as chief palaeontologist in Dr. Roy Chapman Andrews' great expedition to Mongolia.

Dr. Granger and I agreed to visit Chou K'ou Tien in order to see Dr. Zdansky, and to give Dr. Granger some idea of working conditions in China, whilst at the same time Dr. Granger very kindly offered to acquaint us with the extraordinarily developed technique of excavations which had been one of the factors in the phenomenal progress of the American vertebrate palaeontologists.

Zdansky had taken up his headquarters in the same little village temple in which I had lived in 1918. Dr. Granger and I installed ourselves with Zdansky and went with him to Chicken Bone Hill, where we pointed out some of the small bones. Whilst we were sitting at our work a man of the neighbourhood came and looked at us.

"There's no use staying here any longer. Not far from here there is a place where you can collect much larger and better dragons' bones," said he.

Knowing well that in the matter of search for dragons' bones in China we must never neglect any clue, I immediately began to question the man. His information seemed so reliable that after a few minutes we packed up our kit and followed him in a northerly direction over the limestone hills. It appeared that the new discovery also lay in an abandoned quarry 150 metres west of, and at a higher level than, the railway station at Chou K'ou Tien. In an almost perpendicular wall of limestone, about 10 metres high, which faced north, the man showed us a filled-up fissure in the limestone consisting of pieces of limestone and fragments of bones of larger animals, the whole bound together by sintered limestone. We had not searched for many minutes before we found the jaw of a pig, which showed that we were in the presence of a discovery with much greater possibilities than Chicken Bone Hill. That evening we went home with rosy dreams of great discoveries.

Granger sat that evening and pondered over a toothless jaw which he had found and which I guessed to belong to a stag. The learned palaeontologist would assuredly have laughed at me if he had not been such a far-sighted and kindly man, for this remarkable lower jaw showed such a marked thickening that it was almost circular in section and consequently far from the type of a normal stag's jaw. Now it so happened that in the late autumn of 1918 I had found in red clay on the Huai Lai plain north of Peking well-preserved jaws with the teeth intact, which convinced me that I had to do with a stag with an extreme development of the mysterious phenomenon of bone thickening which the learned call hyperostosis.

The following day broke in brilliant sunshine and we wandered along the straight road from our temple to Lao Niu Kou, as the new place of discovery is called, and which will one day become one of the most sacred places of pilgrimage for investigations into the history of the human race.

The day's harvest exceeded all expectations. Not only did we find the jaws, with all the teeth intact, of the hyperostotic animal and were able to confirm that it really was a stag. Rhinoceros teeth, the jaws of a hyena and pieces of jawbone belonging to the bear genus were also some of the finds of the day. When we raised our glasses at the beginning of dinner, our happy trio was able to drink to a certain discovery. Dr. Granger had during the course of the day instructed Dr. Zdansky and myself in the excellent American bandaging system and we now decided to leave the completion of our new discovery to Dr. Zdansky, who probably had weeks of work in front of him on this spot. The next day it poured with rain and Granger and I, who were to take the train back to Peking, were helplessly flooded in, for the little stream which flows out into the Chou K'ou Tien valley, and which during the preceding days had been an insignificant purling rill, was now a wild foaming mountain stream which nobody dared to cross so long as the cloudbursts continued to hurl new masses of water into the valleys.

We drank grog and told stories of almost every part of the world and tried to guess what Zdansky would find during his further excavations at Lao Niu Kou. Then came the evening of the third day and when the sun rose on the fourth day Granger and I prepared for our return home. But right opposite the station we had to strip almost naked and wade across the stream, which had carried away the footbridge and which rose breast high, even though the turbulence of the day before had subsided considerably.

Thus ends the history of the discovery of the Chou K'ou Tien deposit.

Dr. Zdansky remained several weeks at Lao Niu Kou and continued his digging. . . . Zdansky's investigations clearly proved that the Lao Niu Kou find fills a cavity in the Ordovician limestone, and that consequently it is essentially of the same kind as the Chicken Bone Hill, only of much greater dimensions. . . .

I give below Dr. Zdansky's measurements, from which it appears that the large central part of the cave was clearly stratified and consisted primarily of clay and clayey sand as well as breccia and yellowish sandstone.

The succession of strata from the top to the bottom is as follows:

8. Breccia of angular sandstone fragments, unstratified. Binding material sandy limestone. Contains land molluscs and pieces of bone.
7. 80 cm. bright red clayey sand with sandstone inlays. Land molluscs.
6. 33 cm. brown clay, slightly banded.
5. 21 cm. dark brown, banded fat clay.

4. 6.5 cm. light yellow clay.
3. 4.5 cm. black-brown fat clay. Bones and occasionally much corroded teeth. Contains flakes of quartz.
2. 15 cm. light yellow sandy clay with numerous bone remains. Contains angular pieces of quartz.
1. Yellow sandstone of unknown thickness. Contains numerous bone remains, bits of limestone and of travertine.

Section B

9. Like A 8.
8. 80 cm red. stratified sand.
7. 16 cm. clay deposit, yellow at the bottom.
6. 15 cm. red sandstone.
5. 30 cm. red banded, partially hardened sand.

4. 6 cm. light yellow clay.
3. Like A 3.
2. 17 cm. light yellow sandy clay with numerous bone remains. Contains flakes of quartz.
1. Like A 1.

On studying these descriptions of the two sections the reader will observe that in both cases deposits 2 and 3 contain angular pieces of quartz. During my visit to Chou K'ou Tien in order to follow the progress of Zdansky's work I was especially interested in these pieces of quartz, which had often such sharp edges that they might very well have been used as cutting tools.

I also observed that the limestone beside the cave is streaked with narrow veins of quartz, which are cleft in such a manner that it is quite conceivable that the edged pieces of quartz in deposits 2 and 3 simply fell down from the roof.

This is perhaps the most probable, or at any rate the least sensational, interpretation of the occurrence of the flakes of quartz. But, if we begin to reflect on the origin of the human species we are inevitably forced to the conclusion that the very earliest and extremely simple implements *were not prepared* by the "Hominid," but were picked up and selected from the bits of wood and stone which came his way.

In accordance with this compelling conclusion it seemed entirely reasonable that if a hominid had lived in or near the Chou K'ou Tien cave, he would have made use of these flakes of quartz, in order, for example, to cut up the animals which he had succeeded in killing.

This was the train of thought which led me on one of my visits to Zdansky to knock on the wall of the cave deposits and say:

"I have a feeling that there lie here the remains of one of our ancestors and

*Workmen carry a basket while excavating at Zhoukoudian, China, in the 1930s.
The markings on the rock face denote squares in the excavation.*

it is only a question of your finding him. Take your time and stick to it till the cave is emptied, if need be."

The Chou K'ou Tien deposits were more difficult than we at first supposed, and Zdansky concluded his excavations in the late summer of 1921, when he had reached a stage when it would have been dangerous, without large scaffoldings, to dig farther into the now overhanging wall of the cave deposits.

But I could never forget the thought of hominid remains in this cave, and thus it happened that Zdansky, at my request, returned to Chou K'ou Tien for further excavations in the summer of 1923. We shall soon come to the result of his search for the expected hominid remains, but we must first survey the other discoveries of bones which were made in the cave deposit. On the whole the fossil bones of the Chou K'ou Tien cave are rather badly preserved. Whole skulls are scarcely ever to be found and still less complete skeletons. It thus appears as if these animals had been completely broken up, possibly by some beast of prey, and that the bone remains had been exposed to soaking, with the result that only those parts with the greatest powers of resistance, such as teeth and jaws, had been preserved. . . .

On the whole the Chou K'ou Tien fauna reveals many features which indicate that it is not younger than the earliest part of the Pleistocene age.

When the Crown Prince and Crown Princess of Sweden set out in May 1926 on their journey round the world via North America and the countries of the Far East, they invited Dr. Lagrelius and me to meet them in Peking and to me was entrusted the special mission of arranging the archaeological and art studies of the Crown Prince in China. I then conceived the idea of trying to arrange, among other things, a scientific meeting in Peking at which some of the scholars living there might communicate something of the results they had achieved.

What was to me personally of much the greatest interest was a communication from Zdansky that in working on the Chou K'ou Tien material he had found a molar and a pre-molar of a creature resembling a human being, which he designated merely *Homo sp?* He had dug out the molar himself and identified it at Chou K'ou Tien as belonging to an anthropoid ape. The pre-molar he had discovered only while cleaning the material in Upsala.

So the hominid expected by me was found.

On October 22nd the scientific meeting was held in the auditorium of the Medical High School in Peking. After the president of the Geological Society, Dr. Wong Wen-hao, had welcomed the royal guests, the Crown Prince in reply recalled the thousand-year-old traditions of archaeological research in China. The first address was given by a famous political reformer and author, Liang Chi Chao, who also spoke of archaeological research in China. The next speaker was Professor Teilhard de Chardin, who described Father Licent's and his own great discovery of the early Stone-age man in the Ordos desert. The last contribution to the programme of the evening was reserved for me, and I reported, on behalf of Professor Wiman, the latest results of the great palaeontological work done in Upsala. When, finally, I showed in a lantern picture the hominid teeth discovered by Zdansky, I suggested that this in itself extremely incomplete discovery might come to be the most important result of the whole of our Swedish work in China. I further explained that we had no plan to follow up this result by further investigations, but that we would gladly see a large-scale examination of the Chou K'ou Tien cave organized by the Geological Survey of China, in co-operation with Dr. Black, as representative of the Peking Union Medical College, and with the Rockefeller Foundation.

I now remember with pleasure that the far-reaching importance of this announcement was fully appreciated by the leading scientists of China, such as Dr. Ting, Dr. Wong, Dr. Black and Dr. Grabau. Dr. Black worked up Wiman's pictures and text in a short notice on the discovery, which was published in *Nature* in November 1926. My proposal to continue work in the field found active support on all sides and the three institutions which together organized the new undertaking showed so much confidence in us Swedes as to invite Professor Wiman, through Dr. Black and myself, to engage one of his students to conduct the new campaign of excavation at Chou K'ou Tien. Dr. Grabau, who invents such excellent scientific terminology, immediately named the new discovery *The Peking Man*, and it it was under this name that this hominid discovery became known throughout the world.

During the first days, nay months, after the communiqué of October 22nd, a shadow of doubt fell upon the hominid discovery at Chou K'ou Tien. The two French scholars, Licent and Teilhard, were present at the reception in the Peking auditorium, and two days later Teilhard wrote a little note to me, of which I take the liberty of reproducing the brief contents.

Dear Dr. Andersson,

I have reflected much on the photographs which you so kindly showed me and I feel that it would not be right, and still less friendly, to conceal from you what I think of them.

As a matter of fact I am not fully convinced of their supposed human character. Even the rootless assumed pre-molar, which at first sight seemed most convincing, may be one of the last molars of some carnivore, and the same is true of the other tooth, unless the roots are distinctly four in number.

Even if, as I hope, it can never be proved that the Chou K'ou Tien teeth belong to a beast of prey, I fear that it can never be absolutely demonstrated that they are human. It is necessary to be very cautious, since their nature is undetermined.

I have not seen the specimens, however, and since I place great reliance on Zdansky's palaeontological experience I hope most intensely that my criticism will prove unfounded. I have only wished to be absolutely frank with you.

Sincerely yours,
P. Teilhard.

I need scarcely point out that the French scientist, who is one of the most far-seeing and most delightful men I have ever met, expressed this warning in a spirit of candour and warm friendship, with the sole purpose of checking a too optimistic faith and one which might prove erroneous. I knew only too well that this learned palaeontologist had good reasons for his hesitation, since certain teeth of beasts of prey may, when worn to a certain extent, easily be confused with human teeth. My only reply to this criticism was that I had complete confidence in Zdansky's critical acumen, the more so as he had conducted extensive investigations into the fossil carnivores of China and should thus be proof against the danger suggested by Teilhard.

The Discovery of
Australopithecus

RAYMOND ARTHUR DART

Raymond Arthur Dart (1893–1991) was born the fifth of nine children to a merchant couple in Queensland, Australia. A bright and precocious student, Dart won a scholarship to attend the University of Queensland in its inaugural year, 1910, and embarked on a long and fruitful academic career. He went on to study medicine at the University of Sydney and eventually became a demonstrator in anatomy at St. Andrew's College, where he studied the evolutionary development of the human brain. During World War I, the young Dart enlisted in the Australian Army Medical Corps and served throughout Australia, England, and France. After a period in Britain at the University of London, Dart became professor of anatomy at the University of Witwatersrand in Johannesburg, South Africa, in 1923.

Dart soon felt isolated from the scientific community in Europe and was depressed to be stuck in an academic backwater. Perhaps to alleviate his ennui and to improve the caliber of his department, he began to share his interest in physical anthropology with his anatomy students and encouraged them to build a comparative fossil collection for the department in their spare time. Thus was set in motion the chain of events that led to the discovery of the famous Taung baby. Fortunately for science, fate placed this fossil in the hands of one of the few men capable of recognizing its unique worth. Were it not for Dart's early training in comparative neurology and past experience in dentistry, the Taung baby would have been classified almost certainly as a fossil ape.

Dart's claim for a new genus of hominid, Australopithecus africanus *(southern ape-human of Africa), was greeted by a storm of controversy, however. Conservative scientists in Europe, who were mesmerized by the Piltdown skull, dismissed* Australopithecus *as an ape immediately. Only Scottish paleontologist Robert Broom saw the Taung fossil for what it was. He is said to have burst into Dart's office and fallen on his knees before the diminutive skull. An eccentric and flamboyant scientist, Broom found many other australopithecine fossils in South African caves during the 1930s, and they provided an impressive body of data about a seemingly elusive ape-human. He recovered both robust-looking and more gracile australopithecine fossils from caves in*

37

South Africa's northern Transvaal before World War II. Dart himself excavated in the Makapansgat caves, where he found not only more hominid fossils, but also cut and smashed animal bones that he claimed to be the first human tool kit, one of bone, horn, and teeth. (More recent researchers have shown that the animal bones were broken not by Australopithecus, *but by hyenas.) Almost alone, Broom and Dart saw* Australopithecus *for what it was—a remote, and perhaps direct, ancestor of modern humanity. Dart's bold claim finally received wide acceptance in the early 1950s, when* Australopithecus africanus *was shown to be close to the early human line. All subsequent research into early human origins has flowed from the Taung discovery.*

In this selection from his book Adventures with the Missing Link, *Raymond Dart describes his first impressions of the Taung child as he opened the crates on the eve of a wedding.*

As soon as I entered the dissection hall and looked at my class of students I could see that my only woman science pupil, Josephine Salmons, who was assisting me as a demonstrator, was excited. Her normally pale face was flushed and when I caught her looking at me appealingly, I asked her, "Did you wish to speak to me, Miss Salmons?"

She gulped nervously with every man's eye in the room on her and said, "Oh, Professor, could I see you sometime today? I came across something last night that I'm sure will interest you."

I asked her to see me during the break and got on with the business of dissecting.

It was the early summer of 1924 and I was in my second year as professor of anatomy at the Medical School in the University of the Witwatersrand in Johannesburg. Since my appointment I had taken a particular interest in anthropology, a subject in which Josephine had become my most enthusiastic pupil. Before the July vacation I had encouraged my students to collect fossils during the holidays, impressing upon them that to be able to study anatomy properly, the school must have an anatomy museum composed of bones and other parts of any and every animal. I offered a prize of five pounds to the student who collected the most interesting finds on the veld during the holidays.

There was no more vigorous collector than Josephine and I well remember her disappointment when she was beaten to the prize by a student who had brought along a crocodile stuffed with straw, an ox and some interesting stones and bones from a cave. This disappointment had not, I knew, soured her enthusiasm, so that I was fairly sure her excitement concerned some bone or fossil probably of no importance.

However, when we had tea together during break I soon realized that she might have stumbled across an interesting find. The previous night she had visited a family friend, Mr. E. G. Izod, a director of the Northern Lime Company, and had noticed a fossil skull on the mantel above the fireplace. It had come from the company's mine at Taungs in the Bechuanaland Protectorate.

She hesitated before expressing an opinion about the fossil but when I pressed her she said, "Well, don't laugh at me if I prove wrong, but I'm pretty certain it's a baboon fossil."

I was equally certain that she must be mistaken.

"I don't wish to dampen your enthusiasm," I told her, "but other than Rhodesian Man and Boskop Man not a single fossil of any of the primates (the order to which man and all apes, monkeys and baboons belong) has ever been reported south of the Fayûm deposit in Egypt. But I'd very much like to see this skull and examine it. If it is a baboon's, it will be of rare interest."

Josephine said she was sure Mr. Izod would let me keep the fossil, adding quite casually the astonishing information that fossil skulls and bones were often turning up at the mine.

The following morning she brought the fossil to me and, to my surprise, it was the skull of a baboon that had been embedded in limestone rock. A baffling feature was a hole in the front part of the roof of the skull, as if it had been struck by a sharp instrument, but I noted this only briefly. Here, I thought, was a new and primitive species of baboon.

Within a few minutes I was careening down the hill in my model-T Ford to discuss the skull and Taungs with my friend and colleague, Dr. R. B. Young, a veteran Scottish geologist. Young not only knew the limestone works at Taungs from which the skull had been recovered, but had been commissioned by the owners of the works to visit a neighboring lime deposit at Thoming. He promised to call on the manager, Mr. A. E. Spiers, and ask his co-operation in sending any further bone-bearing rocks to me.

On his return Young told me that at Taungs he had met an old miner, Mr. M. de Bruyn, who for many years had taken a keen interest in preserving fossils. Only the previous week he had brought quite a number of stone blocks containing bone fragments to Mr. Spiers' office. When Young mentioned my interest to Mr. Spiers, Spiers gave instructions for them to be boxed and railed to me.

I waited anxiously for their arrival, reasoning that if fossilized baboon skulls were such a common feature at Taungs many other, more interesting specimens might be found there. Of course, the packages turned up at the most inopportune time.

I was standing by the window of my dressing room cursing softly while struggling into an unaccustomed stiff-winged collar when I noticed two men wearing the uniform of the South African Railways staggering along the driveway of our home in Johannesburg with two large wooden boxes.

My Virginia-born wife Dora, who was also donning her most formal outfit, had noticed the men with the boxes and rushed in to me in something of a panic.

"I suppose those are the fossils you've been expecting," she said. "Why on earth did they have to arrive today of all days?" She fixed me with a business-like eye. "Now, Raymond," she pleaded, "the guests will start arriving shortly and you can't go delving in all that rubble until the wedding's over and everybody has left. I know how how important the fossils are to you, but please leave them until tomorrow."

Looking back on that summer afternoon of 1924, I can sympathize with her point of view. Our great South African friend, Christo Beyers, past international footballer and now senior lecturer in applied anatomy and operative surgery at the University of the Witwatersrand, was being married in our home to a French widow whom he had met when studying in London at St. Bartholomew's Hospital. My wife had made the most elaborate arrangements possible for the reception in the then small gold-mining town of Johannesburg, and had gone to special pains to ensure that my London-cut morning clothes were extracted from brown paper and mothballs, and that in general my normally casual appearance would be smartened up so as not to disgrace my role as best man.

At the time, however, this seemed of little importance when I considered the exciting anthropological bits and pieces that the boxes from Taungs might contain. As soon as my wife had left to complete her dressing I tore the hated collar off and dashed out to take delivery of the boxes which meanwhile obstructed the entrance to the stoep. I was too excited to wait until my African servants carried them to the garage, and ordered them to leave the crates under the pergola while I went in search of some tools to open them.

(Later on that momentous day, my wife told me that she had twice remonstrated with me but had been ignored. I had no recollection of any interruptions.)

I wrenched the lid off the first box and my reaction was one of extreme disappointment. In the rocks I could make out traces of fossilized eggshells and turtle shells and a few fragmentary pieces of isolated bone, none of which looked to be of much interest.

Impatiently I wrestled with the lid of the second box, still hopeful but half-expecting it to be a replica of its mate. At most I anticipated baboon skulls, little guessing that from this crate was to emerge a face that would look out on the world after an age-long sleep of nearly a million years.

As soon as I removed the lid a thrill of excitement shot through me. On the very top of the rock heap was what was undoubtedly an endocranial cast or mold of the interior of the skull. Had it been only the fossilized brain cast of any species of ape it would have ranked as a great discovery, for such a thing had never before been reported. But I knew at a glance that what lay in my hands was no ordinary anthropoidal brain. Here in lime-consolidated sand was the replica of a brain three times as large as that of a baboon and considerably bigger than that of any adult chimpanzee. The startling image of the convolutions and furrows of the brain and the blood vessels of the skull was plainly visible.

It was not big enough for primitive man, but even for an ape it was a big bulging brain and, most important, the forebrain was so big and had grown so far backward that it completely covered the hindbrain.

Was there, anywhere among this pile of rocks, a face to fit the brain? I ransacked feverishly through the boxes. My search was rewarded, for I found a

Raymond Dart (left) with his ardent supporter Robert Broom, who holds the skull
of a robust Australopithecine. Also in the picture, taken around 1950, are the Abbé
Henri Breuil, a French prehistorian and expert on Stone Age rock art, and C. Van
Riet Lowe, a prominent South African archaeologist.

large stone with a depression into which the cast fitted perfectly. There was
faintly visible in the stone the outline of a broken part of the skull and even the
back of the lower jaw and a tooth socket which showed that the face might still
be somewhere there in the block.

I must emphasize here the particular reason for my excitement. The most
impressive feature of this endocast, or brain cast, as they are sometimes loosely
called, was the marked distance separating the two well-defined and unmistakable furrows at the back of its outer surface.

These two furrows, called the *lunate* (or moon-shaped) and *parallel sulci*, are
found in the brains of apes and often of men—especially primitive men. My old
professor in University College, London, Grafton Elliot Smith, had been the
first to find the *lunate sulcus* in human brains and thus made these landmarks
famous.

In some human brains, however, the brain substance in the territory between
these two furrows expands so much that the *lunate sulcus* becomes greatly separated from the *parallel sulcus* and, especially in very advanced brains, is pushed
back so far that it entirely disappears from the outer aspect of the brain.

In the Taungs cast, so much of this expansion had occurred between the lunate and parallel sulci that they were separated by a distance *three times as great* as in any existing endocast of a living ape's skull, whether chimpanzee or gorilla. So even had I found no trace of the face in the rock, or if it had proved to be defective, I would still have known instantly that the creature whose skull could give a cast of this sort must have been at least three times as intelligent as any living ape.

I stood in the shade holding the brain as greedily as any miser hugs his gold, my mind racing ahead. Here, I was certain, was one of the most significant finds ever made in the history of anthropology.

Darwin's largely discredited theory that man's early progenitors probably lived in Africa came back to me. Was I to be the instrument by which his "missing link" was found?

These pleasant daydreams were interrupted by the bridegroom himself tugging at my sleeve.

"My God, Ray," he said, striving to keep the nervous urgency out of his voice. "You've got to finish dressing immediately—or I'll have to find another best man. The bridal car should be here any moment."

Reluctantly, I replaced the rocks in the boxes, but I carried the endocranial cast and the stone from which it had come along with me and locked them away in my wardrobe.

I could scarcely wait for the ceremony to cease and the guests to leave so that I could re-examine my treasures. When the last couple were walking down the drive to their car I was back in the bedroom tearing off my collar and tie and reaching in the wardrobe.

A long and careful study of the cast confirmed the conclusions I had reached earlier in the day. What could an anthropoid ape with a brain bigger than that of a chimpanzee and rivaling that of a gorilla be doing down here in South Africa away from the tropical forests and jungles, out in the open, grass-covered plains and undulating, treeless prairie lands of the Transvaal?

Only recently, Dr. A. W. Rogers, head of the Geological Survey in South Africa, had pointed out in a paper that there was no evidence to show that climatic conditions in South Africa had varied appreciably since the Cretaceous period, 70 million years ago.

In the Transvaal there was no food for apes unless they lived, like baboons, on insects and scorpions, lizards and birds' eggs, berries and grubs. There were no natural storehouses of nuts and acorns here such as the squirrels of Europe might collect; they could not wrest bulbs from this tough African turf during our rainless, fruitless winters without some type of digging tools.

As I pondered the mystery of how the big-brained creature could have survived in the Transvaal without an anthropoid's natural foods my mind flashed back to Miss Salmons' baboon skull which had come from the same mine. I remembered the neat round hole on top on the right side.

Was it possible that the opening had been made by another creature to extract its brain for food? Did this ape with the big brain catch and eat baboons? If so it must have been very clever to catch them and kill them; and very courageous too.

However, there were more immediate problems to be faced with my new find, the most important of which was how to expose the face if there were one embedded in the matrix. Although I had no experience in doing this, there was nobody to whom I could turn. I had no proper equipment and had to be satisfied with a hammer and chisels purchased from a hardware store.

The shocks of the small hammer were absorbed by the smallest of the chisels, the rock being supported in sand and buttressed by sand-filled tobacco bags. When I had exposed sufficient of the skull to get an idea of its general position I found that my most useful ally was one of my wife's knitting needles.

I sharpened it pyramidally like a trocar and, working during every spare moment for the next two months, pecked, scraped and levered the lime-consolidated earth from the front of the skull and eye sockets. No trace appeared, however, of eyebrow ridges such as one finds in living apes, even in young ones. The upper and lower jaws, instead of jutting far forward, were shortened and retracted under the skull.

My excitement grew as the outer sides of the jaws were exposed and I became more convinced that the whole face would be there. I lay awake at nights, in a fever of thoughts about cave-dwelling apes and impatient for dawn to break. On my visits to town I searched the ill-stocked bookshops for literature, for during those early days of the University of the Witwatersrand there was not even a university library, let alone a medical or an anatomical library. Beyond the books and casts I had brought out with me from England nearly two years earlier, I had no references whatsoever.

When I visited Cape Town in November to mark examination papers, I met for the first time Dr. S. H. Haughton. I then learned of his preliminary paper concerning the baboons from Taungs. These were at the South African Museum in Cape Town and were generously placed at my disposal for examination.

The first thing I noticed was that all these skulls too seemed to have been broken before fossilization in much the same way as the skull brought to me by Miss Salmons.

What could this mean? Had the big-brained creature from Taungs been carnivorous and deliberately killed the baboons, or were they the victims of a series of rockfalls? The first view was too revolutionary even to whisper to anyone else; the second seemed too improbable a series of coincidences to conjecture.

I was soon back in Johannesburg working away with hammer, chisels and knitting needle, in constant fear that the slightest slip of the chisel would shatter the relic within. No diamond cutter ever worked more lovingly or with such care on a priceless jewel—nor I am sure, with such inadequate tools.

But on the seventy-third day, December 23, the rock parted.

I could view the face from the front, although the right side was still embedded. The creature which had contained this massive brain was no giant anthropoid such as a gorilla. What emerged was a baby's face, an infant with a full set of milk (or deciduous) teeth and its first permanent molars just in the process of erupting.

I doubt if there was any parent prouder of his offspring than I was of my "Taungs baby" on that Christmas of 1924.

When I saw the basic difference between the Taungs brain and those of living anthropoids, I knew that at least I had a most advanced type of ape. Although only a child, its skull capacity was 520cc., and thus bigger than the 320–480 cc. of all known adult chimpanzees. Yet, as it was still below the gorilla's (340–685 cc.) it could scarcely be termed overgrown.

But it was the brain's form that was impressive, for the brains of the living apes, like their skulls, are low and broad, and the forebrain has not expanded enough relative to the hindbrain or cerebellum—the organ of equilibration—to cover it completely. The Taungs cast had inhabited a skull that was narrow and high. Its impressive feature was quality and not quantity, with its globular form and forebrain completely covering the hindbrain.

Even more conclusive, however, were the physiognomy and dental formation. Fortunately, I had brought to South Africa from London a copy of Dr. W. L. H. Duckworth's *Morphology and Anthropology* (1915) which carried drawings of an infant gorilla and an infant chimpanzee similar in age to the infant Taungs.

I have little facility in drawing but one of my student demonstrators, Mr. (now Dr.) Henri Le Helloco, made an excellent copy of the Taungs skull, similar in scale to those in Duckworth's book. When the drawings were completed, I compared them with Duckworth's baby gorilla and chimpanzee and found that the Taungs child differed from both even more than the gorilla and chimpanzee differed from each other.

Even at this early age gorilla and chimpanzee skulls slope back from their eye sockets which have pronounced and overhanging beetling eyebrows. The Taungs child had no trace of eyebrow ridges, but a true forehead arched directly upward from the inward-sloping eye sockets. The markedly shortened face, instead of protruding like an anthropoid's, receded. This contrasted with the massive upper and lower jaws of the gorilla and chimpanzee which clothe formidable rows of molar teeth and large canine fangs.

As Darwin, following Rütimeyer and others, insisted, it is the effect of the jaw muscles on the skull that causes anthropoids to differ so greatly from man, especially the males, "who have a truly frightful physiognomy." Even gorilla and chimpanzee infants have obvious fangs in both jaws while behind these, especially in the lower jaws, lie sharp-cutting, infant molars.

In this young creature from Taungs the canine teeth—as in human beings—were quite small, and the teeth behind them seemed to be grinders, not cutters. Consequently its physiognomy could not be called "frightful."

As my investigations continued I grew prouder of my "baby." Here was a creature which, in the exasperating fashion of children throughout the ages, was daring to vie with man. Its forehead, facial form and dental equipment were startlingly similar; its brain was decidedly bigger than an adult chimpanzee's but not so large as an adult gorilla's.

This similarity was unexpected, and contrary to the assumption of all the authorities. Even Darwin had in mind ancestors that were long in the tooth when he wrote:

> The early male forefathers of man were probably furnished with great canine teeth; but as they gradually acquired the habit of using stones, clubs or other weapons for fighting their enemies or rivals, they would use their jaws less and less. In this case the jaws, together with the teeth, would become reduced in size.

I was also convinced from the earliest period of my investigations that these creatures had placed great reliance on their feet for walking and running and that, consequently, their hands must have been freed for other tasks. This was implicit in the globular form of the skull which was obviously balanced on a more vertically placed type of backbone than that of a gorilla or chimpanzee. The improvement in the poise of the head implied a better posture of the whole body framework, since there must have been a relative forward displacement of the *foramen magnum* (the hole in the base of the skull which links the brain with the spinal cord).

It was many years before my belief in its upright posture received support from any but a handful of scientists throughout the world, and I could never have dreamed in even my most pessimistic moods of the doubts—and in some cases scorn—that would be heaped upon my conclusions.

The Discovery of
Zinjanthropus boisei

MARY LEAKEY AND LOUIS LEAKEY

In 1924, anatomist Raymond Dart identified Australopithecus *(southern ape-human) on the basis of a child's skull found in a lump of solidified cave earth at Taung, South Africa. His claims that the australopithecines lay on the direct human line were highly controversial, and they became widely accepted only in the 1950s. Until 1959,* Australopithecus *was known only from South African sites and was estimated to be less than 1 million years old. Meanwhile, archaeologists Louis and Mary Leakey had been searching for early humans far to the north, in East Africa. During the 1930s and 1940s, they located early butchery sites in Kenya's Rift Valley, and excavated for season after season into undisturbed scatters of stone tools and animal bones at Olduvai Gorge in northern Tanzania, but without finding more than a few hominid teeth.*

After nearly thirty years of excavations, the Leakeys were convinced that Olduvai was the place where early human ancestors would be found. They expected to find fossils with stone tools and animal remains at the edge of an ancient shallow lake, whose beds were stratified in the walls of the great gorge. Hampered by lack of funds and other pressing commitments, the Leakeys were unable to excavate on a large scale. But their persistence paid off with the dramatic discovery by Mary Leakey (b. 1913) of Zinjanthropus boisei *in July 1959. This fragmentary skull of a robustly built australopithecine changed the Leakeys' lives. For the first time, they received sufficient funding for major excavations from the National Geographic Society and other sources. Other fossil discoveries soon followed, among them a lightly built, anatomically more advanced hominid, which Louis Leakey (1903–1972) named* Homo habilis *(handy man), on the assumption that this smaller creature had made the tools found on the same prehistoric land surface. Meanwhile, Garniss Curtis of the University of California applied the new potassium–argon dating technique to volcanic rocks from the hominid levels at Olduvai Gorge and dated* Zinjanthropus *to about 1.75 million years ago. With this one date, Curtis more than doubled the date of human origins.*

The discovery of Zinjanthropus boisei *was a turning point in the study of human origins. Today, we know that toolmaking hominids flourished in East Africa nearly 1 million years before* Homo habilis *and* Zinjanthropus. *But we also know that human evolution was a more complex process than the Leakeys imagined when they made their dramatic discovery in 1959.*

Here is the story of the discovery as told by Mary Leakey in her autobiography, Disclosing the Past. *Her self-effacing account understates the impact of* Zinjanthropus *on the world of paleoanthropology. The find reverberated through science like a thunderclap, turning the search for human origins from a sideline of science into a highly sophisticated, multidisciplinary inquiry.*

In July 1959, we had what seemed to be the first stroke of luck for some while. Heslon Mukiri, inspecting Bed I sites on foot some way down the east end of the Main Gorge, came to MK, a *korongo* named after Donald MacInnes, who had found it during the 1931 expedition. There Heslon found a hominid tooth in a block of limestone, and after the matrix had been removed it was found to be still in place in a fragment of lower jaw. Since MacInnes had originally reported that there were stone tools at MK, this seemed an excellent and promising place to begin our investigation of Bed I. I was not fully convinced in 1959 that there really were Oldowan stone tools contemporary with Bed I, but MK would be a test case. We would have started at once, but for one thing. At Langata we had as near neighbours Armand and Michaela Denis, who made African wildlife and topographic films which had proved popular, especially their "On Safari" series, which was then being shown on British television. Their cameraman was Des Bartlett, whom we also knew well, and we had promised to let them come to Olduvai and film one of our excavations from the start, just as soon as we had a site that looked promising. MK seemed to fit the bill, so we held back the start of work there until Des Bartlett could arrive. There was plenty more prospecting at Bed I exposures that could usefully be done, and only a day or two to wait. . . . It all fitted in nicely. Then Louis got an attack of 'flu and retired to bed, and so it came about that on the morning of 17 July I went out by myself, with the two Dalmatians Sally and Victoria, to see what I could find of interest at nearby Bed I exposures. I turned my steps towards a site not far west of the junction of the two gorges, where we knew that bones and stone artefacts were fairly common on the surface of Bed I sediments. The site was known as FLK, one of the two that Louis had named after Frida, before I knew him.

There was indeed plenty of material lying on the eroded surface at FLK, some no doubt as a result of the rains earlier that year. But one scrap of bone that caught and held my eye was not lying loose on the surface but projecting from beneath. It seemed to be part of a skull, including a mastoid process (the bony projection below the ear). It had a hominid look, but the bones seemed enormously thick—too thick, surely. I carefully brushed away a little of the deposit, and then I could see parts of two large teeth in place in the upper jaw. They *were* hominid. It was a hominid skull, apparently *in situ*, and there was a lot of it there. I rushed back to camp to tell Louis, who leaped out of bed, and then we were soon back at the site, looking at my find together. Louis was sad that the skull was not of an early *Homo*, but he concealed his feelings well and expressed only mild disappointment. *"Zinjanthropus"* had come into our lives. Though we were not immediately aware of it, the whole nature of our research operation at Olduvai was about to alter drastically, and we ourselves were going to be profoundly affected.

The reason why "Zinj" was so important to us was that he captured the public imagination rather than merely exciting the human palaeontologists and stirring up scientific controversy. If we had not had Des Bartlett and his film camera on the spot to record the discovery and excavation of the skull, this might have been much harder to achieve. Zinj made good television, and so a very wide public had the vicarious excitement of "being there when he was dug up." It was the general popular impact of the new skull, combined with the tremendous scientific importance of such a find *in situ* on a rich undisturbed living-floor (for that is what the FLK site proved to contain), that convinced the National Geographic Society in the United States that Louis and I and Olduvai were worth financial support on a scale that exceeded our wildest dreams, starting with $20,200 in 1960. That was what they decided to give us, to carry out a proper excavation at FLK, in return for exclusive American publishing rights for the *National Geographic* magazine, and the right to send a writer and photographer to cover the dig.

There was probably no one in the world better able than Louis to exploit the publicity value, and hence the fund-raising potential, of a find like Zinj. Once we had resources of that kind at our disposal, we were able to work on a scale appropriate to the archaeological sites and the geological problems, and we could import the best specialist advice available as and when we needed it. Therefore further outstanding discoveries were made and continued to be made, and so the National Geographic Society continued to support us, year after year, with great generosity. . . . Other institutions were also anxious to become involved and, as the research expanded and gathered strength, so too established scholars and hopeful students alike were all wanting to come and work at Olduvai. This snowball effect lasted right up to the world recession that began in the middle 1970s, and even in the leaner years since then I have been extremely fortunate in the level of support I have enjoyed. Yet it is in no way fanciful to assert that the start of it all was my happening to notice that fragment of skull on a morning in July 1959 when, but for a promise to friends who wanted to make a film, I should instead have been starting a small trial dig at a quite different site away down the Gorge.

Given that events were to turn out the way I have just indicated, with Louis and myself becoming celebrities whose names were known all over the world, it is curious to recall that when Louis first saw what I had found he was rather disappointed. The reason for this was that the general form of the skull, and the great size of the teeth, showed the fossil to be an australopithecine of some sort rather than an early example attributable to the genus *Homo*, for which Louis was always hoping, since he firmly believed that the australopithecines were not on the direct line of human ancestry, but merely a side branch that eventually became extinct. He soon perked up, however, when he saw how much of the skull was preserved and that, although in many pieces, it was in excellent condition and not distorted by earth pressure. We devoted the rest of our time at Olduvai in 1959 to extracting it, recovering every fragment we could find by sieving and washing the soil, and to demonstrating that it was indeed *in situ* on what was clearly part of an extensive living-floor with many stone artefacts and animal bones. Our trench also yielded a hominid tibia (a leg bone), which Des Bartlett found, and we assumed it belonged to Zinj himself. Sieving the deposit on the erosion slope below the Zinj level produced some skull fragments and the crown of a tooth, which was certainly from a different individual since Zinj already possessed that particular tooth himself. As I had done just over ten years before with *Proconsul*, I again devoted myself to the task of fitting the fragments of the skull back together.

I have referred to the newly found skull as "Zinj" because Louis, when he had studied it, decided it was not after all a straightforward species of *Australopithecus* but a new genus within the hominid family, which he decided to name *Zinjanthropus*, the "Zinj" part of the name coming from an ancient Arabic word for East Africa. To denote the species to which this first member of the supposed new genus belonged, Louis chose the name *boisei*, in honour of Charles Boise, who had given us such valuable support and financial aid over the previous twelve years. He quickly wrote an article for the journal *Nature*, announcing and naming the new find. This should have appeared in mid-August, but one of those printing strikes in which the British seem to specialize delayed publication until early September, and the press release accordingly had to be held back until the technical announcement had been made. The delay in the appearance of *Nature* also meant that care had to be taken when Louis announced the discovery verbally to an excited audience of his colleagues in African archaeology at the Third Pan-African Congress, held at Kinshasa (then Léopoldville) in the Congo, beginning in late August. He and I both attended this meeting, and we flew there from Nairobi, I with Zinj on my knee in a box, rather as I had taken *Proconsul* to London. Nowadays, we should never expose a unique and fragile find to such hazards—an accurate cast would be sent instead; but in 1959 we set out optimistically, and later the same year Louis also flew to London with Zinj, who, by then, was known to his immediate circle of admirers as "Dear Boy."

At the Congress, Zinj attracted enormous attention, and small groups of delegates came to our room for a privileged close examination. Already, grave reservations were being expressed at Louis's identification of a new genus, since robust forms of *Australopithecus* had long been known in South Africa; but Louis was unconvinced. Raymond Dart was particularly pleased and delighted with our discovery. He had been the discoverer of the first australopithecines in South Africa, at Taung and in the Transvaal during the 1920s, and he very charmingly said how happy he was that this great discovery had been made by

Louis and Mary Leakey excavating the Zinjanthropus *site at Olduvai Gorge,
Tanzania, in 1960. Their son Philip and one of Mary's dalmatians
watch the excavation.*

Louis and me. Among others who came to see the skull was another South
African physical anthropologist, Phillip Tobias, who had succeeded Dart in the
Chair of Anatomy at the University of Witwatersrand in Johannesburg. After
discussion with me during the Congress, Louis offered Phillip the task of preparing the technical report on Zinj, which he accepted with amazement and
delight.

In his report, Phillip put Zinj back firmly and formally into the australopithecines, and used his opportunity to sort out the whole tangle of nomenclature
surrounding that genus. He allowed Zinj to be a new species of *Australopithecus,
A. boisei,* and by then Louis was quite prepared to accept this, though he had his
reservations about Phillip's view of the broader picture of hominid evolution.
The general public, however, did not care one way or the other about such
niceties, beyond noting that the scientists had been having a good old fight
among themselves. To them, what really appealed was Phillip's phrase "Nutcracker Man," casually given to Zinj at the time of the Congress in Kinshasa,
because of the huge size of his molar teeth. That caught the popular imagination, and to many people Zinj has been "Nutcracker Man" ever since.

In February 1960 the new series of excavations at Olduvai got under way, and that first season, which began with the excavation of the FLK Bed I site where Zinj had been found, lasted for no less than twelve months.

At Olduvai during 1960 we logged more man-hours in concentrated work than had been expended hitherto in the whole history of the research at the Gorge, thanks not least to the energy of the Wakamba workmen. The principal site studied at first was that where Zinj had been found, and we exposed some 3,600 square feet of the living-floor, noting a curious arc of empty space in the otherwise dense distribution of material, which we thought might indicate the position of a simple windbreak, though no structural traces remained. It was Desmond Clark who first made this suggestion. We also found more hominid remains: a fibula, another tooth, and some fragments of a skull whose structure was much thinner than that of Zinj. Jonathan [our son] had now left school and came down to Olduvai to help for a few months. It was actually he who spotted the hominid fibula at FLK: he was sitting above the baulk that I had left standing in the centre of the excavated area, holding a plumb-bob to help me draw the section and watching the workmen uncovering an area of bones a little way away. "Does any animal have a long thin bone like this?" he asked, tracing the shape he could see with a finger in the air. I said that I couldn't think of one. "Oh, then I think it must be hominid," he said, casually. I dropped my drawing and we rushed round to see. He was quite right. But that was only a start.

Not content with helping at the Zinj excavation, Jonathan liked in spare moments to wander by himself in search of interesting fossil bones. One day in mid-May, near the north end of the series of gullies that make up FLK, he found a fragment of the mandible of a sabre-toothed cat. This was a rare enough species to make it worth sieving the deposits on the surface where Jonathan had made his find, to see if there were more fragments. There were none, but instead the sieving produced a hominid tooth, and shortly afterwards a terminal phalanx—the end bone of a finger or toe. We therefore dug a trench at "Jonny's site" as we called it, though its proper name was FLK NN (FLK North North). Jonathan himself directed the dig and during the course of it, in early November 1960, he personally found some important new hominid material, *in situ* on a living-floor, representing remains of two individuals. Of one, a juvenile, there were not only substantial parts of the skull and the lower jaw but also no less than twenty-one of the small bones that together make up a hand. The other was an adult, probably female, and the most important finds in this case were twelve associated bones that were components of a foot. The group of foot bones I found, but almost everything else was found by Jonathan himself, and it should be stressed that these were no casual items picked up on an erosion surface but were found *in situ* on a datable living-floor.

These new discoveries were very exciting for a number of reasons: they were complementary to Zinj and in many ways more important. The two sites were less than 100 yards apart, which meant that correlation between them was very easy since certain key levels within Bed I were present at both. Thus we knew that the new hominid finds occurred a foot or so below the level of Zinj and in a different deposit, and were therefore a little older. The fragments of the new skull indicated that it was quite different from that of Zinj, even allowing for differences between juvenile and adult. Here was a creature with a larger and better-developed brain, contained within a skull shaped rather more like a modern one, and with thinner cranial bones than Zinj. And then there were the hand and foot bones—a completely unprecedented find for this opening period of the Early Stone Age.

It is one thing trying to work out from the size and shape of a skull, and by estimating brain capacity, how skilled an early hominid *might* have been with his hands, but if you can examine directly the degree of mobility of the hand itself, a quite different order of evidence becomes available. Again, if a few fragments of limb bones are all you have on which to base your judgement of whether or not a given hominid type could walk upright, then the sudden availability of much of a fossilized foot is enormously helpful. That particular point did specifically occur to me soon after I began to excavate the foot bones and more and more of them kept appearing. By the time Phillip Tobias had made a preliminary study of the skull parts and lower jaw, and John Napier and his colleague Michael Day, experts on human palaeontology from London, had between them examined the hand and foot bones, we knew for certain what we had guessed from the start: Jonathan had found a quite different type of hominid from Zinj, but one who was contemporary with him, and indeed had been present at Olduvai before the *Zinjanthropus* living-floor had accumulated. And it was a hominid which in terms of human physical evolution seemed to be one of a far more "advanced" type, relatively larger-brained, able to walk fully upright, and possessing considerable manual dexterity. We were now able to attribute to it most of the hominid remains other than the Zinj skull itself, which we had found at the FLK site—those found on the living-floor, and those we had recovered by sieving on the eroded surface a little way below, which had almost certainly been derived from the floor itself. But what were we to call our new hominid type, and what was his relationship to Zinj?

Louis was predictably delighted by the new finds. In 1959 he had regarded Zinj as the maker of the artefacts at FLK, but here was a far better candidate in terms of both brain and hand. This was right in line with his own theories of *Homo* evolving during the earlier Pleistocene. This had to be *Homo*. He directed his considerable powers of eloquent persuasion towards Phillip Tobias and John Napier, and when the three of them made the formal announcement naming the finds, in an article in *Nature* in 1964, they claimed that the material belonged to *Homo habilis*—that is to say, to a new species within the genus *Homo*. The name *habilis* was suggested by Raymond Dart, to denote the hand was capable of a precision grip: there is no very suitable equivalent word in English, so the press and the popular books have usually made do with "Handy Man," which is about on a par with "Nutcracker Man."

Lucy

DONALD JOHANSON

An explosion of fossil discoveries came after the finding of Zinjanthropus boisei *in 1959. Louis and Mary Leakey continued to work at Olduvai Gorge, while Mary branched out to another site at Laetoli, also in Tanzania, where she found some hominid footprints more than 3.6 million years old. Their son Richard made remarkable fossil discoveries on the eastern shore of Lake Turkana, including many forms of hominid, more early humans* (Homo), *and the earliest humanly manufactured tools in the world, dating to about 2.5 million years ago. East Turkana, Laetoli, and Olduvai took the evolutionary story back to before 3 million years ago, but an even earlier chapter began to unfold in Ethiopia during the 1970s, with the discoveries made by a research team headed by Maurice Taieb, Don Johanson, and Tim White.*

The Hadar region of Ethiopia is hot and desolate, but a major treasure house of early human evolution. Between 5 and 4 million years ago (the exact date is uncertain), the first hominids separated from nonhuman primates. Unfortunately, geologic deposits dating to that critical period are very rare, except in the heart of the Afar desert, where a young palaeoanthropologist named Donald Johanson (b. 1943) made one of the most dramatic fossil discoveries of the twentieth century. The Afar is filled with ancient lake sediments, dating to between 3 and 4 million years ago. A French geologist named Maurice Taieb first located the fossil-rich lake beds and suggested that human remains might be found there. In 1974, Johanson started a long-term exploration of the Afar, specifically to find early hominids. On November 30, 1974, he found the fragmentary bones of Lucy, a diminutive hominid, later named Australopithecus afarensis. *Like Zinjanthropus, Lucy pushed back the boundaries of human evolution, back to a time when our earliest ancestors were standing upright, but not yet making stone tools.*

Lucy was found nearly a quarter-century ago. Since then, Johanson and biological anthropologist Tim White have found the remains of other australopithecines in the Afar, most of them dating to about 3 million years. In 1994, White unearthed an even earlier australopithecine, Australopithecus ramidus, *a hominid that stood upright, but possessed a combination of ape- and humanlike features. Ramidus dates to about 3.8 million years, somewhat earlier than Lucy, but clearly related to Johanson's famous discovery. Each discovery adds new complexity to early human evolution, but few ac-*

*counts give a more immediate picture of the moment of discovery than Don Johanson's
tale in* Lucy *of a hot day in November 1974.*

On the morning of November 30, 1974, I woke, as I usually do on a field expedition, at daybreak. I was in Ethiopia, camped on the edge of a small muddy river, the Awash, at a place called Hadar, about a hundred miles northeast of Addis Ababa. I had been there for several weeks, acting as coleader of a group of scientists looking for fossils.

For a few minutes I lay in my tent, looking up at the canvas above me, black at first but quickly turning to green as the sun shot straight up beyond the rim of hills off to the east. Close to the Equator the sun does that; there is no long dawn as there is at home in the United States. It was still relatively cool, not more than eighty degrees. The air had the unmistakable crystalline smell of early morning on the desert, faintly touched with the smoke of cooking fires. Some of the Afar tribesmen who worked for the expedition had brought their families with them, and there was a small compound of dome-shaped huts made of sticks and grass mats about two hundred yards from the main camp. The Afar women had been up before daylight, tending their camels and goats, talking quietly.

For most of the Americans in camp this was the best part of the day. The rocks and boulders that littered the landscape had bled away most of their heat during the night and no longer felt like stoves when you stood next to one of them. I stepped out of the tent and took a look at the sky. Another cloudless day; another flawless morning on the desert that would turn to a crisper later on. I washed my face and got a cup of coffee from the camp cook, Kabete. Mornings are not my favorite time. I am a slow starter and much prefer evenings and nights. At Hadar I feel best just as the sun is going down. I like to walk up one of the exposed ridges near the camp, feel the first stirrings of evening air and watch the hills turn purple. There I can sit alone for a while, think about the work of the day just ended, plan the next, and ponder the larger questions that have brought me to Ethiopia. Dry silent places are intensifiers of thought, and have been known to be since early Christian anchorites went out into the desert to face God and their own souls.

Tom Gray joined me for coffee. Tom was an American graduate student who had come out to Hadar to study the fossil animals and plants of the region, to reconstruct as accurately as possible the kinds and frequencies and relationships of what had lived there at various times in the remote past and what the climate had been like. My own target—the reason for our expedition—was hominid fossils: the bones of extinct human ancestors and their close relatives. I was interested in the evidence for human evolution. But to understand that, to interpret any hominid fossils we might find, we had to have the supporting work of other specialists like Tom.

"So, what's up for today?" I asked.

Tom said he was busy marking fossil sites on a map.

"When are you going to mark in Locality 162?"

"I'm not sure where 162 is," he said.

"Then I guess I'll have to show you." I wasn't eager to go out with Gray that morning. I had a tremendous amount of work to catch up on. We had had a number of visitors to the camp recently. Richard and Mary Leakey, two well-known experts on hominid fossils from Kenya, had left only the day before. During their stay I had not done any paperwork, any cataloguing. I had not written any letters or done detailed descriptions of any fossils. I *should* have stayed in camp that morning—but I didn't. I felt a strong subconscious urge to go with Tom, and I obeyed it. I wrote a note to myself in my daily diary: *Nov. 30, 1974. To Locality 162 with Gray in AM. Feel good.*

As a paleoanthropologist—one who studies the fossils of human ancestors—I am superstitious. Many of us are, because the work we do depends a great deal on luck. The fossils we study are extremely rare, and quite a few distinguished paleoanthropologists have gone a lifetime without finding a single one. I am one of the more fortunate. This was only my third year in the field at Hadar, and I had already found several. I know I am lucky, and I don't try to hide it. That is why I wrote "feel good" in my diary. When I got up that morning I felt it was one of those days when you should press your luck. One of those days when something terrific might happen.

Throughout most of that morning, nothing did. Gray and I got into one of the expedition's four Land-Rovers and slowly jounced our way to Locality 162. This was one of several hundred sites that were in the process of being plotted on a master map of the Hadar area, with detailed information about geology and fossils being entered on it as fast as it was obtained. Although the spot we were headed for was only about four miles from camp, it took us half an hour to get there because of the rough terrain. When we arrived it was already beginning to get hot.

At Hadar, which is a wasteland of bare rock, gravel and sand, the fossils that one finds are almost all exposed on the surface of the ground. Hadar is in the center of the Afar desert, an ancient lake bed now dry and filled with sediments that record the history of past geological events. You can trace volcanic-ash falls there, deposits of mud and silt washed down from distant mountains, episodes of volcanic dust, more mud, and so on. Those events reveal themselves like layers in a slice of cake in the gullies of new young rivers that recently have cut through the lake bed here and there. It seldom rains at Hadar, but when it does it comes in an overpowering gush—six months' worth overnight. The soil, which is bare of vegetation, cannot hold all that water. It roars down the gullies, cutting back their sides and bringing more fossils into view.

Gray and I parked the Land-Rover on the slope of one of those gullies. We were careful to face it in such a way that the canvas water bag that was hanging from the side mirror was in the shade. Gray plotted the locality on the map.

Then we got out and began doing what most members of the expedition spent a great deal of their time doing: we began surveying, walking slowly about, looking for exposed fossils.

Some people are good at finding fossils. Others are hopelessly bad at it. It's a matter of practice, of training your eye to see what you need to see. I will never be as good as some of the Afar people. They spend all their time wandering around in the rocks and sand. They have to be sharp-eyed; their lives depend on it. Anything the least bit unusual they notice. One quick educated look at all those stones and pebbles, and they'll spot a couple of things a person not acquainted with the desert would miss.

Tom and I surveyed for a couple of hours. It was now close to noon, and the temperature was approaching 110. We hadn't found much: a few teeth of the small extinct horse *Hipparion;* part of the skull of an extinct pig; some antelope molars; a bit of a monkey jaw. We had large collections of all these things already, but Tom insisted on taking these also as added pieces in the overall jigsaw puzzle of what went where.

"I've had it," said Tom. "When do we head back to camp?"

"Right now. But let's go back this way and survey the bottom of that little gully over there."

The gully in question was just over the crest of the rise where we had been working all morning. It had been thoroughly checked out at least twice before by other workers, who had found nothing interesting. Nevertheless, conscious of the "lucky" feeling that had been with me since I woke, I decided to make that small final detour. There was virtually no bone in the gully. But as we turned to leave, I noticed something lying on the ground partway up the slope.

"That's a bit of a hominid arm," I said.

"Can't be. It's too small. Has to be a monkey of some kind."

We knelt to examine it.

"Much too small," said Gray again.

I shook my head. "Hominid."

"What makes you so sure?" he said.

"That piece right next to your hand. That's hominid too."

"Jesus Christ," said Gray. He picked it up. It was the back of a small skull. A few feet away was part of a femur: a thighbone. "Jesus Christ," he said again. We stood up, and began to see other bits of bone on the slope: a couple of vertebrae, part of a pelvis—all of them hominid. An unbelievable, impermissible thought flickered through my mind. Suppose all these fitted together? Could they be parts of a single, extremely primitive skeleton? No such skeleton had ever been found—anywhere.

"Look at that," said Gray. "Ribs."

A single individual?

"I can't believe it," I said. "I just can't believe it."

"By God, you'd better believe it!" shouted Gray. "Here it is. Right here!" His voice went up into a howl. I joined him. In that 110-degree heat we began jumping up and down. With nobody to share our feelings, we hugged each

*The fragmentary bones of Lucy
(Australopithecus afarensis)
displayed in the laboratory.*

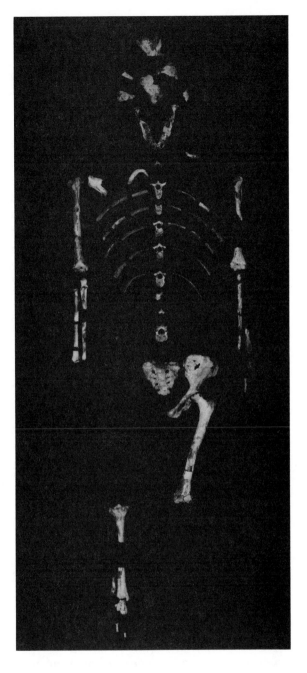

other, sweaty and smelly, howling and hugging in the heat-shimmering gravel, the small brown remains of what now seemed almost certain to be parts of a single hominid skeleton lying all around us.

"We've got to stop jumping around," I finally said. "We may step on something. Also, we've got to make sure."

"Aren't you sure, for Christ's sake?"

"I mean, suppose we find two left legs. There may be several individuals here, all mixed up. Let's play it cool until we can come back and make absolutely sure that it all fits together."

We collected a couple of pieces of jaw, marked the spot exactly and got into the blistering Land-Rover for the run back to camp. On the way we picked up two expedition geologists who were loaded down with rock samples they had been gathering.

"Something big," Gray kept saying to them. "Something big. Something *big*."

"Cool it," I said.

But about a quarter of a mile from camp, Gray could not cool it. He pressed his thumb on the Land-Rover's horn, and the long blast brought a scurry of scientists who had been bathing in the river. "We've got it," he yelled. "Oh, Jesus, we've got it. We've got The Whole Thing!"

That afternoon everyone in camp was at the gully, sectioning off the site and preparing for a massive collecting job that ultimately took three weeks. When it was done, we had recovered several hundred pieces of bone (many of them fragments) representing about 40 percent of the skeleton of a single individual. Tom's and my original hunch had been right. There was no bone duplication.

But a single individual of what? On preliminary examination it was very hard to say, for nothing quite like it had ever been discovered. The camp was rocking with excitement. That first night we never went to bed at all. We talked and talked. We drank beer after beer. There was a tape recorder in the camp, and a tape of the Beatles song "Lucy in the Sky with Diamonds" went belting out into the night sky, and was played at full volume over and over again out of sheer exuberance. At some point during that unforgettable evening—I no longer remember exactly when—the new fossil picked up the name of Lucy, and has been so known ever since, although its proper name—its acquisition number in the Hadar collection—is AL 288-1. . . .

For five years I kept Lucy in a safe in my office in the Cleveland Museum of Natural History. I had filled a wide shallow box with yellow foam padding, and had cut depressions in the foam so that each of her bones fitted into its own tailor-made nest. *Everybody* who came to the museum—it seemed to me—wanted to see Lucy. What surprised people most was her small size.

Her head, on the evidence of the bits of her skull that had been recovered, was not much larger than a softball. Lucy herself stood only three and one-half feet tall, although she was fully grown. That could be deduced from her wisdom teeth, which were fully erupted and had been exposed to several years of wear. My best guess was that she was between twenty-five and thirty years old when she died. She had already begun to show the onset of arthritis or some other bone ailment, on the evidence of deformation of her vertebrae. If she had lived much longer, it probably would have begun to bother her.

Her surprisingly good condition—her completeness—came from the fact that she had died quietly. There were no tooth marks on her bones. They had not been crunched and splintered, as they would have been if she had been killed by a lion or a saber-toothed cat. Her head had not been carried off in one direction and her legs in another, as hyenas might have done with her. She had simply settled down in one piece right where she was, in the sand of a long-vanished lake edge or stream—and died. Whether from illness or accidental drowning, it was impossible to say. The important thing was that she had not been found by a predator just after death and eaten. Her carcass had remained inviolate, slowly covered by sand or mud, buried deeper and deeper, the sand hardening into rock under the weight of subsequent depositions. She had lain silently in her adamantine grave for millennium after millennium until the rains at Hadar had brought her to light again.

That was where I was unbelievably lucky. If I had not followed a hunch that morning with Tom Gray, Lucy might never have been found. Why the other people who looked there did not see her, I do not know. Perhaps they were looking in another direction. Perhaps the light was different. Sometimes one person sees things that another misses, even though he may be looking directly at them. If I had not gone to Locality 162 that morning, nobody might have bothered to go back for a year, maybe five years. Hadar is a big place, and there is a tremendous amount to do. If I had waited another few years, the next rains might have washed many of her bones down the gully. They would have been lost, or at least badly scattered; it would not have been possible to establish that they belonged together. What was utterly fantastic was that she had come to the surface so recently, probably in the last year or two. Five years earlier, she still would have been buried. Five years later, she would have been gone. As it was, the front of her skull was already gone, washed away somewhere. We never did find it. Consequently, the one thing we really cannot measure accurately is the size of her brain.

Lucy always managed to look interesting in her little yellow nest—but to a nonprofessional, not overly impressive. There were other bones all around her in the Cleveland Museum. She was dwarfed by them, by drawer after drawer of fossils, hundreds of them from Hadar alone. There were casts of hominid specimens from East Africa, from South Africa and Asia. There were antelope and pig skulls, extinct rodents, rabbits and monkeys, as well as apes. There was one of the largest collections of gorilla skulls in the world. In that stupefying array of bones, I kept being asked, What was so special about Lucy? Why had she, as another member of the expedition put it, "blown us out of our little anthropological minds for months"?

"Three things," I always answered. "First: what she is—or isn't. She is different from anything that has been discovered and named before. She doesn't fit anywhere. She is just a very old, very primitive, very small hominid. Somehow we are going to have to fit her in, find a name for her.

"Second," I would say, "is her completeness. Until Lucy was found, there just weren't any very old skeletons. The oldest was one of those Neanderthalers I spoke of a little while ago. It is about 75,000 years old. Yes, there *are* older hominid fossils, but they are all fragments. Everything that has been reconstructed from them has had to be done by matching up those little pieces—a tooth here, a bit of jaw there, maybe a complete skull from somewhere else, plus a leg bone from some other place. The fitting together has been done by scientists who know those bones as well as I know my own hand. And yet, when you consider that such a reconstruction may consist of pieces from a couple of dozen individuals who may have lived hundreds of miles apart and may have been separated from each other by a hundred thousand years in time—well, when you look at the complete individual you've just put together you have to say to yourself, 'Just how real is he?' With Lucy you know. It's all there. You don't have to guess. You don't have to imagine an arm bone you haven't got. You *see* it. You see it for the first time from something older than a Neanderthaler."

"How much older?"

"That's point number three. The Neanderthaler is 75,000 years old. Lucy is approximately 3.5 million years old. She is the oldest, most complete, best-preserved skeleton of any erect-walking human ancestor that has ever been found."

The Cro-Magnons

EDOUARD LARTET AND LOUIS LARTET

The establishment of the antiquity of humankind in 1859 left archaeologists with an enormous and undated landscape of the human past. Clearly, Jacques Boucher de Perthes's handax makers of the Somme and the Neanderthal people dated to many thousands of years ago. But what separated these early Stone Age people from the farmers and civilizations of later times? Dramatic archaeological discoveries in southwestern France soon added a new chapter to the European Stone Age.

These finds came at the hands of an amateur scientist with a passion for fossil animals. Edouard Lartet (1801–1871) was a magistrate in the Gers district of southern France. His real enthusiasm was geology, and he eventually abandoned the law for paleontology. In 1852, Lartet heard of a buried cave at Aurignac in the Haute-Garonne, where a roadmaker had found seventeen human skeletons buried with reindeer bones and flint tools. The skeletons were reburied in a local cemetery before Lartet learned of the discovery, but he realized that they were Stone Age finds and searched for more sites in the Pyrenees. He dug up engraved antler and bone objects at the Massat Cave in Ariège, but moved to the Les Eyzies area of the Dordogne in 1863, after recovering a box of flints from a rock shelter near the village. Between 1863 and 1871, Lartet dug into great rock shelters at Gorge d'Enfer, Laugerie Haute, La Madeleine, and Le Moustier, now some of the most famous prehistoric sites in Europe, which eventually gave their names to Stone Age cultures and periods. He was assisted and financed by the English banker Henry Christy, who had traveled widely in Mexico and had a strong interest in archaeology and anthropology.

Lartet's discoveries were not only spectacular, but scientifically of great importance. He soon established that the inhabitants of the Les Eyzies sites had lived along the Vezère River at a time when the climate was much colder than it is today and when mammoth, reindeer, and other cold-loving animals flourished in southwestern France. In a famous monograph, Reliquiae Acquitanicae *(1865–1875), written with his friend Christy, Lartet identified important changes in the Stone Age societies in the caverns, from the simpler culture of the Neanderthals at Le Moustier Cave (later known as the "Mousterian") to the sophisticated tool kits of the people of La Madeleine nearby (the "Magdalenian"). He was able to show that his late Ice Age people had*

*flourished by the Vezère River after the Neanderthals, while the late Ice Age was at its
height. Lartet also discovered magnificent examples of engraved antler—bearing natu-
ralistic depictions of wild horses, reindeer, and other animals—and sophisticated weapons
like antler harpoons and thong straighteners. These superb engravings and sculpted
objects with their minute, often vivid artistry caused a sensation when Lartet exhibited
them in Paris. One of the people who saw the exhibit was an obscure Spanish nobleman,
Don Marcellino de Sautola. A decade later, he and his daughter María discovered the
magnificent paintings of bison in the cave at Altamira.*

*But who were these artists and reindeer hunters? Lartet shoveled his way through
many cubic meters of cave and rock-shelter fill without finding any human remains.
Then, in 1868, as the first parts of* Reliquiae Acquitanicae *were in press, some workmen constructing the new Les Eyzies railroad station uncovered a hitherto unknown
rock shelter, named Cro-Magnon after a large boulder. They found some stone artifacts
and bones, which reached the hands of Edouard Lartet's son Louis, who happened to be
in the village. Louis excavated into the thick deposits at the back of the Cro-Magnon
rock shelter. There he uncovered the skeletons of several "reindeer" people, accompanied
by shell beads, stone artifacts, and other finds.*

*The anatomists who examined the Cro-Magnon skeletons realized at once that they
were of modern appearance, unlike the beetle-browed Neanderthals. But they refused to
believe that these ancient hunters and artists had the same intellectual capacities as
modern humans. The Lartets and their contemporaries believed that the Cro-Magnons
were more primitive than modern humans, perhaps people more akin to the Inuit of
the arctic with their simple culture. Perhaps this is hardly surprising, since Edouard
and Louis lived at a time when doctrines of racial superiority were all-pervasive and
European civilization was regarded as the pinnacle of human achievement. More recent
research has shown that the Cro-Magnons had the same anatomical and intellectual
capacities as twentieth-century humans. The brilliant flowering of their culture was a
highlight of late Ice Age life eighteen thousand years ago.*

*Louis Lartet yielded a more fluent pen than his father, who had many years of legal
writing behind him. Here is Louis's account of the discovery of the Cro-Magnon burials
from* Reliquiae Acquitanicae.

Passing from Limoges to Agen by railway for the first time, and traversing the
tortuous defiles of Périgord, we cannot but feel surprise and admiration on
seeing the Vezère flow in the deep valley whose freshness is in marked contrast
with its bare and rocky escarpments. These picturesque cliffs, sharply limiting
the river's course, and not unfrequently fantastic in shape, attract the traveller's
attention, indifferent though he be, by a succession of unexpected and striking
effects. Soon the eye becomes familiarized with the forms of the rocks, and we
recognize a multitude of cavities in the cliffs. Some of them are natural; others
have been carefully worked out by man, and are sometimes even now used as
portions of the rural habitations. The Romans, Normans, and English have succeeded one another in this little Perigordian Petra; and the chronicles of the

Middle Ages comprise curious documents relative to the part played in the wars of those times by the Roc de Tayac, where we still find, cut in the limestone, rooms, galleries, and stables, constituting indeed a veritable castle.

The cave-dwellers, however, the oldest and strangest of all whom these rocks of Tayac have sheltered, were, without doubt, the hunters of the reindeer, who trod our soil when a crowd of strange animals existed here—such as the mammoth, lion, reindeer, musk ox, aurochs, and others, now extinct or completely driven from our climate. The stations of these hunters are numerous on the banks of the Vezère; and the natural caves which served them for retreats, carefully explored by MM. H. Christy and E. Lartet, have of late years yielded up the secrets of their primitive industry and of their savage life. Little, however, has hitherto been determined as to their ethnic characters—and that only from unsatisfactory specimens, found in possibly abnormal positions. It was therefore with lively curiosity that, towards the end of last March, we were made acquainted with the discovery of some human skeletons in this district, under conditions which cannot fail to prove their high antiquity. . . .

The rocky cliffs out of which are hollowed the caves on the banks of the Vezère consist of the edges of the nearly horizontal strata of Cretaceous limestones, which the river and watercourses have deeply cut in excavating their beds. The faces of the cliffs present great parallel furrows or flutings, at several different levels and of great length. At first sight these chamfered lines seem attributable to the rapid and long-continued passage of strong currents much above the present level of the river; but on further examination we easily see that these parallel flutings have been produced by the incessant degradation of the soft, laminated, and therefore absorbent beds intercalated among harder strata, under the influence of atmospheric agents, particularly frost. This explanation, adopted by my father, has been developed with much sagacity by M. Alain Laganne. Among the proofs which he has advanced, the most conclusive appears to me to be furnished by the fact that at certain places, where the inclination of the limestone bands have a direction different from that of the fall of the river-bed, the flutings follow the dip of the bands, thus showing their independence of the slope of the valley. In accordance with the greater energy of atmospheric action there have been produced in these cliffs the flutings, the rock-shelters, and the true caves, in which the reindeer-hunters could find a refuge and a home.

The accumulation of rubbish detached from the friable strata gives rise, at the foot of these scarped rocks, to the formation of a talus of comminuted débris, lying at the highest "angle of rest"; and these accumulations sometimes entirely mask the flutings and rock-shelters of lower levels. One of these latter, covered by a talus 4 metres thick, has been found 880 metres northwest of the village of Les Eyzies, and 130 metres southeast of the Les Eyzies Railway-station, at a place called Cro-Magnon, and at the foot of a rock the upper part of which stands up detached, roughly resembling a great mushroom.

This newly discovered shelter would perhaps have remained for ever unknown if the construction of the railway-embankment close by had not occasioned the removal of a considerable portion of the talus, and of a gigantic block, detached from the neighbouring rocks and measuring 311 cubic metres, and afterwards the pulling down of a projecting ledge of rock above the talus.

Lastly, towards the end of March, two contractors at Les Eyzies, MM. Bertou-Meyrou and Delmarés, took away still more of the talus, as material for a road near by; and, after having removed 4 metres of the débris covering the shelter, the workmen, digging further beneath the projecting ledge which they had thus exposed, soon came upon broken bones, worked flints, and, lastly, human skulls, the antiquity and scientific importance of which the contractors immediately recognized. With prudence and good feeling, such as are unfortunately too often wanting, but which all lovers of paleoethnological studies will be glad to hear of, the contractors at once stopped the works, and hastened to write to M. Alain Laganne, whose affairs had taken him to Bordeaux. Returning to Les Eyzies, M. Laganne some days after exhumed, in the presence of MM. Galy and Simon, of Périgueux, two skulls and some other fragments of a human skeleton, as well as worked bones of reindeer and many chipped flint implements. It was now that the Minister for Public Instruction sent me to Les Eyzies, where, having surmounted some unexpected difficulties, thanks to M. the prefect of the Dordogne, and to the obliging concurrence of MM. the mayor and the curé of Tayac, I was soon able to proceed with a regular and systematic exhumation of the sepulture and its approaches.

First of all it was necessary to support the vault of the shelter or cave by a pillar; for a deep crack threatened its fall, or at least its giving way. In digging a hole for the base of this pillar, we were able to determine the succession of four black beds of ashes, one on another, the lowest of which contained the stump of the tusk of an elephant; and this, although damaged by the pickaxe, was of sufficient interest to induce the Reverend P. Sanna Solaro, present at the discovery, to help me in disengaging it from the matrix. The pillar having been set up, we methodically excavated the several beds, one by one; and thus determined very exactly their nature, relations, and contents. As, however, in these respects they present a perfect analogy among themselves, excepting that they increase in thickness from below upwards, I shall very briefly describe them in the order of their formation.

The cave of Cro-Magnon is formed by a projecting ledge of Cretaceous limestone, . . . having a thickness of 8 metres and a length of about 17 metres. The bed which it overlies, and the destruction of which has given rise to the cave, abounds with *Rhynchonella vespertilio*, which is a type fossil, fixing the geological horizon. The débris of this marly and micaceous limestone had accumulated on the original floor of the cavern to a great thickness, at least for 0.70 metre, when the hunters of the reindeer stopped here for the first time, leaving as a trace of their short stay a blackish layer, from 0.05 to 0.15 metre thick, containing worked flints, bits of charcoal, broken or calcined bones, and in its upper portion the elephant-tusk before alluded to.

This first hearth is covered by a layer, 0.25 metre thick, of calcareous débris,

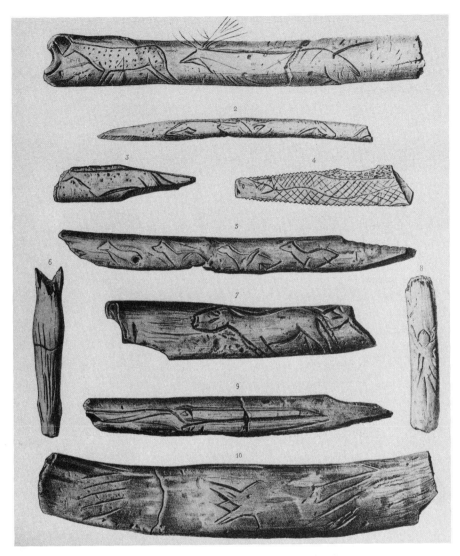

*Engraved antler fragments adorned with horses, reindeer, and other
motifs from rock shelters in the Les Eyzies area of southwestern
France. They belong to the so-called Magdalenian culture, named
after the celebrated La Madeleine shelter, excavated by Louis and
Edouard Lartet, from which they come.*

detached bit by bit from the roof, during the temporary disuse of the shelter.
Then follows another thin layer of hearth-stuff, 0.10 metre thick, also containing pieces of charcoal, bones, and worked flints. This bed is in its turn
overlain by a layer of fallen limestone rubbish, 0.50 metre thick. Lastly there is
over these a series of more important layers, all of them containing, in different
proportions, charcoal, bones (broken, burnt, and worked), worked flints (of dif-

ferent types, but chiefly scrapers), flint cores, and pebbles of quartz, granite, etc. from the bed of the Vezère and bearing numerous marks of hammering. Altogether these layers seem to have reference to a period during which the cave was inhabited, if not continuously, at least at intervals so short as not to admit of intercalations of débris falling from the roof between the different hearth-layers which correspond with the successive phases of this (the third) period of habitation. The first (lowest) of these layers is full of charcoal, and has a thickness of 0.20 metre; it does not touch the back of the cave, but extends a little further than the earlier layers. At its line of contact with the calcareous débris beneath, the latter is strongly reddened by the action of fire.

On the last-mentioned hearth-layer is a bed of unctuous reddish earth, 0.30 metre thick, containing similar objects, though in less quantities. Last in succession is a carbonaceous bed, the widest and thickest of all, having an average thickness of 0.30 metre; at the edges it is only 0.10 metre thick; but in the centre, where it cuts into the subjacent deposits, which were excavated by the inhabitants in making the principal hearth, it attains a depth of 0.60 metre. This bed, being by far the richest in pieces of charcoal, in bones, pebbles of quartz, worked flints, flint cores, and bone implements, such as points or dart-heads, arrow-heads, etc., may be regarded as indicative of a far more prolonged habitation than the previous.

Above this thick hearth-layer is a bed of yellowish earth, rather argillaceous, also containing bones, flints, and implements of bone, as well as amulets or pendants. This appears to be limited upwards by a carbonaceous bed, very thin and of little extent, 0.05 metre thick, which M. Laganne observed before my arrival, but of which only slight traces remained afterwards.

It was on the upper part of this yellow band, and at the back of the cave, that the human skeletons and the accessories of the sepulture were met with; and all of them were found in the calcareous débris, except in a small space in the furthest hollow at the back of the cave. This last deposit also contains some worked flints, mixed up with broken bones, and with some uninjured bones referable to small rodents and to a peculiar kind of fox.

Lastly, above these different layers, and all over the shelter itself, lay the rubbish of the talus (4 to 6 metres thick), sufficient in itself, according to what we have said above about its mode of formation, to carry back the date of the sepulture to a very distant period in the Prehistoric Age.

As for the human remains and the position they occupied in bed, the following are the results of my careful inquiries in the matter. At the back of the cave was found an old man's skull, which alone was on a level with the surface, in the cavity not filled up in the back of the cave, and was therefore exposed to the calcareous drip from the roof, as is shown by its having a stalagmitic coating on some parts. The other human bones, referable to four other skeletons, were found around the first, within a radius of about 1.50 metres. Among these bones were found, on the left of the old man, the skeleton of a woman, whose skull presents in front a deep wound, made by a cutting instrument, but which did not kill her at once, as the bone has been partly repaired within; indeed our physicians think that she survived several weeks. By the side of the woman's skeleton was that of an infant which had not arrived at its full time of foetal development. The other skeletons seem to have been those of men.

Amidst the human remains lay a multitude of marine shells (about 300), each pierced with a hole, and nearly all belonging to the species *Littorina littorea* so common on our Atlantic coasts. Some other species, such as *Purpura lapillus*, *Turritella communis*, etc., occur, but in small numbers. These also are perforated, and, like the others, have been used for necklaces, bracelets, or other ornamental attire. Not far from the skeletons, I found a pendant or amulet of ivory, oval, flat, and pierced with two holes. There were also found near the skeletons several perforated teeth, a large block of gneiss, split and presenting a large smoothed surface; also worked antlers of reindeer, and chipped flints, of the same types as those found in the hearth-layers underneath.

To resume: —The presence, at all levels, of the same kind of flint scrapers, as finely chipped as those of the Gorge d'Enfer, and of the same animals as in that classic Station, evidently shows them to be relics of the successive habitation of the Cro-Magnon shelter by the same race of nomadic hunters, who at first could use it merely as a rendezvous, where they came to share the spoils of the chase taken in the neighbourhood; but coming again, they made a more permanent occupation, until their accumulated refuse and the débris gradually raised the floor of the cave, leaving the inconvenient height of only 1.20 metres between it and the roof; and then they abandoned it by degrees, returning once more at last to conceal their dead there. No longer accessible, except perhaps to the foxes above noticed, this shelter and its strange sepulture were slowly and completely hidden from sight by atmospheric degradation bringing down the earthy covering, which, by its thickness alone, proves the great antiquity of the burial in the cave.

The presence of the remains of an enormous bear, of the mammoth, of the great cave-lion, of the reindeer, the spermophile, etc. in the hearth-beds strengthens in every way this estimation of their antiquity; and this can be rendered more rigorously still if we base our argument on the predominance of the horse here in comparison with the reindeer, on the form of the worked flints and of the bone arrow- and dart-heads, and on the above-mentioned indications of hunting, as well as on the absence of any engraving or carving. Hence we may refer this station of Cro-Magnon to the age immediately preceding that artistic period which saw in this country the first attempts of the engraver and the sculptor.

Whence came these ancient men of the Vezère? Here the geologist must be silent. His duty is to confirm the facts forming the subject of this introductory notice, as far as they belong to his domain. To the anthropologist we look to enlighten us on the characters of the race. It may, however, be remarked that the sea-shells associated with the sepulture at Cro-Magnon are in no wise of Mediterranean origin, but belong only to the Atlantic Ocean, and are notably common on the shores of La Charente. This fact may be taken in consideration together with the circumstance of there being in this sepulture several pebbles of basalt, which could not have been taken from the valley of the Vezère, but might well have been brought from that of the Dordogne. Hence we are led to suppose that before coming to the Cave District, where they found conditions so favourable for their mode of life, the reindeer-hunters had sojourned on our Atlantic coasts, and that they arrived at the banks of the Vezère after having ascended the Valley of the Dordogne.

PART II
GREAT DISCOVERIES

The great tide of civilization has long since ebbed, leaving those scattered wrecks on the solitary shore. Are those waters to flow again, bringing back the seeds of knowledge and wealth that they have wafted to the West? We wanderers were seeking what they had left behind, as children gather up the coloured shells on the deserted sands.

—Austen Henry Layard, *Nineveh and Its Remains*, 1849

rchaeology has long made international headlines: the discovery of Assyrian palaces in Mesopotamia, John Lloyd Stephens and Frederick Catherwood's lyrical descriptions of Mayan cities, Heinrich Schliemann's claims that he found Troy. The headlines began in the adventurous days of nineteenth-century archaeological endeavor and continue to this day, with the tomb of Tutankhamun in the 1920s, the Sumerian royal burial at Ur in the 1930s, and the Lords of Sipán, Peru, in the 1980s and 1990s. Part II explores some of the great archaeological discoveries of the past two hundred years, focusing on both the classic accounts of a century ago and many, often lesser known finds of more recent decades. The selections make no pretense at comprehensive treatment or at geographical balance. I have simply chosen vivid accounts of important finds, as much as possible described by the person who found them. Taken together, they provide a portrait of a rapidly changing archaeology, which began as a nineteenth-century adventure story and ended as a science, with the fieldworker concentrating on the small scale rather than the entire palace or civilization.

The nineteenth century was the classic era of archaeological discovery, of high adventure and breathless searches for priceless finds and lost civilizations. One could describe it as the "Indiana Jones" period, for the stereotypes of archaeology and archaeologists that fascinated the Victorian public are with us to this day. They form part of the essential legacy of what Elizabethan antiquarian William Camden once called the "backward looking curiosity." It is no coincidence that many of the selections in this section come from the early days, when an archaeologist was as much a traveler as a scholar, a popular writer as an excavator.

Our story begins with General Napoleon Bonaparte's invasion of Egypt in 1798. The scientists he took with him to document ancient and modern Egypt revealed exotic Egyptian civilization to an astounded Europe. Their findings sparked intense competition for all kinds of antiquities from the Nile Valley. Both Britain and France appointed consuls in Egypt in 1815, their task to collect mummies and antiquities for museums at home. A motley crowd of adventurers and opportunists descended on the country, among them circus strongman turned archaeologist Giovanni Belzoni. Belzoni used his expertise with levers and gunpowder to assemble fabulous collections of antiquities, many of which ended up in the British Museum. "Those were the great days of excavating," wrote Howard Carter of Tutankhamun fame in the 1920s. "If there was a difference with a brother excavator, one laid for him with a gun." Belzoni fled Egypt in fear of his life.

Adventure, plunder, and spectacular lost civilizations: the three went hand in hand during much of the nineteenth century. Many early archaeologists were diplomats or little more than professional adventurers. In their train came scholars, such as French linguistic genius Jean François Champollion, who deciphered hieroglyphs in 1822. Englishman John Gardner Wilkinson followed in his footsteps and devoted a lifetime to unspectacular scholarship, to recording inscriptions on stone and papyri and using them to paint the first portraits of ancient Egyptian life. There have always been self-effacing archaeologists who have labored quietly out of the limelight, often salvaging vital historical crumbs from the devastation wrought by their more ambitious brethren.

Buoyed by its success in Egypt, the French government established a diplomatic presence in Mesopotamia for purely archaeological purposes in 1840. Paul Emile Botta was appointed French consul in Mosul, northern Iraq, and was ordered to find biblical Nineveh. Three years later, he unearthed Assyrian king Sargon's palace at Khorsabad, with its superb bas-reliefs of royal processions and human-headed animals. "Nineveh est découvert," he announced to a fascinated world, but he was wrong. Englishman Austen Henry Layard upstaged Botta handsomely with enormous excavations at the biblical city of Nimrud and at Nineveh itself, where Botta had found nothing by digging in the wrong place. Layard was an unashamed adventurer, looking for spectacular finds for public display in London. His employers were not disappointed.

Archaeology was still very much an adventure in the 1840s. When New York lawyer and travel writer John Lloyd Stephens and artist Frederick Catherwood set off in search of lost cities in Central America in 1839, they did so with a firm objective of eventual profit in mind. Their best-selling books and pictures brought classic Mayan civilization (A.D. 200–900) into the public eye as the Boston historian William Prescott published his *Conquest of Mexico* in 1843. But the main preoccupation of Victorians was biblical and classical archaeology. The first biblical excavations were in French hands, while British army engineers tunneled surreptitiously beneath Jerusalem. German archaeologist Heinrich Schliemann became obsessed with Homer's epics and with discovering the site of Homeric Troy. His obsession was crowned with triumph when he trenched into the Hissarlik mound in northwestern Turkey. He found what he proclaimed to be Priam's Troy, although he was not the first to dig there and make such a claim. Most archaeologists worked in Europe and the Near East at the time. But every find, however remote, was tied to the Mediterranean world, wherever possible. Such was the case with Great Zimbabwe in central Africa in 1871, where German geologist Carl Mauch became convinced that he had found the queen of Sheba's lost palace, on the grounds that a wooden lintel smelled the same as his cedarwood pencil!

A more sophisticated generation of discoveries came with the new century, by which time Egyptologist Flinders Petrie and others were insisting on the importance of small finds as much as spectacular monuments. The discoveries of Herbert Winlock, Howard Carter, and others in Egypt brought more refined excavation methods and a greater appreciation of the importance of hieroglyphs in studying Egyptian civilization. Late-nineteenth-century Mesopotamian archaeology had been little more than a race for clay tablets, but gradually more scientific approaches prevailed, notably in the research of the Germans and of Leonard Woolley at Ur. His excavations at this most famous of early cities were one of the last heroic digs with large teams of workers and a minimal number of trained supervisors. But Woolley's results were a spectacular vindication of his methods and laid the foundations for the more specialized, slower-moving excavations and surveys of the post–World War II era.

Twentieth-century archaeology began as a provincial, often largely amateur enterprise in the hands of small numbers of often wealthy scholars. But the character of the discipline changed during the 1930s, when professional archaeologists and professional training became more commonplace, especially in Europe, the Near East, and North America. No longer did one learn by informal apprenticeship. And many of the new professionals left their homelands and worked in distant lands, often as employees of colonial governments, in Africa, Asia, and the Pacific. At the same time, American archaeology became a truly international activity, as long-term research projects began in Central and South America, often supported by private philanthropy.

Since World War II, the small world of archaeology has expanded dramatically. Today, there are thousands of archaeologists in Europe and North America, more than four hundred Egyptologists, and several hundred archaeologists in Australia and New Zealand. The pace of archaeological discovery has accelerated with the number of excavators, but, inevitably, archaeology itself has become more specialized, more focused on narrower problems. This intense specialization is a product both of the impact of the sciences on archaeology, with radiocarbon and potassium–argon dating techniques, and of a host of high-tech and just downright ingenious methods for reconstructing the past. Thus many of the unusual discoveries of recent years have been in distant lands or have resulted from the application of specialized methods. For example, careful study of ancient tree rings has led to the reconstruction of major drought cycles in the American Southwest, while the analysis of tiny beetle remains provides clear proof of the presence or absence of houses in waterlogged settlements. There seems to be no limit to the ingenuity of modern archaeologists.

A century ago, archaeology encompassed a vast time scale from human origins to classical times. Today, the archaeologist is at work not only on early sites dating to long before written history, but also on historical sites, where a combination of documents and archaeology provides unique perspectives on the complex interactions between different social groups and levels of ancient society. Archaeology is a priceless, dispassionate eye into the past, for the artifacts of ancient times provide a telling record of human behavior, of the ways in which different members of a society negotiated with one another and coped with prevailing conditions. In the final analysis, the human past is not just a record of rulers and statesmen going about their business. It is a complex record of individuals and groups living and dying, being happy or unhappy, quarreling or trying to understand one another. It is a record of continual, ever changing interactions between people, rich and poor, important and humble, literate or anonymous because they could not write. The challenge for the archaeologist is to reconstruct and understand the past using only the durable and surviving remains of ancient behavior. This is why some of them have chosen to investigate modern urban landfills, to learn more about the behavior of modern humans as a basis for understanding that of our predecessors.

As the selections in Part II show, archaeologists have been brilliantly successful at this task—working not only in royal tombs, but on small, long-forgotten settlements where almost nothing remains to be found. Indeed, some of the "great discoveries" in the pages that follow come from the most unspectacular of sites and are known to us only because of the ingenuity and instinct of those who found them.

Tomb Robber by the Nile

GIOVANNI BELZONI

Of all the early archaeologists, none is more compelling than the circus strongman turned excavator Giovanni Belzoni (1778–1823). His exploits along the Nile immediately after the Napoleonic Wars epitomize the free and easy ways of antiquities collecting in the early years of archaeology.

Belzoni was born in Padua, Italy, and made his early living throughout Europe as a salesman of religious objects. In 1803, he went on the stage in London as a strongman, acquiring the honorific title "The Patagonian Sampson." Tall, handsome, and gifted with prodigious strength, Belzoni became a fixture in circuses and theaters during the Napoleonic Wars. During these years, he became expert with levers, "hydraulicks," and weights, useful skills for a fledgling tomb robber. A chance encounter with one of Pasha Mohammed 'Ali's sea captains in Malta in 1814 brought Belzoni and his family to Egypt, where he attempted to sell the ruler a mechanized water pump. The venture foundered, and Belzoni found himself penniless. British consul Henry Salt employed him to remove a recumbent head of Ramesses II from a temple near Thebes to Alexandria, a task that Belzoni performed with the aid of levers, rollers, and hundreds of men. He went on to collect a rich haul of antiquities from the Thebes area and far upstream, soon acquiring a reputation as an efficient and ruthless acquisitor.

By all accounts, Belzoni was adept with the local villagers, but he did not hesitate to use force to get his way with minor officials, if need be. During his three-year sojourn along the Nile, he opened the Abu Simbel temple for the first time since antiquity, penetrated the burial chamber of the Second Pyramid of Giza, and recovered the alabaster sarcophagus of Seti I from its resting place in the pharaoh's tomb in the Valley of the Kings. He also acquired a vast collection of antiquities and papyri (manuscripts written on papyrus reed "paper") for Henry Salt and his own account. Born with a wanderlust, Belzoni also traveled across the desert to the ancient port of Berenice on the Red Sea and to the famous Temple of Jupiter Amun in the western desert.

By 1819, Belzoni was in serious trouble with his rivals. He fled Egypt in fear of his life, exhibited his finds to popular acclaim in London's Egyptian Hall, and then, ever looking for a new challenge, perished in an abortive attempt to discover the source of West Africa's River Niger, a great geographical prize of the day. Belzoni was little more

*than a tomb robber, but he was more responsible than many of his competitors, taking
the trouble to record the wall paintings in Seti I's tomb with unusual care.*

*Most of what we know about Giovanni Belzoni comes from his own account of his
adventures along the Nile, written in 1820. He is said to have spoken broken English
"with a pretty accent." Belzoni's* Narrative of Operations and Recent Discoveries
. . . in Egypt and Nubia *is a plodding account except for this memorable tale of an
accident deep in a mummy cave.*

It took us three days to reach Thebes, when we moored our bark at Luxor, and
I recommenced my operations with what fellahs I could obtain. . . . Could it
but be accurately known, with what a wretched set of people in these tribes
travellers have to deal, their mean and rapacious dispositions, and the various
occurrences that render the collection of antiquities difficult, whatever came
from thence would be the more prized, from the consideration of these circumstances. . . .

Gournou is a tract of rocks, about two miles in length, at the foot of the
Libyan mountains, on the west of Thebes, and was the burial-place of the great
city of a hundred gates. Every part of these rocks is cut out by art, in the form
of large and small chambers, each of which has its separate entrance; and,
though they are very close to each other, it is seldom that there is any interior
communication from one to another. I can truly say, it is impossible to give any
description sufficient to convey the smallest idea of these subterranean abodes,
and their inhabitants. There are no sepulchres in any part of the world like
them; there are no excavations, or mines, that can be compared to these truly
astonishing places; and no exact description can be given of their interior, owing
to the difficulty of visiting these recesses. The inconveniency of entering into
them is such that it is not everyone who can support the exertion. . . .

Of some of these tombs many persons could not withstand the suffocating
air, which often causes fainting. A vast quantity of dust rises, so fine that it
enters into the throat and nostrils, and chokes the nose and mouth to such a
degree that it requires great power of lungs to resist it and the strong effluvia
of the mummies. . . . In some places there is not more than a vacancy of a foot
left, which you must contrive to pass through in a creeping posture like a snail,
on pointed and keen stones that cut like glass. After getting through these passages, some of them two or three hundred yards long, you generally find a
more commodious place, perhaps high enough to sit. But what a place of rest!
surrounded by bodies, by heaps of mummies in all directions; which, previous
to my being accustomed to the sight, impressed me with horror. The blackness
of the wall, the faint light given by the candles or torches for want of air, the
different objects that surrounded me, seeming to converse with each other, and
the Arabs with the candles or torches in their hands, naked and covered with
dust, themselves resembling living mummies, absolutely formed a scene that
cannot be described. In such a situation I found myself several times, and often

Giovanni Belzoni dressed in Turkish costume, as seen in a portrait from his Narrative of Operations and Recent Discoveries . . . in Egypt and Nubia *(1820).*

G. BELZONI.

returned exhausted and fainting, till at last I became inured to it, and indifferent to what I suffered, except from the dust, which never failed to choke my throat and nose: and though, fortunately, I am destitute of the sense of smelling, I could taste that the mummies were rather unpleasant to swallow. After the exertion of entering into such a place, through a passage of fifty, a hundred, three hundred, or perhaps six hundred yards, nearly overcome, I sought a resting place, found one and contrived to sit; but when my weight bore on the body of an Egyptian, it crushed it like a bandbox. I naturally had recourse to my hands to sustain my weight, but they found no better support; so that I sunk altogether among the broken mummies, with a crash of bones, rags, and wooden cases, which raised such a dust as kept me motionless for a quarter of an hour, waiting till it subsided again. I could not remove from the place, however, without increasing it, and every step I took I crushed a mummy in some part or other. Once I was conducted from such a place to another resembling it, through a passage of about twenty feet in length, and no wider than that a body could be forced through. It was choked with mummies, and I could not pass without putting my face in contact with that of some decayed Egyptian; but as the passage inclined downwards, my own weight helped me on: however I could not avoid being covered with bones, legs, arms, and heads rolling from above. Thus I proceeded from one cave to another, all full of mummies piled up in various ways, some standing, some lying, and some on their heads. The purpose of my researches was to rob the Egyptians of their papyri; of which I found a few hidden in their breasts, under their arms, in the space above the knees, or on the legs, and covered by the numerous folds of cloth that envelop the mummy. The people of Gournou, who make a trade of antiquities of this sort, are very jealous of strangers, and keep them as secret as possible, deceiving travellers by pretending that they have arrived at the end of the pits, when they are scarcely at the entrance.

The Decipherment
of Egyptian Hieroglyphs

Jean François Champollion and Tomkyns Turner

The decipherment of Egyptian hieroglyphs by Jean François Champollion in 1822 was a landmark in early archaeology. Early investigators had compared the mysterious hieroglyphs with Chinese script or had assumed they were a form of picture writing. All attempts at decipherment foundered until Napoleon's soldiers found the Rosetta Stone in the Nile Delta in 1799. The stone bears a decree of the Egyptian priesthood in 199 B.C., a script written in three columns. The first is hieroglyphs; the second, demotic, a late form of cursive ancient Egyptian script; and the third, Greek. Everyone, including Napoleon himself, recognized that the Rosetta Stone held the key to decipherment. Despite the state of war between England and France, Napoleon ordered plaster copies of the stone to be sent to savants throughout Europe. But the defeat of his armies meant that the stone ended up in the British Museum, where it remains to this day.

The stone gave up its secrets reluctantly, for the hieroglyphs bore no resemblance to picture writing. Scholars concentrated on the demotic version of the inscription, thought to be an alphabetical version of ancient Egyptian writing. English physician Thomas Young compared the three versions of the Rosetta inscription. By inspired guesswork, he concluded that the demotic script was a cursive form of hieroglyphs, a form of writing that bore little resemblance to the symbolic writing of classic glyphs. But final decipherment came at the hands of Jean François Champollion (1790–1832), a brilliant linguist who had mastered several Eastern languages, including Coptic, before he was out of his teens. In 1807, he moved to Paris, where he spent fifteen years working on hieroglyphs. In September 1822, he identified Ramesses II's cartouche (an elliptical circle encircling the name of an Egyptian king) at the temple of Abu Simbel in Nubia and realized that the king's name was spelled out phonetically. A few days later, he announced his discovery in his famous "Lettre à M. Dacier." His theories generated furious controversy, but independent checks soon showed that he had deciphered hieroglyphs beyond all reasonable doubt. Within two years, Champollion had completed a précis of the script, which showed it was a combination of ideographic (characters symbolizing ideas) and phonetic signs. In 1828, the egotistical and headstrong Champollion led a trium-

phant tour of Egypt and was the first visitor to read the inscriptions in the field. Cham-
pollion died at a tragically early age four years later. All modern Egyptology is based on
his decipherment.

The extracts that follow are a translation of Jean François Champollion's original
letter, announcing the decipherment, and a report on the situation by Tomkyns Turner,
a fellow of the Society of Antiquaries in London.

Letter to M. Dacier concerning the alphabet of the phonetic hieroglyphs.

Sir,

It is to your generous patronage that I owe the indulgent attention which the Académie Royale des Inscriptions et Belles-Lettres has been pleased to accord to my work on the Egyptian scripts, in allowing me to submit to it my two reports on the *hieratic*, or priestly, script and the *demotic*, or popular one: after this flattering trial, I may at last venture to hope that I have successfully shown that these two types of writing are neither of them composed of alphabetic letters, as had been so widely supposed, but consist of ideograms, like the hieroglyphs themselves, that is, expressing the concepts rather than the sounds of a language; and to believe that after ten years of dedicated study I have reached that point where I can put together an almost complete survey of the general structure of these two forms of writing, the origin, nature, form, and number of their signs, the rules for their combination by means of those symbols which fulfil purely logical and grammatical functions, thus laying the first foundations for what might be termed the grammar and dictionary of these two scripts, which are found on the majority of monuments, and the interpretation of which will throw so much light on the general history of Egypt. With regard to the demotic script in particular, there is enough of the precious Rosetta inscription to identify the whole; scholastic criticism is indebted first to the talents of your illustrious colleague, M. Silvestre de Sacy, and successively to the late M. Akerblad and Dr. Young, for the first accurate ideas drawn from this monument, and it is from this same inscription that I have deduced the series of demotic symbols which, taking on syllabic-alphabetic values, were used in ideographic texts to express the proper names of persons from outside Egypt. It is by this means also that the name of the Ptolemies was discovered, both in this same inscription and in a papyrus manuscript recently brought from Egypt.

Accordingly, it only remains, in completing my study of the three types of Egyptian writing, for me to produce my account of the pure hieroglyphs. I dare to hope that my latest efforts will also have a favourable reception from your famous society, whose good will has been so valuable in encouragement to me.

However, in the present condition of Egyptian studies, when relics abound on every side, collected by kings as much as by connoisseurs, and when, too, with regard to these relics, the world's scholars eagerly devote themselves to laborious researches and strive for an intimate understanding of those written memorials which must serve to explain the rest, I do not think I should delay in offering to these scholars, under your honoured auspices, a short but vital list of new discoveries, which belong properly to my account on the hieroglyphic script, and which will undoubtedly spare them the pains I took in establishing them, and perhaps also some grave misconceptions about the various periods of the history of Egyptian culture and government in general: for we are dealing with the series of hieroglyphs which, making an exception to the general nature of the signs of this script, were given the property of expressing word sounds, and served for the inscription on Egyptian national monuments of the titles, names and surnames of the Greek or Roman rulers who successively governed the country. Many truths concerning the history of this famous country must spring from this new result of my researches to which I was led quite naturally.

The interpretation of the demotic text on the Rosetta inscription, by means of the accompanying Greek text, had made me realize that the Egyptians used a certain number of demotic characters, which assumed the property of expressing sounds, to introduce into their ideographic writings proper names and words foreign to the Egyptian language. We see at once the indispensable need for such a practice in an ideographic system of writing. The Chinese, who also use an ideographic script, have an exactly similar provision, created for the same reason.

The Rosetta monument shows us the application of this auxiliary method of writing, which I have termed *phonetic*, that is, expressing the sounds, in the proper names of the kings Alexander and Ptolemy, the queens Arsinoe and Berenice, in the proper names of six other persons, Aetes, Pyrrha, Philinus, Areia, Diogenes and Irene, and in the Greek words ΞΥΝΤΑΞΙΣ and OΥΗΝΝ. . . .

The hieroglyphic text of the Rosetta inscription, which would have lent itself so felicitously to this study, owing to its cracks, yielded only the name Ptolemy.

The obelisk found on the island of Philae and recently brought to London also contains the hieroglyphic name of a Ptolemy, written in the same symbols as on the Rosetta inscription and similarly enclosed in a cartouche, and this is followed by a second cartouche, which must contain the proper name of a woman, a Ptolemaic queen, since this cartouche ends with the feminine hieroglyphic signs which also follow the hieroglyphic proper names of every Egyptian goddess without exception. The obelisk was, as it were, tied to a pedestal bearing a Greek inscription which is a supplication from the priests of Isis at Philae to the king, Ptolemy, his sister Cleopatra and his wife Cleopatra. If this obelisk and its hieroglyphic inscription resulted from the plea of the priests, who actually mention the consecration of a similar monument, the cartouche with the female name could only be that of a Cleopatra. This name, and that of Ptolemy, which have certain like letters in Greek, had to serve for a comparative study of the hieroglyphic symbols which composed the two; and if identical signs in these two names stood for the same sounds in both cartouches, they would have to be entirely phonetic in character.

A preliminary comparison had also made me realize that these same two names, written phonetically in the demotic script, contained a number of identical characters. The resemblance between the three Egyptian scripts in their general principles caused me to look for the same phenomenon and the same correspondences when the same names were given in hieroglyphs: this was soon confirmed by simple comparison of the hieroglyphic cartouche containing the name Ptolemy and that on the Philae obelisk which I believed, according to the Greek text, must contain the name Cleopatra.

The first sign in the name Cleopatra, which resembles a kind of *quadrant*, and which would represent the K, should have been absent from the name Ptolemy. It was.

The second sign, a *lion couchant*, which would give the Λ, is exactly similar to the fourth sign in the name Ptolemy, also a Λ (Πτολ).

The third sign in the name Cleopatra is a *feather* or *leaf*, standing for the short vowel E; we also see two similar leaves at the end of the name Ptolemy, which, from their position, can only have the value of the diphthong AI in ΑΙΟΣ.

The fourth character in the cartouche for the hieroglyphic Cleopatra, the representation of a kind of *flower with a bent stem*, would stand for the O in the Greek name of this queen. It is in fact the third character in the name Ptolemy (Πτο).

The fifth sign in the name Cleopatra, which appears as a *parallelogram* and must represent the Π, is equally the first sign in the hieroglyphic name Ptolemy.

The sixth sign, standing for the vowel A of ΚΛΕΟΠΑΤΡΑ, is a *hawk*, and does not occur in the name Ptolemy, nor should it.

The seventh character is an *open hand*, representing the T; but this hand does not occur in the word Ptolemy, where the second letter, the T, is expressed by a *segment of a circle*, which, none the less, is also a T; for we shall see why these two hieroglyphs have the same sound.

The eighth sign of ΚΛΕΟΠΑΤΡΑ, which is a frontal *mouth*, and which would be the P, does not occur in the cartouche of Ptolemy, nor should it.

Finally, the ninth and last sign in the queen's name, which must be the vowel A, is in fact the *hawk* which we have already seen representing this vowel in the third syllable of the same name. This proper name ends in the two hieroglyphic symbols for the feminine gender: that of Ptolemy ends in another sign, which consists of a bent shaft, equivalent to the Greek . . . as we shall see.

The combined signs from the two cartouches, analyzed phonetically, thus already yielded us twelve signs, corresponding to eleven consonants, vowels, or diphthongs in the Greek alphabet, A, AI, E, K, Λ, M, O, Π, P, Σ, T.

The phonetic value of these twelve signs, already very probable, becomes indisputable if, applying these values to other cartouches or small enclosed panels containing proper names and taken from Egyptian hieroglyphic monuments, we are enabled to read them effortlessly and systematically, producing the proper names of rulers foreign to the Egyptian language. . . .

You, sir, will doubtless share all my astonishment when the same alphabet of phonetic hieroglyphs, applied to a host of other cartouches carved on the same piece of work, will give you titles, names, and even surnames of Roman emperors, spoken in Greek and written with these same phonetic hieroglyphs.

We read here, in fact:

The imperial title Αυτοκρατωρ, occupying a whole cartouche to itself, or else followed by other still persisting ideographic titles, transcribed ΑΟΤΟΚΡΤΡ, ΑΟΥΚΡΥΟΡ, ΑΟΥΑΚΡΥΡ, and even ΑΥΥΟΚΑΤΛ, the Λ being used as a bastard substitute (pardon the expression) for the P.

The cartouches containing this title are almost always next to, or connected with, a second cartouche containing as we shall shortly see, the proper names of emperors. But occasionally we also find this word in absolutely isolated cartouches. . . .

But it remains, sir, for us to survey briefly the nature of the phonetic system governing the writing of these names, to form an accurate estimate of the character of the signs used, and to investigate the reasons for adopting the image of one or another object to represent a particular consonant or vowel more than another. . . .

I am in no doubt, sir, that if we could definitely determine the object represented or expressed by all the other phonetic hieroglyphs comprised in our alphabet, it could be a relatively easy matter for me to show, in the Egyptian-Coptic lexicons, that the names of these same objects begin with the consonant or vowels which their image represents in the phonetic hieroglyph system.

This method, followed in the composition of the Egyptian phonetic alphabet, gives us an idea to what point we could, if we wished, continue multiplying the number of phonetic hieroglyphs without sacrificing the clarity of their expression. But everything seems to indicate that our alphabet, by and large, contains them. We are, in fact, justified in drawing this conclusion, since this alphabet is the result of a series of phonetic proper names carved on Egyptian monuments during a period of about five centuries in various parts of the country.

It is easy to see that the vowels of the hieroglyphic alphabet are used indiscriminately one for another. On this point we can do no more than establish the following general rules:

1. The hawk, the ibis, and three other kinds of birds are consistently used for A:

2. The leaf or feather can stand for both the short vowels A and E, sometimes even O.

3. The twin leaves or feathers can equally well represent the vowels I and H, or the dipthongs IA and AI.

All I have just said on the origin, formation, and anomalies of the *phonetic hieroglyph* alphabet applies almost entirely to the *demotic phonetic* alphabet. . . .

These two systems of phonetic writing were as intimately connected as the *hieratic ideographic* system was with the *popular ideographic*, which was no more than its descendant, and the *pure hieroglyphs*, which were its source. The demotic

The Rosetta Stone.

letters are generally, in fact, as I have said, the same as the hieratic signs for hieroglyphs which are themselves phonetic. You, sir, will have no difficulty in recognizing the truth of this assertion, if you trouble to consult the comparative table of hieratic signs classified beside the corresponding hieroglyph, the table which I presented before the Académie des Belles-Lettres more than a year ago. So there is basically no other difference between the hieroglyphic and demotic alphabets but the actual form of the signs, their values, and even the reasons for those values being identical. Finally I would add that since these popular phonetic symbols were merely unchanged hieratic characters, there cannot, of necessity, have been more than *two* phonetic writing systems in Egypt:

1. The *phonetic hieroglyph* script, used on public monuments.
2. The *hieratic-demotic* script, used for Greek proper names in the middle text of the Rosetta inscription and the demotic papyrus in the royal library . . . and which we shall perhaps see one day used to transcribe the name of some Greek or Roman ruler in the rolls of papyrus written in the hieratic script.

Phonetic writing, then, was in use among every class of the Egyptian nation, and they employed it for a long time as a necessary adjunct to the three ideographic methods. When, as a result of their conversion to Christianity, the Egyptian people received the alphabetic Greek script from the apostles, and then had to write all the words of their maternal tongue with this new alphabet, adoption of which cut them off forever from the religion, history, and institutions of their ancestors, all monuments being, by this act, "silenced" for these neophytes and their descendants, yet these Egyptians still retained some trace of their ancient phonetic method; and we see in fact that in the oldest Coptic texts in the Theban dialect, most of the short vowels are completely omitted, and that often, like the hieroglyphic names of Roman emperors, they consist of no more than strings of consonants interspersed at long intervals by a few vowels, almost always long. This resemblance seemed to me worth noting. The Greek and Latin writers have left us no formal remarks on the Egyptian phonetic script; it is very difficult to deduce even the existence of this system, forcing the sense of certain passages where something of the kind would seem to be vaguely hinted at. So we must abandon the attempt to study through historical tradition the period when the phonetic scripts were introduced into the ancient Egyptian picture-writing.

But the facts speak well enough for themselves to enable us to say with fair certainty that the employment of an auxiliary script in Egypt to represent the sounds and articulations of certain words preceded Greek and Roman domination, although it seems most natural to attribute the introduction of the semialphabetic Egyptian script to the influence of these two European nations, which had long been using a true alphabet.

Here I base my opinion on the two following considerations, which, sir, may seem to you a solid enough weight to tip the scales.

1. If the Egyptians had invented their phonetic script in imitation of the Greek or Roman alphabet, they would naturally have established a number of phonetic signs equal to the known elements of the Greek or Latin alphabet. But there is nothing of the kind; and the incontestable proof that the Egyptian phonetic writing arose for a totally different purpose from that of expressing the

sounds of proper names of Greek or Roman rulers is found in the Egyptian transcription of these very names, which are mostly corrupted to the point of being unrecognizable; firstly by the suppression or confusion of most of the vowels, secondly by the persistent use of the consonants T for Δ, K for T, Π for I; and lastly by the accidental use of Λ for P and P for Λ.

2. I am positive that the same signs in phonetic hieroglyphs used to represent the sounds of Greek and Roman proper names were also used in ideographic texts carved long before the Greeks reached Egypt, and that they already had, in certain contexts, the same value representing sounds or articulations as in the cartouches carved under the Greeks and Romans. The development of this valuable and decisive point is connected with my work on the pure hieroglyphs. I could not set out the proof in this letter without plunging into extraordinarily prolonged complications.

Thus, sir, I believe that phonetic writing existed in Egypt at a far distant time; that it was first a necessary part of the ideographic script; and that it was then used also, after Cambyses, as we have it, to transcribe (crudely, it is true) in ideographic texts the proper names of peoples, countries, cities, rulers, and individual foreigners who had to be commemorated in historic texts or monumental inscriptions.

I dare say more: it would be possible to recover, in this ancient Egyptian phonetic script, imperfect though it may be in itself, if not the source, at least the model on which the alphabets of the western Asiatic nations were framed, above all those of Egypt's immediate neighbours. If you note in fact, sir:

1. that each letter of the alphabets which we term Hebrew, Chaldean, and Syriac bears a distinguishing name, very ancient appellations, since they were almost all transmitted by the Phoenicians to the Greeks when the latter took over the alphabet;

2. that the *first consonant or vowel of these names* is also, in these alphabets, the *vowel or consonant to be read*, you will see, with me, in the creation of these alphabets, a perfect analogy with the creation of the phonetic alphabet in Egypt: and if alphabets of this type are, as everything indicates, primitively formed from signs representing ideas or objects, it is evident that we must recognize the nation who invented this method of written expression in those who particularly used an ideographic script; I mean, in sum, that Europe, which received from ancient Egypt the elements of the arts and sciences, is yet further in her debt for the inestimable benefit of alphabetic writing.

However, I have only tried here to indicate briefly the many important consequences of this discovery, and it arose naturally from my main subject, the alphabet of the phonetic hieroglyphs, the general structure of which, together with some applications, I proposed to expound at the same time. The latter produced results which have already met with a favourable response from the illustrious members of the Académie, whose scholastic studies have given Europe the first principles of solid learning, and continue to offer her the most valuable of examples. My attempts may perhaps add something to the record of definite achievements by which they have enriched the history of ancient peoples; that of the Egyptians, whose just fame still echoes round the world; and it is certainly no little achievement today that we can take with assurance the first step in the study of their written memorials, and thence gather some precise notion of their leading institutions, to which antiquity itself gave a name for wisdom which nothing has yet overthrown. As for the remarkable monuments erected by the Egyptians, we can at last read, in the cartouches which adorn them, their fixed chronology from Cambyses and the times of their foundation or their successive accretions under the various dynasties which ruled Egypt; the majority of these monuments bear simultaneously the names of pharaohs and of Greeks and Romans, the former, characterized by their small numbers of signs, perpetually resisting every attempt to apply to them successfully the alphabet I have just discovered. Such, sir, I hope, will be the value of this work, which I am flattered to produce under your honoured auspices; the enlightened public will not refuse me its admiration or its support, since I have obtained those of the venerable Nestor of scholarship and French literature, whose devoted studies honour and adorn them, and who, with a hand at once protective and encouraging, is ever pleased to support and guide, in the hard course which he has so gloriously covered, so many young imitators who have later wholly justified his enthusiastic patronage. Happy to rejoice in my turn, I would not, however, venture to make a reply but for my deep gratitude, and my respectful affection; permit me, I beg you, sir, to repeat publicly all my assurances of that affection.

J. F. Champollion the younger
Paris, 22 September, 1822.

————

Argyle Street, May 30, 1810

Sir,

The Rosetta Stone having excited much attention in the learned world, and in this society in particular, I request to offer them, through you, some account of the manner it came into the possession of the British army, and by what means it was brought to this country, presuming it may not be unacceptable to them.

By the sixteenth article of the capitulation of Alexandria, the siege of which city terminated the labours of the British army in Egypt, all the curiosities, natural and artificial, collected by the French Institute and others, were to be delivered up to the captors. This was refused on the part of the French general to be fulfilled, by saying they were all private property. Many letters passed; at length on consideration that the care in preserving the insects and animals had made the property in some degree private, it was relinquished by Lord Hutchinson; but the artificial, which consisted of antiquities and Arabian manuscripts, among the former of which was the Rosetta Stone, was insisted upon by the noble general with his usual zeal for science. Upon which I had several conferences with the French general Menou, who at length gave way, saying that the Rosetta Stone was his private property, but, as he was forced, he must comply as well as the other proprietors. I accordingly received from the under secretary of the institute, Le Père, the secretary Fourier being ill, a paper, containing a list of the antiquities, with the names of the claimants of each piece of sculpture: the stone is there described of black granite, with three inscriptions, belonging to General Menou. From the French sçavans I learnt that the Rosetta Stone was found among the ruins of Fort Saint-Julien, when repaired by the French and put in a state of defence: it stands near the mouth of the Nile, on the Rosetta branch, where are, in all probability, the pieces broken off. I was also informed that there was a stone similar at Menouf, obliterated, or nearly so, by the earthen jugs being placed on it, as it stood near the water; and that there was a fragment of one, used and placed in the walls of the French fortifications of Alexandria. The stone was carefully brought to General Menou's house in Alexandria, covered with soft cotton cloth, and a double matting, where I first saw it. The general had selected this precious relick of antiquity for himself. When it was understood by the French army that we were to possess the antiquities, the covering of the stone was torn off, and it was thrown upon its face, and the excellent wooden cases of the rest were broken off; for they had taken infinite pains, in the first instance, to secure and preserve from any injury all the antiquities. I made several remonstrances, but the chief difficulty I had was on account of this stone, and the great sarcophagus, which at one time was positively refused to be given up by the Capitan Pasha, who had obtained it by having possession of the ship it had been put on board of by the French. I procured, however, a sentry on the beach from M. Le Roy, prefect maritime, who, as well as the general, behaved with great civility; the reverse I experienced from some others.

When I mentioned the manner the stone had been treated to Lord Hutchinson, he gave me a detachment of artillerymen and an artillery engine, called, from its powers, a devil cart, with which that evening I went to General Menou's house, and carried off the stone, without any injury, but with some difficulty, from the narrow streets, to my house, amid the sarcasms of numbers of French officers and men: being ably assisted by an intelligent sergeant of artillery, who commanded the party, all of whom enjoyed great satisfaction in their employment: they were the first British soldiers who entered Alexandria. During the time the stone remained at my house, some gentlemen attached to the corps of sçavans requested to have a cast, which I readily granted, provided the stone should receive no injury; which cast they took to Paris, leaving the stone well cleared from the printing ink, which it had been covered with to take off several copies to send to France when it was first discovered.

Having seen the other remains of ancient Egyptian sculpture sent on board the admiral, Sir Richard Bickerton's, ship, the *Madras*, who kindly gave every possible assistance, I embarked with the Rosetta Stone, determining to share its fate, on board the Egyptienne frigate, taken in the harbour of Alexandria, and arrived at Portsmouth in February 1802. When the ship came round to Deptford, [the stone] was put in a boat and landed at the customhouse; and Lord Buckinghamshire, the then Secretary of State, acceded to my request, and permitted it to remain some time at the apartments of the Society of Antiquaries, previous to its deposit in the British Museum, where I trust it will long remain, a most valuable relick of antiquity, the feeble but only yet discovered link of the Egyptian to the known languages, a proud trophy of the arms of Britain (I could almost say *spolia opima*), not plundered from defenceless inhabitants, but honourably acquired by the fortune of war.

I have the honour to be, Sir,

Your most obedient, and most humble servant,

H. Turner, Major General

Assyrian Palaces at Nimrud

AUSTEN HENRY LAYARD

Until the 1840s, the Assyrians of 2 Kings were but a shadowy presence on the frontiers of biblical history who had swooped on Judah "like lions on the fold." Then the French decided to search for Nineveh. They appointed Paul Emil Botta as their consul in the small town of Mosul to search for the biblical city. Botta found not Nineveh, but King Sargon's palace at nearby Khorsabad. The discovery of ancient Nineveh fell to a remarkable young Englishman, Austen Henry Layard, one of the heroic archaeologists of the nineteenth century.

Austen Henry Layard (1817–1894) was destined for a career in law. But he rebelled against the office life and set out with a friend to ride from England to Ceylon. He became captivated with the desert and Mesopotamia, spending a year among the fierce Bakhtiari nomads of Iran. After some years as a diplomatic agent in Constantinople, Layard prevailed on Sir Stratford Canning, British ambassador to the sultan of Turkey, to subsidize excavations on the mounds of northern Mesopotamia. In 1845, he dug into Nimrud, biblical Calah, where he discovered three Assyrian royal palaces and magnificent bas-reliefs very similar to those found by Botta at Khorsabad some years before. Layard's finds caused a sensation in London. He was lionized by high society. His Nineveh and Its Remains *(1849) became a best seller, selling as many copies as "Mrs Rundell's cookbook," Layard wrote with pride.*

Originally, Layard claimed that Nimrud was Nineveh. His later excavations into Kuyunjik mound opposite Mosul unearthed the palace of Sennacherib and the royal archives of King Ashurbanipal. Layard simply shoveled the thousands of clay tablets that composed the archive into wicker baskets and shipped them to London without further ado. It took more than thirty years for experts to decipher them, for cuneiform scholarship was in its infancy in the mid-nineteenth century. A number of scholars, among them a cavalry officer and orientalist named Henry Rawlinson, had begun to decipher cuneiform, which identified Kuyunjik as biblical Nineveh. Layard's excavations were aimed at finding as many spectacular finds as possible. He achieved his goal by tunneling around the walls of palace chambers, doing irreparable damage in the process. At Kuyunjik, Layard's men dug more than three kilometers of tunnels, clearing seventy rooms of their sculptures and contents.

As the Nineveh excavations drew to a close, Layard turned his attention to the mounds of southern Mesopotamia. He dug into Babylon, but his methods were too crude to allow him to distinguish between sun-dried brick and the surrounding soil. On his return to London in 1851, Layard turned from archaeology to politics, ending up as a successful ambassador in Madrid and Constantinople. His second book, Discoveries in the Ruins of Nineveh and Babylon *(1853), was another best seller, and contained the first attempt to interpret Assyrian civilization with cuneiform.*

Austen Henry Layard's Nineveh and Its Remains *tells how he moved a winged bull from Nimrud to the banks of the Tigris. This best seller, still in print after nearly 150 years, also gives a vivid account of an Assyrian palace revealed in his excavation.*

The Trustees of the British Museum had not contemplated the removal of either a winged bull or lion, and I had at first believed that, with the means at my disposal, it would have been useless to attempt it. They wisely determined that these sculptures should not be sawn into pieces, to be put together again in Europe, as the pair of bulls from Khorsabad. They were to remain, where discovered, until some favourable opportunity of moving them entire might occur; and I was directed to heap earth over them, after the excavations had been brought to an end. Being loath, however, to leave all these fine specimens of Assyrian sculpture behind me, I resolved upon attempting the removal and embarkation of two of the smallest and best preserved. I had wished to secure the pair of lions forming the great entrance into the principal chamber of the northwest palace; the finest specimens of Assyrian sculpture discovered in the ruins. But after some deliberation I determined to leave them for the present; as, from their size, the expense attending their conveyance to the river would have been very considerable.

I formed various plans for lowering the smaller lion and bull, for dragging them to the river, and for placing them upon rafts. Each step had its difficulties, and a variety of original suggestions and ideas were supplied by my workmen, and by the good people of Mosul. At last I resolved upon constructing a cart sufficiently strong to bear any of the masses to be moved. As no wood but poplar could be procured in the town, a carpenter was sent to the mountains with directions to fell the largest mulberry tree, or any tree of equally compact grain, he could find; and to bring beams of it, and thick slices from the trunk, to Mosul.

By the month of March this wood was ready. I purchased from the dragoman of the French Consulate a pair of strong iron axles, formerly used by M. Botta in bringing sculptures from Khorsabad. Each wheel was formed of three solid pieces, nearly a foot thick, from the trunk of a mulberry tree, bound together by iron hoops. Across the axles were laid three beams, and above them several cross-beams, all of the same wood. A pole was fixed to one axle, to which were also attached iron rings for ropes, to enable men, as well as buffaloes, to draw the cart. The wheels were provided with moveable hooks for the same purpose.

Simple as this cart was, it became an object of wonder in the town. Crowds came to look at it, as it stood in the yard of the vice-consul's khan; as long as the cart was in Mosul, it was examined by every stranger who visited the town. But when the news spread that it was about to leave the gates, and to be drawn over the bridge, the business of the place was completely suspended. The secretaries and scribes from the palace left their divans; the guards their posts; the bazaars were deserted; and half the population assembled on the banks of the river to witness the manœuvres of the cart. A pair of buffaloes, with the assistance of a crowd of Chaldaeans and shouting Arabs, forced the ponderous wheels over the rotten bridge of boats. The cart was the topic of general conversation in Mosul until the arrival, from Europe, of some children's toys—barking dogs and moving puppets—which gave rise to fresh excitement, and filled even the gravest of the clergy with wonder at the learning and wisdom of the Infidels.

To lessen the weight of the lion and bull, without in any way interfering with the sculpture, I reduced the thickness of the slabs, by cutting away as much as possible from the back. Their bulk was thus considerably diminished; and as the back of the slab was never meant to be seen, being placed against the wall of sun-dried bricks, no part of the sculpture was sacrificed. As, in order to move these figures at all, I had to choose between this plan and that of sawing them into several pieces, I did not hesitate to adopt it.

To enable me to move the bull from the ruins, and to place it on the cart in the plain below, a trench was cut nearly two hundred feet long, about fifteen feet wide, and, in some places, twenty feet deep. A road was thus constructed from the entrance, in which stood the bull, to the edge of the mound. About fifty Arabs and Nestorians were employed in the work. . . .

As the bull was to be lowered on its back, the unsculptured side of the slab having to be placed on rollers, I removed the walls behind it. An open space was thus formed, large enough to admit of the sculpture when prostrate, and leaving room for the workmen to pass on all sides of it. The principal difficulty was of course to lower the mass: when once on the ground, or on rollers, it could be dragged forwards by the united force of a number of men; but, during its descent, it could only be sustained by ropes. If they chanced to break, the sculpture would be precipitated to the ground, and would, probably, be broken in the fall. The few ropes I possessed had been expressly sent to me, across the desert, from Aleppo; but they were small. From Baghdad I had obtained a thick hawser, made of the fibres of the palm. In addition I had been furnished with two pairs of blocks, and a pair of jack-screws belonging to the steamers of the Euphrates expedition. These were all the means at my command for moving the bull and lion. The sculptures were wrapped in mats and felts, to preserve them, as far as possible, from injury in case of a fall; and to prevent the ropes chipping or rubbing the alabaster.

The bull was ready to be moved by the 18th of March. The earth had been taken from under it, and it was now only supported by beams resting against the opposite wall. Amongst the wood obtained from the mountains were several thick rollers. These were placed upon sleepers or half beams, formed out of the trunks of poplar trees, well greased and laid on the ground parallel to the sculpture. The bull was to be lowered upon these rollers. A deep trench had been cut behind the second bull, completely across the wall. A bundle of ropes coiled round this isolated mass of earth served to hold two blocks, two others being attached to ropes wound round the bull to be moved. The ropes, by which the sculpture was to be lowered, were passed through these blocks; the ends, or falls of the tackle, as they are technically called, being led from the blocks above the second bull, and held by the Arabs. The cable having been first passed through the trench, and then round the sculpture, the ends were given to two bodies of men. Several of the strongest Chaldaeans placed thick beams against the back of the bull, and were directed to withdraw them gradually, supporting the weight of the slab and checking it in its descent, in case the ropes should give way.

My own people were reinforced by a large number of the Abou Salman. I had invited Sheikh Abd-ur-rahman to be present, and he came attended by a body of horsemen. The men being ready, and all my preparations complete, I stationed myself on the top of the high bank of earth over the second bull, and ordered the wedges to be struck out from under the sculpture to be moved. Still, however, it remained firmly in its place. A rope having been passed round it, six or seven men easily tilted it over. The thick, ill-made cable stretched with the strain, and almost buried itself in the earth round which it was coiled. The ropes held well. The mass descended gradually, the Chaldaeans propping it up with the beams. It was a moment of great anxiety. The drums and shrill pipes of the Kurdish musicians increased the din and confusion caused by the war-cry of the Arabs, who were half frantic with excitement. They had thrown off nearly all their garments; their long hair floated in the wind; and they indulged in the wildest postures and gesticulations as they clung to the ropes. The women had congregated on the sides of the trenches, and by their incessant screams, and by the ear-piercing tahlehl, added to the enthusiasm of the men. The bull once in motion, it was no longer possible to obtain a hearing. The loudest cries I could produce were lost in the crash of discordant sounds. Neither the hippopotamus-hide whips of the Cawasses, nor the bricks and clods of earth with which I endeavoured to draw attention from some of the most noisy of the group, were of any avail. Away went the bull, steady enough as long as supported by the props behind; but as it came nearer to the rollers, the beams could no longer be used. The cable and ropes stretched more and more. Dry from the climate, as they felt the strain, they creaked and threw out dust. Water was thrown over them, but in vain, for they all broke together when the sculpture was within four or five feet of the rollers. The bull was precipitated to the ground. Those who held the ropes, thus suddenly released, followed its example, and were rolling, one over the other, in the dust. A sudden silence succeeded to the clamour. I rushed into the trenches, prepared to find the bull in many pieces. It would be difficult to describe my satisfaction, when I saw it lying precisely where I had wished to place it, and uninjured! The Arabs no sooner got on their legs again, than, seeing the result of the accident, they darted out of the trenches, and, seizing by the hands the women who were looking on, formed a large circle, and, yelling their war-cry with redoubled energy, commenced a most mad dance. Even Abd-ur-rahman shared in the excitement, and, throwing his cloak to one of his attendants, insisted upon leading off the debkhé. It would have been useless to endeavour to put any check upon these proceedings. I preferred allowing the men to wear themselves out—a result which, considering the amount of exertion and energy displayed both by limbs and throat, was not long in taking place.

I now prepared to move the bull into the long trench which led to the edge of the mound. The rollers were in good order; and, as soon as the excitement of the Arabs had sufficiently abated to enable them to resume work, the sculpture was dragged out of its place by ropes.

Sleepers were laid to the end of the trench, and fresh rollers were placed under the bull as it was pulled forwards by cables. The sun was going down as these preparations were completed. I deferred any further labour to the morrow. The Arabs dressed themselves; and, placing the musicians at their head, marched towards the village, singing their war songs, and occasionally raising a wild yell, throwing their lances into the air, and flourishing their swords and shields over their heads. . . .

This night was, of course, looked upon as one of rejoicing. Sheep were as usual killed, and boiled or roasted whole; they formed the essence of all entertainments and public festivities. They had scarcely been devoured before dancing was commenced. There were fortunately relays of musicians; for no human lungs could have furnished the requisite amount of breath. When some were nearly falling from exhaustion, the ranks were recruited by others. And so the Arabs went on until dawn. It was useless to preach moderation, or to entreat for quiet. Advice and remonstrances were received with deafening shouts of the war-cry, and outrageous antics as proofs of gratitude for the entertainment, and of ability to resist fatigue.

After passing the night in this fashion, these extraordinary beings, still singing and capering, started for the mound. Everything had been prepared on the previous day for moving the bull, and the men had now only to haul on the ropes. As the sculpture advanced, the rollers left behind were removed to the front, and thus in a short time it reached the end of the trench. There was little difficulty in dragging it down the precipitous side of the mound. When it arrived within three or four feet of the bottom, sufficient earth was removed from beneath it to admit the cart, upon which the bull itself was then lowered by still further digging away the soil. It was soon ready to be dragged to the river. Buffaloes were first harnessed to the yoke; but, although the men pulled with ropes fastened to the cart, the animals, feeling the weight behind them, refused to move. We were compelled, therefore, to take them out; and the Tiyari, in parties of eight, lifted by turns the pole, whilst the Arabs, assisted by the people of Naifa and Nimroud, dragged the cart. I rode first, with the Bairakdar, to point out the road. Then came the musicians, with their drums and fifes, drumming and fifing with might and main. The cart followed, dragged by about three

Austen Henry Layard supervises the lowering of a winged bull found at Nimrud, Iraq, that is now in the British Museum.

hundred men, all screeching at the top of their voices. The procession was closed by the women, who kept up the enthusiasm of the Arabs by their shrill cries. Abd-ur-rahman's horsemen performed divers feats round the group, dashing backwards and forwards, and charging with their spears. . . .

Layard now employed a raft contractor to build a watercraft to ship his finds to Busrah.

I did not doubt that the skins, once blown up, would support the sculptures without difficulty as far as Baghdad. The journey would take eight or ten days, under favourable circumstances. But there they would require to be opened and refilled, or the rafts would scarcely sustain so heavy a weight all the way to Busrah. However carefully the skins are filled, the air gradually escapes. Rafts, bearing merchandise, are generally detained several times during their descent, to enable the raftmen to examine and refill the skins. If the sculptures rested upon only one framework, the beams being almost on a level with the water, the raftmen would be unable to get beneath them to reach the mouths of the skins when they required replenishing, without moving the cargo. This would have been both inconvenient and difficult to accomplish. I was therefore desirous of raising the lion and bull as much as possible above the water, so as to leave room for the men to creep under them.

It may interest the reader to know how these rafts, which have probably formed for ages the only means of traffic on the upper parts of the rivers of Mesopotamia, are constructed. The skins of full-grown sheep and goats are used. They are taken off with as few incisions as possible, and then dried and prepared. The air is forced in by the lungs through an aperture which is afterwards tied up with string. A square framework, formed of poplar beams, branches of trees, and reeds, having been constructed of the size of the intended raft, the inflated skins are tied to it by osier and other twigs, the whole being firmly bound together. The raft is then moved to the water and launched. Care is taken to place the skins with their mouths upwards, that, in case any should burst or require filling, they can be easily opened by the raftmen. Upon the framework of wood are piled bales of goods, and property belonging to merchants and travellers. When any person of rank, or wealth, descends the river in this fashion, small huts are constructed on the raft by covering a common wooden *takht*, or bedstead of the country, with a hood formed of reeds and lined with felt. In these huts the travellers live and sleep during the journey. The poorer passengers seek shade or warmth, by burying themselves amongst bales of goods and other merchandise, and sit patiently, almost in one position, until they reach their destination. They carry with them a small earthen *mangal* or chafing-dish, containing a charcoal fire, which serves to light their pipes, and to cook their coffee and food. The only real danger to be apprehended on the river is from the Arabs; who, when the country is in a disturbed state, invariably attack and pillage the rafts.

The raftmen guide their rude vessels by long oars—straight poles, at the end of which a few split canes are fastened by a piece of twine. They skilfully avoid the rapids; and, seated on the bales of goods, work continually, even in the hottest sun. They will seldom travel after dark before reaching Tekrit, on account of the rocks and shoals, which abound in the upper part of the river; but when they have passed that place, they resign themselves, night and day, to the sluggish stream. During the floods in the spring, or after violent rains, small rafts may float from Mosul to Baghdad in about eighty-four hours; but the large rafts are generally six or seven days in performing the voyage. In summer, and when the river is low, they are frequently nearly a month in reaching their destination. When the rafts have been unloaded, they are broken up, and the beams, wood, and twigs are sold at a considerable profit, forming one of the principal branches of trade between Mosul and Baghdad. The skins are washed and afterwards rubbed with a preparation of pounded pomegranate skins, to keep them from cracking and rotting. They are then brought back, either upon the shoulders of the raftmen or upon donkeys, to Mosul or Tekrit, where the men engaged in the navigation of the Tigris usually reside.

On the 20th of April, there being fortunately a slight rise in the river, and the rafts being ready, I determined to attempt the embarkation of the lion and bull. The two sculptures had been so placed on beams that, by withdrawing wedges from under them, they would slide nearly into the centre of the raft. The high bank of the river had been cut away into a rapid slope to the water's edge.

The beams of poplar wood, forming an inclined plane from beneath the sculptures to the rafts, were first well greased. A raft, supported by six hundred skins, having been brought to the river bank, opposite the bull, the wedges were removed from under the sculpture, which immediately slided down into its place. The only difficulty was to prevent its descending too rapidly, and bursting the skins by the sudden pressure. The Arabs checked it by ropes, and it was placed without any accident. The lion was then embarked in the same way, and with equal success, upon a second raft of the same size as the first; in a few hours the two sculptures were properly secured, and before night they were ready to float down the river to Busrah. Many slabs, and about thirty cases containing small objects discovered in the ruins, were placed on the rafts with the lion and bull.

After the labours of the day were over, sheep were slaughtered for the entertainment of Abd-ur-rahman's Arabs, and for those who had helped in the embarkation of the sculptures. The Abou Salman returned to their tents after dark. Abd-ur-rahman took leave of me, and we did not meet again; the next day he continued his march towards the district of Jezirah. I heard of him on my journey to Constantinople; the Kurds by the road complaining that his tribe were making up the number of their flocks, by appropriating the stray sheep of their neighbours. I had seen much of the sheikh during my residence at Nimroud; and although, like all Arabs, he was not averse to ask for what he thought there might be a remote chance of getting by a little importunity, he was, on the whole, a very friendly and useful ally.

I watched the rafts until they disappeared behind a projecting bank of the river. I could not forbear musing upon the strange destiny of their burdens; which, after adorning the palaces of the Assyrian kings, had been buried unknown for centuries beneath a soil trodden by Persians under Cyrus, by Greeks under Alexander, and by Arabs under the first successors of their prophet. They were now to visit India, to cross the most distant seas of the southern hemisphere, and to be finally placed in a British Museum. Who can venture to foretell how their strange career will end?

———

We will descend into the principal trench, by a flight of steps rudely cut into the earth, near the western face of the mound. As we approach it, we find a party of Arabs bending on their knees, and intently gazing at something beneath them. Each holds his long spear, tufted with ostrich feathers, in one hand; and in the other the halter of his mare, which stands patiently behind him. The party consists of a Bedouin sheikh from the desert, and his followers; who, having heard strange reports of the wonders of Nimroud, have made several days' journey to remove their doubts and satisfy their curiosity. . . .

We descend about twenty feet, and suddenly find ourselves between a pair of colossal lions, winged and human-headed, forming a portal. In the subterraneous labyrinth which we have reached, all is bustle and confusion. Arabs are running about in different directions; some bearing baskets filled with earth, others carrying the water-jars to their companions. The Chaldaeans or Tiyari, in their striped dresses and curious conical caps, are digging with picks into the tenacious earth, raising a dense cloud of fine dust at every stroke. The wild strains of Kurdish music may be heard occasionally issuing from some distant part of the ruins.

We issue from between the winged lions, and enter the remains of the principal hall. On both sides of us are sculptured gigantic winged figures; some with the heads of eagles, others entirely human, and carrying mysterious symbols in their hands. To the left is another portal, also formed by winged lions. One of them has, however, fallen across the entrance, and there is just room to creep beneath it. Beyond this portal is a winged figure, and two slabs with bas-reliefs; but they have been so much injured that we can scarcely trace the subject upon them. Further on there are no traces of wall, although a deep trench has been opened. The opposite side of the hall has also disappeared, and we only see a high wall of earth. On examining it attentively, we can detect the marks of masonry; and we soon find that it is a solid structure built of bricks of unbaked clay, now of the same colour as the surrounding soil, and scarcely to be distinguished from it.

The slabs of alabaster, fallen from their original position, have, however, been raised; and we tread in the midst of a maze of small bas-reliefs, representing chariots, horsemen, battles, and sieges. Perhaps the workmen are about to raise a slab for the first time; and we watch, with eager curiosity, what new event of Assyrian history, or what unknown custom or religious ceremony, may be illustrated by the sculpture beneath.

Having walked about one hundred feet amongst these scattered monuments of ancient history and art, we reach another door-way, formed by gigantic winged bulls in yellow limestone. One is still entire; but its companion has fallen, and is broken into several pieces—the great human head is at our feet.

We pass on without turning into the part of the building to which this portal leads. Beyond it we see another winged figure, holding a graceful flower in its hand, and apparently presenting it as an offering to the winged bull. Adjoining this sculpture we find eight fine bas-reliefs. There is the king, hunting, and triumphing over, the lion and wild bull; and the siege of the castle, with the battering-ram. We have now reached the end of the hall, and find before us an elaborate and beautiful sculpture, representing two kings, standing beneath the emblem of the supreme deity, and attended by winged figures. Between them is the sacred tree. In front of this bas-relief is the great stone platform, upon which, in days of old, may have been placed the throne of the Assyrian monarch, when he received his captive enemies, or his courtiers.

To the left of us is a fourth outlet from the hall, formed by another pair of lions. We issue from between them, and find ourselves on the edge of a deep ravine, to the north of which rises, high above us, the lofty pyramid. Figures of captives bearing objects of tribute—earrings, bracelets, and monkeys—may be seen on walls near this ravine; and two enormous bulls, and two winged figures above fourteen feet high, are lying on its very edge.

As the ravine bounds the ruins on this side, we must return to the yellow bulls. Passing through the entrance formed by them, we enter a large chamber surrounded by eagle-headed figures: at one end of it is a doorway guarded by two priests or divinities, and in the centre another portal with winged bulls. Whichever way we turn, we find ourselves in the midst of a nest of rooms; and without an acquaintance with the intricacies of the place, we should soon lose ourselves in this labyrinth. The accumulated rubbish being generally left in the centre of the chambers, the whole excavation consists of a number of narrow passages, panelled on one side with slabs of alabaster; and shut in on the other by a high wall of earth, half buried, in which may here and there be seen a broken vase, or a brick painted with brilliant colours. We may wander through these galleries for an hour or two, examining the marvellous sculptures, or the numerous inscriptions that surround us. Here we meet long rows of kings, attended by their eunuchs and priests—there lines of winged figures, carrying fir-cones and religious emblems, and seemingly in adoration before the mystic tree. Other entrances, formed by winged lions and bulls, lead us into new chambers. In every one of them are fresh objects of curiosity and surprise. At length, wearied, we issue from the buried edifice by a trench on the opposite side to that by which we entered, and find ourselves again upon the naked platform. We look around in vain for any traces of the wonderful remains we have just seen, and are half inclined to believe that we have dreamed a dream, or have been listening to some tale of Eastern romance.

Some, who may hereafter tread on the spot when the grass again grows over the ruins of the Assyrian palaces, may indeed suspect that I have been relating a vision.

Cracking Cuneiform's Code

Henry Creswicke Rawlinson

Cuneiform, the wedgelike script stamped on to clay tablets, was the lingua franca of the eastern Mediterranean world three thousand years ago. All important diplomatic correspondence was conducted in this near-universal writing system. For example, the famous El-Amarna letters from Egypt, in Akkadian cuneiform, are a priceless archive of pharaonic diplomacy in the fourteenth century B.C. They throw much light on the fortunes of Egypt abroad during the tumultuous period of the heretic pharaoh Akhenaten's reign. Unlocking the secrets of this wedge-shaped script required infinite patience, a comprehensive knowledge of ancient and modern Eastern languages, and a passion for obscure detail.

The decipherment of cuneiform was the second great epigraphic prize after the decoding of ancient Egyptian hieroglyphs. Three scholars finally unlocked cuneiform's secrets: an Irish priest named Edward Hincks; French orientalist Jules Oppert, famous for his identification of the Sumerian civilization of southern Mesopotamia, which flourished long before the Assyrians; and an English cavalry officer turned linguist, Henry Creswicke Rawlinson. It was Rawlinson who copied the famous trilingual inscription of the Persian monarch Darius (548–486 B.C.) inscribed high above the ground on the Great Rock at Behistun, in present-day Iran.

Sir Henry Creswicke Rawlinson (1810–1895) was born in Oxfordshire and appointed an officer cadet in the East India Company in 1827. He soon demonstrated a remarkable ability at languages, mastering five oriental tongues in a very short time. In 1833, he was one of a party of British officers sent to reorganize the shah of Persia's army. Posted to Kurdistan, he decided to attempt a decipherment of King Darius's trilingual inscription, commemorating that monarch's victory over five rebel chiefs. Over the next decade, Rawlinson copied and deciphered the Old Persian, Elamite, and Babylonian texts, establishing that Babylonian was a Semitic, polyphonic language.

Rawlinson was appointed British consul in Baghdad in 1843. This gave him ample time to work on cuneiform tablets found by Austen Henry Layard at Nimrud and Nineveh, which he identified as Assyrian cities. In 1850 and 1851, Layard unearthed Assyrian monarch Ashurbanipal's royal archives at Nineveh. It was Rawlinson who realized the crucial importance of this unique library, with its grammars and rich archives, and arranged for their study in the British Museum. Rawlinson excavated on his own account but once, at Borsippa near Babylon in southern Mesopotamia in 1853, where he unearthed the commemorative cylinders that recorded how Nebuchadnezzar, king of Babylon, had rebuilt and repaired the temple in that city in the early sixth century B.C. He resigned from the East India Company in the same year. In later life, Rawlinson encouraged long-term research on the Ashurbanipal collection, which yielded the celebrated "Deluge Tablets," deciphered by one of his protégés, George Smith, in 1872. This contained an account of a great flood that bore a remarkable resemblance to the Old Testament deluge.

But Henry Rawlinson's greatest feat was the copying of the inscription at Behistun with the assistance of a "wild Kurdish boy." Years later, his precious copies, duly deciphered, were stored in the British Museum, where they were eaten by rats. Here is his firsthand account of the mountaineering required to scale the sheer cliff face, originally delivered as a lecture to the Society of Antiquaries of London and then published in its journal in 1852.

The rock, or, as it is usually called by the Arab geographers, the mountain of Behistun, is not an isolated hill, as has been sometimes imagined. It is merely the terminal point of a long, narrow range which bounds the plain of Kermanshah to the eastward. This range is rocky and abrupt throughout, but at the extremity it rises in height, and becomes a sheer precipice. The altitude I found by careful triangulation to be 3,087 feet, and the height above the plain at which occur the tablets of Darius is perhaps 500 feet, or something more.

Notwithstanding that a French antiquarian commission in Persia described it a few years back to be impossible to copy the Behistun inscriptions, I certainly do not consider it any great feat in climbing to ascend to the spot where the inscriptions occur. When I was living at Kermanshah fifteen years ago, and was somewhat more active than I am at present, I used frequently to scale the rock three or four times a day without the aid of a rope or a ladder; without any assistance, in fact, whatever. During my late visits I have found it more convenient to ascend and descend by the help of ropes where the track lies up a precipitate cleft, and to throw a plank over those chasms where a false step in leaping across would probably be fatal. On reaching the recess which contains the Persian text of the record, ladders are indispensable in order to examine the upper portion of the tablet; and even with ladders there is considerable risk, for the foot ledge is so narrow, about eighteen inches or at most two feet in breadth, that with a ladder long enough to reach the sculptures sufficient slope cannot be given to enable a person to ascend, and, if the ladder be shortened in order to increase the slope, the upper inscription can only be copied by standing on the topmost step of the ladder, with no other support than steadying the body against the rock with the left arm, while the left hand holds the notebook, and

Henry Creswicke Rawlinson, decipherer of cuneiform.

the right hand is employed with the pencil. In this position I copied all the upper inscriptions, and the interest of the occupation entirely did away with any sense of danger.

To reach the recess which contains the Scythic translation of the record of Darius is a matter of far greater difficulty. On the left-hand side of the recess alone is there any foot ledge whatever; on the right-hand, where the recess, which is thrown a few feet farther back, joins the Persian tablet, the face of the rock presents a sheer precipice, and it is necessary therefore to bridge this intervening space between the left-hand of the Persian tablet and the foot ledge on the left-hand of the recess. With ladders of sufficient length, a bridge of this sort can be constructed without difficulty; but my first attempt to cross the chasm was unfortunate, and might have been fatal, for, having previously shortened my only ladder in order to obtain a slope for copying the Persian upper legends, I found, when I came to lay it across to the recess in order to get at the Scythic translation, that it was not sufficiently long to lie flat on the foot ledge beyond. One side of the ladder would alone reach the nearest point of the ledge, and, as it would of course have tilted over if a person had attempted to cross in that position, I changed it from a horizontal to a vertical direction, the upper side resting firmly on the rock at its two ends, and the lower hanging over the precipice, and I prepared to cross, walking on the lower side, and holding to the upper side with my hands. If the ladder had been a compact article, this mode of crossing, although far from comfortable, would have been at any rate practicable; but the Persians merely fit in the bars of their ladders without pretending to clench them outside, and I had hardly accordingly begun to cross over when the vertical pressure forced the bars out of their sockets, and the lower and unsupported side of the ladder thus parted company from the upper, and went crashing down over the precipice. Hanging on to the upper side, which still remained firm in its place, and assisted by my friends, who were anxiously watching the trial, I regained the Persian recess, and did not again attempt to cross until I had made a bridge of comparative stability. Ultimately I took the casts of the Scythic writing . . . by laying one long ladder, in the first instance, horizontally across the chasm, and by then placing another ladder, which rested on the bridge, perpendicularly against the rock.

The Babylonian transcript at Behistun is still more difficult to reach than either the Scythic or the Persian tablets. The writing can be copied by the aid of a good telescope from below, but I long despaired of obtaining a cast of the inscription; for I found it quite beyond my powers of climbing to reach the spot where it was engraved, and the craigsmen of the place, who were accustomed to track the mountain goats over the entire face of the mountain, declared the particular block inscribed with the Babylonian legend to be unapproachable.

At length, however, a wild Kurdish boy, who had come from a distance, volunteered to make the attempt, and I promised him a considerable reward if he succeeded. The mass of rock in question is scarped, and it projects some feet over the Scythic recess, so that it cannot be approached by any of the ordinary means of climbing. The boy's first move was to squeeze himself up a cleft in the rock a short distance to the left of the projecting mass. When he had ascended some distance above it, he drove a wooden peg firmly into the cleft, fastened a rope to this and then endeavoured to swing himself across to another cleft at some distance on the other side; but in this he failed, owing to the projection of the rock. It then only remained for him to cross over to the cleft by hanging on with his toes and fingers to the slight inequalities on the bare face of the precipice, and in this he succeeded, passing over a distance of twenty feet of almost smooth perpendicular rock in a manner which to a looker-on appeared quite miraculous. When he had reached the second cleft the real difficulties were over. He had brought a rope with him attached to the first peg, and now, driving in a second, he was enabled to swing himself right over the projecting mass of rock. Here, with a short ladder, he formed a swinging seat, like a painter's cradle, and, fixed upon this seat, he took under my direction the paper cast of the Babylonian translation of the records of Darius which is now at the Royal Asiatic Society's rooms, and which is almost of equal value for the interpretation of the Assyrian inscriptions as was the Greek translation on the Rosetta Stone for the intelligence of the hieroglyphic texts of Egypt. I must add, too, that it is of the more importance that this invaluable Babylonian key should have been thus recovered, as the mass of rock on which the inscription is engraved bore every appearance, when I last visited this spot, of being doomed to a speedy destruction, water trickling from above having almost separated the overhanging mass from the rest of the rock, and its own enormous weight thus threatening very shortly to bring it thundering down into the plain, dashed into a thousand fragments.

The method of forming these paper casts is exceedingly simple, nothing more being required than to take a number of sheets of paper without size, spread them on the rock, moisten them, and then beat them into the crevices with a stout brush, adding as many layers of paper as it may be wished to give consistency to the cast. The paper is left there to dry, and on being taken off it exhibits a perfect reversed impression of the writing.

The Tomb of Tutankhamun

Howard Carter

Tutankhamun, who reigned over Egypt from 1333 to 1323 B.C., is a shadowy historical figure, overshadowed by his heretic predecessor, Akhenaten, and by illustrious successors like Ramesses II and Seti I. He ascended to the throne of Egypt while still a boy at a time of political and religious controversy caused by Akhenaten's espousal of new religious cults. Tutankhamun's officials worked hard to restore the ancient cult of the Sun God Amun, returning the royal capital to Thebes and erasing all traces of heresy. Tutankhamun died suddenly in 1323, of causes that elude us, although the possibilities of death in battle and murder have been raised. Obscure in life, he achieved immortality in death, not the immortality expected by Egyptian kings in the Otherworld, but worldwide fame from the discovery of his tomb, intact after more than three thousand years. Tutankhamun's tomb ranks among the most spectacular discoveries ever made. It came at the hands of a gifted but moody archaeologist, Howard Carter.

Originally trained as an artist and a draftsman, Howard Carter (1873–1939) arrived in Egypt in 1891 and was trained in excavation methods under the great British Egyptologist Flinders Petrie. Between 1891 and 1899, Carter conducted excavations on behalf of the Egypt Exploration Fund and later joined the Antiquities Service of the Egyptian government as a chief inspector. Carter did not suffer fools gladly and was forced to resign after an altercation with some French tourists in 1905. He eked out a living as a freelance artist, guide, and excavator, until he began work under the patronage of George Herbert, Lord Carnarvon, a wealthy aristocrat whose health forced him to spend the winters in Egypt's dry climate. In 1917, Carnarvon was granted the coveted permit to excavate in the Valley of the Kings, where Carter was convinced that the tomb of Tutankhamun awaited discovery.

Carter spent five unrewarding seasons shifting rubble in a patient search for the missing tomb. A skeptical Lord Carnarvon was ready to call the entire project off. Carter convinced him to finance one last season, however, and returned to the valley in November 1922. He decided to reexcavate to the site of some preliminary first-season trenching near the tomb of Ramesses VI that had yielded nothing but the mud-brick foundations of workmens' huts. Within four days, the laborers had discovered a sunken stairway cut directly into the stone floor of the valley. The story of how Carter drilled a hole in the sealed doorway and peered into the undisturbed tomb is one of the classic stories of archaeology, so much so that it deserves repeating here.

The clearance of the tomb involved specialists from several countries and miracles of ingenuity, artifact conservation being in its infancy. It took two and a half months of painstaking work to clear the antechamber alone of all its treasures. And another three years would pass before the king's coffin was ready to be removed from the burial chamber. Carter's work in the Valley of the Kings was not completed until 1928 and was clouded by the unexpected death of Carnarvon from a septic mosquito bite and bitter disputes with the Egyptian government over the ownership of the finds. But Tutankhamun and his burial furniture have cast a magnetic spell ever since their discovery on that warm November day in 1922.

The following account, from Howard Carter's The Tomb of Tut-ankh-Amen, *of the "wonderful things" uncovered on that "day of days" is charged with the powerful, firsthand excitement of archaeological discovery at its most dramatic. It was written in 1923, when memories of the great discovery were still fresh in his mind.*

This was to be our final season in the valley. Six full seasons we had excavated there, and season after season had drawn a blank; we had worked for months at a stretch and found nothing, and only an excavator knows how desperately depressing that can be; we had almost made up our minds that we were beaten, and were preparing to leave the valley and try our luck elsewhere; and then—hardly had we set hoe to ground in our last despairing effort than we made a discovery that far exceeded our wildest dreams. Surely, never before in the whole history of excavation has a full digging season been compressed within the space of five days.

Let me try and tell the story of it all. It will not be easy, for the dramatic suddenness of the initial discovery left me in a dazed condition, and the months that have followed have been so crowded with incident that I have hardly had time to think. Setting it down on paper will perhaps give me a chance to realize what has happened and all that it means.

I arrived in Luxor on October 28, and by November 1 I had enrolled my workmen and was ready to begin. Our former excavations had stopped short at the northeast corner of the tomb of Rameses VI, and from this point I started trenching southwards. It will be remembered that in this area there were a number of roughly constructed workmen's huts, used probably by the labourers in the tomb of Rameses. . . . By the evening of November 3 we had laid bare a sufficient number of these huts for experimental purposes, so, after we had planned and noted them, they were removed, and we were ready to clear away the three feet of soil that lay beneath them.

Hardly had I arrived on the work next morning (November 4) than the unusual silence, due to the stoppage of the work, made me realize that something out of the ordinary had happened, and I was greeted by the announcement that a step cut in the rock had been discovered underneath the very first hut to be attacked. This seemed too good to be true, but a short amount of extra clearing revealed the fact that we were actually in the entrance of a steep cut in the rock, some thirteen feet below the entrance to the tomb of Rameses VI, and a similar depth from the present bed level of the valley. The manner of cutting was that of the sunken stairway entrance so common in the valley, and I almost dared to hope that we had found our tomb at last. Work continued feverishly throughout the whole of that day and the morning of the next, but it was not until the afternoon of November 5 that we succeeded in clearing away the masses of rubbish that overlay the cut, and were able to demarcate the upper edges of the stairway on all its four sides.

It was clear by now beyond any question that we actually had before us the entrance to a tomb, but doubts, born of previous disappointments, persisted in creeping in. There was always the horrible possibility, suggested by our experience in the Thothmes III valley, that the tomb was an unfinished one, never completed and never used: if it had been finished there was the depressing probability that it had been completely plundered in ancient times. On the other hand, there was just the chance of an untouched or only partially plundered tomb, and it was with ill-suppressed excitement that I watched the descending steps of the staircase, as one by one they came to light. The cutting was excavated in the side of a small hillock, and, as the work progressed, its western edge receded under the slope of the rock until it was, first partially, and then completely, roofed in, and became a passage, ten feet high by six feet wide. Work progressed more rapidly now; step succeeded step, and at the level of the twelfth, towards sunset, there was disclosed the upper part of a doorway, blocked, plastered, and sealed.

A sealed doorway—it was actually true, then! Our years of patient labour were to be rewarded after all, and I think my first feeling was one of congratulation that my faith in the valley had not been unjustified. With excitement growing to fever heat I searched the seal impressions on the door for evidence of the identity of the owner, but could find no name: the only decipherable ones were those of the well-known royal necropolis seal, the jackal and nine captives. Two facts, however, were clear: first, the employment of this royal seal was certain evidence that the tomb had been constructed for a person of a very high standing; and second, that the sealed door was entirely screened from above by workmen's huts of the Twentieth Dynasty was sufficiently clear proof that at least from that date it had never been entered. With that for the moment I had to be content.

While examining the seals I noticed, at the top of the doorway, where some of the plaster had fallen away, a heavy wooden lintel. Under this, to assure myself of the method by which the doorway had been blocked, I made a small peephole, just large enough to insert an electric torch, and discovered that the passage beyond the door was filled completely from floor to ceiling with stones and rubble—additional proof this of the care with which the tomb had been protected.

It was a thrilling moment for an excavator. Alone, save for my native workmen, I found myself, after years of comparatively unproductive labour, on the threshold of what might prove to be a magnificent discovery. Anything, literally anything, might lie beyond that passage, and it needed all my self-control to keep from breaking down the doorway, and investigating then and there.

One thing puzzled me, and that was the smallness of the opening in comparison with the ordinary valley tombs. The design was certainly of the Eighteenth Dynasty. Could it be the tomb of a noble buried here by royal consent? Was it a royal cache, a hiding place to which a mummy and its equipment had been removed for safety? Or was it actually the tomb of the king for whom I had spent so many years in search?

Once more I examined the seal impressions for a clue, but on the part of the door so far laid bare only those of the royal necropolis seal already mentioned were clear enough to read. Had I but known that a few inches lower down there was a perfectly clear and distinct impression of the seal of Tut-ankh-Amen, the king I most desired to find, I would have cleared on, had a much better night's rest in consequence, and saved myself nearly three weeks of uncertainty. It was late, however, and darkness was already upon us. With some reluctance I re-closed the small hole that I had made, filled in our excavation for protection during the night, selected the most trustworthy of my workmen—themselves almost as excited as I was—to watch all night above the tomb, and so home by moonlight, riding down the valley.

Naturally my wish was to go straight ahead with our clearing to find out the full extent of the discovery, but Lord Carnarvon was in England, and in fairness to him I had to delay matters until he could come. Accordingly, on the morning of November 6 I sent him the following cable: "At last have made wonderful discovery in Valley; a magnificent tomb with seals intact; recovered same for your arrival; congratulations."

My next task was to secure the doorway against interference until such time as it could finally be reopened. This we did by filling our excavation up again to surface level, and rolling on top of it the large flint boulders of which the workmen's huts had been composed. By the evening of the same day, exactly forty-eight hours after we had discovered the first step of the staircase, this was accomplished. The tomb had vanished. So far as the appearance of the ground was concerned there never had been any tomb, and I found it hard to persuade myself at times that the whole episode had not been a dream.

I was soon to be reassured on this point. News travels fast in Egypt, and within two days of the discovery congratulations, inquiries, and offers of help descended upon me in a steady stream from all directions. . . . On the 8th I had received two messages from Lord Carnarvon in answer to my cable, the first of which read "Possibly come soon," and the second, received a little later, "Propose arrive Alexandria 20th."

. . . On the night of the 18th I went to Cairo for three days, to meet Lord Carnarvon and made a number of necessary purchases, returning to Luxor on the 21st. On the 23rd Lord Carnarvon arrived in Luxor with his daughter Lady

Evelyn Herbert, his devoted companion in all his Egyptian work, and everything was in hand for the beginning of the second chapter of the discovery of the tomb. . . .

By the afternoon of the 24th the whole staircase was clear, sixteen steps in all, and we were able to make a proper examination of the sealed doorway. On the lower part the seal impressions were much clearer, and we were able without any difficulty to make out on several of them the name of Tut-ankh-Amen. This added enormously to the interest of the discovery. If we had found, as seemed almost certain, the tomb of that shadowy monarch, whose tenure of the throne coincided with one of the most interesting periods in the whole of Egyptian history, we should indeed have reason to congratulate ourselves.

With heightened interest, if that were possible, we renewed our investigation of the doorway. Here for the first time a disquieting element made its appearance. Now that the whole door was exposed to light it was possible to discern a fact that had hitherto escaped notice—that there had been two successive openings and reclosings of a part of its surface: furthermore, that the sealing originally discovered, the jackal and nine captives, had been applied to the reclosed portions, whereas the sealings of Tut-ankh-Amen covered the untouched part of the doorway, and were therefore those with which the tomb had been originally secured. The tomb then was not absolutely intact, as we had hoped. Plunderers had entered it, and entered it more than once—from the evidence of the huts above, plunderers of a date not later than the reign of Rameses VI—but that they had not rifled it completely was evident from the fact that it had been resealed.

Then came another puzzle. In the lower strata of rubbish that filled the staircase we found masses of broken potsherds and boxes, the latter bearing the names of Akh-en-Aten, Smenkh-ka-Re and Tut-ankh-Amen, and, what was much more upsetting, a scarab of Thothmes III and a fragment with the name of Amenhotep III. Why this mixture of names? The balance of evidence so far would seem to indicate a cache rather than a tomb. . . .

So matters stood on the evening of the 24th. On the following day the sealed doorway was to be removed. . . . Mr. Engelbach, chief inspector of the Antiquities Department, paid us a visit during the afternoon, and witnessed part of the final clearing of rubbish from the doorway.

On the morning of the 25th the seal impressions on the doorway were carefully noted and photographed, and then we removed the actual blocking of the door, consisting of rough stones carefully built from floor to lintel, and heavily plastered on their outer faces to take the seal impressions.

This disclosed the beginning of a descending passage (not a staircase), the same width as the entrance stairway, and nearly seven feet high. As I had already discovered from my hole in the doorway, it was filled completely with stone and rubble, probably the chip from its own excavation. This filling, like the doorway, showed distinct signs of more than one opening and reclosing of the tomb, the untouched part consisting of clean white chip, mingled with dust, whereas the disturbed part was composed mainly of dark flint. It was clear that an irregular tunnel had been cut through the original filling at the upper corner on the left side, a tunnel corresponding in position with that of the hole in the doorway.

As we cleared the passage we found, mixed with the rubble of the lower levels, broken potsherds, jar sealings, alabaster jars, whole and broken, vases of painted pottery, numerous fragments of smaller articles, and water skins, these last having obviously been used to bring up the water needed for the plastering of the doorways. These were clear evidence of plundering, and we eyed them askance. By night we had cleared a considerable distance down the passage, but as yet saw no sign of a second doorway or of a chamber.

The day following (November 26) was the day of days, the most wonderful that I have ever lived through, and certainly one whose like I can never hope to see again. Throughout the morning the work of clearing continued, slowly perforce, on account of the delicate objects that were mixed with the filling. Then, in the middle of the afternoon, thirty feet down from the outer door, we came upon a second sealed doorway, almost an exact replica of the first. The seal impressions in this case were less distinct, but still recognizable as those of Tut-ankh-Amen and of the royal necropolis. Here again the signs of opening and reclosing were clearly marked upon the plaster. We were firmly convinced by this time that it was a cache that we were about to open, and not a tomb. . . . We were soon to know. There lay the sealed doorway, and behind it was the answer to the question.

Slowly, desperately slowly it seemed to us as we watched, the remains of passage debris that encumbered the lower part of the doorway were removed, until at last we had the whole door clear before us. The decisive moment had arrived. With trembling hands I made a tiny breach in the upper left-hand corner. Darkness and blank space, as far as an iron testing-rod could reach, showed that whatever lay beyond was empty, and not filled like the passage we had just cleared. Candle tests were applied as a precaution against possible foul gases, and then, widening the hole a little, I inserted the candle and peered in. . . . At first I could see nothing, the hot air escaping from the chamber causing the candle flame to flicker, but presently, as my eyes grew accustomed to the light, details of the room within emerged slowly from the mist, strange animals, statues, and gold—everywhere the glint of gold. For the moment—an eternity it must have seemed to the others standing by—I was struck dumb with amazement, and when Lord Carnarvon, unable to stand the suspense any longer, inquired anxiously, "Can you see anything?" it was all I could do to get out the words, "Yes, wonderful things." Then widening the hole a little further, so that we both could see, we inserted an electric torch.

I suppose most excavators would confess to a feeling of awe—embarrassment almost—when they break into a chamber closed and sealed by pious hands so many centuries ago. For the moment, time as a factor in human life has lost its meaning. Three thousand, four thousand years maybe, have passed and gone since human feet last trod the floor on which you stand, and yet, as you note the signs of recent life around you—the half-filled bowl of mortar for the door,

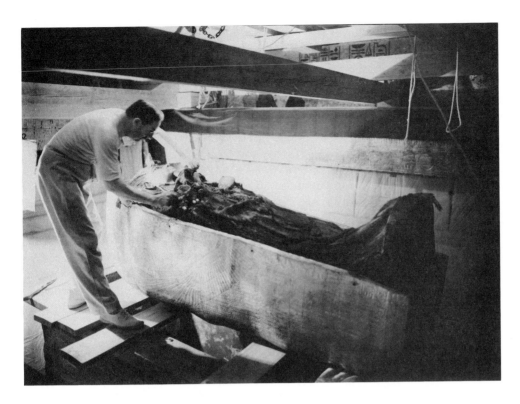

*Howard Carter in 1925 removing the linen shroud that covered the
second of Tutankhamun's three nested coffins.*

the blackened lamp, the finger mark upon the freshly painted surface, the fare-
well garland dropped upon the threshold—you feel it might have been but yesterday. The very air you breathe, unchanged throughout the centuries, you share
with those who laid the mummy to its rest. Time is annihilated by little intimate
details such as these, and you feel an intruder.

That is perhaps the first and dominant sensation, but others follow thick and
fast: the exhilaration of discovery, the fever of suspense, the almost overmaster-
ing impulse, born of curiosity, to break down seals and lift the lids of boxes, the
thought—pure joy to the investigator—that you are about to add a page to
history, or solve some problem of research, the strained expectancy—why not
confess it?—of the treasure seeker. Did these thoughts actually pass through our
minds at the time, or have I imagined them since? I cannot tell. . . .

Surely never before in the whole history of excavation had such an amazing
sight been seen as the light of our torch revealed to us. . . .

Gradually the scene grew clearer, and we could pick out individual objects.
First, right opposite to us—we had been conscious of them all the while, but
refused to believe in them—were three great gilt couches, their sides carved in
the form of monstrous animals curiously attenuated in body, as they had to be

to serve their purpose, but with heads of startling realism. Uncanny beasts enough to look upon at any time; seen as we saw them, their brilliant gilded surfaces picked out of the darkness by our electric torch, as though by limelight, their heads throwing grotesque distorted shadows on the wall behind them, they were almost terrifying. Next, on the right, two statues caught and held our attention: two life-sized figures of a king in black, facing each other like sentinels, gold kilted, gold sandalled, armed with mace and staff, the protective sacred cobra upon their foreheads.

These were the dominant objects that caught the eye at first. Between them, around them, piled on top of them, there were countless others—exquisitely painted and inlaid caskets; alabaster vases, some beautifully carved in open-work designs; strange black shrines, from the open door of one a great gilt snake peeping out; bouquets of flowers or leaves; beds; chairs beautifully carved; a golden inlaid throne; a heap of curious white oviform boxes; staves of all shapes and designs; beneath our eyes, on the very threshold of the chamber, a beautiful lotiform cup of translucent alabaster; on the left a confused pile of overturned chariots, glistening with gold and inlay; and peeping from behind them another portrait of a king. . . .

By the middle of February our work in the antechamber was finished. With the exception of the two sentinel statues, left for a special reason, all its contents had been removed to the laboratory, every inch of its floor had been swept and sifted for the last bead or fallen piece of inlay, and it now stood bare and empty. We were ready at last to penetrate the mystery of the sealed door.

Friday, the 17th, was the day appointed, and at two o'clock those who were to be privileged to witness the ceremony met by appointment above the tomb. . . . In the antechamber everything was prepared and ready. . . .

My first care was to locate the wooden lintel above the door: then very carefully I chipped away the plaster and picked out the small stones which formed the uppermost layer of the filling. The temptation to stop and peer inside at every moment was irresistible, and when, after about ten minutes' work, I had made a hole large enough to enable me to do so, I inserted an electric torch. An astonishing sight its light revealed, for there, within a yard of the doorway, stretching as far as one could see and blocking the entrance to the chamber, stood what to all appearance was a solid wall of gold. For the moment there was no clue as to its meaning, so as quickly as I dared I set to work to widen the hole. This had now become an operation of considerable difficulty, for the stones of the masonry were not accurately squared blocks built regularly upon one another, but rough slabs of varying size, some so heavy that it took all one's strength to lift them: many of them, too, as the weight above was removed, were left so precariously balanced that the least false movement would have sent them sliding inwards to crash upon the contents of the chamber below. We were also endeavouring to preserve the seal impressions upon the thick mortar of the outer face, and this added considerably to the difficulty of handling the stones. . . .

With the removal of a very few stones the mystery of the golden wall was solved. We were at the entrance of the actual burial chamber of the king, and that which barred our way was the side of an immense gilt shrine built to cover and protect the sarcophagus. It was visible now from the antechamber by the light of the standard lamps, and as stone after stone was removed, and its gilded surface came gradually into view, we could, as though by electric current, feel the tingle of excitement which thrilled the spectators behind the barrier. . . . We who were doing the work were probably less excited, for our whole energies were taken up with the task in hand—that of removing the blocking without an accident. The fall of a single stone might have done irreparable damage to the delicate surface of the shrine, so, directly the hole was large enough, we made an additional protection for it by inserting a mattress on the inner side of the door blocking, suspending it from the wooden lintel of the doorway. Two hours of hard work it took us to clear away the blocking, or at least as much of it as was necessary for the moment; and at one point, when near the bottom, we had to delay operations for a space while we collected the scattered beads from a necklace brought by the plunderers from the chamber within and dropped upon the threshold. This last was a terrible trial to our patience, for it was a slow business, and we were all of us excited to see what might be within; but finally it was done, the last stones were removed, and the way to the innermost chamber lay open before us.

In clearing away the blocking of the doorway we had discovered that the level of the inner chamber was about four feet lower than that of the antechamber, and this, combined with the fact that there was but a narrow space between door and shrine, made an entrance by no means easy to effect. Fortunately, there were no smaller antiquities at this end of the chamber, so I lowered myself down, and then, taking one of the portable lights, I edged cautiously to the corner of the shrine and looked beyond it. At the corner two beautiful alabaster vases blocked the way, but I could see that if these were removed we should have a clear path to the other end of the chamber; so, carefully marking the spot on which they stood, I picked them up—with the exception of the king's wishing cup they were of finer quality and more graceful shape than any we had yet found—and passed them back to the antechamber. Lord Carnarvon and M. Lacau now joined me, and, picking our way along the narrow passage between shrine and wall, paying out the wire of our light behind us, we investigated further.

It was, beyond any question, the sepulchral chamber in which we stood, for there, towering above us, was one of the great gilt shrines beneath which kings were laid. So enormous was this structure (seventeen feet by eleven feet, and nine feet high, we found afterwards) that it filled within a little the entire area of the chamber, a space of some two feet only separating it from the walls on all four sides, while its roof, with cornice top and torus moulding, reached almost to the ceiling. From top to bottom it was overlaid with gold, and upon its sides there were inlaid panels of brilliant blue faïence, in which were represented, repeated over and over, the magic symbols which would ensure its strength and safety. Around the shrine, resting upon the ground, there were a number of funerary emblems, and, at the north end, the seven magic oars the king would need to ferry himself across the waters of the underworld. The walls of the chamber, unlike those of the antechamber, were decorated with brightly painted scenes and inscriptions, brilliant in their colours, but evidently somewhat hastily executed.

The last details we must have noticed subsequently, for at the time our one thought was of the shrine and of its safety. Had the thieves penetrated within it and disturbed the royal burial? Here, on the eastern end, were the great folding doors, closed and bolted, but not sealed, that would answer the question for us. Eagerly we drew the bolts, swung back the doors, and there within was a second shrine with similar bolted doors, and upon the bolts a seal, intact. This seal we determined not to break, for our doubts were resolved, and we could not penetrate further without risk of serious damage to the monument. I think at the moment we did not even want to break the seal, for a feeling of intrusion had descended heavily upon us with the opening of the doors, heightened, probably, by the almost painful impressiveness of a linen pall, decorated with golden rosettes, which drooped above the inner shrine. We felt that we were in the presence of the dead king and must do him reverence, and in imagination could see the doors of the successive shrines open one after the other till the innermost disclosed the king himself. Carefully, and as silently as possible, we reclosed the great swing doors, and passed on to the farther end of the chamber.

Here a surprise awaited us, for a low door, eastwards from the sepulchral chamber, gave entrance to yet another chamber, smaller than the outer ones and not so lofty. This doorway, unlike the others, had not been closed and sealed. We were able, from where we stood, to get a clear view of the whole of the contents, and a single glance sufficed to tell us that here, within this little chamber, lay the greatest treasures of the tomb. Facing the doorway, on the farther side, stood the most beautiful monument that I have ever seen—so lovely that it made one gasp with wonder and admiration. The central portion of it consisted of a large shrine-shaped chest, completely overlaid with gold, and surmounted by a cornice of sacred cobras. Surrounding this, free-standing, were statues of the four tutelary goddesses of the dead—gracious figures with outstretched protective arms, so natural and lifelike in their pose, so pitiful and compassionate the expression upon their faces, that one felt it almost sacrilege to look at them. One guarded the shrine on each of its four sides, but whereas the figures at front and back kept their gaze firmly fixed upon their charge, an additional note of touching realism was imparted by the other two, for their heads were turned sideways, looking over their shoulders towards the entrance, as though to watch against surprise. There is a simple grandeur about this monument that made an irresistible appeal to the imagination, and I am not ashamed to confess that it brought a lump to my throat. It is undoubtedly the Canopic chest and contains the jars which play such an important part in the ritual of mummification.

There were a number of other wonderful things in the chamber, but we found it hard to take them in at the time, so inevitably were one's eyes drawn back again and again to the lovely little goddess figures. Immediately in front of the entrance lay the figure of the jackal god Anubis, upon his shrine, swathed in linen cloth, and resting upon a portable sled, and behind this the head of a bull upon a stand—emblems, these, of the underworld. In the south side of the chamber lay an endless number of black shrines and chests, all closed and sealed save one, whose open doors revealed statues of Tut-ankh-Amen standing upon black leopards. On the farther wall were more shrine-shaped boxes and minia- ture coffins of gilded wood, these last undoubtedly containing funerary statu- ettes of the king. In the centre of the room, left of the Anubis and the bull, there was a row of magnificent caskets of ivory and wood, decorated and inlaid with gold and blue faïence, one, whose lid we raised, containing a gorgeous ostrich-feather fan with ivory handle, fresh and strong to all appearance as when it left the maker's hand. There were also, distributed in different quarters of the chamber, a number of model boats with sails and rigging all complete, and, at the north side, yet another chariot.

Such, from a hurried survey, were the contents of this innermost chamber. We looked anxiously for evidence of plundering, but on the surface there was none. Unquestionably the thieves must have entered, but they cannot have done more than open two or three of the caskets. Most of the boxes, as has been said, have still their seals intact, and the whole contents of the chamber, in fortunate contrast to those of the antechamber and the annex, still remain in position exactly as they were placed at the time of burial.

How much time we occupied in this first survey of the wonders of the tomb I cannot say, but it must have seemed endless to those anxiously waiting in the antechamber. Not more than three at a time could be admitted with safety so . . . it was curious as we stood in the antechamber, to watch their faces as, one by one, they emerged from the door. Each had a dazed, bewildered look in his eyes, and each in turn, as he came out, threw up his hands before him, an unconscious gesture of impotence to describe in words the wonders that he had seen. They were indeed indescribable, and the emotions they had aroused in our minds were of too intimate a nature to communicate, even though we had the words at our command. It was an experience which, I am sure, none of us who were present is ever likely to forget, for in imagination—and not wholly in imagination either—we had been present at the funeral ceremonies of a king long dead and almost forgotten. At a quarter past two we had filed down into the tomb, and when, three hours later, hot, dusty, and disheveled, we came out once more into the light of day, the very valley seemed to have changed for us and taken on a more personal aspect. We had been given the Freedom.

The Nubian Kings of Kerma

GEORGE REISNER

Nubia, the mysterious land of the blacks, lay upstream of ancient Egypt, above the first cataract at Aswan, in modern-day Sudan. From the earliest dynasties of pharaonic rule, the Egyptians traded with Nubia, sending expeditions in search of ivory and semiprecious stones. Eventually, Middle Kingdom pharaohs garrisoned this remote land to control its trade routes. But as Egyptian influence waned in times of political instability, the Nubians themselves formed independent states on their own account. The Kingdom of Kerma flourished during the early second millennium B.C., a powerful state ruled by kings who lived in some style in their capital in the heart of the Kingdom of Kush. The New Kingdom pharaohs turned Nubia into a colony, but the tables were turned during the eighth century B.C., when a dynasty of Nubian pharaohs conquered and ruled Egypt before being overthrown by Assyrian invaders.

Archaeology in Nubia has lagged far behind that in Egypt. Some of the most spectacular discoveries came in the early decades of the twentieth century, when several large-scale expeditions explored ancient towns along the Nile. Like Howard Carter, Egyptologist George Reisner (1867–1942) was a student of the pioneer British Egyptologist Flinders Petrie, who dug extensively in Egypt before World War I. Like his illustrious mentor, he believed that every object recovered, no matter how small or insignificant, should be recorded and published if possible. Between 1904 and 1927, Reisner led the Harvard–Boston Museum of Fine Arts expedition that cleared the great mastaba cemetery near the pyramids of Giza. In 1925, he went on to discover the tomb of Queen Hetep-heres, mother of the Old Kingdom pharaoh Khufu. Although the floor of the tomb was littered with many gold museum-quality treasures, Reisner resisted the temptation to collect them immediately. Instead, he carefully excavated the tomb inch by inch, noting the positions of the artifacts and maintaining a high standard of recording throughout.

Later in his career, Reisner turned his attention to Nubia, the so-called Land of Kush. In this account of his excavations at Kerma in 1913, Reisner describes everything exactly as he found it, and then moves beyond mere description in his discussion of the sacrificial rites, with, at times, gruesome consideration of the victims' final feelings. In so doing, Reisner exhibits more of a humanistic concern with the people who produced

116

the artifacts than an antiquarian's obsession with the artifacts themselves. To brush the dust from the miraculously preserved, delicate sandals of a buried slave girl the way Reisner did at Kerma affords us the opportunity to walk a mental mile in her shoes, imagine the world as she may have seen it, and, in so doing, forge an otherwise impossible connection to human beings who lived long before we did. Reisner's Nubian excavation is early-twentieth-century archaeology at its best.

Here George Reisner describes the royal cemetery and its major burials in a report written for the Peabody Museum at Harvard University in 1923.

When the facts presented by the large tumuli are taken under examination, they are found to be exactly the same as in the subsidiary and independent graves, but on a much larger scale. In these, the chief burial [was anciently] without exception entirely cleared out, and the accompaniments scattered in the debris. . . . From the fragments found in the debris disturbed by the plunderers, a series of unusual objects were recorded which I assign without hesitation to the chief burial and which show that the equipment of that body was of the same general character as that of the chief bodies in the subsidiary graves but much more expensive and of finer materials. The parallel is continued by the contents of the other rooms in these tumuli which, according to the form, I call sacrificial corridors or sacrificial chambers. These apartments contain a large number of bodies in the same variety of attitudes and positions as the extra bodies in the subsidiary graves and resting also on the floor of the room, sometimes in almost regular rows but more often in quite irregular groups. The number of the extra bodies were as follows. I give also the estimated original number, as all these sacrificial apartments had been more or less plundered, although many individual bodies were quite intact:

| | Number of Sacrificial Bodies | |
| | --- | --- |
Tumulus	Actually Found	Estimated Original Number
K III A	45 ±	100 ±
K IV B	95	110–120
K X B	322	400
K XVI B, C	30 ±	100 ±
K XVIII B	42	80 ±
K XIX	none	80 ±
K XX, one chamber	12	50 ±

These numbers, although astonishingly large, correspond more or less to the proportions of the large tumuli as compared with other graves. Even in the graves, the number of sacrifices usually increased approximately in proportion to the size of the grave; which means that the graves were made of a size to contain the expected burials. It may be remarked that the estimated number of burials is based on the organic stains on the floor in plundered areas, and would by no means entirely fill these ample apartments. Nor is even the estimated number for K X, 400 bodies (based on concrete evidence of 322 bodies), too large for the size of the hareem of the family of the Egyptian governor of the Sudan. They include a large proportion of women and children, but also some males, no doubt bodyguards or hareem servants. That some of them were eunuchs is of course possible but indeterminable. The man was the governor of a country which controlled the main trade lines and the gold supply of Egypt and, at the distance of so many days' journey from Thebes and Memphis, must have held the position of a nearly independent but tribute-paying viceroy to the king of Egypt. Under such circumstances, a hareem with all its dependents, servants, and miscellaneous offspring would in the Orient easily amount to five hundred persons or more. Thus all the statements in regard to the extra bodies in the smaller graves apply in equal degree to those of the great tombs. These enormous burials also represent family interments made on one and the same day, differing only in scale which was proportionate to the place and power of the chief personage. Concluding that the burial represents a family group of attendants, females, and children together with the chief body; that all were buried in one day and in the same grave; that this occurred not in one grave but in every grave in a vast cemetery, containing in the Egyptian part alone about four hundred graves; and that the practice must cover a period of several hundred years; it may well be asked of human experience under what conditions such a custom can exist. The chances of war become at once an absurdity; the possibility of the continual extermination of family after family by execution for criminal or political offences cannot be seriously considered; and there is certainly no microbe known to modern science which could act in so maliciously convenient a manner as to deliver family after family through so many generations simultaneously at the grave-side. In all the range of present knowledge, there is only one custom known which sends the family or a part of it into the other world along with the chief member. That is the custom, widely practiced but best known from the Hindoo form called *satî* or *suttee*, in which the wives of the dead man cast themselves (or are thrown) on his funeral pyre. Some such custom as this would explain fully the facts recorded in the graves of Kerma, and after several years of reflection I can conceive of no other known or possible custom which would even partially explain those facts. It remains only to determine in what manner the victims of this custom met their death; that is, whether they were put to death before burial, given poison or a mortal wound which caused them to die after entering the grave, or whether they died by suffocation in the grave. In another form the question becomes: whether they died voluntarily by the compulsion of traditional duty or by the act of other hands.

The attitudes of the bodies in the grave and their positions answer at once a part of these questions. If the victims had been killed before entering the grave, they would have been placed all in the same position neatly arranged on the right side, head east, with the right hand under the cheek and the left hand on or near the right elbow. The location and various attitudes of the bodies show that they must have entered the grave alive on their own feet and taken their positions as they could find place. The most casual examination of the photographs will convince anyone of this fact. The only possible conclusion is that these persons died in the grave. A more careful examination of the evidence given in detail in the descriptive chapters reveals the fact that many of these bodies are in attitudes which could only be the result of fear, resolution under pain or its anticipation, or of other movements which would naturally arise in the body of perfectly well persons suffering a conscious death by suffocation. It must be remembered that in those cases where the body was covered directly, the close pressure of the earth would have prevented all but the smallest movements, even those produced by convulsion, and death, or at any rate unconsciousness, would have been a matter of a few minutes. Whatever movements took place would have been mainly the result of fear acting at the last moment before the living body was covered with earth. If a person had the fortitude to withstand the emotion of being covered with earth, subsequently little movement was possible and death came quickly. That there were such persons is clearly shown by a small number of bodies, usually of mature age, which lie approximately in the attitude of those who were buried as corpses. Then there were a few bodies, probably males, who lay in a similar attitude but with the left hand resting on the hilt or the scabbard of their dagger. Even under the hide, the pressure was quite as great, but slightly less close. Only very minor movements, such as those of the extremities, would have been possible after the filling in of the lower part of the grave, but owing to the very slightly greater amount of air, death would have been a little slower. The most unfortunate persons were those, usually younger females, who crept under the bed and being thus enclosed in an air-space of about 0.175 cubic meter died much more gradually by the exhaustion of the air. Thus in the great majority of cases, the movements to be expected are those of emotion in anticipation of death, stirred by the feel of the falling earth. The convulsive movements which take place in a body dying of suffocation will only have been possible in a few cases by accidents of position and chance inequalities in the process of filling the grave.

As a fact, the movements exhibited are largely those of emotion at the prospect of death by burial under earth. The most common thing was for the person to bury the face in the hands. It was also not unusual for one hand to be over the face and the other pressed between the thighs. But most of the better preserved graves presented a case or two of unusual attitudes. In K XX, three bodies have one arm passed around the breast clasping the back of the neck from the opposite side, and indeed that whole group is particularly worthy of attention. In K X B, the very well preserved body AC has the head bent down into the crook of the elbows in a manner most enlightening as an indication of her state of mind at the moment of being covered. Near that body is another lettered PB, which lies on the right side, head west, but with the shoulder turned on the back, while the right hand clutches and presses an ostrich-feather fan against

Pyramids at Meroe, Sudan.

the face which is bent down towards the breast; the left arm passes across the breast so that the left hand holds the right forearm. In K 444, the two bodies, G and H, lie with their foreheads pressed against each other as if for comfort. In K 1026, body B has the fingers of the right hand clenched in the strands of the bead head-circlet, and this was not uncommon. The more unusual conditions are presented by the following examples. In K 3501, the principal sacrifice, a woman who was on a bed under the hide, is turned on her back, legs spread wide apart (probably partly by pressure of filling), left hand half closed on breast, right grasping tightly the right pelvic bone, head bent down against left shoulder. In K 1000A, the woman B, who had been under the bed and is shown by the position of her legs to have been originally on her right side, head east, has turned her body over on the stomach with the head twisted around to lie on its left cheek, facing south instead of north; the arms are stretched down with the left hand on the buttocks and the right apparently grasping the left foot; owing to the lowness of the bed she was unable to turn her legs over without straightening them out and she could not straighten them because they projected beyond the foot of the bed and were held fast by the filling. Another most instructive example is body B in K 1047, a woman lying at the foot of the grave and under a hide; she has turned slightly on her back with the right hand against the right leg and clutches the thorax with the left hand as if in agony. But it is unnecessary to multiply these grewsome evidences further. No one of normal mentality who will read the detailed evidence in the descriptions will escape the conviction that these extra bodies are the remains of persons who died in the places where we found their bones, and who had been in fact buried alive.

Together with these human sacrifices, there were in almost all graves from one to a dozen rams also buried entire and often with the tips of their horns protected by knobs of ivory or wood to prevent goring. Towards the eastern part of the cemetery and in the Nubian graves, the rams become more numerous and the human sacrifices fewer, until in the northern Nubian cemetery most of the graves have only ram sacrifices. In a few cases, the ram was clearly attached by a lead or thong. They were all buried under conditions similar to those of the human beings and therefore probably alive. But in their case the question has less importance. Whether buried alive as I believe or not, these rams are not ordinary food offerings such as were placed in Egyptian graves in all periods; nor have we more than a few similar cases in Egypt. Perhaps the presence of mummified animals in the tombs of human beings may be based on a similar idea.

Much must remain uncertain. It may be suggested that the human sacrifices were more or less stupefied at the great funeral feast, the remains of which I would see in the crescent of ox-skulls about the southern edge of the tumulus. But I judge that feast to have taken place after the burial. . . . I am personally convinced that these people died simply by suffocation. But the question is not of great importance as compared with the general and obvious features of the burial custom here revealed.

. . . But whether the spirit of Prince Hepzefa [who was buried in tomb K III], for example, was setting out on the long journey to Egypt or was remaining to face the unknown spirit-world of the Sudan, his need for the company of his family was more urgent than in Egypt. The family itself was in a still more difficult situation. If they lived on and died singly, whatever perils the after-life might bring, whether those of the journey to Egypt or those of a shadow-world filled with the spirits of the wild tribes and the raging gods of the south, all must face it alone without the aid and protection of their master. Only a few moments of present pain separated them from his familiar presence. Existence was not to cease. The fact of continued existence under the accustomed habits of life on earth was not a matter of doubt. From their point of view manifestly the safest and the most desirable act was to pay the small price and to enter the future life in their familiar family environment. . . . Thus self-sacrifice as practiced in the *satî*-burials at Kerma was not a cruel inhuman thing, but rather a kindly custom, an act of loyalty which provided both him who had died and those who offered themselves to a living death, with the assurance of the continuation of the long-accustomed family life in the other world.

Under such circumstances, the mind attempts to reconstruct the funeral of Prince Hepzefa, probably the first of the Egyptian governors to be buried in Ethiopia. Many of the preliminaries are quite beyond our ken—whether the chapel, K II, and the skeleton of the tumulus had been built before the actual death; to what extent the body was mummified or prepared for burial, whether it lay in state in the thick-walled chapel for some days with the funeral equipment gathered about it; and many similar details. It was entirely in accordance with Egyptian custom to slaughter cattle for a great funeral feast, and the skulls of over a hundred oxen laid on the surface and buried by drift sand around the southern circumference of the tumulus form ocular evidence of such a feast at the funeral of Hepzefa. The disposal of these skulls without rather than within the tumulus seems to indicate that the actual eating took place after the burial. A meat-feast was and remains among primitive people a rare occasion of which advantage was taken by every person within reach and such a ceremonial feast as was provided at the funeral of Hepzefa must have called together almost the whole population of the district for more than fifty miles around, if the delay between death and burial was greater than a few days. I imagine the procession filing out of the chapel, K II, and taking the short path to the western entrance of the long corridor of the tumulus, K III; the blue-glazed quartzite bed, on which the dead Hepzefa probably already lay covered with linen garments, his sword between his thighs, his pillow, his fan, his sandals in their places; the servants bearing alabaster jars of ointments, boxes of toilet articles and games, the great blue faience sailing boats with all their crews in place, the beautifully decorated faience vessels and the fine pottery of the prince's daily life; perhaps the porters straining at the ropes which drew the two great statues set on sledges, although these may have been taken to the tomb before this day; the bearers who had the easier burden of the statuettes; the crowd of women and attendants of the hareem decked in their most cherished finery, many carrying some necessary utensil or vessel. They proceed, not in the ceremonial silence of our funerals, but with all the "ululations" and wailings of the people of the Nile. The bed with the body is placed in Chamber C, the finer objects in that chamber and in the anteroom, the pottery among the statues and statuettes set in the corridor. The doors of the chambers are closed and sealed. The priests and officials withdraw. The women and attendants take their place jostling in the narrow corridor, perhaps still with shrill cries or speaking only such words as the selection of their places required. The cries and all movements cease. The signal is given. The crowd of people assembled for the feast, now waiting ready, cast the earth from their baskets upon the still, but living victims on the floor and rush away for more. The frantic confusion and haste of the assisting multitude is easy to imagine. The emotions of the victims may perhaps be exaggerated by ourselves; they were fortified and sustained by their religious beliefs, and had taken their places willingly, without doubt, but at that last moment, we know from their attitudes in death that a rustle of fear passed through them and that in some cases there was a spasm of physical agony.

The corridor was quickly filled. With earth conveniently placed, a few hundred men could do that work in a quarter of an hour; a few thousands with filled baskets could have accomplished the task in a few minutes. The assembled crowd turned then probably to the great feast. The oxen had been slaughtered ceremonially to send their spirits with the spirit of the prince. The meat must be eaten, as was ever the case. If I am right in my interpretation of the hearths, consisting of ashes and red-burned earth, which dot the plain to the west and south of the tumulus, the crowd received the meat in portions and dispersed over the adjacent ground in family or village groups to cook and eat it. No doubt the wailing and the feasting lasted for days, accompanied by games and dances.

Ukhaidir and Assur

Gertrude Bell

Women have played a leading role in twentieth-century archaeological discovery, but rarely have received credit for their finds. One woman did—the redoubtable Gertrude Bell, who enjoyed minor celebrity as a desert traveler and archaeologist before World War I. She also achieved fame as a founder of modern archaeology in Iraq.

Gertrude Bell (1868–1926) was the daughter of a wealthy Yorkshire ironmaster. She was one of the first women to attend Oxford University, graduating in 1888 with a first-class degree in modern history. Bell then began to travel seriously and became one of the foremost women mountain climbers of her generation. In 1899, she spent seven months in Jerusalem to perfect her Arabic, developing a passion for archaeology and desert travel. By 1909, she had published two acclaimed travel books and a definitive study of the Thousand and One Churches at Birbinkilise in Byzantine Anatolia, a unique record of sites that no longer exist. That year, she set off from Aleppo across the desert to the Euphrates River, her destination the late-eighth-century walled Abbasid palace of Ukhaidir, a huge castle with a fortified enclosure. Bell spent four days planning and photographing the site for the first time, hampered by an armed escort, men who refused to put down their rifles, even when holding tapes. Ukhaidir held a deep appeal for Gertrude Bell. She also thoroughly enjoyed her visit to the German excavations at the Assyrian city of Assur (occupied during the early and middle first millennium B.C.) on the Tigris River, where she befriended the eminent archaeologist Walter Andrae. Her most famous book, Amurath to Amurath *(1911), described her adventures. In it, Bell hinted at the rising tide of Arab nationalism that she encountered in her travels.*

Bell's knowledge of the Near East caused her to be sent to intelligence headquarters in Cairo in 1916. She became an assistant to Sir Percy Cox, the first British civil commissioner in Baghdad after World War I. One of her responsibilities was antiquities, both the administration of new laws protecting sites and controlling the export of artifacts, and the development of a new Iraq Museum. She exercised enormous power over foreign expeditions in Iraq, including the early stages of Leonard Woolley's work at Ur. Of striking appearance and prodigious learning, Bell was resented by many Iraqi nationalists, who accused her of giving away their patrimony. But she was one of the founders of modern archaeology in Iraq. Her writings about the desert were widely read more than three-quarters of a century ago.

125

———————

Great Discoveries

In this selection from her best seller Amurath to Amurath, *Gertrude Bell describes Ukhaidir and her visit to the German excavations at Assur.*

Of all the wonderful experiences that have fallen my way, the first sight of Kheidir is the most memorable. It reared its mighty walls out of the sand, almost untouched by time, breaking the long lines of the waste with its huge towers, steadfast and massive, as though it were, as I had at first thought it, the work of nature, not of man. We approached it from the north, on which side a long low building runs out towards the sandy depression of the Wâdî Lebai'ah. A zaptieth caught me up as I reached the first of the vaulted rooms, and out of the northern gateway a man in long robes of white and black came trailing down towards us through the hot silence.

"Peace be upon you," said he.

"And upon you peace, Sheikh 'Alî," returned the zaptieh. "This lady is of the English."

"Welcome, my lady Khân," said the sheikh; "be pleased to enter and to rest."

He led me through a short passage and under a tiny dome. I was aware of immense corridors opening on either hand, but we passed on into a great vaulted hall where the Arabs sat round the ashes of a fire.

"My lady Khân," said Sheikh 'Alî, "this is the castle of Nu'mân ibn Mundhir."

Whether it were a Lakhmid palace or no, it was the palace which I had set forth to seek. It belongs architecturally to the group of Sassanian buildings which are already known to us, and historically it is related to the palaces, famous in pre-Mohammadan tradition, whose splendours had filled with amazement the invading hordes of the Bedouin, and still shine with a legendary magnificence, from the pages of the chroniclers of the conquest. Even for the Mohammadan writers they had become nothing but a name. Khawarnak, Sadîr, and the rest, fell into ruin with Ḥîrah, the capital of the small Arab principality that occupied the frontiers of the desert, and their site was a matter of hearsay or conjecture. "Think on the lord of Khawarnak," sang 'Adî ibn Zaid prophetically,

> eyes guided of God see clear—
> He rejoiced in his might and the strength of his hands, the encompassing
>   wave and Sadîr;
> And his heart stood still and he spake: "What joy have the living to death
>   addressed?
> For the open cleft of the grave lies close upon pleasure and power and rest.
> Like a withered leaf they fall, and the wind shall scatter them east and west."

But for all its total disappearance under the wave of Islâm, the Lakhmid state had played a notable part in the development of Arab culture. It was at Ḥîrah that the desert came into contact with the highly organized civilization of the Persians, with the wealth of cultivated lands and the long-established order of a settled population; there, too, as among the Ghassânids on the Syrian side of the wilderness, they made acquaintance with the precepts of Christianity which exercised so marked an influence on the latest poets of the Age of Ignorance, some of whom, like 'Adî ibn Zaid himself, are known to have been Christians, and prepared the way for the Prophet's teaching. So little have the eastern borders of the Syrian desert been explored that except for the ruin field of Ḥîrah, a town which was destroyed in order to furnish building materials for the Moslem city of Kûfah, and a cluster of mouldering vaults, said to represent the castle of Khawarnaḳ, not one of the famous pre-Mohammadan sites has been identified, and it is possible that important vestiges of the Lakhmid age may lie unsuspected within a few days' journey from regions familiar to travellers and even to tourists. Meanwhile Kheiḍir (the name is the colloquial abbreviation of Ukheiḍir = a small green place) is the finest example of Sassanian architecture which has yet been discovered. Its wonderful state of preservation is probably due to the fact that it was some distance removed from the nearest inhabited spot. Shetâteh is separated from it by three hours of naked desert; the canals that feed Kerbelâ are yet further away, and the water supply of Ukheiḍir, derived from wells in the Wâdî Lebai'ah, is too small to have tempted the fellaḥîn to establish themselves there. Nowhere in the vicinity, so far as I could learn, are there more abundant springs, and the palace has therefore been allowed to drop into a slow decay, forgotten in the midst of its wildernesses, save when a raiding expedition brings the Bedouin into the neighbourhood of Shetâteh.

Most of us who have had opportunity to become familiar with some site that has once been the theatre of a vanished civilization have passed through hours of vain imaginings during which the thoughts labour to recapture the aspect of street and market, church or temple enclosure, of which the evidences lie strewn over the surface of the earth. And ever, as a thousand unanswerable problems surge up against the realization of that empty hope, I have found myself longing for an hour out of a remote century, wherein I might look my fill upon the walls that have fallen and stamp the image of a dead world indelibly upon my mind. The dream seemed to have reached fulfilment at Ukheiḍir. There the architecture of a by-gone age presented itself in unexampled perfection to the eye. It was not necessary to guess at the structure of vaults or the decorative scheme of niched façades—the camera and the measuring-tape could register the methods of the builder and the results which he had achieved. . . .

. . . A more wonderful sight was in store for us on the next day's march. We had travelled barely two hours when we splashed into a pool of rain-water, and then into another; there was grass round them, green, abundant grass: "More than we have seen all the way from Aleppo!" exclaimed Jûsef. The region of the drought was over, and when our path led us to the top of the Jebel Ḥamrîn, here sunk to a low hog's back, I was scarcely surprised to see the slopes down to the Tigris red with poppies. But even the poppies could not withhold the eye from the great mound of Ḳal'at Shergât by the river's edge, the mound of Asshur, crowned with the crumbling mass of a huge zigurrat, the temple pyramid of the tutelary god of the Assyrians. With the general aspect of the first capital of Assyria I was already familiar, thanks to the excellent photographs published by the German Orient-Gesellschaft, but I was not prepared for so magnificent a prospect. The Tigris in high flood washed the foot of the temple mound; far away to the north ran the snow-clad barrier of mountains whence its waters flow—a barrier which Nature planted in vain against the valour of the Assyrian armies; and across the river the fertile plain stretched away in long undulations to where Arbela lies behind low hills. Bountiful gods had showered their gifts upon the land. . . .

A site better favoured than Ḳal'at Shergât for excavations such as those undertaken by Dr. Andrae and his colleagues could scarcely have been selected. It has not given them the storied slabs and huge stone guardians of the gates of kings with which Layard enriched the British Museum; they have disappeared during the many periods of reconstruction which the town has witnessed; but those very reconstructions add to the historic interest of the excavations. Asshur was in existence in the oldest Assyrian period, and down to the latest days of the empire it was an honoured shrine of the gods; there are traces of Persian occupation; in Parthian times the city was re-built, walls and gates were set up anew, and the whole area within the ancient fortifications was re-inhabited. . . .

The temple of the god Asshur, of which the zigurrat is the most notable feature of Ḳal'at Shergât, goes back to the earliest Assyrian times, but the greater part of it is occupied by a Turkish guard-house, and has not yet been excavated. The court between temple and zigurrat lies open; in a later age the Parthians adorned it with a splendid colonnade, and it is here that Dr. Andrae has succeeded in piecing together large fragments of Parthian architectural decoration which throw a new light both upon the arts of Parthia and upon the succeeding era of the Sassanians. Fortunately there exist upon the mound other temples of the Assyrian period which he has been better able to study. Chief of these is the double shrine of the gods Anu and Adad, lords of heaven and of the thunderstorm, the excavation of which cost him many months of difficult work. The temple was finished by Tiglathpileser at the end of the twelfth century before Christ, but in the course of some three hundred years it fell into complete decay; Shalmaneser II, he who received the homage of Jehu, as is recorded on the Black Obelisk in the British Museum, filled in the ruins of the earlier shrine and set a new edifice upon them, preserving almost exactly the plan of the old. No Assyrian temple has hitherto been studied accurately, save one of Sargon's at Khorsabâd, later by more than a century than the second temple of Anu and Adad; it was therefore necessary to get an exact record of both the periods at Asshur, and in order to leave Shalmaneser's work undisturbed, Dr. Andrae was compelled to trace that of Tiglathpileser by means of a system of underground tunnels. "I have never," he observed, as he surveyed his handiwork, "done anything so mad." But the results have more than justified the labour. The scheme of the Assyrian temple has now been established by examples ranging over a period of four hundred years, and it is conclusively proved that it

A panoramic view of the German excavations at Assur.

differed in a remarkable degree from the Babylonian temple plan, and was related to the plan adopted by Solomon. In Babylonia the chambers are all laid
broadways in respect of the entrance; that is to say, the door is placed in the
centre of one of the long sides, so that he who enters has only a narrow area in
front of him, and must look to right and left if he would appreciate the size of
the hall. At Jerusalem and in Assyria the main sanctuary ran lengthways, an
immense artistic advance, inasmuch as the broadways-lying hall was at best a
clumsy contrivance which could never have given the sense of space and dignity
conveyed by the other. To the genius of what builders are we to attribute this
masterly comprehension of spatial effect? The question cannot as yet be answered, but Dr. Andrae is inclined to seek outside Syria and Mesopotamia for
the prototypes of Asshur and Jerusalem. In the palaces, be it noted, the
lengthways hall was never adopted, but palace architecture is not well illustrated
at Asshur, those buildings having been the first to suffer at the hands of the
spoiler.

The walls to the north of the temples are perhaps the most impressive part
of the excavations. The mound on which the city is built reaches here its greatest elevation, and the gigantic masses of the fortifications rear themselves up
from its very base. Time after time the kings of Assyria renewed these bulwarks,
setting them forward further and further against the river, which once washed
their foundations—its bed runs now a little more to the east, where the stream
still flows under the eastern quays of Asshur. The upper parts of the walls are
of unburnt brick, but the lower, as Xenophon observed at Nimrûd, are cased in
massive stone. The stonework was not in reality as durable as the brick, for the
Assyrians had no binding mortar, and the stones, being set together with mud,
could not resist a pressure from behind, such as that which was offered by the
mound itself. A mortar of asphalt is sometimes used in sun-dried brick, but
binding mortar seems to have been a discovery of the age of Nebuchadnezzar,
since it is first found in constructions of his time at Babylon. The fortifications
sweep round southwards to the Gurgurri Gate, well known in inscriptions, and
identified by epigraphic evidence. Between the gate and the temple and palace
area, a great part of the ground is covered with a network of streets and houses
belonging to a late Assyrian period. The larger houses consist of an outer court

Gertrude Bell in Arab headdress surveying at Ukhaidir,
accompanied by an armed escort.

with rooms for servants and dependents, roughly floored with big cobblestones and traversed by a pathway of smaller cobbles whereon the masters could cross to the inner paved court round which their chambers lay. Every house, however small, is provided with a bath-room. The whole complex has the appearance of another Pompeii, though it is more ancient than the Italian Pompeii by six or seven hundred years. Down in the plain, outside the city walls, stood a magnificent building which has been christened by the excavators the Festhaus. It is a fine open court, surrounded on two sides by a colonnade, while on the side opposite to the gate there is a raised platform of solid masonry. The court must have had the aspect of a formal garden, for at regular intervals there are holes in the hard conglomerate of the floor which the excavators conjecture to have been filled with earth and planted with shrubs. In this colonnaded garden was celebrated the spring sacrifice, the annual festival in honour of the fruitful earth. The plan of the building is not Assyrian—the column itself is a non-Mesopotamian feature—but whence it was derived it would be impossible as yet to say.

Throughout the area of the city a series of deep trial trenches have been dug, cutting through the Parthian period, through the late Assyrian, and down to the earliest times. These trenches afford materials for the most fascinating studies. One of the earliest cities that stood upon the mound of Asshur is, curiously enough, the easiest to trace. The houses are in an unusually perfect state; their walls, preserved not infrequently to a height of several feet, enclose little cobbled courtyards with narrow cobbled streets between. These worn and ancient ways, emerging from under the steep sides of the trench and disappearing again into the earth at its furthest limit, give the observer a sense as of visualized history, as though the millenniums had dropped away that separate him from the busy life of the antique world. It is probable that the city to which they belong was destroyed by some overwhelming catastrophe, laid desolate, perhaps by an onslaught of the Mitanni kings of northern Mesopotamia or of the Babylonians from the south, and so left in age-long ruin until a later generation completed the filling up of court and street which had been begun by time, levelled the whole and built their dwellings upon foundations of the past. The Assyrians were content to leave their story inscribed on clay cylinder or on stone; they did not, like the Egyptians, rear for their dead enduring monuments, but each man in turn was thrust into a clay sarcophagus or sepulchral jar lying immediately below the floor of his own dwelling—we counted as many as fifteen burials in one of the smaller houses—or placed, with a slightly greater regard for the comfort of the living, in an adjoining subterranean chamber vaulted with brick.

As Dr. Andrae led me about the city, drawing forth its long story with infinite skill from wall and trench and cuneiform inscription, the lavish cruel past rushed in upon us. The myriad soldiers of the Great King, transported from the reliefs in the British Museum, marched through the gates of Asshur; the captives, roped and bound, crowded the streets; defeated princes bowed themselves before the victor and subject races piled up their tribute in his courts. We saw the monarch go out to the chase, and heard the roaring of the lion, half paralyzed by the dart in its spine, which animates the stone with its wild anguish. Human victims cried out under nameless tortures; the tide of battle raged against the walls, and, red with carnage, rose into the palaces. Splendour and misery, triumph and despair, lifted their head out of the dust.

One hot night I sat with my hosts upon the roof of their house. The Tigris, in unprecedented flood, swirled against the mound, a waste of angry waters. Above us rose the zigurrat of the god Asshur. It had witnessed for four thousand years the melting of the Kurdish snows, flood-time and the harvest that follows; gigantic, ugly, intolerably mysterious, it dominated us, children of an hour.

"What did they watch from its summit?" I asked, stung into a sharp consciousness of the unknown by a scene almost as old as recorded life.

"They watched the moon," said Dr. Andrae, "as we do. Who knows? they watched for the god."

I have left few places so unwillingly as I left Ḳal'at Shergât.

The Royal Cemetery at Ur

LEONARD WOOLLEY

Few archaeological discoveries rival those of Tutankhamun in Egypt and the Royal Cemetery at Ur of the Chaldees, commonly called Ur, in Iraq. In both cases, we are fortunate that the excavators involved were extremely skilled by the standards of the day. And, in the case of Ur, we are also lucky that Leonard Woolley was a gifted writer for a popular audience.

Sir Charles Leonard Woolley's excavation of the royal cemetery at Ur earned him a reputation as one of the greatest excavators of this century. Woolley (1880–1960) got his professional start following in the footsteps of his famous predecessor, Sir Arthur Evans, by working at the Ashmolean Museum at Oxford. After learning the techniques of excavation in Nubia, he excavated at Carchemish on the Euphrates River in Syria before World War I. The British Museum and the University of Pennsylvania Museum appointed Woolley to the Ur excavations in 1921. From 1922 to 1934, he excavated large parts of the ancient biblical city, which was in its heyday in the third millennium B.C., working with a large number of workers and assisted by only a handful of trained specialists.

Woolley practiced a cautious stratigraphic excavation method, following natural layers in the soil the better to observe the depositional history of the site. He uncovered residential quarters of the city, excavated the great ziggurat, and probed to the base of the city mound, where he found a tiny farming village. This particular test excavation took him through a thick, sterile layer of river silt, which he attributed to the biblical Flood, a conclusion based more on enthusiasm than on scholarly argument. Woolley had no illusions about the difficulty of excavating at Ur, believing that caution would yield rich dividends. He kept careful records of the pottery types he found in every layer, using them to form comparative chronologies across different parts of the site.

His men first found gold and graves in the 1922 season. Realizing that he had found a royal cemetery, Woolley waited for four years to resume work on the graves, reasoning that his men needed more practical excavation experience before attempting to unearth a cemetery. He wanted also to be certain of the chronology he was developing before proceeding any further. By waiting, too, Woolley managed to avoid competing for international publicity with the Tutankhamun discovery, which at the time had a vir-

tual monopoly on archaeological news headlines. Woolley's discussion of the mass sacrifices in the royal tombs bears witness to a careful and logical reconstruction of past events based on the smallest details of his finds. The Royal Cemetery throws dramatic light on the life and rituals surrounding a Sumerian ruler, who expected to take his entire retinue with him to the next life. Woolley's vivid descriptions, published in popular accounts such as Ur of the Chaldees *(1929), made archaeology accessible to the lay reader and did much to promote the budding science and the thrill of discovery as well. One of Woolley's colleagues, archaeologist Max Mallowan, met detective novelist Agatha Christie at the excavations. He subsequently married her, and her book* Murder in Mesopotamia *is based on her experiences at Ur and on her complex relationship with Woolley's wife, Katherine, a controversial figure who brooked no rivals.*

Here is Woolley's reconstruction of a royal funeral at Ur, re-created from months of painstaking archaeology. His Ur of the Chaldees, *from which this selection comes, remains a classic of archaeological writing. But it should be noted that his excavation notes are sufficiently incomplete to make it nearly impossible for modern-day archaeologists to check his reconstruction.*

In 1927–1928, soon after our disappointment with the plundered stone tomb, we found, in another part of the field, five bodies lying side by side in a shallow sloping trench; except for the copper daggers at their waists and one or two small clay cups, they had none of the normal furniture of a grave, and the mere fact of there being a number thus together was unusual. Then, below them, a layer of matting was found, and tracing this along we came to another group of bodies, those of ten women carefully arranged in two rows; they wore head-dresses of gold, lapis lazuli, and carnelian, and elaborate bead necklaces, but they too possessed no regular tomb furnishings. At the end of the row lay the remains of a wonderful harp, the wood of it decayed but its decoration intact, making its reconstruction only a matter of care; the upright wooden beam was capped with gold, and in it were fastened the gold-headed nails which secured the strings; the sounding box was edged with a mosaic in red stone, lapis lazuli, and white shell, and from the front of it projected a splendid head of a bull wrought in gold with eyes and beard of lapis lazuli; across the ruins of the harp lay the bones of the gold-crowned harpist.

By this time we had found the earth sides of the pit in which the women's bodies lay and could see that the bodies of the five men were on the ramp which led down to it. Following the pit along, we came upon more bones, which at first puzzled us by being other than human, but the meaning of them soon became clear. A little way inside the entrance to the pit stood a wooden sledge chariot decorated with red, white, and blue mosaic along the edges of the frame-work and with golden heads of lions having manes of lapis lazuli and shell on its side panels; along the top rail were smaller gold heads of lions and bulls, silver lionesses' heads adorned the front, and the position of the vanished swinglebar was shown by a band of blue and white inlay and two smaller heads of lionesses in silver. In front of the chariot lay the crushed skeletons of two asses with the bodies of the grooms by their heads, and on the top of the bones was the double ring, once attached to the pole, through which the reins had passed; it was of silver, and standing on it was a gold "mascot" in the form of a donkey most beautifully and realistically modeled.

Close to the chariot were an inlaid gaming board and a collection of tools and weapons, including a set of chisels and a saw made of gold, big bowls of grey soapstone, copper vessels, a long tube of gold and lapis which was a drinking tube for sucking up liquor from the bowls, more human bodies, and then the wreckage of a large wooden chest adorned with a figured mosaic in lapis lazuli and shell which was found empty but had perhaps contained such perishable things as clothes. Behind this box were more offerings, masses of vessels in copper, silver, stone (including exquisite examples in volcanic glass, lapis lazuli, alabaster, and marble), and gold; one set of silver vessels seemed to be in the nature of a communion service, for there was a shallow tray or platter, a jug with tall neck and long spout such as we know from carved stone reliefs to have been used in religious rites, and tall slender silver tumblers nested one inside another; a similar tumbler in gold, fluted and chased, with a fluted feeding bowl, a chalice, and plain oval bowl of gold lay piled together, and two magnificent lions' heads in silver, perhaps the ornaments of a throne, were amongst the treasures in the crowded pit. The perplexing thing was that with all this wealth of objects we had found no body so far distinguished from the rest as to be that of the person to whom all were dedicated; logically our discovery, however great, was incomplete.

The objects were removed and we started to clear away the remains of the wooden box, a chest some 6 feet long and 3 feet across, when under it we found burnt bricks. They were fallen, but at one end some were still in place and formed the ring vault of a stone chamber. The first and natural supposition was that here we had the tomb to which all the offerings belonged, but further search proved that the chamber was plundered, the roof had not fallen from decay but had been broken through, and the wooden box had been placed over the hole as if deliberately to hide it. Then, digging round the outside of the chamber, we found just such another pit as that 6 feet above. At the foot of the ramp lay six soldiers, orderly in two ranks, with copper spears by their sides and copper helmets crushed flat on the broken skulls; just inside, having evidently been backed down the slope, were two wooden four-wheeled waggons each drawn by three oxen—one of the latter so well preserved that we were able to lift the skeleton entire; the waggons were plain, but the reins were decorated with long beads of lapis and silver and passed through silver rings surmounted with mascots in the form of bulls; the grooms lay at the oxen's heads and the drivers in the bodies of the cars; of the cars themselves only the impression of the decayed wood remained in the soil, but so clear was this that a photograph showed the grain of the solid wooden wheel and the grey-white circle which had been the leather tyre.

Against the end wall of the stone chamber lay the bodies of nine women wearing the gala headdress of lapis and carnelian beads from which hung golden pendants in the forms of beech leaves, great lunate earrings of gold, silver "combs" like the palm of a hand with three fingers tipped with flowers whose petals are inlaid with lapis, gold, and shell, and necklaces of lapis and gold; their heads were leaned against the masonry, their bodies extended onto the floor of the pit, and the whole space between them and the waggons was crowded with other dead, women and men, while the passage which led along the side of the chamber to its arched door was lined with soldiers carrying daggers, and with women. Of the soldiers in the central space one had a bundle of four spears with heads of gold, two had sets of four silver spears, and by another there was a remarkable relief in copper with a design of two lions trampling on the bodies of two fallen men which may have been the decoration of a shield.

On the top of the bodies of the "court ladies" against the chamber walls had been placed a wooden harp, of which there survived only the copper head of a bull and the shell plaques which had adorned the sounding box; by the side wall of the pit, also set on the top of the bodies, was a second harp with a wonderful bull's head in gold, its eyes, beard, and horn tips of lapis, and a set of engraved shell plaques not less wonderful; there are four of them with grotesque scenes of animals playing the parts of men, and while the most striking feature about them is that sense of humour which is so rare in ancient art, the grace and balance of the design and the fineness of the drawing make of these plaques one of the most instructive documents that we possess for the appreciation of the art of early Sumer.

Inside the tomb the robbers had left enough to show that it had contained bodies of several minor people as well as that of the chief person, whose name, if we can trust the inscription on a cylinder seal, was A-bar-gi; overlooked against the wall we found two model boats, one of copper now hopelessly decayed, the other of silver wonderfully well preserved; some 2 feet long, it has a high stern and prow, five seats, and amidships an arched support for the awning which would protect the passenger, and the leaf-bladed oars are still set in the thwarts; it is a testimony to the conservatism of the East that a boat of identical type is in use today on the marshes of the Lower Euphrates, some 50 miles from Ur.

The king's tomb chamber lay at the far end of his open pit; continuing our search behind it we found a second stone chamber built up against it either at the same time or, more probably, at a later period. This chamber, roofed like the king's with a vault of ring arches in burnt brick, was the tomb of the queen to whom belonged the upper pit with its ass chariot and other offerings: her name, Shub-ad, was given us by a fine cylinder seal of lapis lazuli which was found in the filling of the shaft a little above the roof of the chamber and had probably been thrown into the pit at the moment when the earth was being put back into it. The vault of the chamber had fallen in, but luckily this was due to the weight of earth above, not to the violence of tomb robbers; the tomb itself was intact.

At one end, on the remains of a wooden bier, lay the body of the queen, a

Leonard and Katherine Woolley at work in the Royal Cemetery at Ur, Iraq.

gold cup near her hand; the upper part of the body was entirely hidden by a mass of beads of gold, silver, lapis lazuli, carnelian, agate, and chalcedony, long strings of which, hanging from a collar, had formed a cloak reaching to the waist and bordered below with a broad band of tubular beads of lapis, carnelian, and gold: against the right arm were three long gold pins with lapis heads and three amulets in the form of fish, two of gold and one of lapis, and a fourth in the form of two seated gazelles, also of gold.

The headdress whose remains covered the crushed skull was a more elaborate edition of that worn by the court ladies: its basis was a broad gold ribbon festooned in loops round the hair—and the measurement of the curves showed that this was not the natural hair but a wig padded out to an almost grotesque size; over this came three wreaths, the lowest, hanging down over the forehead, of plain gold ring pendants, the second of beech leaves, the third of long willow leaves in sets of three with gold flowers whose petals were of blue and white inlay; all these were strung on triple chains of lapis and carnelian beads. Fixed into the back of the hair was a golden "Spanish comb" with five points ending in lapis-centred gold flowers. Heavy spiral rings of gold wire were twisted into the side curls of the wig, huge lunate earrings of gold hung down to the shoulders, and apparently from the hair also hung on each side a string of large square stone beads with, at the end of each, a lapis amulet, one shaped as a seated bull and the other as a calf. Complicated as the headdress was, its different parts lay in such good order that it was possible to reconstruct the whole and exhibit the likeness of the queen with all her original finery in place.

For the purposes of exhibition a plaster cast was made from a well-preserved female skull of the period (the queen's own skull was too fragmentary to be used), and over this my wife modelled the features in wax, making this as thin as possible so as not to obliterate the bone structure; the face was passed by Sir Arthur Keith, who has made a special study of the Ur and al 'Ubaid skulls, as reproducing faithfully the character of the early Sumerians. On this head was put a wig of the correct dimensions dressed in the fashion illustrated by terra-cotta figures which, though later in date, probably represented an old tradition. The gold hair ribbon had been lifted from the tomb without disturbing the arrangement of the strands, these having been first fixed in position by strips of glued paper threaded in and out between them and by wires twisted round the gold; when the wig had been fitted on the head, the hair ribbon was balanced on the top and the wires and paper bands were cut, and the ribbon fell naturally into place and required no further arranging. The wreaths were restrung and tied on in the order noted at the time of excavation. Though the face is not an actual portrait of the queen, it gives at least the type to which she must have conformed, and the whole reconstructed head presents us with the most accurate picture we are likely ever to possess of what she looked like in her lifetime.

By the side of the body lay a second headdress of a novel sort. Onto a diadem made apparently of a strip of soft white leather had been sewn thousands of minute lapis lazuli beads, and against this background of solid blue were set a row of exquisitely fashioned gold animals—stags, gazelles, bulls, and goats—with between them clusters of pomegranates, three fruits hanging together shielded by their leaves, and branches of some other tree with golden stems and fruit or pods of gold and carnelian, while gold rosettes were sewn on at intervals, and from the lower border of the diadem hung palmettes of twisted gold wire.

The bodies of two women attendants were crouched against the bier, one at its head and one at its foot, and all about the chamber lay strewn offerings of all sorts, another gold bowl, vessels of silver and copper, stone bowls and clay jars for food, the head of a cow in silver, two silver tables for offerings, silver lamps, and a number of large cockleshells containing green paint; such shells are nearly always found in women's graves, and the paint in them, presumably used as a cosmetic, may be white, black, or red, but the normal colour is green. Queen Shubad's shells were abnormally big, and with them were found two pairs of imitation shells, one in silver and one in gold, each with its green paint.

The discovery was now complete and our earlier difficulty was explained: King A-bar-gi's grave and Queen Shub-ad's were exactly alike, but whereas the former was all on one plane, the queen's tomb chamber had been sunk below the ground level of her grave pit. Probably they were husband and wife: the king had died first and been buried, and it had been the queen's wish to lie as close to him as might be; for this end the gravediggers had reopened the king's shaft, going down in it until the top of the chamber vault appeared; then they had stopped work in the main shaft but had dug down at the back of the chamber pit in which the queen's stone tomb could be built. But the treasures known to lie in the king's grave were too great a temptation for the workmen; the outer pit where the bodies of the court ladies lay was protected by 6 feet of earth which they could not disturb without being detected, but the richer plunder in the royal chamber itself was separated from them only by the bricks of the vault; they broke through the arch, carried off their spoil, and placed the great clothes chest of the queen over the hole to hide their sacrilege.

Nothing else would account for the plundered vault lying immediately below the untouched grave of the queen; and the connecting of Shub-ad's stone chamber with the upper "death pit," as we came to call these open shafts in which the subsidiary bodies lay, made an exact parallel to the king's grave and, in a lesser degree, to the other royal tombs. Clearly, when a royal person died, he or she was accompanied to the grave by all the members of the court: the king had at least three people with him in his chamber and sixty-two in the death pit; the queen was content with some twenty-five in all. Here we had a single stone chamber and an open death pit; where there was a larger stone building with two or four rooms, then one of these was for the royal body and the rest for the followers sacrificed in precisely the same way; the ritual was identical, only the accommodation for the victims differed in different cases.

On the subject of human sacrifice more light was thrown by the discovery of a great death pit excavated last winter. At about 26 feet below the surface we came upon a mass of mud brick not truly laid but rammed together and forming, as we guessed, not a floor but the stopping, as it were, of a shaft. Immediately below this we were able to distinguish the clean-cut earth sides of a pit, sloping inward and smoothly plastered with mud; following these down, we found the largest death pit that the cemetery has yet produced. The pit was roughly rectangular and measured 37 feet by 24 at the bottom, and was approached as usual by a sloped ramp. In it lay the bodies of six men-servants and sixty-eight women; the men lay along the side by the door, the bodies of the women were disposed in regular rows across the floor, every one lying on her side with legs slightly bent and hands brought up near the face, so close together that the heads of those in one row rested on the legs of those in the row above. Here was to be observed even more clearly what had been fairly obvious in the graves of Shub-ad and her husband, the neatness with which the bodies were laid out, the entire absence of any signs of violence or terror.

We have often been asked how the victims in the royal graves met their death, and it is impossible to give a decisive answer. The bones are too crushed and too decayed to show any cause of death, supposing that violence had been used, but the general condition of the bodies does supply a strong argument. Very many of these women wear headdresses which are delicate in themselves and would easily be disarranged, yet such are always found in good order, undisturbed except by the pressure of the earth; this would be impossible if the wearers had been knocked on the head, improbable if they had fallen to the ground after being stabbed, and it is equally unlikely that they could have been killed outside the grave and carried down the ramp and laid in their places with all their ornaments intact; certainly the animals must have been alive when they dragged the chariots down the ramps, and, if so, the grooms who led them and the drivers in the cars must have been alive also: it is safe to assume that those who were to be sacrificed went down alive into the pit.

That they were dead, or at least unconscious, when the earth was flung in and trampled down on top of them is an equally safe assumption, for in any other case there must have been some struggle which would have left its traces in the attitude of the bodies, but these are always decently composed; indeed, they are in such good order and alignment that we are driven to suppose that after they were lying unconscious someone entered the pit and gave the final touches to their arrangement—and the circumstance that in A-bar-gi's grave, the harps were placed on the top of the bodies proves that someone did enter the grave at the end. It is most probable that the victims walked to their places, took some kind of drug—opium or hashish would serve—and lay down in order; after the drug had worked, whether it produced sleep or death, the last touches were given to their bodies and the pit was filled in. There does not seem to have been anything brutal in the manner of their deaths.

None the less, the sight of the remains of the victims is gruesome enough with the gold leaves and the colored beads lying thick on the crushed and broken skulls, but in excavating a great death pit such as that of last winter we do not see it as a whole, but have to clear it a little at a time. The soil was removed until the bodies were almost exposed, covered only by the few inches of broken brick which had been the first of the filling thrown over the dead; here and there a pick driven too deep might bring to view a piece of gold ribbon or a golden beech leaf, showing that everywhere there were bodies richly adorned, but these would be quickly covered up again and left until more methodical work should reveal them in due course. Starting in one corner of the pit, we marked out squares such as might contain from five to six bodies, and all these were cleared, noted, and the objects belonging to them collected and removed before the next square was taken in hand.

It was slow work, and especially so in those cases where we decided to remove the entire skull with all its ornaments in position on it. The wreaths and chains and necklaces restrung and arranged in a glass case may look very well, but it is more interesting to see them as they were actually found, and therefore a few heads on which the original order of the beads and goldwork was best preserved were laboriously cleaned with small knives and brushes, the dirt being removed without disturbing any of the ornaments—a difficult matter as they are loose in the soil—and then boiling paraffin wax was poured over them, solidifying them in one mass. The lump of wax, earth, bone, and gold was then strengthened by waxed cloth pressed carefully over it, so that it could be lifted from the ground by undercutting. Mounted in plaster, with the superfluous wax cleaned off, these heads form an exhibit which is not only of interest in itself but proves the accuracy of the restorations which we have made of others.

Of the sixty-eight women in the pit, twenty-eight wore hair ribbons of gold. At first sight it looked as if the others had nothing of the kind, but closer examination showed that many, if not all, had originally worn exactly similar ribbons of silver. Unfortunately silver is a metal which ill resists the action of the acids in the soil, and where it was but a thin strip and, being worn on the head, was directly affected by the corruption of the flesh, it generally disappears altogether, and at most there may be detected on the bone of the skull slight traces of a purplish colour, which is silver chloride in a minutely powdered state: we could be certain that the ribbons were worn, but we could not produce material evidence of them.

But in one case we had better luck. The great gold earrings were in place, but not a sign of discolouration betrayed the existence of any silver headdress, and this negative evidence was duly noted; then, as the body was cleared, there was found against it, about on the level of the waist, a flat disk a little more than 3 inches across of a grey substance which was certainly silver; it might have been a small circular box. Only when I was cleaning it in the house that evening, hoping to find something which would enable me to catalogue it more in detail, did its real nature come to light: it was the silver hair ribbon, but it had never been worn—carried apparently in the woman's pocket, it was just as she had taken it from her room, done up in a tight coil with the ends brought over to prevent its coming undone; and since it formed thus a comparatively solid mass of metal and had been protected by the cloth of her dress, it was very well preserved and even the delicate edges of the ribbon were sharply distinct. Why the owner had not put it on one could not say; perhaps she was late for the ceremony and had not time to dress properly, but her haste has in any case afforded us the only example of a silver hair ribbon which we are likely ever to find.

Another thing that perishes utterly in the earth is cloth, but occasionally on lifting a stone bowl which has lain inverted over a bit of stuff and has protected it from the soil, one sees traces which, although only of fine dust, keep the texture of the material, or a copper vessel may by its corrosion preserve some fragment which was in contact with it. By such evidence we were able to prove that the women in the death pit wore garments of bright red woollen stuff; and as many of them had at the wrists one or two cuffs made of beads which had been sewn onto cloth, it was tolerably certain that these were sleeved coats rather than cloaks. It must have been a very gaily dressed crowd that assembled in the open mat-lined pit for the royal obsequies, a blaze of colour with the crimson coats, the silver, and the gold; clearly these people were not wretched slaves killed as oxen might be killed, but persons held in honour, wearing their robes of office, and coming, one hopes, voluntarily to a rite which would in their belief be but a passing from one world to another, from the service of a god on earth to that of the same god in another sphere.

This much I think we can safely assume. Human sacrifice was confined exclusively to the funerals of royal persons, and in the graves of commoners, however rich, there is no sign of anything of the sort, not even such substitutes, clay figurines, etc., as are so common in Egyptian tombs and appear there to be a reminiscence of an ancient and more bloody rite. In much later times Sumerian kings were deified in their lifetime and honoured as gods after their death: the prehistoric kings of Ur were in their obsequies so distinguished from their subjects because they too were looked upon as superhuman, earthly deities; and when the chroniclers wrote in the annals of Sumer that "after the Flood kingship again descended from the gods," they meant no less than this. If the king, then, was a god, he did not die as men die, but was translated; and it might therefore be not a hardship but a privilege for those of his court to accompany their master and continue in his service.

Excavating Under Jerusalem

CHARLES WARREN

By the 1850s, the Holy Land was on the regular itinerary of affluent tourists traveling to Mediterranean lands. Americans Edward Robinson and Eli Smith's Biblical Researches in Palestine, Mount Sinai, and Arabia Petraea *had set the stage, conjuring up biblical lands from what was then an obscure province of the Ottoman Empire. Thousands made the pilgrimage to Palestine, and archaeologists were among them. The French were early on the scene. Félicien de Saulcy, gunnery officer and scholar, dug into ruins outside Jerusalem's city walls and proclaimed that he had found the sarcophagus of David, king of the Jews. When French troops intervened in a civil war in Lebanon in 1860, the government followed the Napoleonic tradition in Egypt and sent an archaeological mission along. Hundreds of soldiers dug into ancient Phoenician cities like Byblos, Tyre, and Sidon in what cannot even charitably be called scientific excavations. A small team of British army engineers under Captain Charles Wilson surveyed the topography and hydrology of Jerusalem in 1864. Wilson and his men were obliged to carry out much of their work underground, examining channels and cisterns deep beneath the modern city. They discovered a Roman arch, part of King Herod's temple.*

Wilson's finds caused so much interest that the Palestine Exploration Fund was organized in London to investigate further. Another Royal engineer, Lieutenant Charles Warren (1840–1927), was sent out in 1867 to dig under the foundations of the Haram esh Sharif, a compound that housed some of Islam's most sacred shrines. The pounding of Warren's sledge hammers outraged worshipers in the mosque above, so they showered the soldiers with stones. Forbidden to work near the Haram, Warren rented privately owned land and then tunneled toward the Haram, tracing its walls more than thirty meters below ground. Warren sunk twenty-seven shafts and traced much of the northern and southern limits of the city over a period of four months, the first scientific research carried out in Jerusalem.

This extract, from Warren's book Underground Jerusalem, *published to wide acclaim, describes the difficulties of the work.*

The magnitude of our proposed operations at Jerusalem was never thoroughly realised until *after* we had commenced work; writers and speakers, when in a poetic frame of mind, *had* alluded to the "sixty feet of rubbish" on which the modern city was built; but even this depth was mentioned with a certain uneasy reservation: and it was not until we had clearly demonstrated the great accumulation of rubbish, down even to depths of 130 feet—covering massive walls, even now over 200 feet in height—that the full grasp of the great work we were engaged in became apparent, and efforts were made to assist me in a manner in any degree proportionate to the work in hand.

I was told I must get results; not to go where I thought best for the work, but to go where every basketful unearthed would give information. I had to choose. My first efforts were about the southern wall of the Temple inclosure. I was told by Izzet Pacha not to work near it; but that I could work elsewhere.

However, his successor, Nazîf Pacha, who arrived in March 1867, rescinded all the former permission, and insisted that I must not open a pit anywhere without first obtaining his sanction. This was so contrary to the spirit of the open instructions he had received (he may possibly have received confidential directions) that I refused to notice the rules he laid down, for it put me into a worse position than anybody in the city; any proprietor of land could dig in his own ground, and if I made my bargain with the proprietor I was really only digging for him.

Accordingly, I picked out a spot along the south wall, about eighty feet from the south-west angle, concealed behind some prickly pears, where we worked down along the wall in security; at the same time I also commenced another shaft at the south, about forty feet from the wall in the open, for at that distance it was not supposed I could get near the wall itself. We mined in this case down to the rock, and then ran along its surface until we reached the great wall, and there we commenced our work, examining the masonry. All this time our men were being threatened by the Pacha with imprisonment and driven away; but after they discovered that I looked after their interests, they came back again, though sometimes intimidated, for a few days: all except the nervous ones—men that were not required.

The people of Siloam are a lawless set, credited with being the most unscrupulous ruffians in Palestine; perhaps such qualities make them good workmen in dangerous places. This at least I can say for them, that they were industrious, willing, and good-tempered, easily made to laugh.

Siloam and Lifta, villages north of Jerusalem, supplied our works, from twenty to fifty men daily; we also employed a few Nubians and men from the city. They were not allowed to work by families, but were mixed up as much as possible, so that in case anything was found they would not be able to keep it secret. In the hands of these men we were constantly intrusting our lives, and always felt secure with them so far as their intentions were concerned; but the accidental dropping of a stone, or even a crow-bar down a shaft, at the bottom of which we were working, was rather treated as a joke among them than as a matter for serious consideration.

It took many weeks to drill these men into order; at first they would do just as they chose, but gradually they learnt obedience. First it was necessary to establish three rates of pay, so as to encourage the industrious: and this was a very difficult matter to arrange, for it was contrary to their feeling of justice. Allah had made one man stronger than another; why should the weak receive less than the strong? This had to be met in their own form. "Allah had made one man stronger than another, therefore, Allah intended that one man should receive more wages than another." Though this did not satisfy them at first, they gave way by our perseverance.

Our first result was a general strike, and most of them took themselves off; but next week those who came in their place were paid at a lower rate than some who had remained and knew what to do, and so the strike assisted our efforts. When everything worked fairly, the rates were about 1*s*. 3*d*. to 1*s*. 5*d*. per diem for work from sunrise to sunset. We paid about a penny a day more than the market price, so as to secure our men, and soon found that a tight hold could be kept over them, especially when they discovered that they received the full amount, instead of having a percentage deducted by a middleman.

Praying was a favourite excuse. A man, when he got tired of shouldering the basket, would suddenly face Mecca, and go through his formulae. Now we observed that they never prayed either before or after hours, or when they were working for themselves; in fact, that it was only an excuse for idleness; and accordingly they were mulct pay for each prayer until they desisted. The villagers do not frequently go to the Friday prayers in the mosque, but they found they should like to do so while with us; this was very undesirable, because, when there, they were liable to be cross-questioned by the Turkish authorities. I therefore arranged that one of their number, the head of a family, who enjoyed the distinction of wearing a green turban, should take the sins of the whole party each Friday, and carry them to the mosque: this had a very good effect, for he was paid for this service, and he liked it, and being of the family of the Prophet he was much respected, and had influence among his clan. A little deference thus paid to the old heads of families allowed me to be stricter with the younger branches.

The fellahs, or villagers, have a very simple dress, a white skull cap, with a handkerchief rolled round it of red and yellow or white, to form a turban; a cotton shirt fastened at the waist by a leathern pouch, and over this a woollen abba. Sometimes they wear a coloured cotton waistcoat under the abba, and in cold weather a sheep-skin coat, wool inside, with the leather coloured bright blue or crimson; leather slippers completed their costume. When they go beyond their villages they always carry arms, generally a very long gun with a flint lock. When working hard they take off the abba and throw down their shirt, which remains suspended by the leather band, and in extreme heat they work naked.

Lieutenant Charles Warren (left), with Dr. Joseph Barclay of the London Jews Missionary Society and Corporal Henry Phillips, in August 1867. The man in the foreground is a traveler, F. A. Eaton; the figure standing in the rear is a dragoman, Jerius Salame. Phillips took the photograph.

The fellahîn, like other Easterns, do not know the use of the spade; they only use the mattock; striking towards them when they work: thus the muscles for throwing from them are not developed, neither are those for wheeling a barrow; the consequence was that those men who were initiated into English working ways complained bitterly at first that they felt as though they had been well beaten; gradually, however, the younger ones became used to the work, and were proud of their proficiency. A great deal of the work, however, had to be done according to the manners of the people: that is to say, by means of a mattock and basket and rope. The baskets are made of rushes at Lydd, and will carry about twenty-five pounds of earth; the man draws the earth into the basket with the mattock, and then carries it off on his head, or fastens a rope to it, and allows it to be hauled up by his companion.

In some cases, where the ruins were near the surface, the earth all around was carried off: but where we had to go to great depths, shafts had to be made use of, and galleries driven; both these ought properly to have been sheeted with wood, but owing to the want of frames we had to do much of the work without frames. Of course if the earth we mined through had been hard and tough, as it is in some parts of the city, frames would not have been so necessary; but about the places where we worked there were often layers of stone chips many feet deep, through which we had to make our way, which had no cohesion and would run like water. The shafts were generally four feet square, outside the city, but smaller in the streets; gallery frames three feet wide and four feet high.

In commencing a shaft, the first four cases or sets of frames would be laid in together, and then we began putting each frame one below the other as the earth was taken out: often the stones were so loose that it ran down along the exterior of the frames and up again into the shafts, leaving the frames in the most perilous condition. In these cases wooden sticks were driven in and brushwood stuffed in also, but this did not always prove successful, and often when the workmen were left alone for an hour or two, it would be found that there was alongside the shaft a hole running from top to bottom, quite unsupported in any way, into which masses of chips would continually fall until some large stone would be laid bare and lose its equilibrium. This would descend with a crash, dragging tons of débris with it, smashing one side of the shaft flat against the other, and breaking up the boards like so many sticks; on these occasions it happened fortunately that no men were killed. They ran up the sides of the shafts at the first indication of the danger and escaped.

Nothing could be done to prevent such accidents; they were simply inevitable. But we took every precaution to prevent loss of life, and had it not been for the very stringent rules acted up to, there is no doubt that we should have lost many lives.

I had in each shaft proper ropes for the men to come up by, but to save themselves trouble they would sometimes climb up by the frames alone, or else be hauled up by their companions, by the thin rope which held the basket; both these methods were most dangerous and strictly against orders.

I had on one occasion to be very hard, on an accident occurring, owing to a disobedience of orders; the man had insisted on climbing up by the boards alone, when the corporal was elsewhere, and when near the top fell back and broke his back. In a previous accident I had sent the man home, and paid his wages while he was ill, but now the man had to get his friends to take him home and receive no pay during his illness. This tended somewhat to check the careless, but still not very much. They are a remarkably fearless set of men when engaged on such work: and had they been more attentive to regulations, perhaps they would not have done such excellent work.

I have often stated since my return to England that we were frequently in danger of being *blown up* by the loose shingles, which in an instant would destroy all our galleries or shafts, and I have found much difficulty in making myself properly understood. The stones or chips which form so great a portion of the débris around the old temple area have not only no cohesion, but they slide one on another with great facility, and the consequence is they approach

A drawing of the Roman arch discovered by Charles Wilson under Jerusalem.

in some degree to the character of a fluid. As for example, on a tank full of those stones being broken into a few feet from the bottom, the stones flowed out of the small hole we had made for days as we cleared them away, until the mass inside reached nearly the level of our hole: just in the manner that corn flows out at the lower opening in an Indian granary, or in an English stable, only the stones flow much more freely and vigorously.

It follows, then, in driving a shaft through several feet of this stuff (sometimes twenty or thirty feet), that the stones will flow through every little hole, and that thus gradually around the shaft the whole mass is moving slowly but surely. Should any untoward event occur, a frame break, or a large stone, often fifteen to twenty tons weight, get dislodged, there will be a general movement, the shaft will become skewed, the loose stones blow up through the bottom and sides, and in an instant the whole becomes a wreck. Generally the men knew by a trembling of the whole fabric a few seconds before this took place and got clear; but it was a very hazardous work and gave me intense anxiety: for apart from the desire to prevent loss of life, there is no doubt that if I had met with any serious accident in which we were not ourselves killed, there would have been a very strong feeling raised in the city against us by the Turkish authorities, and it would have at least stopped the work.

The strain on the nerves during this work was intense, and required of the men the greatest amount of fortitude and self-control; again and again they would entirely lose all power of restraining the involuntary movement of the muscles, so that their limbs refused to obey them, and again they would come to the work cool and collected.

I was quite aware and familiar with this strange loss of power over the muscles, for I have found the same occur with men engaged in climbing over precipices for any length of time; a day would come when the man would lose his nerve, often without any apparent cause, and it would be necessary to put him at other work for a week or so until he regained it. It was the same with these men; they were put to work above ground, or at less perilous places, for three or four days, and on their return would have their nervous system restored.

I was very fortunate in having Corporal Birtles with me. He had served with me for many years, and we exactly understood each other. I had taken great pains in former years in teaching him his duties in a meteorological observatory, of which I had the superintendence, and he had early learnt to be an accurate and close observer. I knew that all the instructions I gave him would be carried out implicitly, and that everything left to him would be done well. When I had asked him whether he would go out with me to Palestine, he had expressed his willingness to go with me anywhere, and I can confidently say that if my ten years' previous experience of his worth had not enabled me to be certain of his acting exactly as I required, I should have been obliged more than once to pack up hastily and retire from the field: for matters were at times in so delicate a position that a slight divergence from the instructions given would have enabled Nazîf Pacha to have put me in a false position, and thus have stopped our work entirely at Jerusalem.

In paying this tribute to Corporal Birtles' merits, I do not in any way wish to detract from the sterling work of those corporals who followed him; they all worked well as good men in their position would be expected to do: but they were young, untried, and inexperienced; and even if fully equal in other respects to Corporal Birtles, they could not to me be the same, as in matters of so much delicacy as I had to deal with it was necessary to know beforehand how a man would act under different circumstances, and I could not expect to know any of them sufficiently well for this for several months. But I must not weary the reader with these matters, although they actually strongly influenced our work at Jerusalem.

It is no easy matter for people in a civilised land to understand the difficulty of getting stores in Jerusalem; we could get nothing but pickaxes and mattocks. There were a few planks to be obtained certainly, but the dealer, directly he heard we wanted them, put a double price on them, so that they were far cheaper to get from England. When I found that my necessities were not understood at home, I sent to Malta for some and received them, on payment, from the War Department Stores; the storekeeper being most ready to facilitate matters for re-payment. The mining frames, however, which were sent from Malta, would not stand the Syrian climate; they rotted in a few weeks, so that they could not be used again, while those from England, eventually obtained, after continued applications for them, could be used over and over again.

Palestine is utterly destitute of timber, and the extremes to which we were often reduced at our work for want of proper materials made me on one occasion liken ourselves to the ancient Scythians cooking their victuals, according to Herodotus: who in their destitution—in want of firewood, pots and such like— stripped the flesh from the bones of their victims, stuffed it into the paunch with a little water, and burnt the bones underneath, thus making the ox or other victim cook himself. But I found it hard to get anybody to understand our difficulties. If I had had the money available, I could of course have ordered stores for myself from England; but I was always unavoidably kept several hundred pounds in arrears, which I had to advance myself to pay the men on the spot.

There were no less than twenty-seven shafts and excavations carried on during the time that I was away from Jerusalem, off and on, that is to say between March and June, before I had come back and regularly settled down to the work at the end of August. During the greater part of July and August, we did nothing in Jerusalem, pending the expected receipt of gallery frames from England, and an amended vizierial letter or firman. I will refer only to the more important results obtained during these first four months, scattered about in various directions.

The rock-cut steps were examined near the English cemetery, in the scarp, which there can be no doubt, formed portion of the ancient wall of the Upper City: the first wall spoken of by Josephus. These steps are just at the turn of the wall towards Siloam: the steps had originally been laid bare by Major Wilson. We followed them to the bottom, and there ran a gallery along the foot of the scarp without frames, as the earth here was very firm.

It was proved without doubt that this was a portion of the old city scarp, twenty-nine feet in height, a goodly bulwark to present to the enemy. "Mark well her bulwarks" might well be applied to a city wall built on such a rocky cliff; for no doubt the wall itself rose many feet above the rock. One of the old bastions has been made use of as a foundation for the Bishop's School, and Mr. Maudeslay, C. E., in his benevolent work in adding to the school, has since laid bare another tower or bastion further to the south, so that now we have a most complete idea of the appearance of this wall built by King David.

Thus year by year we find fresh items added to our knowledge until we may hope even in our own day to know Jerusalem as it once existed from one end to the other. What a store of knowledge would exist if the work of every builder were jotted down as carefully as that done by Mr. Maudeslay. It would well repay the trouble (and would that the Palestine Exploration Fund could afford it!), if there were a paid agent in Jerusalem, to take sections and depths at the building of every house in the city. Depend upon it there is the most valuable information covered in every month, which only requires to be noted down; but money is not forthcoming for everything that is desirable.

At the Damascus Gate, the northern gate of the city, we also made an important discovery. Baring a huge massive drafted stone wall in front of the gate, we found what was probably the wall of the asnerie or donkey-house, used by the Knights of St. John in the twelfth century in the execution of one of their three-fold duties, viz., that of conducting pilgrims between Jerusalem and the sea coast.

In the execution of this work we laid bare the wall of the Damascus Gate; and though difficulties were raised, and we had quickly to cover it up again, sufficient was seen to enable us to be certain that the present wall is of drafted stones, similar to those at the south-west corner of the Temple area, evidently of the same date nearly, and thus the wall of Herod Agrippa, or third wall of the city: this established the northern bounds of the city just as the excavation at the English cemetery settles the southern limits, and so both to north and south we had the boundary of the old city.

Our next view of the ancient topography was obtained in the deep valley lying between the Temple and Olivet, commonly called the Kidron Valley. Though, as I shall hereafter relate, the real Kidron Valley runs into this one further north, and is now quite choked up with rubbish to a height of over 150 feet. However, accepting the ordinary name as Kidron, I have to relate how we found that the present bottom is not the true bed; but that so enormous is the accumulation of rubbish on the east side of the Temple, so many millions of tons have fallen down the steep slopes, that the bottom of the valley has been quite filled up, and that the present bed is really the side of the opposite hill of Olivet, some 100 feet to east of, and about 40 feet above, the true bottom.

During the rains water still flows along the true bed of the Kidron, so far underground, and in such volumes, that during a heavy storm our gallery frames were damaged and partly washed away. We also partially examined the slope leading up to the Temple, now covered up to a depth of nearly 100 feet, and found it terraced with masonry walls: in all probability the walls which existed before the building of the Temple, when wheat was threshed on Mount Moriah, and its sides sown with corn, or garnished with the vine.

Nothing could give a more complete idea of the total change which had taken place than this section through the Kidron; after this, I was prepared to find all modern Jerusalem a sham and a delusion, covering unknown valleys and hills, and such to a great extent it has been shown to be. If in one valley the old watercourse should still run with water through many months of the year, deep under the present surface, what was there to prevent the same being found to prevail elsewhere? Why was not the brook flowing through the midst of the land to be discovered and again made use of, notwithstanding its depth? Reader, that brook has been discovered and might again flow with water, were it not cut through by the foundations of modern houses.

The Discovery of the
Dead Sea Scrolls

JOHN ALLEGRO

In 1947, a Bedouin youth searching for a lost goat came across a cave full of jars containing scrolls wrapped in linen cloth near Qumran, by the Dead Sea. A few reached scholarly hands. To everyone's astonishment, they included a copy of most of the book of Isaiah. The Dead Sea Scrolls were once the treasured possessions of a Jewish community at nearby Khirbat Qumran. The Qumran community was austere, enjoined to "seek God and do what is good and upright before him." Excavations showed that Qumran had flourished twice, the first time for about seventy years until an earthquake drove the people away in A.D. 31, and again until A.D. 68, when Roman persecution made life unbearable. It was then that the Qumran community buried its precious scrolls in a nearby cave.

The Dead Sea Scrolls are important religious texts. They bear witness to the historical milieu in which Christianity was to emerge. But soon after their discovery, they became revered relics, sacred texts reclaimed and proudly exhibited by the new state of Israel. To many people, they were tangible tokens, now venerated, not necessarily to be studied, icons of sanctity. They became political symbols of immense value, religious tourist attractions commemorated in the Shrine of the Book. At the same time, Middle Eastern politics placed Qumran in Jordan, not Israel. On both sides of the border and overseas, insiders, establishment figures, and government officials controlled access to and study of the scrolls for many years. Archaeology became a weapon in a generations-long political battle. The scrolls came under the control of learned men more interested in paleography, analyzing texts, and protecting their intellectual preserves. It is only in recent years that their control has been challenged and the texts have been made available to scholars and others everywhere.

The story of how archaeologists "discovered" the scrolls entails all the excitement of a spy thriller and murder mystery rolled into one. At the same time, John Allegro's The Dead Sea Scrolls, *written by an archaeologist with firsthand knowledge of the discovery, is a telling commentary on the role that greed and financial gain play in far too many important archaeological discoveries. Here we learn of the discovery itself.*

Muhammad Adh-Dhib had lost a goat. The lad was a member of the Taʻamireh tribe of semi-Bedouin who range the wilderness between Bethlehem and the Dead Sea, and he had been out all this summer's day tending the animals entrusted to his care. Now one of them had wandered, skipping into the craggy rocks above. Muhammad pulled himself wearily up the limestone cliffs, calling the animal as it went higher and higher in search of food. The sun became hotter, and finally the lad threw himself into the shade of an overhanging crag to rest awhile. His eye wandered listlessly over the glaring rocks and was suddenly arrested by a rather queerly placed hole in the cliff face, hardly larger than a man's head. It appeared to lead inwards to a cave, and yet was too high for an ordinary cave entrance, of which there were hundreds round about. Muhammad picked up a stone and threw it through the hole, listening for the sound as it struck home. What he heard brought him sharply to his feet. Instead of the expected thud against solid rock, his sharp ears had detected the metallic ring of pottery. He listened a moment, and then tried again, and again there could be no doubt that his stone had crashed among potsherds. A little fearfully the Bedouin youth pulled himself up to the hole, and peered in. His eyes were hardly becoming used to the gloom when he had to let himself drop to the ground. But what he had seen in those few moments made him catch his breath in amazement. On the floor of the cave, which curved back in a natural fault in the rock, there were several large, cylindrical objects standing in rows. The boy pulled himself up again to the hole, and holding on until his arms and fingers were numb, saw, more clearly this time, that they were large, wide-necked jars, with broken pieces strewn all about them. He waited no longer, but dropped to the ground and was off like a hare, his goat and flock forgotten in a frantic desire to put as much distance between himself and this jinn-ridden cave as possible. For who else but a desert spirit could be living in such a place with an entrance too small for a man?

That night Muhammad discussed his discovery with a friend who, being the elder, was entitled to scoff at the superstitions of his junior. He urged Muhammad to take him to the spot, and the next day the two of them went to the cave, and this time squeezed through the hole and dropped inside. It was just as the younger lad had described. The jars stood in rows on each side of the narrow cave, and, in the middle, broken sherds lay amidst debris fallen from the roof. There were seven or eight of the jars all told, and some had large, bowl-like lids. They lifted one and peered in, but found it empty. And so with another, and another, until in the third they saw a bundle of rags and under it two more. If they had hoped for the glitter of gold and precious stones they were sorely disappointed, for the bundles crumbled at a touch, and, pulling away some of the folds, they could see only some black tarry substance and, below that, folds of smooth brown leather. When, later, the boys had taken this booty back to their camp, they took off all the wrappings from the large bundle, and unrolled the scroll it contained, until, as they later recounted wonderingly, it stretched from one end of the tent to the other. It seems certain that this must have been the larger of the two manuscripts of Isaiah, the news of which was to set the biblical world astir. However, at the time it evoked little interest among its new owners who could neither read the strange writing inscribed on it, nor think of anything useful to which they could put the leather, fragile as it was. So for a time the Bedouin carried the scrolls about with them as they pastured their flocks and made what trade they could with their neighbours. . . . It was [to Bethlehem] that they made regular visits to sell their milk and cheese, and there, one market day, they took the three scrolls. Their general dealer happened to be an Assyrian Christian, by name Khalil Iskander Shahin, known locally as Kando, who, besides the small general store patronized by the Ta'amireh, owned a cobbler's shop next door. When the Bedouin showed him the scrolls, he evinced little interest, but thought they might serve as raw material for his cobbler's business. Later, after they had been kicking about the floor of the shop for some days, he picked one up and looked more closely at the surface. The writing was as meaningless to him as to the Bedouin, but it occurred to him that his spiritual guardians in Jerusalem might know more about it, and accordingly one day when he was going up to the city, he took the scrolls along with him, to the Syrian Convent of St. Mark in the Old City. This much is certain, but it must be confessed that from here on the story begins to disintegrate, as love of truth on the parts of the chief actors in the drama gives way before fear and cupidity. One thing is certain, however; Kando began to realize that the scrolls had some monetary value and found out that the Bedouin had by no means cleared the cave. He and his accomplice George accordingly launched a minor archaeological expedition to the cave indicated by the Bedouin and collected at least a number of large fragments and probably at this time the remainder of the scrolls, making seven in all. After they had taken all they could find, they seem to have let the Syrian authorities of St. Mark's into the secret. In any case the Metropolitan organized his own expedition to the cave, which proceeded to ransack the place, making a large opening near the ground, and pulling out everything they could lay their hands on. Of course, it will be realized that all such excavations were and are completely illegal under the laws of the country, whether of the Mandate or of the succeeding Jordan government. All such archaeological material remains the property of the country in which it is found, until the government directs otherwise. So complete secrecy shrouded all these operations, and much harm was done as a result. It is certain that the Syrians found some more fragments, but valuable archaeological data like linen wrappings and sherds from the broken jars they threw on to a rubbish dump outside. Kando had meanwhile deposited the scrolls in his possession with the Metropolitan, on a security, he now says, of £24; and these and some fragments the church leader began to hawk round the various scholastic institutions of Jerusalem to get an idea of their worth. It seems that one of the scrolls was shown to the late Professor E. L. Sukenik of the Hebrew University, who kept it for some time and then set about finding the rest of the scrolls, which he had realized were very old and of considerable value. He made a perilous journey to Bethlehem, for by now the Jewish–Arab hostilities had become open warfare following on the withdrawal of the Mandate. There he seems to have contacted Kando and brought away three more scrolls. This gentleman now began to get scared since he was afraid that the news of the illegal excavations would leak out, and he would rightly be held responsible by the authorities. He therefore took the precaution of burying some of the largest fragments from the cave in his garden at Bethlehem! Unfortunately, the soil of Kando's back garden is somewhat different from the parched dust of the Qumran caves, and when later he went to retrieve them he found only several lumps of sticky glue.

Meanwhile, in Jerusalem, the Syrian Metropolitan was continuing his rounds trying to discover if the scrolls were really old. Finally, on 18 February 1948 he called up the American School of Oriental Research and spoke to Dr. John C. Trever, who had been left in temporary charge of the establishment during the absence of the director. He told Trever that during a clear-out of his library at the convent, he had found some old Hebrew manuscripts on which he would like his advice. An appointment was made for the next day, and the Metropolitan sent round the scrolls packed in an old suitcase, by the hand of a Father Butros Sowmy and his brother. After some hasty comparing of pictures of other ancient Hebrew manuscripts, and complicated research into dictionaries and concordances, Trever discovered that he was looking at a scroll of Isaiah, and that as far as he was able to tell, it was genuinely very old. He asked permission to make photographs of the scroll, and after some negotiations did so. As he worked he became more and more excited, for if it was as old as a favourable comparison with a photograph of a pre-Christian Hebrew papyrus fragment would seem to indicate, then he was handling the oldest manuscript of the Bible ever known. It was only with great difficulty that Trever could restrain his impatience when, half way through the work of photography, he had to fulfil a long-standing engagement with the curator of the Palestine Museum, then Mr. Harry Iliffe, to go to Jericho and take photographs of a local excavation. But if any mention of the discovery was made at the time to the authorities responsible for the control of antiquities in Palestine, little attention seems to have been paid the story, and nothing was done to organize adequate and immediate steps to safeguard the treasures and seal the cave until a properly equipped expedition could probe its secrets. Trever urged the Metropolitan to take the documents out of the city, since the situation was fast deteriorating, and war was beginning to stalk the streets and hills of that unhappy land. The archaeologists themselves were obliged to leave Jerusalem, and it was not until November of 1948, when the April copies of the *Bulletin of the American Schools of Oriental Research* reached Jerusalem, that Mr. G. Lankester Harding, newly responsible for the archaeological interests of Arab Palestine as well as Trans-Jordan, learnt that eighteen months before, a fabulous discovery had been made by the Dead Sea. By now photographs of the scrolls had been examined by competent palaeographers like Professor W. F. Albright and pronounced definitely pre-Christian, probably dating to the first or second centuries before our era. Excitement ran high all over the scholarly world, and in Jordan Harding was now faced with an extremely difficult and urgent problem. The source of these scrolls had to be found, and if any related archaeological material remained, it had to be expertly examined at the first opportunity, not only to confirm the palaeographical dating but to determine the community from whose library they had come. Furthermore, it seemed not improbable that there might be more scrolls, and certainly fragments, since apparently some of the documents found were in a fragile condition with pieces missing from the outside and edges. But the original discovery had taken place so long ago that the chances of finding the source relatively free from tampering were very slight. The Metropolitan had succeeded in smuggling the scrolls in his possession out of the country, and had taken them to America. The Jordan government, of course, demanded their immediate return, but by now the monetary values being accorded them in the popular press were so astronomical as to persuade the Syrian church leader that the chances of his returning were well worth sacrificing for the sake of the money he could expect to raise in their sale. The one bright light in the whole miserable affair at this stage was that he had agreed with Trever and the American Schools to allow them to photograph and publish the scrolls immediately, whilst their sale was being negotiated. The Americans had told him that if they were published quickly their value would be much enhanced. In fact, momentarily, it declined, since once they were readily available in printed form the need for the originals became less urgent. The American scholars did, in fact, publish them, extraordinarily well and quickly, putting the scholarly world greatly in their debt.

Back in Jordan, Harding had gone immediately to the Palestine Archaeological Museum in Jerusalem, and in his capacity as acting curator instructed Joseph Saad, the new secretary, to spare no effort in discovering the whereabouts of the fabulous cave and any other information he could about the find and the personalities involved. Saad's first call was to the American School, and there Dr. O. R. Sellers, that year's director, immediately offered all the help in his power. Together they went to St. Mark's Monastery, despite the extremely dangerous nature of the journey through the Old City, where Jewish shells and sniping were making it near suicide to be out of doors during daylight. Slipping from shelter to shelter they finally arrived at the building which backs on to the dividing wall between Arab and Jewish Jerusalem, and there interviewed a person by the name of George Isaiah. It became clear from the beginning that he was not going to be very helpful, and, although he did not deny that the monastery had organized an excavation of the cave, refused point-blank to disclose its whereabouts. Saad argued, cajoled, and bullied, but all to no effect, and he was just about to give up hope of gaining any useful information at all when, out of the corner of his eye, he saw one of the Syrian fathers approaching, a venerable saint called Father Yusif. When the old man had drawn quite near, Saad suddenly turned from George and asked Yusif what he knew about the cave. Before George could stop him, the old man began to describe the excavations and their whereabouts. George turned on him fiercely, but could not silence him before he had given at least a general idea of the cave's position. It seemed that it was somewhere south of the junction of the roads to Jericho and the Dead Sea, amongst the cliffs which border the sea to the west. Now those limestone cliffs are honeycombed with caves and clefts in the rock, and the mountains rise nearly a thousand feet from the marly plateau, so that with a southern limit at Ras Feshkha about six miles to the south, a good deal more detailed pin-pointing was going to be necessary for the cave to be discovered. As Saad and his companion retraced their steps through the Old City, they discussed the next move. It seemed obvious that they would have to try the great stand-by of the East, bribery. Most things out there have their price, and it only remained to find out how high it was going to be. So on their return, negotiations with George Isaiah were opened, on the general principle that, if he would lead a party to the cave, he would receive a cash payment and the custody of any further scrolls found would be equally shared between them. These negotiations took a considerable time, involving many trips to the monastery through gun-fire. Finally, when it seemed that arrangements were sufficiently far advanced, Saad arranged for the mayor of Jerusalem and his dignitaries to accompany them to St. Mark's to witness the formal agreement. The party arrived on the day appointed and took their seats. Everybody asked after everybody else's health, and were asked in return, and Allah duly thanked. Coffee was passed round, and, after that, the customary small talk ensued, without which no Arab meeting is considered opened. Sellers was beginning to get restless, but Saad, raised in the traditions of the East, played the game in all its formality and was patient. At last, after the seventh round of thanking Allah for their individual good health, the main subject was broached, the terms stated, and nothing but the clasping of hands remained to seal the bargain. And George Isaiah would have nothing to do with it.

Sellers and Joseph parted gloomily at the gates of the American School, and Saad carried on to the museum. Weeks of negotiation had produced practically nothing and, apart from its general locality, they knew little more about the cave than what had been learnt from the American *Bulletin*. Now it happened that the museum at this time was in the hands of the Arab Legion, and Saad had to pass a ring of sentries to reach his quarters. He made a perfunctory greeting to the man on duty at the gate and then something prompted him to hesitate and look at the soldier more closely. He was a lean, dark-skinned Arab of the desert, of the type Glubb always chose for his picked troops, and Saad studied his face for a moment, noticing his long, straight Semitic nose, his short curly beard, and black smouldering eyes. He was a true son of the desert from the sandy wastes of the Hijaz, trained from his boyhood in desert lore and with eyes as keen as an eagle's. It occurred to Saad that if anybody could find that cave, given general directions as to its whereabouts, men like this soldier could. They would be able to perceive from an amazing distance any disturbance of the ground round the illicit excavations, and so detect the cave perhaps even from ground level. The idea crystallized into a plan of campaign, and waiting only to collect Sellers from the American School, Saad went in search of the officer in charge of the troops in the Jerusalem area, a Major-General Lash. He found this officer well prepared, for only a night or two before he had been discussing the problem with a Belgian United Nations observer, Captain Lippens, and had that day

Kando and George Isaiah.

telephoned to Harding in Amman, asking if he would like him to send a few of his desert troops down to the area and search for the caves. Harding had agreed, and now with the added information Saad was able to provide, no further time was lost and a detachment of troops under the direction of an English officer, Brigadier Ashton, and a Jordanian Captain (now Major) Akkash el Zebn, was sent down to the road junction by the Dead Sea. Deploying from this point, in such a way that as far as possible no section of the cliffs at all visible from the littoral plain would miss their scrutiny, they set off slowly, working their way south. Within seventy-two hours, Akkash was on the phone reporting that they had found the cave, and asking for further instructions. Whilst waiting for Harding's arrival, Ashton plotted the cave and started collecting the pottery which lay round about, making accurate notes and drawings which were of the greatest help to the excavators later. Then Harding arrived, and together they made the first preliminary excavation. Harding confesses that when he first saw the cave he was dubious of its being the source of the scrolls, but the presence of undoubtedly ancient pottery made it worth investigating further. He asked Ashton to mount a guard on the cave until such time as a properly equipped archaeological party could be assembled. This was done, but the expedition was dogged by bad luck for days. Every time they gathered at the road junction it rained, which made the tracks completely impassable to their transport, and once it even snowed! Ashton could not leave his men standing about outside a cave by the

Dead Sea for long, however, and it became urgent to mount the expedition, which finally started work on 15 February 1949, a fortnight after the rediscovery of the cave. Father De Vaux of the French School of Archaeology, Joseph Saad, and two others joined the excavation, and the early finding of scores of small inscribed fragments of leather, together with pieces of the linen wrappings, and the sherds of dozens of the characteristic large scroll jars, in which it was said that the original scrolls had been found, soon made it plain that this was certainly a scroll cave, if not the original one. The damage caused by illegal excavations was all too plain; no hope could now be entertained of any stratification of the remains, and some of the most valuable of the pottery and wrappings had been tossed outside on to a dump. The number of jars originally placed in the cave was now seen to have been between forty and fifty, and if, as it was then thought, each of those jars had held several scrolls, then it became a matter of extreme urgency to find the rest which might still be in the country and perhaps suffering damage. In any case, there must clearly have been hundreds of fragments and these had also to be found and studied together, if they were to be of any use at all.

Another detective inquiry was instituted, and Saad given *carte blanche* to find and, if necessary, buy those pieces regardless of cost. It was clear now, as more and more reports came in from scholars studying the first scrolls, that every word of these documents was going to be worth its weight in gold, and, indeed, that was just about what they were going to cost before they were all finally in safe hands.

Saad went again to the Monastery of St. Mark's, this time accompanied by Harding himself. The object of this inquiry was to find out the name of the dealer in Bethlehem who had continually cropped up in reports, but had never been named. If there were more scrolls and fragments about, he was the most likely person to know about them, and he would also know the names and tribe of the Bedouin who had found the cave. George Isaiah was a little more informative this time, but could not or would not describe the cave in sufficient detail to make its identification with the legion's discovery certain, and refused to disclose the name of the dealer. Saad knew better this time than to waste much time over him. After the inevitable coffee, and inquiries after each other's health, with no more useful information forthcoming, they rose to leave, keeping their eyes open all the time for Father Yusif. It was as they were leaving the gate of the monastery that they saw the frail figure approaching, and immediately engaged him in conversation on the cave. Unfortunately, they now seemed to know more than he, and still they lacked the name of the Bethlehem dealer. Then they had an amazing piece of luck. Harding had noticed that as they had been speaking to Father Yusif, a woman across the road had been showing keen interest in their conversation. Finally, she came across to them and spoke. Were they talking about the excavations of the Dead Sea cave which George Isaiah had organized about a year ago? Her husband had taken part in the "dig," and had even been rewarded for his pains with a leather fragment, which the priests had told him was most valuable, although he had not yet discovered a way of converting it into hard cash. However, if they would like to wait a moment she would see if she could find him; he could not be far away. Saad and Harding looked at each other, and then to heaven. They finally ran the man, Jabra by name, to earth in a nearby coffee shop, and induced him to come along to the museum. In the basement, the spoils of the official excavation of the cave were arranged on large trestle tables, and, bringing him near, Harding asked Jabra if he could see anything there that he recognized. The man looked long and earnestly over the table, and then a broad smile lit his face. Yes, this. Amidst the broken pottery and linen wrappings, the Roman lamp and the cooking pot, he had spied his own dear, long-lost but never forgotten cigarette roller. So another link in the chain was forged, the cave was now definitely identified, and it now remained to find out how much more Jabra knew. An Arab who realizes that he has partaken, however unwittingly, in an illegal act, is a wary creature. Harding and Saad had somehow to win his confidence, if they were to obtain the information they so desperately wanted. Bribery was of course inevitable, and a generous tip went far towards loosening Jabra's tongue. He admitted that they had found some scroll fragments, and the Metropolitan had taken most of them away with him when he left. They tackled him about the name of the Bethlehem dealer; but at once he shut up like a clam, and for a long time would say nothing on the subject. Harding saw the fear of death in his eyes, and the man confessed that he was literally scared for his life. It took a great deal of alternate threatening and reassuring before they finally forced the truth from him, and when they had let him scurry off home, Saad and Harding sat down and faced one another. Events now had taken a sinister turn. If Jabra's fears were justified, it meant that this dealer and his confederates were willing to go to any length to avoid interference in their territory. It was clear that from now on the game would be played to very high stakes, perhaps to higher values than mere money.

The journey to Bethlehem was an adventure in itself. Today it takes only half an hour of smooth driving on a new tarmac road to go from Jerusalem to Bethlehem, and before the troubles a more direct road took only half that time. In 1949, with this in Jewish hands, as it still is, the make-shift route was long and dangerous, a dirt track which snaked far out into the Judaean hills by the monastery of Mar Saba. Transport was by donkey, and the journey took half a day. The morning following the interview with Jabra, Saad set out, taking with him two of the museum guards, and reached Bethlehem shortly after midday. Leaving the guards and the animals on the outskirts of the town, he walked into the centre, feeling suddenly lonely and unprotected. From now on he would be working alone; any sign of official support, and every way would be blocked; the dealer, scrolls, and everything else would go underground and nothing ever recovered. But Bethlehem in those days, cut off from a central government by the fighting, was no place for an unprotected man to face a gang of desperate brigands, and Joseph hesitated a moment outside the shop which had been pointed out to him as Kando's. It opened, like all such eastern shops, straight on to the street, and behind the piles of vegetables and hanging kuffiyas, the bright sunlight did not penetrate. Joseph peered into the shadows but could see nothing from outside. Then he entered.

His eyes took a little time to accustom themselves to the gloom, so he did not at first see the men standing at the back of the room, watching him. One of them was rather portly, heavy-jowled, and dressed in the long Arab night-shirt type of garment, with a red tarbush on his head. His companion was an older man who stared at Joseph suspiciously from beneath heavy eyebrows, and glanced from time to time at his companion and the door standing ajar behind him. Saad realized from their manner that news of his arrival had preceded him and came straight to the point. He had heard that Kando knew something about the scrolls which had been found in a cave, and furthermore, had some of the illegally excavated fragments in his possession. There was a moment's heavy silence, and then the old man flew at him, calling him a government spy, traitor, and worse, pushing Saad against the wall as he hurled abuse at him. Joseph raised his arms to fend off his assailant, but, even as he did so, saw the other man slip out of the open door and shut it behind him. Almost immediately the old man calmed down, glancing behind him to ensure that Kando had got clear, but Saad knew now that there was nothing to be gained by waiting longer and left the shop to return to his friends. Now the fat was really in the fire. Kando knew what he was after and suspected him of being in league with the government. The chances were that either he would try and silence Saad, or smuggle the incriminating evidence out of the country and make off, until things had quietened down. The safest thing for Saad to do would have been to make tracks for Jerusalem and his well-guarded museum. Instead he sent his men away, and took lodgings in Bethlehem, determined to try and win his way into Kando's confidence. It was the act of a brave man.

Day after day Joseph returned to the little shop, engaging Kando in conversation at first on anything but the scrolls. He made the acquaintance of George, who appeared to be Kando's right-hand man, and had certainly co-operated with him in the illicit digging. Slowly he won their confidence, and one day brought up the subject of the scrolls again. He hastened to reassure them that no ill would come to them from working with him; indeed, if they would trust him he would find them a market for their fragments which would pay well and be perfectly safe. After all, if they tried to smuggle them out of the country they might lose everything, including their freedom. They would lose nothing doing things Saad's way. The logic of Joseph's reasoning gradually had its effect, and the first suspicion gave way to a wary, but nevertheless, genuine friendship. When he finally left Bethlehem, it was with a promise from Kando that he would come and visit him at the museum. On the journey back, Joseph reflected rather ruefully that he had not seen a single fragment during all those days in Bethlehem; yet, on balance, he was not displeased with progress.

Kando kept his word and soon after appeared at Jerusalem, and Saad in due course paid a return visit. This went on for some weeks without further mention being made of the fragments, and Joseph was almost beginning to wonder if

Kando had already sold them or, indeed, had ever possessed any. Then one day, in the gardens of the museum, Kando took Saad over to a shady corner, looked at him hard, and then thrust his hand into the grimy "night-shirt" and brought out a wallet. Inside, as he slowly opened it, there lay a piece of inscribed parchment, about the size of three or four fingers. Saad took the piece in his hand and studied it. There could be no doubt that the writing was very similar to that on the fragments he had already seen and the leather on which it was written was genuinely old. He replaced it carefully in the folds of Kando's wallet, knowing that one false move now could forfeit in a moment all the confidence he had built up over these trying weeks. Nevertheless, as he watched the wallet go back into its home, he wondered if he would ever see that precious fragment again. However, the game had to be played out the hard way; if Kando had that piece he would probably have a lot more, and Harding had told him to get the lot. Saad showed his interest in buying the piece and any more that Kando might have, and on this they parted, Joseph reporting the new development to Harding. In a few days Kando returned, ready to take negotiations further. Who was Saad acting for? Joseph answered that an English professor visiting the country was anxious to buy these fragments, but wanted more than this one piece; how much had he to offer? Kando rather warily replied that he had "quite a lot," and arranged a rendezvous at which Saad would bring the "English professor" and where Kando would have all the pieces in his possession. The place appointed was to be in Jericho, and, when the date and time had been arranged, Saad went off to find the mythical financier. It so happened that, working with Harding at this time as a non-technical assistant, was an Englishman, Mr. Richmond Brown, who willingly agreed to take the part. At a preliminary meeting Harding handed over a thousand pounds in one dinar notes (1 Jordan dinar = 1 pound sterling), but told Saad to try and obtain all the fragments in Kando's possession for eight hundred pounds. The absolute maximum was fixed at a pound per square centimetre of fragment, but to try and ascribe any monetary value at all to this priceless material was extremely difficult. If this price seems outrageously high, it must be remembered that, at that time, the Syrian Metropolitan was asking something like a million dollars for the scrolls in his possession, and reports to this effect were being heard all over Jordan on the radio. The Bedouin and Kando were now well aware that these scrolls were considered beyond price by the outside world, and that their recovery was worth almost any amount of money. It should be also recognized that behind all these negotiations there lay the shadow of irresponsible people who were willing to buy illegally smuggled pieces for their collections or as souvenirs, or in order to make a profit on a further transaction. The danger of such loss was ever present forcing the pace, and thus raising the price. It was bad enough that the complete scrolls should be taken from the country, but at least they could be published as a unity, as the American scholars were doing so admirably. But with fragments, it was different. They could only be made of use to scholarship if they were kept together, and as far as possible reunited with their parent documents. A small piece of Dead Sea Scroll may look very nice framed and hung over the mantel-piece, but it may well ruin the value of other larger pieces, depending for their sense on the inscription on the "souvenir." Furthermore, irresponsibility is not the sole prerogative of tourists and dealers. At a later stage, one world-famous museum was willing to consider buying fragments smuggled from Jordan in order to have them in their cases, even though to have taken them would have delayed the publication of thousands of others, or, at least, reduced their value for want of the additional evidence. Happily the possibility was then foiled by the more responsible attitude of an Eastern university who procured the fragments and returned them immediately to Jordan. Thus at this stage there was little quibbling about price; the main thing was to rescue the fragments and give them to the world in as complete a form and as soon as possible.

Kando's choice in hotels ran pretty low. This was a dirty, fifth-rate hovel, and, as the two drew near, Saad could see that Kando was fearing a trap and taking no chances. Lounging on both sides of the street and round the entrance were some of the grimmest, toughest-looking characters one could wish not to meet anywhere, and they watched Saad and his companion through every move and gesture as they approached. Joseph felt the thick wad of notes bulging in his pocket, and thought they could not have been more conspicuous if he had carried them in his hand. The hairs on their necks bristled as they walked through the porch, trying to look unconcerned. Casually they asked a shifty-looking proprietor if Kando was there, and he motioned them to a room leading off the main entrance hall. Saad put his hands on the notes in his pocket, squared his shoulders, and the two of them walked in.

Kando was standing with George at the far side of the room. A table covered with a greasy cloth stood in the centre, and Saad noticed that, as usual, Kando had prepared for a quick exit with a window standing wide open behind him. It idly crossed Joseph's mind to wonder if they were as well prepared. A brief greeting did nothing to relieve the tension, and Saad asked abruptly if Kando had got the fragments. The man nodded and raised his eyebrows questioningly in return. In answer, with studied carelessness, Joseph brought out the bundle of notes, stripped off the band, and fanned them out on to the table. It was a magnificent gesture and Kando hesitated no longer but laid on to the table beside the notes a pile of decrepit-looking pieces of skin, torn and rotted at the edges, and covered with a fine white dust through which the ancient writing could just be seen. Saad passed them over to the "English professor" who at once began measuring them with a pocket rule. The tension had now decreased considerably, and whilst Richmond Brown was at work, Saad engaged Kando in conversation. Brown's calculations actually brought the figure to 1,250 sq. cm., but following his instructions he said "I can only give eight hundred pounds for this lot." Saad looked at Kando expectantly, but the latter jerked his head and gave the click of the tongue which is the Arabic refusal. Then he began to collect the fragments together, and Saad after a while did the same with the notes. Each delayed the process as long as possible, hoping for the other to give way, but when they both had finished the silence remained unbroken. Saad walked to the door, followed by Brown, both wondering if Kando would let them go through that grim circle of henchmen with a thousand pounds in their pockets. However, they passed unmolested and started to walk towards the Winter Palace Hotel where Harding awaited them. Certainly they were alive, and had handled the precious fragments, but were they to lose them all for the sake of two hundred pounds? Harding, however, having heard their story supported their action, and was sure that the next day would see Kando at the museum with his pieces, more than willing to sell them for eight hundred pounds.

The next day, sure enough, Kando appeared. But he seemed curiously certain of his ground, and would not go below a thousand pounds. Saad said he would go and ask the "professor" and stepped next door to where Harding sat in the board room, awaiting developments. Harding agreed to the price and Saad returned and gave Kando the money. Then part of the cause of his confidence became apparent, for as Kando handed him the fragments, he looked at Joseph and said, "and give my greetings to Mr. Harding." Saad remembered then that, when the three of them had left the Winter Palace in Jericho that day, a bystander had stared curiously into the windows of the car. Of course, Kando now knew the secret of Saad's relationship with the director of antiquities, and probably realized that the "English professor" had been a fake. He knew too that the government meant to deal leniently with him so long as he played their game. Indeed, Harding still had much to learn about the finding of that cave, and wanted badly to know the names of the Bedouin lads who had climbed through the hole. It was by no means certain that with Kando's collection all the fragment material from the cave had been exhausted, and there was always the possibility that new caves in the vicinity might be found any day, now that the Bedouin were on the look-out.

Eventually, Kando told Saad the names of the Bedouin and their tribe, and in due course they were persuaded to leave their desert camps and come to Amman. There Harding learned the full story of the discovery, and the Bedouin found a new friend in the director of antiquities. Well dined and liberally tipped, the lads returned to their shepherding to enliven the camp fires of their tribe with marvellous tales of the great city across the Jordan, and of an English official of their government who spoke their tongue as well as they, and knew their customs and their lore better than any foreigner they had ever met. The wise administrator knows when to put the letter of the law into second place, and to the fact that Harding is such a person, the world owes much of the light which further discoveries in the Judaean desert were to throw upon this important Jewish sect by the Dead Sea.

Digging Up Jericho

KATHLEEN KENYON

Until ten thousand years ago, human societies everywhere lived by hunting, fishing, and gathering wild plant foods of every kind. Then, about eight thousand years before Christ, some communities in the Near East began cultivating wild cereal grasses and herding wild sheep and goats. Within a few centuries, the new food-producing economies had spread throughout the Near East, transforming hunter-gatherers into village farmers. Within five thousand years, farming had led to the appearance of urban civilizations in Mesopotamia and Egypt. The origin of agriculture has been one of the great controversies of archaeology for more than a century. Until 1956, most archaeologists believed that farming had begun along the Nile, and perhaps farther afield in about 4000 B.C.—that is to say, about one thousand years before the appearance of Egyptian and Sumerian civilization. But Kathleen Kenyon's excavations into the lowest levels of the city mound of Jericho, in modern-day Jordan, and the new radiocarbon dating technique revolutionized thinking about the beginnings of farming almost overnight.

Dame Kathleen Kenyon (1906–1978), one of the great woman archaeologists of this century, learned the techniques of excavation in the Near East and at Great Zimbabwe, where she worked with Gertrude Caton-Thompson in 1929. Subsequently, she dug with Mortimer Wheeler on the Roman town at Verulameum, England, and served as the first secretary of the London Institute of Archaeology. An expert, no-nonsense excavator, Kenyon ran her large-scale excavations into the great city mound at Jericho with brilliant panache. A previous excavator, John Garstang, had trenched deep into the tell, exposing Bronze Age levels and traces of even earlier Stone Age farming occupation. Kenyon began by reopening Garstang's rather carelessly excavated and poorly reported trenches, and then dug down to the very base of the biblical city. To her surprise, she exposed two small farming communities, the earlier of which boasted of massive stone walls, at least one watchtower, and a deep outer ditch. At the very base of the mound lay a small shrine by a spring.

Kenyon's excavations between 1952 and 1956 coincided with a new interest in the origins of agriculture and animal domestication, driven by the use of not only multidisciplinary research teams in the field, but also a new dating technique, radiocarbon dating. Samples from Jericho's earliest levels were processed by Willard Libby's pioneer radiocar-

163

bon laboratory at the University of Chicago. To everyone's astonishment, they gave readings in the eighth and seventh millennia B.C., far earlier than conventional estimates for early agriculture in the 4000 B.C. range. The Jericho dates agreed well with readings from another early farming village at Jarmo in the Zagros highlands to the northwest, and helped set the stage for excavations at many other early farming sites, among them Abu Hureyra in Syria and Çayönu in Turkey.

Kenyon also recovered a series of human skulls, delicately modeled with the features of their owners. She believed that they were evidence of one of the earliest ancestor cults in the world. In the passage from her book Digging Up Jericho *that follows, Kathleen Kenyon describes the finding of the skulls and the early farming settlements of which they were a part.*

The next finds were far more exciting. In the area in the centre of the west side of the mound, Site D I in Square H₄, a portion of a human skull had, in the 1953 season, for some time been visible in the side-wall of the excavation. But . . . it is most important that the sides of cuttings are kept straight, so that the stratification, the lines of the floors, walls and so on, can be clearly seen. Also, it looks most untidy to have the sides of the excavation pock-marked by pits dug into them. So excavators are trained not to go burrowing into the walls of the trench or square to get out objects, however inviting they look.

So the skull remained where it was until after digging had stopped. But a skull of an individual perhaps some seven thousand years old is something of a special case, so, after I had one morning finished drawing the section of the stratification, I rather unwillingly gave permission for the site supervisor to get it out. I then went off to draw a section in another area. In the course of the day, the site supervisor came over with a mysterious report that the skull seemed to be covered with a coating of clay. He was told to proceed as carefully as possible, but we were none of us prepared for the object he produced in the evening. . . . What we had seen in the side of the trench had been the top of a human skull. But the whole of the rest of the skull had a covering of plaster, moulded in the form of features, with eyes inset with shells.

What was more, two further similar plastered skulls were visible at the back of the hole from which the first had come. When these were removed, three more could be seen behind them, and eventually a seventh beyond. The whole timetable of the end of the dig was disrupted. The furniture had all been packed up, the kitchen cleared and the servants dismissed, the dark-room and repair room dismantled and most of the material packed up. For nearly a week we lived in considerable discomfort, sitting on the floor and eating picnic meals, while the photographer and repair assistant did wonders of improvisation. The excavation of the heads was a very difficult and tricky business. They lay in a tumbled heap, one skull crushed firmly on top of another, with stones and very hard earth all round. Each successive group was farther back from the face of the section and increasingly difficult to get at, and the bone surfaces were exceedingly fragile, so the greatest gentleness had to be used.

It took five days to extract them all, and it was a triumph of patient work to do so. We heaved a sigh of relief when no more were visible behind. But the family group of seven heads was well worth our trouble. They were all most remarkable as realistic human portraits. One was very much more beautiful than the rest. . . . The reason that it stands out from the rest is that it alone has the lower jaw in position. In the others, the plaster representing the lower jaw is actually modelled over the upper teeth, and the heads therefore have a somewhat squat and chubby appearance. Six of the seven have eyes composed of two segments of shell, with a vertical slit between, which simulates the pupil. The seventh has eyes of cowrie shell, and the horizontal opening of the shells gives him a somewhat sleepy appearance. The state of preservation of five was excellent, but the other two were less good, one having little more than the eyes surviving intact.

Each head has a strongly marked individual character, though the features and method of manufacture is similar. The interior of the head was packed solidly with clay, and a clay filling put into the eye-sockets as setting for the shell eyes. The lower part of the skull was then enveloped in plaster from the level of the temples, the crown of the skull being left bare. In one specimen there are bands of brown paint on the skull, perhaps indicating a head-dress. In all the intact specimens, the base of the skull was completely covered, with a flat finish to the plaster, so there is no question that they could ever have formed part of complete figures. The features, nose, mouth, ears, and eyebrows, are moulded with extraordinary delicacy. The plaster of one head is coloured to represent a fine ruddy flesh-colour; others show some colouring, but not so pronounced.

Modern anthropology provides the only close parallel for such a use of human skulls. In New Guinea, and especially in the Sipek River Valley, skulls were similarly given features up to comparatively modern times, though the features take the form of masks rather than the complete encasing of the skull. In some cases these heads seem to be those of venerated ancestors, in others those of enemies, preserved as trophies. It would be possible to interpret the Jericho skulls in either sense. I have personally always been convinced that they are the heads of venerated ancestors, largely owing to the impression they give of being portraits, and to the loving care which the skilful modelling of the features suggests. There is now some archaeological evidence to support this view.

The sources from which the skulls were derived would allow of their interpretation either as those of venerated ancestors or of enemies. They were found in a discarded heap, beneath the plastered floor of a house. That they were typical of this phase is proved by the discovery in 1956 of two more, some 10 feet away from the others, but beneath the floor of the same house. They lay in the debris of an earlier house, presumably the one in which they had been treasured. Beneath the floor of this lower house, we came upon an extraordinary number of skeletons, about thirty in a comparatively small area. From many of these bodies the skull had been removed, often leaving a displaced lower jaw. In some cases, where the bodies were very tightly packed, the bones seem literally to have been ransacked to remove the skulls, at a stage when the bodies were sufficiently decayed to allow of the separation of limbs from the trunk, but the ligaments were still sufficiently intact for the individual bones of the limbs to remain in articulation. . . . Burial beneath the floors of the houses was certainly the normal custom, but this number of burials was quite exceptional. It suggests a disaster, a plague or massacre, and other circumstances, to which I will refer, do make a massacre a possibility, though there was no evidence of violent deaths from the actual skeletons. If this were the case, it would still leave the two possibilities. If the attackers were the victors, the heads might be trophies taken from the bodies of massacred defenders, while if the defenders drove off the attackers, though with casualties to themselves, the heads might be those of important individuals, whose memory was preserved in this manner.

But though in this instance the evidence is ambiguous as to the interpretation to be put upon the custom, further excavation has shown that the custom was not confined to this single stage. As we have cleared layer after layer of superimposed houses in the various areas excavated, beneath almost every single floor we have found burials. In a large number of instances, the skull has been removed. The action of enemies can obviously not be involved in all these cases. It does therefore seem probable that the removal of the skull was a general practice, and that they were kept as mementoes of dead members of the family. It is true that the instances that I have described are the only ones of this phase in the history of Jericho in which we have found the detached skulls. They may have been removed to some central sanctuary lying outside the excavated area, or they might be in parts of the houses not excavated, for in no case does the complete plan of a house lie within any of our areas.

From this treatment of the skulls it may be deduced that these early inhabitants of Jericho had already developed a conception of a spiritual life as distinct from the bodily one. They must have felt that some power, perhaps protective, perhaps of wisdom, would survive death, and somehow they must have realised that the seat of these extracorporeal powers was the head. They perhaps believed that the preservation of the skull secured the use of the power to succeeding generations, perhaps that it placated the spirit, perhaps controlled it.

A further fascinating aspect of this find is the artistic and technical skill shown in the moulding of the plaster features. People who could do this moulding certainly did not lack the technical skill to make pottery; it can only be that they did not feel the need for it.

Our finds have thus shown that the people of Jericho were both culturally and technically highly developed. We have also established the fact that the settlement of the period was of considerable size.

The settlement is quite clearly on the scale, not of a village, but of a town. Its claim to a true civic status is established by the discovery, the first of the exciting finds to be produced by the present excavations, that it possessed a

*The Jericho town wall found during Kathleen Kenyon's
excavations, with the foundations of oval-shaped houses to
the left.*

massive defensive wall. . . . It was built of large, undressed stones, and survived
to the height of 2.50 metres. It looked most impressive as one peered down at
it, with its base at what then seemed to us the great depth of 7 metres. In this
area, we uncovered a length of 20 metres, and 25 metres to the north, in Site
M I, we subsequently picked up what is very probably its continuation. We
cannot as yet say whether it enclosed the whole settlement, as it is of course not
impossible that it enclosed only a citadel area. But whether or not it enclosed
the whole town, it is clear evidence of community organisation. No one small
group or family could have carried out an undertaking of this sort, and someone
or some corporate body must have provided the organisation to bring the great
boulders from the stream beds at the foot of the mountains, half a mile or so
away, someone must have ordained its line, and someone have supervised its
construction.

The wall was free-standing only on its outer side. On the inner side, the
contemporary level was 2.80 metres higher than the external one. This terrace
was constructed by cutting away the earlier levels on the outer side, and piling

them up on the inside, the wall being built against this pile. The wall must originally have stood at least 2 metres higher than the surviving top, giving a total minimum height of about 5 metres, for on the inside it served also as a house wall, and the additional 2 metres is necessary to give head-room within the house.

It was in this house that the plastered skulls must have been preserved, for they were found discarded in its debris, beneath the floor of the next succeeding building. In the fill beneath the floor of the house, put in when the wall was built, was found the surprising number of burials, from which the skulls must have been derived. It is the association of the great defensive wall with the mass burial that makes it tempting to interpret as a massacre the disaster which the number of burials suggests. If a violent attack on a town at that time undefended had resulted in the death of a large number of the citizens, it would be reasonable that when it was rebuilt, a defensive wall should be added. But this can only be a hypothesis, for the surviving portions of the skeletons do not show any identifiable signs of injuries.

After a period, this wall apparently collapsed. After the first collapse, it was rebuilt on the same line. But after a second collapse, a new wall was built 6.50 metres in advance, against the debris which buried the face of the original one. The new one was on the same principle as the old one, with a free-standing outer face and a higher terrace inside, and the internal house was extended over the new fill, probably up to the new wall, but erosion has destroyed the actual junction. This same erosion makes it impossible to say whether the eight succeeding house levels belonging to the pre-pottery Neolithic period, all with the same type of plan, structure, and plastered floors, also run up to the new wall, or to some successor.

As I have just said, the town in the stages preceding the first of these two walls was undefended. But in 1954 we found that they were not the earliest on the site. Beneath the first of them was a deep tipped fill, partly bricky and partly ashy. This dipped down steeply to the west, over the face of a yet earlier wall. As this gradually emerged, it became clear that it was much more impressive than the later one which overlay it. It was not built of such large stones, but it had a considerably more regular face, though the stones were likewise undressed. Moreover, it survived to a height of 6 metres, with its foundations resting on bedrock at a depth of 15 metres (nearly 50 feet) from the surface of the mound. Like the later one, it was free-standing only on the outer face, and was built on a slight batter against an interior fill.

In the following two seasons, further details of the system of fortification to which this wall belongs have emerged. On the outer side was a great rock-cut ditch, 9 metres wide and 3 metres deep. The labour involved in excavating this ditch out of the solid rock must have been tremendous. As we have discovered nothing in the way of heavy flint picks, one can only suppose that it was carried out with stone mauls, perhaps helped by splitting by fire and water.

Still more remarkable is the adjunct to the wall on the inner side. This is a massive tower, 9 metres in diameter, and solidly built of stone. In conception and construction, this tower would not disgrace one of the more grandiose medieval castles. In its centre is a stone-built staircase with twenty steps, leading down to a horizontal passage. The treads of the stairs are formed by great stone slabs more than .75 metre across, hammer-dressed to a smooth finish, and the roofs of the staircase and the passage are formed of still larger slabs, .95 metre across and up to a metre long, similarly dressed. The whole thing is excellent in both architecture and masonry, and everyone who sees it finds it impossible to believe that it was built eight thousand years or more ago.

We have not yet solved the problem of the purpose of the staircase. The passage at its base most unfortunately leads to just that point in the circumference of the tower which lies beyond the edge of our excavations, and to clear down to its entrance on the outside will mean shifting some 50 feet of filling, as well as 20 feet of our own dump on top. As found, the passage was full of skeletons, twelve in all, jammed in extremely tightly. But this was certainly not the primary purpose, since when they were put in, the fill in the passage had risen to within 2 feet of the roof. For this same reason, one cannot give the dramatic interpretation that they were the last heroic defenders of the tower. Clearly the passage had ceased to be functional at that stage, and the bodies were put in, after it had gone out of use, simply because it was a convenient hole.

Even the stage of this great wall, ditch, and tower is not the beginning of the story of the defences of Jericho. The tower has two outer skins surrounding a stone core. The outermost is not continuous, but is associated with some curiously shaped rooms on the north-west side. These skins proved to represent successive building phases, and it is only to the last of these that the town wall just described belongs, for it is built against the outermost skin, with which it was structurally contemporary. To the north of the tower, the town wall was built against a filling of stone chips, clearly derived from the cutting of the ditch, which is therefore contemporary with it. These chips were piled up against a yet earlier massive stone wall, which survives, free-standing on both faces, to a height of 4 metres. This wall was cut through by the inner skin surrounding the tower. It is therefore earlier than it, and it almost certainly is the town wall going with the core of the tower, which must represent its earliest phase. The wall contemporary with the intermediate phase, in which the inner skin was added to the core, may be represented by the lower part of the later wall, which is in a different and rather rougher style of building.

We have, therefore, indications that the elaborate system of defences has a very long history. The earlier stages have not yet been fully traced, and it will indeed be difficult to do so without disturbing more than is desirable of the stage at present exposed, which must represent the climax of this remarkable achievement. But the earliest so far traced, with the nucleus of the tower, and a free-standing stone wall must in itself have been sufficiently magnificent, and again and again one returns to the feeling of amazement at the very great antiquity of the remains, and at the evidence they provide for the high degree of organisation and technical ability of their builders.

The Aegina Marbles

SAMUEL PEPYS COCKERELL

Greek and Roman antiquities cast a powerful spell over wealthy noblemen as they traveled in classical lands. They returned from their Grand Tours laden with statuary and painted vases, which they displayed in "cabinets of curiosities" at home. In the eighteenth century, Greece was still a remote land, difficult of access except to diplomats and the most ambitious travelers. But its temples attracted adventurers and collectors like a magnet, as did Egypt, Mesopotamia, and other areas a few generations later. The most notorious was Lord Elgin (1766–1841), appointed British ambassador to Constantinople, who employed hundreds of laborers to remove the sculptor Phidias's frieze from the Parthenon. He shipped the reliefs to London in 1803 and sold them to the British government, which displayed them in the British Museum, where they have been ever since. Interestingly, many people were disappointed in the marbles, for their style was not in keeping with the artistic taste of the times, which was strongly conditioned by Roman art. The Greek government has tried repeatedly to have the frieze returned, but to no avail.

Others followed in Elgin's footsteps, among them Charles Robert Cockerell (1788–1863), an English architectural student with a passion for classical architecture, who arrived in Athens in 1811. He and three other young men sailed to the island of Aegina as sightseers, to sketch and paint. But they soon unearthed sculptures at what was then called the Temple of Jupiter Panhellenius. On the second day, one of the diggers found the head of a helmeted warrior. The Aegina marbles were from the early classical period and were carved before those on the Parthenon. Cockerell realized their value at once, bought the marbles from the islanders for £40, and shipped them to Athens under cover of darkness.

A bidding war over the marbles started at once, pitting the British, French, and Germans against one another. The final sale was advertised in European newspapers and was won by Prince Ludwig of Bavaria. The Aegina marbles are now in Munich, but were, alas, heavily restored during the late nineteenth century. Cockerell subsequently removed the frieze of Amazons, Centaurs, and Lapiths from the Temple of Phigaleia and sold it to the British government for £15,000. The local administrator received £400 as his share of the spoils.

Cockerell's son's account of his father's three idyllic weeks on Aegina gives a wonderful impression of what it was like to dig lightheartedly for antiquities in Greece nearly two centuries ago. Today, it is hard to imagine what Cockerell must have experienced. The temple is now a major tourist attraction mobbed by thousands of visitors daily during the summer. The selection comes from Samuel Pepys Cockerell's Travels in Southern Europe and the Levant *(1903), which was based on his father's diaries.*

I told you we were going to make a tour in the Morea, but before doing so we determined to see the remains of the temple at Aegina, opposite Athens, a three hours' sail. Our party was to be Haller, Linckh, Foster, and myself. At the moment of our starting an absurd incident occurred. There had been for some time a smouldering war between our servants and our janissary. When the latter heard that he was not to go with us, it broke out into a blaze. He said it was because the servants had been undermining his character, which they equally angrily denied. But he was in a fury, went home, got drunk, and then came out into the street and fired off his pistols, bawling out that no one but he was the legitimate protector of the English. For fear he should hurt some one with his shooting, I went out to him and expostulated. He was very drunk, and professed to love us greatly and that he would defend us against six or seven or even eight Turks; but as for the servants, "Why, my soul," he said, "have they thus treated me?" I contrived, however, to prevent his loading his pistols again, and as he worked the wine off, calm was at length restored; but the whole affair delayed us so long that we did not walk down to the Piraeus till night. As we were sailing out of the port in our open boat we overtook the ship with Lord Byron on board. Passing under her stern we sang a favourite song of his, on which he looked out of the windows and invited us in. There we drank a glass of port with him, Colonel Travers, and two of the English officers, and talked of the three English frigates that had attacked five Turkish ones and a sloop of war off Corfu, and had taken and burnt three of them. We did not stay long, but bade them "bon voyage" and slipped over the side. We slept very well in the boat, and next morning reached Aegina. The port is very picturesque. We went on at once from the town to the Temple of Jupiter, which stands at some distance above it; and having got together workmen to help us in turning stones, etc., we pitched our tents for ourselves, and took possession of a cave at the northeast angle of the platform on which the temple stands—which had once been, perhaps, the cave of a sacred oracle—as a lodging for the servants and the janissary. The seas hereabouts are still infested with pirates, as they always have been. One of the workmen pointed me out the pirate boats off Sunium, which is one of their favourite haunts, and which one can see from the temple platform. But they never molested us during the twenty days and nights we camped out there, for our party, with servants and janissary, was too strong to be meddled with. We got our provisions and labourers from the town, our fuel was the wild thyme, there were abundance of partridges to eat, and we bought kids of the shepherds; and when work was over for the day, there was a grand roasting of them over a blazing fire with an accompaniment of native music, singing and dancing. On the platform was growing a crop of barley, but on the actual ruins and fallen fragments of the temple itself no great amount of vegetable earth had collected, so that without very much labour we were able to find and examine all the stones necessary for a complete architectural analysis and restoration. At the end of a few days we had learnt all we could wish to know of the construction, from the stylobate to the tiles, and had done all we came to do.

But meanwhile a startling incident had occurred which wrought us all to the highest pitch of excitement. On the second day one of the excavators, working in the interior portico, struck on a piece of Carian marble which, as the building itself is of stone, arrested his attention. It turned out to be the head of a helmeted warrior, perfect in every feature. It lay with the face turned upwards, and as the features came out by degrees you can imagine nothing like the state of rapture and excitement to which we were wrought. Here was an altogether new interest, which set us to work with a will. Soon another head was turned up, then a leg and a foot, and finally, to make a long story short, we found under the fallen portions of the tympanum and the cornice of the eastern and western pediments no less than sixteen statues and thirteen heads, legs, arms, etc. (another account says seventeen and fragments of at least ten more), all in the highest preservation, not three feet below the surface of the ground. It seems incredible, considering the number of travellers who have visited the temple, that they should have remained so long undisturbed.

It is evident that they were brought down with the pediment on the top of them by an earthquake, and all got broken in the fall; but we have found all the pieces and have now put together, as I say, sixteen entire figures.

The unusual bustle about the temple rapidly increased as the news of our operations spread. Many more men than we wanted began to congregate round us and gave me a good deal of trouble. Greek workmen have pretty ways. They bring you bunches of roses in the morning with pretty wishes for your good health; but they can be uncommonly insolent when there is no janissary to keep them in order. Once while Foster, being away at Athens, had taken the janissary with him, I had the greatest pother with them. A number that I did not want would hang about the diggings, now and then taking a hand themselves, but generally interfering with those who were labouring, and preventing any orderly and businesslike work. So at last I had to speak to them. I said we only required ten men, who should each receive one piastre per day, and that that was all I had to spend; and if more than ten chose to work, no matter how many they might be, there would still be only the ten piastres to divide amongst them. They must settle amongst themselves what they would choose to do. Upon this what did the idlers do? One of them produced a fiddle; they settled into a ring and were preparing to dance. This was more than I could put up with. We should get no work done at all. So I interfered and stopped it, declaring that only those who worked, and worked hard, should get paid anything whatever.

The Temple of Jupiter, Aegina.

This threat was made more efficacious by my evident anger, and gradually the superfluous men left us in peace, and we got to work again.

It was not to be expected that we should be allowed to carry away what we had found without opposition. However much people may neglect their own possessions, as soon as they see them coveted by others they begin to value them. The primates of the island came to us in a body and read a statement made by the council of the island in which they begged us to desist from our operations, for that heaven only knew what misfortunes might not fall on the island in general, and the immediately surrounding land in particular, if we continued them. Such a rubbishy pretence of superstitious fear was obviously a mere excuse to extort money, and as we felt that it was only fair that we should pay, we sent our dragoman with them to the village to treat about the sum; and meanwhile a boat which we had ordered from Athens having arrived, we embarked the marbles without delay and sent them off under the care of Foster and Linckh, with the janissary, to the Piraeus, and from thence they were carried up to Athens by night to avoid exciting attention. Haller and I remained to carry on the digging, which we did with all possible vigour. The marbles being gone, the primates came to be easier to deal with. We completed our bargain with them to pay them 800 piastres, about 40*l.*, for the antiquities we had found, with leave to continue the digging till we had explored the whole site. Altogether it took us sixteen days of very hard work, for besides watching and directing and generally managing the workmen, we had done a good deal of digging and handling of the marbles ourselves; all heads and specially delicate parts we

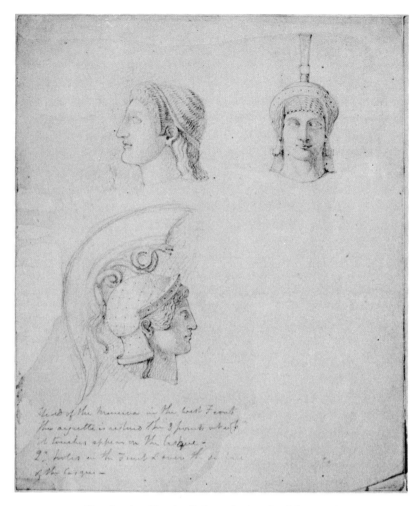

*Sketches by Charles Robert Cockerell of figures from
the Temple of Aphaia, Aegina.*

were obliged to take out of the ground ourselves for fear of the workmen ruining them. On the whole we have been fortunate. Very few have been broken by carelessness. Besides all this, which was outside our own real business, we had been taking measurements and making careful drawings of every part and arrangement of the architecture till every detail of the construction and, as far as we could fathom it, of the art of the building itself was clearly understood by us. Meanwhile, after one or two days' absence, Foster and Linckh came back; and it then occurred to us that the receipt for the 800 piastres had only been given to the names of Foster and myself (who had paid it), and Linckh and Haller desired that theirs should be added. Linckh therefore went off to the town to get the matter rectified. But this was not so easy. The lawyer was a crafty rogue, and pretending to be drunk as soon as he had got back the receipt into his hands, refused to give it up, and did not do so until after a great deal of persuasion and threatening. When we fell in with him at dinner two days later he met us with the air of the most candid unconcern. It was at the table of a certain Chiouk aga who had been sent from Constantinople to receive the rayah tax. Linckh had met him in the town when he went about the receipt, and the Chiouk had paid us a visit at the temple next day and dined with us, eating and especially drinking a great deal. A compliment he paid us was to drink our healths firing off a pistol. I had to do the same in return. The man had been to England, and even to Oxford, and had come back with an odd jumble of ideas which amused us but are not worth repeating. Next day, as I have said, we dined with him and the rogue of a lawyer. He was very hospitable. Dinner consisted mainly of a whole lamb, off which with his fingers he tore entire limbs and threw them into our plates, which we, equally with our fingers, *à la Turque*, ate as best we could. We finished the evening with the Albanian dance, and walked up home to our tent.

Homeric Troy

Heinrich Schliemann

A nineteenth-century classical education was firmly based on Homer's Iliad *and* Odyssey, *epic poems recited and written centuries before Athens ruled ancient Greece. But were these poems records of actual historical events, or were they pure fable? The controversy raged for generations and spilled far from the small world of academe.*

German-born Heinrich Schliemann (1822–1890) was a pastor's son who amassed a great fortune from indigo, the California gold rush, and the Crimean War. He became obsessed with the Homeric epics and retired from business at the age of forty-six to devote his life to archaeology. Schliemann was convinced that the Iliad *and* Odyssey *were the literal historical truth. He traveled extensively in Greece and Turkey and, with the aid of American Frank Calvert, who lived nearby, decided that the Hissarlik mound in northwestern Turkey was the site of Homeric Troy. Schliemann dug Hissarlik for four seasons. In 1871 to 1873 and 1879, he worked alone with his wife, Sophia; in 1882 and 1883 and again in 1889 and 1890, he had the expert assistance of Wilhelm Dorpfeld, a German archaeologist trained in excavation techniques at Olympia by Ernst Curtius, a pioneer in accurate recording.*

All Schliemann's excavations were on a massive scale. At Hissarlik, he employed engineers who applied methods used in digging the Suez Canal. He identified seven cities at Hissarlik, the second being Homeric Troy, "the citadel of Priam." (In 1893, Dorpfeld proved that the sixth city was the Homeric settlement.) At the end of the 1873 season, he claimed to have discovered a hoard of superbly crafted gold objects in the ruins of the Homeric city. He smuggled the artifacts out of Turkey, thereby incurring the wrath of the authorities, who declared him persona non grata. While Schliemann decked out his wife with "Priam's Treasure" like Helen of Troy, many scholars believe that the collection was excavated from many levels of the dig and never formed a single treasure. The finds vanished during World War II, but have recently turned up in Russia.

In the intervals of digging Hissarlik, Schliemann also dug at Mycenae, fabled citadel of Agamemnon. He unearthed a series of magnificently decorated shaft graves from a small area just inside the Lion Gate, proclaiming the richest to be the sepulchers of Agamemnon and Clytemnestra. Schliemann's Mycenae claims were disputed immedi-

ately, with many scholars arguing that they were of pre-Homeric date. Subsequent researches have confirmed this hypothesis.

Heinrich Schliemann was a prolific author, and his account of the first Hissarlik excavations, taken from his book Ilios *(1873), is still the best of his writing. But reader beware: history has not been kind to Schliemann, who fabricated many details of his life story for popular consumption, lied consistently about the discovery and makeup of "Priam's Treasure," and took all the credit for locating Troy at Hissarlik. Recent researches have shown that local resident Frank Calvert had dug into the mound before Schliemann and was certain that he had found Troy. But Schliemann claimed all the credit for himself and has passed into history as the discoverer of the Homeric city.*

At last I was able to realize the dream of my life, and to visit at my leisure the scene of those events which had always had such an intense interest for me, and the country of the heroes whose adventures had delighted and comforted my childhood. I started therefore, in April 1868, by way of Rome and Naples, for Corfu, Cephalonia, and Ithaca. This famous island I investigated carefully; but the only excavations I made there were in the so-called Castel of Ulysses, on the top of Mount Aëtos. I found the local character of Ithaca to agree perfectly with the indications of the *Odyssey*. . . .

I afterwards visited the Peloponnesus, and particularly examined the ruins of Mycenae, where it appeared to me that the passage in Pausanias in which the Royal Sepulchres are mentioned, and which has now become so famous, had been wrongly interpreted; and that, contrary to the general belief, those tombs were not at all understood by that writer to be in the lower town, but in the Acropolis itself. I visited Athens, and started from the Piraeus for the Dardanelles, whence I went to the village of Bounarbashi, at the southern extremity of the Plain of Troy. Bounarbashi, together with the rocky heights behind it, called the Bali Dagh, had until then, *in recent times*, been almost universally considered to be the site of the Homeric Ilium, the springs at the foot of that village having been regarded as the two springs mentioned by Homer, one of which sent forth warm, the other cold water. But, instead of only two springs, I found thirty-four, and probably there are forty. . . . The distance of Bounarbashi from the Hellespont is, in a straight line, 8 miles, whilst all the indications of the *Iliad* seem to prove that the distance between Ilium and the Hellespont was but very short, hardly exceeding 3 miles. Nor would it have been possible for Achilles to have pursued Hector in the plain round the walls of Troy, had Troy stood on the summit of Bounarbashi. I was therefore at once convinced that the Homeric city could not possibly have been here. Nevertheless, I wished to investigate so important a matter by actual excavations, and took a number of workmen to sink pits in hundreds of different places, between the forty springs and the extremity of the heights. But at the springs, as well as in Bounarbashi and everywhere else, I found only pure virgin soil, and struck the rock at a very small depth. At the southern end of the heights alone there are some ruins belonging to a very small fortified place, which I hold with the learned archaeologist, my friend Mr. Frank Calvert, United States vice-consul at the Dardanelles, to be identical with the ancient city of Gergis. . . .

Bounarbashi having thus given negative results, I next carefully examined all the heights to the right and left of the Trojan plain, but my researches bore no fruits until I came to the site of the city called by Strabo New Ilium, which is at a distance of only 3 miles from the Hellespont, and perfectly answers in this, as well as in all other respects, to the topographical requirements of the *Iliad*. My particular attention was attracted to the spot by the imposing position and natural fortifications of the hill called Hissarlik, which formed the northwestern corner of Novum Ilium, and seemed to me to mark the site of its Acropolis as well as of the Pergamus of Priam. . . . The elevation of this hill is 49.43 metres or 162 feet above the level of the sea.

In a hole dug here at random by two villagers, some twenty-five years ago, on the brink of the northern slope . . . there was found a small treasure of about 1,200 silver staters of Antiochus III (223–187 B.C.).

The first recent writer who asserted the identity of Hissarlik with the Homeric Troy was Maclaren. He showed by the most convincing arguments that Troy could never have been on the heights of Bounarbashi, and that, if it ever existed, Hissarlik must mark its site. . . . Such weighty authorities as George Grote, Julius Braun, and Gustav von Eckenbrecher have also declared in favor of Hissarlik. Mr. Frank Calvert further, who began by upholding the theory which placed Troy at Bounarbashi, became, through the arguments of these writers, and particularly, it appears, through those of Maclaren and Barker Webb, a convert to the Troy–Hissarlik theory and a valiant champion of it. He owns nearly one half of Hissarlik, and in two small ditches he had dug on his property he had brought to light before my visit some remains of the Macedonian and Roman periods, as well as part of the wall of Hellenic masonry, which, according to Plutarch (in his Life of Alexander), was built by Lysimachus. I at once decided to commence excavations here, and announced this intention in the work *Ithaque, le Péloponnèse et Troie*, which I published at the end of 1868. Having sent a copy of this work, together with a dissertation in ancient Greek, to the University of Rostock, that learned body honoured me with the diploma of Doctor of Philosophy. With unremitting zeal I have ever since endeavoured to show myself worthy of the dignity conferred on me.

In the book referred to I mentioned . . . that, according to my interpretation of the passage of Pausanias . . . in which he speaks of the sepulchres at Mycenae, the Royal Tombs must be looked for in the Acropolis itself, and not in the lower town. As this interpretation of mine was in opposition to that of all other scholars, it was at the time refused a hearing; now, however, that in 1876 I have actually found these sepulchres, with their immense treasures, on the very site indicated by me, it would seem that my critics were in the wrong and not myself.

Circumstances obliged me to remain nearly the whole of the year 1869 in the United States, and it was therefore only in April 1870 that I was able to return to Hissarlik and make a preliminary excavation, in order to test the depth to which the artificial soil extended. I made it at the northwestern corner, in a place where the hill had increased considerably in size, and where, consequently, the accumulation of debris of the Hellenic period was very great. Hence it was only after digging 16 feet below the surface that I laid bare a wall of huge stones, 6½ feet thick, which, as my later excavations have shown, belonged to a tower of the Macedonian epoch.

In order to carry on more extensive excavations I needed a firman from the Sublime Porte, which I only obtained in September 1871. . . .

At length, on the twenty-seventh of September, I made my way to the Dardanelles, together with my wife, Sophia Schliemann, who is a native of Athens and a warm admirer of Homer, and who, with glad enthusiasm, joined me in executing the great work which, nearly half a century ago, my childish simplicity had agreed upon with my father. . . . But we met with ever recurring difficulties on the part of the Turkish authorities, and it was not until the eleventh of October that we could fairly commence our work. There being no other shelter, we were obliged to live in the neighbouring Turkish village of Chiblak, a mile and a quarter from Hissarlik. After working with an average number of eighty labourers daily up to the twenty-fourth of November, we were compelled to cease the excavations for the winter. But during that interval we had been able to make a large trench on the face of the steep northern slope, and to dig down to a depth of 33 feet below the surface of the hill.

We first found there the remains of the later Aeolic Ilium, which on an average, reached to a depth of 6½ feet. . . . Below these Hellenic ruins, and to a depth of about 13 feet, the debris contained a few stones, and some very coarse handmade pottery. Below this stratum I came to a large number of house walls, of unwrought stones cemented with earth, and, for the first time, met with immense quantities of stone implements and saddle querns, together with more coarse handmade pottery. From about 20 feet to 30 feet below the surface, nothing was found but calcined debris, immense masses of sun-dried or slightly baked bricks and house walls of the same, numbers of saddle querns, but fewer stone implements of other kinds, and much better handmade pottery. At a depth of 30 feet and 33 feet we discovered fragments of house walls of large stones, many of them rudely hewn; we also came upon a great many very large blocks. The stones of these house walls appeared as if they had been separated from one another by a violent earthquake. My instruments for excavating were very imperfect: I had to work with only pickaxes, wooden shovels, baskets, and eight wheelbarrows.

I returned to Hissarlik with my wife at the end of March 1872, and resumed the excavations with 100 workmen. But I was soon able to increase the number of my labourers to 130, and had often even 150 men at work. I was now well prepared for the work, having been provided by my honoured friends Messrs. John Henry Schröder & Co. of London with the very best English wheelbarrows, pickaxes, and spades, and having also procured three overseers and an engineer, Mr. A. Laurent, to make the maps and plans. The last received monthly £20, the overseers £6 each, and my servant £7 4s.; whilst the daily wages of my common labourers were 1 franc 80 centimes, or about 18 pence sterling. I now built on the top of Hissarlik a wooden house, with three rooms and a magazine, kitchen, etc., and covered the buildings with waterproof felt to protect them from the rain.

On the steep northern slope of Hissarlik, which rises at an angle of 45°, and at a perpendicular depth of 46½ feet below the surface, I dug out a platform 233 feet wide, and found there an immense number of poisonous snakes; among them remarkably numerous specimens of the small brown adder called *antelion* . . . which is hardly thicker than an earthworm, and gets its name from the vulgar belief that the person bitten by it only survives till sunset.

I first struck the rock at a depth of about 53 feet below the surface of the hill, and found the lowest stratum of artificial soil to consist of very compact debris of houses, as hard as stone, and house walls of small pieces of unwrought or very rudely cut limestone, put together so that the joint between two of the stones in a lower layer is always covered by a single stone in the course above it. This lowest stratum was succeeded by house walls built of large limestone blocks, generally unwrought, but often rudely cut into something resembling a quadrangular shape. Sometimes I came upon large masses of such massive blocks lying close upon one another, and having all the appearance of being the broken walls of some large building. There is no trace of a general conflagration, either in this stratum of buildings built with large stones or in the lowest layer of debris; indeed, the multitudinous shells found in these two lowest strata are uninjured, which sufficiently proves that they have not been exposed to a great heat. I found in these two lowest strata the same stone implements as before, but the pottery is different. The pottery differs also from that in the upper strata.

As the cutting of the great platform on the north side of Hissarlik advanced but slowly, I began on the first of May a second large trench from the south side; but the slope being there but slight, I was forced to give it a dip of 14°. I here brought to light, near the surface, a pretty bastion, composed of large blocks of limestone, which may date from the time of Lysimachus. The southern part of Hissarlik has been formed principally by the debris of the later or Novum Ilium, and for this reason Greek antiquities are found here at a much greater depth than on the top of the hill.

As it was my object to excavate Troy, which I expected to find in one of the lower cities, I was forced to demolish many interesting ruins in the upper strata. . . .

With the consent of Mr. Frank Calvert, I also began on the twentieth of June, with the help of seventy labourers, to excavate in his field on the north side of Hissarlik, where, close to my large platform and at a perpendicular depth of 40 feet below the plateau of the hill, I dug out of its slope another platform, about 109 feet broad, with an upper terrace and side galleries, in order to facilitate the removal of the debris. No sooner had I commenced the work than I struck against a marble triglyph with a splendid metope, representing Phoebus Apollo and the four horses of the Sun. This triglyph, as well as a number of drums of Doric columns which I found there, can leave no doubt that a temple of Apollo of the Doric order once existed on the spot, which had, however, been so completely destroyed that I did not discover even a stone of its foundations _in situ_.

When I had dug this platform for a distance of 82 feet into the hill, I found that I had commenced it at least 16½ feet too high, and I therefore abandoned it, contenting myself with cutting into its centre a trench 26 feet wide at the top and 13 feet wide at the bottom. At a distance of 131 feet from the slope of the hill, I came upon a great wall, 10 feet high and 6½ feet thick, the top of which is just 34 feet below the surface. It is built in the so-called Cyclopean manner, of large blocks joined together with small ones; it had at one time been much higher, as the quantity of stones lying beside it seemed to prove. It evidently belonged to the city built with large stones, the second in succession from the virgin soil. At a depth of 6 feet below this wall I found a retaining wall of smaller stones, rising at an angle of 45°. This latter wall must of course be much older than the former; it evidently served to support the slope of the hill, and it proves beyond any doubt that, since its erection, the hill had increased 131 feet in breadth and 34 feet in height. As my friend Professor A. H. Sayce was the first to point out, this wall is built in exactly the same style as the house walls of the first and lowest city, the joint between two of the stones in the lower layer being always covered by a third in the upper layer. Accordingly, in agreement with him, I do not hesitate to attribute this wall to the first city. The debris of the lower stratum being as hard as stone, I had very great difficulty in excavating it in the ordinary way, and I found it easier to undermine it by cutting it vertically, and with the help of windlasses and enormous iron levers, nearly 10 feet in length and 6 inches in circumference, to loosen and so break it down in fragments 16 feet high, 16 feet broad, and 10 feet thick. But I found this manner of excavating very dangerous, two workmen having been buried alive under a mass of debris of 2,560 cubic feet, and having been saved as by a miracle. In consequence of this accident I gave up the idea of running the great platform 233 feet broad through the whole length of the hill, and decided on first digging a trench, 98 feet wide at the top and 65 feet at the bottom.

As the great extent of my excavations rendered it necessary for me to work with no less than from 120 to 150 labourers, I was obliged, on the first of June, on account of the harvest season, to increase the daily wages to 2 francs. But even this would not have enabled me to collect the requisite number of men, had not the late Mr. Max Müller, German consul at Gallipoli, sent me 40 workmen from that place. After the first of July, however, I easily procured a constant supply of 150 workmen. Through the kindness of Mr. Charles Cookson, English consul at Constantinople, I secured 10 hand-carts, which are drawn by two men and pushed by a third. I thus had 10 hand-carts and 88 wheelbarrows to work with, in addition to which I kept 6 horsecarts, each of which cost 5 francs or 4 shillings a day, so that the total cost of my excavations amounted to more than

Some of Heinrich Schliemann's workers at Hissarlik.

400 francs (£16) a day. Besides screw jacks, chains, and windlasses, my implements consisted of 24 large iron levers, 108 spades, and 103 pickaxes, all of the best English manufacture. I had three capital foremen, and my wife and myself were present at the work from sunrise to sunset; but our difficulties increased continually with the daily augmenting distance to which we had to remove the debris. Besides this, the constant strong gale from the north, which drove a blinding dust into our eyes, was exceedingly troublesome.

On the south side of the hill, where on account of the slight natural slope I had to make my great trench with an inclination of 76°, I discovered, at a distance of 197 feet from its entrance, a great mass of masonry, consisting of two distinct walls, each about 15 feet broad, built close together, and founded on the rock at a depth of 46½ feet below the surface. Both are 20 feet high; the outer wall slopes on the south side at an angle of 15°, and is vertical on the north side. The inner wall falls off at an angle of 45° on its south side, which is opposite to the north side of the outer wall. There is thus a deep hollow between the two walls. The outer wall is built of smaller stones cemented with clay, but it does not consist of solid masonry. The inner wall is built of large unwrought blocks of limestone; it has on the north side solid masonry to a depth of only 4 feet, and leans here against a sort of rampart 65½ feet broad and 16½ feet high, partly composed of the limestone which had to be removed in order to level the rock for building the walls upon it. These two walls are perfectly flat on the top, and have never been higher; they are 140 feet long, their aggregate breadth being 40 feet on the east and 30 feet at the west end. The remnants of brick walls and masses of broken bricks, pottery, whorls, stone implements, saddle-quern stones, etc., with which they were covered, appear to indicate that they were used by the inhabitants of the third or burnt city, as the substructions of a great tower; and I shall . . . call these walls . . . "the Great Tower," though they may originally have been intended by their builders for a different purpose. . . .

Up to the beginning of May 1873, I had believed that the hill of Hissarlik, where I was excavating, marked the site of the Trojan citadel only; and it certainly is the fact that Hissarlik was the acropolis of Novum Ilium. I therefore imagined that Troy was larger than the latter town, or at least as large; but I thought it important to discover the precise limits of the Homeric city, and accordingly I sank twenty shafts as far down as the rock, on the west, southwest, south-southeast, and east of Hissarlik, directly at its foot or at some distance from it, on the plateau of the Ilium of the Greek colony. As I found in these shafts no trace of fragments either of pre-historic pottery or of pre-historic house walls, and nothing but fragments of Hellenic pottery and Hellenic house walls; and as, moreover, the hill of Hissarlik has a very steep slope toward the north, the northeast, and the northwest, facing the Hellespont, and is also very steep on the west side towards the plain, the city could not possibly have extended in any one of these directions beyond the hill itself. It therefore appears certain that the ancient city cannot have extended on any side beyond the primeval plateau of Hissarlik, the circumference of which is indicated on the south and southwest by the Great Tower and the double gate; and on the northwest, northeast, and east, by the great boundary wall. . . .

The inhabitants of the five pre-historic sites of Hissarlik seem generally to have burnt the dead, as I found in 1872 two tripod urns with calcined human remains on the virgin soil in the first city; and in 1871, 1872, and 1873, a vast number of large funeral urns, containing human ashes, in the third and fourth cities. I found no bones however except a single tooth, and on one occasion among the ashes a human skull, which is well preserved, with the exception of the lower jaw, which is missing: as I found a brooch of bronze along with it, I suppose it may have belonged to a woman. . . .

It is true that nearly all the pottery found in the pre-historic ruins of Hissarlik is broken, and that there is hardly one large vessel out of twenty which is not in fragments; nay, in the first two cities the pottery has all been shattered by the weight and pressure of the stones with which the second city was built. But still, even if all the funeral urns with human ashes ever deposited in Hissarlik had been well preserved, yet, judging from the fragments of them—in spite of the abundance of these fragments—I can hardly think that I could have found even a thousand entire urns. It is, therefore, evident that the inhabitants of the five prehistoric cities of Hissarlik buried only a small part of their funeral urns in the city itself, and that we must look for their principal necropolis elsewhere.

Whilst these important excavations were going on, I neglected the trenches

*Sophia Schliemann wearing
"Priam's Treasure."*

on the north side, and only worked there when I had workmen to spare. But I brought to light here the prolongation of the great wall which I agree with Professor Sayce in attributing to the second stone city.

Wishing to investigate the fortifications on the west and northwest sides of the ancient city, in the beginning of May 1873 I also commenced making a trench, 33 feet broad and 141 feet long, on the northwest side of the hill, at the very point where I had made the first trench in April 1870. I broke first through an Hellenic circuit wall, probably that which, according to Plutarch in his Life of Alexander, was built by Lysimachus, and found it to be 13 feet high and 10 feet thick, and to consist of large hewn blocks of limestone. Afterwards I broke through an older wall, 8¾ feet high and 6 feet thick, composed of large blocks cemented with earth. This second wall is attached to the large wall which I brought to light in April 1870, and the two form two sides of a quadrangular Hellenic tower, a third wall of which I had to break through later on.

This part of the hill was evidently much lower in ancient times, as seems to be proved not only by the wall of Lysimachus, which must at one time have risen to a considerable height above the surface of the hill, whereas it is now covered by 16½ feet of rubbish, but also by the remains of the Hellenic period, which are here found to a great depth. It appears, in fact, as if the rubbish and debris of habitations had been thrown down on this side for centuries, in order to increase the height of the place.

In order to hasten the excavations on the northwest side of the hill, I cut a deep trench from the west side also, in which, unfortunately, I struck obliquely the circuit wall of Lysimachus, here 13 feet high and 10 feet thick. . . .

While following up this circuit wall, and bringing more and more of it to light, close to the ancient building and northwest of the Gate, I struck upon a large copper article of the most remarkable form, which attracted my attention all the more as I thought I saw gold behind it. On the top of it was a layer of red and calcined ruins, from 4¾ to 5¼ feet thick, as hard as stone, and above this again the above-mentioned wall of fortification (5 feet broad and 20 feet high), built of large stones and earth, which must have been erected shortly after the destruction of Troy. In order to secure the treasure from my workmen and save it for archaeology, it was necessary to lose no time; so, although it was not yet the hour for breakfast, I immediately had *païdos* called. This is a word of uncertain derivation, which has passed over into Turkish, and is here employed in place of $\alpha' \nu \alpha' \pi \alpha \nu \sigma \iota \varsigma$ or time for rest. While the men were eating and resting, I cut out the treasure with a large knife. This required great exertion and involved great risk, since the wall of fortification, beneath which I had to dig, threatened every moment to fall down upon me. But the sight of so many objects, every one of which is of inestimable value to archaeology, made me reckless, and I never thought of any danger. It would, however, have been impossible for me to have removed the treasure without the help of my dear wife, who stood at my side, ready to pack the things I cut out in her shawl, and to carry them away. . . .

As I found all these articles together, in the form of a rectangular mass, or packed into one another, it seems certain that they were placed on the city wall in a wooden chest. This supposition seems to be corroborated by the fact that close by the side of these articles I found a copper key. It is therefore possible that someone packed the treasure in the chest, and carried it off, without having had time to pull out the key; when he reached the wall, however, the hand of an enemy, or the fire, overtook him, and he was obliged to abandon the chest, which was immediately covered, to a height of 5 feet, with the ashes and stones of the adjoining house.

Perhaps the articles found a few days previously in a room of the chief's house, close to the place where the treasure was discovered, belonged to this unfortunate person. These articles consisted of a helmet and a silver vase, with a cup of electrum. . . .

That the treasure was packed together at a moment of supreme peril appears to be proved, among other things, by the contents of the largest silver vase, consisting of nearly 9,000 objects of gold. . . . The person who endeavoured to save the treasure had, fortunately, the presence of mind to place the silver vase, with the valuable articles inside it, upright in the chest, so that nothing could fall out, and everything has been preserved uninjured. . . .

I now perceived that the trench which I had made in April 1870 had exactly struck the right point for excavating, and that, if I had only continued it, I should, in a few weeks, have uncovered the most remarkable buildings in Troy.

Minoan Civilization at the Palace of Knossos

Arthur Evans

Who ruled Greece before classical times? Heinrich Schliemann found the Greek Bronze Age at Mycenae, uncovering a civilization of warriors and traders who lived long before the Homeric epics were set down in writing. But it was left to another archaeologist, Arthur Evans, to find evidence of an earlier civilization on Crete.

Sir Arthur Evans (1851–1941) was exposed to the thrill of discovery at an early age through the work of his father, the distinguished antiquary Sir John Evans, famous for his role in the establishment of the antiquity of humankind. Arthur's studies in classical history and particularly his interest in ancient coins and seals drew his attention to the island of Crete, where he would eventually uncover the Minoan civilization. But before settling into his career as an archaeologist, the young Evans was an accomplished journalist and political activist. While visiting the Dalmatian coast in the early 1880s, Evans sympathized with the Slavs and Albanians of Bosnia and Herzegovina who were struggling for their independence from Turkey and wrote a book about their plight. He later became a news correspondent for the Manchester Guardian *in the Balkans. His vociferous criticism of the Austrian occupation of Bosnia led to his imprisonment and subsequent banishment from the country.*

In 1884, Evans became keeper of the Ashmolean Museum at Oxford University, a moribund institution that he revived against almost insurmountable odds. Shortly before, Evans had met Heinrich Schliemann, fresh from his triumphs at Mycenae and Troy, an encounter that rekindled his interest in ancient Greek scripts. Blessed with microscopic eyesight, Evans pored over tiny prehistoric seals that he purchased in the Athens flea market and was told they came from Crete. He soon decided to dig at Knossos, but the Cretan revolution interrupted his plans. None other than Schliemann had attempted to purchase Knossos and dig there, but the same political unrest deterred him. Characteristically, Evans threw his support to the rebels, and then began excavating in 1900 when Crete won its independence from Turkey. His research, which would span three and a half decades, yielded most of what we know about Minoan civilization and brought to light the palace of the fabled King Minos.

How old were the Minoans? Evans was able to cross-date the Knossos palace with Egypt using Minoan vessels found in Egyptian deposits of known age to do so. He found that the Minoan civilization flourished before 1500 B.C. He also established that the Minoan civilization was older than the Mycenaean state of the Greek mainland unearthed by Schliemann a quarter century earlier. Evans's pioneering but unsuccessful work on the mysterious Minoan written scripts, inscribed on clay tablets, laid the groundwork for the eventual decipherment of the "Linear B" script in 1952. Linear B was used to record Mycenaean Greek, which was used at Knossos in the Late Bronze Age. It derives from earlier Linear A, which is still undeciphered.

Between 1921 and 1935, Evans published his life's work in his monumental four-volume Palace of Minos at Knossos. *This selection comes not from this monograph, but from an early article on the preliminary discoveries at Knossos published in the* Monthly Review *(1901). Evans's account of the events that led him to the ancient palace highlights the political realities that constrained his research early on. It also has an immediacy resulting from recent discovery, which sets it apart from Evans's later writings. His early journalistic experience also shows through here.*

Less than a generation back the origin of Greek civilization, and with it the sources of all great culture that has ever been, were wrapped in an impenetrable mist. That ancient world was still girt round within its narrow confines by the circling "Stream of Ocean." Was there anything beyond? The fabled kings and heroes of the Homeric age, with their palaces and strongholds, were they aught, after all, but more or less humanized sun myths?

One had had faith, accompanied by works, and in Dr. Schliemann the science of classical antiquity found its Columbus. Armed with the spade, he brought to light from beneath the mounds of ages a real Troy; at Tiryns and Mycenae he laid bare the palace and the tombs and treasures of Homeric kings. A new world opened to investigation, and the discoveries of its first explorer were followed up successfully by Dr. Tsountas and others on Greek soil. The eyes of observers were opened, and the traces of this prehistoric civilization began to make their appearance far beyond the limits of Greece itself. From Cyprus and Palestine to Sicily and southern Italy, and even to the coasts of Spain, the colonial and industrial enterprise of the "Mycenaeans" has left its mark throughout the Mediterranean basin. Professor Petrie's researches in Egypt have conclusively shown that as early at least as the close of the Middle Kingdom, or, approximately speaking, the beginning of the second millennium B.C., imported Aegean vases were finding their way into the Nile Valley. By the great days of the Eighteenth Dynasty, in the sixteenth and succeeding centuries B.C., this intercourse was of such a kind that Mycenaean art, now in its full maturity of bloom, was reacting on that of the contemporary Pharaohs and infusing a living European element into the old conventional style of the land of the Pyramids and the Sphinx.

But the picture was still very incomplete. Nay, it might even be said that its central figure was not yet filled in. In all these excavations and researches the very land to which ancient tradition unanimously pointed as the cradle of Greek civilization had been left out of count. To adapt the words applied by Gelon to slighted Sicily and Syracuse, "The spring was wanting from the year" of that earlier Hellas. Yet Crete, the central island—a halfway house between three continents—flanked by the great Libyan promontory and linked by smaller island steppingstones to the Peloponnese and the mainland of Anatolia, was called upon by Nature to play a leading part in the development of the early Aegean culture.

Here, in his royal city of Knossos, ruled Minos, or whatever historic personage is covered by that name, and founded the first sea empire of Greece, extending his dominion far and wide over the Aegean isles and coastlands. Athens paid to him its human tribute of youths and maidens. His colonial plantations extended east and west along the Mediterranean basin till Gaza worshipped the Cretan Zeus and a Minoan city rose in western Sicily. But it is as the first lawgiver of Greece that he achieved his greatest renown, and the Code of Minos became the source of all later legislation. As the wise ruler and inspired lawgiver there is something altogether biblical in his legendary character. He is the Cretan Moses, who every nine years repaired to the Cave of Zeus, whether on the Cretan Ida or on Dicta, and received from the God of the Mountain the laws for his people. Like Abraham, he is described as the "friend of God." Nay, in some accounts, the mythical being of Minos has a tendency to blend with that of his native Zeus.

This Cretan Zeus, the God of the Mountain, whose animal figure was the bull and whose symbol was the double axe, had indeed himself a human side which distinguishes him from his more ethereal namesake of classical Greece. In the great Cave of Mount Dicta, whose inmost shrine, adorned with natural pillars of gleaming stalactite, leads deep down to the waters of an unnavigated pool, Zeus himself was said to have been born and fed with honey and goat's milk by the nymph Amaltheia. On the conical height immediately above the site of Minos' City—now known as Mount Juktas—and still surrounded by a Cyclopean enclosure, was pointed out his tomb. Classical Greece scoffed at this primitive legend, and for this particular reason, first gave currency to the proverb that "the Cretans are always liars." . . .

If Minos was the first lawgiver, his craftsman Daedalus was the first traditional founder of what may be called a "school of art." Many were the fabled works wrought by them for King Minos, some gruesome, like the brass man Talos. In Knossos, the royal city, he built the dancing ground, or "Choros," of Ariadne, and the famous Labyrinth. In its inmost maze dwelt the Minotaur, or "Bull of Minos," fed daily with human victims, till such time as Theseus, guided by Ariadne's ball of thread, penetrated to its lair, and, after slaying the monster, rescued the captive youths and maidens. Such, at least, was the Athenian tale. A more prosaic tradition saw in the Labyrinth a building of many passages, the idea of which Daedalus had taken from the great Egyptian mortuary temple on the shores of Lake Moeris, to which the Greeks gave the same name; and recent philological research has derived the name itself from the *labrys*, or double ax, the emblem of the Cretan and Carian Zeus. . . .

When one calls to mind these converging lines of ancient tradition it becomes impossible not to feel that, without Crete, "the spring is taken away" indeed from the Mycenaean world. Great as were the results obtained by exploration on the sites of this ancient culture on the Greek mainland and elsewhere, there was still a sense of incompleteness. In nothing was this more striking than in the absence of any written document. A few signs had, indeed, been found on a vase handle, but these were set aside as mere ignorant copies of Hittite or Egyptian hieroglyphs. In the volume of his monumental work which deals with Mycenaean art, M. Perrot was reduced to the conclusion that "as at present advised, we can continue to affirm that, for the whole of this period, neither in Peloponnese nor in Central Greece, no more upon the buildings nor upon the thousand-and-one objects of domestic use and luxury that have come forth from the tombs, has anything been discovered that resembles any form of writing."

But was this indeed, the last word of scientific exploration? Was it possible that a people so advanced in other respects—standing in such intimate relations with Egypt and the Syrian lands where some form of writing had been an almost immemorial possession—should have been absolutely wanting in this most essential element of civilization? I could not believe it. Once more one's thoughts turned to the land of Minos, and the question irresistibly suggested itself—was that early heritage of fixed laws compatible with a complete ignorance of the art of writing? An abiding tradition of the Cretans themselves, preserved by Diodorus, shows that they were better informed. The Phoenicians, they said, had not invented letters, they had simply changed their forms—in other words, they had only improved on an existing system.

It is now seven years since a piece of evidence came into my hands which went far to show that long before the days of the introduction of the Phoenician alphabet, as adopted by the later Greeks, the Cretans were, in fact, possessed of a system of writing. While hunting out ancient engraved stones at Athens I came upon some three- and four-sided seals showing on each of their faces groups of hieroglyphic and linear signs distinct from the Egyptian and Hittite, but evidently representing some form of script. On inquiry I learnt that these seals had been found in Crete. A clue was in my hands, and like Theseus, I resolved to follow it, if possible to the inmost recesses of the Labyrinth. That the source and centre of the great Mycenaean civilization remained to be unearthed on Cretan soil I had never doubted, but the prospect now opened of finally discovering its written records.

From 1894 onwards I undertook a series of campaigns of exploration chiefly in central and eastern Crete. In all directions fresh evidence continually came to light. Cyclopean ruins of cities and strongholds, beehive tombs, vases, votive bronzes, exquisitely engraved gems, amply demonstrating that in fact the great days of that "island story" lay far behind the historic period. From the Mycenaean sites of Crete I obtained a whole series of inscribed seals, such as I had first noticed at Athens, showing the existence of an entire system of hieroglyphic or quasi-pictorial writing, with here and there signs of the co-existence of more linear forms. From the great Cave of Mount Dicta—the birthplace of Zeus—the votive deposits of which have now been thoroughly explored by Mr. Hogarth, I procured a stone libation table inscribed with a dedication of several characters in the early Cretan script. But for more exhaustive excavation my eyes were fixed on some ruined walls, the great gypsum blocks of which were engraved with curious symbolic characters, that crowned the southern slope of a hill known as Kephala, overlooking the ancient site of Knossos, the city of Minos. They were evidently part of a large prehistoric building. Might one not uncover here the palace of King Minos, perhaps even the mysterious Labyrinth itself?

These blocks had already arrested the attention of Schliemann and others, but the difficulties raised by the native proprietors had defeated all efforts at scientific exploration. In 1895 I succeeded in acquiring a quarter of the site from one of the joint owners. But the obstruction continued, and I was beset by difficulties of a more serious kind. The circumstances of the time were not favourable. The insurrection had broken out, half the villages in Crete were in ashes, and in the neighbouring town of Candia the most fanatical part of the Mahomedan population were collected together from the whole of the island. The Faithful Herakles, who was at that time my "guide, philosopher and mule-teer," was seized by the Turks and thrown into a loathsome dungeon, from which he was with difficulty rescued. Soon afterwards the inevitable massacre took place, of which the nominal British "occupants" of Candia were in part themselves the victims. Then at last the sleeping lion was aroused. Under the guns of Admiral Noel the Turkish commander evacuated the government buildings at ten minutes' notice and shipped off the sultan's troops. Crete once more was free.

At the beginning of this year I was at last able to secure the remaining part of the site of Kephala, and with the consent of Prince George's government at once set about the work of excavation. I received some pecuniary help from the recently started Cretan Exploration Fund, and was fortunate in securing the services of Mr. Duncan Mackenzie, who had done good work for the British School in Melos, to assist me in directing the works. From about 80 to 150 men were employed in the excavation which continued till the heat and fevers of June put an end to it for this season.

The result has been to uncover a large part of a vast prehistoric building—a palace with its numerous dependencies, but a palace on a far larger scale than those of Tiryns and Mycenae. About two acres of this has been unearthed, for by an extraordinary piece of good fortune the remains of walls began to appear only a foot or so, often only a few inches, below the surface. This dwelling of prehistoric kings had been overwhelmed by a great catastrophe. Everywhere on the hilltop were traces of a mighty conflagration; burnt beams and charred wooden columns lay within the rooms and corridors. There was here no gradual decay. The civilization represented on this spot had been cut short in the fulness of its bloom. Nothing later than remains of the good Mycenaean period was found over the whole site. Nothing even so late as the last period illustrated by the remains of Mycenae itself. From the day of destruction to this the site has been left entirely desolate. For three thousand years or more not a tree seems to have been planted here; over a part of the area not even a ploughshare had passed. At the time of the great overthrow, no doubt, the place had been methodically plundered for metal objects, and the fallen debris in the rooms and passages turned over and ransacked for precious booty. Here and there a local bey or peasant had grubbed for stone slabs to supply his yard or threshing floor. But the party walls of clay and plaster still stood intact, with the fresco painting on them, still in many cases perfectly preserved at a few inches' depth from the surface, a clear proof of how severely the site had been let alone for these long centuries.

Who were the destroyers? Perhaps the Dorian invaders who seem to have overrun the island about the eleventh or twelfth century before our era. More probably, still earlier invading swarms from the mainland of Greece. The palace itself had a long antecedent history and there are frequent traces of remodelling. Its early elements may go back to a thousand years before its final overthrow, since, in the great Eastern Court, was found the lower part of an Egyptian seated figure of diorite, with a triple inscription, showing that it dates back to the close of the Twelfth or the beginning of the Thirteenth Dynasty of Egypt; in other words approximately to 2000 B.C. But below the foundation of the later building, and covering the whole hill, are the remains of a primitive settlement of still greater antiquity, belonging to the insular Stone Age. In parts this "Neolithic" deposit was over twenty-four feet thick, everywhere full of stone axes, knives of volcanic glass, dark polished and incised pottery, and primitive images such as those found by Schliemann in the lowest strata of Troy.

The outer walls of the palace were supported on huge gypsum blocks, but there was no sign of an elaborate system of fortification such as at Tiryns and Mycenae. The reason of this is not far to seek. Why is Paris strongly fortified, while London is practically an open town? The city of Minos, it must be remembered, was the centre of a great sea power, and it was in "wooden walls" that its rulers must have put their trust. The mighty blocks of the palace show, indeed, that it was not for want of engineering power that the acropolis of Knossos remained unfortified. But in truth Mycenaean might was here at home. At Tiryns and Mycenae itself it felt itself threatened by warlike continental neighbors. It was not till the mainland foes were masters of the sea that they could have forced an entry into the House of Minos. Then, indeed, it was an easy task. In the Cave of Zeus on Mount Ida was found a large brooch (or *fibula*) belonging to the race of northern invaders, on one side of which a war galley is significantly engraved.

The palace was entered on the southwest side by a portico and double doorway opening from a spacious paved court. Flanking the portico were remains of a great fresco of a bull, and on the walls of the corridor leading from it were still preserved the lower part of a procession of painted life-size figures, in the centre of which was a female personage, probably a queen, in magnificent apparel. This corridor seems to have led round to a great southern porch or *Propy-laeum* with double columns, the walls of which were originally decorated with figures in the same style. Along nearly the whole length of the building ran a spacious paved corridor, lined by a long row of fine stone doorways, giving access to a succession of magazines. On the floor of these magazines huge store jars were still standing, large enough to have contained the "forty thieves." One of these jars, contained in a small separate chamber, was nearly five feet in height.

Here occurred one of the most curious discoveries of the whole excavation. Under the closely compacted pavement of one of these magazines, upon which the huge jars stood, there were built in, between solid piles of masonry, double tiers of stone cists lined with lead. Only a few were opened and they proved to be empty, but there can be little doubt that they were constructed for the deposit of treasure. Whoever destroyed and plundered the palace had failed to discover these receptacles, so that when more come to be explored there is some real hope of finding buried hoards.

On the east side of the palace opened a still larger paved court, approached by broad steps from another principal entrance to the north. From this court access was given by an anteroom to what was certainly the most interesting chamber of the whole building, almost as perfectly preserved—though some twelve centuries older—as anything found beneath the volcanic ash of Pompeii or the lava of Herculaneum. Already a few inches below the surface freshly preserved frescoes began to appear. Walls were shortly uncovered decorated with flowering plants and running water, while on each side of the doorway of a small inner room stood guardian griffins with peacocks' plumes in the same flowery landscape. Round the walls ran low stone benches, and between these on the north side, separated by a small interval and raised on a stone base, rose a gypsum throne with a high back, and originally coloured with decorative designs. Its lower part was adorned with a curiously carved arch, with crocketed mouldings, showing an extraordinary anticipation of some most characteristic features of Gothic architecture. Opposite the throne was a finely wrought tank of gypsum slabs—a feature borrowed perhaps from an Egyptian palace—approached by a descending flight of steps, and originally surmounted by cyprus wood columns supporting a kind of *impluvium*. Here truly was the council chamber of a Mycenaean king or sovereign lady. It may be said today that the youngest of European rulers has in his dominions the oldest throne in Europe.

The frescoes discovered on the palace site constitute a new epoch in the history of painting. Little, indeed, of the kind even of classical Greek antiquity has been hitherto known earlier at least than the Pompeian series. The first find of this kind marks a red-letter day in the story of the excavation. In carefully uncovering the earth and debris in a passage at the back of the southern propy-laeum there came to light two large fragments of what proved to be the upper part of a youth bearing a gold-mounted silver cup. The robe is decorated with a beautiful quatrefoil pattern; a silver ornament appears in front of the ear, and silver rings on the arms and neck. What is specially interesting among the orna-

*The Throne Room in the Palace of Minos at Knossos, exposed during
Arthur Evans's excavations.*

ments is an agate gem on the left wrist, thus illustrating the manner of wearing
the beautifully engraved signets of which many clay impressions were found in
the palace. . . .

To the north of the palace, in some rooms that seem to have belonged to
the women's quarter, frescoes were found in an entirely novel miniature style.
Here were ladies with white complexions—due, we may fancy, to the seclusion
of harem life—*décolletées*, but with fashionable puffed sleeves and flounced
gowns, and their hair as elaborately curled and *frisé* as if they were fresh from a
coiffeur's hands. *"Mais,"* exclaimed a French savant who honoured me with a
visit, *"ce sont des Parisiennes!"* . . .

Very valuable architectural details were supplied by the walls and buildings
of some of the miniature frescoes. In one place rose the façade of a small temple,
with triple cells containing sacred pillars, and representing in a more advanced
form the arrangement of the small golden shrines, with doves perched upon
them, found by Schliemann in the shaft graves at Mycenae. This temple fresco
has a peculiar interest, as showing the character of a good deal of the upper
structure of the palace itself, which has now perished. It must largely have consisted of clay and rubble walls, artfully concealed under brilliantly painted plas-

*Evans with the same throne and a Minoan vase displayed
at an exhibition at the Royal Academy in London, October 1936.*

ter, and contained and supported by a woodwork framing. The base of the small temple rests on the huge gypsum blocks which form so conspicuous a feature in the existing remains, and below the central opening is inserted a frieze, recalling the alabaster reliefs of the palace hall of Tiryns, with triglyphs, the prototypes of the Doric, and the half-rosettes of the "metopes" inlaid with blue enamel, the Kyanos of Homer. . . .

But manifold as were the objects of interest found within the palace walls of Knossos, the crowning discovery—or, rather, series of discoveries—remains to be told. On the last day of March, not far below the surface of the ground, a little to the right of the southern portico, there turned up a clay tablet of elongated shape, bearing on it incised characters in a linear script, accompanied by numeral signs. My hopes now ran high of finding entire deposits of clay archives, and they were speedily realized. Not far from the scene of the first discovery there came to light a clay receptacle containing a hoard of tablets. In other chambers occurred similar deposits, which had originally been stored in coffers of wood, clay, or gypsum. The tablets themselves are of various forms, some flat, elongated bars, from about 2 to 7½ inches in length, with wedgelike ends; others, larger and squarer, ranging in size to small octavo. In one particular magazine tablets of a different kind were found—perforated bars, crescent and scallop-like "labels," with writing in the same hieroglyphic style as that on the seals found in eastern Crete. But the great mass, amounting to over a thousand inscriptions, belonged to another and more advanced system with linear characters. It was, in short, a highly developed form of script, with regular divisions between the words, and for elegance hardly surpassed by any later form of writing.

A clue to the meaning of these clay records is in many cases supplied by the addition of pictorial illustrations representing the objects concerned. Thus we find human figures, perhaps slaves; chariots and horses; arms or implements and armor, such as axes and cuirasses; houses or barns; ears of barley or other cereal; swine; various kinds of trees; and a long-stamened flower, evidently the saffron crocus, used for dyes. On some tablets appear ingots, probably of bronze, followed by a balance (the Greek τάλαντον), and figures which probably indicate their value in Mycenaean gold talents. The numerals attached to many of these objects show that we have to do with accounts referring to the royal stores and arsenals.

Some tablets relate to ceramic vessels of various forms, many of them containing marks indicative of their contents. Others, still more interesting, show vases of metallic forms, and obviously relate to the royal treasures. It is a highly significant fact that the most characteristic of these, such as a beaker like the famous gold cups found in the Vapheio tomb near Sparta, a high-spouted ewer, and an object, perhaps representing a certain weight of metal, in the form of an ox's head, recur—together with the ingots with incurving sides among the gold offerings in the hands of the tributary Aegean princes—on Egyptian monuments of Thothmes III's time. These tributary chieftains, described as Kefts and People of the Isles of the Sea, who have been already recognized as the representatives of the Mycenaean culture, recall in their dress and other particulars the Cretan youths, such as the cupbearer described earlier, who take part in the processional scenes on the palace frescoes. The appearance in the records of the royal treasury at Knossos of vessels of the same form as those offered by them to Pharaoh is itself a valuable indication that some of these clay archives go back approximately to the same period—in other words, to the beginning of the fifteenth century B.C.

Other documents, in which neither ciphers nor pictorial illustrations are to be found, may appeal even more deeply to the imagination. The analogy of the more or less contemporary tablets, written in cuneiform script, found in the palace of Tell-el-Amarna, might lead us to expect among them the letters from distant governors or diplomatic correspondence. It is probable that some are contracts of public acts, which may give some actual formulas of Minoan legislation. There is, indeed, an atmosphere of legal nicety, worthy of the House of Minos, in the way in which these clay records were secured. The knots of string which, according to the ancient fashion, stood in the place of locks for the coffers containing the tablets were rendered inviolable by the attachment of clay seals, impressed with the finely engraved signets, the types of which represent a great variety of subjects, such as ships, chariots, religious scenes, lions, bulls, and other animals. But—as if this precaution was not in itself considered sufficient—while the clay was still wet the face of the seal was countermarked by a controlling official, and the back countersigned and endorsed by an inscription in the same Mycenaean script as that inscribed on the tablets themselves.

Much study and comparison will be necessary for the elucidation of these materials, which it may be hoped will be largely supplemented by the continued exploration of the palace. If, as may well be the case, the language in which they were written was some primitive form of Greek we need not despair of the final decipherment of these Knossian archives, and the bounds of history may eventually be so enlarged as to take in the "heroic age" of Greece. In any case the weighty question, which years before I had set myself to solve on Cretan soil, has found, so far at least, an answer. That great early civilization was not dumb, and the written records of the Hellenic world are carried back some seven centuries beyond the date of the first known historic writings. But what, perhaps, is even more remarkable than this is that, when we examine in detail the linear script of these Mycenaean documents, it is impossible not to recognize that we have here a system of writing, syllabic and perhaps partly alphabetic, which stands on a distinctly higher level of development than the hieroglyphs of Egypt or the cuneiform script of contemporary Syria and Babylonia. It is not till some five centuries later that we find the first dated examples of Phoenician writing.

A Bronze Age Town in Gournia, Crete

MARY ALLESBROOK AND HARRIET BOYD HAWES

Arthur Evans's magnificent discoveries at Knossos overshadowed much valuable work on the Minoan civilization carried out by other scholars of the day. One of them was a woman, the first female archaeologist to excavate on the island of Crete.

Harriet Boyd Hawes (1871–1945) is something of an unsung heroine in early-twentieth-century archaeology. Only now, a half century after her death, is the discoverer of the Minoan town of Gournia receiving the credit she has long been due, thanks to the publication of her biography, Born to Rebel, *by her daughter Mary Allesbrook. Harriet was born shortly after the American Civil War to a middle-class family in Boston. Her mother died while Harriet was very young, an experience that taught her self-reliance early on. She was educated at Smith College, where she discovered a passion for ancient art, and soon ended up studying at the American School in Athens (now the American School of Classical Studies). But Boyd had a second calling. During the 1897 war between Turkey and Greece, she volunteered her services as a nurse. Boyd would periodically interrupt her archaeological work throughout her life, and she served as a nurse in three wars. These field experiences made a lasting impression on her. Shortly after World War I, she gave up excavation to lecture about the horrors she had witnessed and to campaign for peace. But for many years, she taught a course in ancient art at Wellesley College, maintaining at least a tenuous link with the archaeological world.*

Boyd made the most of her short time in the field. Having earned a Yale fellowship to study ancient inscriptions near Athens, she traveled to Europe. She was soon longing for more than the quiet museum work that was permissible for women in archaeology at that time. Encouraged by Arthur Evans and the redoubtable Sophia Schliemann, she made arrangements to search for a site on Crete. Boyd made a quick adjustment to field life, traveling everywhere on muleback without complaint, accompanied by her companion and cook, making the meanest of accommodations hospitable. Her curiosity and perseverance paid off: in May 1901, with the help of a local peasant, Boyd found the ruins of a Bronze Age town. In three short seasons, Gournia and its treasures were brought to light. Boyd directed and commanded the respect of a labor force of more than a hundred persons, kept meticulous records of her finds, and published them in a beauti-fully illustrated, and now very rare, monograph. It is difficult to believe that, until recently, the discipline of archaeology had forgotten one of its most significant daughters and ascribed the discovery of Gournia to a male colleague. Her work becomes all the more remarkable when one remembers that she accomplished what she did in the cum-bersome outfits of a Victorian lady at a time when women's professional opportunities were seriously restricted.

Here, her daughter Mary Allesbrook, in her biography Born to Rebel, *uses Harri-et's diaries and notes to relive life at the Gournia excavations.*

Fifty enthusiastic workmen reported at the site the next morning, and during the day nineteen trial pits were dug. One worker hit rock right away; others dug down until they reached house floors or corridors. The ninth hole was so rich in finds that it was immediately nicknamed the Treasury. There was no gold, but it bore all the household gadgets of 3,500 years ago.

Three days after first reconnoitring at Gournia, [Harriet] was sure they had found the settlement she had been searching for. She sent Aristides to the tele-graph office sixty miles away to cable the American Exploration Society: "Dis-covered Gournia Mycenaean site, street, houses, pottery, bronzes, stone jars." Mycenaean was the term then used to describe the Cretan period now known as Minoan.

Within a week the payroll jumped to a hundred men and ten girls—the average force during her campaigns of 1901, 1903 and 1904. It was exhilarating to ride back the four miles to Kavousi each evening with the marching workers in a triumphal procession. But she and Blanche [her companion] felt they had to be close to such a promising site. So they found two rooms over a storehouse at the coastguard station of Pachyammos, which they shared with a colony of rats.

An outside wooden staircase led up to the first room, which was converted into a kitchen-bedroom for Manna. The second, a narrow triangular one with a single small window, became their bedroom. Meals were served on the roof of an adjoining shed, "reached in rather undignified fashion by crawling through the kitchen window!" There the men made an arbour of oleanders for shade. This arrangement was no help in dispensing graceful hospitality to visiting ar-chaeologists. Even Harriet realised the disadvantage of wriggling through a kitchen window in a dress of the 1900s fashion, despite the attraction of dining amidst a bower of blossom.

As well as these quarters

two adjacent storehouses were hired, one for the antiquities, the other for those workmen who did not wish to trudge home to Kavousi every night, but . . . the greater number of young men preferred to build shelters of boughs at the diggings within which they slept and did their simple cooking over a fire of sticks.

After a full day of directing the men from six in the morning to six at night, with two hours off for siesta, she had to burn the midnight oil (literally and figuratively) preparing the payroll. It was not simply a matter of doling out dollars. When she first started excavating

> wages were reckoned in "grossia" (piastres), a coin which did not exist in Crete and were paid in Turkish, French, Italian, and English currency in accordance with an elaborate system of equivalents. Once a fortnight, much time was consumed in calculating wages and in convincing the employee that with, for example, 2 medjidies, 2 half-crowns, 3 francs and 10 metalliks, he had received his just due of 96 grossia at the rate of 8 grossia per day.

Fortunately a Cretan currency was established in 1902.

The payroll list itself was a problem. There was a serious shortage of names to help identify the men. They had Christian names, but out of a hundred men fifteen might step forward to the call of Manoles. Harriet therefore decreed "severely that a man would be dismissed the following night if in twenty-four hours he had not provided himself with a distinctive name."

Success brought a new difficulty. As the hundreds of small objects were unearthed there was a serious danger that the men might be tempted to smuggle some to collectors. So Harriet had to decide how best to discourage dishonesty. At many sites, rewards were given for each article found. Another possibility was to raise the wages slightly and pay a reward only for a sealstone. She put both options to her "Firsts" (those who had worked longest for her), and they voted for the higher wages. This pleased her because she felt it put the men on their honour not to make off with history, and it seemed fairer. Otherwise, the men would jostle for the job of excavating a craftsman's home, in the hope of receiving a reward, and shirk the important chore of digging to find an unpromising site for a dump.

Sealstones were made an exception to encourage the workmen to keep a sharp lookout for them. These smallest and most saleable of objects, which Cretan women wore around their necks as milk-charms, carried a five franc reward. They were a favourite with Arthur Evans, who had collected scores of them when touring Crete before he could excavate there. Back in his study in Oxford, he used to take them from his pockets and examine them with the utmost care.

All the work force were warned that anyone who held back anything would be discharged and handed over to the law if possible. Members of their family would also be dismissed. In a close community this Old Testament justice was a great incentive to honesty. Fortunately there was never any call to carry out the threat.

Labour was cheap in Crete and the average daily wage bill for 110 people working at the Gournia site was about US$32.00, or $200 a week. Most of the workers were happy with what they got; there was only one dispute in three years, when forty discontents demanding better pay downed tools for twenty minutes. Their employer explained that she had a fixed fund, took no salary for herself, and that if she gave higher wages some of the force would have to be discharged. This mollified most of the men. Thirty-eight went back for the old wages, and they laughed at one of the two ringleaders who would have been promoted that very day but was temporarily discharged for making trouble "without first seeking redress." Harriet considered the proper time to protest was at the evening roll-call, when "the men were invited to make known their grievances."

She also considered it proper to consult the workers on certain subjects and, wanting their discussions to be conducted in a democratic way, arranged for them to use

> a form of government invented by the Greeks long before Christ. . . . Our force was divided into a Senate of the older workmen and an Assembly of the younger men—experience vs. numbers. The two voted separately, the Senate first, . . . it being understood that both bodies must agree before action could be taken."

So when a stranger wanted to set up a café near the excavations the men took a vote. The Senate was unanimously against it, and the Assembly fell into line. Their decision delighted her, for she had feared the men might waste their wages in "treating."

For nearly thirty-five centuries the town of Gournia had lain dormant. Archaeologists had passed along the highway several hundred feet away never suspecting it was there, and she had herself previously picnicked two minutes' walk from the site. But its discovery was perhaps most surprising to her work force, who had lived all their lives within walking distance, never dreaming a whole town with streets and houses lay buried there.

One of the first fellow archaeologists to visit the site was Mr. Hogarth, who only two months before had unknowingly passed it by. He was astonished to find now a little town beside the road, and described Gournia in the *London Times* of August 10, 1901, as

> the most perfect example yet discovered of a small "Mycenean" town . . . and at this moment after the two great palaces, is the "sight" best worth visiting in Crete. . . . Unobserved till now, though close to the main road . . . it was discovered by the perseverance of the American lady, Miss Harriet Boyd, who has been directing its excavation.

Gournia was, in fact, the oldest town discovered in Europe, and soon became known as the "Cretan Pompeii," even though centuries older than the Roman Pompeii.

Every hour brought fresh excitement. Four days after the first pick struck ground, the men started looking for places to dump their baskets of earth, but this was no easy task. Before deciding on a location they had to dig down to bed rock to ensure no hidden treasure would be covered. But each trial hole led to more finds.

Next day they were still searching for a suitable spot when a workman struck a block of trimmed stone. It was much more elegant than the rubble and brick walls of the ordinary town dwellings. Could it belong to a special building, perhaps a provincial palace? It did.

During the second week the diggers found a Minoan status symbol, a double axe, and also a more worldly one, a roulette table. But particularly revealing and gratifying was Room 7. When in about 1500 B.C. the town was destroyed by fire, the lime plaster fell and was burnt. It was then soaked by rain and "solidified into a mass which was firm on the surface but was still soft and even moist at some points inside." Picking into this mass, the workmen found thirty vases completely embedded. Some had fallen from the upper storey and cracked into a score of pieces, but they had been kept in shape as if within a mould. This was very lucky, because otherwise no one could possibly have puzzled out the reconstruction of a peculiar double-jug.

The following week a small shrine was unearthed in the centre of the town—the first Minoan sanctuary discovered intact. Slowly there emerged a little low altar table, several crude cult vases vaguely reminiscent of Egypt, and a modernistic-looking image of the Earth Goddess, intertwined with snakes. How appropriate that a woman should be the first to find a shrine sacred to the Mother Goddess of the Minoans!

As experience grew, the process of uncovering the past began to take on the appearance of a production line. The most skilled and best-paid men—fourteen to eighteen in number—were entrusted with the picks and knives; an equal number wielded the shovels; one or two carpenters and a few masons attended to wood and stone work; and most of the others carried away the stones and earth in barrows and baskets. When small articles were being found, the soil had to be sifted handful by handful.

Ten girls cleaned the potsherds, which eventually numbered tens of thousands. First they were washed in water, then soaked in a dilute solution of nitric acid, next rinsed in ammonia, and finally washed again in water. Once clean, the sherds were very patiently pieced together, and no one was more skilled at this than Aristides, who assembled the eighty-six bits of the finest find of all—a vase showing two sprawling octopuses entwined with coral and seaweed.

Gournia was ancient in history but modern in spirit. It spread over the hillside, with no fortifications, and a ring road almost encircled the inner part of the town, intersected by radial roads. The streets measured only five feet from house wall to house wall. But they were neatly paved and better than many of the twentieth-century roads she had travelled along. Some were stepped and led up the hill to the public courtyard and the palace.

Although in the most prominent position, Gournia's provincial palace was not stand-offish; all the town houses were clustered around it. But it was by far the largest building; about 130 feet square, or twelve times the size of the ordinary dwellings. In miniature it had many of the features of the great palaces of Crete, with a large pillared central hall, magazines, storerooms, and separate apartments for the men and women of the Court. But a feature more in tune with the twentieth century than 3,500 years ago was the split-floor levels built on three rock terraces, which followed the contour at the crest of the hill. In places the palace had risen to two, and possibly three, storeys. Elsewhere there was only one level with a flat roof that the household probably used as a terrace from which to look out at the headlands of Mirabello Bay and the surrounding silhouetted mountain ranges. The luxury of the view, however, was not matched by basic amenities. There was only one bath in the whole palace, and that was in the men's quarters.

The palace's majestic, commanding setting also turned out to be its ruin. Exposure to the ravages of the elements and the attention of looters had left the palace only an outline of its former glory, and it was almost stripped of finds, but not quite. Some ceremonial lamps were unearthed which have a lasting grace and simplicity that might today win them design awards as birdbaths.

During the three campaigns of digging, two to three acres of Gournia were uncovered. In some places the picks struck floor level within a matter of inches; in others they dug to a depth of fifteen feet. Sixty to seventy houses were exposed, each abutting the next and flush with the streets, following the lay of the land rather than any conventional plan. The houses averaged about eight rooms; some had stairs to upper storeys; others had cellars and basements.

The workmen, although themselves mostly peasants, proudly called Gournia an "industrial town" because of the large number of tools found there. And it was indeed a do-it-yourself community, almost isolated from outside influence.

Towards the harbour and highway a smith had set up his forge for working bronze. Here he had a stone mould for casting nails and chisels, and it was so valuable to him that he had carefully mended a crack with bronze strips. Over towards the palace was a well-built house which clearly had belonged to a carpenter. His tools—five chisels, a saw, and an axe—were hidden under the floor of the corridor. His wife was obviously a weaver; thirteen loom weights lay on the floor, after the shelf on which they had been kept had been burnt. Other artisan tools included a cobbler's last; a fisherman's hooks, sinkers, and netweights; and an artist's paint-box and pallets. The stone pestle used for grinding the colours at Gournia exactly resembled one used by a Boston firm 3,500 years later in making prize-winning plates for the book *Gournia*.

In some rooms the workmen unearthed so many stacked cups they nicknamed them "Coffee Houses." In other homes tiny vases of varied shapes were more common—only suitable, it seemed, for Lilliputians, or as toys for children.

The pottery style in vogue (Late Minoan I) showed that Gournia flourished before the heyday of Knossos and the rise of Mycenae. Decoration was simple and spontaneous and not sophisticated, as in the period that followed. The favourite designs were crocuses, lilies, ivy leaves, seaweeds, and shells, sometimes

true to nature, sometimes stylized, usually in black or red paint on a buff background.

Six weeks of excited excavating uncovered only a portion of the site. Work had to stop, and it stopped without anyone knowing that the main entrance to the palace was close at hand. Digging had been halted scores of times by church festivals, but it was a rather different occasion that marked the conclusion of this year's campaign—the celebration of American Independence, July 4. A sports day was held on the great, lonely, curving beach nearby, in view of majestic mountains. No wonder the Venetians who held Crete for four centuries called that gulf Mirabello—"wonderfully beautiful." The workmen vied in running and jumping for "a branch of wild olive," and the winner of this coveted prize was entitled to carry home "an amphora of oil or wine." At the feast that followed, the schoolmaster proposed a toast "To the Memory of George Washington and may God have Mercy on his Soul." This was such a successful ending to the first campaign that they celebrated American Independence Day again in 1904, ironically while Crete itself was still under a multiple foreign yoke. . . .

They made a round trip through eastern Crete, searching again for a possible site, preferably a pre-Mycenean one. Harriet was determined to find something larger than tombs and older than the Iron Age. Other archaeologists—all men—

had staked out their claims to the most promising places. So the first woman treasure hunter allowed herself to be drawn back to the remoter isthmus.

On reaching the northwest shore of Mirabello Bay, the party left their horse and three mules and crossed to Kavousi, tossing about in a sponge diver's caïque. There they were enthusiastically received by the villagers and housed again in the cobbler's shop.

The Ag. Antonios clue to a possible Minoan settlement was such a slight ray of hope that she had kept it from other archaeologists. And when word got around that she had permission to go back to the area—presumably to look for relics of the Dark and not the Golden Age of Crete—she was pitied. Mirabello Bay might be very beautiful, but living conditions there were thought to be appalling and archaeological prospects comparatively poor.

The following day a priest came to sanctify a piece of ground where they could put any Christian bones disturbed by their digging, and then the twenty-five men started work. They found ancient walls, probably belonging to a fortified homestead; a number of household bits and pieces, so ordinary that in the absence of decoration it was hard to date them; and no iron but some bronze. They also discovered ancient tombs nearby. But their employer was discouraged. Her hopes sank and she confessed to her diary to being "a little homesick."

The feeling of being awash was added to by the weather. The skies opened and it rained for twelve, twenty-four, thirty-six hours. Manna spent the whole night bailing out the kitchen, and a nearby hut was wrecked. Water loosened the walls of their main room, while inside Harriet tried to console herself by reading *The Clouds* by Aristophanes. She longed for a silver lining.

Progress was slow. There were days too wet for digging and holidays—or holy days—so numerous and so rigidly adhered to that one English archaeologist considered complaining to the local bishop. On these days off the two ladies went down onto the plain to search for a settlement of earlier, more artistic times. Up and down they rode. With rocks strewn everywhere, the eager archaeologists began to see ancient walls "in every chance grouping." But the area seemed cursed with shallow soil too thin to cover buried treasure.

Then one day a peasant who made a hobby of antiquities heard of the search. George Perakis, who lived a few miles from Kavousi at Vasiliki, told the local schoolmaster he would lead Miss Boyd to a low hill where there were old walls and sherds; as evidence he sent an excellent sealstone picked up there.

On May 19 the two women met Perakis at the roadside khan near the little harbour of Pachyammos. He led them three-quarters of a mile westward to a pretty cove called Gournia, where they saw traces of massive walls and then, turning inland, they crossed the highway and climbed a low hill covered with carob trees. There they peered and pried into the thick undergrowth, finding what might be the tops of ancient walls and bits of broken pottery of the Bronze Age like that thrown into the walls at Ag. Antonios. It was worth exploring.

At four the next morning they made ready to leave their mountain home. The overseer was sent ahead to muster thirty-six workmen to Gournia. Harriet ran up to the little chapel to say her prayers and to "kiss the hand of the Christ, and coming out found the sun just touching the top of the mountains." In the half-light they wound down the gorge, chief sleuth ahead with measuring rod and drawing board; the tea basket brought up the rear. She reported: "We tried to steal a march on the village through the grey gloom and surprise it without finding the roads and housetops beset with women—but impossible!"

They took over their old house in Kavousi, and after the hill hut it seemed a haven of comfort. But the first evening the floor gave way.

Harriet and Blanche longed to be with the men as they started work at the new site, but it was mail day and so they had to stay in the village and write important letters. At last, in the afternoon, they were able to ride over. Men were scattered all over the hillside excitedly clamouring to show their finds— many fragments of vases, a bronze knife, a spear point, house walls and, best of all, a well-paved road with a threshold and a gutter. The workers swelled with pride as, wielding picks and shovels, they amassed basket-loads of history. This was clearly something big and, judging from the pottery, it was of the Bronze Age, or Minoan. The evidence was so promising that Harriet went back to Kavousi and hired fifteen new hands. There was no difficulty in getting them; few could resist the appeal of unknown treasure.

Earthquake at Kourion, Cyprus

DAVID SOREN AND JAMIE JAMES

Early on July 21, 365, a powerful earthquake hit the eastern Mediterranean, leveling entire cities and bringing monstrous tidal waves in its train. This major natural disaster came at a time when pagan Rome was collapsing and Christianity was becoming the dominant spiritual and intellectual power of the West.

The earthquake of 365 is well known from contemporary writings. The fourth-century Roman historian Ammianus Marcellinus said that "the firm and stable mass of the earth trembled and shook, and the sea withdrew." But until classical archaeologist David Soren (b. 1946) of the University of Arizona dug the Greco-Roman city of Kourion on the southern coast of Cyprus in 1984 and 1985, no physical traces of the disaster remained. His research team uncovered the remains of a family, lying where the earthquake had buried them alive. A girl of thirteen lay crushed to death in a courtyard next to a mule tethered to a stone trough. Her parents were in a nearby room, the husband holding a lamp, as if he was getting up to see what the commotion was about. An adjoining dwelling yielded another family: a man, a woman, and an eighteen-month-old child. The woman was trying to shield the baby from falling debris; the man, his entire family, but to no avail. They died under the weight of massive stone blocks as the building collapsed. The man wore a bronze ring inscribed with a Christian symbol, clear evidence that the new religion flourished in Kourion.

Cyprus was an early center of Christianity, being converted by none other than Saint Paul himself. By the time of the great earthquake, it was probably the dominant religion on the island. Certainly, the new city of Kourion, which rose on the rubble of the earlier town, was an entirely Christian community. Today, Kourion is one of the best preserved archaeological sites on Cyprus and a major tourist attraction. The remains of the Christian city mantle the even earlier settlement, which contains dramatic evidence of the terrible destruction wrought by an earthquake remembered for centuries. So detailed were Soren's excavations that he used the tilt angles of masonry and roof tiles to estimate that the epicenter lay about thirty-two kilometers southwest of Kourion, between the city and the neighboring community of Paphos.

Soren describes the discovery of earthquake victims in this passage from Kourion, *a popular account of his excavations written with Jamie James.*

Like a Texas wildcatter, we needed to find a good place to dig. Our license to return to Kourion was granted to us by Karageorghis specifically for the purpose of testing my hypotheses about the quake that had destroyed the city, especially my ideas about dating it. In fact our circumstances were exactly like a wildcatter's, for we did not have the time or the money for a "dry hole"; if we came away from this season with nothing, it would be very difficult indeed to go back to Karageorghis to ask for a permit for another year, or, what was more to the point, to raise money. In archaeology, as in any field, nothing succeeds like success. You are only as good as your last trench, and people wait with appalling glee to destroy your career through gossip. After one has made one's name, one is much more of a target: make a single mistake, and all of your successes cease to exist.

To tell us where to dig, in place of a wildcatter geologist's report, we had the rather disorganized field diaries and photographs of the Penn expeditions in the 1930s and McFadden's brief, sporadic publications in *The Illustrated London News* and the *University of Pennsylvania Museum Bulletin*. We found many tantalizing tidbits, but the difficulty was in translating the various crumbs of data into an X on the spot where we could plant our spade. As we pored over them, one passage kept jumping out at me, this paragraph from one of McFadden's contributions to the Penn museum bulletin: "Both of the settlements which we have found, Greek and Roman, met with sudden catastrophes due to earthquakes. . . . In one of the rooms of a house which was part of the second floor, preserved in the walls, we found two skeletons, of a man and a woman, entangled in such a way as to suggest a Romeo and Juliet tragedy. On the girl's finger was a bronze and quite a lovely gold ring."

In another piece for the Penn museum bulletin, published in October 1940, McFadden, who for unknown reasons had changed his mind, described the same skeletons as two women "caught in the earthquake that brought down the house." The skeletons have been lost, but it later became clear, from the drawings and photographs we found, that there never was any Romeo and Juliet death embrace. Only one skeleton was intact, an adult lying on his side in the fetal position, both arms bent across the chest and the hands placed over the face for protection. The skull was facing toward the west, approximately the direction from which the earthquake emanated. A second adult skeleton was indeed present, but it survived only in part. Again oriented in a westerly direction, of this specimen only the legs and feet were recovered. As the skeletons were not correctly, or at least not completely, identified when first unearthed, it is possible that the rest of the second skeleton was shoveled away by the laborers in 1943 before anyone realized it was happening.

While McFadden did not fully understand the significance of the human remains—not at all unusual for an archaeologist of his era—he did make this astute observation: "That none returned to retrieve or bury the dead testifies to the magnitude and extent of the earthquake, and explains the catastrophe that overcame the Sanctuary of Apollo at the same time."

It sounded like the perfect place to test our theories about the earthquake: everything we knew about what McFadden and Daniel had found there in 1934, particularly the photographs of the skeletons, suggested that the area had not been disturbed by grave robbers in the period immediately following the earthquake. We were reasonably sure that no one had disturbed the area since the 1930s, for it had been under official control ever since then, and, as we have seen, no one had shown interest in digging there in the intervening fifty years. An intact postquake site was just what we needed, but Daniel in his diary had neglected to mention one critical point: where this house and trench were located. All we knew was that it was somewhere on the seaside edge of Kourion City. Without more specific information, we might be digging for years before we found it. . . .

After our success in room one, we decided to expand. We moved to the next room to the northwest, which had never been excavated. We called it—what else?—room two, in the great archaeological tradition of drearily prosaic names. After removing the meter or so of sandy soil, we hit the jackpot, in the form of virgin collapse. Here we found twenty-four coins and fragments of the glass vessel that may have held them. The range of dates in these coins was the same as among those we had unearthed in room one. Pressing on to room three, along the same northwest axis, we found more evidence of the temblor's power. At least half a dozen pots had exploded in the quake and scattered all over the room. A threshold weighing more than a hundred pounds had been ripped loose from the ground and rotated ninety degrees from its original position.

Several meters below the surface, the earthen floor of the room appeared. Here we discovered a silver-plated bone hairpin, a well-preserved spatula, an olive pit—and more copper coins, this time 113 of them. As before, the coins all fitted the pattern that my theory of the earthquake's date had predicted: a few were of earlier date, but several were early issues of the reign of Valens, and nothing had to be dated after 365. By this time we were feeling quite confident, if not altogether vindicated. It was only thirty days into the campaign, and we had already proved our point. Now we were ready for even bigger game, and we found it, right under our noses in room two: our first human victim of the disaster.

Room two was the only space that we were able to excavate completely in that first return season, and we soon deduced that it was not a room at all but a hastily improvised stable. Originally, rooms one and two had been one larger space, but a crudely built cross wall had been inserted and the animal feeding trough introduced. This hypothesis was verified when we found the remains of a mule, still tethered by an iron chain to a stone feeding trough. This trough provided us with the most graphic testimony yet to the awesome power of this quake. Weighing more than eight hundred pounds, the trough had been lifted up by the shock wave and hurled against the southeast wall of the stable, denting the wall. A pulse also snapped the trough in two like a candy cane. The hind legs of the mule had given out under it as the ground turned to Jell-O beneath its feet, disorienting and terrifying the animal. And next to the mule's hindquarters, we found the remains of a young girl.

As we slowly and carefully extracted the child's bones from the earth, the picture of her last moments of life began to take shape. We all shared a deep sense of intimacy with her as we lifted her remains from the ground. If our conclusions are right, it had been very early in the morning, before dawn, when the temblor occurred. Camelia (our name for the girl) must have woken up when she heard the mule whinnying anxiously, for it is well known to seismologists, folklorists, and zoologists alike that animals are sensitive to seismic upheavals long before humans notice anything. She went out to calm the beast, who was perhaps her workmate. Then the disaster struck. The earth trembled sickeningly, the glass jar of coins fell from the shelf with a crash, the half-roof of the stable collapsed. As her world came crashing down over her, as she was buried alive in stone, her hairpin, perhaps a gift from her mother ("Juliet," in the adjoining room, wore one identical to it), came flying out of her hair. The last sounds she heard were the hysterical neighing of her mule and the screams of "Romeo and Juliet," who might well have been her parents, inside the house.

Next, our multifarious scientific team moved into place to do its work. Our forensic anthropologists, Walter Birkby and Alison Galloway, reconstructed the girl's shattered skeleton. They determined that when Camelia fell, she was turning her head toward the southwest—the direction from which the shock wave and most of the flying debris were coming. She probably died very quickly from severe trauma. After the first wave she was most likely still alive and crawling through the rubble. When the second wave hit about four seconds later, she fell face down, her hands covering her face. Most of her bones must have been broken and crushed in the shower of stone.

We had all supposed that she was a girl by the presence of the hairpin, but because of differences in size and formation between men's and women's teeth, Birkby and Galloway were able to sex the skeleton beyond any doubt through a comparative analysis. A dental study also made her age approximately thirteen; but after the forensic anthropologists measured her bones, they found them to be quite small, the size of a modern eleven-year-old's. Proceeding logically, Galloway and Birkby at first inferred that the girl's diminutive stature had resulted from the fact that she was crippled. However, as more bodies have come to light, it has become apparent that ancient Cypriots were simply quite small people, many less than five feet tall, and they now think that Camelia was in relatively good health.

Her teeth, at least, were in good shape, which suggests that her diet was a fairly coarse one; Camelia, like most Greek peoples of this era, had no cavities. In the recent spectacular archaeological discoveries at the seaside edge of Herculaneum, dozens and dozens of human victims were studied by paleoosteologist Sarah Bizell. She observed the same extremely fine degree of dental health and attributes it at least in part to the relative lack of sugar in the diet. Another factor contributing to the soundness of ancient teeth is the fact that their owners got more jaw exercise from chewing because food tended not to be cut up into little pieces. (There were no forks until the seventeenth century.)

The one abnormality that did turn up was a remarkable thickening of the victims' parietal bones, the back plates of the skull. That may be the result of iron-deficient anemia, which could have been caused by an episode of malaria, a disease that has afflicted Cypriots since the Stone Age; alternatively, it may have been caused nutritionally. A trace-element analysis carried out by atomic spectrophotometry at the Analytical Laboratory of the University of Arizona showed a high level of arsenic. The elder Pliny tells us, however, that that poisonous element, used as a liniment, was a favorite Roman cure for coughs and sore throats.

The reason that most of these conclusions must be so heavily larded with "mights" and "maybes" is that, until we began to unearth some of Camelia's neighbors, Galloway and Birkby had virtually nothing with which to compare her remains. The essence of forensic work is comparative analysis, setting an unidentified bone side by side with one of which the whole story is well known. Only by a comparison of the chemical analysis of one corpse with the findings for a large population can a forensic scientist say whether a certain substance exists overabundantly or is deficient.

One of the valuable contributions that the Kourion dig may ultimately make is to provide anthropologists for the first time with a reliable and complete cross section of an ancient Mediterranean city. Any skewing of the specimen population will undermine the accuracy of the identification in a particular case, as happened to our own excellent forensic anthropologists, who were temporarily thrown off by Camelia's small size compared with modern girls her age but perhaps not with other Cypriot girls of the latter fourth century.

With the exception of Herculaneum, human skeletal analyses in the ancient Mediterranean have had to be based primarily on burial populations, which are not especially accurate because they contain an excessively high proportion of babies and elderly people. Because everyone in this district of Kourion was trapped at the same moment, the excavation offers an unprecedented opportunity for compiling the first trustworthy sample of a classical society in situ. The victims of Vesuvius at Herculaneum had such a long warning time that many people were able to escape and thus were not found in their usual habitats. (No complete skeletons were recovered at Pompeii. There, decayed human remains left molds in the volcanic ash, which could then be filled with plaster.) At Kourion, however, death came without warning, burying the fleet and the halt side by side, which means that after we have unearthed more we shall have a representative census of this estimable city. Further, we shall be able to break it down by age, sex, health, and even in some cases by religious affiliation.

In terms of artistic finds, Kourion has not yet yielded a great trove of museum-ready artifacts. Nonetheless, we have come up with a number of quite nice items, and among the most pleasing are some copper-alloy lamps. While copper lamps can be helpful in the cause of dating, they can also be deceptive:

because they did not break and were often of great artistic value, they were frequently kept as heirlooms, just as fine jewelry will generally be passed down in a family while costume jewelry perhaps will not. Nonetheless, copper lamps are of considerable artistic interest, representing a much higher level of artisanship than their clay counterparts. Lamps of this era came in any number of different forms, but the basic function of all was the same: a wick floating in a bowl of oil will burn where it surfaces, and a fist-sized lamp could burn for an entire dinner party. The oil could be extracted from sesame seeds, nuts, or fish, but olive oil was the principal fuel employed throughout the Mediterranean. Wicks could be made from linen, papyrus, flax, and possibly even asbestos, oddly enough.

Here in Camelia's stable, we found an elegantly wrought copper-alloy volute lamp (one having a spout that is bordered with spiral decorations), with a separately manufactured finial in the shape of a leaf. It was found near the surface, at the beginning of our excavation, just below the southeastern wall of the room, which made it difficult to fix its location in the room. The experts who have examined it say it is in the Italian style and date it to the first century of the Christian era, which would have made it a three-hundred-year-old heirloom to its owner at the time of the quake—the equivalent of a Louis XIV chair to us. A lamp specialist from the University of Delaware named Steven Sidebotham has found analogues in two clay lamps from Carthage, both dated to the first century. When our team conservator cleaned this lamp, some well-preserved wicks were found in the interior. Examination by scanning-electron microscopy at the Metropolitan Museum of Art in New York City showed them to be made of bast fiber, probably flax, which is what the elder Pliny is talking about in his *Natural History* when he writes: "[The part of the flax] nearest the skin is called oakum. It is flax of inferior quality, and mostly . . . fit for lamp wicks." We were all very buoyed up by this discovery. It is rare indeed to find organic matter in a state of preservation that permits such a precise identification. . . .

On the eastern side of the paved courtyard we found two more rooms, which might have been the original entrance to the house. Room twenty, which occupied the better part of this side of the patio, resembles a propylon, or arched gateway, and room twenty-five (our numbering scheme having by now lapsed into a hither-and-yon yet nonetheless serviceable chaos), at its side, could have been a guardroom, servant's quarters, or storage room. The evidence seems to point in the direction of the two rooms having been converted after the first earthquake, or at least sometime prior to the quake of 365 into yet another self-contained living space. Thus, the main entrance to the house would have been shifted from here to room eighteen, the recessed part of the porch around the Camelia complex, which would have meant that the portico was not as necessary as before.

We were not able to finish excavating these rooms in the 1986 season, but what we found was of exceptional interest and high quality. In room twenty-five we came up with two amphorae, a unique red slip bowl with elaborate stamped decoration, and a copper knife. Yet the major discovery awaited us in room twenty.

There, on the very last day of the excavation as we were preparing to head back to the States, we unearthed the Christian family. McFadden had his Romeo and Juliet, at least for a while, but here was something even more moving, a young man and woman and a baby. The female, according to Walt Birkby, was about nineteen years old, with a height of four feet eight and one-half inches. Her neck had been broken and snapped to a right angle by falling rock debris, a large chunk of mortar and several rocks had entered her skull. Three arched blocks of stone, originally part of a decorative facade (perhaps belonging to the hypothetical gateway), had fallen on her. These fragments were in a remarkable state of preservation, still bearing traces of the original purple, yellow, and red paint.

In her arms she held an eighteen-month-old baby to her breast and face; when we found the child, its skull was still cradled in her bent arms, and its right hand was grasping the mother's left elbow joint. The child's legs were bent, the right leg resting on the mother's right leg. Next to and behind the woman was the skeleton of the man. At five feet three inches, he was a bit larger, though the two of them support the idea that the ancient Cypriots were a diminutive race. His crushed skull was pressed against her shoulder near the area where her neck had been broken; and his spine was crushed by falling rocks.

We shall never know if this was indeed a young married couple and their baby. It is possible that they are not; indeed it falls within the realm of the theoretically possible that they are all complete strangers. Yet the presumption that they are a family is supported by the circumstantial evidence. The man was clearly attempting to shield the woman and the baby at the time of their deaths. His left arm was covering her breast, while his left hand enfolded the baby's lower back. His right leg was drawn up over the legs and pelvis of the woman. As we removed the earth from them clod by clod, we could plainly see that the adult skeletons were pressed close to each other, with the male in the protective position. Both of them struggled to shield the baby, surely *their* baby, as enormous blocks, cobbles, and mortar exploded above and finally entombed them. There was also evidence of rodent action. The soft flesh of the adults' hands and the child's entire body had been disturbed.

And then we found the bronze ring inscribed with the chi rho and the alpha and omega. There were two rings, actually, just above the man's hands. (The other one, plain, was wrought of iron.) In every dig, out of the tons of pottery and bones and ancient garbage, and above all dirt, there is always one object that stands out as the most important, the most telling. There are famous cases, like the golden mask of Mycenae that prompted Heinrich Schliemann, when he found it, to cable the king of Greece, "I have gazed upon the face of Agamemnon!" (Of course, the mask antedates a historical Agamemnon by several centuries.) Yet more often, the pièce de résistance, the key to the puzzle, is something humble. At Kourion, it was that bronze ring incised with the simple symbol denoting the name of Christ.

This ring, in the moment we unearthed it, told us more than the thousand spadefuls that came before: it gave us the context, the theme, the motif of everything else at the site. Of course, we "understood" what we were excavating before we found the ring, but our understanding existed in a vacuum, or at least in thin air. While a coin or a thigh bone belonging to a Christian in no way differs from a pagan thigh bone or coin, it nonetheless changes everything to know which condition obtains. Although we know, comparatively, a great deal about the daily life of pagans in this part of the Mediterranean, the Christian world remains more elusive. Although the empire had become officially Christian, . . . in the hinterlands like Cyprus (in other words, in most places that constituted the empire), the Christians themselves were still by and large poor people, like the settlers who appropriated this earthquake-ruined house, and while they left a formidable legacy of literature, archaeologically speaking they were a fugitive race.

Now, at last, we have the chance to study the life of an early Christian community in this part of the world. And it is exactly its fugitiveness, its lack of "civilization" in the sense that an archaeologist ordinarily uses the word, that interests us. We know from the literature and above all from history how viable and strong was their civilization; yet it would seem that they took Christ at his word when he said that his kingdom was not of this world. What one may discern in the spare remains of these early Cypriot Christians is a hardy people who must have been sustained by a rich spiritual life, for their temporal life, it seems, was hard indeed.

The Sutton Hoo Ship Burial

CHARLES GREEN

Archaeology has added much to our knowledge of the Anglo-Saxons, who ruled Britain after the Romans. But few discoveries from cemeteries or settlements rival the spectacular finds from Sutton Hoo.

When British archaeologist James Brown asked Suffolk landowner Elizabeth Pretty in 1939 which of the burial mounds on her Sutton Hoo property in eastern England she wanted opened, she pointed to the largest. "What about this?" she remarked. Her casual choice epitomized the archaeology of sixty years ago. The work began that very May afternoon with the cutting of a wide trench across the tumulus. Brown soon found five iron ship nails and suspected that he was uncovering a funerary boat. With trowels and brushes, he and his workmen cleared the bow and first eleven frames of an Anglo-Saxon vessel. A sealed bulkhead now appeared. Brown wisely stopped the dig and called in Charles Phillips of Cambridge University, an expert on Anglo-Saxon sites and on timber structures. From the very beginning, one of the most important excavations of the century was in the hands of a well-trained, experienced observer. Phillips followed gray discolorations in the mound, tracing the lines of the boat and the planked burial chamber. He established that the twenty-seven-meter ship was dragged nearly a kilometer from a nearby river to its final resting place. It was seaworthy at the time of its burial. The diggers even found traces of repairs to the hull. With infinite care, they opened the burial chamber, recording and conserving each plank and each find, however small. The boat was actually the larger of two vessels uncovered in the mounds. It had no mast and was propelled by thirty-eight oars. The burial chamber contained a rich variety of metalwork treasures, including cauldrons, bowls, spears, a sword, axes, bottles, and a magnificent cloisonné purse. The entire find was dated to within twenty-five years of A.D. 650 by the presence of thirty-seven coins of known age. The identity of the deceased is still uncertain, but he was probably a member of the historically known Wuffing family.

In 1939, seventh-century Anglo-Saxon England was still a shadowy entity. The Sutton Hoo ship chronicled a well-established kingdom that traded with European towns across the North Sea. Phillips reported on his finds with scrupulous care. His sober reports were models of cautious interpretation, so much so that later generations of archaeologists have been able to return to Sutton Hoo with a much more sophisticated scientific armory at their disposal. They use metal detectors to find tiny buttons, ground-penetrating radar to map subsurface features, and ultraviolet light to detect the fragile outlines of ghostly bodies in the soil and chemicals to consolidate them. They hope one day to be able to establish the sex, age, and perhaps individual identity of their owners.

The formal reports on the Sutton Hoo excavations are sober reading, but Charles Green gives us a popular account of this remarkable excavation, taken from his book Sutton Hoo.

Mrs. Pretty . . . was determined to know more about the contents of her barrows. She held further discussions with Mr. Maynard and, in Mr. Brown's own words, "On April 4, 1939, I received a letter from Mr. Guy Maynard containing the following: 'If you would like another spell at Sutton Hoo, Mrs. Pretty is willing to resume work on the barrows.' On Monday, May 8, I arrived at Sutton Hoo and had an interview with Mrs. E. M. Pretty, during which arrangements were made regarding personnel and equipment for the excavation. We then went to the barrows and upon my asking Mrs. Pretty which mound she would like opened, she pointed to the largest of the group (Tumulus I) and said: 'What about this?' and I replied that it would be quite all right for me. After a preliminary survey of the mound, work was commenced in the afternoon and the technique decided upon was similar to that adopted for dealing with the tumuli explored in 1938." So simply and almost casually was the decision made which led to the dramatic finding of the unique treasure-ship.

The story may now be continued in Mr. Brown's own words.

The original form of the barrow had been greatly altered by various disturbances; on the west many tons of material had been removed and had it not been prevented by the late Colonel Frank Pretty, who turned down a proposal to use material from the mound to make up the farmyards, more would have gone, while on the east material had also been taken for bunkers of a private golf course. Also, evidence was forthcoming from a gamekeeper who had dug into the mound at the request of a former owner of the estate in the hope of finding treasure. Lastly there was damage from the rabbits which had burrowed into the mound for centuries. The mound which before excavation presented a hogback appearance, especially when observed from the west, was in plan an elongated oval. . . .

An initial or exploratory trench 6 feet wide was cut east to west across the mound down to the old ground surface, care being taken to note any inequality in the level of the sand which might serve to indicate a grave beneath and also for ship-nails in view of the data obtained from the 1938 excavations. On May 11, I was able to deduce with certainty the existence of a pit or grave below the old ground surface and explained the indications to Mrs. Pretty and that our trench was practically following the same alignment.

I proceeded to widen our exploratory trench to 12 feet to admit of clearing the grave pit.

The first find was a loose ship-nail and then five others in position. We were definitely at one end of a ship which was protruding a little above the old ground surface which here had been much disturbed by rabbits, fortunately without destroying the end or displacing the iron nails which remained in their original places. It was at first thought that this was the stern end of the ship and that its bow would be pointing to the Deben, but it was not until the vessel had been almost completely excavated that this point was elucidated and that her bow was known to point to the east.

From now on extreme care had to be practised and the ship's interior was gradually cleared, frame by frame, with small tools and bare hands, the spoil being removed with the kitchen dustpan from Little Sutton. As soon as the rust of a ship's nail showed in the sand or the black and grey dust from wood decomposition, these features were left. As work progressed and the ship gradually opened out, drastic cut-backs were made and timbering with terraces became necessary to avoid landslides; the cutting through the mound proper assumed a width of 40 feet. It now became evident from the indications that a larger craft than the Snape ship was to be expected with a strong possibility of a length of at least 70 feet. . . .

When Mr. Phillips took over the direction of the excavation, Mr. Brown and his team had just cleared from the bows of the ship to the eleventh frame, where they had seen what appeared to be a timber partition across the interior of the vessel. From this it had been inferred, as has been said, that the central part had contained some sort of burial-chamber, built to protect the body and its accompanying grave-goods. This inference was later shown to be true but, as what evidently had been a substantial timber partition now showed merely as a "slight dark discoloration in the sand not more than a quarter of an inch thick . . . only the most careful watch made it possible to get any idea of what had formerly existed."

In order to ascertain the structural detail of this chamber, a different method of clearance was adopted. The sides of the cutting in the mound were further cut back and the central area, for a length of some 25 feet, was cut away horizontally. This was done with long-handled coal shovels with which the sand could be shaved away in very thin slices. Any trace of discoloration in the area could then be noted and, as successive slices were removed, could be followed downward in whatever direction it might trend. By some trick of the packing or of the collapse, one fragment of wood, apparently from this structure, had not been disintegrated by decay. This carbonised oak was left in position on a supporting pillar of sand and so provided a "control section" for the rest of the chamber. It also showed that the roof of the chamber had been covered with turf, though whether this was a special covering or just a part of the ordinary structure of the overlying mound was not quite clear. Mr. Phillips thought that the first explanation might well be true.

Excavation by this careful shaving-method was soon to be rewarded for, some 17½ feet to the west of the first cross-partition, the second was exposed, again as a slight stain in the sand. The extent of the chamber having now been defined, the clearance progressed more confidently and quickly gave further results. On the south side of the chamber, another line of decayed wood appeared, this time running parallel to the ship's side. When followed downward, this was seen to slope outward towards the side of the ship. A column of filling, containing this sloping line, was left standing for a time until the rest of the clearance had been finished. It could then be seen that, when the sloping roof of the chamber had collapsed, a small part on the south side had remained in position. From this, of course, it was possible with some confidence to calculate the pitch and, from that, the height of the roof. The two ends of the chamber, therefore, were gabled, the peak standing some 12 feet above the keel-plank, with the eaves of the roof resting on the ship's gunwale.

At a later stage of the work, the grave-goods were seen to be overlain in places by decayed planking, apparently fallen fragments of the roof. These remnants lay pointing in two directions at right angles to each other. From this it was inferred that the roof itself was of double thickness, one layer of planks running from gable to gable, the other from eaves to ridge. No trace of a door could be discerned at either end and nothing could be inferred of the timber framework which must have supported the planked ends and roof. At one end, however, a rusted angle-iron was found; this probably had a place in the structure. And later, when the burial deposits had been cleared, a number of metal cleats forming a line on either side of the ship's floor was seen; they may also have served some structural purpose in this hut. Sawn-off scraps of planking were also found on the flooring; these, it was thought, were fallen pieces left by the chamber-builders. When the mound had been constructed over the chamber, the latter of course had not been filled with sand. The filling removed by the excavators was that which had fallen in after the collapse of the roof which seems not to have happened until many years after the burial. Outside the chamber, however, the ends of the ship had been completely filled at an early stage in the erection of the mound.

Above the grave-goods in this collapsed chamber-filling was found a curious clay structure. This was an oval slab of clay with a saucer-shaped hollow in its upper surface. The slab was about 36 inches by 18 inches by 5 inches deep and showed no traces of fire, so that it could not have been used as a hearth. It was, therefore, suggested that after the lower part of the mound had been built around and over the chamber, this receptacle had been laid above the roof where, perhaps, it received libations as a part of the burial ceremony. No exact parallel for this clay-pan is known. It will, however, be remembered that, in Barrow No. 3, the upper filling of the grave-pit contained a slightly concave clay layer though, as our record of this is inadequate, a close comparison cannot be made.

The emptying of the lower part of the burial-chamber now proceeded rapidly and soon the first objects began to show above the damp sandy filling. . . .

The work now demanded even greater care and forethought than before. Gold, as is well known, is little subject to chemical corrosion and the objects of gold in the hoard were in essentially good condition. But the other objects, whether of silver, bronze, iron, or leather and woven fabric, were in parlous condition, partly due to the corrosion of the damp sand and partly to the pressure of the overlying collapsed roof and mound.

The method of clearing now had to be changed and the long-handled shovel gave place to paint-brush and packing needle. With these new tools, the topmost layer of sand on and around each object was removed, exposing the damper sand below. This soon dried in the hot sun and was then removed in similar fashion until the object was completely exposed and undercut as far as was possible. Such precise treatment, with its resulting slow progress, was very necessary as, in their flimsy and corroded condition, the slightest adhesive contact of wet sand increased the strains on the thin and distorted metals and so lessened the chances of removing each object without further damage.

But some of the objects could not be allowed to dry in this way. Leather, the gourds and fabrics, as well as other things, began to distort and crumble as they dried and so these were frequently removed in a block and, wrapped carefully in damp coverings often of moss, were then transported to be individually cleaned and sorted when they had reached the laboratory. Though this meant that the precise nature of each object was not recognised at the time and the very existence of some was not suspected, the true shapes and relationships were better able to be worked out in the more suitable environment of the laboratory, where also were the resources required for the rapid treatment which sometimes was so urgently needed during the unpacking.

Not only in the uncovering and packing was this care exercised; equally important was the record-making as the objects emerged. For, grouped and disintegrated as they were, it was frequently difficult or impossible to be sure to which object a detached fragment might belong. For example, during the uncovering of the group under the great silver dish, a fluted bowl lay by the remains of a leather bag. This bag was equipped with a "strap fitted with bronze buckle and slider to pass round it for support when full" and to this bag was also attributed a pair of silver handles. But later, in the laboratory, it was seen that the silver handles were, in fact, a part of the fluted bowl, from which they had become detached. And so, stage by stage and detail by detail, sketches and descriptive notes were multiplied. In this work the camera also proved its importance. While this part of the clearance was in progress Mr. O. G. S. Crawford made his very full photographic record, capturing each group as, little by little, they were exposed and so supplementing the notes with a permanent pictorial record of the precise position of each fragment. In the subsequent work of restoration all this was to prove invaluable.

Much of the work of removing the objects from the chamber, as has been said, was done by Mr. W. F. Grimes. In 1940 he published a description of that work, so that we may now follow him into the excavated pit and see what he saw. He says that the dominant feature in my first view of the ship was a great three-foot purple-grey disk; the silver dish, beneath which the lip of at least one other vessel was promise of more treasure to come. Other things there were already exposed—especially the two bronze bowls at the southwest corner of the burial deposit. But the urgent interest was centred on the dish and on the problem of whether it could be lifted entire, or whether steps should be taken by means of drawings and photographs to record its complete character before the hazardous work of lifting it began.

Now this dish was lying right way up and it could be seen that it bore a complicated engraved ornament so that, to record it fully, all this ornament would have had to be drawn and photographed in detail, a task of great difficulty. Fortunately, so much preliminary work was judged to be unnecessary as "the metal was thick and seemed to be strong, in spite of a crack along one side." The dish was safely lifted on July 26 and, as Mr. Grimes says, "Beneath it was an assortment of articles, most of them in a fragile and parlous state, the recording, removal, and packing of which took the undivided attention of all working on the site."

In the fluted bowl, for example, were several small cups with metal mounts; the cups themselves at first were thought to be of wood, though later it was realised that they were hollowed gourds. Warped and damaged as they were, no delay in their treatment could be allowed, sun-drying in particular being the greatest danger. Into boxes they went at once, tightly packed in damp moss, which served to maintain their condition until laboratory treatment made them safe. Immediately under the great dish and around the fluted bowl were masses of leather and woven textile fabrics; the leather objects included bags and shoes. All these were decayed, the cloth being very rotten; to permit them to dry would have meant their complete loss. They were accordingly placed at once in bowls of water where they were kept until they could be properly packed for travelling. Also here were a small silver cup and what later proved to be a silver ladle, a small ivory gamespiece, and two badly decayed bronze hanging-bowls.

When all these varied objects had been removed, it was seen that they had been resting on a great wooden tray, a part only of which remained. On this, protected by the cloth and leather, were found an iron axe and a mass of rusted iron chain-mail. The tray fragment, some at least of which was still in condition to be lifted, was finally dealt with. As so much of the wood in the ship and chamber had completely decayed, it was rather surprising that a part of this tray had, comparatively speaking, survived; it is thought that this was due largely to the protection given by the leather and cloth over which lay the great dish.

The greatest concentration of grave-goods was certainly that at the west end of the chamber; they lay packed close to the wooden wall. The first to be found was a giant whetstone with carved and bronze-decorated ends. This, of course, was in sound condition and was lifted with ease. But soon, more complex objects began to be exposed. Still closer to the wall lay a mass of rusted iron which, as it was cleared, was revealed as a long iron rod with various structural attachments. Though so heavily rusted, this "lamp-stand," as it was named, was by no means destroyed and, when completely cleared of sand, was quite strong enough to be lifted by three persons on to a plank; on this it was suitably supported by packing and made fast. Near the upper part of this stand there lay an iron ring on which was a beautifully modelled image in bronze of an antlered stag. It was at the time thought perhaps to be a helmet-crest.

On the other side of the stand was the collapsed ruin of a large wooden bucket with iron mountings. But sufficient of this was left to make its removal as a unit worth while. When the sand was cleared away, the remnants of the bucket were swathed in strong webbing. By slow degrees a thin iron plate was then slipped beneath, space for it being cleared by trowelling. It was now realised that the plate was too thin to carry the weight without bending, so that whole complex of plate and swaddled bucket was picked up on a spade and lifted on to a strong wooden base where it was made secure without any of its parts having suffered serious disturbance.

To the south of this bucket lay a complex group composed apparently of two bronze bowls, one inside the other, and a number of spear and angon heads of iron. The latter were even resting in one of the handles of the outer bowl and were rusted both to the handle and the body of the bowl with which they were in contact. Accordingly, the whole group was lifted as a single unit, to be treated and disengaged in the laboratory. Later, at a little distance, the iron ferrules from the butts of the spear-shafts were also found; from the position of heads and ferrules, of course, the overall length of the weapons could be approximately calculated; the spears were in fact some 9 feet long.

To the east of the bucket lay, in Mr. Grimes' words, "a smudge of purple indicating silver, of which we had been conscious for some time. It was roughly circular in shape and near it was what appeared to be the end of a slender moulded bar." Cleaning this silver was perhaps one of the most difficult tasks undertaken by Mr. Grimes. It proved finally to be a nest of inverted silver bowls and the silver rod was the handle of a spoon, below which lay another similar spoon. One of the bowls had slipped from the pile and was completely disintegrated, so that a photographic record only was possible. The remainder were lifted *en bloc* on an iron plate similar to that under the bucket and packed to be isolated in the laboratory. At first it was thought that this pack contained eight bowls, but later analysis proved that it held nine, six only of which were in good condition. Altogether therefore a stack of no less than ten of these bowls was deposited in the grave.

Near the north end of the stand was what Mr. Grimes himself claimed was "perhaps the most intricate piece of cleaning: that of the remains of the shield," though this task, which took almost a whole day, he dismissed in comparatively few words.

The central feature was the massive boss, which was solid and unlikely to cause trouble. But radiating irregularly from it were several richly decorated bronze mounts: some of almost paper thinness, some face upwards, some

The Sutton Hoo ship exposed during excavations immediately before World War II.
The outline of the ship was traced from the positions of iron nails and outlines of
ribs and planks left in the sandy soil.

reversed, at all angles and presenting a picture of complete confusion. . . .
To add to the difficulties this complex was partly covered with the remains
of a fine wooden object ornamented with gold leaf. None of the material of
the shield itself appeared to remain. The *umbo* was lifted without difficulty,
but freeing the various adhesions of the mounts was a slow and tedious business. Each was lifted separately on two or more trowels after it had been
drawn in on the plan.

In this very brief account, slight mention only is made of what was thought
to be a thin wooden "tray" with gilt gesso edging and animal-head decoration,
which seemed to overlie the heavier mountings of the shield. It was not until
the whole complex began to be analysed and studied in the British Museum that
these, too, seen to be a part of the shield itself.

To the east of the shield lay what was called the "nucleus" of a helmet. It is
not certain where this helmet was originally placed, for fragments of it were
scattered over a much larger area, and it seems that it must have been damaged
and dispersed by the fall of the roof. To the present writer it seems not unlikely
that it may have hung on the gabled west wall of the chamber, to be flung down
and broken when the first fall happened. But sufficient remained to make its
unusual character evident and the description of the gathered fragments, made
when they were unpacked, and the final reconstruction, serve to show its magnificence.

Close to the silver bowls and just to the south of the centre-line of the ship,
were an iron blade and a sword. The blade was heavily rusted and appeared to
be a scramasax, a characteristic weapon of the times, best described as a small
cutlass. The sword itself had been a magnificent weapon, but it had been seriously damaged by the fall of the roof, as well as by rusting. It apparently had a

wooden scabbard, bound with fabric at the lower end. Its hilt was decorated with gold and garnets.

Both over the sword and between it and the "helmet nucleus" were scattered the gold and jewelled objects which formed the most costly part of the deposit; they were described by Mr. Phillips as "the finest collection of Anglo-Saxon jewellery yet known." These pieces comprised buckles, purse, clasps, and small mounts of various types which, it seems, must have been attached to a complex leather harness made to be worn by a man, though its disposition was not what it would have been if worn by a body at the time of the burial. As Mr. Phillips records, most of these pieces lay face downward and he suggests that the harness may originally have been hanging up in the chamber, to be thrown down at the time of the collapse. The beautifully jewelled purse contained a number of Merovingian (Frankish) gold coins and two small gold ingots. These coins, as we shall see, were to provide a fairly close date for the burial.

Immediately to the east of the jewellery lay another complex which again, owing to its sadly decayed condition, was lifted *en bloc* to be treated and analysed in the laboratory. This complex had probably been in part protected by a layer of roof-planking, but at the time of the fall, the wood must have pressed the underlying objects flat. These very puzzling objects were finally seen to be a collection of drinking-horns with silver-gilt mounts. In two only was any of the original horn preserved. The others showed merely as flat triangles like the "rays" of a starfish and there was some indication that these horns had originally been wrapped in cloth. The metal itself of the mounts had been converted to a salt of the element, but enough remained for the designs, or some of them, to be recorded, though permanent preservation was not possible.

On the south side of the chamber, a single object lay outside the H-pattern made by the others. This was a second iron-bound wooden bucket, generally similar to that lifted from the west end. And, near to the east end, close to the great silver dish, lay a wheel-turned pottery bottle and a small iron lamp. Finally, across the eastern end lay a further group of large objects. These comprised three bronze cauldrons of different sizes, a large iron-bound wooden bucket or tub and a mass of iron chainwork and bars. Of the wooden bucket nothing remained but the very rusty binding. The largest of the three cauldrons was much crushed, but the metal was still in fairly good condition, giving some hope of its future restoration. But the smaller cauldrons were so crushed and corroded that the thin sheet bronze of which they were made had fallen away into "hundreds of small pieces," leaving little hope of a successful reconstruction.

Now in the layout of these grave-goods, the "place of honour" would seem to have been on the central line towards the west end, below the gold and jewelled harness-fittings. Here the buried body would be expected to lie. But neither here nor, indeed, anywhere in the chamber could the slightest trace of a body be discovered. It is well known that, in some sandy soils, the acid moisture destroys bone. But even had this happened in the ship the teeth, or some of them, would be expected to have survived. Even had the body been toothless and so left no bony trace at all, there would have been its outline or at least the blank space it had occupied, surrounded by the weapons, personal articles such as finger-rings and armlets, and the small metal fittings of the clothing, to mark its position. Of this there was no evidence at all. Later, it may be said, further tests were carried out in the British Museum laboratory. These were designed to reveal, if indeed they existed, traces of a decayed body left on the remaining grave-goods. All these tests have failed to produce the slightest positive evidence. It is, therefore, now certain that an unburnt body never lay in this burial-chamber. The other possibility, that of a cremated body, is equally negatived. Calcined bone might be destroyed in the same way by soil acids; the presence of cremated bones in two of the other excavated barrows confirms that it has not happened here. Not a single receptacle in the chamber contained the smallest fragment of burnt bone nor was any found lying in the filling of the chamber. It is therefore generally agreed that this burial is a memorial, or *cenotaph*, burial for a person, clearly a man, whose body for one reason or another lay elsewhere.

The Horsemen of Pazyryk

SERGEI RUDENKO

Classical writers identified a number of nomadic peoples in Central Asia after the seventh century B.C. Their constant movements have frequently been correlated with early migrations of Indo-European peoples, but little is known about their life-style. They left no written records of their own or many permanent material remains. Only the occasional spectacular, and well-preserved, grave provides a portrait of these most elusive of all ancient peoples. One such group of horsemen, quite possibly the Scythians described by Herodotus, has been identified from a series of remarkably well preserved graves of the fifth century A.D. in the Altai mountain region of Siberia.

Soviet archaeologists Yuri Gryaznov and Sergei Rudenko (b. 1904) first investigated burial mounds in the area in 1929 and returned at last to excavate them thoroughly forty years later. The mounds concealed approximately sixty graves built directly into the permafrost: long earthen shafts leading to wooden chambers at the bottom. Grave robbers had ravaged some of the tombs in antiquity, breaking through the timber roofing of the burial chambers. Rainwater later seeped into the chambers and soaked their fragile, organic contents. They were deep frozen almost immediately, preserving them for twenty-four centuries. The tombs, with their lavish grave offerings, acted like time capsules, providing clues about many different facets of the Pazyryk horsemens' lifeways. Rudenko and his colleagues found clothing, leather, felt, food, splendidly decorated horses, carriages, tents, wall hangings, and exotic goods acquired through trade from faraway places such as China and Persia. The finds confirmed what classical writers had recorded: the nomads lived in large part off their animals and animal products. But the Pazyryk excavations also revealed a lively art style that was found on artifacts and horse trappings, and even perpetuated in the intricate tattooed designs on the horsemens' bodies. Since the breakup of the Soviet Union, more frozen horsemen have come to light at other locations, so Pazyryk is no longer unique.

Here Sergei Rudenko describes the burials in an extract from The Horsemen of Pazyryk, *translated by English archaeologist M. W. Thompson.*

Besides the adornments worn on the ears, hands, and possibly legs, tattooing of the body was also practised in the period under review. The tattooing revealed on the chief's body buried in barrow 2 at Pazyryk was one of the most remarkable discoveries made by the 1948 expedition.

The tattooing had not survived intact, as the body was in a poor state of preservation, particularly the left side of the chest where the skin and muscle fibre had perished. However, here above the heart the forepart of a monster was depicted, more exactly the head (the basic feature in all the tattooing) of a lion-griffin or some other imaginary creature. The body of the beast passed under the man's left arm, and over the left shoulder-blade lay its back part with long raised tail, twisting into a spiral and terminating with a bird's, or a snake's, head. Although the head and front portion of the animal did not survive, and the forepaws were severely deformed, some idea of the lost parts can be gained from the right arm or right leg below the knee. Excepting part of the right shoulder, the tattooing on the right arm survived, which it covered entirely from shoulder to hand. At the bottom is a donkey or onager with back twisted round; at the same level is a winged monster with a feline tail; above is a mountain ram with twisted crupper; then in the same attitude comes a deer with eagle's beak, long antlers, the tines terminating in birds' heads, which also run along its neck and tip of its tail. Above the deer is a fanged carnivore, not winged, but resembling that found on the left side, and, at the top on the shoulder, a deer with crupper twisted round, antlers with birds' heads, and long tail on the tip of which is a bird's head.

The tattooing on the left arm is worse preserved, and, in so far as we can interpret it, consisted of three independent figures, two deer and one mountain goat, with front legs in a springing position, crupper twisted round and back legs raised in the air. The most interesting and best preserved of these is the central figure of a deer.

On the right leg the tattooing was clearly discernible. The left leg had been severely hacked by the robbers, and the undamaged parts of the tattooing were insufficient to make sense of the figures. The basic figure on the outside of the right shin, running from knee-cap to ankle, was a fish. Below the fish on the foot running from the top surface round under the inner ankle and behind over the heel was the figure of a fanged and horned monster with feline tail, which has three birds' heads on its neck. Several little balls are noticeable flying, as it were, out of its mouth. I think these disks have no direct connection with the creature; similar disks, one long and one short row, are tattooed on the man's back, following the general line of the vertebrae down to the waist. These and the others were probably put there with a therapeutic aim, to counteract pains in this area from one or another cause. Such a use of tattooing is well known to ethnologists; I have personally seen it among Siberian peoples, particularly among Khanty and Eskimos. On the inner shin parallel to the fish is a row of four hurrying mountain rams or goats with horns pressed down. These animals, with legs touching one another, form a single dynamic composition. Above this

*A felt wall hanging from Pazyryk shows a rider in the presence of a
goddess who is sitting on a throne and holding a branch in bloom.*

there is yet another, not properly intelligible, figure of a squatting horned and
winged animal with a long tail terminating in a bird's head.

The tattooing just described could be done either by stitching or by pricking
in order to introduce a black colouring substance, probably soot, under the skin.
The method of pricking is more likely than sewing, although the Altaians of
this time had very fine needles and thread with which to have executed this. In
the preparation of clothes of exceptionally fine squirrel and sable skin, as we
have seen, minute stitches were passed through the material from the inside.
Sinew thread was used only in the most superficial skin layer and never taken
through to the external furry side. The considerable depth of the colouring
substance in the body inclines one to the view that the tattooing was done not
by sewing but by pricks. Undoubtedly also it had been carried out on the ageing

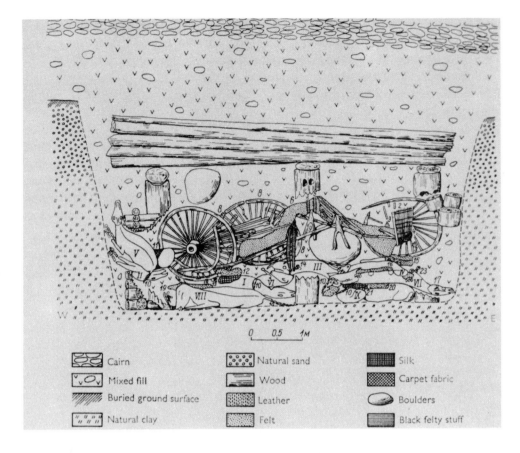

*A diagram showing horses, a carriage, and other artifacts found in the
northern part of the burial shaft in barrow 5.*

chief long before his death, possibly in his youth. We are dealing with a stout
man with strongly developed subcutaneous fat tissue. The ordinary fat layer,
directly under the skin, was not coloured, although the muscles under them in
the area directly below the tattooing were intensely blackened. At the time he
was being tattooed the chief, if not exactly thin, was not as stout as he became
before his death.

During life the soot or black matter of the tattooing always looked lightish
blue on white, and dark blue on swarthy skin. At its discovery the tattooing was
almost black on the grey skin of the body.

What was the purpose of this tattooing?

At that period tattooing had a varying significance among different people.
According to Herodotus, among the Thracians "cuts in the skin signified noble
birth; not having them, absence of it." Xenophon relates that among the sons
of the rich Mossynoeci "their bodies were drawn over and the front part tattooed in colours." According to Pomponius Mela the Agathyrsi "bore drawings

over the face and body, more or less according to their degree of noble blood." At a later date this custom was noticed among the Din-Lin and their successors, the Kirgiz, among whom being tattooed is a privilege for the very brave.

The tattooing of the chief in barrow 2 at Pazyryk most probably signified noble birth or was a mark of manhood or perhaps both. Furthermore the lion's or griffin's head depicted on the chest over the heart is not coincidental, since it is the basic figure of all the tattooing. In addition the majority of the other figures are monsters including in themselves signs of the tiger, deer, eagle, and snake (its head on the tip of the tail). These figures all had some kind of magical significance not yet understood; they were perhaps protective (apotropaic) signs. However, apart from these the presence of a row of running mountain rams would seem to indicate that at the level reached by Altaian society tattooing could be used purely decoratively.

The Discovery of Tollund Man

PETER GLOB

For the most part, archaeologists deal with a relatively anonymous past: entire sites, communities, and societies rather than individuals. Only rarely do excavators gaze on the countenance of a perfectly preserved corpse. When they do, it is almost invariably because they are working in very dry, cold, or waterlogged conditions. The arid tombs of the Nile Valley have preserved Egyptian mummies, including those of the pharaohs, in remarkable condition. The deserts of coastal Peru have yielded thousands of desiccated corpses, tightly wrapped in matting and cloth shrouds. The bogs and swamps of low-lying Denmark have been a fruitful source of all manner of organic finds for centuries, among them wooden dugout canoes, bows and arrows, and timber houses. From time to time, a well-preserved corpse has come from deep in thick peat deposits, none in better condition than Tollund Man, a sacrificial victim hanged and cast into a shallow pond two thousand years ago.

Tollund Man came to light during peat-digging operations in central Jutland in May 1950. Two men digging blocks of peat for winter fuel stumbled across the body. Thinking they had uncovered a murder victim, they reported their find to the local police. Fortunately, the police were aware of other prehistoric bodies that had come from the peat, so they invited scientists from the local museum to join them. The local archaeologists, in turn, contacted Peter Glob (b. 1911) at the University of Aarhus, the leading authority on such discoveries. Glob not only was an expert archaeologist, but was gifted with writing ability. He describes how he was struck by the peaceful expression on the man's face, and then horrified to see that he had been hanged. The victim lay on his side in a crouched position, a serene expression on his face and his eyes tightly closed. He wore a pointed skin cap and a hide belt, nothing else. By examining the contents of Tollund Man's stomach, a botanist established that the victim had eaten a gruel of barley, linseed, and several wild grasses and weeds about twelve to twenty-four hours before his death. No one knows why Tollund Man was hanged. Perhaps he was a sacrificial victim, possibly part of a fertility cult that ensured successful crops and the continuation of life. Bog corpses are not unusual finds in European marshes, but few are as well preserved as the Tollund body.

Here, Peter Glob himself describes the events surrounding the discovery and excava-

tion of Tollund Man in his popular book The Bog People, *published many years after the find. But he still manages to communicate the excitement of finding an intact prehistoric body.*

An early spring day—8 May 1950. Evening was gathering over Tollund Fen in Bjaeldskov Dal. Momentarily, the sun burst in, bright and yet subdued, through a gate in blue thunder-clouds in the west, bringing everything mysteriously to life. The evening stillness was only broken, now and again, by the grating love-call of the snipe. The dead man, too, deep down in the umber-brown peat, seemed to have come alive. He lay on his damp bed as though asleep, resting on his side, the head inclined a little forward, arms and legs bent. His face wore a gentle expression—the eyes lightly closed, the lips softly pursed, as if in silent prayer. It was as though the dead man's soul had for a moment returned from another world, through the gate in the western sky.

The dead man who lay there was two thousand years old. A few hours earlier he had been brought out from the sheltering peat by two men who, their spring sowing completed, had now to think of the cold winter days to come, and were occupied in cutting peat for the tile stove and kitchen range.

As they worked, they suddenly saw in the peat-layer a face so fresh that they could only suppose they had stumbled on a recent murder. They notified the police at Silkeborg, who came at once to the site. The police, however, also invited representatives of the local museum to accompany them, for well-preserved remains of Iron Age men were not unknown in Central Jutland. At the site the true context of the discovery was soon evident. A telephone call was put through straightaway to Aarhus University, where at that moment I was lecturing to a group of students on archaeological problems. Some hours later— that same evening—I stood with my students, bent over the startling discovery, face to face with an Iron Age man who, two millennia before, had been deposited in the bog as a sacrifice to the powers that ruled men's destinies.

The man lay on his right side in a natural attitude of sleep. The head was to the west, with the face turned to the south; the legs were to the east. He lay fifty yards out from firm ground, not far above the clean sand floor of the bog, and had been covered by eight or nine feet of peat, now dug away.

On his head he wore a pointed skin cap fastened securely under the chin by a hide thong. Round his waist there was a smooth hide belt. Otherwise he was naked. His hair was cropped so short as to be almost entirely hidden by his cap. He was clean-shaven, but there was very short stubble on the chin and upper lip.

The air of gentle tranquillity about the man was shattered when a small lump of peat was removed from beside his head. This disclosed a rope, made of two leather thongs twisted together, which encircled the neck in a noose drawn tight into the throat and then coiled like a snake over the shoulder and down across his color portfolio commemorates some of archaeology's most spectacular discoveries. Some, such as Ramesses II, came at the hands of tomb robbers. Others, such as the Han burials, were accidental finds. And many, such as Tutankhamun and Kourion, resulted from deliberate search. All of them have added immeasurably to our knowledge and understanding of the past.

An earthquake leveled the Roman port of Kourion in A.D. 365, killing victims with falling debris while they slept. The excavations at Kourion are an example of first-rate archaeology: they were so precise that they identified the direction of the earthquake's epicenter.

The mummy of Ramesses II, who died in 1213 B.C.

Tutankhamun's gold funerary mask.

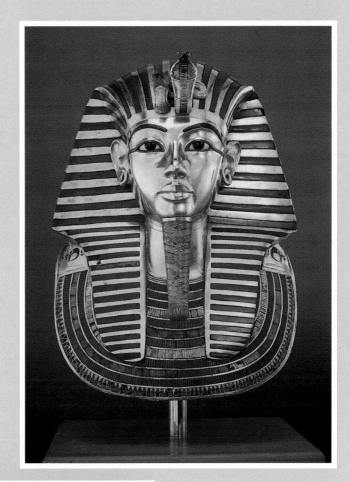

Han noblewoman Tou Wan's burial suit, made of jade plaques woven together with gold thread.

Lords of the Supernatural

Nighttime excavation of a warrior priest's tomb at Sipán, Peru.

A gold representation of a Moche deity found at the Sipán site.

"The Arraignment of the Prisoners," one of the
Bonampak murals from Mexico, conveys the lavish,
and often bloody, ceremonies of Maya lords.

A Moche warrior priest buried with funerary mask,
elaborate ear plugs, and necklace of gold and silver.

Horsemen, Laborers, and Soldiers

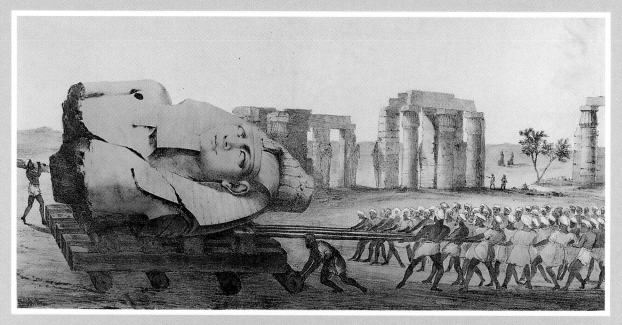

Giovanni Belzoni and his army of laborers transport the head of Ramesses II—now in the British Museum—to the Nile.

A Pazyryk horseman, depicted in felt and preserved by the Siberian permafrost.

The Terracotta regiment of Chinese Emperor Qiunshishiuangdi, guarding its master for eternity.

S pectacular archaeological discoveries continue unabated in the late twentieth century in both familiar and remote lands. The Uluburun ship, a Bronze Age ship discovered in nearly 100 feet (30m) of water off southern Turkey, is a triumph of modern archaeological discovery. Thanks to painstaking recovery methods and research, the find has revolutionized our knowledge of ancient trade 3,000 years ago.

Recovering an amphora from the Uluburun ship in Turkey.

the back. After this discovery the wrinkled forehead and set mouth seemed to take on a look of affliction.

Proper study of such an interesting find, and the need to preserve it for the future, called for its immediate removal to the National Museum in far away Copenhagen. Preparations were quickly begun. In the gathering dusk a local saw-mill was visited and asked to supply planks for a box to be built in the bog round the dead man and his bed of peat, so that everything could be despatched for investigation intact. As darkness encroached, this task had to be postponed. Next day a strong team from the Silkeborg Museum moved in under the direction of two museum curators, Peter Nielsen and H. Hansen, assisted by the police. The dead man and the surrounding peat were first tightly walled in between the sides of the box. Next, boards were pushed in underneath the whole. When the box had been filled right up to the top with peat blocks so that there was no possibility of its contents shifting during the journey, a lid was nailed on.

The heavy plank box weighed almost a ton when filled. It had to be raised nearly ten feet vertically from the bottom of the bog and on to a horse-drawn cart which was to take it to the nearest railway station, in the village of Engesvang. The soft surface of the bog made it impossible to bring a crane up to the spot, and everything had to be done by hand. This was not accomplished without loss. One of the helpers overstrained himself and collapsed with a heart attack. The bog claimed a life for a life; or, as some may prefer to think, the old gods took a modern man in place of the man from the past.

A unique feeling of antiquity still rests over the landscape around Tollund Fen and the Bjaeldskov valley. A ravine with sandy wheel-tracks leads down between high heather-covered slopes to the sacrificial bog, passing through vegetation in which the red trunks and dark caps of fir, and willows—with light golden catkins and slender pointed green leaves in the early spring—predominate. Wild cherry, blackthorn, crabapple, and briar grow on the sloping banks, and with them the ancient Danish forest tree, the aspen, its leaves still shivering from the winter's cold. It is the primeval northern woodland, not very different from the oldest Jutland forests of which we have knowledge.

The valley debouches into the fen, which is still covered with a wild profusion of flora in spite of two thousand years of peat-cutting. The sides of modern peat-cuttings show vertical stripes, the marks made in cutting the good solid peat-mass. In them, however, lighter-coloured areas are to be seen, the smaller-scale peat-workings of earlier ages. It was in one of these that the man had been deposited. A peat-spade made entirely of wood and belonging to the same remote period had in fact been found a few days before the discovery of the Iron Age man.

The bog at Tollund opens out into a great tract of fenland, the old Bølling lake, now grown over, and reflecting the blue sky no more. Some of Jutland's earliest hunters once lived on its shores. In the north of the region lies the ancient hunting station of Klosterlund, about ten thousand years old, and to the south, at Hesselhus, a somewhat later habitation-site with thousands of small geometrically struck flint flakes belonging to a culture with affinities over wide tracts of Central and Eastern Europe. Ancient burial mounds can be seen in rows on the high ground surrounding the fenland. They mark the line of ancient highways. Some three or four hundred of these bowl-shaped memorials of the distant past once existed in the immediate neighbourhood. Only a third of them still survive in the grass and heather, or overgrown with trees. These mounds date from the Stone and Bronze Ages and are therefore between one and two thousand years earlier than the Iron Age man. The oldest are the funeral monuments of the "battle-axe people," who invaded Eastern and Central Europe about four thousand years ago from the far-off steppes of Central Asia. Some branches of these people penetrated as far north as Jutland and settled there. They were of Indo-European stock, and it was their incursion into the Scandinavian lands so long ago that more than anything else gave the northern peoples the special physical characteristics which persist to this day. The battle-axe people formed a solid foundation in these regions for the development of the culture of the period which followed—the Bronze Age, in which bronze was the most important metal for weapons, tools, and ornaments.

The Tollund man represents the population of the succeeding period, the Iron Age, in this area; but he is not the only Iron Age man from these bogs. In June 1938, again during peat-cutting, and only sixty yards further out in the bog to the north-east, a remarkable discovery had been made—a man wrapped in an animal skin. Because of the skin, the peat-cutters at first thought they had come upon a roe-deer and continued digging until they saw woven material. Only then was the assistance of the National Museum called for. By this time the legs and lower part of the body had been almost completely dug away.

This dead man lay about five feet below the surface of the fen, with his head to the south and his legs to the north. It was clear that he lay in an old excavation in the bog, probably an ancient peat-working. The way in which the hair was dressed was interesting. Locks from the forehead and neck were gathered up in a knot on the left side of the back of the head. The animal skin in which the man was wrapped was some kind of sheepskin with pieces of cow hide sewn on to it. A leather strap, about sixteen inches of which were preserved, was threaded through a buckle; and this suggested that the man was either strangled or hanged before being deposited in the bog. The woven material which had led to the suspension of peat-cutting turned out to be a belt twenty-six inches long and about one and a half inches wide.

Yet another body was found in May 1898 in a little bog two and a half to three miles further north. . . .

A rich find of gold of Iron Age date occurred in the same district near the ancient highway, marked by prehistoric burial mounds, along the terminal moraine of central Jutland, where, twenty thousand years ago, the edge of the ice-cap remained stationary for a long period during the last glaciation. The find, at Stenholt, comprised ten gold discs with representations of a dragon-like bird, five pieces of ring-money, eighteen glass beads, and a bar of silver. Such a discovery tells us that this highway already existed in the Early Iron Age. It was still in use throughout the Middle Ages, following the same track. The pilgrims' way from distant Iceland to the Holy City of Rome also followed this route, and it has remained in use up to our own day as a drove-way for cattle to the south. The two Romanesque parish churches of Kragelund and Funder have fine granite sculptures: Christ blessing, animal figures resembling lions and dragons, and runic inscriptions. These inscriptions name the patrons and builders of the churches and, together with some of the animal representations, establish similar links between the use of this highway and the final pagan phase of the Iron Age.

The name Tollund, which appears in the form *Torlund* in a document of 1481, may have ancient origins. It probably indicates a grove sacred to one of the best-known gods of the Viking age, Thor, described in the *Poetic Edda* as the strongest of all gods and men. Thor is the sky god, Asiatic in origin. His symbol is a hammer, the handle of which he grasps with iron gloves. He derives the power he uses in hurling it at his enemies from a special belt which doubles his divine strength when he fastens it round his body. When he moves from place to place, in a waggon drawn by a team of goats, the heavens thunder. He wishes all men well and stands by them in the face of their enemies and against the new God, Christ. "Tor's Grove," however, was not situated where the bog lies in Bjaeldskov Dal, but probably near Tollund farm, closer to Funder Kirkaby.

The journey of the Tollund man by rail through Denmark took a week. As soon as he reached the National Museum's laboratory in Copenhagen a thorough investigation was begun under Dr. Knud Thorvildsen, the head of the laboratory. The long journey had gone well. When the plank box was taken apart the dead man was found lying on his peat bed exactly as when he was first uncovered. Examination of the block of peat which surrounded the body confirmed that he had been deposited in an old peat-cutting at some time in the Early Iron Age, that is, about two thousand years ago. Underneath the whole body was a very thin layer of sphagnum moss, a reddish peat-stratum which was formed in Danish bogs precisely in the Early Iron Age. Danish peat-cutters call it "dogs' flesh" because of its colour and its relatively poor quality as fuel.

The Iron Age man's head and body were exceptionally well preserved, particularly the side which lay downwards and so was first subjected to the action of the bog water. Bog water, saturated with soil-acids, is an essential factor in the preservation of this type of ancient find. If the soil-acid is not too strong, the bones are preserved. On the other hand, they may disappear completely in certain circumstances, dissolved in the water by the action of the acid and further decalcified by the roots of bog plants. This point is illustrated by a find made at Damendorf, in Schleswig. Here only the skin survived; but it was so well preserved that it might have been taken from a living man.

The Tollund man's head was especially well preserved, the best-preserved human head, in fact, to have survived from antiquity in any part of the world. Majesty and gentleness still stamp his features as they did when he was alive.

*Tollund Man's body when first
recovered from the surrounding
bog deposits. He wears a cap, and
the strangling cord can be clearly
seen.*

His cropped hair, up to two inches long, was not dressed in any way. His eyebrows were partially preserved, and the very short stubble already mentioned covered his upper lip, chin, and cheeks. It is the dead man's lightly closed eyes and half-closed lips, however, that give this unique face its distinctive expression, and call compellingly to mind the words of the world's oldest heroic epic, *Gilgamesh*, "the dead and the sleeping, how they resemble one another."

As to the condition of the body, Dr. Thorvildsen writes that most of its upper part was still covered with skin. The left part of the chest and the left shoulder, however, were slightly decomposed, the epidermis being absent from considerable areas. A succession of sharp cuts could be seen down the back. These had been caused by peat-cutting. The left hip-bone protruded from the skin and the stomach lay in folds. The sexual organs were in a good state of preservation.

The naked body was clad only in cap and girdle, with a skin rope fastened tightly around the neck. The pointed cap was made of eight pieces of leather sewn together, the hair side inwards, and was fastened to the head by two thin leather laces, fixed at the temples with knots and tied off in a bow, which was tucked in under the cap at the right temple. The belt lay low on the hips, in folds at the back but tight across the stomach. Made of thin hairless skin, it had one end drawn through a slot in the other and wider end and was secured with a slip-knot on the left side.

The plaited skin rope round the dead man's neck was knotted at one end to form an eyelet through which the other end was drawn, forming a noose which could be tightened from the back. It had left clear impressions in the skin under the chin and at the sides of the neck, but no mark at the nape of the neck, where the knot rested. The rope was skilfully plaited from two strips of hide about half an inch wide, and measured five feet from the curve of the eyelet to the opposite extremity. It had, however, been cut at this point and must originally have been longer.

The Tollund man most probably met his death by means of this rope. The vertebrae of the neck did not appear to be damaged, but the doctors and medico-legal experts who took part in the examination judged, nevertheless, from the way the rope was placed that the Tollund man had not been strangled, but hanged. An attempt was made to decide the point by radiography, carried out by a senior medical officer at Bispebjerg Hospital, Dr. Baastrup. The result was indeterminate, because of the decalcified state of the vertebrae. A radiograph of the skull was taken at the same time. This showed clearly that the head was undamaged. The wisdom teeth had developed, indicating that the man must have been appreciably over twenty years old. The brain was intact but shrunken. An autopsy showed that the inner organs such as the heart, lungs, and liver were very well preserved. So was the alimentary canal, which was removed by the palaeo-botanist, Dr. Hans Helbaek, with the object of determining the nature of the dead man's last meal. This was still contained in the stomach and in the larger and smaller intestines which, though somewhat flattened by the weight of the overlying peat, were otherwise intact.

These organs were carefully rinsed externally, to remove contamination from the surrounding peat. Their contents were then washed out and proved to consist of a blend of finely reduced plant remains and particles of seeds. The contents of the stomach and the smaller intestine were inconsiderable, occupying in volume barely 0.5 and 10 cubic centimetres respectively. The contents of the larger intestine, on the other hand, amounted to 260 cubic centimetres. All was of the same character. It was not possible to establish with certainty the proportions of the different ingredients because the plants had varied in their resistance to the digestive juices which had acted on them from the time the meal was eaten and for some while after death.

By the time it has been crushed in a hand-mill and between the teeth a meal of this kind, consisting largely of grains and seeds, is reduced to myriads of small particles. The basis of the investigation was a sample of 50 cubic centimetres taken from the larger intestine.

In collaboration with the anatomists, Drs. Bjøvulf Vimtrop and Kay Schaurup, a point of great interest was established. Investigation showed that although the contents of the stomach consisted of vegetable remains of a gruel prepared from barley, linseed, "gold-of-pleasure" *(Camelina sativa)*, and knotweed, with many different sorts of weeds that grow on ploughed land, it could not have contained any meat at the time of death, since recognizable traces of bone, sinew, or muscular tissue would certainly have remained. It was further established, from the degree of digestion of the remains of the meal in the alimentary canal, that the Tollund man had lived for between twelve and twenty-four hours after eating his last meal.

In addition to the varieties of cultivated grain, it is worth noticing the unusual quantity of knotweed *(Pale persicaria)* in the stomach. It must have been gathered deliberately and other plants represented may have been gathered along with it incidentally; for example, blue and green bristle-grass, dock, black bindweed, camomile, and gold-of-pleasure. The gruel made from this mixture of cultivated and wild grains was no doubt the normal diet in the Early Iron Age, around the time of Christ, when the Tollund man was alive. Fish and meat were also eaten. Rich furnishings of bowls and dishes, with ribs of ox and sheep, and carving knives lying ready, are known in the graves of the time. But meat was certainly not the daily diet as it was in the time of the Stone Age hunters. Milk and cheese, on the other hand, probably were, as the forms of the pottery vessels would seem to indicate.

It is not surprising that this two-thousand-year-old "recipe" for gruel from the Iron Age (consisting primarily of various cultivated grains together with the seeds of many types of weeds known at that time) should have been tried out in our own day, and in front of a big audience at that. Gruel made to this recipe was served up on an English television programme, in the summer of 1954, to two well-known archaeologists—Sir Mortimer Wheeler and Dr. Glyn Daniel. Reports tell us that these gentlemen were not particularly smitten with the taste and had to wash it down with good Danish brandy, drunk from a cow-horn. Sir Mortimer finished up by saying that it would have been punishment enough for the Tollund man to have been compelled to eat this gruel for the rest of his life, however terrible his crime might have been. The Tollund man, though, would not have had brandy to help it down, as the archaeologists did. It was not until about a thousand years later that people learned to distil something stronger from fermented drinks. However, there was an alcoholic drink in the Iron Age, as has been revealed by analysis of sediments in bronze vessels of the period. It was half way between beer and a fruit wine. Barley and the wild plants cranberry and bog myrtle were used in its manufacture. The alcoholic content may have been increased by the addition of honey. This agrees with the account given in the Roman historian Tacitus' *Germania*, a work contemporary with Denmark's Early Iron Age. It says of the Germani that "they drink a fluid made from wheat or barley, fermented so as to give it some resemblance to wine."

When the exhaustive study of the Tollund man had been concluded, a decision was taken on preserving him for the future. Unfortunately it was only thought practicable to undertake the conservation of the splendid head. This was first of all placed for six months in a solution of water to which formalin and acetic acid had been added. The solution was then changed for one of 30 per cent alcohol, which was later replaced by one of 99 per cent alcohol to which toluol had been added. Finally, it was put into pure toluol progressively mixed with paraffin, for which wax heated to different temperatures was later substituted. After more than a year's treatment the head was sent to the Silkeborg Museum in Central Jutland, a bare six miles from the spot where it had come to light in Tollund fen. It can be seen there, alongside other discoveries of the Iron Age.

In the process of conservation the proportions of the head and the features of the face were happily completely retained, but the head as a whole had shrunk by about 12 per cent. In spite of this it has emerged as the best preserved head of an early man to have come down to us so far. The majestic head astonishes the beholder and rivets his attention. Standing in front of the glass case in which it is displayed, he finds himself face to face with an Iron Age man. Dark in hue, the head is still full of life and more beautiful than the best portraits by the world's greatest artists, since it is the man himself we see.

Otzi the Ice Man

KONRAD SPINDLER

Many spectacular archaeological discoveries come about by accident, such as when two hikers found the mummified body of a five-thousand-year-old man exposed under an eroding glacier high in Europe's Tyrolean Alps. His survival and discovery were a miracle, for only three days after he was found, the area was again mantled in snow. Otzi the Ice Man caused an international sensation, as well as a diplomatic flurry, for he lay on a poorly defined frontier line between Austria and Italy. Otzi is as important an archaeological find as Tutankhamun, for he is the earliest European corpse to have survived. Once research is complete, his deep-frozen body will yield a mine of information about Bronze Age diet, disease, and genetic makeup.

Otzi survived in remarkable anatomical condition, thanks to the protection afforded by the natural hollow in which he lay. An international team of scientists is poring over his body, clothing, and equipment. They believe that he climbed the mountains from the south, following the only logical route in this area to an altitude of 3,200 meters. The cause of his death is unknown, but he may have been surprised by a sudden weather change, which prevented him from descending the mountains before snow came. Perhaps Otzi was a shepherd, grazing his flocks on summer pastures high in the mountains. He wore leggings and a loincloth, a deerskin coat, and an outer cape of woven grass or reeds. Calfskin shoes filled with grass held in place by an inner skin "sock" protected his feet. Otzi carried an unfinished yew long-bow, a quiver of arrows, a copper ax with yew handle, a small flint knife, fire-making equipment, and two birch-bark containers. He was in good health, but had broken several ribs during his life and suffered from some hardening of the arteries. Radiocarbon dates place his death at about 3200 B.C., at the beginning of the European Bronze Age.

Konrad Spindler describes the finding of the "Ice Man" in 1991 and the controversies surrounding the discovery in this selection from The Man in the Ice, *a popular account of Otzi. (This account has been heavily edited to shorten it.)*

Erika and Helmut Simon live in Nuremberg, the provincial capital of Franconia. All around that ancient imperial city, which suffered such destruction in the war, extends the flat Nuremberg countryside, resembling nothing so much as a sandpit. Helmut Simon is a caretaker; his wife works on a newspaper. They are a modest couple who radiate contentment. Never in their wildest dreams did they imagine that one day they would be seen on television screens around the world. Although the Simons are no longer young, they go to the Alps every year.

From 15 to 23 September 1991 the couple were on holiday in the Italian South Tyrol, in the popular little resort village of Unserfrau im Schnalstal. From there it is not far to the peaks of the main Alpine ridge. As always they planned their daily excursions with care. Both of them are experienced mountaineers, unafraid of even the most difficult routes, but they like to be back in their village by nightfall.

Their destination for Wednesday, 18 September, was the Similaun summit, at 3,607 metres above sea level a normal day's climb of medium difficulty for a trained mountaineer. The Simons are a capable pair. They chose a little-used route across an icefield. Unexpectedly, they found themselves faced with wide crevasses, disappearing down into darkness. Laborious detours became necessary. Already the midday sun was beating down on them. Their schedule was falling apart. But like all true mountaineers they wanted to reach their objective. At last they stood on the summit—but by then it was 3:30 P.M.

It became clear that a full descent would be impossible before dusk. They consulted their tourist map to locate the nearest refuge. An unplanned night in the mountains was inevitable, and the descent to the Similaunhütte, the Similaun refuge, took about two hours. On the way they were joined by two Austrian mountaineers, who had made reservations there. The sun was just dipping below the crest as they reached the hut.

The early morning heralded a radiant day. This is Thursday, 19 September 1991. The Simons had really intended to return directly to the car park, but such brilliant mountain weather is irresistible. The peaks beckon. Their programme has been abandoned anyway. On the spur of the moment the Simons decide to climb the 3,516-metre Finailspitze. At the peak they rest for about an hour, beginning their descent around 12:30 P.M.

Once more they leave the marked path and choose a route to the Similaun refuge, where they have left their rucksacks. They cross a wide, slightly inclined snowfield that ends at a small rocky ridge, behind which lies a narrow gully. Its base is filled partly with glacier ice and partly with meltwater. To avoid it they make an arc towards the left. The time is 1:30 P.M.

Later, Helmut Simon would describe their discovery to us like this: "From a distance of 8 or 10 metres we suddenly saw something brown sticking out of the ice. Our first thought was that it was rubbish, perhaps a doll, because by now there is plenty of litter even in the high mountains. As we came closer, Erika said: 'But it's a man!' " Helmut Simon immediately ran back to get the

Austrian couple, from whom they had parted shortly before. But they were no longer in sight.

Sticking out of the ice is a leather-brown round bald skull with a medallion-sized injury. Also visible are the shoulders and back, draped against a rock. The face is immersed in water, with dirt around the chin. The arms cannot be seen, and seem to be missing. Because of its delicate proportions, Erika suggests that it is the body of a woman.

> We thought it was a mountaineer who died here. We were shocked and didn't touch the body. There was a blue ski-clip lying nearby, the rubber strap used for tying skis for transport. We thought the accident probably happened ten or twenty years ago. Not far from the body we saw a piece of birch bark, which used to be a tube but had been squashed flat, wound round with string or leather and open at both ends. Helmut picked it up, looked at it carefully and put it back. We memorized the exact position of the body before we left. Helmut took a photograph as a record, in case the place couldn't be found again from our description.

It was the last frame of his film—the photograph of the year.

The Simons still have a descent of about an hour ahead of them. After ten minutes they meet a walker who intends to climb the Finailspitze. They exchange greetings—but they do not tell him of their discovery. For a long while they watch him move on. He sticks closely to the path and so is unlikely to see the body. Some twenty minutes later they meet another man who has lost his way on the ridge. They do not reveal anything to him either.

The Simons reach the Similaun refuge towards 2:30 P.M. The guests are sitting outside, enjoying the sunshine. Only the innkeeper, Markus Pirpamer, is busy inside. Tormented by thirst, but even more so by the need to recover from their shock, they go into the kitchen and order a beer. Then Helmut Simon asks if anyone from the hut is missing. Pirpamer says no, and the Nuremberg couple tell him of their discovery. Immediately there is great excitement. Pirpamer questions them meticulously about the spot. He even steps outside with Helmut Simon and gets him to describe the route. A few tourists prick up their ears and ask what has happened, and the Simons tell of their find below the Hauslabjoch. Markus Pirpamer undertakes to notify the police.

The Nuremberg couple wait for the rescue helicopter. But when it fails to arrive they set off again at about 4:30 P.M. They spend a few more enjoyable days in the mountains before returning home on Monday, 23 September. The reporters are already lying in wait. . . .

Of course, rumours abound. It is said that the body has burn marks on its back and an open wound on its head, even that the dead man was in fetters. . . . Back at the police station, Schöpf first deals with the axe, depositing it in the air-raid shelter. Then he sits down to type his report:

Alpine incident: body discovered at Hauslabjoch (Niederjochferner)—supplement. On 20.9.1991 District Inspector Koler of the Imst police was flown to the Hauslabjoch by the helicopter of the Federal Ministry of the Interior in order to effect the recovery of the body. Because of unfavourable weather conditions the recovery operation had to be cut short. It was only possible to free the corpse from the ice up to the region of its hips. The dead man's identity has not as yet been established. On the strength of the articles found near the body it may be assumed that the accident happened as long ago as the nineteenth century. According to information from Alois Pirpamer, the mountain rescue chief from Vent, the body cannot be Capsoni's as this person's body was recovered some years ago. Given appropriate weather conditions recovery will be continued and/or completed. When further details become known a report will again be submitted. . . .

Even before the axe disappeared behind the heavy steel doors of the air-raid shelter below the police station in Sölden, it had been seen by many people. Wooden hafts of that kind have been found in many prehistoric pile-dwellings of the circum-Alpine region. Similar picks with the characteristic elbow-shafting are known, especially in Austria, from the Iron Age salt mines of Hallstatt and Hallein. They should be familiar to people outside the narrow circle of specialist academics. But never once did it occur to anyone who had seen it that the Hauslabjoch axe might be a prehistoric artefact which should, in the first instance, have been reported to the Ancient Monuments Office. . . .

The metal analyses later conducted on the axe showed that the blade consists of almost pure copper. The original guess that it was iron is understandable. Objects made from copper, as from bronze, if left lying in a damp environment for any length of time develop a so-called water patina. As a rule, this is a wafer-thin layer of brownish, occasionally rust-coloured, rarely greenish, hue on the metal. But prehistoric finds in water are not very frequent. A prehistoric axe found in glacier ice is unprecedented. Infinitely more common are articles of copper or its alloys found in mineral soils. Generally these have a thick covering of verdigris, sometimes called "noble patina," which has become the common mental picture of prehistoric artefacts. The finds at the Hauslabjoch were not strictly compatible with any of the previous theories, which was one reason why the authorities decided to exercise extreme caution. Messner alone had come close to the truth.

Markus Pirpamer then exhibits the piece of birch bark. Discussion is brief. They all want to visit the site of the mystery. Together the three mountaineers and the Haids set out. Messner, Kammerlander, and Fritz choose a short-cut over some scree and only take half an hour. Hans Haid arrives some fifteen minutes later. Gerlinde Haid finds herself in quite dangerous fog and takes an additional half hour. The old mountaineers' rule that the pace should be set by the weakest member of the party seems to have been somewhat modified in this instance.

Messner and Kammerlander pull aside the plastic sheet. The dead man looms above the ice and water. Through the meltwater they see that he is wearing something rather like trousers on his legs. For that reason, and in order to look for more pieces of equipment, they hack open the ice around the man's buttocks and along his thighs. Messner uses a ski-pole. Kammerlander has nothing suitable to hand and so picks up a piece of wood lying nearby. Not until later does he realize that this was the thinner strut of the frame of the back pannier on which, 5,000 years ago, the man had dragged his possessions up to the Hauslabjoch. The hazel switch is still serviceable. The birch-bark vessel and its contents have by now been crushed underfoot. Nevertheless the mountain guide Kurt Fritz notices "wilted leaves whose veining was still clearly recognizable."

These leaves were subsequently identified by our botanists as those of the Norway maple *(Acer platanoides)*. They also noticed that numerous flakes of charcoal were adhering to the leaves, a fact which provided vital proof that the function of the birch-bark container had been to carry embers. Hunter-gatherer peoples usually took some embers along from the hearth-fires of their last camp, as nomads do today. The charcoal fragments were wrapped in fresh leaves or grass, and the lot placed in a container of wood or ceramic material. A leather pouch, a basket, or, as in our case, a bark vessel could serve the same purpose. This keeps the embers live for a long time. Even today Austrian housewives will wrap a briquette in damp newspaper and shove it in a tile stove. This helps to kindle the fire quickly the following morning.

The visitors to the Hauslabjoch endeavour to pull what was later found to be a bow clear of the ice. A conical hole about 20 centimetres deep is hacked around the lower end of the stave. But the glacier refuses to give it up. The attempt is abandoned, especially as meltwater continues to flow in.

Attention is also focused on the body itself. The leatherlike leggings are inspected, and fine seams are detected. Fritz reaches into the water and picks up a piece of leather. One of the man's feet is likewise wrapped in leather, with grass spilling out. It reminds Messner of the footwear of the Lapps. Then Fritz raises the dead man's head, so that his crumpled features are visible for the first time. A fibrous "mat" is revealed frozen to the boulder against which the man's torso is resting.

This matted grass was found again during the second archaeological examination at the beginning of October 1991. Only then was the exact position of the body at the point of discovery accurately determined. The so-called mat formed part of a straw, or rather grass, cloak in which the man had wrapped himself against the bad weather. As recently as this century pastoral peoples used the same kind of straw cloak as protection against cold and rain.

A piece of wood barely 20 centimetres long is found floating near the body in the meltwater pool. It has holes at regular intervals—a flute springs to mind. However, Gerlinde Haid, the folk-music expert, disagrees. In fact, it is a broken-off piece of the quiver stiffening. The fact that this fragment was found not near the quiver, but right next to the dead man, is an important clue to the drama which, over 5,000 years ago, occurred near the main ridge of the Alps. But more of this later.

A little way behind the rocky ledge against which the bow rests Gerlinde Haid finds numerous pieces of birch bark. This spot is about 5 metres from the corpse. As their presence at this altitude strikes her as odd she pockets the scraps and takes them away.

A few weeks later Gerlinde Haid handed the birch-bark fragments to us. Without a doubt they too belong to a container. Some of the pieces even show clear signs of stitch-holes. She also described to us their precise location. Subsequent examination showed that the fragments were all natural-coloured on the inside; the birch bark found near the body, on the other hand, was all stained black, which was one of the main arguments in favour of its identification as a cinder carrier. The pieces collected by Gerlinde Haid evidently came from a second container which the man had been carrying. These details show how important it was to question every visitor to the Hauslabjoch site minutely about what they had seen. The piece which Markus Pirpamer picked up on the morning of the same day, some 20 metres away, is the base of the second container. Obviously the wind must have moved some of the lighter items once they were released from the ice, and some of them will probably never be found.

The visitors again carefully cover up the corpse. They place lumps of snow and ice and a few stones on the black plastic sheet before, about half an hour later, they leave the Hauslabjoch. . . .

On Sunday, 22 September 1991, Alois Pirpamer and Franz Gurschler, a retired joiner who helps with the maintenance of the goods lift to the Similaunhütte, set out at sunrise for the Hauslabjoch. The time is 7:00 A.M. In his capacity as mountain rescue chief Alois Pirpamer intends to free the corpse entirely from the glacier ice, ready for its official recovery which is planned for Monday. The ascent takes about an hour. The corpse lies before them, exposed. The plastic sheet, presumably lifted off by the wind, now lies near the bow. Overnight an ice crust roughly 2 centimetres thick has formed on the meltwater pool surrounding the dead man's torso. Systematically they set about freeing the body with their ice-picks.

There are no longer any clothes to be seen on the man's back, buttocks or thighs. Only below the knees can they still detect remnants of his trousers. His left foot can only be freed with great difficulty, as meltwater keeps running in. The right arm cannot be freed at all. It sticks down diagonally into the ice. They assume that the dead man might be holding something that obstructs movement. As they try to lift the body, remains of fur stay clinging to the ice. It is not impossible that the lesions in the genital area, which will be noted in the forensic examination, were caused then. Once more they cover the body with the plastic sheet. Once more the sheet is weighed down with chunks of ice and stone slabs.

Next the two men collect all the loose objects. Into a plastic refuse bag they place the pieces of wood, the rod with the holes, the remains of cord, and the scraps of fur, which are lying on or beside the rocky shelf. Another attempt is made to hack the stave out of the ice, but again it fails. After two hours' work Pirpamer slings the bag over his shoulder and they leave the Hauslabjoch. That same afternoon Pirpamer takes the bag with the finds down to his hotel in Vent.

Rainer Henn usually arrives at his office in the Forensic Medicine Institute very early. This morning he finds two fax messages waiting on his desk. A body has been found in a glacier at the Hauslabjoch—nothing out of the ordinary this year. He arranges a flight because he wants to be present at the recovery. He also gets in touch with the public prosecutor. They agree to meet as soon as the body has been brought to Innsbruck. At about 8:30 A.M. a professor of archaeology named Spindler telephones, claiming that the find could be exceedingly old and of historical interest. He even wants to fly to the site himself, but Henn dissuades him.

With a slight improvement in the weather the helicopter takes off at 11:40 A.M. The pilot Anton Prodinger, the air rescue operator Roman Lukasser, and Henn first fly to Vent for an operational briefing. At 12:05 P.M. the machine touches down. A curious crowd has gathered, as well as the police from Sölden and a few journalists. Alois Pirpamer reports that the dead man is already clear of the ice and so stretcher, ice-picks, and shovels are off-loaded as useless ballast. The press photographer Werner Nosko and an unknown individual press their cameras into the hands of Prodinger and Lukasser, begging them to take pictures up in the mountains. Fifteen minutes later they take off again, circle over the gully, and touch down at the Hauslabjoch at 12:37 P.M.

Much to his surprise, Henn is welcomed by a freezing camera team. (As the recovery that followed was filmed from first to last, it is exceptionally well documented.) Henn trudges through the snow to the site of the find. Lukasser walks ahead, dragging the body bag. They have to clamber over a few boulders. Henn carries his black bag with his special instruments and his camera round his neck. Then he stands in front of the plastic sheet. He pulls it aside a little to reveal the dead man. Lukasser doesn't want to touch the corpse with his bare hands, so Henn hands him some rubber gloves. Then he spreads out the zipped transparent-plastic body bag, while Lukasser removes the black sheet completely. Henn tries to move the dead man's head. But something unexpected has happened—overnight the body has once more frozen into its base and can be neither moved nor shaken free. What's to be done? No ice-picks, no shovels. Henn takes photographs, Lukasser considers bringing up the tools. Henn turns up the collar of his steel-grey anorak. It is bitterly cold. The camera is still rolling.

Hölzl seizes the opportunity for an interview. He tries to get Henn to make a guess at the date of the corpse, but the forensic expert refuses to speculate before he has seen the results of scientific examinations. Only when he is asked how it is at all possible to date a corpse does he give a precise answer. He explains that if very long periods of time are involved, the carbon-14 method can be used. Conclusions could also be drawn from the nature and degree of conversion into grave-wax. If the location of the discovery is taken into account, deductions could be made, with the help of glaciologists, from the speed of flow of the glacier ice.

Fortunately a mountaineer, the South Tyrolean Markus Wiegele, happens to arrive at the site. He carries an ice-pick and a ski-pole. Of course he did not simply turn up out of the blue. The previous evening, at the Schöne Aussicht refuge, the conversation had turned to Messner, who was said to have discovered a body near the Similaunhütte the previous day. Wiegele is resting on the crest when he sees the helicopters circling. Immediately he connects them with the story he heard the night before and makes his way down. He willingly offers his pick and ski-pole and enthusiastically lends a hand.

While Lukasser works with the ice-pick, Henn kneels down and recovers tatters of leather, stacking them up beside the corpse. Meltwater keeps running in. The tools ring on the ice. Gradually the body is loosened. Lukasser pulls at the corpse's arm with the ice-pick; Wiegele helps with the ski-pole. Henn takes hold of the feet. And so they ease the body out of the ice and lay it on its back by the hole. It is a shocking sight. Everyone stands silent around the dead man. Henn is the first to speak, and takes a businesslike approach: "What matters now is that we bring out a few more things for the archaeologists." Items of equipment are duly fished out of the trough in which the body has lain.

Hölzl conducts a second interview: "Herr Professor, what can you say now that you can see the body as a whole?" Henn sums up: "Teeth worn down from chewing, rather ground down. Partially mummified. Must have been exposed to the air for some time before he got into the ice. Clothes? Unfortunately nothing left. That's all we can say at this point."

Henn turns the body back onto its stomach. Then follows its insertion into the body bag. Henn takes the feet, Lukasser the shoulders. The zip is fastened. Lukasser keeps hacking with the ice-pick in order to recover more items of equipment, while Henn wipes his hands with snow. The ÖRF helicopter starts up its engine. Markus Pirpamer, the refuge keeper, is brought along to the Hauslabjoch for an interview. He reports how, having been notified of the discovery by the Simons, he had informed both the Italian and Austrian authorities. He describes the location of the find, his observations at the spot, and the equipment of the dead man. He too has no idea of the age of the corpse, but thinks it can hardly be more than a hundred years old.

The helicopter which has brought the refuge keeper now brings further tools, including a shovel. Henn uses it to make a channel in the snow to let the meltwater drain away from the ice trough. Lukasser continues to dig for further items of equipment. A large scrap of leather or hide appears. Then Henn joins in, probing with the ski-pole. Meanwhile Wiegele has taken over the shovel to drive the water through the drainage channel. Lukasser works untiringly with the pick, throwing bits and pieces on a pile. Then Henn bends down and frees a small oblong article from the ice, roughly at the spot where the dead man's

Scientists carry the body of the Ice Man after dislodging it from the ice.

hip or belly had lain. Henn lifts the object, and part of it falls away. It is the Iceman's miniature dagger with its short flint blade and wooden handle. Only the scabbard drops back into the water. Henn shows the find to Lukasser. Then he places it with the rest of the things on the heap. The others also scrutinize the object and Matthis takes a close-up of it. The television people have now finished and they fly back down to the valley.

Those left behind pack their things. The implements found are also stowed away in the body bag. It is not zipped up completely because the corpse has begun to smell. Wiegele meanwhile makes a last attempt to pull the bow out of the ice—in vain. It is therefore broken off and stuffed into the body bag. The end left in the ice will not be salvaged until the following year. The bundle is dragged to the helicopter and shoved into the orange recovery bag. . . .

Afterwards, especially when the television pictures were transmitted around the world, fierce accusations were levelled against the forensic examiner. But these accusations only began to circulate once the find had been classified as prehistoric and assigned an age of at least 4,000 years. It is easy to be wise after the event. The Viennese, in particular, voiced loud accusations without knowing the circumstances. Naturally enough, traditional rivalries between Vienna and the Tyrol played their part. At least, it was argued, a prehistorian should have been brought in on the recovery, which in any case had been performed in a most unprofessional manner. However, prior to the recovery there was no real contact between Henn and myself. Neither he nor I expected a prehistoric find, nor could we have anticipated its sensational nature. According to the press reports I have seen, modern archaeology should at least have been involved— but this is a young discipline often still not taken seriously in professional circles. . . . The man from the Hauslabjoch is the 619th body which fate has placed on the forensic dissection table in 1991, so it is given the reference number 91/619. Public Prosecutor Wallner and Examining Magistrate Böhler arrive after being summoned by telephone. They bring along a junior lawyer, Marlene Possik, to act as secretary. The refuse bag with the secondary finds lies on a second dissection table; the items have yet to be tipped out. The top of the bag is merely rolled down a little to allow a view of the contents.

Böhler dictates:

Public prosecutor Dr. Wallner on 23.9.1991 reported the following state of affairs: In the Ötztal, near the Finailspitze, a body was found. According to rumour the body is said to have been fettered and to have burn marks on its back. Possibly it is a very ancient corpse. Upon application of public prosecutor Dr. Wallner I ordered a forensic examination of the body with a view to establishing its identity and the possibility of culpability by a third party. This instruction was passed on by Dr. Wallner to the security authorities. In the afternoon I participated jointly with Dr. Wallner and Magistrate Böhler in the forensic examination. Purely external examination of the mummified corpse revealed that it is evidently several hundred years old. The alleged fetters are remnants of clothes or footwear. No burn marks could be identified on the back. With the corpse some primitively wrought tools (knife with stone blade and wooden handle, a kind of "ice-pick" with stone point) were found, as well as hand-sewn clothing (leather parts crudely sewn), so that it may be assumed that the corpse had been lying at the place of discovery for several hundred years. The reason why there was no grave wax formation is probably that the body was already mummified before being frozen into the ice. In the opinion of Dr. Unterdorfer the body discovered is historical. I have given instructions that the body should be handled with care and that, after examination, it should be made available to the historians, seeing that there are no indications of third-party culpability or of a culprit still pursuable. I have raised no objections to the corpse being photographed by the press, etc. Innsbruck, 23.9.1991.

Henn telephones the Institute for Pre- and Protohistory. After all, we had spoken on the phone earlier that morning. But it is outside office hours and I am on my way home. So the involvement of the "historian" is postponed to the following day. The material of the axe, described by the examining magistrate as "a kind of ice-pick," is carefully inspected and the blade scraped with a scalpel; from its colour and softness the material is thought to be copper.

Unterdorfer dictates the following report to his secretary, Uta Halper:

Name XY [the pre-printed boxes for Sex, Date of birth, Occupation, and Address are left empty].

Identity: not yet established; unknown mummified mountain corpse from the Niederjochferner, Ötztal.

External diagnosis:

1. The body, along with scraps of greyish-black sodden material, was delivered in a colourless body bag and placed on the table by the undertaker Klocker from Längenfeld. The other items brought with it are contained in a black bag.

2. Sodden body of a largely mummified, externally ochre-coloured to brownish-black person. The body displays local blackish-grey sandy encrustations, along with remnants of interspersed fur-like patches. A clump of ice adheres to the area of the crotch and the buttocks. In the area of the back there are likewise similar, partially ice-impregnated, deposits.

3. As far as can be judged, no head-hair, body-hair or pubic hair; evidently the epidermis is no longer present; as far as can be seen, there are no nails left either.

4. In the area of the right foot and ankle joint: remnants of evidently simple footwear. As far as can be judged, this is dried straw and grass with leather-like footwear wrapped around it. This in turn is tied with a twisted cord; some interlacing recognizable.

5. The body relatively light, its weight is provisionally estimated at between 20 and 30 kg. Its length is given at 153 cm along the left leg.

6. With the body lying on its back, the left arm is extended from the shoulder joint at an angle upwards to the right. The right arm, with the shoulder area angled upwards, is extended outwards at an angle of approximately 60 degrees, the right hand held as though gripping a round object.

7. The body is lightly rinsed down with cold water; it is evidently a very, very old corpse.

8. In the eye sockets the dried-up eyeballs are still recognizable, with major damage; the chewing surfaces are clearly diagonally worn down by chewing.

9. The front and side of the neck without outwardly visible indications of fatal injuries.

10. Chest and abdomen sunken, the skeletal parts clearly identifiable; as far as can be judged from the outside, without injuries.

11. The lump of ice between the legs detaches itself; in it are thong-like leathery materials.

12. The external genitals foliated, as far as can be judged most probably male, desiccated. In the region of the left thigh and hip extensive damage. As far as can be seen, the muscle tissue fibrously transformed, torn

out in hide-like scraps: one third of the left thigh-bone (the third nearest to the trunk) sticks out, the head of the bone without identifiable degenerative changes, in the sciatic area of the back some degree of damage noted, evidently as a result of being eaten by animals.

13. In the area of the outer and rear side of the left leg superficial soft-tissue damage, evidently as a result of being eaten by animals.

14. The body is carefully turned to lie on its stomach and cleansed with cold water of the adhering blackish-grey sandy encrustations.

15. In the occipital area there is damage about 3 × 4 cm to the scalp, evidently made by a carrion-eating animal (bird of prey?), jagged along the edges, towards the left scratch-like superficial defects. The cranium, as far as can be seen, does not exhibit a corresponding fracture. The area of the nape without external indications of injury of an especially fatal nature.

16. In the left-hand lower dorsal region there are four groups of longitudinal, blackish-grey linear discolorations of the skin. The individual lines are arranged in parallel series, in four groups slightly below each other. They show discolorations of the skin. The individual lines have a length of about 2.8 cm to 3.0 cm, and a width between 2 mm and 3 mm. From top to bottom, first a group of four, then at closer intervals two groups of three, and finally, faintly identifiable, another group of four. This one, considerably fainter, localized in the area of the left sacro-iliac joint.

17. In the area of the sacro-coccygeal region and the left rear half of the pelvis, as well as in the adjoining left thigh region, there is extensive damage to the soft tissue suggesting that the flesh has been eaten by animals (dog-like predator). Ice still at this spot. As far as observable, the skeletal parts are also affected, exhibiting something like clipped marginal areas. More detailed assessment not possible because the deeply ingrained ice has not yet melted.

18. In the area of the hollow of the right knee a cross with a length of bars of 2.8 cm and 2.7 cm and a bar width of between 3 mm and 4 mm dyed-in or tattooed in blackish colour.

19. In the area of the lower extremities no indication of major injuries.

20. The hay-upholstered footwear remains on the right foot are left in place.

21. In the area of the right lower dorsal region, more feebly, another group of four lines in the shape of longitudinal blackish parallel skin discolorations as on the left side.

22. In the area of the back of the left hand, near the wrist, two transverse parallel linear skin discolorations, 4.2 cm in length at a distance of 7 mm to 8 mm.

23. The Institute of Forensic Medicine is informed that, on the strength of its external appearance, independently of the accompanying articles, this

is a corpse at least many hundreds of years old. Following consultation with Professor Henn the accompanying items are laid out on the second dissection table and the entire find left as it is to await the arrival, after notification, of Professor Spindler of the University Institute for Pre- and Protohistory.

24. In view of the circumstances Dr. Böhler, the examining magistrate, issues no instruction for an autopsy. After further telephone consultation, no prohibition of photography is issued.

Great Zimbabwe

CARL MAUCH

The Great Zimbabwe ruins first came to the attention of the European world in 1514, when a pardoned Portuguese convict named António Fernandes heard rumors of exotic stone buildings in the far interior of southeastern Africa. The masonry structures were said to be the palace of a powerful chief of the Shona tribe named Mwene Mutapa. The Portuguese traded sporadically with the Shona people between the Limpopo and Zambezi Rivers from 1514 until the nineteenth century, but they never visited the legendary Zimbabwe (Shona for "buildings of stone"). No European visited the ruins until the late nineteenth century when an obscure German geologist named Carl Mauch explored the overgrown site. Zimbabwe did not receive archaeological attention until 1890, but has been the subject of occasional excavation and controversy ever since. It is one of the best known archaeological sites in sub-Saharan Africa.

Carl Mauch (1837–1875) was hungry for fame and fortune, one of the many Europeans who flocked to the northern frontiers of South Africa in 1871. The lure was gold, ancient mines in the still-remote country between the Limpopo and Zambezi Rivers. Rumors of fabulous wealth, of long lost civilizations, circulated freely. Mauch himself heard stories of glittering palaces north of the Limpopo River, in the heart of gold country, so he decided to investigate. After an arduous journey, he met an American named Adam Render, who had married an African woman and settled close to Zimbabwe. Render arranged for local guides to take Mauch to the overgrown ruins. The serious-minded geologist was astounded by the high, freestanding walls of the Elliptical Building, with its mysterious conical tower, and by the secluded enclosures nestled among granite boulders on a low hill overhead. Mauch was in no doubt that he had stumbled across the palace of the biblical queen of Sheba. Proof, he said, came from the scent of a wooden lintel in one of the buildings, which was identical to that given off by his cedarwood pencil!

Mauch published his findings in an obscure German periodical, but they were forgotten until the 1950s. In 1890, though, Cecil Rhodes's Pioneer Column passed close to Zimbabwe. When reports of the imposing ruins filtered back to Rhodes, he commissioned European antiquarian Theodore Bent to investigate, hoping that he would demonstrate that a Mediterranean civilization had once occupied his new colony, thereby justifying

251

white colonization. Bent and his successors did indeed claim that Zimbabwe had been built by Phoenicians and other exotic peoples. But these claims never stood up to serious scientific scrutiny, despite efforts of white settler governments to perpetuate them in the 1960s. Modern archaeological researches have shown that Great Zimbabwe was built by Shona-speaking Africans around A.D. 1000, with its heyday in the fifteenth century A.D., long after the Phoenicians had vanished into history. In recent years, Zimbabwe has become an important symbol of African nationalism and nationhood. The modern country of Zimbabwe is named after the ruins.

Carl Mauch's journals remained untranslated and unpublished until 1969. His firsthand account of his discoveries at Zimbabwe, reprinted here, is little known outside the narrow coterie of African archaeologists.

TUESDAY, 5 SEPTEMBER 1871

The start was early and we proceeded on a considerable detour so as not to be discovered by Mangapi's people on whose land the ruins lie. At last, after 2½ hours walking, a bare, large, and rounded granite hill was reached, from the summit of which a preliminary view of the mountain could be had. But only a very small site could be made out which was not a rock but which could be a wall. Only a short stop was made and another ½ hour led us along a little valley and along the foot of the hill, about 400 feet high, which was regarded by all with great awe. A long line of tumbled-down stones guided us and in places one could still recognise the former shape of a wall. The stones are granite and about double the size of our bricks. On three sides of the oblong they are smoothly cut, the fourth, facing inwards, has been left unworked. Nowhere is the wall higher than 3 to 4 feet and it has usually fallen down or is covered. The western slope of the rocky mountain is likewise covered with similar stone fragments. Nothing further could be noticed, but that these probably had been walls of a fortification. So as not to act contrary to custom a halt was made close to the wall and one of my companions was sent up the hill to the chief whose huts could be made out on its summit. Till the return of this messenger I ambled around a little between extensive ruinous walls and saw, a short distance away, an apparently round edifice and so I directed my steps towards it. Presently I stood before it and beheld a wall of a height of about 20 feet, of similar granite bricks. I did not have to look for an entrance for long, for very close by there was a place where a kind of foot-path, which apparently is used quite frequently, led over rubble into the interior. Following this path I stumbled over masses of rubble and parts of walls and dense thickets, and big trees prevented me from gaining an overall view from any point. Several attempts to obtain such were in vain and, finally, I stopped in front of a tower-like structure which was built quite near to the opposite side from where I entered. It stood there apparently quite undamaged. Altogether it rose to a height of about 30 feet. The lower 10 feet are cylindrical with a diameter of 15 to 16 feet, the upper 20 feet are conical with a diameter of about 8 feet at the top; completely similar kind of building with trimmed granite bricks without any mortar, but with bonding according to the art of building. In vain did I look for an entrance or a walled-up opening, in vain did I try to discover the reason for this structure. Now I am called from outside and I have to discontinue my archaeological endeavours and follow the call. However, it was not easy to find the exit again in this labyrinth and only after having climbed, or fallen, through the dense thicket and over walls and rubble and having reached my path of entry did I emerge from these very sombre environments into the open air. Here I learned that the chief had come down from the mountain and that he was a very friendly fellow. This was a consolation. Led by him we all went up the hill to his huts. He did not appear to be upset at all by our inquisitiveness, he even made us a present of a goat ram. As this was only a casual visit to initiate the establishment of friendship, we hardly mentioned the ruins in our conversation. Suffice it that I obtained visual sight of their existence and permission to return again in a few days' time. . . .

MONDAY, 11 SEPTEMBER 1871

Early in the morning we started for the ruins which were reached after 1¾ hours walking. A strong southeast wind makes my companions shiver. Mangapi presents me with an ox which I send back with some of Pike's people. Without stopping at the ruins in the plain the summit of the hill is climbed and there breakfast, consisting of rice and Arachis, is prepared. After this began the inspection of the hill ruins. The assertions of the blacks were such that they made the heart burn with eagerness. There was supposed to exist a tin bowl filled with various things and a great quantity of beautiful white linen was supposed to be hidden at a certain place. At another place, it was said, large iron rods were to be seen, then again, inscriptions and, further, drawings of birds' feet and carved heads of children, etc., etc. Small wonder that I presented the chief, who had promised to show me all, with many beads which should now be thrown down this kloof or on to that crag as sacrifice. He left everything to me and my companions while he himself rested once again and showed great fear of going any farther. So I went through a narrow entrance between boulders into the interior of the ruins. After prolonged wandering over and between rocks and rubble, after troublesome and dangerous pushing through dense undergrowth in which a shrub-like nettle played a not minor role, I came to the definite conclusion that these ruins must be the fallen remains of a very strong fortification of earlier times. I noticed some very narrow corridors (hardly 2 feet wide) formed by 15- to 20-foot high walls still standing, as well as another covered one which leads into the ruins below a large boulder, but it is partly in ruins, partly walled up. The cross-beams are of trimmed stone and, indeed, of a peculiar, easily split, mica slate. Wood appears to have been used only exceptionally. Most of the walls join one another and the outer wall in a curve. This [outer wall] is best preserved on the southern slope and is 30 feet high over a length of about 120 feet and, from the bottom to the top, 12 to 6 feet thick. It is built

*At Great Zimbabwe, the Elliptical Building is seen from the Acropolis, the low hill
that overlooks the site, once an important rain-making shrine.*

on the extreme edge of a mighty rock precipice so that only sufficient room is
left for one man walking barefoot or for a baboon, to proceed along the foot of
the wall. It is especially remarkable how strongly this wall had been built without any mortar and that it is succumbing only very slowly, in spite of wind and
decay. From several walls there still protrude vertical beams of stone, from 8 to
12 feet in height and 4 to 6 inches in diameter. From their firmness when being
shaken one can surmise that their overall length is about 20 feet. They probably
served to give greater strength to the individual sections of the wall. None of
them had any inscriptions and only one showed some decoration. It was still 8
feet long with an elliptical section of $4 \times 2\frac{1}{2}$ inches. Its material was greenish
grey, scaly soapstone.

Another relic is a bowl of the above shape, of soft soapstone of greenish-
grey colour. It is broken in half and lies underneath a large boulder where definite signs of walling are to be seen which must have been built to close the cave.

Besides these two items I could not discover anything else and it may be that
either much has been stolen already or that such things are hidden in caves and
kloofs. In some places it is evident that walls have been built in front of caves
by the Kaffirs according to their sense of art, for they have no notion of the
regular laying of stones or of bonding. They even think that the walls were built
at a time when the stones were still very soft, otherwise it would have been

impossible for the whites who built these walls to form them into a square shape!

The whole of the western slope is strewn with rubble from the walls and the few remains still visible point to the fact that there were once terraces which served either as gardens or [as platforms] for huts. But there is no clue which would allow one to come to a final conclusion in this matter. I expected greater success from the investigations in the ruins in the plain. A cultivated piece of land at the southern foot of the mountain also appears to have been made use of in the same way by the former inhabitants and a small, now dry, or rather periodical, river-bed may have contained the water necessary for irrigation. Remains of walls, however, seem to point to a one-time connection between the two fortifications. In any case, there did exist out-buildings connected with the round main building, but these are destroyed to such an extent that nothing positive can be stated. The principal item of the investigation remained the well-preserved tower in the interior of the *rondeau*. An ascent to the summit by means of creepers which grow all over it, taught me that it is not hollow from the top but filled with small stones, and on none of its sides could a walled-up entrance be discovered. That it, actually, was the most important object is shown by some nearby decorations and attempts to reinforce it. For it stands between two very high walls which are only 10 feet apart. A narrow path of access, coming from the north through one of them, shows alternate double layers of grey or white granite and black phonolite, that is, on either side of the access but only covering a length of about 6 feet. As well, the outer wall shows on about one-fourth of its circumference, with the tower as its approximate centre, a decoration on its upper part. . . .

On this occasion, too, it was impossible to draw a plan of the whole building and I postpone this till the next visit. The petty chief on the hill had recalled me. On my way back I looked at what I believed to be out-buildings and found an object which was of iron. Its use was a complete riddle to me, but it proves most clearly that a civilised nation must once have lived here. It consists of two triangularly shaped shells which are connected by an iron arc. A further visit may possibly elicit more. As it was already past sunset, it was necessary to remain on the mountain for the night. No further information about the "when" and "how" could be obtained. The name of the hill with the ruins is Zimbabye or, possibly Zimbaoë. The former is the name given to it by the local Makalakas or Banyais. . . .

Tuesday, 22 March 1872

. . . I went alone with my sketch-book and armed with my revolver to the House of the Great Wife. I was well hidden from possible observers by the tall grass, and I soon found, struggling through thick grass intertwined with leguminous creepers, a suitable boulder from which I could obtain an over-all sketch in the shortest of time. Always taking advantage of the tall grass which, unfortunately, prevented a clearer inspection of the area between the mountain and the *rondeau*, I crept into the interior of the latter and commenced drawing a rough sketch-map. However, the ruined walls were hidden to such an extent by trees, thorns, nettles, creepers, shrubs, grass, and dry branches, that I had to do the sketch without accurate measurements. No fixed point relative to the sometimes visible parts nor a fixed segment of a wall could be obtained because of the thick undergrowth. While the outer wall up to a height of 24 feet presents the best-preserved part, it appears that none of the inner ones ever attained that height. Trunk-like, split beams of mica slate were also used in the building of the outer [wall]. Its thickness is very much greater at the bottom than at the top. The inner walls are generally only 2 feet thick and are not reinforced by similar stone beams. . . . the ground is everywhere covered with fragments of ruined walls.

One of the largest of the central trees, the only one of its kind, has a diameter of 2½ feet and a beautiful trunk reaching up to a height of about 20 feet. I could not find out what name belongs to it. My stay would have lasted too long and so I desisted from further investigations. I did cut some splinters off the cross-beam over the northern entrance. This beam is as old as the building itself and had only been damaged a little by at least 2,500 grass fires. Equally strange is the fact that none of the numerous borers ever tried to attack it. The wood is still quite healthy, of reddish colour, exudes a weak odour, but burns with a strong one, similar to a torch. A comparison of it with the wood of my pencil shows great similarity and therefore I suppose, strengthened by further hypotheses, that it must be cedar-wood. This would be a dead, though very telling witness to the fact that these ruins are an imitation of Salomo's buildings. . . . It can be taken as a fact that the wood which we obtained actually is cedar-wood and from this that it cannot come from anywhere else but from the Libanon. Furthermore only the Phoenicians could have brought it here; further Salomo used a lot of cedar-wood for the building of the temple and of his palaces: further: including here the visit of the Queen of Seba and, considering Zimbabye or Zimbaöe or Simbaöe written in Arabic (of Hebrew I understand nothing), one gets as a result that the great woman who built the *rondeau* could have been none other than the Queen of Seba.

The Oudepost Discovery

CARMEL SCHRIRE

In 1488, Portuguese sea captain Bartolomeu Dias rounded the Cape of Good Hope at the southernmost tip of Africa. He anchored his storm-battered ships in Mossel Bay some distance to the east, in a quiet berth surrounded by rolling hills where herdsmen grazed large-horned cattle. These Khoikhoi herders wore few clothes; spoke in an exotic, clicklike tongue; and seemed to wander aimlessly between coast and interior. For two centuries, European sea captains would stop at the site of modern Cape Town, replenish their water casks, and trade beads, iron tools, tobacco, and other trifles for cattle to feed their crews. Then, in 1652, the Dutch colonized the Cape, establishing farms and soon encroaching on Khoikhoi lands. By this time, the Khoikhoi had acquired a reputation as the most primitive people on earth, folk who wandered across the landscape with their herds, had few material possessions, and, most cardinal sin of all, apparently had no religion at all. They were called "Hottentots," barbarians considered perhaps half-human.

The Khoikhoi did not stand a chance against aggressive European settlement. Dutch farmers seized their lands and established permanent cattle ranges, cutting off the herders from critical segments of their annual grazing range. Within a few generations, most Khoikhoi had lost their breeding stock to the cattle trade or had moved far inland. By the end of the seventeenth century, their traditional lifeway had effectively vanished at the Cape.

Contemporary European documents chronicled many of the interactions between Dutch colonists and Khoikhoi at the Cape from the settlers' perspective. But what of the voices of Khoikhoi themselves? Archaeology provides some clues, for fragmentary sheep bones document the presence of herds at the Cape at least 1,800 years ago. Only in recent years have archaeologists combined archaeology and historical records to study the silent dimensions of colonist–Khoikhoi interactions, with remarkable results.

South African archaeologist Carmel Schrire spent years studying the interactions between Australian Aborigines and white colonists, and was struck by the similarities between these exchanges and those between the Khoikhoi and Dutch settlers at the Cape of Good Hope in her homeland. She located the long-lost site of a provisioning outpost for visiting ships on Saldhanha Bay's Churchhaven Peninsula, occupied from 1669 to

1732, where she unearthed what she calls a "rough frontier settlement occupied by lads working off their contract to the Dutch East India Company." But Schrire's main concern was with the interactions between colonists and local Khoikhoi at Oudepost, which she inferred from associations of indigenous and colonial artifacts, especially animal bone fragments, which gave graphic proof of the devastating effect of firearms on game, birds, and other animals—a shift from the Khoikhoi's small, persistent culling to wholesale onslaught. But the remains found in the site itself were misleading, for the colonists dumped the butchered carcasses of larger animals, including large numbers of cattle, into the nearby ocean. The bones at water's edge documented the deep inroads the colonists made into the Khoikhoi's herds and breeding stock, which was one of the primary causes of the breakdown of their society. And the glass beads found in the excavations dramatized the inequitable nature of a trade in worthless baubles on one side and basic commodities on the other, a barter system that ensured the Khoikhoi could never compete as equals.

In a brilliant study of Oudepost, Carmel Schrire used a series of intersecting scenarios to create a portrait of the settlement and the interactions that took place there. She juxtaposed archaeological evidence, extended quotation from historical documents, and her own fictional reconstructions to flesh out the story. She recounts how the excavation unfolded in Digging Through Darkness, *a work that is part history, part archaeology, part fictional reconstruction, and a unique chronicle of an archaeologist at work.*

The settlement consisted of several ruined structures built on the beach sand of a small rocky promontory, between the high-water mark and a point about 40 meters inland. We defined three main structures. The lodge, named for its designation in the archival records, was a rectangular building facing the beach. The fort, or redoubt, was an irregular-shaped structure with a series of small enclaves, one of which stood so close to the sea that it was periodically percolated by the high tide. Finally, GCL was a small structure separated from the north wall of the fort by a curtain wall. All three were made from the local undressed granite rocks such as currently litter the shoreline, making it likely that the small sandy beach in front of the lodge was in fact created by clearing building materials off its former rocky stretch.

The lodge stood about 30 meters from the water's edge, its front door set in the narrow end, facing the sea. It was built by digging long trenches 0.7 meter wide, which were then filled with rocks to serve as footings for the walls. The structure measured about 19.85 by 5.65 meters, dimensions that translate into more simple vernacular readings of about 62 by 18 Rhineland feet. But the makers made an error laying out the walls, and as a result they produced a building without a single right angle in the entire affair! Likewise, though most of the walls stood on footings, short stretches were missing, and parts of the walls stood directly on the sand. The walls were generally 0.54 meter thick, built as a double tier, with occasional slabs laid across the entire width for added strength. It had two rooms, the larger open to the sea in front and the smaller rear room through a door in its north wall. There were no paved surfaces or other evidence of floors inside, but fragments of shell plaster sticking to the joint between the footings and the wall suggested that the walls were once covered with plaster. No chimneys were found, but heaps of charcoal reveal that fires were lit directly on the sand up against the walls. In the back room several well-placed rocks and iron bars showed where a rough grid once supported a kettle or pot.

The fort, its curtain wall, and parts of GCL rested directly on sand or on the bedrock of the rocky beach. The fort walls and the curtain wall were generally between 1.4 and 2 meters thick and consisted for the most part of two outer walls filled in with broken rocks. Paved surfaces were found in three parts of the fort, with granite and sandstone slabs interspersed with an occasional yellow brick. Crude though these floors were, they were not laid haphazardly. The floor in the northern side of the fort was laid from the walls inwards, whereas the southwest one grew from a few central stones, outwards. Fragments of shell plaster clinging to the cracks suggest that it might originally have covered the entire floor. Finally, GCL lay just beyond the curtain wall. It measured 3.55 by 2.85 meters, with walls 0.50 to 0.75 meters thick. Two walls rested directly on the sand; the others lay partly on the sand and partly on a dense secondary fill of charcoal, rubble, and broken bricks. The origin of this fill is unknown, but if it was generated on this site, its stratigraphic position suggests that GCL was not the first structure built here.

Architectural similarities suggest that all the buildings were part of a single settlement. Provision lists specify that beams, slats, rafters, and rattan were sent to build the station, but since we found no postholes to suggest the presence of upright roof supports, it seems that the roofs rested directly on the low walls. Fragments of shell plaster imprinted with reeds imply that they were thatched. Then too, various lines of evidence suggest that this settlement was built after the colonists had been living here long enough to accumulate some garbage. The floor in the northeast section of the fort was set in sand stuffed with broken pipes and bones, and two walls of GCL rested, in part, on a fill of charcoal and broken bricks that must have been generated in the ruins of a previous structure. An earlier foundation lay alongside the dividing wall of the lodge, running under the outer walls of the back room. Finally, the footings at the entrance of the lodge were packed with ash and garbage that accumulated while the men built the lodge.

In and around the structures lay broken bits of glass, stoneware, earthenware, porcelain, iron, and tin. Two large rusty locks and some broken pintles suggest doors or hinged windows. Activity areas were evident in the predominance of gun flints, shot, and metalware in the fort, as opposed to more broken glass and earthenware in the lodge. The reconstructed squalor says that this was not a Dutch home of the sort immortalized in genre paintings but, rather, a rough frontier settlement occupied by lads working off their contract to the Dutch East India Company. They trampled their garbage underfoot or broadcast it all over the place, rather than placing it into pits, as was customary in colonial sites of the later eighteenth century. Soldiers melted lead and poured it into bullet molds, dropping blots of molten metal and lead pulls in the sand. They wrote on slates with stone pencils as similar to those found in wrecks of the VOC [Dutch East India Company] ships dated from 1629 and 1656 as they are to modern ones, used in Holland today. They cut patches out of tin sheets and riveted them with nails to mend their rusted kettles. Behind them they left masses of snarled, metal cutouts, as an archaeological signature of distant frontier outpost, where broken pots and pans were conserved rather than dumped. The men stewed fish in kettles, tossing out a mass of cleanly defleshed bones and scales when they were done. They butchered their meat with hatchets and knives and grilled it over embers, throwing away the charred bones with their tell-tale cut-marks. Their hearths sat directly on the sand floor of the lodge, and the men probably coughed and hawked inside, as the smoke percolated slowly through the damp, thatched roof.

Historical sources told us that we were dealing with a discontinuous occupation spread over some sixty years, but we needed a stratigraphic time frame to draw the archaeology closer to the documents. Since there were no direct stratigraphic links between the buildings, we carefully examined the artifacts to see if they would help us infer a sequence. Beads and coins, though promising, were rare, so we turned to ceramics. Here too the Oudepost collections were small when compared to those found in other colonial sites, especially in old privies, where hundreds of broken vessels might be recovered from a single pit, as opposed to a total of 280 vessels from the entire Oudepost dig!

Nevertheless, using what we had, we began with the earthenwares. Plates, small tripod dishes, porringers, colanders, and bowls were decorated with dull green, yellow, rust, and red tin glazes. Although these seemed potentially definitive of time and space, they were not. Similar wares were made since medieval times in Europe and without microscopic analyses of sherds and clay sources, we could not even distinguish imported vessels from those which were made at the kilns that operated at the Cape since 1665.

Turning next to stonewares, the jars and bottles, which probably held wine, liquor, vinegar, and medicines, were certainly not made at the Cape, but any expectation that these, or other vessels like them, might be tightly seriated according to the stamps on the necks and bottles had been dashed some years earlier when a shipment of stoneware bottles, or bellarmines, excavated from the 1629 wreck of the East India Company ship *Batavia*, was found to include every style formerly thought to form a succession over several centuries.

This left Oriental porcelain. Despite its predominance at Oudepost, where it made up almost 50 percent of the sherds and over 70 percent of the minimum number of vessels present, porcelain never appears on the supply lists to the post. This is probably because the tea bowls, dishes, bowls, and plates at Oudepost did not come overland from the Cape but, rather, from ships sailing home from the East, who called in here for supplies. Incongruous though it may be to imagine soldiers on a rough frontier outpost sipping from a porcelain tea-bowl, one must recall that for all its rarity in Europe, coarse South Chinese provincial wares were so common in Asia that they probably occupied the same role on a homeward voyage as did earthenware and tin vessels on the outbound run. Records attest that company men were entitled to export a certain amount as private trade, but contraband far exceeded the allowance, so that the weight of these shipments was, on occasion, enough to sink a homebound ship! Porcelain draws its name from the white cowrie shell called *porcella*, or little pig. Its deep, drowning blue set on a white sheen and the sweep of the bowl up from the small, neat, foot to the prim everted lip excite the prospective seriator. For all their elegant features, the best way to date porcelain is in reference to dated cargoes from shipwrecks. But unfortunately there are, at present, too few such wrecks to provide appropriate fine-tuned comparisons with the Oudepost material, so that its porcelains cannot provide a key to the relative age of different parts of the site.

So we turned to the key to such chronological conundrums, namely, the clay tobacco pipes. Briefly, after tobacco was introduced to Europe from America and the West Indies, smoking became fashionable, and pipe-making guilds sprang up in England and Holland in the late sixteenth century. The earliest pipes were short stemmed, with small, squat bowls to hold small amounts of this valuable product. As shipments of tobacco proliferated, pipe stems grew longer, terminating in large bowls, for a more leisurely, cooler smoke. Unfortunately these very general stylistic trends do not serve as a tight dating device. Turning from form to decoration, makers stamped their names and coded dates of manufacture on the bowl, stem, or heel, but these signs usually provide a relatively long time range that brackets the duration of the factory, rather than specifying the year, or decade, of manufacture of the pipe. If this were all the information encoded in clay pipes, they would be no different from other artifacts, such as porcelain bowls, stamped with the mark of a Chinese dynasty, and glass bottles that were fashionable for a sixty-year span. But clay pipes carry a potent and subtle time code in the diameter of the bore that runs the length of the stem, from the bowl to the mouthpiece.

Over forty years ago, "Pinky" Harrington observed of colonial sites in Virginia that the older the site, the larger the holes in the broken clay pipe stems that littered the ground. Since stem bores grew smaller as a direct function of time, the average diameter of a set provides both a relative and an absolute age, to a decade or so, for assemblages of pipes. Most subsequent conclusions about stem-bore chronology were established using English pipes, and since the Oudepost yielded about 7,000 fragments of clay pipes, almost all of which were made in Gouda, Holland, the question was whether the Dutch pipe stem bores had shrunk over time like the English ones. It turned out to be so, possibly because pipemakers interacted across the Channel, even to the point of shipping clays from England to France.

Jim Deetz and I started to analyze the pipes while the dig was still in progress. He set up a table at the University of Cape Town and stuck graded drill bits into the stems of thousands of pipes. He lined up a series of nine styrofoam cups and labeled each one according to the diameter of the stem bores. A tenth cup was filled with their modern equivalent, namely, the butts of his filter-tipped cigarettes. We then persuaded two successive statisticians to explore the nuances of stem-bore distribution in different parts of the site. They concluded that although we could use the pipes to show the relative age of different parts of the site, using stem bores to calculate the mean age of a site was intrinsically doomed unless pipes there were deposited in a constant, unbroken rate over time.

Typologists expanded on the limits of heel-stamp dating. I traveled to Leiden in the winter of 1988 to consult Don Duco, the world's expert on Dutch clay pipes. We were especially concerned about a small collection of fragments stamped with the arms of the city of Delft that lay at the very bottom of the deposits in the lodge, in close association with hearths there. According to Duco's published list of heel marks, these pipes were made in a very narrow time range, between 1744 and 1749, a date which threw our entire site into confusion, if, as we believed, Oudepost I was occupied from 1669 to 1732. Duco's scholarship and passion for pipes had led me to expect an old man with nicotine-stained fingers. The youthful scholar in his unheated Georgian museum threw me off guard. We sat at a polished table and pored over the Oudepost pipes. Duco was in shirt sleeves, I huddled in my coat. I trembled, in part from the cold, and partly from apprehension, as I drew the "Wapen van Delft gekrooned" specimens from their plastic bags.

Duco took a quick look. He seemed unmoved.

"Oh, forget it," he drawled. "I must have got the date wrong!"

"Wrong?"

"Sure," he snapped. "The old lists are often full of errors."

I turned to more immediate concerns.

"Tell me," I said, "are you warm in here?"

Duco looked puzzled.

"Oh no," he replied, "if I were warm, I would take off my shirt."

The published report on pipe analysis confirmed and supported the documentary sources which said that whole site was occupied from the late seventeenth century to about 1730. It also showed that despite the ravages of wind, water, and burrowing moles, a succession still survived, with the lower levels having more, older, large-bored pipes than the upper ones. It revealed that the lodge and fort were occupied around the same time, in contrast to the small square structure, GCL, which was the latest building on the site. It told us nothing about the age of the burial, however, because the fill there was too shallow and mixed to lend itself to dating.

Now we could try to reconstruct what happened at Oudepost and what the behavior and events signaled by the artifacts meant in the larger framework of Dutch–Khoikhoi existence.

Historical archaeology seeks to tighten the embrace of archaeology and history beyond the confines of each discipline by relating objects first to context and then to behavior. The actual evidence under review is often so tenuous that the enterprise resounds with disputes and disagreement. Interpretations at Oudepost are no exception as may be seen in the following controversies over the archaeological evidence for Dutch–Khoikhoi interaction at this site and the impact of the Dutch settlers and soldiers on the land.

Archaeological interactions between colonists and Khoikhoi at Oudepost are inferred primarily from the association of patently indigenous artifacts with colonial rubbish. Stone tools, coarse-tempered pottery, bone points, a tortoiseshell bowl, and ostrich eggshell beads lie cheek-by-jowl with colonial hoes, bottles, and porcelains. They cluster in and around the buildings, suggesting that the post was in use when the debris was dropped. Simple though these observations may appear, they merit deeper scrutiny because Later Stone Age people probably lived in this region for more than 35,000 years, raising the question whether the association of artifacts signals interactions at the post or merely reflects an accidental intermixture of colonial and indigenous refuse.

We argue that it denotes interaction and, moreover, that the indigenous material represents the material signature of contact people. For starters, this particular little beach was not viable real estate until about 2,000 years ago, when the slightly raised sea level fell to its present position and exposed the sandy land on which the post was erected. But if geology rules out 33,000 years of Stone Age presence, we still need to prove that the indigenous artifacts excavated at Oudepost are a mere 300 years old. Some prehistoric archaeologists were disturbed by the fact that the chipped stone tools at Oudepost are different from those found at the only well-attested Cape Khoikhoi camp at Kasteelberg, some 40 kilometers away. They argued that the Oudepost association is fortuitous, that the outpost stands on the site of an earlier herder encampment, similar to those on the coast nearby, and that the indigenous artifacts were churned upwards by wind, rain, and moles, to end up in apparent association with the colonial garbage. When confronted with a total absence of any underlying indigenous deposits, or for that matter any typically indigenous debris, such as a dense shell midden, coupled with the presence of patently undisturbed Stone Age artifacts—including an ostrich eggshell necklace buried against the lodge and a typical Khoikhoi bone spear point stuck deep into the fort wall—they retract momentarily. Regrouping, they argue that the concentration of indigenous debris around the Dutch buildings does not signify interaction but rather, separation, in that the Khoikhoi must have occupied the ruins when the Dutch were gone, either in the twelve years immediately after the massacre of 1673 or later, after the post was abandoned in 1732.

The passion of published exchanges on these matters hints that what we might be seeing here are different rules of evidence in prehistoric, as opposed to historical, archaeology. Colonial artifacts are seldom found in prehistoric caves, kraals, and rock shelters because after Europeans drove hunters and herders off their traditional territories, these sites fell into a different ambit. They accumulated only the odd glass flake, bead, or pipe when used peripatetically by Khoikhoi shepherds out pasturing their new employers' sheep. In contrast, colonial expansion drew indigenous people into new towns, farms, and trading posts

*Dutch colonists trading with
Khoikhoi fisherfolk in the
seventeenth century.*

where they became transformed from herder-landowners into an underclass within the new colonial society. Their imprimature now changed, as, for example, when traditional arrows and spear points were chipped from superior materials like glass and porcelain. The archaeological implications of artifacts such as these are neatly expressed in Tasmania, where an excavator needed to prove that natives reoccupied a colonial stock camp *after* it was destroyed by fire. Flaked tools made of glass and gun flints, coupled with traditional bone points fashioned from introduced dog and horse bones, proved his case, pointing as they do to Aboriginal scavenging for their raw materials in an abandoned colonial midden. A more subtle expression of indigenous presence, which is often more difficult to read, is the signature of this underclass in inferior ceramics, cheap cuts of meat, bottles of cheap liquor, and reused pipes.

Where evidence of contact at Oudepost is concerned, although indigenous tools lie in direct and on occasion patently undisturbed association with colonial ones, there are no scrapers fashioned from glass and porcelain, no iron spear points, no bones butchered with stone tools, nor any points made of the bones of colonial imports, like pigs and horses. The only cultural swop that we have found is a small collection of chipped stone tools made from local silcrete with tell-tale iron stains lodged in their crevices that seem to be gun flints or strike-a-lights. Since the Khoikhoi seldom, if ever, had guns, we infer that these objects were made by the garrison when their normal, imported flint ones ran short. But if the colonists were so inventive, why not the Khoikhoi? Surely they perceived the advantages of iron and glass over stone? If they had no chance to try it while the garrison was emplaced, they certainly would have had all the time in the world, had they camped for any length of time in the ruins. But there are no porcelain or glass scrapers and no iron spear heads in the Oudepost collections. Thus lacking all such indications, the demand of purists that each and every stone tool at Oudepost be shown to represent an actual artifact dropped by a particular Khoikhoi person at a documented instant in time simply cannot be fulfilled.

The second issue concerns the interpretation of the archaeological food remains. Oudepost I was littered with mammal, fish, reptile, and bird bones, some burned in cooking fires, others bearing the marks of butchery with iron hatchets and knives similar to those found on the site. There are many ways to estimate the relative importance of different animals, but a favored tactic is to count MNI (Minimum Numbers of Individuals) present by grouping all the bones that could possibly have come from one creature. Analysis of the large excavated collection reveals that soldiers ate three times as many wild as domesticated mammals, as well as large numbers of tortoises, fish, and game birds.

This pattern of hunting is consistent with the records on some frontier stations but utterly at odds with the majority of dispatches regarding Oudepost I. Frontier farmers tended to save their stock for the market, and consequently they hunted and gathered wild food all the time. The cull was monitored in principle, if not in practice, by a series of proclamations and rules, duly noted in the Game Books. The garrison at Saldanha Bay, who had to provision ships, bought and traded meat on the hoof from nearby Khoikhoi herders, from colonial farmers, and from company stock posts all year round, but the archaeology suggests that they did not rely on this to any great extent, where their own needs were concerned. This discrepancy prompted a closer look at the primary records. The Company Meat Books—great sheets of parchment housed today in the Royal Archives at The Hague—record shipments of butchered meat made to various outposts. The quarterly rations for the troops were dispatched according to a weight formula per man, but between 1725 and 1732 we find that significantly less meat was sent to Oudepost as compared with other posts. This suggests one of two things: either the passage of stock here was so effective that the men did not need any more meat or else the garrison at Saldanha Bay hunted so efficiently that they had no need of the company's provisioning.

The predominance of wild foods at Oudepost is therefore not surprising, but it does carry ominous implications where the local Khoikhoi people were concerned. They were herders who hunted and foraged for food year round, especially in those seasons when pastures were sparse and the stock grew thin. They slaughtered their stock when they could afford to do so, and they relied on wild foods to buffet their losses in hard times. The colonial stock trade probably seemed feasible to them at first, but as its demands escalated and as their stock was confiscated for infractions, Khoikhoi herders lost more animals than they were accustomed to cull. Analysis of the Oudepost sheep bones confirms the documentary evidence that sheep were consumed all year round, and, as such, it contrasts with the situation found on many indigenous sites of the past 2,000 years, where sheep were consumed only at specified times of the year, when the flock was largest. After the famous conversation of 1660, when native chiefs begged for access to forage on land they had lost in what the company regarded as a just war, the Khoikhoi came to realize that from then on the land and its yield were no longer the province of the spear, bow, and poisoned arrow but of the gun and the horse. The residues at Oudepost afford chilling confirmation in a comparison of the minimum number of game birds there, as opposed to those commonly found in food debris on precontact Khoikhoi sites in the same region. Prehistoric sites generally yield around ten species, some of which were probably "wash-ups"—exhausted or dead birds thrown up on the shore. In striking contrast, the Oudepost series, boasts forty-two different species of birds, a startling tribute to the gun and bird shot.

The bottom line, then, is that the Oudepost bones illustrate in detailed material terms one aspect of the colonial grab of native resources in this newly invaded land. Extrapolating beyond this post to the long chain of other posts and farms along the frontier, we may envisage in very specific terms, how the new settlers cut a broad swathe through the wild food base, swamping the old Khoikhoi pattern of a small persistent cull with a sudden vigorous onslaught.

This is a very satisfying conclusion because it refocuses the bland archival record into a tighter, simpler vision.

The only problem, where Oudepost is concerned, is that it is wrong.

Three years after digging ended, in the winter of 1990, [we] wandered down to the site again to check what the sea might have washed up during some particularly high tides. We noticed a large bone, glinting in the mud of a shallow rock pool. Scraping off the sand, we pulled, and watched in astonishment, as a huge bone sighed reluctantly out of the mud, revealing a dense mass of other bones below. We crouched down at the pool, digging with bare hands before the tide returned. The dark ocher fragments were waterlogged and heavy, and some showed scars where they had been smashed by repeated blows from iron hatchets. Sandwiched alongside were bits of porcelain, glass, clay pipes, a gun flint, a coin, a few bits of Khoikhoi pottery, and stone tools. [We] stared at each other. We began laughing wildly as the tide crept in and covered the pool. We stuck a pole in the mud to mark the spot, and returned on the following two days to retrieve the rest.

The contents of the rock pool, which we unceremoniously labeled "DP," for "Dump," were jammed into an area of about 4 square meters, down to a depth of about 30 centimeters. The accumulation seemed to be the lowermost level of a large heap of colonial garbage that was dumped into the sea. It fell onto the rocky platform, where most of it was washed away, leaving only the bottommost stuff wedged between the rocks. Comparison of its 61 pipe stems with the other 7,000 from the site suggests that the event took place around the end of the seventeenth century. A single coin, dated 1658, does not dispute this claim, nor do the associated fragments of porcelain, earthenware, glass, and iron. One particular piece of porcelain was originally part of a Kang XI Chinese bowl, whose other fragments lay scattered around the fort. Its translucent white body sported bright cerulean designs of the eight horses of the emperor Mu Wang outside and pine trees inside, all utterly characteristic of bowls made in the second half of the seventeenth century.

But although the dump contained the same mix of colonial and indigenous artifacts as we found in the land-based collections, its 1,700 bones looked quite unlike those found in the rest of the site. The dump contained the partial remains of twenty-one mammals, including a hippo, a probable hartebeest, five cows, six sheep, three seals, a pig, a few buck, and a rabbit. These were represented by numerous large bones, that contrasted with the many small ones in the land-based collections. In addition, while wild mammals outnumbered domesticates three to one on land, there were twice as many domesticated as wild mammals in the dump.

The most obvious question is whether the colonists habitually dumped the different parts of different animals on land and in the sea. To answer this, we need to rule out postdepositional winnowing by asking whether the dump once contained the remains of many smaller animals, which were subsequently washed away, leaving mainly large ones behind. An analysis of body parts of cows and sheep suggests that this was not the case. The sheep are represented largely by twenty-eight small teeth, and had whole sheep been dumped there, the teeth should have been winnowed away every bit as easily as the rest. The cows, on the other hand, are represented by five solitary teeth and a mass of postcranial bones. Had whole cows' skeletons been dumped, the resilient heads and jaws should have withstood the tidal effects better than they did. In other words, winnowing notwithstanding, it seems that where this episode was concerned, sheep heads, and cow bodies were dumped in the sea.

The next question is whether people dumped different butchered residues on land and in the sea. The dump contains proportionally more large bones, and twice as many domesticates—cows, sheep, and pigs—as were found on land. Assuming that this dump was representative of the garbage that the soldiers customarily threw into the sea, then clearly the garrison butchered many farm animals at one time, threw most of the big, beef bones in the sea, and scuffed the smaller pork and mutton elements underfoot.

But since it is clear that the garrison also ate a lot of wild animals, we need to ask when periodic butchering of large numbers of domesticated animals cropped up. Historical records note the arrival of ships all year round, crammed with sick and starving men who demanded fresh water, meat, and herbs from the Saldanha Bay post. The corporal was repeatedly instructed to attend to these demands at once, buying or bartering stock from local herders, nearby farmers, and from the company abattoir at the outpost of Groene Kloof (modern Mamre), 50 kilometers away. The garrison was ordered to butcher very carefully, saving heads, plucks, and other offal. These provisioning episodes must have generated large piles of bones, guts, and hides. Excavations show that they did not dump rubbish in pits, nor could they rely on carnivores to clean up the mess, for according to the rare incidence of gnaw marks, it seems that there were few dogs or wild animals scavenging around the site. The only way to avoid accumulating fly-blown heaps all around their living quarters was to gather it up, or load it in a wheelbarrow, walk a few steps down to the beach or across to the fort wall, and tip the lot into the sea, leaving the tides to do the rest.

Assuming that the episode, whose debris ended up in our little dump, was only one of many such moments of disposal, it opens a window on the taphonomy, or postdepositional history, of the residues at Oudepost I. If butchered remains of cows and sheep were selectively removed and dumped in the sea, then clearly the excavated collection does not tell the entire story of what people hunted, butchered, and consumed at Oudepost. The land-based remains give a misleading impression that the colonists depended heavily on smaller wild animals, hunting and fishing in the former ranges of the pastoral foragers. At the same time, the remains fail fully to reveal the dependence of the colonists on domesticated stock. But does this realization, when extrapolated to other posts and settlements, diminish the degree to which the Dutch colonists invaded the food base of the indigenous people? Had the indigenous Khoikhoi been purely hunter-gatherers, we might have had to back-track pretty smartly from our original conclusions. But the Khoikhoi were pastoralists, and as such they were locked into a demanding trade in stock. Consequently, the large numbers of butchered sheep and cows that must have been consigned to the waves point every bit as strongly to colonial inroads into the indigenous food base as do the residues of wild animals scattered around the site. For although many of the sheep at Oudepost were brought there from colonial farms and outposts, they were mixed breeds, the outcome of persistent cross-breeding of a small imported pool with a larger indigenous one obtained through trade and capture. As for the cows, cattle were not imported in any quantities until the late eighteenth century, so that all the cow bones may be traced to an ultimate indigenous source. In other words, whether we argue that the animal bones from Oudepost reflect the way the Dutch invaded the wild food *or* the domesticated food base of the Khoikhoi, the process of colonial conquest and domination still emerges strongly from these findings. . . .

The Oudepost dig, like any other research project, started off clear and bright and gradually became convoluted, contradictory, and complex. The deeper we dug, the more we choked on the artifacts of conquest and the bones of subjugation. But for all the ominous messages of beads and pipes, there is a sweeter side to material things, one that breeds a gentler view. At Oudepost, such a vision is construed from two ostrich eggs excavated on the site, one bored with a single hole, the other carved with visions of an empire that extended far beyond this trivial rocky spur.

The bored egg is identical to those used to hold water by traditional hunters and herders to this day. It was excavated in the sand just beyond the lodge. Perfectly intact, stained dark from the soil, it lay there, as though in wait for later retrieval. The carved one came to us in fragments, washed out of the fort wall by the sea. It is decorated with a tree, not a pine or oak, such as may have grown in Europe or even by then at the Cape, but with a composite of tropical leaves, bracts, and trunk of palm trees, cycads, and tree ferns, such as flourish in low latitudes on the African and Indian coasts and the islands of Southeast Asia.

Both eggs evoke visions of their makers. A small Khoikhoi woman crests the dunes along the bay as the dawn mist rises from the sea. She squats in the sand, pulls two sticks from her bag, and makes a small fire. Warming her hands at the blaze for a moment, she reaches into the bag and removes an ostrich egg. She stands it carefully in the hot sand, then taps the top until it cracks, and, taking a pointed stick, chews it, and pushes the frayed end into the egg. She twirls the yolk until it curdles, sending forth a fragrant steam that announces that the meal is ready. Eating done, she scuffs the fire out and walks delicately to the water's edge to rinse the egg. Then she sets off toward the watering place. The fountain is muddy, but she digs into the sand until it pools and clears and, bending carefully, so as not to dislodge any of the beads around her forehead, she fills the egg, plugging its hole with a twist of grass.

Water slaps around as the egg bobs in her skin bag. It bumps up against a parcel of honey that she hopes to exchange for three glass beads. Later, as the day cools, she squats near the wall of the lodge and, lifting the egg, drinks deeply. She uses the last of the water to wash the soldiers' musk from her legs. She smiles at the thought of the sparkling beads tied carefully into a corner of her kaross, scoops a hollow in the sand, and carefully buries the empty egg, to wait there until she returns next week.

The soldier is tired. Inside he is still glowing a little, yet his legs ache as he sits on the fort wall watching the sea come in. Humming tunelessly, he turns to the egg that he and his mates ate last night. He reaches for the dagger that he keeps tucked into his belt, and begins to carve, imitating as he does the Danish sailor he once met, who decorated a walrus tooth, scoring the cream surface with lines and curves. A tree emerges under his blade. It looks like those he saw in Macassar last year. He wonders when he will smell the cardamom again, whether he will ever again taste a clove, and he smiles, remembering the veiled women, who seemed to tinkle as they minced past.

A sudden wave splashes against his leg. He starts. The egg smashes on the rocks below. Cursing, he turns back to the lodge. The woman is running toward some herders who have appeared over the hill. She calls out their names, skimming across the dunes like a curlew as she hastens home.

The Terracotta Army of Emperor Shihuangdi

ARTHUR COTTERELL

King Zheng, "the Tiger of Qin," was the first sovereign emperor (Shihuangdi) of China. He became ruler of Qin at the age of thirteen in 246 B.C., unifying China after a series of ruthless military campaigns in 221 B.C. Work may have begun on the emperor's tomb as early as 246 B.C., but intensified with unification. The emperor considered himself unique, so his sepulcher was to be the largest ever built. Later court histories write of more than 700,000 conscripts, many of them convicts, who worked on the tomb, the capital, and the royal palace. Shihuangdi's great burial mound measures more than 335 meters on each side and rises 43 meters above the surrounding country-side 40 kilometers east of Xianyang on the banks of the Wei River. Inside is said to lie a replica of the royal domains, with China's great rivers re-created in mercury flowing by some mechanical device into the ocean.

No one has yet excavated Shihuangdi's mound, which once lay in the middle of a large funerary park surrounded by a 5-kilometer outer wall. Instead, Chinese archaeologists have turned their attention to the surrounding features of the funerary landscape, with spectacular results. In the 1970s, they excavated a regiment of terracotta soldiers, armed cavalrymen, kneeling archers, and their officers—perhaps a ceremonial guard assigned to protect the eastern side of the tomb. The molded figures were finished with individual hairstyles, mustaches, and other features and were fully armed. Other finds near the tumulus include two half-scale bronze chariots and their horses as well as underground stables, some with mangers containing horses buried alive. Only a portion of the terracotta garrison has been excavated, and it is uncertain whether the royal tomb has been looted. Chinese scholars are taking their time and will not open the burial mound until they are satisfied that they have the facilities and expertise to do it scientific justice. We can confidently expect Shihuangdi's tomb to be one of the most spectacular excavations of the twenty-first century.

In the absence of a good firsthand account of the discovery in English, we use writer Arthur Cotterell's clear description of the army after partial excavation, from his book The First Emperor of China. *(This account has been heavily edited to shorten it.)*

Looking eastwards from the top of this mound, we could see the hangar-like roof covering Pit No. 1 of the terracotta army 1.5 kilometres away. We scrambled down the footpath, paused for a backward glance at the foot of the slope, then rejoined our companions in the car. Within a few minutes we turned into the forecourt of the museum, to find Mr. Yang Chen Ching, the curator, awaiting our arrival. On his head was the soft broad-rimmed hat worn by Shensi farmers, who know the power of the summer sun. After introductions and tea in his office, he kindly answered our questions about the amazing finds under his care.

As he explained, there are four pits altogether. Three of them contain pottery figures and horses; the other is empty. The largest one—known as Pit No. 1—was discovered in March 1974, when a series of wells was excavated in search of water to supply the local community. The pit's shape is rectangular, and it measures about 210 metres from east to west and 60 metres from north to south. It consists of a series of eleven parallel corridors, nine measuring 3 metres by 200 metres, and two measuring just under 2 metres by 200 metres. The narrower corridors run along the outside. At the east and west ends, a gallery runs from north to south, with five earthen ramps leading to the surface. There may have been two other entrances on the north and south sides as well. These subterranean chambers were skilfully built: the rammed earth surrounding the corridors and galleries prevented subsidence, while each chamber was paved with bricks and its wooden roof was supported by stout timber pillars and cross-beams. To prevent moisture seeping down from the surface, the roof was covered by woven matting and then a layer of clay.

No. 1 Pit is a military formation. The chambers are arranged in the battle order of an infantry regiment, which faces eastwards. Altogether it is estimated that there are 3,210 terracotta foot soldiers. They do not wear helmets; only Ch'in officers have these. But most of the infantry soldiers wear armour. These armoured men are divided into forty files; they stand four abreast in the nine wide corridors, and form two files in each of the narrow ones. The head of the regiment in the eastern gallery comprises a vanguard of unarmoured bowmen and crossbowmen, nearly 200 sharpshooters, drawn up in three north–south ranks. Their clothing is light cotton because they are fast moving, long-range fighters—the ancient equivalent of artillery. They would have fired their arrows from a distance, keeping away from hand-to-hand engagements, once contact was made with the enemy. The three ranks would have taken turns at firing, so as to keep up a continuous stream of arrows. The majority carried crossbows with a 200-metre shooting range.

Between these sharpshooters and the armoured infantry are six chariots and three unarmoured infantry squads. Each chariot is pulled by four terracotta horses and manned by a charioteer and one or two soldiers. The guards would have wielded long flexible lances, possibly bamboos measuring as much as 6 metres, in order to stop enemy soldiers from cutting off the heads of the horses. Two of the six chariots, however, seem to have had a special function. They were command vehicles, equipped with drums and bells. The officers riding on them could order the regiment to advance or retreat by striking these instruments. Officers wore headgear, mainly rode in chariots, and displayed badges of rank. Besides the groups of twelve unarmoured footmen who precede the six chariots, there are in the other three corridors squads containing thirty-two spearmen. Their spears might have been longer than the 2-metre ones belonging to the armoured infantry in the rear. Again these lightly dressed soldiers were probably mobile auxiliaries who co-operated with both the crossbowmen and the chariots.

In each of the narrow north and south corridors a line of soldiers faces outwards. Although these men were guarding the flanks, they have no shields. Ch'in soldiers did not use shields at all: their vigilance and bravery would have been thought sufficient protection on the battlefield. Even the armour worn by Ch'in troops covered only a relatively small portion of the body. This means that a regiment like the one in Pit No. 1 always took the offensive, always attacked. We know of the ferocity of Ch'in armies from the historical records, but not until these pottery figures were unearthed was it appreciated how much the strategy of Ch'in generals depended on taking the initiative on the battlefield. The troops under their command were certainly the most mobile of the time. They were also the best disciplined since the officers would not have hesitated to decapitate any soldier who disobeyed orders.

The terracotta soldiers definitely had real arms, Mr. Yang Chen Ching believed, and they were probably made from bronze. Little iron has been recovered from the pits. All the pits, however, were plundered for weapons by the rebel forces after the downfall of the Ch'in dynasty. Despite all the looting and destruction, various bronze weapons such as arrow heads, halberds, spear heads, swords, and crossbow triggers have been found. Over 1,400 bronze arrow heads have been recovered in the trial excavation of Pit No. 2 alone. On the other hand, the armour of the terracotta soldiers, sculpted in detail on the pottery figures, suggests that iron may have been used for this purpose. Even the heads of the rivets on the coats of mail have been modelled. The histories tell us that during the Chan Kuo period both iron mail coats and iron weapons existed; furthermore, the remains of an actual coat of mail were excavated in 1965 in Hopei province. It consisted of numerous iron slates, joined so that the top pieces pressed on the ones below them. At Mount Li seven different styles of mail coat have been found. They are excellently designed and reveal the advanced nature of ancient Chinese protective weapons. The Chinese investigators have concluded that a mail coat was put on and taken off over the head, the button for fastening it tight being on the upper right side, where the coat opens and closes.

The statues in Pit No. 1 are made from the heavy clay found in the vicinity of Mount Li. The advantage for the Ch'in potter-sculptor was that this type of clay was strong enough for large-scale pieces. Although some people find this difficult to believe, no two faces are alike. Each head is a personal portrait, and so far the excavators have not discovered two faces which are the same. Unlike the stereotyped funerary statues of other ancient rulers, these soldiers are modelled on living men. This individual portraiture of the soldiers is unique and remains unexplained. Mr. Yang Chen Ching suggested that the First Emperor might have wished to celebrate the unification of China, a country of many peoples, and that is why the statues buried in the pits exhibit all the varying physical features of the inhabitants of mainland East Asia. He also argued that they not only represent the multi-racial Ch'in empire, but also bear witness to the power of the ordinary people. And the time and energy spent on the figures in the pits—the largest ones ever discovered in China—show how important they were to the First Emperor. But as one might expect, a degree of standardization is apparent in the treatment of the torso. The body of each statue was manufactured separately. From the abdomen downwards the figure is solid, the weight being supported by the legs. The upper part of the body, including the head, is hollow and the forearms and hands, as well as the head, were added later. Each head is attached to the torso by an elongated cylindrical neck. Moulds must have been used, according to Mr. Yang Chen Ching. Individual details such as ears, beards, and head decoration were then sculpted, and finally the complete statue was brightly painted. In Pit No. 1 there were probably two colour schemes for the armoured infantrymen. One group had black armour slates with white rivets, gold buttons, and purple cords. Their cloaks were green, their trousers dark blue, and their shoes black with red laces. A second group wore brown slated armour with red rivets and orange buttons. . . .

Pit No. 2, situated about 20 metres north of Pit No. 1, holds slightly more than 1,400 warriors and horses divided into four groups. The construction of the second pit is similar to the first, but its more complicated layout reflects the greater variety of military personnel it contains. A projecting area at the northeastern corner is filled by a group of kneeling armoured archers, around which stand ranks of unarmoured spearmen. Immediately behind this vanguard come two units, one essentially a mixture of chariots and armoured cavalry, the other chariots and armoured infantry. The fourth and largest unit consists of sixty-four chariots. In their limited excavation of this pit the Chinese have unearthed two generals, or at least two unit commanders. One stood with the infantry at the back of the vanguard, the other on a command vehicle towards the rear of the chariots and armoured infantry unit. They both wear distinctive mail coats.

Pit No. 3 was dug from March to December 1977. It is a small irregular chamber, about one-seventh of the area of the first pit. It was pillaged in 206 B.C., but not burned by the rebels and appears to have been the place where the commander-in-chief was stationed. His war chariot is there, along with sixty-eight soldiers, many of whom are officers. The height of his guards is exceptional, being 1.9 metres (6 feet 2 inches) as opposed to an average of 1.8 metres (5 feet 9 inches) in Pit No. 1. Only the vanguard commander in the second pit is taller; he reaches 1.96 metres (6 feet 4 inches). The figure of the commander-in-chief, however, has not been discovered. There may be a connection between this fact and the huge Ch'in period tomb just 15 metres to the west of the third pit, though no one yet knows whether it will contain an actual interment or a terracotta statue. From the arrangement and personnel of Pit No. 3 there can be little doubt that it was the command headquarters of the pottery army. The soldiers are deployed to protect the commander-in-chief. Their armour is of two kinds: a light mail suited to rapid movement, and a heavier mail advantageous in close combat. Several of the weapons recovered had a ceremonial rather than a practical use, a fact which strengthens the argument for the importance of the third pit. Indeed, the pits can be seen as a single creation, although the fourth one is unfinished. Pit No. 3 is the controlling one for the entire 7,000-piece force. The rank of its missing commander would have been a high one, at least a foremost Ch'in minister, but until further investigations have been made, no one can be sure of his identity.

Han Burials in China

BRIAN FAGAN

The Chinese believe that archaeology has many lessons for the present. For thousands of years, Chinese philosophers speculated about the legendary past. More recently, Chairman Mao actively encouraged archaeological research. "Make use of the old ways for present purposes," he proclaimed, considering archaeology a way of promoting understanding of contemporary society in terms that are readily intelligible to everyone. For this reason, and because of endemic tomb robbing, archaeological research and conservation are tightly controlled in China. Long before Mao, archaeologists carried out lengthy excavations in the Huanghe Valley and recovered the legendary Shang civilization from the shadows of history. The same close government control brought scientists from the same academy to a hillside near Man-Zh'ieng in June 1968, when a detachment of soldiers discovered the subterranean burial chamber of Liu Sheng under a hill near the town. A few days later, the same soldiers came across the sealed tomb of his wife, Tou Wan, on a neighboring hillside.

The Han emperors were the longest-lived dynasty of Chinese rulers, assuming power in 206 B.C. and ruling China without interruption for four hundred years. They expanded their territory deep into Central Asia, developed the Great Silk Road, and sent trading missions deep into Southeast Asia. The emperor himself was the "Son of Heaven," and he presided over a despotic government administered by a vast bureaucracy of nobles and officials. He appointed his own relatives—who ruled harshly and in great state—to maintain the imperial presence throughout his domains. Liu Sheng was Emperor Wu-ti's elder brother and was appointed prince of Zhou-shan principality. He ruled for nearly forty years until his death in 113 B.C. Tou Wan survived him by about ten years. Their richly decorated tombs provide an extraordinarily detailed record of life at a Han court and of the wealth of the Chinese nobility more than two thousand years ago. The jade suits worn by the deceased noble and his wife, designed to ensure immortality, were made of thousands of finely crafted jade plaques joined with gold wire. Each suit alone, quite apart from the lavish artifacts that lay with the noble couple, probably took most of the lifetimes of several artisans to fabricate and fit.

I wrote this account of the discovery of the tombs in 1977, as part of Quest for the Past, *a book on major archaeological discoveries. The Chinese authorities have since* _reported the excavation of another jade-suited nobleman believed to be of somewhat earlier date._

The Han principality nearest Peking had a population of 600,000. Emperor Wu-ti appointed his elder brother Liu Sheng to be prince of this Chung-shan principality. Liu Sheng ruled for nearly forty years until his death in 113 B.C. His wife Tou Wan survived him for about ten years. Both were buried with elaborate imperial ceremony in royal graves dug deep into the barren Lingshang hillsides near the town of Man-Ch'eng. There they rested until June 1968, when a detachment of the People's Liberation Army made a dramatic archaeological discovery.

"One evening," wrote one of the soldiers involved, "comrades of the 12th Troop on night patrol discovered a subterranean structure." The excited soldiers immediately reported the find to their company headquarters. "When the company commander, Comrade Kou Chou-lin, heard the news, he leaped from his bed and drove many miles to the scene of the report," continued the soldier. Kou Chou-lin and his men made their way cautiously into the newly discovered cavern. They found themselves inside a vast chamber, "big enough to hold a thousand men, a feat of careful engineering, a veritable underground palace." The feeble light of their flashlights could not even reach the end of the tomb.

Kou Chou-lin stared in amazement. Everywhere he turned, his flashlight caught the glint of gold, silver, and jade. Bronze and clay pots stood in long, orderly rows. Kou Chou-lin trod delicately between the pots and peered at the inscriptions on the vessels. "Palace treasure of Chung-shan," he spelled out aloud. "This must be a very ancient tomb. We must report it at once." The soldiers retreated in awe, mounted an armed guard over their remarkable find, and reported the discovery to higher authority.

Within hours, the Academy of Sciences in Peking had archaeologists on the scene. They entered the tomb with bright lights and emerged in a state of great excitement. "This is the tomb of Liu Sheng, Prince of Chung-shan of the former Han," one archaeologist exclaimed. "It dates to about two thousand years ago."

Meanwhile, soldiers eagerly exploring further in the area noticed huge piles of rocky chips on a neighboring hillside. They poked around the piles and came across a sealed entrance to another cavern, a massive fortification of stone blocks sealed with molten iron. Was this another tomb? Under careful supervision, army demolition experts blasted open the entrance. It proved to be the sepulchre of Liu Sheng's wife Tou Wan. . . .

The archaeologists soon realized they had a formidable task ahead, one fully as complex and demanding as that facing Howard Carter when he cleared the tomb of Tutankhamun half a century before. Fortunately, by government fiat, they were able to rely on assistance from the military as well from experts on preservative methods. The best archaeological technicians in China were soon on the scene.

Liu Sheng's tomb was sealed by two brick walls. The cavity between them had been filled with molten iron that must have been smelted on the site. This task alone would have been a formidable undertaking. An entrance passageway blocked with earth and rocks led into the tomb itself. The excited archaeologists organized the clearance of the passage, then measured the dimensions of the huge rock cavern before them. Liu Sheng's sepulchre was 171 feet long, Tou Wan's somewhat larger. More than 64,000 cubic feet of rock had been laboriously dug from the solid hillsides to form the sepulchres. Even with modern equipment, it would require several hundred men at least a year to excavate the chambers. Liu Sheng and his wife employed thousands of laborers at enormous cost. . . .

Once through the passage, the archaeologists found themselves in an antechamber, off of which led two side passages. Liu Sheng's six carriages, sixteen horses, and eleven dogs lay in these defiles. He also took with him a horse-driven grindstone, complete with horses, and ample food and wine for a long journey. The antechamber itself led into a central chamber, originally hung with finely embroidered curtains that had decayed over the centuries. Both chambers had wooden walls and tiled roofs.

The central chamber held hundreds of fine vessels and figurines, laid out in rows. This chamber in turn led to a stone doorway and the burial chamber itself. Liu Sheng's coffin lay on a platform on the north side of the chamber; a bathroom was situated on the south side. A walkway extended around the stone-lined burial chamber. Tou Wan's sepulchre was of similar design.

For several incredible months, the archaeologists and their military assistants worked on clearing the two tombs. They removed more than 2,800 funerary objects from the sepulchres, an unbelievable treasure. There were magnificent bronze and gold vessels, gold, silver, and jade ornaments, fine clay vessels, lacquered vases, even fine silks. Everything was of the finest quality, of a magnificence that could only be associated with royalty. The soldiers looked on incredulously as the contents of the tombs were carefully cataloged and moved into the open air. Every piece bore signs of many hours of painstaking craftsmanship. Some were inscribed with details regarding their place of origin and cost.

Two bronze jugs from Tou Wan's tomb had come all the way from Shansi province. One of them was inscribed with a price: 840 cash. This, Chinese sources tell us, was twice the annual poll tax on a family of two adults and three children. . . .

Perhaps the most beautiful pieces from the two-thousand-year-old tombs are a lamp and an incense burner. Tou Wan's body was watched over by a gilt-bronze lamp modeled in the form of a young serving girl. The servant is kneeling, a lamp in her hands. Both the lamp and its shade are adjustable, so that the direction and intensity of its rays can be changed at will. The girl's head can be removed to fill the lamp. Smoke from the lamp was diverted into the body through the hollow right arm, so that the room remained clear of fumes. The lamp bears the words "Lamp of the Palace of Eternal Trust." We know that Tou Wan's grandmother lived in a palace of that name; the lamp may have been a wedding present to her granddaughter.

Liu Sheng took a magnificent incense burner with him to the next world. The bronze burner was shaped in the form of a precipitous mountain peak. Hunters cavort on its slopes as they pursue wild animals. The peak appears to float in clouds of inlaid silver and gold. When the incense was lit, the pungent smoke would swirl out through numerous holes in the burner to wreathe the mountain scene. It is an exquisite piece, far more refined than any burners found in earlier excavations.

Some of the other bronze vessels were equally magnificent. Two gilded wine containers modeled with intricate dragon and knob designs still glowed with lustrous color after two thousand years. A flying bird holding a round dish with three candlesticks formed an elegant lamp. The bronzes bore intricate patterns and the glitter of gold and silver inlay was to be seen everywhere. . . .

The corpses of Liu Sheng and Tou Wan . . . wore magnificent jade suits sewn together with gold thread. Although the Han emperors and their nobles were known to have been buried in such suits, this was the first time complete jade burial clothes had been found. Funeral superstitions about jade dated far back in China. Even simple farmers placed jade rings with the dead over four thousand years ago. The Han emperors and their nobles believed in Taoist magical traditions, traditions that called for the use of jade to stop up the nine orifices of the human body. Taoists believed that jade prevented the body from decaying. Many people apparently were content to place one jade object in each of the nine openings, but Liu Sheng and his wife went to the limit. They were buried in complete jade suits, evidently a privilege of only the most important and noble aristocrats. The rank of the corpse was also indicated by the material used to wire together the thousands of thin jade plaques that made up the suit. The emperor and his chosen favorites were allowed gold-threaded suits; slightly less prestigious people were accorded silver or bronze, according to their rank.

The experts who examined the intricate suits were amazed at the painstaking craftsmanship. Liu Sheng's suit consisted of 2,690 pieces of jade sewn together with 39,025 lengths of gold thread. Each piece of jade was cut into a small rectangular or square wafer 0.125 inch thick and perforated at each corner. Many were shaped to different angles of the body. The workmen used tiny saws with delicate teeth to saw the jade into pieces. The 0.03-inch corner holes were drilled with tubelike drills filled with abrasive sand. The gold thread was intricately woven into twelve-stranded wire, tied together with nine different knots. Each suit, carefully made to measure, was assembled in twelve separate sections, such as the head, gloves, or legs. Each section was then edged with red cloth and set aside until the death of its intended wearer. Before burial, the suits were tightly sewn together around the corpse, so that no part of the body was left exposed. The suited prince and princess were laid to rest in their coffins, their heads reposing on bronze pillows inlaid with gold. Liu Sheng was accompanied by an iron knife and two swords. Each corpse grasped two ceremonial jade crescents.

When first discovered, the jade-suited corpses were in a state of total disarray. As the bodies decomposed and the wooden coffins rotted to dust, the jade suits collapsed and the gold threads broke. All that remained was a tightly compacted jumble of dusty jade and gold. With infinite care, the excavators sorted the piles of priceless jade and removed the fragments to a laboratory in Peking for restoration. Laboratory experts tried to record the original position of each jade square. They fitted many of them in groups, using networks of wire, paper, and plaster of paris to solidify the fragile assemblages. Once in the laboratory, every piece was photographed and cleaned and the gold wire restored to its original state. Then Liu Sheng and Tou Wan's suits were reassembled piece by piece on aluminum frames from the reconstructed fragments. The experts estimated that each jade suit took a single craftsman more than ten years to complete. The price of eternity came high for royalty in Han China. But it was all in vain: all that remained of Liu Sheng, a man who ruled over and taxed 600,000 people, was a handful of teeth. . . .

The archaeologists recalled that Liu Sheng was a corrupt and depraved man. Historians wrote that he was "fond of wine and women." One of the bronze wine jars found among the many in his tomb bore a revealing inscription, a prayer for prosperity: "May good food fill your gate, expand your girth, extend your life, keep illness at bay." Both Liu Sheng and his wife enjoyed lavish funerals at a time when thousands of their people were starving as a result of terrible floods. But by destroying their bodies, history has exacted a just retribution.

The Princess of
Khok Phanom Di, Thailand

CHARLES HIGHAM

Southeast Asia remains one of the great archaeological gaps on the world map. Yet humans have flourished there for almost 2 million years. Exciting discoveries await archaeologists in the great river valleys of the region, which were home to small groups of hunter-gatherers throughout the Ice Age. In 8000 B.C., the Southeast Asian main-land extended far offshore, most of it low-lying marshland intersected by several major river systems. As sea levels rose as a result of global warming, so the continental shelf shrank, forcing Stone Age hunter-gatherer populations back toward higher ground. The major river systems of Southeast Asia are much reduced versions of earlier rivers, each with its own fertile delta. All of them flood seasonally, inundating large areas of farm-land with shallow water in which long-stalked, fast-growing rice can be grown. These river valleys have been the homelands of complex societies for many centuries, fertile enclaves surrounded by higher ground where deciduous, drought-resistant forest and moist tropical forest flourish. The same rivers formed important communication arteries for many thousands of years.

The staple crop in ancient Southeast Asia was rice, domesticated somewhere in south-ern or southeastern Asia and southern China well before 5000 B.C. For more than four thousand years, autonomous rice-farming societies flourished throughout Southeast Asia, but we still know little about them, as few archaeological sites of this period have been discovered or excavated. Charles Higham (b. 1939), professor of anthropology at the University of Otago, Dunedin, New Zealand, has spent many years investigating the early peoples of Southeast Asia, researching the origins of farming and more complex societies. One of his early excavations was at Khok Phanom Di in Thailand, an early rice-farming community that lay close to coastal mangrove swamps between 2000 and 1400 B.C. The site, now nineteen kilometers from the sea, covers almost five hectares and is twelve meters deep. It contains abundant evidence for rice cultivation, already a staple of Southeast Asian life for centuries.

Many people assumed that early rice farmers lived in simple, egalitarian communi-ties, with little differentiation in wealth between different members of society. Burials often provide evidence of social ranking, for the dead were often buried with all their ornaments and prized possessions, many of them symbols of rank. To Higham's surprise, he discovered the grave of a wealthy woman, perhaps a potter, whom he named the "Princess of Khok Phanom Di." This important find provided the first indications that Southeast Asian society had been quite complex long before Indian merchants made contact with the region more than two thousand years ago. As this cultural influence strengthened, local rulers assumed the role of divine kings, as a patchwork of volatile but prosperous states arose in lowland areas, supported by rice cultivation and fishing. Between 800 and 1430, the dazzling and glittering Khmer civilization flourished in the central basin of Cambodia, marked by a frenzy of temple and palace building, by great structures like Angkor Wat and Angkor Thom, which replicated the heavenly world in stone. But some of the roots of these spectacular civilizations lay in much humbler, and hitherto unknown, societies, like that at Khok Phanom Di.

Charles Higham kindly wrote this firsthand account of the Princess of Khok Phanom Di specially for this volume.

In 1957, I anticipated two years in the army before going up to Cambridge to study archaeology. But in the nick of time, the government of the day decided that anyone born after 1 October 1939 would be excused national service. So my parents had wisely seen to it that I was on the right side of the ledger by nineteen days, and they cast about for some way of keeping me out of mischief. Their research led to the discovery that the Institute of Archaeology offered a two-year postgraduate diploma course, so fresh from school and only seventeen years old, I found myself studying the archaeology of Iron Age and Roman Europe at London University.

The Institute of Archaeology was then situated in St. John's Lodge, a Regency home of stately proportions in Regent's Park. I count myself very lucky indeed to have studied there, for under the aegis of Sir Mortimer Wheeler, we were taught not only the theory, but the practice of archaeology in the field. I was soon introduced by my teachers to the excitement of discovery. Kathleen Kenyon was then digging at Jericho, and Max Mallowan came back after each summer season from his excavations at Nimrod. I well remember the laboratory where we could see at first hand the magnificent ivories from Fort Shalmaneser. It was an egalitarian institution, staff and students sharing tables at morning and afternoon tea. On one such occasion, I found myself beside Mallowan's wife, Agatha Christie. On another, I met Margaret Murray, then aged ninety-nine, who had worked with Flinders Petrie in Egypt.

As if this were not enough to whet a young and impressionable appetite, I was also able to help with fieldwork in a Roman city, a French hill fort, and painted caves, and to tour sites in Sicily. I soon learned two cardinal principles: excavation can be terminally tedious if you find nothing, and one of the most absorbing and exciting of activities if you are lucky enough to uncover something rare, beautiful, or significant hidden from human gaze for centuries.

Having finished my postgraduate diploma, I moved fifty miles north to Cambridge to begin my degree. It was certainly different. No mixing of young and old in the tea room, but still plenty of opportunities for further fieldwork. One long summer was spent excavating at Nea Nikomedia, a small Neolithic mound on the Plain of Macedon. Every day, we drove out to the site and through a village called Vergina. I recall passing a large, grass-covered mound in that village, but never gave it much thought. It was only later that I read that a Greek archaeologist had discovered within it the tomb of Philip of Macedon, father of Alexander the Great, along with a treasure trove of wonderful grave offerings. The track for aspiring archaeologists then was to complete your first degree, complete your doctoral dissertation, and then, the most difficult of hurdles, seek your first academic post.

After achieving the first two objectives, I found myself part of a diaspora of young archaeologists who colonised new or growing university departments in Australia, New Zealand, Africa, and America. My destination was Otago, the world's most southerly university. Soon after my arrival in 1967, I received a letter from Chester Gorman, then a young graduate student in Hawaii: would I look at some material which he had excavated in Thailand? This introduced me to Southeast Asia and its prehistoric past. I excavated with him in the remote jungles of northern Thailand, and at the prehistoric cemetery of Ban Chiang. It was in 1981, just after finishing my excavations at another Bronze Age cemetery at Ban Na Di, that my Thai colleague Pisit asked if I would like to visit a newly discovered site situation about an hour's drive from Bangkok. This was Khok Phanom Di.

Like a Middle Eastern tell, you can see the mound from miles away; it lies like a great stranded whale, dominating the flat flood plain of the Bang Pakong River. We drove up the steep track and alighted in the grounds of the Buddhist temple on the top. There, surrounded by a bamboo fence, was a small square just excavated by a Thai archaeologist. A ladder provided an invitation to explore, and, rung by rung, I descended into the gloom.

My eyes traced layer after layer, each downward step representing centuries of occupation. I found myself at one stage looking into the hollow eye sockets of a prehistoric person, whose skull lay embedded still in the walls of the excavation. Finally, about nine metres down, I came across the thick shell middens laid down by the first settlers. At that time, the sea lapped the site, for the shellfish came from cockles which live on mudflats. During my ascent to the sunlight, I made a resolution: one day I would return and excavate a large area of this mound. I had a hunch that it might provide some vital clues on the early development of rice farming, for one pottery vessel found deep in the deposits had already provided a sample of charred rice grains.

But one of the lessons I had imbibed at the Institute of Archaeology is that one does not start an excavation until any previous fieldwork is fully published. So for three years, my Thai students and I dedicated ourselves to the analysis of the material we had unearthed at Ban Na Di. Over eighty burials and all the grave goods, figurines, complete pots, and rice remains had to be given due attention. But by 1984, I felt able to put together grant proposals, for Khok Phanom Di would require considerable resources. One by one, my approaches met with success, and I could plan an excavation square covering an area of ten by ten metres, covered with a huge steel roof with a thirteen-metre span. My former Thai students, now back in their own country and working for the Fine Arts Department, joined the field team and at last, in late December 1984, we began. I was particularly fortunate that Rachanie Thosarat agreed to join me as codirector of the excavation. Time and again, her sharp eye and meticulous skill turned up discoveries that most would have missed.

Our square was located in the middle of the mound, placed there by the orders of the abbot, for it would not involve cutting down any of the trees. The first few weeks saw us digging down through the latest deposits, during which time the occupants had used the area for fashioning and firing their pottery vessels. But at a depth of a metre or so, we came across a change in the soil texture: it became lighter and more sandy. And before long, our careful cleaning of the surface revealed a promising shape, for there we picked out a silhouette of marbled dark soil cut into the sand in the form of a human grave. That was not all, for alongside it we detected a line of clay, looking like a wall foundation.

As the days progressed, and we gradually continued on our way down, we began to pick up a pattern. The first grave was one of a row; the wall turned out to be part of a building, raised on a platform behind the line of graves. We were becoming increasingly absorbed as our trowels traced out the form of whole pottery vessels, some beautifully decorated with curvilinear designs, and polished to a lustrous black finish. Structures of any form are rare in prehistoric Southeast Asia, because people sensibly lived in stilt houses to avoid monsoon flooding. So our keen anticipation in finding the raised platform chamber quickened as we identified a central grave, containing the remains of a woman. She was interred with several pots, thousands of small disc beads, and a clay anvil in the form of a mushroom which she had used to fashion pots. Alongside her lay the skeleton of a child, whose head rested on a large circular disc of shell. Viewed from the platform, I could look down the row of skeletons and see the remains of men, women, children, and even a tiny grave with the intertwined bones of two newly born infants, probably twins. It looked like a family group, running through a couple or more generations.

We recorded, drew, measured, and lifted the bones before proceeding on our downward journey. It was now February, the weather was getting hotter with every passing day but under our roof, we entered a world of our own. One of the prehistoric women had been buried directly over a headless man, and other burials began to appear: a circular grave containing an infant resting within two large pottery vessels, more silhouettes. It was on 13 March that my Thai colleague Amphan and I found ourselves tracing a straight line: on one side, white ash from a prehistoric fire; on the other, the marbled soil that promised to be another grave. He was always the optimist, I the pessimist, so we wagered on whether this would indeed turn out to be our fifteenth burial. We inched our way along the line. At the point where, by all our past experience it should have

Skeletons in the grave of the "Princess of Khok Phanom Di," Thailand.

turned left or right, it obstinately carried on, straight as a die. We passed the three-metre mark before it finally wavered, and turned to the left. Amphan grinned: it must be a grave, and a big one too. After another metre on its new course, it turned again and finally, we traced its complete course. It was the largest grave cut we had ever seen in prehistoric Thailand. Now came the exciting bit, to inch our way down through the marbled fill and seek the person within.

Of course, I wanted to do this, but running an excavation, even with as skilled a codirector as Rachanie, involves many responsibilities. Twenty or more people would be working in other parts of the excavation square, and there was a constant flow of questions and decisions to be taken. Bernard Maloney was coming and going from the area round the site, where he was taking cores through the soft sediments to procure pollen samples. These would later enable him to reconstruct the ancient environment. Jill Thompson was running the flotation apparatus, and processing a sample of each layer into order to extract the tiny fragments of plants, including the precious remains of rice. Then there were the people cleaning and packing all the finds. It was rather like a military operation, where the general rarely wields a rifle. All I wanted was to be left alone with a trowel and this monster grave. But instead I watched as I passed by, as Jacqui Pilditch and Rachanie delicately picked away at the fill.

I had imagined that we would find a deep grave, but felt rather disappointed when the outline of a pot rim, and then a second, emerged only twenty centimetres down. The pots were different from others too. Rather than reflecting with a lustrous black burnish, they were rather dull earthenware. But then came the first of many surprises, for these pots turned out to be balanced on top of a growing pyramid of circular cylinders of clay, each of which, we felt, was destined 3,500 years before to be fashioned into a vessel. It as at one of these heaps that Rachanie came across a hint of red, which swelled into a pool of what looked like blood. But it was in fact, powdered red ochre. A gentle probe with one of our dental picks, and there, revealed, was a patch of yellowish bone, part of a human skull.

Now that we knew where we were, the time had come to uncover the whole skeleton. First, the overlying clay cylinders and pots were catalogued and removed and then, by gradual degrees, we brushed, picked, and scraped away. By the right ankle, we found a shell containing two round smooth pebbles, lying beside a clay anvil. The pebbles had flattened facets, the result of constantly polishing and smoothing clay pots before firing, to give them their lustrous sheen. The legs were covered in the broken remains of several such pots, which had been used as vehicles for complex incised decorative motifs. As Jacqui uncovered the pots, Barbara Friedell and Mardys Whiteman, two volunteers, followed down the length of the body from the skull. The person who was now a central object of interest for all the excavation team had been buried with a headdress, for we found the shell components attached to the skull. Over the chest, we gradually revealed two matching shell discs, each with a central horn-like projection, and each so thin as to be translucent. But it was the chest area that attracted most attention, for it was literally covered with a carpet of tiny shell disc beads, over which lay a set of large white I-shaped beads still lying as if strung together into a necklace. A shell bangle covered the left wrist. By now, we had uncovered enough of the pelvis to indicate that the grave had contained a woman, who was immediately christened the Princess.

As luck would have it, the following day the director general of the Thai Fine Arts Department, and his extensive entourage, were coming to visit the excavation. I decided to place a shroud over the grave, and invite Khun Taweesak to introduce her to the television cameras and the press. Reporters crowded round and the cameras rolled and, to my consternation, I found myself marshaling every word of my halting Thai to describe the burial to an audience of millions on the Thai national television news. But such publicity raises security problems.

I am asked from time to time if I ever feel it wrong to excavate in prehistoric cemeteries, and my answer is that, if there are no known living descendants who object, I see my role as being that of a scientist, trying to illuminate an extinct society. But I must admit that I felt a pang as I looked down on the body of our Princess, particularly when I had to review overnight security. Looting is a serious problem as artefacts are always in demand to satisfy the jackdaw mentality of ignorant tourists or greedy collectors. So I decided that after photography and recording, it would be prudent to remove the unique ornaments from the grave. As I eased her bangle from her wrist, I felt an uneasy kinship with this long dead woman.

There remains the thousands of beads on her chest, disposed in row after row. Jacqui Pilditch recorded the direction and number of layers of these rows, and came to the conclusion that she was buried wearing at least two upper garments. When the time came to remove her bones, I decided to take out the upper body in a block and turn it over for excavation in well-lit conditions. And as we pared away the soil, we discovered that the rows of beads continued across her back. Still iridescent, the Princess must have dazzled in reflected sunlight in life. When we finally returned all these finds, along with the human remains, to the laboratory, we counted 120,787 shell disc beads.

Nancy Tayles is our project biological anthropologist, and she has found that the Princess died when in her mid-thirties. She had well formed wrist muscles, perhaps as a result of preparing clay for making pots, and had borne one or more children. I have already mentioned a circular grave containing an infant buried within two pots. This lay to the south of the Princess. In a northerly direction and just two metres away, we found another grave. This one lay on exactly the same orientation, with the head pointing to the rising sun, and was the right size for an adult burial. Stratigraphically, it was an exact contemporary of the Princess. We wondered what sort of person it might reveal.

Archaeology is full of surprises, and this grave, burial 16, was no exception. Again, we encountered a heap of round clay cylinders, below which lay an almost exact replica of the Princess's burial, except that it involved an infant aged about fifteen months at death. There was the same generous application of red ochre over the body, the same profusion of shell disc beads, this time numbering 12,247, and a shell bangle had been placed over the left wrist. Remarkably, a tiny clay anvil lay beside the right ankle. We speculated at the time, and still feel strongly, that this was the Princess's daughter.

We could easily have stopped excavations at this point and still have obtained enough information for a long and demanding period in the laboratory. But in fact, the excavation season was still young. Ahead, we faced the searing heat of April and May, and the breaking of the monsoon. We had only reached a depth of 2.5 metres, and knew we still had at least another 3.5 to go before reaching the natural substrate. I had reached a tally of 16 burials, but when, in July, we reached the last grave, it was to bring our total to 155. We found that under the Princess, graves were concentrated in clusters. There were some remarkable and most unusual finds to come. The pelvic area of one woman contained a ball of partially digested food, the remains of her last meal. This together with some excrement found with another person allowed us unique insight into the diet of these early inhabitants of Southeast Asia, for we extracted rice husks, fish bones and scales, the hair from mice, even a beetle which prefers life in rice stores. Did the people store their rice and have trouble with vermin infestation?

In many cases, we found the remains of beaten-bark or asbestos-fibre shrouds, and the wooden biers on which the dead were laid in their graves. We found the pattern of postholes suggesting burial in collective wooden tomb structures, and identified the ebb and flow of grave wealth as the generations succeeded each other. But when finally, in July 1985, we struck the natural soil under the mound at a depth of 6.8 metres, it was with relief and a wonderful sense of achievement. I could look back on seven months of constant but rewarding work, and forward to at least a decade of analysis as we published our finding volume by volume. We would find that the site was occupied from 2000 to 1500 B.C., that our superimposed burials represented about seventeen to twenty generations, and that, indeed, the inhabitants grew rice in the marshland behind the mangrove fringe. I think that the wealth of the Princess reflects her expertise as a potter, and that the loss of her infant daughter, already the owner of a miniature potter's anvil, was a serious blow to the future of her line, for the people of Khok Phanom Di employed pots in an exchange network to obtain, in return, exotic shell jewellery.

Whenever I return to Thailand to conduct further excavations, I always try and visit my friends, the monks and villagers of Khok Phanom Di. But I reserve a special affection for the abbot, whose decision it was to excavate where we did. But for him, the Princess would still lie, undisturbed in her oblivion, sleeping there for I wonder how many more millennia before archaeologists return to Khok Phanom Di.

Late Ice Age Hunters
in Tasmania

RHYS JONES

Archaeologists still make fascinating discoveries in the most remote and unlikely terrain. Southwestern Tasmania is mantled with dense rain forest, forest so thick as to be practically impenetrable. At the time of the first European settlement in the early nineteenth century, the sparse Aboriginal population lived on Tasmania's coasts, not in the rain forest. But when archaeologists Don Ranson and Rhys Jones went up the Gordon River into the heart of the forest in 1981, they were astounded to find stone artifacts in one of the riverbanks. They were following up a report from geomorphologist Kevin Kiernan, who had visited a cave on the nearby Fraser River in which he had picked up stone artifacts. The cavern itself had been occupied at a time during and immediately after the late Ice Age when southwestern Tasmania was open tundra and the climate much colder than it is today.

Over the past decade, excavations in the heart of the rain forest, largely supplied by helicopter, have produced evidence of human occupation in southwestern Tasmania as early as 29,000 years ago. Humans continued to live in this rugged terrain throughout the coldest millennia of the late Ice Age, hunting red wallabies and visiting at least twenty caves in the region. These people, the contemporaries of the well-known Cro-Magnon of western Europe, lived on Tasmania at a time when the island was joined to the mainland by a land bridge resulting from the low sea levels of the late Ice Age. When European explorers first landed on Tasmania in the late 1770s, the Aborigines who greeted them had been living in complete isolation for more than nine thousand years, cut off from the mainland by rising post–Ice Age sea levels.

Archaeologist Rhys Jones (b. 1946) was interviewed by Hemisphere *magazine soon after his initial investigations in the rain forest. His remarks provide a sense of the excitement and immediacy of unexpected archaeological discovery in a very tough environment.*

Southwest Tasmania is nowadays covered by an extremely dense rain forest. It is probably one of the most inhospitable parts of the world, so dense that in one hard morning's walking through it recently we covered only three hundred metres. Often, if you are making a survey with a twenty-metre tape you can't see the person on the other end, because there are trees everywhere—horizontal rain forest. When the first white men came to Tasmania in the early 1800s, no Aborigines lived within this country. Aboriginal occupation was tightly coastal: that is, you had a narrow coastal rim a few hundred metres wide kept open by fire, with the people able to live on the sea shore. Inland, in the mountains, with this very dense rain forest and huge rivers, there was just no occupation whatever.

Now, earlier this year, we went up the Gordon River—one of the swiftest-flowing rivers in all Australia, that just tears through this extremely wild country—right up to its junction with the Denison River. In the heartland of the south-west wilderness area, I noticed that on a bank a great tree, a *nothotasus*, had fallen down, taking some of the earth with it. We stopped the little boat we were in, walked up to the bank, and found stone implements, stone tools. After-wards we found more, *in situ*, buried in a clay deposit on the high river bank.

Now this was the first evidence we have had of any prehistoric occupation of this region by man—a very interesting discovery. But since, this discovery has triggered off a series of other searches, leading to our joint expedition when we went to a huge limestone cave just off the Franklin River, also in the heartland of the south-west wilderness area of Tasmania. The cave is one of the richest archaeological sites ever found in Australia. . . . For example, in one small exca-vation we made, about a metre square, we were getting of the order of 100,000 flakes per cubic metre. A flake is a piece of stone formed when you take a chert, or very fine-grained stone, and you strike it with a hammer stone, perhaps a piece of quartzite. The force of the percussion or blow detaches a flake of stone which has very sharp edges and which can be used to cut, say, meat, sinew, or fur, or which can be used as a scraper. With a bevelled edge it can be used for taking bark from trees and sticks and used for making spears and so on. It was with these flakes or stone tools that the Aborigines were able to make all their other tools—all their wooden tools. . . .

The cave itself is in a limestone cliff, about thirty metres off the Franklin River. Almost all of the caves I have seen in Australia are sink holes—Koonalda Cave, a sink hole! Devil's Lair, a sort of sink hole! and so on. A sink hole is formed when water, say a river, gets into limestone and works its way down to the next layer and successive layers, forming a vertical trap. These caves are often animal traps. Although you often find animal bones in such caves, it is something totally natural, and nothing to do with man. It is very rare indeed that you get any human occupation of any limestone cave in Australia, and when you do, the occupation is of brief episodes, with odd visits over say ten thousand years.

In this cave, however, it is totally different. The cave is like an aircraft hangar. You can walk erect into it for almost two hundred metres into the cliff. The hole is on the side of a vertical cliff and is about forty metres wide and fifty metres high. Inside, it opens into a cavern, about the size of a house.

When I first saw the cave, I was following the person who first found it, Kevin Kiernan, a geomorphology student at the University of Tasmania. A group of speleologists—people interested in caves—had found it in 1977, but not realised that it contained evidence of human occupation. But Kevin went back to the cave early in 1981 and found these objects he thought might be stone tools. He showed them to my colleague, Don Ranson, who works with the Tasmanian National Parks and Wildlife Service. Don said they were definitely stone tools and that this was an extremely interesting and exciting site.

So we got together. As I said, I was following Kevin; it was getting dark, the rain was pouring down and I was getting cold; we had been going up the river all day, up the rapids, and carrying our gear on portage, having to take stuff out of the boat, climb with it over wet slippery rocks and around waterfalls, then repack the boats, and so on.

. . . We were up to our waists in water—cold water—pushing the rubber dinghy. Anyway, we eventually stopped on the side of a limestone cliff—it was getting dark—and we had to take our packs and gear out of the rubber boat, climb up a slippery, wet muddy slide and into the forest. I had closed my mind to everything, I was just following the person in front and trying to avoid these wet branches hitting me in the face. Suddenly I was aware of this light in front— as if I was in a huge clearing in the middle of the forest. I thought, "that's funny"—what I had not realised was that I had actually walked into the cave without knowing it, that I was already thirty metres inside. You can see how easy it is to get in—it is like a huge, curved shell.

Now what we had to do was to try to find the depth of deposit in the cave and get some idea of the content. We laid out a little square and began to excavate and when we did, found what I have already said is one of the richest sites in Australia. To give you some idea of the richness: we put stuff into a sieve and washed the sieve in the Franklin River, and just one sieve would have something like one thousand or two thousand flakes—beautiful sharp, shiny little flakes—and between a hundred and three hundred bones of animals the people had hunted. I estimate that the whole site could have of the order of 10 to a 100 million artefacts in it and that makes it one of the richest sites ever found in Australia.

. . . This was probably a base camp in which between thirty and fifty people camped for say a few weeks a year. If you are camping on the floor and the flakes are there they get covered by the dirt and clay. When you come on to the place next you have to make them again. So this is the pattern. You get a build-up of deposits through the thousands of years, with each group coming in bringing their own new materials.

When we excavated, we found on the top a whole series of hearths, where people had been camping. These were charcoal hearths, very, very rich, with lens-like pieces of black charcoal and underneath, burnt earth.

*Archaeologist Don Ranson fights his way through dense
Tasmanian rain forest.*

. . . When the people lit a fire, they would make a shallow depression and
light their fire inside, then leave it. The next people who came along made a
fire, making their own depression and so on. You get an adding-up effect, one
depression on top of another, one set of raw cinders and charcoal on top of the
other.

Now underneath these hearths, we found something most interesting and
exciting—a series of angular deposits of limestone. These angular fragments had
fallen from the roof, and we believe, under different climatic conditions than at
present.

We have not done the tests yet; I have right here . . . the charcoal to be
carbon dated. What we want to test is whether this rubble was formed in different climatic conditions—in particular during the last Ice Age, between twelve
and eighteen thousand years ago.

During the Ice Age this country was quite different: in the immediate area
of this cave there were glaciers in the high mountain valleys all around and
instead of having trees everywhere, you had open country, like the tundra of

northern Russia, Alaska, or northern Canada. In such tundra conditions, it is cold and dry, though with the glaciers up above. The only trees would have been a gallery of rain forest just on the side of the rivers, where they were sheltered and irrigated by the water.

Now the marvellously interesting analogue is that in this region, this arctic—no, antarctic region—equivalent to the tundra of the arctic, you again have large numbers of stone tools and the bones of the animals that have been killed. So we are going to test the idea that here we have evidence of Ice Age man in south-west Tasmania. . . .

Almost nowhere in Australia do you get a very good picture of what the hunting strategy was like in the time we are talking about, say more than ten thousand years ago. In most caves we can find owl pellets or the bones of Tasmanian Devils. But we do not find the prey of humans. Now in this site we have got the prey of humans. The bones suggest that what the people were doing was hunting one or two species only. It was an extremely narrow targetting strategy. They were eating several sorts of wallaby, mostly red-necked wallabies, and some wombats, and that's about all. . . . We can tell this from the bones. What we have are jaw-bones—upper and lower jawbones—and the long bones of the leg, leg-bones of wallabies. These have all been smashed in half or in bits; you can see the smash marks where the bones have been put between two stones to get to the marrow. A large proportion of the bones has been charred, forming a bone charcoal. There is no way you could have that combination—of broken bones of only certain body parts with quite a large percentage charred: these are the remains of human middens. These middens are going to give us a tremendously interesting picture—almost a unique one—of the hunting way of life of the people in this area, perhaps during the Ice Age. . . .

Before 23,000 years ago, Tasmania was an island, much as now, with the sea more or less at its present level. But around that time the world was getting colder. More and more water was being locked up in the ice sheets, the ice sheets expanded and the level of the sea dropped one hundred metres, exposing a great dry plain between Tasmania and Australia. Calculations from world temperature curves show this plain was opened up about 24,000 years ago.

Now what Sandra Bowdler has are remains of man in this cave off north-west Tasmania about 23,000 years old—a marvellous conjunction of events. It shows that as soon as this gate was opened people took the opportunity to go there.

What interests me about these south-western sites is that here you have the extreme climatic place. Think of the great adventure of man coming out of Asia, early man from, say, Java or South China, managing to cross the great water barriers between Asia and Australia, getting to the great tropical areas of New Guinea and northern Australia, then eventually colonising the continent, and coming to south-eastern Australia. Eventually the great route to Tasmania opens and they take it. Somehow here they are, having gone from the tropics down through the deserts and into the high latitudes, and suddenly here is the extreme colonisation. Here are people, moving inexorably, impelled into empty space. Here they find themselves in full Arctic conditions. No other people out of Asia, if Aborigines are that, experienced the southern ice sheets. This is the one place in the southern hemisphere where human beings lived on the edge of the great ice sheet. Recent research on deep sea cores suggests that about eighteen thousand years ago the full unbroken ice sheet was as close to southern Tasmania as Canberra is: the ice sheet was about a thousand kilometres to the south. You can imagine that in front of this ice sheet you have a whole sea of icebergs floating up past the Tasmanian coast.

Here we have then in a cave like this: human beings who are experiencing the great climatic event, the only ones in the south because only Tasmania is that far south. What I find most interesting is to think of the world, the globe, back in the last Ice Age, twelve to eighteen thousand years back. Everywhere in the world men were hunters: there was no agriculture or industry. In the northern hemisphere you can go to the Magdalenian Caves of France, where the great cave artists were, and find evidence of cave men. The northern ice sheet was as close to them in the north as the southern ice sheet would have been to early men in Tasmania.

A Paleo-Indian Bison Kill

Joe Ben Wheat

Who were the first Americans? When did they cross from Siberia into North America, what route did they take, and how did they survive in an uninhabited continent? These questions are among the most controversial in all archaeology. Even after more than a century of scientific investigations, we still lack definitive answers. A broad consensus among archaeologists places first settlement at the very end of the Ice Age, perhaps some fifteen thousand years ago, with small groups of Paleo-Indians (as they are called) moving southward into the heart of the continent as the northern ice sheets retreated. For years, archaeologists assumed that the first settlers were little more than big-game hunters who preyed on herds of now-extinct large Ice Age mammals, such as the mammoth, mastodon, and steppe bison. This misleading portrait came from excavations of big-game kill sites on the North American Plains, where hundreds, sometimes thousands, of large animal bones give an almost overwhelming impression of hunting at the expense of all other activities. But recent research in other parts of North America has provided abundant evidence that Paleo-Indians subsisted off a very wide range of plant and animal foods indeed. Just like later Native Americans, they had an encyclopedic knowledge of wild plant foods and different environments, which enabled them to live successfully in a wide variety of harsh and demanding climates.

Even if the stereotype of big-game hunters is misleading, some of the most spectacular archaeological finds in North America result from successful large mammal hunts thousands of years ago. Such events, conducted for millennia on foot, were probably rare events, involving close collaboration between several small Paleo-Indian bands. Bison are difficult animals to stalk and drive, so a successful hunt was an important occasion, providing food for nomadic hunting bands for many weeks. The techniques for butchering dozens of animals at once were as efficient as ancient hunting methods, for much of the meat was dried or pounded up to make pemmican, a vital food on the march.

Joe Ben Wheat's (b. 1916) excavation of a successful Paleo-Indian bison hunt of eight thousand years ago at the Olsen–Chubbuck site in Colorado reconstructs all the drama of a long-forgotten game drive from a silted-up and bone-filled gully. This is painstaking archaeological discovery, involving meticulous excavation techniques, precise three-dimensional recording, months of animal-bone analysis, and plain common sense to relive a dramatic hunt at a time when only a few thousand people lived in North America. Wheat's account comes from his monograph "The Olsen–Chubbuck Site."

Down in the valley the little stream flowed gently southward. Pleasant groves of trees were heavy with their new burden of early summer leaves. Here and there small herds of bison were drinking. In the lush prairie bottoms, paralleling the stream and occasionally crossing it, were the main bison trails. Those currently in use were narrow grooves cut into the sod. Older abandoned trails were visible; some had become small rivulets emptying runoff water into the stream, but others had become filled with earth and grass, and were visible as narrow, bright green ribbons against the paler green of the less well fertilized prairie. For countless years, the bison each spring had moved gradually northward and eastward, along similar trails, up the smaller tributaries such as this one, into their summer grazing ranges. To the east, the prairie sloped gently upward to the level High Plains country, and narrow, undulating, bison trails led to the grassland there. Out of the valley bottom, other trails led westward to grazing grounds in the uplands near a low divide. On the approach to this western divide, the slope at first steepened sharply, then flattened out into a small basin before rising gradually again to a low pass into the valley beyond. At one time, this narrow basin had been drained by a small stream which carried runoff waters to the southeast. However, an abandoned bison trail had gradually diverted the flow of this stream, and in the process had become a gully, or arroyo, some 2 or 3 meters wide and about 2 meters deep. Seeps and small pools lined the sides and bottom of this arroyo. To the north, a small herd of 200 to 300 long-horned bison—cows, bulls, yearlings, and young calves—were grazing in the small valley. A gentle breeze was blowing from the south.

As the bison grazed, a party of hunters approached from the north. Quietly, under cover of the low divide to the west and the steep slope to the east, the hunters began to surround the grazing herd. Moving slowly and cautiously, keeping the breeze in their faces so as not to disturb the keen-nosed animals, they closed in on the herd from the east, north, and west. Escape to the south was blocked by the arroyo. Now the trap was set.

Suddenly the pastoral scene was shattered. At a signal, the hunters rose from their concealment, shouting and yelling, and waving robes to frighten the herd. Spears began to fall among the animals, and at once the bison began a wild stampede toward the south. Too late, the old cows leading the herd saw the arroyo and tried to turn back, but it was impossible. Animal after animal pressed from behind, spurred on by the shower of spears and the shouts of the Indians now in full pursuit. The bison, impeded by the calves, tried to jump the gully, but many fell short and landed in the bottom of it. Others fell kicking, twisting, and turning on top of them, pressing those below ever tighter into the confines of the arroyo. In a matter of seconds, the arroyo was filled to overflowing with a writhing, bellowing mass of bison, forming a living bridge over which a few animals escaped. Now the hunters moved in and began to give the coup de grace to those animals on top, while underneath, the first trapped animals kept up the bellows and groans and their struggle to free themselves, until finally the heavy burden of slain bison above crushed out their lives. In minutes the kill was over.

One hundred ninety bison lay dead in and around the arroyo. Tons of meat awaited the knives of the hunters—meat enough for feasting, and plenty to dry for the months ahead—more meat, in fact, than they could use. Immediately, the hunters began to butcher their kill. From the top of the heap, they dragged the carcasses back and rolled them onto their bellies, flexed the forelegs alongside and extended the hind legs behind the body, to help support the great bulk. They slit the skin the length of the back, and, peeling the skin down, began to strip the meat away from the hump and ribs. A foreleg cut from another animal was used as an adze to break the ribs near their juncture with the backbone, to give access to the interior where the vital organs were delicacies awaiting them. The shoulders were removed, then the backbone was severed just behind the rib cage. The neck was cut just in front of the ribs. Jaws were cut away from the skull and broken apart at the joint to free the tongue, or else the throat was slit and the tongue pulled through and cut off. The hind quarters were disjointed and stripped of their meat. As it was cut off, some of the flesh was eaten raw, but most of the meat was laid on the skin to keep it clean. Animal after animal was butchered. As the days passed, amid the feasting on internal organs and fresh meat, the drying of meat went on, assuring a supply to last until the next kill. While the meat was drying, skins were prepared for use as robes, and containers were made from the horns, which had been removed by breaking off the core from the skull. Many of the leg bones were broken and the marrow removed. Some carcasses were wedged well down into the arroyo, and these were too heavy for the hunters to move. The beautifully flaked spear points which had killed these animals went unretrieved. Wherever a leg jutted up, it was cut off, and other accessible parts were butchered; but much remained which could not be cut up. No attempt was made to salvage the bison trapped in the very bottom of the arroyo.

For many days, the butchering, feasting, preparation of hides, and meat-drying went on. In time, however, the meat remaining on the carcasses became too "high" for use, and the hunters had dried as much meat as they could carry; so finally they moved on, leaving the gully filled with bones and rotting flesh. As the summer wore on, rain water drained into the arroyo, carrying sediment with it, but the carcasses blocked free flow of the water and caused the stream to dump its load of silt and sand, covering the mass of rotting flesh and bones. Within a few years, the upper part of the arroyo was filled, although there continued to be a shallow wash to the eastward.

Several thousand years passed before this last remnant of the arroyo was filled, and the climate became drier and hotter. During this time, another group of hunters and gatherers moved into the area and camped for a time on the hill to the west and on the ridge to the north. Their campsites were marked by the remains of pit ovens and by a few of their characteristic indented-base, stemmed dart points, as well as some scrapers and other crude tools. One or two of their tools were lost in the, by now, nearly filled wash.

Still later, other groups camped and hunted near the old bison kill, but by this time no evidence of the old arroyo was left on the surface.

By 1880, there were no bison left, and the last Indians began to be replaced by white cattlemen. In 1947, the sod was broken for planting; shortly thereafter, the combination of drought and fierce winds that marked the early 1950s began to erode away the upper deposits that had covered the gully and the terrace through which it had been cut. By 1957, the bones that filled the one-time arroyo were once again exposed on the surface.

The foregoing is a reconstruction and interpretation of events which transpired over a period of some 10,000 years. In over a quarter of a century of practicing archaeology, I have, from time to time, discovered evidence which made real and immediate the people whose remains and relics were being uncovered. For the most part, these instances have been minute fragments of a continuum whose whole was too diffuse, whose time span too long, and whose practitioners too alien, to call to mind a picture of events which could be sustained from more than moments.

However, at the Olsen–Chubbuck site there was unfolded a picture so complete within itself, whose action was so brief and self-contained, that, except for minor details, one could almost visualize the dust and tumult of the hunt, the joy of feasting, the satisfaction born of a surplus of food, and finally, almost smell the stench of the rotting corpses of the slain bison as the Indians left the scene of the kill to seek other game in other places. Time seemed, indeed, to be stilled for an interval, and a microcosm of the hunters' life preserved. This is what I have tried to convey. The evidence from which I have drawn, in perhaps too firm lines, a picture of the kill, constitutes the body of this study. . . .

Before the University of Colorado Museum took over excavation of the Olsen–Chubbuck site, a furrow had been plowed lengthwise through the outcropping of bones. This had damaged the upper bones to a certain extent, but it had shown the deposit to be linear, and had defined the orientation of the bone bed. This furrow, in addition to the pits excavated by Olsen and Chubbuck, enabled us to estimate closely the course of the ancient gully which contained the bone bed.

A base line, oriented 80° magnetic (June 19, 1960) was established along the south side of the bone bed and generally parallel to it. This base line was divided into 2-meter sections numbered consecutively beginning with Section 1, well beyond what we believed to be the eastern end of the bone deposit, and continuing westward beyond the known extent of the site. These sections were then staked out at right angles to the base line. The width of each section was determined by the width of the arroyo and its contained bone deposit. Each section took its number from the stake at its southeastern corner.

The pits dug by Chubbuck and Olsen lay between the east end of Section

16 and the west end of Section 10, thus encompassing all or part of Sections 10, 11, 12, 13, 14, 15, and 16. The eastern extremity of this pit was not dug in a vertical face but, rather, sloped from the surface, beginning some 30 centimeters east of the line dividing Sections 10 and 11, and sloping some 50 centimeters westward into Section 11.

Eastward, beyond the Olsen and Chubbuck pit, the bone bed did not outcrop on the surface but sloped down as the bottom of the arroyo sloped. Thus, from Section 10 eastward, there was an ever-increasing overburden of fill above the bone bed.

A contour map of the site was made, including the surrounding area. A hand level mounted on a tripod, and a surveying rod were used for this purpose. A plane table and alidade were used during the 1960 season to plot in additional excavations and features.

When we began excavation of the site, we had the impression, gathered from the surface outcrop and the exposed faces of the Olsen–Chubbuck pit, that the bone bed consisted almost entirely of disarticulated bones which the Indians, in an excess of tidiness, had tossed into the arroyo following the butchering. Hence, we planned to excavate the site by arbitrary 30-centimeter levels within each section, and to record the bones merely by section and level. However, it very quickly became apparent that, while there was a quantity of disarticulated bones, there were also many articulated segments of skeletons. These segments consisted of varying numbers of bones—two or three articulated vertebrae, a whole foot, and so on, including, as we later discovered in the lower deposits, whole animals. It seemed clear that these segments represented portions of the bison which were cut off during the butchering process. We reasoned that, if we could recover enough of these segments, we should have considerable first-hand data as to the butchering techniques of the Indians.

The Olsen–Chubbuck site preserved a classic example of the mass slaughter of a herd of bison by stampeding them across a natural obstacle, in this case an arroyo. Whether or not the arroyo was formed by the erosion and deepening of an abandoned bison trail, as appears likely, the part it played in the kill is clear: it constituted the trap into and across which the bison were stampeded by the Indians.

The evidence for the role the stampede, itself, played in the kill lies in the orientation of the skeletons and in the massed, violently twisted and contorted positions in which they were found; approximately the position where they met death by suffocation, by being trampled to death, or by injury suffered from the spears of the hunters, perhaps terminated with the coup de grace. In Hind's description of the destruction of a bison herd in a pound, it is clear that, to a certain extent, some animals were able to mill around until they were killed by the Indians. Hence, some of the bodily positions were the result, not of the stampede into the pound, but of the frenzied milling of the bison in the pound. In a natural trap such as an arroyo, the confines of the trap itself would at least partly determine the position of the animals, for there was no chance of milling about. The relative narrowness and linearity of the Olsen–Chubbuck arroyo would, of necessity, force some of the trapped bison into an orientation parallel to that of the arroyo. Nevertheless, there should be evidence of violent death in the positions of the bodies of the bison trapped as a result of being stampeded into the arroyo.

While the majority of the bison in the upper half of the Olsen–Chubbuck arroyo had been butchered, and thus are not pertinent to this problem, the lower half of the arroyo, particularly from Section 20 eastward, contained the skeletons of forty whole or nearly whole animals, or animals which, because of their position in the arroyo, had been only partly butchered, in addition to those that may have been in the section dug by Olsen and Chubbuck.

Almost without exception, every whole or nearly whole skeleton overlies or is overlain by skeletons of other whole or nearly whole animals, often by two or three others. This would suggest that those first into the arroyo had no chance to get out and were covered by those following so rapidly and so violently that they were simply wedged into the position they landed in, only to be pushed, twisted, and torn by the impact of those following.

Of the forty bodies still approximately in the position in which they met death, fifteen had been violently twisted on or around the axis formed by the vertebral column. In many of these, the back appeared to have been broken just behind the rib cage and the forepart of the animal rotated up to 45°. In a few cases the neck appeared to have been broken and twisted forward of the rib cage. Eleven other bodies had been forced into a violent curve. Of this number three were completely doubled up into a "U" shape, with the rear end wedged against the north side of the arroyo and the fore-quarters and head wedged against the south side, the vertebral column making a continuous arc across the width of the arroyo. In still other units, it was not possible to determine whether or not the bodies had been twisted because the forepart of the body had been removed, presumably for butchering.

Eighteen of the bodies had their rear legs in an abnormal position. In some, it would seem that the animal had simply squatted to get into position to leap out of the arroyo but was foiled because, before it could jump, it was pinned down by another animal. In a few cases the animal hit or slid into position with the rear legs extended and was not able to return them to a normal flexed position. In still others, the twisting of the forepart of the animal had resulted in extension of the rear legs to one side while the forelegs extended to the other. Eleven bodies had forelegs in an abnormal position, in some cases extended to the front or side of the body, and in others extended to the rear, parallel to the body, as if they had hit on the chest or head and had not been able to pull the legs back into a flexed position before they were buried by the avalanche which followed them.

When the bison jumped, the positions in which they landed depended in part on the positions of the bodies they landed on, or on the shape of the arroyo at that particular point. About half of the bodies either landed in a horizontal position, or we lack data in our records on the point. However, ten animals landed front downward and were held in that position, head down and rear end up. Another ten landed with the rear end down and the head and forepart up. Two bodies lay on the back, one in the very bottom of the arroyo. The other had evidently been spun around in mid-air and had hit the south bank of the arroyo, then had slid clear to the bottom with one rear leg jackknifed up the north side of the arroyo, the other extended at right angles to the body along the arroyo bottom. Altogether, three animals were found in a vertical position, being held upright by the surrounding press of other bodies. One of these was a calf only a few days old, head down, that was pressed against the north side of the arroyo. Another was a large mature bull which had landed against the south wall of the arroyo with the rear legs and pelvis oriented east and the front legs and shoulder girdle oriented west. This animal had collapsed into a vertical heap of bones after the meat had decayed.

There can be no doubt that the stampede ran from north to south, or, perhaps more accurately from northwest to southeast. Of the thirty-nine whole or nearly whole bodies for which orientation data were recorded, not a single animal was oriented to the northern half of the compass. Nine animals were oriented to the southeast, and nine to the south, including three whose bodies lodged in a "U" shape across the arroyo. Three bodies were oriented to the southwest. Twelve animals were oriented to the east, including most of those from Section 10 eastward, and six were oriented to the west. It is important to note, in connection with those oriented to the east or west, that they were all in the narrow inner channel of the arroyo, and that they were forced to assume an easterly or westerly orientation by having been wedged into the channel. Thus, without exception, those animals, the orientation of whose bodies was without constraint from the physical limitations of the arroyo, were oriented southeast, south, or rarely, southwest.

There is, of course, very little direct evidence of the surround or partial surround which normally would have accompanied and precipitated the stampede across the arroyo. We discovered no physical evidence for the construction of wings of "deadmen" to direct the stampeding herd into and across the arroyo. Nevertheless, there is some evidence which suggests that hunters were stationed along the sides of the moving herd as well as to the rear of it.

This evidence consists of the fact that projectile points were found associated with bodies in the lowest part of the arroyo as well as those in the middle and upper parts. Point 10,972 lay inside the rib cage of Unit 272, a nearly complete animal which lay on the very bottom of the arroyo. Point 10,486 had apparently lodged in Unit 148, which also lay in the lowest part of the arroyo. Unit 131 had been penetrated from the side by Point 10,485 which ultimately had lodged inside the pelvic girdle. This animal lay somewhat above the lowest level but was clearly not one of the last into the arroyo. Olsen and Chubbuck found their Points F-6, F-9, and F-12 at depths near 1.3 meters, and their Points F-10 and F-7 among bones at a depth of almost a meter, which would have placed the animals with which they were associated near the bottom of the deposit.

Given the size and speed of the stampeding herd, it would appear highly unlikely that these points could have lodged where they struck their quarry had they been shot from the rear of the herd. On the other hand, spears shot from the flanks of the moving herd would normally have struck some of the lead animals, coercing the herd into a narrower path and across the arroyo. These animals would have been the first into the arroyo, where they were found. That the shooting continued until the arroyo was completely filled is evidenced by the finding of points embedded in one animal in the sternum of Unit 152 and near the bones of other units near the top of the bone bed, and representing, therefore, some of the last animals to be trapped.

These data can only be suggestive, but coupled with the knowledge that the conditions only suggested by the distribution of the projectile points in the bone bed would have been the normal, rather than exceptional, hunting technique employed in a kill such as the Olsen–Chubbuck, they lend weight to the idea that a partial surround preceded the actual stampede which eventuated in the kill itself.

The catchment basin to the north and northwest was the only place where general concealment of the hunters could have been effected until they were ready to start the stampede. The ridge to the west, the low divide to the northwest, and the ridge to the northeast and east afforded a physical cover for most of the area north of the arroyo, behind which the hunters could work their way into position. If there was, in addition, plant cover, and if the breeze was blowing from the south or southeast, as would be normal for late spring and early summer, then the classic conditions would be met for the Olsen–Chubbuck kill. . . .

The composition of bison herds and the time of calving both have a bearing on the time of year that the Olsen–Chubbuck bison kill occurred. The skeletons in the bone bed were from nearly 200 animals of both sexes and of all ages. Sex was determined on a total of 58 units, of which 42 were adult and 16 immature. Sex was not determined on any of the juvenile skeletons. Of these 58 units, 25 (43.10%) were male and 33 (56.90%) were female. Age was determined for 269 units. It will be noted that this figure includes some cases where determinations were made on what must have been different elements of the same animal. Of the 269 age determinations, 153 (56.88%) were adult, 100 (37.17%) were immature, and 16 (5.95%) were juvenile. Of the latter, 1 or 2 appeared to be not more than a few days old, while most appeared, from the stage of growth, to be a month or possibly two months old. No fetal calves were found.

From evidence based on the sex and age ratios in the bone bed, it appears that the kill could have occurred as early as April or as late as August, with most data suggesting a time fairly late in the calving season but before the onset of the rutting season. The ages of the calves found point to late May or early June. The absence of fetal calves may be due to accident of either preservation or excavation, since we do not have detailed information on the skeletons excavated by Chubbuck and Olsen. In passing, it should also be noted that fetal calves were considered to be a great delicacy by some of the historic Plains tribes, and the absence of them in the bone bed could be due, in part, to their having been taken as food. In any case, their absence suggests a time toward the end of the calving season.

Finally, there is no way to establish the total size of the herd which was stampeded across the Olsen–Chubbuck arroyo (since you can't count the ones that got away), but the number of animals trapped was near the optimum size of the small grazing herds expectable prior to the rutting season. While this does not preclude the possibility of the trapping of a small segment of the huge aggregations of animals normal during the rutting season, it does not support it.

In summary, it would appear that a date of late May or early June best accommodates the known biological evidence as to the time of year that the Olsen–Chubbuck bison kill occurred.

Ethnographic sources concerning seasonal variation in the utilization of bulls and cows also point to a time prior to the rutting season. According to most observers, . . . bulls were normally consumed only during May and June, since they were then in prime condition. During the calving season, the cows tended to be poor in flesh, but by the end of the season, that is, late May or early June, they, too, were once again becoming good to eat. Since there is ample evidence in the Olsen–Chubbuck site that both bulls and cows were butchered, a date of late May or, more probably, early June is suggested. . . .

The analysis of the bone bed at the Olsen–Chubbuck site has produced a considerable amount of evidence of the process of butchering followed there. It will be recalled that at the beginning of excavations, the assumption was made that most of the articulated skeletal segments which we found in fact represented those parts of the animals that were cut off during the butchering, and that the essential uniformity of such segments reflected a standardized pattern of butchering. . . .

When the kill was finished, the area in and around the arroyo must have been strewn with dead bison of all ages and sexes. Access for butchering those on the flats on either side of the arroyo presented few problems, but the contorted mass of animals actually caught in the arroyo had to be pulled, shoved, rolled, or otherwise moved so that the cutting-up could proceed. In part, this may have been done by some preliminary butchering before the major part of the carcass was moved, a technique mentioned in some of the historical literature. In any event, a point was reached in the removal or clearance process when the hunters were unable or unwilling to move the carcasses from their constricted positions in the arroyo. It would be difficult, if not impossible, to say whether this point was reached because the manpower available made it impossible to lift more of the huge animals up and out of the arroyo, or whether there were more animals killed than could be utilized. In either case, when this point was reached, it left a number of whole animals along the bottom of the arroyo which were not butchered at all. However, those parts which could be reached without moving the whole animal were cut off, resulting in what we have termed

The bison bone bed at the Paleo-Indian Olsen–Chubbuck
site, Colorado. The densely packed bones are from bison
that were stampeded into a narrow gully.

partly butchered units. The variety of the parts butchered out, in relation to the position of the partly butchered units in the bone bed, makes this rather clear.

There is some minor evidence of the impromptu feasting on tidbits, probably in part uncooked, which was a standard part of historic bison kills. The fact that almost 40 percent of the disarticulated hyoids were found in the lowest level, and another 30 percent in the middle level, suggests that before the heavy butchering got under way, the tongue was removed in the classic Plains method of slitting the throat, pulling the tongue through, and cutting it off. This was often eaten raw in historic times, as were the liver, spiced with gall, the lips, the udder, and some of the organs and glands, none of which would leave evidence in the archaeological record. However, since some 40 percent of the disarticulated scapulae were found in the lower levels, it suggests that the carcass was opened early in some animals, perhaps to give access to the internal organs. The distribution of disarticulated ribs, almost half of which were found in the lower levels, supports this interpretation, as well as suggesting that scapulae and humps, which had to be removed before the ribs could be taken, were among the first items to be cut off of individual animals, as they were in historic times. Ribs and humps were normally cooked, although we found no evidence of fire at the Olsen–Chubbuck site. The fact that we did not find such evidence is not conclusive, however, because it will be remembered that wind deflation had removed some of the top layers of the soil.

It appears that when the heavy butchering began, a number of bison were butchered simultaneously rather than that single animals were butchered in succession. When these were finished, another group would be butchered. The evidence for this is that the segments which were cut off and stripped of their meat were discarded in groups of like units rather than individually, helter-skelter. The occurrence in groups also suggests that the butchers were working fairly close together, but whether this implies a family group working together, a larger kin group, or simply a number of individuals, I can discern no sure way of determining. . . .

In butchering an individual bison, the first step seems to have been to roll the animal onto its belly with the legs positioned to serve as props to maintain the carcass in an upright position. Then, the skin was cut along the back and stripped off the sides. As among the historic bison hunters, the skin was probably cut into halves along the belly and used as a "table" to receive the meat as it was cut away from the bones. The "blanket of flesh" which immediately underlies the skin was probably removed next, to expose the front leg. The front leg was then removed, the meat stripped off by laying open the muscles, . . . the bones removed and, minus any bones saved for particular purposes, discarded, still articulated, in a heap.

The evidence for this sequence of events is that wherever the order of deposition in the bone piles was clear, the first bone units to be emplaced were front-leg units, showing that they were the first skeletal elements to be cut off and processed. In order that the front leg could be removed, it was first necessary to remove the "blanket of flesh" and the skin which covered it. Many of the front-leg units found together in the groups appear to be pairs, suggesting that both front legs were removed at nearly the same time, a feat only to be accomplished by having the animal propped up on the belly. In this position, the skin was usually cut down the back. The fact that this procedure was the most widely used Plains Indian technique also tends to give weight to this interpretation.

The various cuts of meat over the ribs and along the vertebral column were next removed. At this point, the ribs were frequently broken away near their point of articulation to the vertebral column. A number of instances of ribs being broken near the head and, conversely, of rib-heads still articulated to the vertebral column, are evidence of this procedure. The distribution of foot units, centering near the vertebral-column units, suggests that feet were cut off and used as hatchets in this process, as in historic times. The removal of the meat along the vertebral column exposed the backbone behind the rib cage, and it appears that the backbone was severed somewhere between the rib cage and the pelvis, and the rear end separated.

The flesh was then cut away from the pelvis and the head of the femur was exposed. Once the rear legs were cut off, the pelvic girdle was discarded onto the growing bone pile, where it fell on top of or among the previously discarded front-leg units. The meat was then cut away from the bones, and the rear legs, again minus those bones saved for particular uses, were discarded, still articulated, on the bone pile overlying the pelvic-girdle units. . . .

It appears that when the rear part of the animal had been butchered, the head and neck were separated from the vertebral column, usually just in front of the rib cage. Probably at this point the sinews that lined the backbone were removed and the vertebral-column units discarded. At about the same time, the head was being processed and the neck meat stripped off the cervical vertebrae. Evidence that the neck meat was taken is that in several cases the cervical vertebrae were pulled forward and lay over the frontal portion of the skull, something possible only if all the meat had been removed from the neck. Furthermore, the fact that less than half of the skulls still retained any cervical vertebrae suggests that, in the process of removing the neck meat, the neck was often severed from the skull.

The tongue was then removed, if it had not been taken previously. While some may have been removed by the throat-slitting process, most, at this point in the butchering process, seem to have been removed in different fashion. The lower jaw was cut away from the skull, entirely or on one side, and the mandibles broken at the symphysis, thus permitting the tongue to be removed entire. That this was the common method is evidenced in the fact that more than half of the skulls had both mandibles removed, and four others had only one mandible still articulated.

Horns appear to have been broken off occasionally and the cores removed and thrown onto the bone pile. On the other hand, there is virtually no evidence that the brain case was deliberately broken open to get at the brains. The two or three instances in which the skull was broken open may have been the result of accident rather than intention.

When the skull was stripped of all desirable parts, it, too, was discarded on the bone pile, among and on top of the vertebral-column units. . . .

In summary, it will be noted that the butchering techniques evidenced at the Olsen–Chubbuck site, with few exceptions, adumbrate the pattern observed and recorded by the early explorers and by the ethnographers. One difference is in one of the methods of removing the tongue, since mandible breakage is not recorded for the historic Indians. The apparent lack of use of the brains, either as food or for tanning at the Olsen–Chubbuck site, also differs from the usual pattern. Perhaps the most striking apparent difference, however, is degree of organization noted in the butchering at the Olsen–Chubbuck site, in contrast to the general individual approach to butchering by the later Indians. It is possible that such organized butchering was practiced in historic times, but if so, it does not appear strongly in the literature. . . .

The ethnographical and historical literature demonstrates that the amount of edible meat on a bison carcass should never be taken as an indication that the amount available was, in fact, always utilized. There were many factors involved in the amount of meat actually taken. In a mass slaughter obtained by the various forms of surrounding and impounding, frequently there were simply more bison killed than could be utilized. Individual and tribal preferences must often have dictated those parts of each animal to be taken, or even whether a particular animal would be butchered at all. Spoilage caused by weather elements such as rain, temperature, and humidity, and time itself, would certainly have rendered a portion of the kill unfit for use. Even the earliest historic records, Hennepin, for example, indicate that frequently only the tongue and choice parts were taken, especially if there was no current shortage of meat. Therefore, it is impossible to say, as a generalization, that each buffalo killed provided a definite quantity of meat produce. Conversely, the quantity of bison bone found in a habitation site should never be taken as indicative of the quantity of meat consumed there, since most of the meat would have been transported as boneless fresh or preserved meat unless the kill had been very near the camp. . . .

In an interpretation of a bison kill, a number of factors must be considered. These include the length of time necessary to process the kill, as well as the length of time that the meat remained edible for fresh consumption; the amount of meat consumed daily under "feasting" conditions and the number of people to feast; the weight of the preserved produce, the weight a person would carry under aboriginal conditions, and the number of persons to carry that weight. If dogs were present they would both shorten the time necessary to consume the fresh meat and enable the transport of larger quantities of produce, as well as the camp gear of the hunting group. . . .

When a kill was "heavy" butchered, as was the Olsen–Chubbuck kill, it was primarily for the purpose of laying in a supply of preserved meat and skins. At such times, the hunting party, which usually included the whole camp, band, or even several bands together, men, women, and children, would normally remain in residence at or near the kill site until the major part was consumed and processed, when the entire group would move in search of other game. Times ranging from a few days to more than a month for the processing of a single kill have been recorded in historic times. Apart from butchering, there are few data on the length of time necessary to process an animal, but many activities such as drying meat, making pemmican, and preparing skins were carried on simultaneously by various members of the camp, and a period of a month or even less would appear adequate for the processing of the Olsen–Chubbuck kill. Historical data on the amount of meat consumed under "feasting" conditions such as apparently prevailed at the Olsen–Chubbuck kill record amounts ranging from about 10 pounds (4.5 kg) per person per day to more than 30 pounds (13.6 kg). Considering the probable variation in the amounts consumed by women and children, and the fact that some waste must have occurred, I have used 4.5 kilograms as the basis for computing fresh meat consumption at the Olsen–Chubbuck kill. A train dog's ration of fresh meat was 8 pounds (3.6 kg) per day. With the exception of Lewis H. Morgan, who provides a ratio of 1 pound (0.45 kg) of dried meat for every 12 pounds (5.4 kg) of fresh meat, every observer records a ratio of 1:5, or 20 pounds (9.07 kg) of dried meat to 100 pounds (45.5 kg) of fresh meat, which is the figure I have used. Data on tallow are unsatisfactory. I have used the Belcourt and Ross figures for one set of computations, but because the "depuyer" or "back fat" is consistently mentioned as having been taken by the Indians of historic times, I have computed for this also, using a value of 4.5 kilograms per animal, for both the "heavy" and "light" butchered animals in the Olsen–Chubbuck site. Marrow seems to have been consistently taken, so, on the basis of historical pattern, as well as the evidence of broken and missing marrow bones in the Olsen–Chubbuck site, I have assumed that it was taken there, and have used the figure 3.3 kilograms (7.5 lb) per animal butchered. Although the average dressed buffalo robe weighed about 4.5 kilograms, because of the larger *B. occidentalis* hide, I have computed half-robes at 7 pounds (3.28 kg) each for this reconstruction. Among the early historic Buffalo Indians, the woman and the dog were the usual burden bearers, a woman's normal load being about 45.5 kilograms. Men usually carried only their weapons for hunting and ready protection along the way, although they might carry some burden when moving camp or at other times, as might also the children. Loads of from 13.6 kilograms to 45.5 kilograms have been recorded for dogs, but the average figure is about 50 pounds (22.7 kg), and that is the figure I have used. . . .

Because of the complete and systematic butchering at the Olsen–Chubbuck site, and because of the taking of some meat usable only in dried-meat or pemmican form, there is every reason to assume that the maximum possible use was made of the kill there, both with regard to the consumption of fresh meat and the preservation of meat. Obviously, it is impossible to control all of the variables, but of all the possibilities cited, some appear inherently more plausible than others because they fall within the known limits of time, amount of meat consumed, and the amount of produce which, together with the camp gear, could be transported. Conversely, some of the groups posited may be eliminated because they could not reasonably have carried out the evident exploitation of the kill. Thus, a group of 50 persons alone could neither have consumed half or two-thirds of the meat butchered while the meat remained edible, nor have been able to transport the preserved produce of the remaining half or third. A hundred persons could have consumed half of the meat fresh, but transport of the remaining half would have been at the very limit of possibility; while they could, with some difficulty, transport the produce from one-third of the kill, they could have consumed the remaining two-thirds only with great difficulty. One hundred fifty, or 200, persons could have consumed half or two-thirds of the kill easily, and could have as easily transported the remaining half or third in the form of preserved meat. If, therefore, the hunters who made the Olsen–Chubbuck kill were without dogs to help in the transport of the produce and the camp equipment, I believe a group of not less than 150 to 200 persons were involved, for fewer than that could hardly have carried out the observed utilization of the kill. On the other hand, if the hunters had 100 or so dogs, a band of no more than 50 persons could have accomplished the observed results, although a somewhat larger group of 75 to 100 would fit better in terms of the probable time span involved. That the butchering operation was organized there can be little doubt. Because of the season of the kill, and the pattern of utilization, it would appear reasonable that the hunt was an organized, cooperative spring kill, of the sort commonly observed on the Plains in early historic times, but it may have been only the highly organized utilization of a random kill.

Ozette, Washington

RICHARD DAUGHERTY AND RUTH KIRK

In 1947, Richard Daugherty (b. 1922) of Washington State University conducted a survey of coastal sites on the Olympic Peninsula in the extreme northwestern United States. He identified a large midden in a sheltered location at Ozette, south of Cape Flattery, but was unable to excavate there until 1966, when he discovered numerous whale bones and some well-preserved wooden house planks, along with traces of human settlement going back more than 2,500 years.

Three years later, the local Makah Tribal Council alerted Daugherty, after a storm cut into the midden and exposed all manner of wooden artifacts. During the next ten years, Daugherty and a large research team exposed four collapsed cedarwood longhouses and their perfectly preserved contents. The excavations were fraught with difficulty. High-pressure hoses and fine sprays were used instead of shovels and trowels to clear the liquid mud away from delicate basketry, wooden boxes with their contents intact, fishhooks, bowls, and other artifacts. The white muck that mantled the houses had engulfed them suddenly in a damp blanket that preserved everything except flesh, feathers, and skins. One longhouse exposed in 1972 was twenty-one meters long and fourteen meters wide. There were separate hearths and cooking platforms. Hanging mats and low walls served as partitions.

Ozette is a classic example of how much can be recovered from an archaeological site under waterlogged conditions. But the settlement is also important in other ways. The Makah Indians who lived at Ozette until the 1920s possessed oral traditions that went back to only about A.D. 1800. Daugherty's excavations traced this village of whale catchers and fisherfolk back at least 2,500 years, giving the Makah a much longer history. As a direct result of this excavation, a Makah Tribal Museum was constructed in nearby Neah Bay, where the artifacts from the excavation are displayed.

Writer Ruth Kirk worked closely with Richard Daugherty on a popular account of the excavations, Hunters of the Whale. *This selection describes some of the house contents and artifacts.*

Three years passed, and the calendar showed February 1970, when Daugherty received a phone call urging him back to Ozette. It came from Ed Claplanhoo, chairman of the Makah Tribal Council at the time and formerly a student at Washington State University. Storm waves driven high onto the beach had undercut the bank at Ozette, Claplanhoo reported, and wet midden had slumped. Deep layers within the bank now were exposed, and old-style fish-hooks of wood and bone, parts of inlaid boxes, and a canoe paddle had washed out from where they had lain buried for centuries. Hikers had found the arti-facts. They were even carrying them away—and once such items are gathered up and taken off by collectors, they no longer reveal the life of the people who made them and used them. They become mere things.

Daugherty listened to the tribal chairman's full account; then he headed al-most straight from the phone to his car. He had to get to the coast and see for himself. If the discoveries were as important as they sounded, he would need to raise finances, hire a crew, round up the necessary field equipment, and begin excavating as soon as possible.

The drive took ten hours. Daugherty slept what was left of the night at the head of the trail and at dawn hiked the familiar three miles through the forest to the beach. Ed Claplanhoo and a delegation of Makahs met him. Together the men examined the slump—not a large one and completely without drama for most eyes. Banks along beaches the world over give way as a normal part of erosion. But Daugherty and the Makahs knew the special nature of this bank, and Daugherty even more than the others knew how much evidence of the coastal prehistory already had been lost. Sites mentioned in a 1917 report cov-ering the Washington coast were nowhere to be found when he made his 1947 site survey as a graduate student. They had been swept into the ocean. Daugh-erty couldn't let this happen at Ozette. Not just as the preliminary work of 1966 and 1967 had given the keys needed to unlock the full archaeological story. . . .

The slumped bank was about five meters high. Wild crabapple trees, elder-berry, and sword ferns had slid with the mud and now formed a junglelike tan-gle. Daugherty climbed in among the roots and limbs, sinking over his boot tops in the ooze. His eye lit on planks that were sticking out end on, and a basketry rain hat of the kind women twined from spruce roots in the old days. There were also bone points used for shooting birds, halibut hooks, a harpoon shaft, and part of a carved wooden box.

Daugherty felt a familiar excitement. If this much had been brought to the surface, what must still lie hidden? Obviously these were the remains of a house. Not the one he had located in 1967. Another. How many more might lie buried with their contents preserved by the wet mud of the ages? How many of the missing pieces needed to understand the whale-hunting Indians of the North-west lay beneath his feet? It was as if the house had been delivered specially for study. A major expedition was needed, and right away. . . .

At the site new excavation techniques were called for. Machines could not be used. The old house and its contents were too delicate. Not even hand shovels were possible. A metal edge would cut through a buried basket before even the most careful excavator could know it was there. Water seemed to be the answer. Pumped up from the ocean and blasted out through fire hoses, it would wash away the heavy mud on top of the house. Then the spray of garden hoses could be used when the crew reached the house and its artifacts. The method has decided advantages when working in saturated deposits. With a trowel, mud tends to ball up, and this may cause an archaeologist to scrape aside and lose small artifacts such as wooden arrow points, fishhooks, or shell beads. Working gently with water allows him to expose objects without disturbing them, and also the artifacts show up well because the mud has been washed off them. . . .

Tons of equipment were needed, and again the Coast Guard made airlifts. Later the Marine Air Reserve took over. The flights gave practice in loading and unloading all manner of materials—hoses, pumps, barrels of gasoline, lumber, roofing paper, stoves, propane tanks. Reservists could learn the techniques of suspending heavy cargo under the belly of a helicopter and gain experience in the logistics problems of remote areas.

Even with materials in hand at Ozette, getting them into operation challenged ingenuity and patience. Time and again waves rolling in over the reef tore out the hoses that served the pumps, and a crewman would have to put on a wet suit and struggle out through the surging water to salvage what he could, then reset it all when calm had been restored. Sometimes seaweed clogged the pumps. Once stinging jellyfish spattered out of the hoses, burning and scarring Grosso's arms as he washed the mud from above the buried house. . . .

The project was like opening a time capsule. Here was an Indian home from the time before Columbus set sail for America. Everything was present—sleeping benches, cooking hearths, storage boxes, harpoons, bows and arrows, baskets, mats, tool kits. All the household possessions of a family of whale hunters—and all of it tossed into a muddy jumble. The crew's job was to untangle the mess and discover its meaning. Find the roof planks and distinguish them from the wall planks. Hose away more of the mud slide and locate the north end of the house (so far work had been only in the south end). Keep notes and make drawings and photographs. Preserve each piece as it was lifted from the mud—the splintered boards the house was built of, the wooden bowls that once held seal oil and whale oil, the mussel-shell lance blades, the elk-antler wedges—everything.

The house still held its original wooden and fiber materials, complete to wooden needles and pieces of string. There were even alder-tree leaves still green when first uncovered, although with exposure to the air they turned brown within seconds. Probably the house had been lived in for several generations, perhaps for a century or more. Parts of the wall showed damage from termites or carpenter ants, and the crew found several places where repairs had been made. A whalebone had been jammed in among the planks to close a break in the wall, and in another place part of a canoe paddle had been added as support. There was also a wide board that must originally have been intended as a roof board but was used in the wall. Parallel grooves ran the length of its surface, and these were how Daugherty recognized it as belonging originally to a roof. The purpose of the grooves was to direct rain runoff.

Some planks measured nearly a meter wide and were five or six centimeters thick. Splitting them from cedar logs was slow and hard, so householders naturally salvaged them whenever possible. An example of this was found in the house. One of the largest planks was badly cracked but had been repaired. Holes were drilled along each side of the crack, and a cord was laced through them. . . .

Discoveries came one on another. Some items were small and could easily have been missed or gone unrecognized except for the expert care being taken. There were finger-sized pieces of whittled wood that had been used as plugs in sealskin floats. Several bone barbs from harpoons lay close by and with them were spirals of cherry bark, which had been wrapped around ropes made of sinew and fastened to the harpoon heads. The ropes had decayed and were gone, but the bindings remained. There was also a piece of bone roughed out and begun as a comb but never finished—the sort of find that archaeologists treasure because it gives both the article itself and a look at how it was made.

"Continued excavation in the house," reads the log. "Found several flattened wooden boxes in Square 70, Unit VI, one with remains of what seems to be a blanket, white with blue-black plaid design."

Something appeared to be folded inside, but Daugherty gave orders against opening it, much as everybody wondered what the contents would be. The blanket was so fragile that the mud couldn't even be thoroughly cleaned off it, although what inspection was possible seemed to show that it was made of cattail fluff or the fuzzy seeds of fireweed. Perhaps dog wool or mountain-goat wool had once been spun in with the plant fluff, but it was gone now.

The crew wrapped the blanket in plastic to keep it moist, then put it into a backpack. Three students headed down the beach to the trail and began the long trip to the Laboratory of Anthropology in Pullman. There they would see if X rays would reveal the mysterious contents. If not, they would treat the blanket with a mold preventative and put it into a freezer for safekeeping. Seeing what lay inside was tempting, but not worthwhile if unfolding the blanket would destroy it. The wrapping was unique; the contents might not be. No other plaid pattern was known along the Northwest Coast from such an early time. Daugherty wanted to save it even though it probably meant never knowing about the contents.

Tests seemed to bear out that fear. The X rays showed nothing. "It's like having a Christmas present you can't open," Daugherty said with a sigh.

On another day, not long after the blanket had been discovered, the entry in the log read, "Found a piece of carved wood set with teeth. Appears to be part of a feast bowl. Box removed from under it, also a canoe paddle."

Four days later the carving had been worked free and the log recorded, "Big wooden object assembled and photographed. It's not a bowl, but a carving in the shape of a whale's fin. Size, about eighty centimeters wide and eighty high with Thunderbird and other designs set in teeth and painted red and black."

*Richard Daugherty with a whale fin carved of cedar and inlaid
with more than 700 otter teeth found in a plank house at Ozette,
Washington. The teeth at the base depict a mythical bird carrying a
whale in its talons.*

The teeth were sea otter—700 of them. Most were molars, although there also were canines set in along the edge to give a jagged, saw-blade effect. A ceremony of some sort must have been associated with such an elaborate piece, but nobody could say what the rituals were or what importance the decorated fin held for the man who owned it. Written records make no mention of such an item, and none of the Makahs could remember their elders speaking of similar carvings. The only available clue came from an historical source. An etching made by the official artist for Captain James Cook's voyage of discovery in the late 1700s shows a carved fin in an Indian house on Vancouver Island, north of Ozette.

Tragedy at Utqiagvik, Alaska

ALBERT A. DEKIN, JR.

Archaeologists who excavate in the North American arctic work under harsh conditions, enjoying a field season that lasts but two or three months. All too often, their finds are confined to the stone foundations of winter houses or some animal bones and stone artifacts from a shallow midden. But the permafrost conditions of the far north have resulted in some remarkable archaeological discoveries: entire houses and even settlements have survived, organic remains and all. Thanks to excellent preservation conditions, we can enjoy the rich artistic traditions of the sea-mammal hunters of the Bering Strait region and explore minute details of ancient dwellings or bone and ivory artifacts.

But occasionally, long-forgotten ancient tragedies come to light, preserved by the natural refrigeration of the permafrost. One stormy night in the 1540s, two Inupiat women—one in her forties, the other in her twenties—and three children slept in a small driftwood house on a bluff overlooking the Arctic Ocean at Utqiagvik, Alaska. The subzero winds swept over the bluff, sending sea ice crashing against the nearby shore. High waves drove the pack violently toward the bluff. Suddenly, a giant mass of ice chunks broke free in a violent surge and was carried over the bluff, crashing tons of ice down on the tiny dwelling. The roof collapsed, killing the sleeping inhabitants immediately. At dawn, neighbors found the crushed house and left it buried under the massed ice. Sometime later, other members of the family recovered some utensils and food from the edges of the ruins, and the timber uprights projecting through the ice were salvaged. The rest of the hut remained undisturbed for more than four centuries, deep-freezing a prehistoric tragedy.

Four centuries ago, Utqiagvik was a sizable settlement of at least sixty houses, but it is now buried under much of the expanding city of Barrow, Alaska. When the collapsed house came to light, archaeologists were soon on the scene, treading a delicate path between the need to respect the spiritual beliefs of the local people and the objectives of scientific research. This is the story of how two worlds met and collaborated in the rediscovery of a long-forgotten traumatic event. In an essay written for this book, Albert Dekin (b. 1944), who headed the investigations, tells the story of the discovery of the tragedy, and discusses some of the challenges and intricacies of conducting archaeological research in cooperation with Native Americans and government agencies.

314

"Uh-oh," I muttered to no one in particular, standing in the open door of our field laboratory. As I looked out, I saw two young men walking down the road toward us. I recognized them as having been digging in the archaeological deposits exposed along the eroding bluff edge above the ocean, looking for artifacts on private land next to the historic preserve where our archaeological team was digging. The cause of my concern was the green garbage bag dangling from the closest man's hand, with a conspicuously rounded, heavy object within, swinging back and forth as they walked.

As they approached, I turned to my colleagues and said, "If they come in here, you talk to 'em and I will go talk to the engineers." They came. As I had worried, they opened the bag to reveal a human skull, wet and still partly frozen, with long, black hair adhering to it. I went. Thus began the events leading to our excavations of the "Frozen Family."

Late June 1982 was a very busy time. Our crew of nearly twenty archaeologists had just begun the excavation of several low mounds containing remains of ancient houses from the centuries old Inupiat village of Utqiagvik—part of the present city of Barrow, Alaska. As the summer sun gradually thawed the exposed surfaces we had outlined, we worked carefully, but quickly. Each day we scraped off several inches of thawed soil, knowing it would take at least a month before we knew what the perennially frozen mounds contained. Our goal was to record and interpret historical and archaeological information about the Utqiagvik site that might be threatened by the continuing expansion of the city of Barrow. Our research design had begun with broad, ethnohistorical research among the Inupiat people of Barrow to provide a context for understanding the archaeology of the site. We had concentrated our excavations on areas where the federal and borough governments were constructing sewer, water, and natural-gas facilities through the area of the ancestral village.

I was excited to be back in Barrow with my colleagues from the previous field season, including Raymond Newell, from the Rijksuniversiteit Groningen in the Netherlands. The National Park Service (with Jim Thomson's wise administrative guidance) and the Bureau of Indian Affairs had provided funding for the previous year's broad villagewide studies. These had given us a general knowledge of the nature and extent of the historic and prehistoric occupations of this locale. This second year, the North Slope Borough funded more detailed and focused studies that built on the knowledge we had gathered in 1981. Drs. Raymond Newell and Claudia Chang interviewed the elders in the community, trying to learn about past land use and artifact deposits both from present practices and from recollections of the recent past. We tested our preliminary archaeological interpretations of the community structure of artifacts and activities in the areas among the mounds. We divided our excavation crew efforts between the extensive excavation of a *qargi*, or men's house, and several smaller mounds.

This unprecedented opportunity for two years of staged, large-scale excavations of a well-preserved prehistoric and historic village was one that had not come quickly or easily. We had submitted our proposal in a nationwide competition, and it took several months for the review process. When we were awarded the research contract, the research potential was well worth the effort and the wait. Glenn Sheehan was collecting data for his doctoral dissertation at the *qargi* excavation, while Greg Reinhardt and Dale Slaughter directed other mound excavations. This second year, with a much better understanding of the nature and distribution of the archaeological deposits, we could concentrate our efforts on specific research problems in two or three of the more than sixty mounds we had mapped the previous year. These included studies of how people had used the areas around their houses and how the houses themselves were occupied and reoccupied through time.

Each mound contained remains of rectangular winter houses, dug partly into the frozen ground and roofed with driftwood. People entered the house through a hole in the floor reached through a covered trench, or tunnel. Alcoves along the trench contained stored tools, clothing, and food. The alcove closest to the house was a kitchen. The walls and roof were insulated with blocks of dried sod, and the tunnel alcove floors were covered with whalebone. Even with this insulation, the little heat generated by the oil lamps and kitchen fires seldom raised the house floor temperature much above freezing. The tunnel floor was always frozen.

Each mound contained evidence of many winters of occupation, with remains of plank floors often left one on top of another as the winter houses were reconstructed in successive seasonal reoccupations. When the summer meltwater filled each house and many people traveled from the village to hunt and fish along the coast, parts of these floors were sometimes left in place. When this happened, the artifacts stored beneath them were also left behind where they had been stored, well preserved by the frozen ground.

As we recovered the many stone, bone, ivory, wood, and other organic artifacts from the excavations, we took them to our field laboratory on the site. There, Randy Peterson directed the cataloging of each specimen as it was brought in. The lab crew applied conservation solutions to protect any fragile artifacts that might otherwise be damaged in shipment to our Binghamton University laboratories at the end of August. He also maintained collections to show to visitors, including objects difficult for us to interpret. The steady stream of elders to the laboratory had been a big help, since they could often identify even fragments of artifacts and tell us how they were traditionally used. The archaeologists were fascinated by the elders and their affinity with the materials being excavated.

By late June, with the midnight sun and good weather making the workdays as long as we wished, we had settled into a routine of excavations and interviews. The daily flow of information, artifacts, and records had become a steady and predictable torrent to the lab people. Then, one sunny afternoon, two young men stopped by unexpectedly to show us their finds. Our research went off in a new direction.

Although we had worked closely with the community in 1981 and were funded by them in this second year, we were still separated by the fact that our anthropological perspective viewed both them and their ancestors as objects of study. We were acutely aware of people's interest in our work and a heightened awareness of archaeology, as we were aware of the community's growing influence on us and on our research.

When we first set up tents in town and began to do archaeology in 1981, there were occasional misunderstandings, some hostility and not a little resentment from some people in the Inupiat community as our field party of more than thirty people suddenly started publicly digging up their heritage. People constantly watched us work as they went about their business or walked around town. We spent the Fourth of July excavating 1,500-year-old ancestral Inupiat burials while holiday shoppers and revelers paused to watch and offer advice on their way to the grocery store next to our excavations. In 1982, our work was more focused on the Historic Preserve and the *qargi*, our staff was smaller, and we were sponsored by the borough. We were less of an oddity, though still intrusive and pegged as "white scientists."

Many people had dug for artifacts in the eroding bluff edge (as long as the ground was thawed and weather allowed) during all the time we had been in Barrow these two summers. We tried to stay away from their digging, intending neither to encourage them nor to encourage the market for antiquities that led people to destructive digging in archaeological sites across coastal Alaska. Nonetheless, we knew they were there and what they were doing. They knew we were here, and what we were doing. We each had kept to ourselves.

Then, when two young men brought us a human skull and mandible, several of our archaeologists returned with the clandestine diggers to what we had enumerated as Mound 44, observing the protruding legs and feet of an intact body. I quickly notified the engineering firm that managed our contract for the borough and borough representatives. Later that evening, Ray Newell, Ed Hall, and I (the three coprincipal investigators on the project) and our site director, Dale Slaughter, accompanied the local magistrate to Mound 44 at her request.

The diggers had chopped down through the ground surface and thrown the sods and charcoal-darkened soil down the slope toward the beach. Scattered through this loose peaty soil, we saw many human bones, but very few artifact fragments and no architectural remains save for a single upright, wooden post. As we troweled through the loose debris, we uncovered a tightly flexed, desiccated body, intact except for portions of both hands, held tightly in front of the chest. The body had turned brown from the soil, and the shrunken skin was wrinkled, but intact.

The magistrate declared the body and the scattered bones to be "forensic specimens" and asked us to help her by collecting the specimens and putting them in "body bags." We agreed, and later collected all the human remains we could find at or near the surface of the talus slope. The magistrate took these bags back to facilities where they were kept in cold storage. The magistrate's jurisdiction clearly resulted from the understanding that these were "modern" remains, based in large part because we observed no evidence of intact archaeological context for the remains and no associated archaeological deposits.

We went back to work. I was puzzled by the finds but not surprised. Traditional Inupiat treatment of the dead included placing them formally in exposed locations on the tundra inland from the village and leaving them in houses when they had died there, whether from accident, starvation, or disease. The finding of exposed bones had been quite common, and bodies in house ruins should be expected.

For the next three weeks, we dug deeper into the large, complex mound that contained the *qargi* and collected more information on the spatial patterns of discard and storage on the periphery of houses. With the field season in good order, I returned to Binghamton to manage other projects. Meanwhile, the clandestine diggers returned to the location where they were chopping away the bluff edge, continuing to dig deeper in their search for artifacts. On July 19, they visited our laboratory again—now they had found another frozen body, just inland from the first. This time, inside what remained of a traditional Inupiat house, surrounded by artifacts and skins.

When Raymond Newell called me, it was clear that the archaeologists were excited by the unusual nature of the finds and by the potential to study both the archaeological remains and the remains of the humans who created them. After all, this was what archaeologists are trained to do. Ray and I had previously considered how to study catastrophically abandoned Alaskan coastal houses in a proposal to the National Science Foundation (unfortunately, not funded) submitted in 1977. We were already predisposed to the research potential that might exist. As word of the discovery spread, there was considerable local interest and concern for finding out how the people died and whether their uncovering was a health risk. Some Barrow residents even wanted to view the bodies in case they could recognize the facial features as those of relatives!

With Ray taking the initiative to explain the potential significance of these finds to our sponsors and managers, we initially received permission from the landowner to visit the location and to record and evaluate the finds. The combination of research potential from well-preserved human and archaeological remains in established archaeological context, and the threats from clandestine digging and from bluff-edge erosion, all heightened our archaeological concern. The archaeological team understood that if we could, we should change the thrust of our intended research to take advantage of this unprecedented opportunity. However, we were initially stymied by the reluctance by our project manager–engineers to approve such a radical departure from our contracted obligations.

Thus began a whirlwind week of complicated negotiations and discussions, made difficult by my being in New York, transcontinental phone calls with five-hour time differences, and a multitude of interests and perspectives among the constituencies involved. Fortunately, Ray and I had already designed an approach to investigate such a find. To change our contractual research design and

This three-inch-high wood figurine from a house in Utqiagvik village, Barrow, Alaska, may have been a charm or a child's doll.

investigate the finds on Mound 44, we needed the approval (or, at least, not the disapproval) of the landowner, the sponsor, the engineering management firm, and, most important, the elders. Fortunately, we had been working closely with the elders and the sponsors, both in our ethnohistorical research and in preparation for an upcoming conference of elders from across the North Slope Borough. Nonetheless, with lines of authority and responsibility vague and with public interest and attention so high, none of the parties wanted to make a unilateral decision to approve or to disapprove the research design change we proposed. We talked. We waited. We proposed. We listened. Finally, nobody said no, and we were authorized to proceed.

On July 26, we finally began a month-long excavation of Mound 44, directed by Greg Reinhardt under the supervision of Dale Slaughter and Raymond Newell. Much of the work was accomplished by the volunteered extra hours of our excellent field crew, especially Beth Turcy and Jake Kilmarx.

The excavations were difficult. On the one hand, there was a need for haste so that the still-frozen body and associated artifacts and remains would not deteriorate such that they would be biologically unanalyzable. On the other hand, there was a need for care such that the fragile organic remains were not further damaged. We tried several unusual techniques, including squirting hot water from spray bottles and chiseling the ice matrix. There was a broad sense of commitment and dedication among the crew, as they labored night and day to excavate the still-frozen body to protect any biological information preserved within the body's tissues.

While the excavations proceeded, Jack Lobdell, our consulting archaeologist, was arranging for an autopsy of the frozen bodies, obtaining funding from the Atlantic Richfield Foundation and ARCO Alaska, and the cooperation of Drs. Michael Zimmerman and Arthur Aufderheide and a team of medical scholars and scientists to study the remains. The borough and the elders were in agreement that the skeletons and preserved bodies should be studied as long as they were treated with respect and not disfigured. I arrived back in Alaska in time to attend the autopsies in Fairbanks and then to proceed to Barrow. This whirlwind of media attention and autopsy procedures was new and exciting. It was sometimes difficult to keep from referring to the bodies as "specimens" and their organs as "data."

The preliminary autopsy results and our initial interpretations of the archaeological context were made public at a press conference, resulting in several Alaskan newspaper, television, and radio reports. Zimmerman and Aufderheide concluded that the bodies were of two women. One died in her mid-twenties, and the other in her early forties; the latter had recently given birth. Both suffered from anthracosis (from inhalation of soot from fires), atherosclerosis, and osteoporosis. They each died within minutes of the house collapse, from chest injuries. Their bladders were distended, the colons had contents, and the stomachs were empty, suggesting that death occurred in the middle of the night. The associated finds confirmed this view, since the women had been naked, in repose, and covered with skins or robes.

We returned to Barrow, where Raymond and I made presentations to the Borough Commission on Inupiat History, Language and Culture; the Elders Conference; and the community, the last through appearances on KBRW radio. Our excavation of the house had continued, going sufficiently deep to reveal that there was clear ice in the tunnel under the house, implying an abandonment that might contain other remains associated with the events that crushed the house. Because the excavation of the house was completed without identification of adult males, an infant, or stone lamps, there was speculation that these "missing remains" might be found in the tunnel.

Somewhat naively, we had hoped to study a family's behaviors "frozen in time," with artifacts in the position of their last use before the house collapse. With the time of the collapse fixed in the middle of the night, we soon realized that the last use of artifacts was placement in "storage," rather than "dinner" or "needle manufacture" or "butchering." This meant that the unique research opportunity was to study frozen archaeological evidence for storage, caches, and the nighttime organization of house contents—sleeping was the principal human activity that was "frozen in time."

The borough purchased the landowner's rights to the collection and encouraged us to submit a proposal for an excavation in 1983 of the tunnel features associated with the house. We completed our excavations, removed the structural wood for the borough to collect and stabilize in preparation for museum exhibition, and began to think about what the tunnel area might reveal. The archaeologists left the field at the end of August, having completed their research and organized the further study of the artifacts and data and preparation of reports. On September 15, 1982, the bodies and skeletons were formally reburied in a Barrow cemetery.

In March 1983, the research results of the excavations and autopsies were presented at a special symposium at the annual meeting of the Alaska Anthropological Association. Here for the first time, the scientists who had studied samples taken from the bodies at autopsy reported that while the individuals were generally in good health when they died, they had suffered from illnesses that left their mark. These include pneumonia, trichinosis, and malnutrition. In conjunction with these meetings, the participants were interviewed for several media and television productions, and also traveled to Barrow for presentations within the community.

When the borough brought us back to Barrow in 1983, we had great expectations for the excavation of the tunnel and kitchen of the Mound 44 house. We first drilled a number of soil borings where we expected to find the tunnel. The core profiles revealed the nature of the subsurface deposits. Once we found a core with "clear ice," we knew that it contained part of the tunnel and we could outline our excavations properly. While we did not find any human remains or lamps, we did discover a number of important characteristics of tunnel architecture and storage. The tunnel was really a trench dug into the frozen ground. The roof consisted of horizontally stacked sods on top of a ceiling framed with wood and whale bone, supported at intervals with bone uprights along the margins of the tunnel. More sods were stacked along the tunnel outside the trench to make walls for the alcoves, storage areas, and kitchen.

In the alcoves along the tunnel, we found many skin bags full of clothing, artifacts, and raw materials. Several had part of their contents spilled onto the tunnel floor and the bag tossed among them. I was surprised to find little stored food anywhere. These finds and the lack of stone lamps suggest that someone had gone through part of the house after the collapse and removed some items, apparently undeterred by traditional sentiment that houses in which people had died should be left alone. Because the clear ice that covered all these remains was homogeneous from top to bottom without layered evidence of several filling and cutting events, it seems likely that the artifact and food removal occurred sometime in the several months after the collapse but before the next spring thaw.

Again this season, we were visited by the elders and others from the borough and community, including a television crew from the University of Alaska, Anchorage. We also reburied the skeletal materials recovered in the 1981 excavations of formal burial areas of the Birnirk culture, which predated the Mound 44 finds by perhaps five hundred years. This was a solemn ceremony with lay readers from the borough officiating in a new cemetery. The weather was cold, with snow flurries reminding us that it snows here every month of the year, even in summer.

We left Barrow at the end of August. I have not been back. But the legacy of the "Frozen Family" continues. The currents, tides, and storms still tear against the land and, occasionally, rip it. Twice since 1982, when human bodies have eroded out of the bluff near Mound 44, the community has reacted to try to save them. When a large block of the coast near Mound 44 broke off and portions of archaeological deposits slumped down to the beach, the community sponsored field school excavations to teach and to learn. The borough has installed the 1983 traveling display describing the Frozen Family finds (produced by the Atlantic Richfield Foundation) in its museum facility in the former Naval Arctic Research Laboratory near Point Barrow. The television production *People of Utqiagvik* airs regularly on Alaska public television and is popular among those who borrow videos from the University of Alaska, Anchorage. Reports on these investigations include the special issue of *Arctic Anthropology* describing the 1982 excavations of the Frozen Family and the biological investigations of the human remains, the 1987 article in *National Geographic* that describes the Frozen Family, and the three-volume set of formal reports published by the North Slope Borough in 1990 describing the three summers of excavation at Utqiagvik, including the excavations of Mound 44.

In addition to these publications and programs, the borough has funded archaeological field schools, has committed to public interpretations, and continues to cooperate with archaeologists and medical researchers whenever additional frozen remains have been found. The borough and the archaeologists involved are a model of cooperative effort to an extent not seen elsewhere in Alaska and rarely seen elsewhere.

So what are the lessons, the lasting contributions from the discovery of the Frozen Family? First, archaeological research is a meeting ground for several communities. From conception to publication, this research was conducted within a complex matrix of people and institutions. The discovery of the frozen bodies was serendipitous. The recovery of the Frozen Family was a socially complicated, cooperative effort. Second, it is difficult to prepare to execute complex research designs in situations that can change in ways only dimly anticipated. For good results, we rely on the basic parameters of goodwill and good faith and good communications, finding common cause throughout the community of stakeholders.

Contributions include paving the way for heritage research that balanced the social and scientific requirements for research on human ancestors. This project was remarkable for being able to conduct important and unprecedented research on human remains from within a community that had reason to be concerned that the bodies might be recognized as relatives. This project was among the first archaeological studies of human remains to involve a period of sanctioned research with agreed-on protocols followed by a respectful reburial within the community of descendants. This project reversed a half century of exploitative archaeology, leading to a strong program of community-based heritage research, one component of which continues to be archaeological. We now know a great deal about the organization of winter houses, their construction, and their abandonment. We have an emerging understanding of the prehistoric health of northern Alaska and its people. We understand the importance of grounding the

Inupiat future in their understanding of the past, and we respect the knowledge that the elders and their ancestors are able to provide.

For my part, I was gratified to have directed the conception, design, and execution of research; managed the tortuous course of the project through three field seasons; and worked closely with so many people who each had a key role to play in achieving successful results.

An African Cemetery in Manhattan

Spencer Harrington

Dutch colonists founded Nieuw Amsterdam in 1624 to capitalize on the fur trade. The settlement prospered, especially after the British takeover of 1664. In 1674, Nieuw Amsterdam became New York. From the late seventeenth century until the American Revolution, southern Manhattan Island became a bustling seaport. The growing metropolis of New York has always been portrayed as being peopled by enterprising European immigrants, carving out a new life in an alien land, with close ties to their homeland across the Atlantic. The Statue of Liberty and Ellis Island carefully preserve this image, yet reality for many was very different. Much of New York's bustling seaport was built on reclaimed land. For most of the heavy reclamation work, landfill contractors used black slaves, people rarely mentioned in the archives of the day, but reclaimed for history by archaeological discovery.

A chance discovery of an African-American cemetery near Water Street in 1991 caused furious controversy. The General Services Administration planned to build a thirty-four-story office building to house a number of federal offices in lower Manhattan. When archaeologists retained to study the building site examined city maps of the day, they found that a "Negros Burial Ground" had existed at this location in the mid-eighteenth century. As many as twenty thousand Africans and poor whites could have been buried in this five- to six-acre lot. Experts assumed that the digging of several deep basements in the nineteenth century had destroyed most, if not all, of the burials in the abandoned cemetery. Six weeks before construction was scheduled to begin, the cautious General Services Administration hired a group of archaeologists to check the lot just in case one or two odd burials still remained. Dozens of undisturbed graves appeared over the next two months. From just this small portion of the cemetery came 420 skeletons, often stacked one on top of the other, the largest sample of historic African remains ever discovered in North America. Intense controversies surround the exhumed skeletons. The dispute over the African Burial Ground epitomizes the profound ethical debates surrounding the excavation of human remains by archaeologists.

Spencer Harrington's investigative article "Bones and Bureaucrats" ably summa-

The bones of 420 enslaved Africans found last year under a parking lot two blocks north of New York's City Hall comprise the largest and earliest collection of African-American remains, and possibly the largest and earliest collection of American colonial remains of any ethnic group. The excavation of the old Negros Burial Ground has challenged the popular belief that there was no slavery in colonial New York, and has provided unparalleled data for the Howard University scholars who will study the remains of New York's first African Americans. But as archaeologists removed the remains one by one, they dug up age-old resentment and suspicion with every trowel-full of earth. Scholarly excitement was tempered by the protest of the city's black community, which felt its concerns were not being addressed in decisions about the excavation and disposition of the remains. In the flurry of protests, negotiations, and political maneuverings, the controversy took on an undeniably racial cast. The African Burial Ground, as it is known today, became a "microcosm of the issues of racism and economic exploitation confronting New York City," says Michael L. Blakey, a Howard University anthropologist and the burial ground's scientific director.

In a national context, the controversy over the burial ground excavation became an important episode in a larger struggle of descendant communities to reclaim their heritage. But more specifically, the story was about African-American empowerment: about how a black congressman, acting on the advice of New York City's first black mayor, stopped the excavation of the burial ground; about how the African-American community chose Washington D.C.'s Howard University, the country's most prestigious black research university, as a venue for the study of the remains, thereby ensuring that black researchers and students would study and interpret the remains of their ancestors; and about how the city's black community lobbied for and received a $3 million appropriation from Congress for a memorial and commemorative museum. Equally important were the hard lessons learned by the General Services Administration, the federal agency that supervised the excavation—lessons about the importance of descendant-community involvement in salvage archaeology.

The story of the African Burial Ground begins in 1626, when the Dutch West Indies Company imported its first shipment of slaves, eleven young men from today's Congo-Angola region of Africa. Two years later, the company brought over three African women "for the comfort of the company's Negro men," according to Dutch West Indies records. Like the British who governed Manhattan after them, the Dutch encountered difficulties attracting European settlers to the new colony. Grave manpower shortages threatened the profitability of the Dutch West Indies trading enterprise, and the company was quick to import slave labor to farm its fields. In 1664, just before the Dutch ceded Manhattan to the British, enslaved Africans made up about 40 percent of the colony's total population. The British continued the slave trade, importing as many as 6,800 Africans between 1700 and 1774, many of whom had worked previously on Caribbean plantations. By the mid-eighteenth century, New York had become a thriving port town, and enslaved Africans loaded and unloaded cargo at the docks, wharves, slips, and warehouses along the East River. They also piloted boats ferrying produce from the farming villages of Long Island, repaired and expanded city streets, and worked in shipbuilding and construction. On the eve of the American Revolution, New York City had the largest number of enslaved Africans of any English colonial settlement except Charleston, South Carolina, and it had the highest proportion of slaves to Europeans of any northern settlement. Though seldom acknowledged, Africans were essential to the functioning, as well as the building, of colonial New York.

In November 1697, New York City adopted a policy of mortuary apartheid, declaring lower Manhattan churchyards off-limits to blacks. Forced to look for a place to bury its dead, New York's African population, which then numbered about 700, chose unappropriated property outside city limits two blocks north of today's City Hall. There, from 1712 until 1790, in an area characterized by David Valentine, an early city historian, as "unattractive and desolate," Africans conducted last rites for their people. "So little seems to have been thought of the race that not even a dedication of their burial place was made by church authorities," wrote Valentine of what was known then as the Negros Burial Ground. Under the British, Africans were subject to a sunset curfew and city ordinances that prohibited unsupervised gatherings of more than three slaves. They were, however, allowed to gather in large numbers and with regularity at the burial ground. Some 10,000 to 20,000 people, both black and lower-class white, are believed to have been buried in the five- to six-acre plot of land.

The growth of the city's population in the late eighteenth and early nineteenth centuries led to a northward expansion along main thoroughfares such as Broadway. Street plans were drafted, and blocks over the burial ground were divided into lots for residential and commercial development. By the end of the century, ten- and fifteen-story buildings with deep foundations and with vaults that were used for storage and coal delivery were going up. The Negros Burial Ground, now paved or built over, was all but forgotten, noted only in a few historical maps and documents. Meanwhile, African Americans were now burying their dead on the Lower East Side, near what are now Chrystie and Delancey streets.

Nearly 200 years later a section of the burial ground lay beneath a parking lot between Duane and Reade streets. In December 1990, New York sold this property and another plot on nearby Foley Square to the General Services Administration (GSA), the federal agency charged with constructing and managing government buildings. The GSA paid $104 million for both properties, which it hoped to develop simultaneously. It planned to build a $276 million, thirty-four-story office tower and adjoining four-story pavilion on the parking lot area. A federal courthouse was envisioned for the Foley Square property. The tower, designated 290 Broadway, would contain the offices of the United States Attorney, a regional office of the Environmental Protection Agency, and the downtown district office of the Internal Revenue Service. The pavilion would house a day-care center, an auditorium, and a pedestrian galleria.

Five months before the GSA bought the sites from the city, the agency hired Historic Conservation and Interpretation (HCI), an archaeological salvage and consulting firm, to write the archaeological portion of an environmental impact statement for the 290 Broadway site. Such statements are a legal requirement before any new construction using federal funds can begin. HCI's report identified the area as a section of the old Negros Burial Ground and included historical maps indicating its approximate location. But the impact statement predicted that nineteenth- and twentieth-century construction at the site would have destroyed any significant archaeological deposits. It read in part: "The construction of deep sub-basements would have obliterated any remains within the lots that fall within the historic bounds of the cemetery."

Still, the statement left open the possibility of some human remains being preserved under an old alley that once bisected Duane and Reade streets. That the GSA purchased the land despite this possibility suggests that the agency was betting on HCI's overall assessment that few, if any, human remains would be found there. In retrospect, GSA regional director William Diamond admits that the agency would never have bought the land if it had known it would have to remove hundreds of skeletons before sinking the office tower foundation.

In May 1991, six months after purchasing the land, the GSA hired HCI to investigate the possibility that there were undisturbed burials in the alley area. By the end of the summer the firm started to find human bones. In September a full-scale excavation was under way, and on October 8 Diamond held a press conference to announce the discovery of the remains. One year later, the last of some 420 skeletons had been removed from the site to Lehman College in the Bronx, where they were undergoing conservation before being transferred to Howard University for more detailed study.

African-American outrage over the handling of the excavation stemmed from a perception that the black community had no control over the fate of its heritage—that decisions about the burial ground were being made by white bureaucrats with little insight into African-American history and spiritual sensitivities. "Religious, Afrocentric people believe that to disturb burials in any way is the highest form of disrespect," says Gina Stahlnecker, an aide to State Senator David Patterson, who represents Harlem and the Upper West Side. "There were some people who believed the archaeologists were releasing evil." According to Peggy King Jorde, of the Mayor's Office of Construction, an early monitor of the project, the GSA initially was calling the site a "potters' field," which she felt divorced it from its African origin and diminished its importance. There were even rumors, she says, that the bones were to be removed without any archaeological study. Jorde says that the GSA had only vague ideas about what to do with the remains that were coming to light.

The black community was also upset because it was not alerted at the outset to what might lie beneath the parking lot between Duane and Reade streets. While the GSA did distribute both draft and final environmental impact statements to more than 200 federal, state, and city agencies and local community groups, the agency did not alert civic groups in predominantly black neighborhoods that the buildings would be constructed on top of the old burial ground. "I spoke to hundreds and hundreds of people in the black community, and no one had ever heard about it," says Stahlnecker. While distributing environmental impact statements to descendant communities may seem like a good idea, it is not customary for private or government developers to do so. Peter Sneed, the GSA's planning staff director, argues that the distribution list was formulated in accordance with federal regulations. "We didn't include the Harlem community board because the project isn't in Harlem, it's in lower Manhattan," he says. "We felt it was incumbent upon the Mayor's office to spread the word. It's unreasonable to expect a federal agency to know every interest group in the community."

African-American fury over the excavation increased dramatically after a backhoe operator digging the tower's foundation accidentally destroyed several of the burials. The incident was reported by Dan Pagano, an archaeologist for the city's Landmarks Preservation Commission, who was photographing the site through a telephoto lens when he spotted HCI archaeologists sifting through human remains outside the excavation area, where the backhoe had scooped up earth so that a concrete footing could be poured for the tower. Pagano says jawbones and leg and arm bones were among the remains scooped up by the backhoe. The GSA blamed the accident on an out-of-date drawing that the construction crews were using to determine which part of the site was "culturally sterile." Diamond halted tower construction pending further investigation by archaeologists. The incident led State Senator David Patterson to form an oversight committee to monitor the burial ground excavation.

Miriam Francis, a member of Patterson's committee, says that the involvement of African-American anthropologists in the excavation was among the group's most pressing concerns. "If it was an African find, we wanted to make sure that it was interpreted from an African point of view," she says. But the committee soon learned that the GSA had picked physical anthropologists from the city's Metropolitan Forensic Anthropology Team (MFAT) to conduct field analyses of the remains and that the bones would be stored at the group's Lehman College facility. "We didn't know anything about MFAT, whether they were butchers, bakers, or candlestick makers," says Francis. She notes that when the committee introduced the GSA to African-American specialists like Howard University's Michael Blakey, it was either stonewalled or ignored.

Meanwhile, the GSA was having difficulty getting HCI, its archaeological salvage contractor, to produce a research design stating conservation measures and scientific study goals for the burial project. The GSA had managed to obtain extensions on the report's due date from the Advisory Council on Historic Preservation, the government agency that reviews all federal projects that might have an impact on historic sites. Still, the missing research plan sent further signals

*Broken legs of an African-
American skeleton found in the
African Burial Ground in
Manhattan. The legs may have
been broken at burial to fit the
corpse into the grave.*

Chester Higgins, Jr.

to the black community that something was wrong with the way work was progressing. "Any archaeological excavation is useless without a research design," noted Landmarks Preservation Commission Chair Laurie Beckelman at a congressional hearing on the burial ground. "It's like driving a car in a foreign country without a road map or destination."

HCI's Edward Rutsch, the project's archaeologist, says that although he was responsible for the research design, he felt too overworked to get it done properly. "They [GSA] had us working seven days a week and overtime every day," says Rutsch. "Many times it was expressed to me that millions of dollars of public money were being lost. There was terrific pressure to get the excavation done—to finish it."

Last April [1991], black activists staged a one-day blockade of the site in an effort to prevent the GSA from pouring concrete for the tower's foundation. Among other things, they were concerned that there was little African-American involvement in the scientific aspects of the excavation; they were visibly unhappy at the choice of Lehman College as the site for the conservation of the remains. Bones from the site had been wrapped in newspaper and placed in cardboard boxes before being shipped to Lehman. One problem, according to Dan Baer of Edwards and Kelcey, an engineering firm hired to manage the site, was that "we were digging them out faster than [storage] cases could be made." But in the African-American community there was concern that the bones were being damaged at Lehman. "They had some remains up there in boxes ten or eleven months," says Abd-Allah Adesanya, director of the Mayor's Office of African American and Caribbean Affairs. "They were wrapped in newspaper longer than they should have been. They had to be rewrapped in acid-free paper." Baer says, "The bones were stored in newspaper, which may be scientific protocol, but it didn't appear respectful to those who visited the site. It was a mistake that was made. But the bones were in good shape and Dr. Blakey said so after touring the facility."

Blakey's tour of Lehman resulted from pressure by Senator Patterson's committee. "We kept asking them [MFAT], 'Can we go up there?' And that involved more waiting, more delays," says Miriam Francis. "It wasn't that we were against Lehman, we just wanted to see how our ancestors were being stored." Blakey's visit to the facility confirmed the community's suspicion of inadequate conservation. In a letter to *Archaeology*, Blakey wrote, "We intervened in time to prevent the potential for further deterioration, such as the spread of mold in the skeletal remains due to inadequate environmental controls, and improper storage of skeletal materials on top of fragile bone."

As the excavation progressed, the GSA began briefing the public on the burial project's progress. But there was a widespread perception among African Americans that the GSA was merely paying lip-service to the public, that they were digging the bones as fast as they could so the tower foundation could be poured. "People would tell them [the GSA] their gripes, then they went off and did what they wanted," says Adesanya. "The community wanted to be let in on the decision-making process, to influence the direction of the project." While descendant-community input into decisions about the course of contract excavations seems desirable when human remains are involved, consultation is not part of standard archaeological practice. Nonetheless "the [African-American] community was very unhappy," says Diamond, "and I understood that and kept saying to them, 'I wish I could help you with this but my obligations by law are contrary to your wishes, and the only way we can get this changed is by an act of Congress or an agreement from the administrator of the GSA.' And I was in consultation with them [GSA administrator Richard G. Austin and members of Congress] and they were telling me to continue the construction."

At the GSA's public meetings, African Americans also questioned the propriety of continuing with the removal of remains from the area where the pavilion would be built. They also hoped that the GSA would consider not building the pavilion, or at least modify the plans so there would be no further removals. "There were several conflicting demands," recalls Diamond. "Some wanted the exhumation to stop, others wanted nothing built on the site, and still others wanted a museum built on the site. . . . But I had no authority but to continue under the law with the construction."

The GSA eventually replaced Historic Conservation and Interpretation with John Milner Associates (JMA), a West Chester, Pennsylvania, archaeological contractor. JMA had recently completed a successful excavation of an early-nineteenth-century cemetery associated with the First African Baptist Church in Philadelphia that brought to light information on that city's early black history. "JMA had done this sort of job before," says Baer. "We didn't feel we had involved the community enough and we thought that JMA would improve that situation."

But reports by agencies monitoring the excavation were becoming increasingly critical. One report filed by the Advisory Council on Historic Preservation stated, in part, that "the GSA was proceeding without any clear focus on why the remains were being removed; how they were to be analyzed; how many more bodies were involved; or, what the African-American community's desire was for the treatment of the burials." Mayor David Dinkins sent a letter to Diamond complaining about the lack of a research design and requesting "that the GSA suspend all excavation and construction activities in the pavilion area and bring the project into compliance with the terms outlined in the Memorandum of Agreement [a document specifying the terms of archaeological work to be undertaken in advance of construction]." There is "no basis for discontinuance of ongoing excavations" was Diamond's response a week later. "I would not be put in a position of abrogating important government contracts because of political pressure," he later recalled.

The final act in the drama was played out before the congressional committee that appropriates funds for the GSA, the House Subcommittee on Public Buildings and Grounds. Meeting in New York, the subcommittee was chaired by former Representative Gus Savage, an Illinois Democrat, who heard testimony from the GSA, the Advisory Council, the city's Landmarks Preservation Commission, and concerned citizens. At the meeting, the GSA argued that stopping the excavation would jeopardize the exposed human remains, and it estimated that relinquishing the pavilion site would cost taxpayers as much as $40 million: $5 million in interest payments, $10 million in land acquisition costs, and $25 million in initial construction costs.

Savage then subjected GSA representatives to intense questioning, during which it became apparent that at the outset the GSA was aware that a historic burial ground had once occupied the land it intended to purchase and develop, and that the agency had made no contingency plans for construction in the event that human remains were found. The meeting also revealed that the building prospectus for 290 Broadway the GSA had submitted for congressional approval did not mention the burial ground, nor was Savage's subcommittee alerted by the agency when HCI's impact statement mentioned the possibility of intact graves. Savage ended the hearing early, noting that he would not approve any further GSA projects until he received "a more honest and respectful response" from the agency regarding its excavation of the burial ground. "And don't waste your time asking this subcommittee for anything else as long as I'm chairman, unless you can figure out a way to go around me! I am not going to be part of your disrespect," Savage said.

Three days later, Savage halted excavation on the pavilion site, and last October former President Bush signed Public Law 102-393, ordering the GSA to cease construction of the pavilion portion of the project and approving $3 million for the construction of a museum honoring the contribution of African Americans to colonial New York City. Meanwhile, JMA removed the last of the exposed burials.

In a statement to the House Subcommittee on Public Buildings and Grounds, GSA head Richard G. Austin acknowledged that "in hindsight we could have handled some things better." Austin's statement made it clear to all parties that the GSA recognized the need for descendant-community cooperation in salvage excavations. Its office tower would be built, but African Americans would determine the course of research on the remains. The agency hired Blakey to develop a research design, which he produced in consultation with JMA and numerous black scholars. Blakey was also appointed scientific director of a five-year research program on the remains that will take place at Howard University. Sherill D. Wilson, an urban anthropologist and ethnohistorian, calls the sudden involvement of black scholars "very revolutionary." Such scholarship, she says, "is going to set a precedent for what happens to African burial grounds in the future, and how African heritage will be viewed by the public."

Meanwhile, a chastened GSA has also set up a federal advisory committee chaired by Howard Dodson of New York's Schomburg Center for Research in Black Culture that will address plans for reburial of the remains, an African Burial Ground memorial, a burial ground exhibition in the office tower, and a museum of African and African-American History in New York City. State Senator David Patterson's burial ground oversight committee seeks to create a museum that will honor African-American heritage, "a place similar to Ellis Island, something that can attest to Afro-American history." The city Landmarks Preservation Commission has also proposed that the burial ground be designated a city landmark and has requested that it be considered for National Historic Landmark status. These efforts stemmed in part from a massive petition drive spearheaded by Senator Patterson's oversight committee and jazz musician Noel Pointer that yielded more than 100,000 signatures. Among other things, the petition called for the creation of a museum and landmark status for the burial ground.

The burial ground controversy and its attendant publicity have had important repercussions nationwide. "The media exposure has created a larger, national audience for this type of research," says Theresa Singleton, an archaeologist at the Smithsonian Institution who has done pioneering research on African-American sites. "I've been called by dozens of scholars and laypeople, all of them interested in African-American archaeology, all of them curious about why they don't know more about the field. Until recently, even some black scholars considered African-American archaeology a waste of time. That's changed now."

Things have indeed changed. Public curiosity about this country's African-American past has been aroused by the New York experience. And it is probably safe to assume that in the future government and private developers will take a hard look at how to include descendant communities in their salvage excavations, especially when human remains are concerned. "Everyone could have talked more to everyone else," concludes the GSA's planning staff director Peter Sneed. "There would have been a lot less heartache . . . the GSA has certainly been sensitized to archaeology."

Exploring Maya Copán

JOHN LLOYD STEPHENS

John Lloyd Stephens (1805–1850) was a New York lawyer with a taste for politics who started traveling for his health. His letters home were so eloquent that his family published them, earning him an unexpected reputation as a best-selling author from his travels in Egypt, Russia, and the Holy Land. While in London in 1836, Stephens met Frederick Catherwood (1804–1852), a British architect and artist who had just returned from a lengthy sketching trip in the Near East. Catherwood was another inveterate traveler who had repaired mosques in Cairo and even worked on railroad construction. The two men became friends and prominent members of New York's literary circle, where they heard rumors of unexplored temples in the Central American rain forest. In October 1839, they set out on a journey in search of rumored jungle civilizations.

About five weeks later, they arrived at the tiny village of Copán. While Stephens wandered through plazas and overgrown pyramids, Catherwood stood ankle-deep in mud sketching the elaborate glyphs on Copán's stelae, making copies so accurate that they rival the best photographs. (Both men knew at once that these hieroglyphs were quite unlike Egyptian script and thus of very great interest.) Their first journey then took them from Copán to Palenque and Uxmal in the Yucatán, where Stephens realized he was looking at the remains not of a colonizing European civilization, but of an entirely indigenous American society, whose descendants still lived in nearby villages. His Incidents of Travel in Central America, Chiapas, and Yucatan *appeared in 1841 to critical acclaim and best-sellerdom. It is still in print today.*

The same year, Catherwood and Stephens returned to the Yucatán to study Uxmal, Chichen Itzá, and other now famous ruins. Their second Incidents *book was as successful as the first. Stephens corresponded with the Boston historian William Prescott, whose immortal* History of the Conquest of Mexico *(1843) replaced myth with historical reality and clothed American archaeology with respectability. His views on the Maya played an important role in Prescott's account, the first to take account of archaeology and to attribute a significant time depth to ancient Central American civilization.*

In later life, Catherwood and Stephens were involved in schemes to build a canal across Central America. Stephens died of the aftereffects of fever in 1850, while Cather-

wood perished when the steamship SS Arctic *foundered in the mid-Atlantic two years later.*

    John Lloyd Stephens's lyrical description of Copán, likening it to a shipwreck, is a classic of early archaeological reporting. So is his sober description of the palace at Palenque. But most important of all is his forthright declaration that the civilization that built these stupendous sites was not of Old World origin, but an indigenous society. From his remarks stemmed all subsequent research into the Mayan civilization.

As we gazed on the wall of the city on the opposite side of the river, this account of the city's conquest which the Spanish historians have given us seemed to us most meager and unsatisfactory. It did not appear to us that the massive stone structures before us could have belonged to a city the intrenchment of which could be broken down by the charge of a single horseman. Since at this place the river was not fordable, we returned to our mules, mounted, and rode to another part of the bank, a short distance above. Here the stream was wide, and in some places deep, rapid, and with a broken and stony bottom. Fording it, we rode along the bank by a footpath encumbered with undergrowth, which José opened by cutting away the branches. At the foot of the wall which we had seen from the opposite bank we again dismounted and tied our mules.

    The wall was of cut stone, well laid, and in a good state of preservation. We ascended by large stone steps, only some of which were well preserved, and reached a terrace, the form of which it was impossible to make out because of the density of the forest in which it was enveloped. Following a path which our guide cleared for us with his machete, we passed a large fragment of stone elaborately sculptured and half buried in the earth, and came to the angle of a structure with steps on the sides, which in so far as the trees allowed us to make them out, resembled the sides of a pyramid in form and appearance. Diverging from the base of the structure, and working our way through the thick woods, we came upon a square stone column, about fourteen feet high and three feet on each side, sculptured on all four of the sides, from the base to the top, in very bold relief. On the front side was carved the figure of a man (evidently a portrait) curiously and richly dressed, whose face was solemn, stern, and well fitted to excite terror. The design on the opposite side was unlike anything we had ever seen before; the remaining two sides were covered with hieroglyphics. About three feet in front of the column was a large block of stone, also sculptured with figures and emblematical devices. From our guide we learned that the square column was an "idol" and the block of stone an "altar." The sight of this unexpected monument put at rest once and forever all uncertainty in our minds as to the character of American antiquities, and gave us the assurance that the objects we were in search of were not only interesting as the remains of an unknown people, but were works of art as well, proving, like newly discovered historical records, that the people who once occupied the American continents were not savages.

With an interest perhaps stronger than we had ever felt in wandering among the ruins of Egypt, we followed our guide, who, sometimes missing his way, with a constant and vigorous use of his machete conducted us through the thick forest, among half-buried fragments, to fourteen more monuments of the same character and appearance, some with more elegant designs, and some in work-manship equal to the finest monuments of the Egyptians. One, we found, had been displaced from its pedestal by enormous roots; another, locked in the close embrace of branches of trees, was almost lifted out of the earth; and still another had been hurled to the ground and bound down by huge vines and creepers. One with its altar before it stood in a grove of trees which grew around it, seemingly to shade and shroud it as a sacred thing; in the solemn stillness of the woods, it seemed a divinity mourning over a fallen people. The only sounds that disturbed the quiet of this buried city were the noise of monkeys moving among the tops of the trees and the cracking of dry branches broken by their weight. They moved over our heads in long and swift processions, forty or fifty at a time. Some with little ones wound in their long arms walked out to the end of boughs and, holding on with their hind feet or a curl of the tail, sprang to a branch of the next tree; with a noise like a current of wind, they passed on into the depths of the forest. It was the first time we had seen these mockeries of humanity and, amid these strange monuments, they seemed like wandering spir-its of the departed race guarding the ruins of their former habitations.

We returned to the base of the pyramidal structure and ascended by regular stone steps, which in some places had been forced apart by bushes and saplings and in others thrown down by the growth of large trees. In parts they were ornamented with sculptured figures and rows of death's heads. Climbing over the ruined top, we reached a terrace overgrown with trees and, crossing it, de-scended by stone steps into an area so covered with trees that at first we could not make out its form. When the machete had cleared the way, we saw that it was a square with steps on all the sides almost as perfect as those of the Roman amphitheatre. The steps were ornamented with sculpture, and on the south side, about halfway up, forced out of its place by roots, was a colossal head, again evidently a portrait. We ascended these steps and reached a broad terrace a hundred feet high overlooking the river and supported by the wall which we had seen from the opposite bank. The whole terrace was covered with trees, and even at this height were two gigantic ceibas (kapok trees), over twenty feet in circumference; their half-naked roots extended fifty or a hundred feet around, binding down the ruins and shading them with their wide-spreading branches.

We sat down on the very edge of the wall and strove in vain to penetrate the mystery by which we were surrounded. Who were the people that built this city? In the ruined cities of Egypt, even in the long-lost Petra, the stranger knows the story of the people whose vestiges he finds around him. America, say historians, was peopled by savages; but savages never reared these structures, savages never carved these stones. When we asked the Indians who had made them, their dull answer was "Quién sabe? (Who knows?)" There were no associ-ations connected with this place, none of those stirring recollections which hallow Rome, Athens, and "The world's great mistress on the Egyptian plain." But architecture, sculpture, and painting, all the arts which embellish life, had flourished in this overgrown forest; orators, warriors, and statesmen, beauty, ambition, and glory had lived and passed away, and none knew that such things had been, or could tell of their past existence. Books, the records of knowledge, are silent on this theme.

The city was desolate. No remnant of this race hangs round the ruins, with traditions handed down from father to son and from generation to generation. It lay before us like a shattered bark in the midst of the ocean, her masts gone, her name effaced, her crew perished, and none to tell whence she came, to whom she belonged, how long on her voyage, or what caused her destruction—her lost people to be traced only by some fancied resemblance in the construction of the vessel, and, perhaps, never to be known at all. The place where we were sitting, was it a citadel from which an unknown people had sounded the trumpet of war? or a temple for the worship of the God of peace? or did the inhabitants worship idols made with their own hands and offer sacrifices on the stones before them? All was mystery, dark, impenetrable mystery, and every circumstance increased it. In Egypt the colossal skeletons of gigantic temples stand in unwatered sands in all the nakedness of desolation; but here an immense forest shrouds the ruins, hiding them from sight, heightening the impression and moral effect, and giving an intensity and almost wildness to the interest. . . .

Of the moral effect of the monuments themselves, standing as they do in the depths of a tropical forest, silent and solemn, strange in design, excellent in sculpture, rich in ornament, different from the works of any other people, their uses and purposes and whole history so entirely unknown, with hieroglyphics explaining all but being perfectly unintelligible, I shall not pretend to convey any idea. Often the imagination was pained in gazing at them. The tone which pervades the ruins is that of deep solemnity. An imaginative mind might be infected with superstitious feelings. From constantly calling them by that name in our intercourse with the Indians, we regarded these solemn memorials as idols—deified kings and heroes—objects of adoration and ceremonial worship. We did not find on either the monuments or sculptured fragments any delineations of human, or, in fact, any other kind of sacrifice, but we had no doubt that the large sculptured stone invariably found before each idol had been employed as a sacrificial altar. The form of sculpture most frequently met with was a death's head, sometimes the principal ornament and sometimes only accessory. There were whole rows of them on the outer wall, adding gloom to the mystery of the place, keeping death and the grave before the eyes of the living, presenting the idea of a holy city—the Mecca or Jerusalem of an unknown people.

In regard to the age of this desolate city I shall not at present offer any conjecture. Some idea might perhaps be formed from the accumulations of earth and the gigantic trees growing on the top of the ruined structures, but it would be uncertain and unsatisfactory. Nor shall I at this moment offer any conjecture in regard to the people who built it; or to the time when or the means by which it was depopulated to become a desolation and ruin; or as to whether it fell by the sword, or famine, or pestilence. The trees which shroud it may have sprung from the blood of its slaughtered inhabitants; they may have perished howling with hunger; or pestilence, like the cholera, may have piled its streets with the dead and driven forever the feeble remnants from their homes. Of such dire calamities to other cities we have authentic accounts, in eras both prior and subsequent to the discovery of the country by the Spaniards. One thing I believe: its history is graven on its monuments. No Champollion has yet brought to them the energies of his inquiring mind. Who shall read them?

> Chaos of ruins! who shall trace the void,
> O'er the dim fragments cast a lunar light,
> And say "here was or is," where all is doubly night?

––––––––

The palace was constructed of stone, with a mortar of lime and sand, and the whole front was covered with stucco and painted. The piers were ornamented with spirited figures in bas-relief. One stands in an upright position and in profile, exhibiting an extraordinary facial angle of about forty-five degrees. The upper part of the head seems to have been compressed and lengthened, perhaps by the same process employed upon the heads of the Choctaw and Flathead Indians of our own country. Supposing the statues to be images of living personages, or the creations of artists according to their ideas of perfect figures, they indicate a race of people now lost and unknown. The headdress is evidently a plume of feathers. Over the shoulders is a short covering decorated with studs, and a breastplate; part of the ornament of the girdle is broken. The tunic is probably a leopard's skin. He holds in his hand a staff or sceptre, and opposite his hands are the marks of three hieroglyphics, which have decayed or been broken off. At his feet are two naked figures seated cross-legged, and apparently suppliants. A fertile imagination might find many explanations for these strange figures, but no satisfactory interpretation presents itself to my mind. The hieroglyphics doubtless tell its history. The stucco is of admirable consistency, and hard as stone. It was painted, and in different places about it we discovered the remains of red, blue, yellow, black, and white.

The principal doorway is not distinguished by its size or by any superior ornament, but is only indicated by a range of broad stone steps leading up to it on the terrace. The doorways have no doors, nor are there the remains of any. Within, on each side, are three niches in the wall, about eight or ten inches square, with a cylindrical stone about two inches in diameter fixed upright, by which perhaps a door was secured. Along the cornice outside, projecting about a foot beyond the front, holes were drilled at intervals through the stone. Our impression was, that an immense cotton cloth, running the whole length of the building, perhaps painted in a style corresponding with the ornaments, was attached to this cornice, and raised and lowered like a curtain. Such a curtain is used now in front of the piazzas of some haciendas in Yucatán.

The tops of the doorways were all broken. They had evidently been square, and over every one were large niches in the wall on each side, in which the lintels had been laid. These lintels had all fallen, and the stones above formed broken natural arches. Underneath were heaps of rubbish, but there were no remains of lintels. If they had been single slabs of stone, some of them must have been visible and prominent; and we made up our minds that these lintels were of *wood*. We had no authority for this. We should not have ventured the conclusion but for the wooden lintel which we had seen over the doorway at Ocosingo; and by what we saw afterward in Yucatán. The wood, if such as we saw in the other places, would be very lasting; its decay must have been extremely slow, and centuries may have elapsed since it perished altogether.

The builders were evidently ignorant of the principles of the arch, and the support was made by stones lapping over as they rose, as at Ocosingo. The long, unbroken corridors in front of the palace were probably intended for lords and gentlemen in waiting. Or perhaps the king himself sat in it to receive the reports of his officers and to administer justice.

From the centre door a range of stone steps thirty feet long leads to a rectangular courtyard, eighty feet long by seventy broad. On each side of the steps are grim and gigantic figures, carved in basso-relievo, nine or ten feet high, and in a position slightly inclined backward from the end of the steps to the floor of the corridor. They are adorned with rich headdresses and necklaces, but their attitude is that of pain and trouble. The design and anatomical proportions of the figures are faulty, but there is a force of expression about them which shows the skill and conceptive power of the artist.

On each side of the courtyard the palace was divided into apartments, probably for sleeping. On the right the piers have all fallen down. On the left they are still standing, and ornamented with stucco figures. In the centre apartment are the remains of a wooden pole about a foot long. It was the only piece of wood we found at Palenque, and we did not discover this until some time after we had made up our minds in regard to the wooden lintels over the doors. It was much worm-eaten, and probably, in a few years, not a vestige of it will be left.

The courtyard was overgrown with trees, and encumbered with ruins several feet high, so that the exact architectural arrangements could not be seen. Having our beds in the corridor adjoining, when we woke in the morning, and when we had finished the work of the day, we had it under our eyes. Every time we descended the steps the grim and mysterious figures stared us in the face, and it became to us one of the most interesting parts of the ruins. We were exceedingly anxious to make excavations, clear out the mass of rubbish, and lay the whole platform bare; but this was impossible. It is probably paved with stone or cement; and from the profusion of ornament in other parts, there is reason to believe that many curious and interesting specimens may be brought to light.

*Frederick Catherwood's drawing
of a stela at the Maya city of
Copán, Honduras.*

This agreeable work is left for the future traveller, who may go there better
provided with men and materials, and with more knowledge of what he has to
encounter; and, in my opinion, if he finds nothing new, the mere spectacle of
the courtyard entire will repay him for the labour and expense of clearing it.

The floor of the corridor fronting the courtyard sounded hollow, and a
breach had been made in it which seemed to lead into a subterraneous chamber;
but in descending, by means of a tree with notches cut in it, and with a candle,
we found merely a hollow in the earth, not bounded by any wall. In the farther
corridor the wall was in some places broken, and had several separate coats of
plaster and paint. In one place we counted six layers, each of which had the
remains of colours. In another place there seemed a line of written characters
in black ink. We made an effort to get at them; but, in endeavouring to remove
a thin upper stratum, they came off with it, and we desisted.

So far the arrangements of the palace are simple and easily understood; but
on the left are several distinct and independent buildings. The principal of these
is the tower, conspicuous by its height and proportions. The base is thirty feet
square, and it has three stories. Entering over a heap of rubbish at the base, we
found within another tower, distinct from the outer one, and a stone staircase,

so narrow that a large man could not ascend it. The staircase terminates against a dead stone ceiling, closing all farther passage, the last step being only six or eight inches from it. For what purpose a staircase was carried up to such a bootless termination we could not conjecture.

East of the tower is another building with two corridors, one richly decorated with pictures in stucco. In the centre [is an] elliptical tablet four feet long and three wide of hard stone set in the wall, and the sculpture is in bas-relief. Around it are the remains of a rich stucco border. The principal figure sits cross-legged on a couch ornamented with two leopards' heads. The attitude is easy, the expression calm and benevolent. The figure wears around its neck a necklace of pearls, to which is suspended a small medallion containing a face; perhaps intended as an image of the sun. Like every other subject of sculpture we had seen in the country, the personage had earrings, bracelets on the wrists, and a girdle round the loins. The headdress differs from most of the others at Palenque in that it wants the plumes of feathers. Near the head are three hieroglyphics.

The other figure, which seems that of a woman, is sitting cross-legged on the ground, apparently in the act of making an offering. In this supposed offering is seen a plume of feathers. Over the head of the sitting personage are four hieroglyphics. This is the only piece of sculptured stone about the palace except those in the courtyard. Under it formerly stood a table, of which the impression against the wall is still visible.

At the extremity of this corridor there is an aperture in the pavement, leading by a flight of steps to a platform; from this a door, with an ornament in stucco over it, opens by another flight of steps upon a narrow, dark passage, terminating in other corridors. These are called subterraneous apartments; but they are merely a ground-floor below the pavement of the corridors. In most parts, however, they are so dark that it is necessary to visit them with candles. There are no bas-reliefs or stucco ornaments. The only objects which our guide pointed out or which attracted our attention were several stone tables, one crossing and blocking up the corridor, about eight feet long, four wide, and three high. One of these lower corridors had a door opening upon the back part of the terrace, and we generally passed through it with a candle to get to the other buildings. In two other places there were flights of steps leading to corridors above. Probably these were sleeping apartments.

It was impossible to form any conjecture for what uses these different apartments were intended; but if we are right in calling it a palace, it seems probable that the part surrounding the courtyards was for public and state occasions, and that the rest was occupied as the place of residence of the royal family. This room with the small altar, we may suppose, was what would be called, in our own times, a royal chapel.

From the palace no other building is visible. Passing out by what is called the subterraneous passage, you descend the southwest corner of the terrace, and at the foot immediately commence ascending a ruined pyramidal structure, which appears once to have had steps on all its sides. The interior of the building is divided into two corridors, running lengthwise, with a ceiling rising nearly to a point, and paved with large square stones. The front corridor is seven feet wide. The separating wall is very massive, and has three doors, a large one in the centre, and a smaller one on each side. In this corridor, on each side of the principal door, is a large tablet of hieroglyphics, each thirteen feet long and eight feet high, and each divided into 240 squares of characters or symbols. Both are set in the wall so as to project three or four inches. In one place a hole had been made in the wall close to the side of one of them, apparently for the purpose of attempting its removal, by which we discovered that the stone is about a foot thick. The sculpture is in bas-relief.

In the right-hand tablet one line is obliterated by water that has trickled down and formed a sort of stalactite. In the other tablet, nearly one half of the hieroglyphics are obliterated. When we first saw them both tablets were covered with a thick coat of green moss, and it was necessary to wash and scrape them, clear the lines with a stick, and scrub them thoroughly, for which last operation a pair of blacking-brushes that Juan had picked up in my house at Guatimala, and disobeyed my order to throw away upon the road, proved exactly what we wanted and could not have procured. On account of the darkness of the corridor, it was necessary to burn torches while Mr. Catherwood was drawing.

In the centre apartment, set in the back wall is another tablet of hieroglyphics, four feet six inches wide and three feet six inches high. The roof above it is tight; consequently it has not suffered from exposure, and the hieroglyphics are perfect, though the stone is cracked lengthwise through the middle. Captains Del Rio and Dupaix both refer to them, but neither of them has given a single drawing. It is my belief they did not give them because in both cases the artists attached to their expedition were incapable of the labour, and the steady, determined perseverance required for drawing such complicated, unintelligible, and anomalous characters. As at Copán, Mr. Catherwood divided his paper into squares; the original drawings were reduced, and the engravings corrected by himself, and I believe they are as true copies as the pencil can make: the real written records of a lost people.

There is one important fact to be noticed. The hieroglyphics are the same as were found at Copán and Quirigua. The intermediate country is now occupied by races of Indians speaking many different languages, and entirely unintelligible to each other; but there is room for the belief that the whole of this country was once occupied by the same race, speaking the same language, or, at least, having the same written characters.

I have now given, without speculation or comment, a full description of the ruins of Palenque. I repeat what I stated in the beginning, there may be more buildings, but, after a close examination of the vague reports current in the village, we are satisfied that no more have ever been discovered; and from repeated inquiries of Indians who had traversed the forest in every direction in the dry season, we are induced to believe that no more exist. It is proper to add, however, that, considering the space now occupied by the ruins as the site of palaces, temples, and public buildings, and supposing the houses of the inhabitants to have been, like those of the present race of Indians, of frail and perishable materials, and to have disappeared altogether, the city may have covered an immense extent.

The reader is perhaps disappointed, but we were not. There was no necessity for assigning to the ruined city an immense extent, or an antiquity coeval with that of the Egyptians or of any other ancient and known people. What we had before our eyes was grand, curious, and remarkable enough. Here were the remains of a cultivated, polished, and peculiar people, who had passed through all the stages incident to the rise and fall of nations; reached their golden age, and perished, entirely unknown. The links which connected them with the human family were severed and lost, and these were the only memorials of their footsteps upon earth. In the midst of desolation and ruin we looked back to the past, cleared away the gloomy forest, and fancied every building perfect, with its terraces and pyramids, its sculptured and painted ornaments, grand, lofty, and imposing, and overlooking an immense inhabited plain; we called back into life the strange people who gazed at us in sadness from the walls; pictured them, in fanciful costumes and adorned with plumes of feathers, ascending the terraces of the palace and the steps leading to the temples.

———

There is, then, no resemblance in these remains to those of the Egyptians; and, failing here, we look elsewhere in vain. They are different from the works of any other known people, of a new order, and entirely and absolutely anomalous: they stand alone.

I invite to this subject the special attention of those familiar with the arts of other countries; for, unless I am wrong, we have a conclusion far more interesting and wonderful than that of connecting the builders of these cities with the Egyptians or any other people. It is the spectacle of a people skilled in architecture, sculpture, and drawing, and, beyond doubt, other more perishable arts, and possessing the cultivation and refinement attendant upon these, not derived from the Old World, but originating and growing up here, without models or masters, having a distinct, separate, independent existence; like the plants and fruits of the soil, indigenous. . . .

It perhaps destroys much of the interest that hangs over these ruins to assign to them a modern date; but we live in an age whose spirit is to discard phantasms and arrive at truth, and the interest lost in one particular is supplied in another scarcely inferior; for, the nearer we can bring the builders of these cities to our own times, the greater is our chance of knowing all. Throughout the country the convents are rich in manuscripts and documents written by the early fathers, caciques, and Indians, who very soon acquired the knowledge of Spanish and the art of writing. These have never been examined with the slightest reference to this subject; and I cannot help thinking that some precious memorial is now mouldering in the library of a neighbouring convent, which would determine the history of some one of these ruined cities; moreover, I cannot help believing that the tablets of hieroglyphics will yet be read. No strong curiosity has hitherto been directed to them; vigour and acuteness of intellect, knowledge and learning, have never been expended upon them. For centuries the hieroglyphics of Egypt were inscrutable, and, though not perhaps in our day, I feel persuaded that a key surer than that of the Rosetta stone will be discovered. And if only three centuries have elapsed since any one of these unknown cities was inhabited, the race of the inhabitants is not extinct. Their descendants are still in the land, scattered, perhaps, and retired, like our own Indians, into wildernesses which have never yet been penetrated by a white man, but not lost; living as their fathers did, erecting the same buildings of "lime and stone," "with ornaments of sculpture and plastered," "large courts," and "lofty towers with high ranges of steps," and still carving on tablets of stone the same mysterious hieroglyphics. If, in consideration that I have not often indulged in speculative conjecture, the reader will allow one flight, I turn to that vast and unknown region, untraversed by a single road, wherein fancy pictures that mysterious city seen from the topmost range of the Cordilleras, of unconquered, unvisited, and unsought aboriginal inhabitants.

In conclusion, I am at a loss to determine which would be the greatest enterprise, an attempt to reach this mysterious city, to decipher the tablets of hieroglyphics, or to wade through the accumulated manuscripts of three centuries in the libraries of the convents.

Pacal's Tomb at Palenque, Mexico

ALBERTO RUZ

Palenque, one of ancient America's greatest cities, lies near the western frontier of the Mayan lowlands in Mexico. Thanks to the decipherment of Mayan glyphs, we know that a long dynasty of talented lords presided over the growing city, starting on March 11, 431, when Chan-Bahlum (Snake-Jaguar) became ruler. The dynasty endured for just under four hundred years, achieving the height of its power under the rule of Pacal (Shield) and his son Chan-Bahlum between A.D. 603 and 702. Pacal and Chan-Bahlum gained control over a large area by political marriages, diplomatic offensives, trade, and conquest. Pacal ruled for sixty-seven years, turning Palenque into a dominant city in the lowlands. As his burial place, he erected the celebrated Temple of the Inscriptions, an elaborately decorated pyramid and shrine constructed over a period of more than fifteen years. The builders dug a large burial chamber with an immense sarcophagus belowground, erecting a pyramid above it. A secret internal stairway led to the sanctuary of the corbeled temple atop the artificial mountain. The elaborately carved sarcophagus lid recited the genealogy of the great Mayan ruler, who lay in the grave below, adorned with a superb jade mask.

John Lloyd Stephens and Frederick Catherwood visited the Temple of the Inscriptions in 1840, during their epic journey of archaeological discovery in Mayan country. Palenque became world-famous through their writings and drawings and was the site of intensive research in later years. But Mexican archaeologist Alberto Ruz (b. 1906) was the first scholar to dig behind the elaborate facades of Palenque's buildings in search of earlier structures. Convinced that a ruler lay buried under the Temple of the Inscriptions, he lifted a floor slab in the sanctuary and followed a rubble-filled stairway into the heart of the pyramid where Pacal's burial chamber lay. No one had deciphered Mayan glyphs in 1949, so the identity of the masked ruler was a mystery. But the now translated glyphs on the sarcophagus leave us in no doubt that Ruz unearthed one of the greatest of all Mayan rulers.

Alberto Ruz's firsthand account of his great discovery comes from the Illustrated London News, *long a widely read source of information on important archaeological sites and finds.*

When in the spring of 1949 the National Institute of Anthropology and History of Mexico appointed me director of research at Palenque, I fully appreciated that this was the most important event in my professional life.

I knew that my predecessors had been explorers, artists, scientists, distinguished men, and that marvellous sculpture had been discovered there during the course of 150 years; but I was convinced that many other archaeological treasures still lay hidden in the rubble of the palaces, temples and pyramids, and beneath the dense and mysterious Chiapas jungle which had been their jealous guardian.

A feature of my working plan was one which should always be present in the plans of archaeologists working in Mexico and Central America: to seek for architectural structures of an earlier date and lying beneath the actually visible building. It has, in fact, been proved that the ancient inhabitants of Central America were in the habit of building on top of older constructions, more with the object of increasing their height and bringing them closer to the heavens in which the gods lived than for any practical purpose.

For various reasons I decided to make such a search in the Temple of the Inscriptions. First, because it was the tallest building in Palenque and therefore the most likely to have been built on top of something older; secondly, because of its importance and its containing some fine, large, sculptured panels and one of the largest Mayan hieroglyphic inscriptions; and thirdly, because it had never been explored and its flooring was more or less intact—owing to its being made of great slabs instead of the more usual simple levelled plaster.

This temple is composed of a portico leading to a sanctuary and two lateral cells; and in the central room of the temple one of the slabs of the flooring caught my eye, as it had done with my predecessors on the site. This slab has round its edges two rows of holes provided with stone plugs. After thinking for some hours on its possible purpose, I came to the conclusion that the answer would be found underneath the stone; and accordingly I began to clear the floor beside it, in a place where the slabs had been already removed or broken by treasure-seekers, who had been discouraged from going on by meeting with a heavy filling of large stones.

Quite soon after beginning to remove the rubble I noticed that the temple's walls were prolonged under the floor instead of stopping at its level—a sure sign that there was "something" to be found underneath. Elated by this prospect, I began excavating and on the next day—May 20, 1949—there appeared that stone which, in Mayan buildings, is always used to close up a vault. The Mayans did not build a true arch, their vaulting being simply the result of bringing walls closer together by means of inclined facings which converge until there remains only a very small space to be closed with a single flat stone. A few days later I found a step, and then more and more steps. What had been found was an interior staircase descending into the pyramid and which, for a reason which we then did not know, had been made impracticable by a filling of large stones and clay.

Four spells of work—each two and a half months long—were needed before we were able to clear the filling from this mysterious staircase. After a flight of forty-five steps, we reached a landing with a U-turn. There followed another flight, of twenty-one steps, leading to a corridor, whose level is more or less the same as that on which the pyramid was built—i.e., some 22 metres under the temple flooring. In the vaulting of the landing two narrow galleries open out and allow air and a little light to enter from a near-by courtyard.

Above one of the first steps we reached we found a box-shaped construction of masonry containing a modest offering: two ear-plugs of jade placed on a river stone painted red. On reaching the end of the flight we found another box of offerings, backing on to a wall which blocked the passage. This time it was a richer offering: three pottery dishes, two shells full of cinnabar, seven jade beads, a pair of circular ear-plugs also of jade, the plugs of which were shaped like a flower, and a beautiful tear-shaped pearl, with its *lustre* pretty well preserved. An offering of this kind, at such a depth, told us without any doubt that we were approaching the object of our search.

And, in fact, on July 13, 1952, after demolishing a solid obstruction some metres thick, made of stone and lime—this was very hard and the wet lime burnt the hands of the workmen—there appeared on one side of the corridor a triangular slab, 2 metres high, set vertically to block an entrance. At the foot of this slab, in a rudimentary stone cist, there lay, mixed together, the largely destroyed skeletons of six young persons, of whom one at least was a female.

At noon on the 15th of the same month we opened the entrance, displacing the stone enough for a man to pass through sideways. It was a moment of indescribable emotion for me when I slipped behind the stone and found myself in an enormous crypt which seemed to have been cut out of the rock—or rather, out of the ice, thanks to the curtain of stalactites and the chalcite veiling deposited on the walls by the infiltration of rain-water during the centuries. This increased the marvellous quality of the spectacle and gave it a fairy-tale aspect. Great figures of priests modelled in stucco a little larger than life-size formed an impressive procession round the walls. The high vaulting was reinforced by great stone transoms, of dark colour with yellowish veins, giving an impression of polished wood.

Almost the whole crypt was occupied by a colossal monument, which we then supposed to be a ceremonial altar, composed of a stone of more than 8 square metres, resting on an enormous monolith of 6 cubic metres, supported in its turn by six great blocks of chiselled stone. All these elements carried beautiful reliefs.

Finest of all for its unsurpassable execution and perfect state of preservation was the great stone covering the whole and bearing on its four sides some hieroglyphic inscriptions with thirteen abbreviated dates corresponding to the beginning of the seventh century A.D., while its upper face shows a symbolic scene surrounded by astronomical signs.

I believed that I had found a ceremonial crypt, but I did not wish to make any definite assertions before I had finished exploring the chamber and, above all, before I had found out whether the base of the supposed altar was solid or not. On account of the rains and the exhausting of the funds available for this phase of the exploration, we had to wait until November before returning to Palenque. I then had the base bored horizontally at two of the corners, and it was not long before one of the drills reached a hollow space. I introduced a wire through the narrow aperture and, on withdrawing it, I saw that some particles of red paint were adhering to it.

The presence of this colouring matter inside the monolith was of supreme importance. The offerings found at the beginning and the end of the secret staircase had borne red paint; and the sides of the great stone showed traces of having been painted red all over. This colour was associated in the Mayan and Aztec cosmogony with the East, but also it is nearly always found in tombs, on the walls, or on objects accompanying the dead person or on his bones. The presence of red in tombs came, therefore, to indicate resurrection and a hope of immortality. The particles of cinnabar adhering to the wire inserted into the centre of the enormous stone block was therefore unquestionable evidence of burial: and our supposed ceremonial altar must therefore be an extraordinary sepulchre.

To prove this it was necessary to lift the sculptured stone, which measured 3.80 metres by 2.20 metres (some 13 by 7 feet), weighing about 5 tons and constituting one of the most valuable masterpieces of American pre-Hispanic sculpture. The preparations lasted two days in the midst of feverish tension. It was necessary to fell in the forest a hard-wood tree of the kind called in that region "bari," and to cut it into sections of different lengths, lift these along a greasy path to the lorry, convey them by motor to the pyramid, move them by manpower to the temple, lower them by cables through the interior staircase and introduce them through the narrow aperture of the crypt.

The four major sections of the trunk were placed vertically under the corners of the stone and on top of each was placed a railway or motor-car jack. On November 27, at dusk, after a twelve-hour working day, the soul-shaking manoeuvre took place. Every kind of precaution was taken to prevent the stone tipping up or slipping, and, above all, to prevent its suffering any damage. Handled simultaneously and without any jerking, the jacks lifted the stone millimetre by millimetre, and while this was happening slabs were placed underneath it to hold it up. When the jacks reached the limit of their extension, other sections of the tree were inserted and the operation was repeated. A little before midnight the stone was resting intact 0.60 metre above its original level on six robust logs of "bari" and a few days later it was lifted to a height of 1.12 metres.

Once the stone left its seating and began to rise it could be seen that a cavity had been cut out of the enormous block which served it as a base. This cavity was of an unexpected shape, oblong and curvilinear, rather like the silhouette in schematised form of a fish or of the capital letter omega (Ω), closed in its lower part. The cavity was sealed by a highly polished slab fitting exactly and provided with four perforations, each with a stone plug. On raising the slab which closed it we discovered the mortuary receptacle.

This was not the first time during my career as an archaeologist that a tomb had been discovered, but no occasion has been so impressive as this. In the vermilion-coloured walls and base of the cavity which served as a coffin, the sight of the human remains—complete, although the bones were damaged—covered with jade jewels for the most part, was most impressive. It was possible to judge the form of the body which had been laid in this "tailored" sarcophagus; and the jewels added a certain amount of life, both from the sparkle of the jade and because they were so well "placed" and because their form suggested the volume and contour of the flesh which originally covered the skeleton. It was easy also to imagine the high rank of the personage who could aspire to a mausoleum of such impressive richness.

We were struck by his stature, greater than that of the average Mayan of to-day; and by the fact that his teeth were not filed or provided with incrustations of pyrites or jade, since that practice (like that of artificially deforming the cranium) was usual in individuals of the higher social ranks. The state of destruction of the skull did not allow us to establish precisely whether or not it had been deformed. In the end, we decided that the personage might have been of non-Mayan origin, though it is clear that he ended in being one of the kings of Palenque. The reliefs, which we have still to uncover on the sides of the sarcophagus and which are now hidden under lateral buttresses, may tell us before long something of the personality and identity of the glorious dead.

Even if he had not been buried in the most extraordinary tomb so far discovered in this continent of America, it would still be perfectly possible to assess the importance of this personage from the jewels which he wore—many of them already familiar in Mayan bas-reliefs. As shown in some reliefs, he was wearing a diadem made from tiny disks of jade and his hair was divided into separate strands by means of small jade tubes of appropriate shape; and we discovered a small jade plate of extraordinary quality cut in the shape of the head of Zotz, the vampire god of the underworld, and this may have been a final part of the diadem. Around the neck were visible various threads of a collar composed of jade beads in many forms—spheres, cylinders, tri-lobed beads, floral buds, open flowers, pumpkins, melons, and a snake's head. The ear-plugs were composed of various elements, which together made up a curious flower. From a square jade plate with engraved petals, a tube, also of jade, projected and this ended in a flower-shaped bead; while on the back of the square plate (which carries a hieroglyphic inscription) a circular plug was fitted. All these elements would be united by a thread and it would seem that there hung as a counterpoise to them, behind the broad part of the ear, a marvellous artificial pearl, formed by uniting two perfectly cut pieces of mother-o-pearl, polished and adjusted to give the impression of a pearl of fabulous size (36 millimetres). Over the breast lay a pectoral formed of nine concentric rings of twenty-one tubular beads in each. Round each wrist was a bracelet of two hundred jade beads, and on each finger of both hands a great ring of jade. We found these still fixed on the phalanges, and one of the rings was carved in the form of a crouching man, with a delicate head of perfect Mayan profile. In the right hand he held a great jade bead of

*Alberto Ruz cleaning the stucco
head of a Mayan lord.*

cubical form, and in the left, another, but this one spherical, the two being perhaps symbols of his rank or magical elements for his journey to another world. Near his feet we found another two great jade beads, one of them hollow and provided with two plugs in the shape of flowers. A jade idol of precious workmanship stood near the left foot and is probably a representation of the sun god. Another little figure of the same material must have been sewn above the breech-clout. From the mouth cavity we extracted a beautiful dark jade bead, which, according to the funeral rites of the Mayans, was placed there so that the dead person should have the means to obtain sustenance in the life beyond the tomb. At the moment of burial, the personage wore over his face a magnificent mask made of jade mosaic, the eyes being of shell, with each iris of obsidian, with the pupil marked in black behind. Of the hundreds of fragments, some remained on the face, adhering to the teeth and the forehead, but the greater part were lying on the left side of the head, clearly as the result of the mask's slipping off during the burial. The corpse must have been set in the sarcophagus entirely wrapped in a shroud painted red, and the same cinnabar colour adhered to the bones, the jewels and the bottom of the sarcophagus when the cloth and the flesh decomposed. The mask was fitted directly on the dead man's face, the fragments being stuck in a thin coating of stucco, the remains of which fitted to the human face. Nevertheless, the mask had to be prepared beforehand and may

*Stucco head of a Mayan lord from the Temple of the Inscriptions,
Palenque, mid- to late seventh century A.D.*

perhaps have been kept on a stucco head. It is perfectly possible that its main traits, realistic as they are, represent more or less those of the actual dead man. After the burial the sarcophagus was closed with its lid and covered with the enormous sculptured stone. Some jewels were thrown upon this—a collar with slate pendants and what was probably a ritual mask made of jade mosaic—and there were placed underneath the coffin various clay vessels, perhaps containing food and drink, and two wonderful human heads modelled in stucco, which had been broken from complete statues. At the closing of the crypt six young persons, perhaps sons and daughters of important persons at court, were sacrificed to act as companions and servants of the dead man in the other world. In the best-preserved of their skulls could be noted the cranial deformation and the mutilation of the teeth which were customary in the nobility alone. A serpent modelled in lime plaster seems to rise straight out of the sarcophagus and ascend the steps which lead to the threshold of the room. Here it is transformed into a tube, running as far as the flooring of the corridor and after this it leads on to the temple, in the form of an echeloned moulding, hollow and superimposed on the steps. This amounts to a magical union, a conduit for the spirit of the dead man to ascend to the temple in order that the priests might continue to be in contact with his deified being and able to explain his mandates. Our search for an older building under the Temple of the Inscriptions could therefore not lead to the expected result, but in exchange it revealed a tomb whose discovery leads to considerable modification of certain established concepts concerning the function of the American pyramid. It was formerly thought that this was solely a solid base for supporting a temple, unlike the Egyptian pyramids, which are vast mausoleums. Palenque's "Royal Tomb," as it is now popularly called—with a certain intuitive propriety, perhaps—brings us a great deal closer to the Egyptian concept once we grant that the pyramid which hid it, although supporting a temple, was also constructed to serve as a grandiose funeral monument. The monumental quality of this crypt, built by thousands of hands to challenge the centuries and enriched with magnificent reliefs; the sumptuousness of the tomb itself, a colossal monument weighing 20 tons and covered all over with bas-reliefs of stupendous quality: the rich jade finery of the buried personage; all this expensive toil and this magnificence suggest to us the existence in Palenque of a theocratic system similar to that of Egypt, in which the all-powerful priest-king was considered during life or after death to be a real god. This Palencan Royal tomb also leads us to suppose that the attitude towards death of the Mayan *halach uinic* was very close to that of the pharaohs. The stone which covers the tomb appears to confirm this obsession and synthesises in its reliefs some essentials of the Mayan religion. The presence here, in a sepulchral slab, of motives which are repeated in other representations gives perhaps the key to interpret the famous panels of the Cross and the foliated Cross (in Palenque) and also some of the paintings in the codices. On the stone in question we see a man surrounded by astronomical signs symbolising heaven—the spatial limit of man's earth, and the home of the gods, in which the unchanging course of the stars marks the implacable rhythm of time. Man rests on the earth, represented by a grotesque head with funereal traits, since the earth is a monster devouring all that lives; and if the reclining man seems to be falling backwards, it is because it is his inherent destiny to fall to the earth, the land of the dead. But above the man rises the well-known cruciform motif, which in some representations is a tree, in others the stylised maize plant, but is always the symbol of life resurgent from the earth, life triumphing over death.

The Murals of
Bonampak, Mexico

KARL RUPPERT

In May 1946, an American archaeologist-photographer named Giles Healey was mak-ing a film about the Lacandon Maya Indians in south-central Chiapas, Mexico. The local people led him to the hitherto unknown Bonampak ceremonial center, erected by the classic Maya in the seventh century A.D. *Healey was astounded to discover three rooms of well-preserved wall paintings in one of Bonampak's temples. The announce-ment of the discovery in 1947 caused an international sensation. The entire surfaces of the three temple chambers are covered with paintings, done in a fresco technique that applies a mixture of paint and water to wet lime plaster.*

At the time the Bonampak murals were discovered, most experts believed that the Maya were a peace-loving people ruled by priest-kings obsessed with astronomy and the measurement of time. The frescoes came as a shock, for they depict war and human sacrifice, the execution of prisoners, and ritual blood-letting. Bonampak showed that the Maya were as bloodthirsty and warlike as their Central American contemporaries, such as the rulers of the great city of Teotihuacán on the Mexican highlands. Through the murals, archaeologists have also gained much insight into Mayan dress, celebration, social organization, gender relations, political hierarchy, and countless other details of daily life not depicted in other art. The murals are also of great interest for their depictions of warfare, weapons, and fighting and sacrifice.

In this selection, archaeologists Karl Ruppert (1895–1960) and J. E. S. Thompson (1898–1975) and artist Tatiana Proskouriakoff analyze the Bonampak mural entitled "Arraignment of the Prisoners," which shows the public display and possible torture of war captives before the local nobility. They offer a detailed interpretation of its imagery, in an account that gives a feeling for the vital importance of the information contained in the murals. This account of the Bonampak murals was written in 1955, well before the decipherment of Mayan script confirmed the warlike and bloodthirsty nature of much Mayan life. The wall paintings are no longer unique, as other sites have subse-quently come to light.

The most important personages are grouped on the summit of the structure. Slightly off-center is a personage clad in a jaguar jerkin and wearing a large jade pectoral; a sweeping panache of long quetzal feathers attached to his headdress attests to his high rank. I think it can be fairly assumed that this is the same *halach uinic*, great chief, whom we saw watching from his dais the preparations for the ceremony in Room 1 and whom we have just encountered in the raid. To left and right of him are three personages wearing jaguar skins and carrying batons. Two of them wear jaguar heads as helmets; the third has donned the head of some unidentified animal. It would appear that these are the same three batabs who were shown in Room 1, first being attired for the ceremony and, subsequently, as participants in the ceremony. On the flanks are, to the left, five other persons of obvious rank; to the right, two women and a fat male attendant. The rather imperious lady presumably is the chief's wife, whom we recognized on the dais in Room 1. One feels that in our culture she would have been an active organizer and clubwoman. The second woman supposedly can be equated with the second woman on the dais; the fat attendant we shall encounter again in Room 3.

Seated at the foot of the chief, and looking up to him in an attitude of fear or entreaty, is a naked man whose coarse face and tow-like hair contrast strongly with those of the persons of rank. On the next two steps are seated seven other individuals, whose gross features, lank matted hair, and lack of ornament or clothing except for the simplest loincloth indicate that they are of the same status as the supplicant just noted. Three gaze, presumably in pain or fear, at their hands from which blood drips; a well-clad individual holds the bleeding hand of one of them as though he had just performed the act which caused the bleeding, but unfortunately, his other hand is not visible because of damage to the mural, thereby depriving us of information on the implement used to cause the bleeding. Others hold out their hands as though they awaited with fear and trepidation the same fate.

It is not easy to explain this scene. The bleeding hands do not seem to have been maimed; at least there is no sign that phalanges have been cut off. Moreover, if the person who holds the hand of one of the captives by the wrist has just completed the operation, as seems to be the case, he could hardly have cut off parts of the fingers, since a severing action would require that the captive's hand be placed on the ground or on something solid. There is no evidence that blood is being drawn for ceremonial purposes, since it is not being collected on strips of bark paper or in vessels. As the Maya are not by nature sadists, I do not think that torture of captives is depicted.

These eight men clearly are enemies captured in the raid, for they are of the same physical type as those being captured in the battle scene and they similarly lack ornament and clothing. Moreover, unless it was the convention to represent all enemies as physically repulsive, one must assume that all eight prisoners are peasants, not members of the ruling class.

Throughout Mesoamerica persons of noble blood were sought as sacrificial victims, particularly, it would seem, when the victim impersonated a god and so had to be without blemish; prisoners of plebian origin often became the slaves of their captors. However, it is clear that many sacrificial victims were not of rank, for slaves were purchased in large numbers for sacrifice both in Yucatán and on the Mexican plateau, and of the huge quantities of prisoners sacrificed by the Aztec not all could have been persons of importance. Moreover, not a few of the captives depicted on Maya stelae, who presumably were to be sacrificed at the dedicatory ceremonies in connection with the erection of those monuments, appear to be of lowly origin. If the eight are to live, as slaves, it is possible, although hardly probable, that they are being marked in some way, perhaps by scarification. To the best of my knowledge there is no report of slaves being branded in any way.

One is inclined to think that the terror of the eight prisoners is not engendered by fear of the cutting or pricking of their fingers or hands, but may be due to their imminent execution. If, however, they are to be sacrificed, what does the finger bleeding portray? Sahagún, in his description of the ceremonies in the month Panquetzaliztli, records that a short time before the slaves were to be sacrificed each dipped both hands in a bowl of dye either of red ocher or of a blue color and imprinted them on the lintels and house posts of the house of his master. It is just conceivable that the preparations for an analogous ceremony are here depicted, with the imprint of the victim's hand to be made in its own blood. Hand imprints in red paint are not uncommon in Maya temples; the Lacandon believe that red hands were imprinted on a building to mark its completion.

In the middle of the eight captives and with his arm almost touching the foot of the great chief lies a man whose posture is rendered with dignity, realism, and wistful beauty. His closed eye and position together indicate that he is dead or, conceivably, has fainted; his features are refined and his hair lacks that towlike quality of the others. Several small gashes on his body seem to represent wounds, although they hardly appear to have been fatal, and there seems to be no sign of blood.

It is hard to surmise what part this handsome man has played in the events. One may, I think, presume that he is one of the enemy. If he died in or immediately after the fight, it is difficult to imagine why his body should have been brought to the scene of this ceremony; if he has just been sacrificed, it is not easy to see how this was done. Moreover, one gets the impression that the events depicted in this scene are not primarily religious, but rather that they are a prelude to the great religious ceremony.

There appears to be a gash below the left breast, but it does not seem to be large enough to have permitted of the removal of the heart. One is mindful of the arrow sacrifice practiced in Yucatán immediately prior to the coming of the Spaniards. That was a late development, and it is almost certain that at the time these murals were painted, the Maya had no knowledge of the bow and arrow. It is probable, however, that the arrow sacrifice derives from an earlier form in which spears were hurled at the victim. The victim on the mural may have been wounded in the genitals, recalling Landa's account of the arrow sacrifice in which he says that at the start of the ceremony the priest wounded the victim in that part. Moreover, it is interesting to note that in a Maya poem on the arrow sacrifice, published with a translation by Barrera Vásquez, the shooters are instructed not to shoot with all their strength but to cause light wounds; the same is true of the Pawnee sacrifice to the morning star. It is, accordingly, possible that this youth has been sacrificially speared, but such an interpretation must be regarded as highly speculative.

At his foot a human head, surrounded by greenery, rests on one of the terraces in a manner strongly reminiscent of the decapitated head of the maize god which rests on the earth symbol on page 34 of Codex Dresden. The green on which the head rests may represent leaves of the wild *Ficus*, the Maya *copo*, which was used to a considerable extent in Maya ceremony. According to Landa, leaves of this tree were strewn on the floor during certain ceremonies. In the Quijada papers it is reported that at a clandestine ceremony at Yaxcaba the victim was sacrificed in front of the idols which had been placed on some leaves of *higuera de infierno*. This is probably the same plant. The same source speaks of the church of Sanahcat being decorated with *copo* leaves for human sacrifice, "which they used to do in their sacrifices of [to] their idols." To the right of this head the wall surface is damaged. The area where the mural has scaled off is perhaps sufficient to have held the body belonging to the head. Conceivably, this is the head of the youth who impersonated the maize god in the dance scene of Room 1. I would hesitate to advance this explanation were it not that decapitation was particularly the fate of impersonators of deities of vegetation and the soil in central Mexico. Completing the scene, various chiefs and attendants to the number of seventeen are ranged on the lower terraces.

The halting interpretation offered for this scene is that it is the preliminary to the great ceremony, which occupies most of the wall space in Room 3. Apparently sacrifices have already been made, as the head resting on the greenery and, apparently, the sprawled body of the young man bear witness. The fate of the group of captives is being pronounced, but whether that is death on the sacrificial stone or slavery is a matter for speculation. For the bleeding of the hands a possible explanation has been offered, but one on which I do not place overmuch confidence, for this is a baffling matter. We may, however, presume with some certainty that the *halach uinic* and the three *batabs* are correctly identified in this scene.

The Aztec Templo Mayor

EDUARDO MATOS MOCTEZUMA

"These great towns and temples and buildings rising from the water, all made of stone, seemed like an enchanted vision . . . indeed some of our soldiers asked whether it was all not a dream." Spanish conquistador Bernal Díaz del Castillo was the last survivor of the tiny band of soldiers and adventurers who accompanied Hernán Cortés on his journey to the heart of the Aztec Empire in 1519. He wrote his account of the conquest when in his eighties, but his memory of the Aztec capital, Tenochtitlán, was as vivid as if he had seen it only recently. The conquistadors wandered through a marketplace larger than that of Constantinople or Seville. The Lord Moctezuma himself climbed with Cortés to the summit of the great temple of Huitzilopochtli and Tlaloc, where the shrines reeked of the blood of human sacrifice. From the summit of the pyramid, the Spaniards gazed out over a city of more than 200,000 people, from a vantage point where a great drum would sound, audible up to eight kilometers away. Cortés and his men witnessed the most elaborate of all Native American civilizations at the height of its powers. Two years later, Tenochtitlán was a smoking ruin, its people decimated by a brutal siege and unfamiliar epidemic disease. And on the site of the once resplendent capital rose Mexico City. All traces of Tenochtitlán and its temples vanished under urban sprawl.

Tenochtitlán is a vast archaeological site that appears from time to time during urban-renewal projects. The digging of the Mexico City Metro yielded rich treasures, including a temple to Ehecatl-Quetzalcoatl, which is now part of a stop on the line. But the most spectacular excavations have uncovered the very Templo Mayor, dedicated to the sun god Huitzilopochtli and rain deity Tlaloc, visited by Cortés in 1519. Between 1978 and 1982, Mexican archaeologist Eduardo Matos Moctezuma (b. 1940) peeled off the remains of at least seven building phases, where successive Aztec rulers vied with their predecessors in embellishing the great temple. Eleven times, the builders erected new temple facades on the face of an earlier one, which was slowly sinking into the underlying swampy soil. On five occasions, they built an entire new temple on the same site. Matos found a superb array of ceremonial artifacts, numerous human remains, and votive gifts brought from every corner of the Aztec Empire. The Templo Mayor is

357

now a popular tourist attraction alongside the Catholic cathedral, built on the ruins of the ancient sacred precincts.

Eduardo Matos Moctezuma described his spectacular excavations in The Great Temple of the Aztecs. *In this selection, he draws on archaeology and historical accounts to reconstruct the appearance of the great temple in its heyday.*

The discovery of the Coyolxauhqui relief in 1978 was a major event in the history of Mexican archaeology. The realization that here was a keystone to the city's history caused the authorities to order intensive work to expose the central area of Tenochtitlán.

The Coyolxauhqui sculpture seemed to form part of the Great Temple itself. It was clear that all the explorations of the Temple undertaken during the first half of the twentieth century had examined only a very small part of the whole complex. To put the Coyolxauhqui Stone in its context, therefore, a research strategy involving thorough investigation of the urban environment surrounding the Temple was considered necessary. This would help to establish the aims of the project, the questions to be answered, and which archaeological techniques should be used. Three phases of research were proposed and eventually adopted.

PHASE ONE: STATING THE PROBLEM

This consisted of gathering all information on the Great Temple currently available from both archaeological and historical sources. . . . [L]imited archaeological investigation [was] carried out on the Temple up until 1978. . . . [M]uch more information about the structure was available from the eyewitness sixteenth-century accounts of chroniclers such as Bernal Díaz del Castillo and Hernán Cortés. According to the chronicles, the Great Temple was a pyramidal edifice facing west, with two stairways leading to its upper part. At the summit were two shrines, one dedicated to Tlaloc—god of rain, water, and the earth's fertility—and the other to Huitzilopochtli—solar and war god. These two gods were enshrined at that important spot because together they represented the Aztecs' most fundamental economic concerns: agriculture and tribute. The need for water was a major preoccupation which was the concern of Tlaloc, while warfare and military conquests, crucial for the maintenance and expansion of the Aztec empire, were overseen by Huitzilopochtli.

If it is accepted that agriculture and tribute were the pillars of Aztec economy and life, then it would seem reasonable to suggest that these things may be reflected in the architecture, sculptures, and offerings associated with the Great Temple. The team of archaeologists and specialists involved in the project, working within the restrictions of the urban setting, had to evaluate which excavation methods would be best for verifying or disproving this idea.

The excavation took place over five years, from 1978 to 1982. The modern urban environment not only presented the problem of how to deal with obstructions such as houses, streets, and drainage systems, but also meant that all the buildings in the proposed excavation area had to be assessed to avoid damaging those of historical significance. The downtown sector of the Great Temple is rich in colonial structures superimposed on Aztec remains. An Advisory Board on Monuments was established to decide which of the houses threatened by the excavation should be saved. As a result, only two of the buildings which were demolished had some sections dating to the colonial period, and these parts were photographed, numbered, and sent to the office in charge of colonial monuments.

Another important consideration was that the prehispanic buildings in the Great Temple area were severely damaged during the Spanish conquest and the stone re-used in colonial structures. For example, the latest construction stage of the Great Temple—there were found to be seven in all—had been leveled down to its foundations, and only traces of this stage were discovered on the flagstone floor of the great plaza of the ceremonial precinct, although at the north side of the square approximately 1 meter of the platform was well preserved. Construction from the earlier six stages, however, was found to be in much better condition, because these older, smaller levels were basically protected by later additions to the Great Temple, and were not intentionally razed; in fact the second construction stage (Stage II, A.D. 1390) was found almost complete.

The high modern water-table presented a further problem. It stands a mere 4–5 meters below present-day street level owing to the city's location over a lakebed. This meant that only the upper parts of the earlier levels of the Great Temple could be excavated, that is, the topmost of the four or five sloping tiers of the pyramidal core, and the remains of two shrines which surmounted it. If we had pumped out the water to reach the lower tiers it might have caused serious problems of stability not only for the Temple but also for the colonial and modern buildings near the precinct. Technological developments in future years may enable this subsurface water to be controlled and permit examination of the earlier levels. For the present, however, work was concentrated on the remains found above the water-table and below the streets of modern Mexico City.

To obtain the maximum information from the site a multidisciplinary approach was adopted. Biologists, chemists, and geologists from the Department of Prehistory of INAH were called in to help the archaeologists. Engineers specializing in soil mechanics were also consulted because of the problems of subsoil water, and they provided useful advice too on how close excavation trenches could be dug to nearby buildings without endangering them.

Anticipation of conservation needs was another important aspect of planning the excavation. Groups of technicians worked with the archaeologists, including photographers, draftsmen, and administrative assistants, to record all the finds. Many of the objects and other remains required conservation, so a laboratory was set up with conservators working alongside archaeologists as they excavated architecture, murals, and offerings; in this way, a large amount of both organic and inorganic material was preserved.

The excavation covered a surface area of between 5,000 and 7,000 square meters and was divided into 2-×2-meter grid squares, each square identified by a letter and number. Depth was gauged by carefully controlled measurements and a fixed starting point or datum. Excavation led to the third and final phase of analysis, that of interpretation of the results.

Phase Three: Results and Interpretation

It appeared that the Great Temple had been constructed in seven stages, several of which could tentatively be dated by the glyphs carved on excavated objects.

Construction Stage I

This can be identified with the sanctuary built by the Aztecs when they reached Tenochtitlán in A.D. 1325. This stage is known only from historical sources, because it was not possible to excavate below the Stage II pyramid owing to the high subsoil water-level.

Construction Stage II

Considerable information has come from the archaeological examination of Construction Stage II, and this is corroborated by historical accounts of the last or Stage VII Temple which the Spaniards saw and described. Numerous chronicles state that the Temple was crowned by two shrines dedicated to the gods Tlaloc and Huitzilopochtli. Bernal Díaz del Castillo describes the Great Temple thus:

> In the shrines there were two figures, as if they were of giants, with very tall bodies, and very corpulent; and about the first, which was on the right side, they said it was Huichilobos [i.e. Huitzilopochtli], their god of war. . . . At the summit of the Temple there was another recess made of richly carved wood, and here was another figure that seemed to be half man and half alligator . . . this body was covered with all the seeds of the earth, and they said this was the god of the fields and of the caves . . . [Tlaloc].

Sahagún also describes the Temple:

> This Temple was divided at the top so that it appeared to be two, and it had two shrines or altars at the summit, each one with its spire. And at the top each of these had its insignia or special emblems. In one of these shrines, the principal one, was the statue of Huitzilopochtli. . . . In the other, there was an image of the god Tlaloc. Before each one of these [images] there was a round stone like a chopping block, called *techcatl*, upon which they killed those who were sacrificed in honor of that god. And from these [sacrificial]

stones to the base of the Temple flowed a stream of blood from those [victims] who were slain on them. And it was the same in all the other temples. These towers [i.e. temples] faced the west. The stairways were narrow and straight, from the base to the summit, on all these temples, all alike, and one ascended [the stairways, to reach the top].

At the Temple's summit and in front of the entrance to Huitzilopochtli's shrine, a stone comparable to the one mentioned by the chroniclers was found *in situ* during the excavation of the Stage II structure, although this sacrificial stone was made of black *tezontle*, a volcanic rock. It was set into the floor 2 meters from the stairway and measured 50×45 centimeters, which is very close to the dimensions given by Sahagún when he refers to the stone used during a sacrifice in honor of Xipe Totec at the annual festival of Tlacaxipehualiztli: "When they reached the sacrificial block, which was a stone three *palmos* [about 60 centimeters] high . . . and two *palmos* wide . . . they threw [the victims] over them, on their backs."

This stone would have served as a visual and functional symbol of Aztec power where war captives were slain. Sahagún would, of course, have seen a later stone to the one which was excavated here, and it may have been slightly larger, as well as of a different color, as Durán indicates:

> Before the two rooms where these gods were found there was a courtyard 40 feet square, very well finished and painted white. In the middle [of this courtyard] and in front of those two rooms there was a green stone, rather pointed [in form], about as high as one's waist. And when a man was thrown on his back on this stone, his body bent over the stone; and thus they sacrificed men.

This semi-precious stone used during the Temple's latest period was brought as tribute payment from areas in the present-day state of Guerrero, where it is very common.

At the entrance to the Tlaloc shrine of the Stage II Temple, and mirroring the location of the sacrificial stone in front of the Huitzilopochtli altar, a second sculpture, the multicolor *chacmool*, was discovered. This is a representation of a man, in a supine position, with a receptacle resting on his abdomen; his knees are bent and his head raised toward those approaching the shrine. The fact that the *chacmool* has been placed at the entrance in this way may corroborate one interpretation of the figure, namely that he represents a divine messenger, an intermediary bearing sacrifices and offerings between the priest and the gods.

It may be that both the sacrificial stone and the *chacmool* served as symbolic guardians for the Temple, and they may also reflect the character of the deity honored within each shrine. The sacrificial stone is more overtly associated with warfare and the fate of war captives, while the supine human figure is a more abstract, religious symbol signifying the divine intermediary.

Both shrines were originally decorated inside and out. Two stone pillars were found at the entrance to the Tlaloc shrine, and the outside faces of these bear geometric mural painting that symbolizes the deity: a band of "goggle-eyes" of Tlaloc painted black on a white background. Below these "eyes" is a horizontal strip of blue, followed by two red bands. The lower part of the pillars are painted with black and white vertical bands which may represent rain.

The remains of a wall were found at both ends of the shrine dedicated to Tlaloc, and it appears that it was originally divided into two long rooms. A banquette or low dividing wall lay in the center of the room, and perhaps the image of Tlaloc was placed on top of this bench.

Some of the interior painting from Tlaloc's shrine has survived. Standing human figures adorn the inner face of each of the two pillars; their bodies are painted yellow and they wear blue and black bracelets and leg ornaments. With legs apart as if striding, each figure extends his left arm with a staff or spear in his hand.

Huitzilopochtli's shrine was probably similar to the one dedicated to Tlaloc, at least in plan. Decoration on the bases of the two pillars has survived, as has some of the interior painting. A banquette was also found in the middle of this sanctuary, partly overlapped by a small altar—aligned with the sacrificial stone—on which the image of Huitzilopochtli once stood. This is corroborated by Durán, who remarks that this idol, thus dressed and adorned, was always placed on a tall altar in a small room.

Pine and cedar wood used for the door-jambs and pillars—and probably initially decorated—was found at the entrance to both shrines, as well as in a few of the offerings. Bernal Díaz del Castillo and Cortés both described richly decorated wood in the Temple interiors.

There are many reasons to believe that Stage II corresponds to the reigns of either Acamapichtli, Huitzilihuitl, or Chimalpopoca, that is, before 1428 (the year of Aztec independence from Azcapotzalco). The size of the Stage II Temple is markedly smaller than later constructions, suggesting an early date. Furthermore, on the top step of the stairway leading to the Huitzilopochtli shrine, and aligned with the sacrificial stone, a sculpted face with two glyphs above it was found. One glyph is almost completely destroyed, but the other represents the date "2 Rabbit," perhaps corresponding to A.D. 1390. Later construction stages were aimed at enlarging the Temple and so were built directly on top of this early edifice. However, only five of these construction stages were total enlargements on all four sides; others were enlargements of the main façade. The Temple described as Construction Stage II is the oldest structure found to date that has four sides.

Clearly a great quantity of fill was needed to cover this Stage II Temple in order to form a base for the following structures, in comparison with the fill required for subsequent building stages. This great surge of building activity gives the impression that, once liberated from the yoke of Azcapotzalco, the Aztecs wanted to construct a magnificent Temple—perhaps as a symbol of freedom.

It is known from historical sources that groups which paid tribute to the

Aztec Eagle Warrior found at Templo Mayor, Tenochtitlán, Mexico.

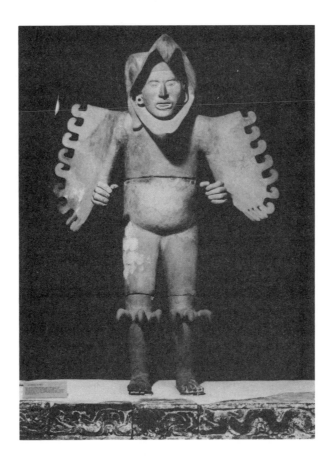

Aztecs brought *tezontle* and earth for constructional fill. The fact that the sacrificial stone was made of the same material used in construction attests to its early date because, as we have seen, greenstone—imported from southern Mexico—was used for the sacrificial block in the latest building stage.

Construction Stage III

Relatively little can be said about the construction of this stage because only the plain pyramidal base, without any adornment or surmounting structures, has survived. The double stairways are well made and the walls forming the tiers of the pyramidal base are vertical. Eight *tezontle* sculptures, representing life-size standard-bearers, were found leaning against the steps near the base of the stairs leading to the Huitzilopochtli shrine. At one time they may have adorned the Temple; perhaps they represent Huitzilopochtli's brothers, the Huitznahua, and, when the new Temple was constructed, they were removed and placed ceremonially in a row on the stairway, to be covered up by the next construction stage.

On the back wall of the pyramidal body of the Great Temple, at the base of the side devoted to Huitzilopochtli, there is a stone carved with the calendrical glyph "4 Reed." This is probably equivalent to A.D. 1431, which would date this construction stage to the reign of Itzcoatl.

Construction Stage IV

The architecture and sculptures of this stage are among the most spectacular known from the Great Temple. Not only is the pyramidal base enlarged, it is also adorned with braziers and serpent heads on all four sides. At the rear of the Tlaloc half of the Temple these over-sized braziers bear his face, while each of those on the Huitzilopochtli side—that is, the south façade—prominently display a large bow which is believed to be a symbol of this deity. Traces of various offerings are still evident, buried at the feet of these braziers and serpents.

Construction Stage IVb is labeled as such because it consists only of a partial enlargement of the Temple: the main façade, on the west side, was amplified and adorned with a wealth of different elements. The Temple from this stage rested on a vast platform with a single, majestic stairway. Enormous, undulating serpent bodies wrapped around the corners and terminated in dramatic snake heads, each one different from the next and several still showing traces of red, blue, and yellow pigment. The rise of the great stairway is broken only by a little altar near the base of the side dedicated to Tlaloc: two frogs rest on this altar, which has its own small steps and is aligned with the stairs leading to the shrine. In the middle of the stairway from the platform on the side of Huitzilopochtli's shrine there is a 2-meter-long tablet that forms part of the fourth step: it is made of andesite and has a serpent engraved on the rise.

At the base of the platform formed by the remains of two stairways that originally rose to the top of the Temple, four serpent heads—two on the balustrades at either end and two in the middle—mark the place where the two structures dedicated to Tlaloc and Huitzilopochtli meet. In the middle of Huitzilopochtli's side, at the foot of the stairway, Coyolxauhqui's dismembered body is preserved in low-relief carved on a huge stone.

The numerous offerings buried beneath this platform were either found around the Coyolxauhqui Stone, or between the two central serpent heads, or else at the base of the stairway on Tlaloc's side. Only Chambers (caches) I and II were found behind this staircase, at the midway point of the sides dedicated to Huitzilopochtli and Tlaloc, respectively. Rooms paved with colored marble were discovered at the north and south ends of the Stage IVb platform, and on the north side of the platform two offerings appeared within a small altar with its own little stairway: one of these offerings contained more than forty skulls and bones of children. Beneath this is the offering known as Chamber III; owing to their location and content, both these offerings appear to be dedicated to Tlaloc.

A stone plaque bearing the glyph "1 Rabbit" was found set in the back wall of the platform on Huitzilopochtli's side, and is believed to be equivalent to A.D. 1454. Chronologically, therefore, it seems that Construction Stage IV corresponds to the reign of Motecuhzoma I. The Coyolxauhqui stone and the serpents may well have been added during Axayacatl's reign, judging from another relief on the south side of the pyramid which bears the glyph "3 House": this seems to relate to A.D. 1469, the year Axayacatl became *tlatoani* [ruler].

Construction Stage V

Very little has survived from this stage. All that has been uncovered is the stucco plaster on the platform, and part of the floor of the ceremonial precinct, the latter formed by stone slabs joined by stucco.

Construction Stage VI

Part of the remains from what we can see of this penultimate building stage belong to the great platform underlying the whole of the Temple structure. As in all the previous periods, the main façade faces west. Part of the stairway is visible, but most of it was destroyed in 1900 when a large drainage ditch was cut through the Great Temple. Three serpent heads and a decorated balustrade adorn the principal façade. . . .

According to Sahagún, there were seventy-eight structures, including the Great Temple, within the sacred space of the ceremonial precinct, which measured 500 meters on each of its four sides. The patio at the rear of the Temple, which would have formed part of this sacred space, is made of flat stones joined by stucco, and dates to Construction Stage VI. Sections of stairway alternating with fragments of balustrade form the eastern limit of the ceremonial precinct, a boundary device similar to that found at Tlatelolco: this archaeological discovery, however, contradicts some of the chroniclers who claimed that a wall in the form of serpents encircled the precinct.

Construction Stage VII

This is the final building stage of the Great Temple and is the one seen by the Spaniards at the beginning of the sixteenth century. All that remains of this period is part of the stone flooring of the ceremonial precinct and traces of where the Temple stood. Part of the platform belonging to Stage VI is still visible on the north side; but the three shrines (A, B, and C) and the Eagle precinct were completely covered by the flooring of this final building stage.

The Great Temple is a microcosm of the Aztec vision of the world, in which both horizontal and vertical dimensions have special cosmic significance. In my view, the platform supporting the Temple corresponds to the terrestrial level; this interpretation is reinforced by the sculptures of serpents—symbols of the earth—located upon it. Two large braziers stand on either side of the serpent-head sculptures, at the center of the north and south façades, and on the east side on an axis with the central line of the Tlaloc and Huitzilopochtli shrines. These braziers indicate that it was on the platform, which signified the earthly level, that ephemeral offerings were usually made.

The celestial levels are represented by the four slightly tapering tiers of the pyramid which rise to the summit where stand the two shrines of the principal gods, the supreme level: Omeyocán or "Place of duality."

The lower levels, corresponding to the underworld, are below the earthly platform. The majority of the offerings—many durable but some perishable—have been found beneath this great floor.

The words addressed to Ahuitzotl, Aztec ruler from 1486 to 1502, by Nezahualpilli, ruler of Texcoco, during the festivities to celebrate the completion of one of the construction stages of the Great Temple, reflect this belief in a sacred center:

> Although you are very young, because you are the sovereign of such a powerful kingdom, which is the root, the navel, and the heart of this entire worldly apparatus, make it your destiny to see that the honor of the Aztecs does not diminish but rather becomes greater.

In vertical terms, the Great Temple is formed of two halves, representing two sacred mountains. The southern half signifies Coatepec Hill, where Huitzilopochtli defeated his opponents, while the northern side represents the "Hill of sustenance," Tonacatepetl, where Tlaloc was patron deity. These two hills or shrines may also symbolize one of the places—where two mountains crashed together and crushed the traveler—through which the deceased passed on the way to Mictlan, according to Sahagún's account. . . .

The entire ceremonial precinct of Tenochtitlán with its seventy-eight structures, described by Sahagún, is also closely related to the Aztec worldview. The placement of each building was significant, often with reference to the Great Temple in the center, and conformed to the Aztec conception of its role within space and time in the universe. Examples are the Temple of the Sun, situated toward the southwest corner of the precinct, and the Temple of Tezcatlipoca, powerful god of Fate, which lay to the south of the Great Temple. Another example is the Temple of Ehecatl-Quetzalcoatl, "God of winds preceding the rains," located, according to the chronicles, in front of the Great Temple. A temple dedicated to this god was placed in a similar position in neighboring Tlatelolco. Perhaps this orientation is related to the myth of the creation of the Fifth Sun at Teotihuacán. According to this myth, all the gods gathered to see from which direction the sun would rise, each facing one of the four cardinal directions. Ehecatl faced east, and it was from here that the sun rose: therefore the Temple of Ehecatl-Quetzalcoatl in the ceremonial precinct has its main façade toward the east.

Adventure at Macchu Picchu

Hiram Bingham

The flamboyant Hiram Bingham (1875–1956) preferred to be recognized as an explorer rather than an academic. At the time of his famous expeditions to South America, he was actually a lecturer in Latin American history at Yale University. Born and raised on his grandfather's mission station outside Honolulu, Hawaii, Bingham was educated at the prestigious Phillips Academy in Andover and eventually attended Yale University. After graduation, he became the pastor at the impoverished Palama Chapel in Hawaii, where he worked for a few months before meeting Alfreda Mitchell, daughter of a local whaling tycoon and heiress to the Tiffany fortune on her mother's side. Bingham promptly abandoned his chaplaincy and saved enough money, by working as a land surveyor for the American Sugar Company, to travel to California and begin his graduate studies in history and social science at the University of California, Berkeley. After completing his master's degree, he married Alfreda and commenced his doctoral work at Harvard, where they were comfortably provided for by her family.

While at Harvard, Bingham became the curator of a collection of Latin American antiquities and literature that he had donated to the university. Soon after, he taught at Princeton at the invitation of Woodrow Wilson, the dean at that time, and made his first trip to Latin America. Upon returning home, his fondest wish, to lecture at his alma mater, was realized when he was appointed as a lecturer at Yale and eventually made full professor. Through his research, Bingham had become enchanted with the idea of discovering the secret capital of the Incas, from which they purportedly led a resistance against the Spanish for some thirty years after they were forced to relinquish Cuzco. In 1911, he led his famous expedition, which rediscovered what he claimed was this very city: Macchu Picchu. While the city was probably never truly lost (for there were local people living in it when he arrived), Bingham put the spectacular ruins back on the archaeological map and captivated the world with his accounts of the magnificent site. After several successful seasons of archaeological exploration, he was forced to flee Peru for violating excavation permit laws and never returned. Soon after, he gave up teaching and became an aviator in World War I. The larger-than-life Bingham moved on to a successful, if at times scandalous, career in American politics and never again dabbled in exploration, but he will always be best remembered as a finder of lost cities, one of the last archaeological adventurers.

Hiram Bingham wove a fast-moving tale. This selection from his Lost City of the Incas *tells of his dramatic excursion to Macchu Picchu at a time when the high Andes were far off the beaten track.*

The morning of July 24th dawned in a cold drizzle. Arteaga shivered and seemed inclined to stay in his hut. I offered to pay him well if he would show me the ruins. He demurred and said it was too hard a climb for such a wet day. But when he found that I was willing to pay him a *sol* (a Peruvian silver dollar, fifty cents, gold), three or four times the ordinary daily wage in this vicinity, he finally agreed to go. When asked just where the ruins were, he pointed straight up to the top of the mountain. No one supposed that they would be particularly interesting. And no one cared to go with me. The naturalist said there were "more butterflies near the river!" and he was reasonably certain he could collect some new varieties. The surgeon said he had to wash his clothes and mend them. Anyhow it was my job to investigate all reports of ruins and try to find the Inca capital.

So, accompanied only by Sergeant Carrasco I left camp at ten o'clock. Arteaga took us some distance upstream. On the road we passed a snake which had only just been killed. He said the region was the favorite haunt of "vipers." We later learned the lance-headed or yellow viper, commonly known as the fer-de-lance, a very venomous serpent, capable of making considerable springs when in pursuit of its prey, is common hereabouts.

After a walk of three-quarters of an hour Arteaga left the main road and plunged down through the jungle to the bank of the river. Here there was a primitive bridge which crossed the roaring rapids at its narrowest part, where the stream was forced to flow between two great bowlders. The "bridge" was made of half a dozen very slender logs, some of which were not long enough to span the distance between the bowlders, but had been spliced and lashed together with vines!

Arteaga and the sergeant took off their shoes and crept gingerly across, using their somewhat prehensile toes to keep from slipping. It was obvious that no one could live for an instant in the icy cold rapids, but would immediately be dashed to pieces against the rocks. I am frank to confess that I got down on my hands and knees and crawled across, six inches at a time. Even after we reached the other side I could not help wondering what would happen to the "bridge" if a particularly heavy shower should fall in the valley above. A light rain had fallen during the night and the river had risen so that the bridge was already threatened by the foaming rapids. It would not take much more to wash it away entirely. If this should happen during the day it might be very awkward. As a matter of fact, it did happen a few days later and when the next visitors attempted to cross the river at this point they found only one slender log remaining.

Leaving the stream, we now struggled up the bank through dense jungle, and in a few minutes reached the bottom of a very precipitous slope. For an hour and twenty minutes we had a hard climb. A good part of the distance we went on all fours, sometimes holding on by our fingernails. Here and there, a primitive ladder made from the roughly notched trunk of a small tree was placed in such a way as to help one over what might otherwise have proved to be an impassable cliff. In another place the slope was covered with slippery grass where it was hard to find either handholds or footholds. Arteaga groaned and said that there were lots of snakes here. Sergeant Carrasco said nothing but was glad he had good military shoes. The humidity was great. We were in the belt of maximum precipitation in eastern Peru. The heat was excessive; and I was not in training! There were no ruins or *andenes* of any kind in sight. I began to think my companions had chosen the better part.

Shortly after noon, just as we were completely exhausted, we reached a little grass-covered hut two thousand feet above the river where several good-natured Indians, pleasantly surprised at our unexpected arrival, welcomed us with dripping gourds full of cool, delicious water. Then they set before us a few cooked sweet potatoes. It seems that two Indian farmers, Richarte and Alvarez, had recently chosen this eagles' nest for their home. They said they had found plenty of terraces here on which to grow their crops. Laughingly they admitted they enjoyed being free from undesirable visitors, officials looking for army "volunteers" or collecting taxes.

Richarte told us that they had been living here four years. It seems probable that, owing to its inaccessibility, the canyon had been unoccupied for several centuries, but with the completion of the new government road, settlers began once more to occupy this region. In time somebody clambered up the precipices and found on these slopes at an elevation of nine thousand feet above the sea, an abundance of rich soil conveniently situated on artificial terraces, in a fine climate. Here the Indians had finally cleared off and burned over a few terraces and planted crops of maize, sweet and white potatoes, sugar cane, beans, peppers, tree tomatoes, and gooseberries.

They said there were two paths to the outside world. Of one we had already had a taste; the other was "even more difficult," a perilous path down the face of a rocky precipice on the other side of the ridge. It was their only means of egress in the wet season when the primitive bridge over which we had come could not be maintained. I was not surprised to learn that they went away from home "only about once a month."

Through Sergeant Carrasco I learned that the ruins were "a little further along." In this country one never can tell whether such a report is worthy of credence. "He may have been lying" is a good footnote to affix to all hearsay evidence. Accordingly, I was not unduly excited, nor in a great hurry to move. The heat was still great, the water from the Indians' spring was cool and delicious, and the rustic wooden bench, hospitably covered immediately after my arrival with a soft woolen poncho, seemed most comfortable. Furthermore, the view was simply enchanting. Tremendous green precipices fell away to the white rapids of the Urubamba below. Immediately in front, on the north side of the valley, was a great granite cliff rising two thousand feet sheer. To the left was the solitary peak of Huayna Picchu, surrounded by seemingly inaccessible precipices. On all sides were rocky cliffs. Beyond them cloud-capped snow-covered mountains rose thousands of feet above us.

We continued to enjoy the wonderful view of the canyon, but all the ruins we could see from our cool shelter were a few terraces.

Without the slightest expectation of finding anything more interesting than the ruins of two or three stone houses such as we had encountered at various places on the road between Ollantaytambo and Torontoy, I finally left the cool shade of the pleasant little hut and climbed farther up the ridge and around a slight promontory. Melchor Arteaga had "been there once before," so he decided to rest and gossip with Richarte and Alvarez. They sent a small boy with me as a "guide." The sergeant was in duty bound to follow, but I think he may have been a little curious to see what there was to see.

Hardly had we left the hut and rounded the promontory than we were confronted with an unexpected sight, a great flight of beautifully constructed stone-faced terraces, perhaps a hundred of them, each hundreds of feet long and ten feet high. They had been recently rescued from the jungle by the Indians. A veritable forest of large trees which had been growing on them for centuries had been chopped down and partly burned to make a clearing for agricultural purposes. The task was too great for the two Indians so the tree trunks had been allowed to lie as they fell and only the smaller branches removed. But the ancient soil, carefully put in place by the Incas, was still capable of producing rich crops of maize and potatoes.

However, there was nothing to be excited about. Similar flights of well-made terraces are to be seen in the upper Urubamba Valley at Pisac and Ollantaytambo, as well as opposite Torontoy. So we patiently followed the little guide along one of the widest terraces where there had once been a small conduit and made our way into an untouched forest beyond. Suddenly I found myself confronted with the walls of ruined houses built of the finest quality of Inca stonework. It was hard to see them for they were partly covered with trees and moss, the growth of centuries, but in the dense shadow, hiding in bamboo thickets and tangled vines, appeared here and there walls of white granite ashlars carefully cut and exquisitely fitted together. We scrambled along through the dense undergrowth, climbing over terrace walls and in bamboo thickets where our guide found it easier going than I did. Suddenly without any warning, under a huge overhanging ledge the boy showed me a cave beautifully lined with the finest cut stone. It had evidently been a Royal Mausoleum. On top of this particular ledge was a semi-circular building whose outer wall, gently sloping and slightly curved bore a striking resemblance to the famous Temple of the Sun in Cuzco. This might also be a Temple of the Sun. It followed the natural curvature of

*Hiram Bingham took this photograph of Macchu Picchu, after the clearance work
by members of his expedition.*

the rock and was keyed to it by one of the finest examples of masonry I had ever seen. Furthermore it was tied into another beautiful wall, made of very carefully matched ashlars of pure white granite, especially selected for its fine grain. Clearly, it was the work of a master artist. The interior surface of the wall was broken by niches and square stone-pegs. The exterior surface was perfectly simple and unadorned. The lower courses, of particularly large ashlars, gave it a look of solidity. The upper courses, diminishing in size toward the top, lent grace and delicacy to the structure. The flowing lines, the symmetrical arrangement of the ashlars, and the gradual gradation of the courses, combined to produce a wonderful effect, softer and more pleasing than that of the marble temples of the Old World. Owing to the absence of mortar, there were no ugly spaces between the rocks. They might have grown together. On account of the beauty of the white granite this structure surpassed in attractiveness the best Inca walls in Cuzco which had caused visitors to marvel for four centuries. It seemed like an unbelievable dream. Dimly, I began to realize that this wall and its adjoining semicircular temple over the cave were as fine as the finest stonework in the world.

It fairly took my breath away. What could this place be? Why had no one given us any idea of it? Even Melchor Arteaga was only moderately interested and had no appreciation of the importance of the ruins which Richarte and Alvarez had adopted for their little farm. Perhaps after all this was an isolated small place which had escaped notice because it was inaccesible.

Then the little boy urged us to climb up a steep hill over what seemed to be a flight of stone steps. Surprise followed surprise in bewildering succession. We came to a great stairway of large granite blocks. Then we walked along a path to a clearing where the Indians had planted a small vegetable garden. Suddenly we found ourselves standing in front of the ruins of two of the finest and most interesting structures in ancient America. Made of beautiful white granite, the walls contained blocks of Cyclopean size, higher than a man. The sight held me spellbound.

Each building had only three walls and was entirely open on one side. The principal temple had walls twelve feet high which were lined with exquisitely made niches, five, high up at each end, and seven on the back. There were seven courses of ashlars in the end walls. Under the seven rear niches was a rectangular block fourteen feet long, possibly a sacrificial altar, but more probably a throne for the mummies of departed Incas, brought out to be worshipped. The building did not look as though it ever had a roof. The top course of beautifully smooth ashlars was not intended to be covered, so the sun could be welcomed here by priests and mummies. I could scarcely believe my senses as I examined the larger blocks in the lower course and estimated that they must weigh from ten to fifteen tons each. Would anyone believe what I had found? Fortunately, in this land where accuracy in reporting what one has seen is not a prevailing characteristic of travelers, I had a good camera and the sun was shining.

The principal temple faces the south where there is a small plaza or courtyard. On the east side of the plaza was another amazing structure, the ruins of a temple containing three great windows looking out over the canyon to the rising sun. Like its neighbor, it is unique among Inca ruins. Nothing just like them in design and execution has ever been found. Its three conspicuously large windows, obviously too large to serve any useful purpose, were most beautifully made with the greatest care and solidity. This was clearly a ceremonial edifice of peculiar significance. Nowhere else in Peru, so far as I know, is there a similar structure conspicuous for being "a masonry wall with three windows." It will be remembered that Salcamayhua, the Peruvian who wrote an account of the antiquities of Peru in 1620, said that the first Inca, Manco the Great, ordered "works to be executed at the place of his birth, consisting of a masonry wall with three windows." Was that what I had found? If it was, then this was not the capital of the last Inca but the birthplace of the first. It did not occur to me that it might be both. To be sure the region was one which could fit in with the requirements of Tampu Tocco, the place of refuge of the civilized folk who fled from the southern barbarian tribes after the battle of La Raya and brought with them the body of their king Pachacutec who was slain by an arrow. He might have been buried in the stone-lined cave under the semi-circular temple.

Could this be "the principal city" of Manco and his sons, that Vilcapampa where was the "University of Idolatry" which Friar Marcos and Friar Diego had tried to reach? It behooved us to find out as much about it as we could.

The Lords of Sipán

WALTER ALVA AND CHRISTOPHER DONNAN

The Moche state flourished on Peru's arid northern coast between the first and eighth centuries A.D. Moche lords presided over a kingdom centered on several intensely culti-vated coastal river valleys. Highly organized irrigation systems produced beans, maize, cotton, and other crops, sufficient to support dense valley populations. As in all Peruvian states, the Moche nobility formed a tiny minority, whose secular authority rested on their abilities as priests and warriors. Until the 1980s, almost everything known about the Moche came from their ceramics, sculpted vessels, and painted pots, which depict not only the portraits of important lords, but ritual and battle scenes. Then, in 1987, grave robbers unearthed a spectacular, gold-laden burial near the village of Sipán in the Moche heartland. Fortunately for science, Peruvian archaeologist Walter Alva (b. 1940) was soon on the scene. Since then, he has recovered three unlooted royal burials. Each contained an elaborately costumed man, buried in complete ceremonial regalia, including crescent-shaped headdresses and superbly crafted body ornaments. The treasures from these graves rival those from the tomb of Tutankhamun, and, in some cases, the artistry is vastly superior.

American archaeologist Christopher Donnan has spent a lifetime studying the rituals and other scenes depicted on Moche vessels. He believes that the Lords of Sipán were warrior priests who reenacted a complex sacrificial ceremony at prescribed times of the year, when prisoners of war were sacrificed to the gods. When lords died, they were interred wearing the formal regalia and objects they used in the sacrificial ceremonies. Their successors assumed their roles, wearing new sets of the same costumes and artifacts, not only perpetuating the official religion, but also guaranteeing work for the dozens of skilled artisans who manufactured precious objects for the nobility. The Sipán burials are remarkable for their sophisticated artifacts, which presented a major challenge to conservators in Germany and Peru. And thanks to decades of research on Moche ceram-ics, Alva was able to describe the religious context of the tombs.

In the following extract from their book Royal Tombs of Sipán, *Walter Alva and Christopher Donnan describe their discovery of the tomb and some of the problems encountered in excavating the undisturbed royal sepulchers. They also discuss the identity of the mysterious lords.*

For months, as the contents of the plank coffin were being excavated, we had been working and moving equipment around all four of its sides. We had absolutely no idea that we had been walking only centimeters above hundreds of ceramic vessels, and the burials of six other individuals!

Over the next six months, we painstakingly excavated these remains. Only then did we understand the full complexity of the remarkable tomb, and the nature of its construction. The burial chamber was actually a room, with solid mud-brick benches along its sides and at the head end. Niches had been created in these benches—two in each of the sides and one at the head. The benches reduced the floor space of the burial chamber to an area 2.40 meters north–south by 3.25 meters east–west. The plank coffin had been placed in the center of this area, aligned parallel to the side walls. The contents of the coffin were then placed inside it, and the coffin lid was securely fastened with copper straps.

Hundreds of ceramic vessels were subsequently lowered into the burial chamber and arranged in groups that filled the niches in the side benches. Some ceramics were also placed on the floor near the head of the coffin, and along the right and left sides of the interred lord.

The ceramics were predominantly mold-made jars, sculpted in the form of nude prisoners with ropes around their necks, warriors holding warclubs and shields, and seated figures with their hands on their knees or chests. Most were neither painted nor polished, and appear to have been mass-produced. . . .

Somewhat finer ceramics were placed in the niche at the head of the burial. These included stirrup spout bottles in the form of seated humans, owls, and lizards. This selection presumably meant something special to the Moche people, but its meaning is unknown to us today. In one side niche, there was a fragmented stirrup spout bottle depicting a seated figure with inlaid eyes and copper ear ornaments.

At about the time the ceramics were being placed in the burial chamber, two sacrificed llamas were put on the floor—one on each side adjacent to the foot of the coffin. The body of a child was also placed on the floor near the head of the coffin. The child was seated with its back leaning against the southwest corner of the burial chamber, and its legs extended forward along the floor.

The child had died at age nine or ten. The dentition suggests several episodes of either illness or dietary deficiency from which the child had recovered, but which left a permanent record in the developing tooth crowns. A cavity in the deciduous upper second molar also suggests that this child may have been in poor health.

Once the ceramics, llamas, and child were placed in the funerary chamber, five cane coffins, each containing one adult, were lowered into position. One of these coffins, containing the body of an adult male, was placed on the east side of the plank coffin, directly on top of one of the sacrificed llamas. The body was fully extended, lying on its back with the head to the south. The left foot was missing. The man was between thirty-five and fifty years old at the time he died. Although shorter in stature than the lord in the plank coffin, he was more powerfully built, with a massive square chin and large teeth. His body was covered with copper objects, including a large crescent-shaped headdress ornament and a circular shield. Alongside his body was a large warclub, completely encased in copper sheet. His body had been wrapped in a coarsely woven shroud, and placed inside a rectangular box-like coffin made of cane.

On the other side of the plank coffin was another cane coffin, placed on top of the other sacrificed llama. It also contained an adult male lying extended on his back. In this instance, however, the head was to the north. His age at death has been estimated as between thirty-five and forty-five years. He was wearing a beaded pectoral, and had several unidentified copper objects on top of his body. Inside his coffin was a dog, stretched out with its head near the man's feet and its tail by the man's waist.

Three other cane coffins contained adult females. Two of these were stacked one on top of the other at the head of the plank coffin. The lower coffin had been placed over the extended legs of the child seated in the southwest corner of the burial chamber. Both females were fully extended with their heads to the east. The lower individual lay on her back, while the upper one was lying face down.

The third cane coffin containing a female was at the foot of the plank coffin. She lay on her side with her head to the west, facing the plank coffin.

All three women were between fifteen and twenty years old when they died. They exhibited no sign of illness or violent death, but the upper female at the head of the plank coffin was missing her left foot. These women had relatively few objects in their coffins, although the woman at the foot of the plank coffin was buried wearing a large copper headdress, and the upper individual at the head of the plank coffin was wearing a beaded pectoral.

As the burials around the plank coffin were being excavated, we thought they were individuals who had been sacrificed in order to accompany the principal figure in the afterlife. Perhaps the flanking males were his bodyguards, or members of his court, and the females were his wives, concubines, or servants.

While this supposition may be valid concerning the males, we were to learn that it may not have been true for the females. Their skeletal remains suggest that they had died long before the principal figure, and that their bodies were partially decomposed at the time they were put in his tomb. Their bones were disarticulated and jumbled in ways that could not have occurred with *in situ* decomposition of the bodies. This was most apparent in the torso, where the ribs and vertebrae were completely out of position. This state suggests that the bodies were placed in the burial chamber *after* substantial soft tissue decomposition, when the bones were free to move about inside the textile wrappings that formed the burial shrouds.

We do not know how long the women had been dead prior to their placement in the royal tomb. They may have died during the life of the principal male, although it is also possible that they had been dead long before he was born. Whatever the case, their bodies were probably wrapped in burial shrouds, placed in cane coffins, and subsequently stored in a dry, sheltered place for many years while the soft tissue decomposed, freeing the ribs and vertebrae. This may have occurred in a palace, or in a temple at the summit of one of the pyramids. Then, on the occasion of the death of someone of the importance of the principal male, they were brought out of storage for placement in his tomb. The movement involved in transporting these bodies to the grave site, lowering them into the funerary chamber, and putting them into their final resting place would have caused the bones to fall out of position.

With the coffins in place, the tomb was sealed by the construction of the beam roof. The roof was only slightly higher than the benches that extended along the sides and head of the burial chamber, and would have been only a little more than a meter above the floor—too low to have created a room in which people could have stood upright.

The roof was covered with soil as the area above it was filled. It was in this fill, approximately 50 centimeters above the roof, that the footless first male burial had been located.

High up on the south wall of the chamber, approximately one meter above the roof beams, there was one final burial. The body was seated with its legs crossed and its hands on its knees. It had been placed in a small niche, carved into the south wall, so that it looked out over the royal mausoleum. And so it had remained, undisturbed, for seventeen centuries. . . .

As Tomb 1 was being excavated and its contents catalogued, one question kept recurring to all who participated: "Who was this person?" Analysis of the bones indicated an adult male about forty years of age. The elaborate tomb, with its unusual plank coffin, accompanying male and female burials, and the quantity and quality of grave goods, attested to an individual of high status—a member of the nobility. But a more precise identification of this noble and the role he played in Moche society was possible only through a careful study of Moche art.

The key to this research was a major photographic archive of Moche art, located on the campus of the University of California in Los Angeles (UCLA). This archive, containing more than 125,000 photographs of Moche objects in museums and private collections throughout the world, has served for many years as an important resource for the study of Moche culture. As the tomb was being excavated, photographs of the objects were sent to UCLA for comparative study.

If we assume that the objects in the plank coffin were worn and used by the man during his lifetime, they should tell us about his role in Moche society. Many of the objects in his coffin suggest that he was a warrior. Warriors and warrior activities were very frequently depicted by Moche artists, and the archive of Moche art contains hundreds of these depictions that can be grouped into categories forming a sequential narrative of Moche militarism and the ceremonial activities that follow it.

There are many sculptural depictions of warriors, generally kneeling or standing and holding warclubs diagonally across their chests. Some fineline drawings show processions of warriors, perhaps as they marched toward the field of battle. . . . The essence of Moche warfare appears to have been the expression of *individual* valor in which the warriors engaged in one-on-one combat. In rare instances it is clear that one or more of the combatants was actually killed, but normally only the vanquishing of the enemy is shown. This generally involved hitting the opponent on the head or upper body with the warclub. Defeat is indicated by the enemy receiving such a blow, bleeding profusely from his nose, losing his headdress and possibly other parts of his attire, or by the victor grasping his hair, removing his nose ornament, or slapping his face.

Once an enemy was defeated, some or all of his clothing was removed, a rope was placed around his neck, and his hands were sometimes tied behind his back. The prisoner's clothing and weapons were made into a weapon bundle which was tied to the victor's warclub and slung over his shoulder. The victor held the rope tied to the prisoner's neck and forced the prisoner to walk in front of him. The many fineline drawings of warriors with prisoners suggest that public parading and display of the spoils of war was an important part of Moche militarism.

The prisoners were ultimately taken to a place where they were formally arraigned before a high-status individual. At the arraignment, weapon bundles were often placed on the ground near the prisoners. The arraignment is sometimes shown in the setting of sandy hillsides, perhaps near the field of battle. The prisoners were brought back to Moche settlements or ceremonial precincts. One scene clearly shows them arriving at a large pyramid with a structure at its summit—a setting similar to the pyramids at Sipán.

Following arraignment there was a ceremony in which the prisoners were sacrificed by having their throats cut and their blood consumed by priests and attendants. The prisoners' bodies were then dismembered: their heads, hands, and feet were removed and tied individually with ropes to create trophies. . . .

There are many representations of the Sacrifice Ceremony in Moche art, and these imply that it was an important aspect of Moche religion.

. . . Of the . . . four principal priests who participate in the Sacrifice Ceremony, most important is the Warrior Priest, the large figure on the left, who holds a tall goblet. Rays emanate from his head and shoulders, and he wears a conical helmet with a crescent-shaped ornament at its peak, a crescent-shaped nose ornament, large circular ear ornaments, and a warrior backflap. A dog is adjacent to his feet.

The figure to the right of the Warrior Priest is the Bird Priest. He is always part bird and part human and is always shown wearing either a conical helmet (as in this representation) or a headdress with an owl at its center.

To the right of the Bird Priest is the Priestess, who always wears a dress-like garment and a headdress with two prominent plumes. Her hair is in wrapped braids that hang down over her chest and end in serpent heads.

To the right of the Priestess is the fourth major participant, a priest who always wears a headdress with long streamers having serrated upper edges, and a sash-like garment with a fringe of discs at the end. His headdress is a half-circle of sheet metal with an animal face, perhaps a feline, embossed near its center. This half-circle is flanked by two curved pieces of sheet metal, and at the back of the headdress is a fan of feathers.

In the lower register of this scene two nude prisoners are having their throats cut. Their hands are tied behind their backs and their weapon bundles are placed to one side.

To the left of the prisoners is a litter with rays projecting from its backrest. This is the litter of the Warrior Priest who is seen in the register above. In other scenes the Warrior Priest is actually riding in the litter. Human heads hang from the ends of the litter poles, and a feline is perched in front of the seat. Above the feline and tied to the litter with a cord is a scepter, shown in horizontal view, with its box-like chamber on the left and its spatula-bladed handle on the right.

There are a number of secondary figures and objects in this scene. Of particular relevance to Tomb 1 are the paisley-shaped fruits that appear to float in the background. These are called *ulluchus*, and have been identified as a member of the papaya family. Native people in the tropical forest of South America recognize the anticoagulant property of this fruit, and it is thought that the Moche may have used it to keep the human blood from coagulating during the Sacrifice Ceremony. It is interesting that *ulluchus* are associated with two activities in Moche art that involve the ritual consumption of blood—the Sacrifice Ceremony and deer hunting. Deer are often anthropomorphized, sometimes as warriors or as prisoners with ropes around their necks. The ritual hunting of deer was clearly analogous to the capture and sacrifice of warriors.

PART III

ARCHAEOLOGY BECOMES A SCIENCE

Archaeology is the latest born of the sciences. It has but scarcely struggled into freedom, out of the swaddling clothes of dilettante speculations. It is still attracted by pretty things rather than by real knowledge.

—Flinders Petrie, *Methods and Aims in Archaeology*, 1904

art III approaches archaeological discovery from a different perspective: that of the excavators who turned the investigation of the past from a casual pastime into a science. As we have seen, archaeological excavation began as treasure hunting, conducted with robust panache. Cavaliere de Alcubierre used gunpowder and brute force to tunnel into Roman Herculaneum. English barrow digger William Cunnington used teams of laborers to trench open several burial mounds a day. In Egypt, Giovanni Belzoni was a maestro of the lever and roller, not averse to blowing open a tomb when it suited him. Even today, many people still believe that archaeologists pursue tombs and precious statuary to the virtual exclusion of all other finds. Only a handful of early diggers recorded the layers of the soil or placed their findings in a stratigraphic context. One of them was none other than Thomas Jefferson, politician and renaissance scientist, who investigated an Indian burial mound in Virginia not for treasure, but to find out who built it. He did so in the 1780s, long before archaeology was a household word. Most diggers excavated for adventure, fun, or profit, for archaeology was the province of the professional traveler, the tomb robber, or the leisured gentleman with time to kill on his estate. Jefferson describes his burial mound findings with an elegant logic that would not be out of place in a modern excavation report. But antiquary Thomas Wright's account of a Victorian excavation paints a more realistic picture of much nineteenth-century archaeological discovery. The laborers dug, while the gentry amused themselves with games and never got their hands dirty. As for Austen Henry Layard and other Near Eastern pioneers, they employed hundreds of men and behaved like kings among them. Layard simply tunneled into Nimrud and Nineveh, following the decorated walls of Assyrian monarchs' palaces. His excavations were without finesse and driven by the need to find as much as possible in the shortest time.

The tide began to turn in the 1870s, partly in reaction to Heinrich Schliemann's depredations at Troy, when the Germans excavated on Samothrace and at Olympia with architects and photographers in attendance. Their methods were crude by modern standards and far behind those of General Augustus Lane Fox Pitt-Rivers, who applied military principles to his excavations in southern England in the 1880s and 1890s. "The figure standing at attention in the foreground gives the scale," he wrote in one of his reports. The general's passion for organization, for detail and routine, honed by a lifetime in the military, rubbed off on the first truly modern excavators like Mortimer Wheeler, who finally brought science to archaeological discovery in the 1920s. For while Pitt-Rivers dissected a few sites over years of patient digging, his contemporaries still thought of excavation as a form of dignified treasure hunt. To archaeologists like J. C. Droop, who wrote his manual on fieldwork ten years before Wheeler started digging, excavation was a pastime for gentlemen.

Egyptologist Herbert Winlock was a serious fieldworker early in the century, but his methods were casual by modern standards. Leonard Woolley's excavations at Carchemish before World War I were run with casual aplomb, with more scientific methods than a half century before, but still with a strong undercurrent of adventure. Mary Chubb perfectly captures the atmosphere on an Egyptian excavation of the 1930s, a dig run on a shoestring, but with a much greater concern for detail than exhibited by Flinders Petrie and his contemporaries, who had stressed the importance of small finds. But, as Chubb shows only too well, it was the spectacular find that justified the expense and brought funds for another season, a syndrome that continues to this day.

Mortimer Wheeler's memorable reconstruction of the Battle of Maiden Castle represents the newly sophisticated archaeology of the 1930s and 1940s, a time when science first had a significant impact on the study of the past. Computers, infrared photography, spectrographic analysis, new dating methods— since the 1950s, archaeology has rapidly become a high-technology science concerned as much with explaining why human societies changed as with describing them. Stuart Struever's excavation at the Koster site in the Illinois River Valley in the Midwest was a major project where computers were first used to their full potential and where a whole battery of scientific methods came into play as thousands of years of changing Native American society emerged from the soil. Advancing technology also made possible scientific archaeology underwater, an approach to excavation pioneered by George Bass and brought to a very high pitch with the investigation of the Bronze Age shipwreck at Uluburun off southern Turkey. Archaeology underwater has the same objectives as archaeology on land—the reconstruction of ancient human behavior and societies. It just happens that scuba-diving technology has made the seabed accessible and has allowed archaeologists to develop a now highly refined array of scientific recovery methods for excavating sites as meticulously as on land.

Some of the most fascinating archaeological discoveries of recent years have come from recent centuries; in interpreting these finds, archaeologists work alongside historians, combining the study of material culture with evidence from documentary sources. The archaeologist studies artifacts and food remains, the dispassionate and tangible remains of an entire community, such as Annapolis, Maryland. Annapolis is often portrayed as an aristocratic eighteenth-century town, but archaeological excavations have revealed a city of remarkable social diversity, with its nonliterate citizens known to us, for the most part only from their artifacts. Sometimes, too, the archaeologist unearths an entire historical community that has left few traces in the archives of the day. Such was the case at Martin's Hundred, Virginia, where Ivor Nöel Hume located a forgotten seventeenth-century colonial village from virtual historical oblivion. He used a combination of archaeological and historical detective work to conjure up a vanished hamlet from a jigsaw puzzle of post holes, foundation trenches, and other subsurface features.

But even in today's work, archaeological discoveries have an allure all their own. As I write, a report comes in about a mummy of a man discovered in Spirit Cave, Nevada, in 1940. The man wore moccasins and a skin robe and was wrapped in a shroud of two marsh-reed mats. His undated remains lay in a sealed box in the Nevada State Museum for a half century until Ervin Taylor of the University of California, Riverside, applied accelerator mass spectrometry (AMS) radiocarbon dating to a sample of the mummy's hair. To everyone's surprise, the Spirit Cave burial dated to more than 9,400 years ago, the earliest mummy in North America and far older than Otzi the Ice Man. Nevada archaeologists are now studying the man's intestines to determine his diet and will carry out DNA analysis to establish his genetic makeup. The Spirit Cave discovery is a classic example of how more and more archaeological discoveries come from the laboratory and the high-technology world of science.

The First American Archaeologist

Thomas Jefferson

In 1781, Thomas Jefferson (1743–1826) retired to his Monticello estate in Virginia, exhausted from an arduous term as governor of Virginia. "Surrounded by his farm, his family, and his books," Jefferson sat down to answer a questionnaire about Virginia sent to him by the French government. His responses turned into a lengthy discourse that touched on philosophical matters, local life and lore, natural history, products "animal, vegetable, and mineral," and the "aborigines," the Indians of Virginia ancient and modern. Jefferson described the modern tribes, but it was inevitable that he would probe the question of their origins. Who were the earliest peoples to live in Virginia? At the time, this was the subject of lively speculation, for the settlers moving west across the Allegheny Mountains had come across hundreds of large, deserted earthworks and burial mounds. Who had built these abandoned monuments? Were they the work of long-vanished civilizations, perhaps from Egypt or other far-flung lands? Or were they the work of the Ten Lost Tribes of Israel or of Native Americans?

While others speculated, Jefferson decided to indulge his scientific curiosity by investigating a small burial mound that lay near the Rivanna River. Such tumuli were commonplace in Virginia. Many were the theories advanced to explain the mounds—that they were the resting places of war casualties or the only tangible remains of long-vanished settlements built on the "softest and most fertile meadow-fields on river sides." But Jefferson was the first scholar to excavate for answers. "I wished to satisfy myself whether any or which of these opinions was just," he wrote. The result was one of the first stratigraphic excavations anywhere in the world. Jefferson observed layers of human bones at different depths, recorded the internal structure of the mound, and estimated that more than one thousand skeletons had been deposited in the tumulus over a considerable period of time. This was no ardent hunt for artifacts and buried treasure, but a measured description of a burial mound and its contents for scientific posterity. Jefferson ended by concluding that the Rivanna mound served as a burial place for many generations, a place "of considerable notoriety among the Indians."

Notes on the State of Virginia, *from which this selection is taken, is not only a classic account of Thomas Jefferson's beloved homeland, but one of the first scientific accounts of a burial mound excavation ever written. Here Jefferson describes the layers of the mound in a sober essay, which offers a marked comparison with the picnic-like atmosphere of the Victorian excavation sixty years later described in the next selection. A century was to pass before archaeological excavations were reported so thoroughly.*

I know of no such thing existing as an Indian monument: for I would not honour with that name arrow points, stone hatchets, stone pipes, and half-shapen images. Of labour on the large scale, I think there is no remain as respectable as would be a common ditch for the draining of lands: unless indeed it be the barrows, of which many are to be found all over this country. These are of different sizes, some of them constructed of earth, and some of loose stones. That they were repositories of the dead, has been obvious to all: but on what particular occasion constructed, was matter of doubt. Some have thought they covered the bones of those who have fallen in battles fought on the spot of interment. Some ascribed them to the custom, said to prevail among the Indians, of collecting, at certain periods, the bones of all their dead, wheresoever deposited at the time of death. Others again supposed them the general sepulchres for towns, conjectured to have been on or near these grounds; and this opinion was supported by the quality of the lands in which they are found (those constructed of earth being generally in the softest and most fertile meadow grounds on river sides) and by a tradition, said to be handed down from the Aboriginal Indians, that, when they settled in a town, the first person who died was placed erect, and earth put about him, so as to cover and support him; that, when another died, a narrow passage was dug to the first, the second reclined against him, and the cover of earth replaced, and so on. There being one of these in my neighbourhood, I wished to satisfy myself whether any, and which of these opinions were just. For this purpose I determined to open and examine it thoroughly. It was situated on the low grounds of the Rivanna, about two miles above its principal fork, and opposite to some hills, on which had been an Indian town. It was of a spheroidical form, of about forty feet diameter at the base, and had been of about twelve feet altitude, though now reduced by the plough to seven and a half, having been under cultivation about a dozen years. Before this it was covered with trees of twelve inches diameter, and round the base was an excavation of five feet depth and width, from whence the earth had been taken of which the hillock was formed. I first dug superficially in several parts of it, and came to collections of human bones, at different depths, from six inches to three feet below the surface. These were lying in the utmost confusion, some vertical, some oblique, some horizontal, and directed to every point of the compass, entangled, and held together in clusters by the earth. Bones of the most distant parts were found together, as, for instance, the small bones of the foot in the hollow of a scull, many sculls would sometimes be in contact, lying on the face, on the side, on the back, top or bottom, so as, on the whole, to give the idea of bones emptied promiscuously from a bag or basket, and covered over with earth, without any attention to their order. The bones of

Thomas Jefferson.

which the greatest numbers remained, were sculls, jaw-bones, teeth, the bones of the arms, thighs, legs, feet, and hands. A few ribs remained, some vertebrae of the neck and spine, without their processes, and one instance only of the bone which serves as a base to the vertebral column. The sculls were so tender, that they generally fell to pieces on being touched. The other bones were stronger. There were some teeth which were judged to be smaller than those of an adult; a scull, which, on a slight view, appeared to be that of an infant, but it fell to pieces on being taken out, so as to prevent satisfactory examination; a rib, and a fragment of the under-jaw of a person about half grown; another rib of an infant; and part of the jaw of a child, which had not yet cut its teeth. This last furnishing the most decisive proof of the burial of children here, I was particular in my attention to it. It was part of the right-half of the under-jaw. The processes, by which it was articulated to the temporal bones, were entire; and the bone itself firm to where it had been broken off, which, as nearly as I could judge, was about the place of the eye-tooth. Its upper edge, wherein would have been the sockets of the teeth, was perfectly smooth. Measuring it with that of an adult, by placing their hinder processes together, its broken end extended to the penultimate grinder of the adult. This bone was white, all the others of a sand colour. The bones of infants being soft, they probably decay sooner, which might be the cause so few were found here. I proceeded then to make a perpendicular cut through the body of the barrow, that I might examine its internal structure. This passed about three feet from its center, was opened to the former surface of the earth, and was wide enough for a man to walk through and examine its sides. At the bottom, that is, on the level of the circumjacent plain, I found bones; above these a few stones, brought from a cliff a quarter of a mile off, and from the river one-eighth of a mile off; then a large interval of earth, then a stratum of bones, and so on. At one end of the section were four strata of bones plainly distinguishable; at the other, three; the strata in one part not ranging with those in another. The bones nearest the surface were least decayed. No holes were discovered in any of them as if made with bullets, arrows, or other weapons. I conjectured that in this barrow might have been a thousand skeletons. Every one will readily seize the circumstances above related, which militate against the opinion, that it covered the bones only of persons fallen in battle; and against the tradition also, which would make it the common sepulchre of a town, in which the bodies were placed upright, and touching each other. Appearances certainly indicate that it has derived both origin and growth from the accustomary collection of bones, and deposition of them together; that the first collection had been deposited on the common surface of the earth, a few stones put over it, and then a covering of earth, that the second had been laid on this, had covered more or less of it in proportion to the number of bones, and was then also covered with earth; and so on. The following are the particular circumstances which give it this aspect. (1) The number of bones. (2) Their confused position. (3) Their being in different strata. (4) The strata in one part have no correspondence with those in another. (5) The difference in the time of inhumation. (6) The existence of infant bones among them.

Excavation, Victorian and Edwardian Style

THOMAS WRIGHT AND J. C. DROOP

The Victorians relished archaeological discovery, provided it was not taken too seriously. To the ladies and gentlemen of organizations like the British Archaeological Association and country archaeological societies, a digging excursion was an entertaining day in the open air, often under the benevolent patronage of a wealthy nobleman. Antiquarian Thomas Wright (1810–1877) contributed regular essays called "Wanderings of an Antiquary" to the now long-forgotten Gentleman's Magazine. *His account of a burial excavation in Oxfordshire during August 1844 is a classic of its kind. A few days later, the members of the newly formed British Archaeological Association convened on Lord Albert Conyngham's land nearby to hear formal papers and to witness the opening of burial mounds on nearby Breach Downs. Their meeting also featured the public unwrapping of an ancient Egyptian mummy, a popular antiquarian attraction of the day. The report of the proceedings in the* Archaeological Journal *for 1845 reprinted here gives the flavor of a memorable gathering and of the efforts made to give the membership the thrill of discovery at first hand.*

Little changed in the late nineteenth century. Archaeologist J. C. Droop was a respected classical archaeologist who worked at Sparta in southern Greece before World War I. His manual, Archaeological Excavation *(1915), remains a classic exposition of archaeology as an amiable and gentlemanly pastime. Droop's casual attitudes to digging reflect those of most excavators of the day. No archaeologists received formal field training before World War I. They learned their craft alongside more experienced excavators. Archaeological discovery was considered an art, and record keeping was sufficient to maintain a daybook for entering in the "general trend of the excavation," as Droop charmingly puts it.* Archaeological Excavation *was an anachronism, even in its own day, for German excavators in Greece, the redoubtable General Pitt-Rivers in southern England, Flinders Petrie in Egypt, and Arthur Evans in Crete—to mention only a few fieldworkers—had already moved beyond casual excavation.*

Thomas Wright's charming essay and a selection from J. C. Droop's manual give

387

the flavor of early excavation. The latter is a delicious vignette of Edwardian archaeology, the more so for its forthright statements on the role of women on a dig.

It was in the latter part of the August of 1844 that I accompanied Lord Albert Conyngham (now Lord Londesborough) on a visit to the Friars at Aylesford, for the purpose of opening a large Roman barrow or sepulchral mound in the adjoining museums, and private collections, and to excavate or at least visit excavations. Its first meeting was held in Canterbury under the presidency of Lord Albert Conyngham. . . . The following passages from the report of the meeting published in the first volume of the *Archaeological Journal* (1845) show what went on at these meetings, and what was then involved in excavation. The previous digging took four days; here we seem to have many barrows opened in an afternoon.

Monday, September 9

The proceedings of the general meeting were opened at half past three o'clock by an address from the president upon the objects of the association, and the benefits it was calculated to realize. His lordship remarked that a disposition to cultivate intellectual pursuits was making rapid progress in this country, as well as on the continent, and this growing feeling was especially manifested with regard to archaeology. Most men of cultivated minds were now beginning to take an interest in examining and pondering over the remains of past ages. They were no longer satisfied with taking for truth the baseless vagaries of the human mind; they wished to judge for themselves, and to form theories that would spring from a study of facts, well scrutinized and established by the test of personal examination and severe criticism. Archaeology, thus placed on a sound footing, would go hand in hand with history. The antiquary was no longer an object of ridicule. . . .

The meeting then adjourned to Barnes's rooms, where a conversazione was held. The tables were covered with an interesting variety of antiquities. . . . Lord Albert Conyngham exhibited some ancient gold ornaments found in Ireland, and a variety of amethystine beads, fibulae, and other objects, chiefly from barrows on Breach Downs opened by his lordship. . . .

Between nine and ten o'clock the members assembled on the Breach Downs to be present at the opening of some barrows, under the superintendance of the noble president. The workmen employed had previously excavated the barrows to within a foot of the place of the presumed deposit. Eight barrows were examined. . . . They are generally of slight elevation above the natural chalky soil, the graves, over which the mounds are heaped, being from two to four feet deep. Most of them contain skeletons, more or less entire, with the remains of weapons in iron, bosses of shields, urns, beads, fibulae, armlets, bones of small animals, and occasionally glass vessels. The graves containing weapons are assigned to males; those with beads, or other ornaments, to females. The correctness of this appropriation seems determined by the fact that these different objects are seldom found in the same grave. The deposit in one of the barrows opened this morning presented the unusual association of beads and an iron knife. All contained the remains of skeletons much decayed; in some, traces of wood were noticed, and vestiges of knives.

After the examination of these barrows, the whole party visited the mansion of the noble president, at Bourne, and having inspected his lordship's interesting collection of antiquities, and partaken of a substantial repast, attended the excavation of two barrows in his lordship's paddock, forming part of the group of which some had been recently opened.

————

The time has perhaps gone by when it was necessary, if it ever were, to put forward a defence of the pleasant practice of digging, a defence of it, that is to say, not as a harmless recreation of the idle rich, but as a serious business for a reasonable man. In all ages the maker of history and the recorder of history have alike received due honour. Today a place is found, not equal, of course, in glory but in the same hierarchy, for the reverent discoverer of the dry bones of history; and on Clio's roll of honour next to Homer and Agamemnon there is now a place for Schliemann. . . .

In Greece, at least, and in Egypt it was unavoidably, but none the less deplorably, the case that the great men of the past lacked the experience that is now ours. Excavation, like surgery, is an art, but, unlike the surgeon, the excavator has no unlimited supply of new subjects ready to benefit by his growing skill. The number of sites that have been spoiled will not bear thinking of, sites that bring a vicarious remorse to the mind that remembers by what ignorance they were very lovingly but very shamefully mishandled, so that their secrets, instead of being gathered up, were spilled and lost. The pity of it is that in the old days excavation was not recognized as an art; the excavator took a spade and dug and what he found he found; what could be more simple or more satisfying? . . .

I believe that to be able to dig a stratified site well is to have attained to the highest and most remunerative skill in this particular work. . . . If time and money were of no account there is no doubt that for a productive site the best digging tool would be a kind of bread knife without a point. The use of such a weapon goes nearest to insure the fewest possible breakages, for it is light, and the blunt end does not provide the same strong temptation as a point to use premature leverage. . . .

The keeping of an excavation daybook is sometimes thought advisable. . . . In practice however it happens that reference is seldom made to the daybook, each man preferring to refer to his own notes, and what is felt to be the useless labour of writing it up every night becomes a great burden. The better plan would seem to keep such a book for entering once a week or once a fortnight

*Victorian excavation at its most dramatic (and unscientific). M. De Morgan lifts a
golden crown from the mummy of Queen Khnemit at Dahshur, 1896.*

not the details of every day, which are safe enough elsewhere, but the general
trend of the excavation, and the broad conclusions drawn from the work accomplished to date. . . .

Meticulous care directed by common sense along the lines laid down by past
experience, that is the essence of good digging; yet the ideal man to have charge
of an excavation would be a very versatile person. . . . He should have tact and
social charm both for dealing with his staff, for an unhappy dig is an inefficient

dig, and for negotiating any difficulties that may arise. He should have a good temper, but a stiff jaw. . . .

I may perhaps venture a short word on the question much discussed in certain quarters, whether in the work of excavation it is a good thing to have co-operation between men and women. I have no intention of discussing whether or no women possess the qualities best suited for such work; opinions, I believe, vary on the point, but I have never seen a trained lady excavator at work, so that my view if expressed would be valueless. Of a mixed dig however I have seen something, and it is an experiment that I would be reluctant to try again; I would grant if need be that women are admirably fitted for the work, yet I would uphold that they should undertake it by themselves.

My reasons are twofold and chiefly personal. In the first place, there are the proprieties: I have never had a very reverent care for these abstractions, but I think it is not everywhere sufficiently realized that the proprieties that have to be considered are not only those that rule in England or America, but those of the lands where it is proposed to dig; the view to be considered is the view of the inhabitants, Greek, Turk, or Egyptian. My chief reasons, I said, were personal, but I hasten to add that they have nothing to do with the particular ladies with whom I was associated; should these lines meet their eyes I hope they will believe me when I say that before and after the excavation I thought them charming; during it, however, because they, or we, were in the wrong place, their charm was not seen. My objection lies in this, that the work of an excavation on the dig and off it lays on those who share in it a bond of closer daily intercourse than is conceivable, except perhaps in the Navy where privacy is said to be unobtainable, except for a captain; with the right men that is one of the charms of the life, but between men and women, except in chance cases, I do not believe that such close and unavoidable companionship can ever be other than a source of irritation; at any rate I believe that, however it may affect women, the ordinary male at least cannot stand it. . . . Marriage apart, and I can imagine a man conducting a small excavation very happily with his wife, mixed digging I think means loss of easiness in the atmosphere and consequent loss of efficiency. A minor, and yet to my mind weighty, objection lies in one particular form of constraint entailed by the presence of ladies, it must add to all the strains of excavation, and there are many, the further strain of politeness and self-restraints in moments of stress, moments that will occur on the best-regulated dig, when you want to say just what you think without translation, which before ladies, whatever their feelings about it, cannot be done.

Revolutionizing Excavation

AUGUSTUS LANE FOX PITT-RIVERS

Serious excavation, concerned more with the acquisition of knowledge than of spectacular artifacts, began in the late nineteenth century. The Germans carried out exemplary excavations at Olympia with the official support and encouragement of the kaiser. An architect was always on site, and photography was used to record the trenches and finds. Ernst Curtius, the excavator of Olympia, trained a generation of careful fieldworkers, among them Alexander Conze, who worked at Samothrace, and Walter Andrae, who investigated the Assyrian city of Assur. Wilhelm Dorpfeld learned his craft from Curtius, and then labored alongside Heinrich Schliemann at Troy. These archaeologists worked on large sites, often using near-military organization. And it was no coincidence that another, perhaps even better, Victorian excavator came from an army background.

General Augustus Lane Fox Pitt-Rivers (1827–1900) enjoyed a successful military career. A soldier of restless interests and an omnivorous collector, Lane Fox studied the development of weaponry. He soon became passionately interested in the evolution of artifacts, deciding that all material culture could be studied by arranging changing objects in an evolutionary order. Lane Fox was one of the founding fathers of ethnography. He worked closely with pioneer anthropologist Edward Tylor and demonstrated the great value of ethnography to archaeology. His displayed collections, he said, "were not for the purpose of surprising anyone . . . but solely with a view to instruction. For this reason ordinary and typical specimens rather than rare objects have been selected and arranged in sequence."

In 1880, Lane Fox inherited the vast wealth and landholdings of the Pitt-Rivers family and changed his name accordingly. He had always been interested in archaeology and had excavated in England, Wales, and Germany. His inheritance included much of the vast Cranborne estates in southern England, where he excavated Iron Age and Roman camps, villages, earthworks, and Bronze Age burial mounds without regard to constraints of time or money. Between 1880 and 1900, Pitt-Rivers dug several Cranborne sites totally, observing every detail of their construction and stratigraphy. He recorded the position of every find, described even trivial objects minutely, and published his findings in four lavishly printed volumes. Excavations in Cranborne Chase

*(1887–1898) is the first truly modern excavation report. Pitt-Rivers was years ahead
of his time. His methods were largely ignored until Mortimer Wheeler applied and
refined them in the 1920s. Interestingly, Wheeler had military experience as well.*

In this selection from Excavations in Cranborne Chase, *Pitt-Rivers lays out the
principles of sound excavation.*

Having retired from active service on account of ill health, and being incapable of strong physical exercise, I determined to devote the remaining portion of my life chiefly to an examination of the antiquities on my own property. Of these there were a considerable number, especially near Rushmore, consisting of Romano-British villages, tumuli, and other vestiges of the Bronze and Stone Ages, most of which were untouched and had been well preserved. . . .

I had an ample harvest before me, and with the particular tastes that I had cultivated, it almost seemed to me as if some unseen hand had trained me up to be the possessor of such a property, which, up to within a short time of my inheriting it, I had but little reason to expect. I at once set about organizing such a staff of assistants as would enable me to complete the examination of the antiquities on the property within a reasonable time, and to do it with all the thoroughness which I had come to consider necessary for archaeological investigations.

A permanent residence in the district to be explored is almost necessary for a satisfactory investigation of its ancient remains, and it is needless to say that ownership adds greatly to the power of carrying out explorations thoroughly, for although I have found my neighbours at all times most obliging in giving me permission to dig, it requires some assurance so far to trespass on a friend's kindness as to sit down and besiege a place on another man's property more than a year, which is not at all too long a time to spend in the excavation of a British village.

Whilst living at Kensington, I had carefully examined the drift gravels near Acton and Ealing, and by constantly watching the excavations for buildings made at no great distance from my place of abode, I had been able to make the first carefully recorded discovery of palaeolithic implements in association with the remains of extinct animals that had been made in the Thames Valley near London up to that time . . . in Sussex also I had made some more or less lengthy excavations, in camps at Mount Caburn, Cissbury, and other places, dating from the late Celtic period, the value of which would certainly have been much increased if a permanent residence in the neighbourhood had enabled me to devote more time to them. At Thebes, in Egypt, I had discovered palaeolithic implements in the gravels of the Nile Valley embedded in the sides of Egyptian tombs, a discovery the interest of which consisted in finding these implements for the first time *in situ*. But anthropology has no pet periods, all ages have afforded materials of nearly equal value for the history of the human race, and in the region around Rushmore my attention has been drawn more especially to the Romanized Britons, as being the race for whose study the district appears capable of affording the greatest facilities. . . .

It will, perhaps, be thought by some that I have recorded the excavations of this village [Woodcuts Common] and the finds that have been made in it with unnecessary fullness, and I am aware that I have done it in greater detail than has been customary, but my experience as an excavator has led me to think that investigations of this nature are not generally sufficiently searching, and that much valuable evidence is lost by omitting to record them carefully. That this has been so in the present instance is proved by the fact that this village had before been examined and reported upon in the twenty-fourth volume of the *Journal of the Archaeological Institute*, and not a single pit or skeleton had been found; whilst I have discovered ninety-five pits and fifteen skeletons.

Excavators, as a rule, record only those things which appear to them important at the time, but fresh problems in archaeology and anthropology are constantly arising, and it can hardly fail to have escaped the notice of anthropologists, especially those who, like myself, have been concerned with the morphology of art, that, on turning back to old accounts in search of evidence, the points which would have been most valuable have been passed over from being thought uninteresting at the time. Every detail should, therefore, be recorded in the manner most conducive to facility of reference, and it ought at all times to be the chief object of an excavator to reduce his own personal equation to a minimum.

I have endeavoured to record the results of these excavations in such a way that the whole of the evidence may be available for those who are concerned to go into it, whilst those who confine themselves to an examination of the plates will find each object carefully described on the adjoining page. . . . I have placed all the relics discovered in the ancient villages and tumuli in a museum near the village of Farnham, Dorset, where each object is carefully ticketed and described. Accurate models have been made of the villages, and models on a larger scale of the particular finds. In the case of Rotherley, I have a model of the ground, both before and after excavation, by means of which the results of the exploration are explained in such a way as to require the least possible effort of attention. The museum also includes other objects of husbandry and peasant handicraft, calculated to draw the interest of a purely rural population ten miles distant from any town or railway station, and I am glad to say the interest it has attracted amongst the workingmen of the neighbourhood has exceeded my utmost expectations. On Sunday afternoons the visitors' book often records more than 100 visitors: and on special holidays, between 200 and 300 frequently visit the museum. . . . I have established a pleasure ground and built a temple in the woods, with a private band, . . . where upwards of 1,000 of the villagers and neighbours frequently congregate with their wives and families, between the hours of divine service upon Sunday afternoons.

All the villages and tumuli, after being excavated, have been restored and turfed over, leaving sufficient indication to mark the various parts discovered in the villages, and at the bottoms of the principal excavations I have placed a medallet to show future explorers that I have been there.

It only remains to say something of the way in which the work has been carried out. I saw clearly that it was more than I could accomplish without assistance in the brief space of time allotted to me at my period of life. I therefore determined to organize a regular staff of assistants, and to train them to their respective functions after establishing a proper division of work. It was necessary they should all have some capacity for drawing in order that the relics discovered might be sketched as soon as found, instead of entrusting the drawings to inexperienced lithographers and artists who had little feeling for the subject. Surveying I was able to teach them myself, having always been fond of field sketching as a soldier. The work of superintending the digging—though I never allowed it to be carried on in my absence, always visiting the excavations at least three times a day, and arranging to be sent for whenever anything of importance was found—was more than I could undertake singlehanded, with the management of a property and other social duties to attend to, and I had by ample experience been taught that no excavation ought ever to be permitted except under the immediate eye of a responsible and trustworthy superintendent. The work of clearing and drawing the skeletons on the ground also required to be done by competent hands, although no skeleton has ever been taken out except under my personal supervision. The calculation of the indices, the classification and sorting of the pottery upon so large a scale, and with the care that I considered necessary, involved an amount of labour that I was not able to devote to it alone. . . .

Reserving, therefore, to my share of the work the entire supervision of everything, the description and arrangement of the plates, the writing of the record, checking the calculations and the measurement of every relic discovered in the diggings, and all the bones, I have, after some changes and preliminary trials been able to engage . . . assistants with suitable salaries. . . . All have from time to time been present at the excavations and have acquired much archaeological experience, which, I trust, may be useful to them in after life.

Mr. Martin, the estate carpenter, has shown much ingenuity in constructing wooden models of the villages and pits from plans and sections provided for him by the assistants. Some of the workmen of whom I employed from eight to fifteen constantly, have acquired much skill in digging and detecting the relics in the several villages and tumuli that have been examined, so as to entitle them to be regarded as skilled workmen, upon which no small share of the success of an investigation of this kind depends. . . .

I have endeavoured to keep up in the present volume the minute attention to detail with which investigation commenced. Much of what is recorded may never prove of further use, but even in the case of such matter, superfluous precision may be regarded as a fault on the right side where the arrangement is such as to facilitate reference and enable a selection to be made. A good deal of the rash and hasty generalization of our time arises from the unreliability of the evidence upon which it is based. It is next to impossible to give a continuous

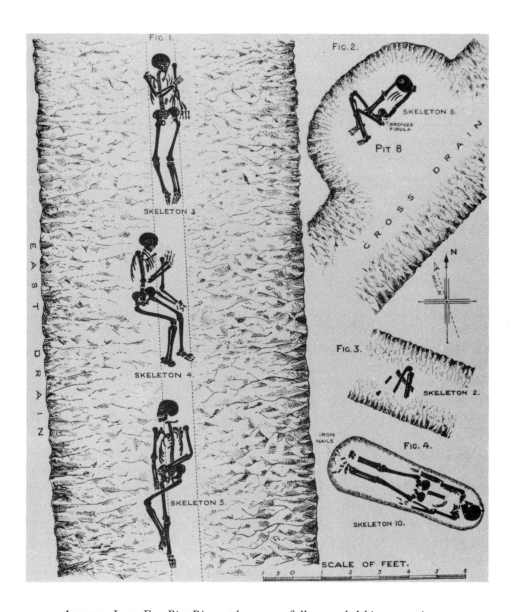

*Augustus Lane Fox Pitt-Rivers always carefully recorded his excavations at
Cranborne Chase. In his "plan showing the position of skeletons found in drains
and graves—Romano-British settlement, Woodyates," he tells us that skeleton
number 10 was that of a young man about twenty-two years of age; 4 feet, 10.6
inches tall; and resting on his back. Iron nails and pottery came from the grave.*

narrative of any archaeological investigation that is entirely free from bias; un-
due stress will be laid upon facts that seem to have an important bearing upon
theories that are current at the time, whilst others that might come to be considered of greater value afterwards are put in the background or not recorded, and
posterity is endowed with a legacy of error that can never be rectified. But when

fulness and accuracy are made the chief subject of study, this evil is in a great measure avoided. . . .

No excavations have been carried out at any time during my absence . . . all the measurements of skulls and bones, human and animal, as well as of all the objects found in the excavations, have been taken by myself personally. All the descriptions, and the letterpress, have fallen to my share as well as the close direction and supervision of the whole, both indoors and out. Nothing has been delegated to the assistants which has not been personally supervised by me. . . . As a rule I visited the diggings from two to three times a day, regulating my time on the ground by the importance of the work that was going on. The excavations in Winkelbury having been carried on before my assistants were sufficiently trained, I never left the ground during any part of them. One or more of the assistants were always engaged in superintending the workmen upon the ground, and the others were employed in planning the ground, or in drawing the objects, in repairs to the skulls and the pots, and in forming the relic tables, by which means the records have been kept up to date; and it has been found important that, as far as possible, everything should be recorded whilst it was fresh in the memory. . . .

The expense of conducting explorations upon this system is considerable but the wealth available in the country for the purpose is still ample, if only it could be turned into this channel. The number of country gentlemen of means who are at a loss for intelligent occupation beyond hunting and shooting must be considerable; and now that a paternal government has made a present of their game to their tenants, and bids fair to deprive them of the part that some of them have hitherto taken, most advantageously to the public, in the management of local affairs, it may not perhaps be one of the least useful results of these volumes if they should be the means of directing attention to a new field of activity, for which the owners of land are, beyond all others, favourably situated. It is hardly necessary to insist upon the large amount of evidence of early times that lies buried in the soil upon nearly every large property which is constantly being destroyed through the operations of agriculture, and which scientific anthropologists have seldom the opportunity or the means of examining.

To render all this evidence available for anthropological generalization is well worth the attention of the owners of property, who may thus render great service to an important branch of science, provided always that it is done properly; for to meddle with and destroy antiquities without recording the results carefully would be a work as mischievous as the converse of it would be useful. . . .

An almost new branch of inquiry has been added to this volume by the careful measurement of all the bones of domesticated animals, of which a large number have been found in the Romano-British villages; fifteen animals have been killed for comparison as test animals after external measurement, and by this means the size of all the animals whose bones have been found in the villages has been ascertained.

Tedious as it may appear to some to dwell on the discovery of odds and ends that have, no doubt, been thrown away by their owners as rubbish, and to refer to drawings, often repeated, of the same kind of common objects, yet it is by the study of such trivial details that archaeology is mainly dependent for determining the dates of earthworks; because the chance of finding objects of rarity in the body of a rampart is very remote. The value of relics, viewed as evidence, may on this account be said to be in an inverse ratio to their intrinsic value. The longer I am engaged in these pursuits, the more I become impressed with this fact, the importance of which has, I think, been too much overlooked by archaeologists. Hereafter it will probably strike future archaeologists as remarkable that we should have arrived at the state of knowledge we now possess about ancient works of high art and yet have paid so little attention to such questions as when iron nails for woodwork were first introduced into Britain, what kind and quality of pottery was in common use at different periods, when red Samian was first introduced from abroad, at what exact period in the world's history flint flakes ceased to be fabricated and used for any purpose, and other matters of that nature. . . .

Next to coins, fragments of pottery afford the most reliable of all evidence, and, on this account, I have elsewhere spoken of pottery as the human fossil, so widely is it distributed. . . . Vessels of pottery in prehistoric and Roman times were subject to breakage, as are now our less fragile and more durable ones; the pieces were not carried away by the dustman, as is now the case, but were scattered and trampled into the soil. . . .

A tumulus is easily dug into and the relics obtained from it are of value, whereas the examination of a town or encampment is a costly undertaking and the relics have seldom any intrinsic value, consisting mostly of common objects that have been thrown away by the inhabitants. It is for this reason that our knowledge of prehistoric and early people is derived chiefly from their funeral deposits, and for all we know of their mode of life, excepting such information as has been obtained from lake dwellings, and crannoges, they might as well have been born dead. Yet the everyday life of the people is, beyond all comparison, of more interest than their mortuary customs. . . .

I hope that these excavations, and the models of them that have been deposited in my museum at Farnham, Dorset, if they serve no better purpose, may at least be a means of showing how much the value of a museum may be enhanced by models, and may serve to stimulate research into ancient sites, in preference to mere relic grubbing; not that I wish to be understood to deprecate continued researches into graves and tumuli. . . .

War Casualties at Thebes

HERBERT EUSTICE WINLOCK

Before World War I, Egypt was a hive of archaeological activity, playing host to expeditions from Canada, many European nations, and the United States. Much of this research was financed by wealthy patrons, who were more interested in spectacular finds than in day-to-day detail. Nevertheless, an enormous amount of valuable fieldwork was carried out, much of it in the hands of artists and epigraphers who recorded tomb art that has now vanished. Howard Carter of Tutankhamun fame was one of the archaeologists regularly employed by the rich visitors who were granted excavation permits by the government. Many of the finds that came from these excavations were of great importance because the arid Nile Valley regularly preserved wooden objects, hair, and other organic substances. But few discoveries rival that of the Theban war casualties.

Herbert Eustice Winlock (1884–1950) was an American Egyptologist who was known for his high standards of excavation and meticulous recording habits. He worked in the Valley of the Kings and excavated the mortuary complex of the pharaoh Mentuhotpe (2061–2010 B.C.). This fourth king of the Eleventh Dynasty captured the city of Herakleopolis in Lower Egypt, which had served as the capital of the rival Ninth- and Tenth-Dynasty Hyksos kings. Mentuhotpe established the authority of Thebes as the capital of a unified Egypt and ushered in the Middle Kingdom period of Egyptian history. One of Winlock's most remarkable discoveries came from a tomb beside Mentuhotpe's mortuary buildings that had been buried by a later landslide. The sepulcher contained the bodies of sixty soldiers killed in battle, sealed in an underground chamber, wearing linen shrouds marked with the cartouche and seals of the pharaoh. Winlock used fragments of linen to date the tomb, and pieced together the fate of the soldiers from both biological and archaeological data. His report on what appears to have been a fierce attack on a fort, which ultimately succeeded, is a model of sober, careful archaeological reporting. Small-scale studies such as this foreshadowed the much more sophisticated archaeology of a generation later, when excavators routinely called on anatomists, biologists, and other scientists to help them reconstruct the past.

In this extract from his account Excavations at Deir el Bahri, 1911–1931, *Herbert Winlock describes his exemplary piece of archaeological detective work and an unusual, yet vivid, discovery.*

The month-long Mohammedan fast of Ramadān was upon us in March that year, and we had kept on only a small gang of men for just such jobs as this. The tomb was re-opened and all of its gruesome tenants brought outside while Hauser measured and planned the crypts and corridor within. Not a single object was discovered in the tomb and although about sixty bodies were in it, we found chips of no more than two or three cheap Eleventh Dynasty coffins. That the bodies were late seemed at first unquestionable. In the hot sun they were extraordinarily unpleasant—to put it mildly—and they had all the look of the dried-up corpses of Copts of whom many had been buried in the neighborhood. Still there was something not quite Coptic about the bandages, and the men were told to start early in the cool of the next morning, sorting out the linen which the thieves had ripped off of the bodies, to see if by any chance it was marked. It seemed unlikely, but to assure a conscientious search a bakshīsh was offered to any man who would discover a bit of inscription.

By seven o'clock next morning the men were down at the house with some thirty bits of marked linen, and by noon the number had been doubled. What we never expected had happened. Here were sixty-two absolutely typical examples of Eleventh Dynasty linen marks, with such familiar names as Amūny, Sebk-ḥotpe, Sebk-nakhte, In-tef, In-tef-oker, Mentu-ḥotpe, and S'en-Wosret, and most striking—and also most numerous, for half of the marked bandages bore it—was a curious, enigmatic ideogram which we had already found on the bandages of 'Ashayet and the women of Neb-ḥepet-Rē''s harīm. Furthermore, only a few weeks before, we had recognized the same mark on a chisel dropped by some stone-cutter in the catacomb tomb at the bottom of the hill, and we had concluded that it must have denoted property of the royal necropolis, or of its dead, in the reign of Neb-ḥepet-Rē'. After all, then, the sixty corpses in the tomb were four thousand years old, preserved in that dry, hermetically sealed, underground corridor in an unbelievable way.

From the point of view of physical anthropology the find had attained an unexpected importance. Of all of the Eleventh Dynasty tombs that we had dug, nearly every one had been plundered, had been re-used in later times, and then been plundered again, until it was impossible, generally, to tell whether the bones we found in them were of the Eleventh Dynasty or later. The result was that we had obtained a disappointingly small amount of information on what physical manner of men had descended from Thebes about 2000 B.C., conquered Memphis, and started the second great period of Egyptian culture. Here, however, were sixty individuals definitely of the very race we wanted to know about, and an urgent telegram was sent off to Dr. Derry to come up from the medical school in Cairo to examine them.

As soon as Derry, Brewster, and I started in on our study, the first and most obvious thing which we remarked about these bodies was the simplicity in which they had been buried. As we had already seen, probably no more than two or three could have had coffins and in the crypts the rest must have been stacked up like cord-wood with no other covering than their linen wrappings. These last, where enough had been left by the thieves to judge, seem to have averaged no more than some twenty layers of sheets and bandages, which are less than one may expect to find on even a middle-class body of the period. As our examination went on, this same hurried cheapness became evident in the embalming—or perhaps more accurately lack of embalming, for at the most little could have been done to these bodies beyond a scouring off with sand, and we differed among ourselves even as to that.

The second striking point was the absolute similarity these bodies bore, one to another. So far as we could see, all of them had been buried under identical conditions and all at the same time. Moreover, all were men, and as Derry's examination proceeded they turned out to be remarkably vigorous men, every one in the prime of life. We found none who showed any signs of immaturity and only one whose hair was even streaked with gray. Another curious point was that there did not seem to have been a single shaven head among the lot. On the contrary, every one of these men had a thick mop of hair, bobbed off square at the nape of the neck as on the contemporary statuettes of soldiers from Assiūt. Sometimes it was curled and oiled in tight little ringlets all over the head.

However, it was broiling hot; Derry's time was short; and ahead of us lay a long unpleasant task. We were wasting no time on theories, therefore, and had methodically measured the first nine bodies when the tenth was put on the table and Brewster noticed an arrow-tip sticking out of its chest.

Physical anthropology immediately lost its interest, and another unexpected chapter was added to the story of the tomb. Up to that time our work-tent had been a mere laboratory. From this moment onward it took on some of the gruesomeness of a field dressing station—only the front was four thousand years away.

Before we were done, we had identified a dozen arrow wounds and we felt certain that we had missed many others. So neat and small were they that they would easily pass unnoticed in the dried and shriveled skin except in those cases where some fragment of the arrow had been left in the bodies. Of head wounds we noted twenty-eight and again we felt that others were probably lost in the rough handling of the ancient thieves. But even so, we had seen two-thirds as many wounds as there were bodies and we felt justified in concluding that every one of these sixty men had met a violent end. This seemed especially likely when we discovered that six of the bodies on which no wound was visible to us had been torn by vultures or ravens, and that could hardly have happened except on a battlefield.

Obviously what we had found was a soldiers' tomb. To judge from the cheapness of their burial perhaps only the three who had had coffins were more than soldiers of the rank and file, and yet they had been given a catacomb presumably prepared for dependents of the royal household, next to the tomb of the Chancellor Khety. Clearly that was an especial honor. If we were right in supposing that all had been buried at once, they must have been slain in a single battle. Considering the especial honor paid them it would follow that this fight

Marks on the linen shrouds of ancient Egyptian warriors.

must have been one which meant much to the King Neb-ḥepet-Rē'. To us, unfortunately, lacking a single line of inscription from the tomb—for the linen marks tell us nothing beyond the date—it was only a nameless battle of the dim past.

And yet, without unduly stretching our imaginations, we can see how it was fought.

It was not a hand-to-hand encounter. We saw nothing that looked like dagger or spear stabs; none of the slashes which must have been inflicted by battle-axes, and no arms or collar bones smashed by clubs, as one might expect from fighting at close quarters. Many of the head wounds—for the moment we will omit a certain class of crushing blows on the left side of the skull—were small, depressed fractures in the forehead and face such as would be given by smallish missiles descending from above. From the same direction must have come several arrows which found their marks at the base of the neck and penetrated vertically downward through the chest, or one which entered the upper arm and passed down the whole length of the forearm to the wrist. Such would have been the wounds received by men storming a castle wall, and with this clue to guide us we had only to turn to the contemporary pictures of sieges at Deshāsheh and Beni Ḥasan. The defenders line the battlements armed with bows and arrows, with slings and with handfuls of stones. The attackers rush up to the walls with scaling ladders, or crouch beneath them with picks, endeavoring to sap the defenses under a rain of missiles falling on their heads and shoulders, only precariously protected by their companions' shields.

It must have been during an assault on a fortress, then, that our unknown soldiers fell, under a shower of sling-shots on heads protected by nothing but a mass of hair, or with lungs and heart pierced by arrows aimed at their uncovered shoulders. The fire had been too hot, and their fellows had scampered away out of range, but not without some of them being overtaken by a storm of arrows. One of them had been hit in the back just under the shoulder blade by an arrow which had transfixed his heart and projected some eight inches straight out in front of his chest. He had pitched forward, headlong on his face, breaking off the slender ebony arrow-tip in his fall, and the ragged end between his ribs was found by us all clotted with his blood. It was only after he was long dead that those who gathered up his body had broken off the reed shaft sticking out of his back, for that end had no trace of blood upon it.

With the attack beaten off there had followed the most barbarous part of an ancient battle. The monuments of Egyptian victories always show the king clubbing his captives in the presence of his god, and the battle pictures show the Egyptian soldiers searching out the enemy wounded to despatch them. Usually they grab the fallen by the hair and dragging them half upright, club or stab them, and as they swing their clubs with their right hands their blows fall upon the left sides of their victim's faces and heads. We recognized at least a dozen who had been mercilessly done to death in this way. One of the wounded had fallen unconscious from a sling-shot which had hit him over the eye; another had been stunned by an arrow which had all but penetrated one of the sutures of his skull; and a third probably lay helpless from loss of blood ebbing from the arteries in his arm torn by an arrow. None of these need have been fatal wounds, but evidently, as soon as the attackers had retired out of range, a party had made a sortie from the castle to mop up the battlefield, and when the last breathing being had been finished off, their bodies were left lying beneath the walls to be worried and torn by the waiting vultures and ravens. The ghastly evidence of their work was plain enough to see and the ancient pictures of the carrion birds devouring the slain were made only too real by these mangled corpses.

Unquestionably a second attack on the castle had been successful or these bodies never could have been recovered for burial in Thebes. Furthermore, the reed arrows with ebony tips used by the defenders show that the castle was in Egypt, and we know that no part of Egypt successfully resisted King Neb-ḥepet-Rē'.

Of Theban bows and arrows we have found a great number. Every one of the great nobles had enough to equip a whole bodyguard, piled up in the crypt of his tomb, and of the lesser fry buried at the bottom of the hill each had his single bow and set of arrows beside him in his coffin. The bow was always of the long type with a twisted gut cord simply hitched around either tip. The arrow had a shaft of reeds with three feathers, and a tip of ebony some eight or nine inches long, almost invariably pointed with a chisel edge of flint set in cement. Of the ebony arrow tips used by the defenders of the castle, remarkably enough, not one had a flint point—and yet they had been driven as cleanly into a man's body as one drives a nail into a pine board. Perhaps, some day, we may discover whether there was any particular part of Egypt where it was usual to dispense with the flint points, and if so, we will be a long way toward knowing where this battle took place.

Bridging Cultures at Carchemish

Leonard Woolley

Sir Charles Leonard Woolley (1880–1960) gained archaeological immortality for his excavations of the Royal Cemetery at Ur. The excavation methods Woolley used at Ur stemmed from his earlier excavation experience in Britain and the Sudan, and at Carchemish, a Hittite and Roman city on the Euphrates River in what is now Syria.

Carchemish guarded a major ford across the Euphrates and acquired considerable commercial and strategic importance as a result, especially in Hittite times. The Hittites first entered history in about 1650 B.C., when they became the rulers of Anatolia, what is now Turkey. Hittite kings were expert diplomats and warriors who exercised enormous influence in the Near East for four centuries, competing with Egypt and Mitanni for control of the wealthy ports of the eastern Mediterranean coast, the Levant. Carchemish was of vital importance to them because of its control of Syrian desert trade routes and its proximity to Mitanni. Archaeologically, the Hittites remained little known until the Germans excavated their capital at Boghazkoy and Woolley excavated Carchemish from 1912 to 1914, immediately before World War I.

The Carchemish excavations were an important turning point in the young Woolley's career. Largely self-taught, he took over the British Museum–sponsored excavation from David Hogarth, an archaeologist who had worked at Knossos with Arthur Evans and was known to his workmen as the "Angel of Death," because of his uncertain temper before breakfast. He also inherited a young man named T. E. Lawrence, who had just graduated from Oxford with an interest in archaeology and especially pottery and was to go on to world fame as Lawrence of Arabia.

Most great discoveries in archaeology owe more to detailed planning and preparation than to mere serendipity. Every field season is a carefully anticipated event constrained by economic, social, and political realities, not the least of which is the management of an extensive and often foreign labor force. Woolley, like other great Near Eastern excavators, got on extremely well with his laborers. Years later, in 1956, he published a lighthearted volume of reminiscences, which recalled those distant and idyllic days. Dead Towns and Living Men *deals more with the social relations of excavation and discovery than with the archaeology itself. Woolley remembered his experiences with maintaining morale and bridging the cultural distance between the British excavation leaders and*

the Arab workers. He offers his readers, presumably the next generation of field archae-
ologists, practical advice on labor relations in non-Western contexts. In so doing, he
reveals a genuine sensitivity to the values of the people he worked among and a deep
respect for their cultural property, attitudes that were rare indeed for Woolley's time.
His treatment of issues such as the desecration of holy ground, the necessity for operating
within the procedural guidelines of foreign governments, and the evils of black marke-
teering marks another development in the transition of archaeology from organized
plunder to scientific exploration. He also reminds us that the spirit of discovery is a
cross-cultural phenomenon and that its excitement is contagious.

In this selection, an excerpt from Dead Towns and Living Men, *Leonard Woolley*
describes his views on his workers. Even taken with a grain of salt, which, we are told,
all Woolley's tales required, there is plenty of common sense here.

The digging of these graves was a very pleasant interlude, and incidentally
showed how important it is to have one's men well disposed. I have mentioned
that the authorities boggled a good deal at granting permission for the work
because part of the ancient cemetery was overlaid by modern burials, and the
sanctity of a Moslem cemetery is far more inviolable than that of a Christian
churchyard. I had promised to respect every possible prejudice, and therefore
started on the far fringe of the ancient graves and worked forwards toward the
forbidden ground. But as we drew nearer to this the old tombs were found to
be richer and more numerous, and the men's interest—and their *baksheesh* accounts—grew in proportion. Now the old graves were dug some six or seven
feet down, deeper than the modern villager thinks necessary for his dead, and
one morning, coming up rather late from breakfast, I was horrified to see one
of the gangs on the very edge of the modern cemetery, and the pick-man, hot
on the scent of a Hittite burial, burrowing right under a modern grave, whose
stone lining hung out above his head. The rest of the gang stopped work and
grinned broadly as I called the man out and told him pretty forcibly that this
sort of thing couldn't be allowed; I would not have the Moslem graves disturbed.
The worker looked sheepish and the rest began to laugh out loud, and then
Hamoudi intervened. "It is really all right, Effendim," he urged, "that's his own
grandfather!" I let him finish what he was doing, but would not repeat the
experiment, and the village cemetery suffered no further desecration. I think
that the men were rather relieved at being stopped, though they professed their
willingness to dig up the whole place; but they added that if anyone other than
the English had worked even near their people's graves they would have made
him pay dearly for it, and I know of more than one instance to prove the genu-
ineness of the threat.

The north Syrian Arab differs from the Egyptian *fellah* in that his horizon is
not limited to piastres; his sense of fun and his personal honour are incentives
almost as strong as money. It is an admirable quality which we have been able

to exploit. Our foreman, Hamoudi, and Lawrence between them worked out a very paying system whereby any really good discovery made in the field is celebrated with a *feu de joie* from the foreman's revolver. This very natural mode of expression was at first indulged in by everybody, the finder thus announcing his good luck to the rest, but now there is a ritual in such matters. As soon as anything of value turns up Hamoudi, our head foreman, is on the spot—if possible without letting Lawrence or myself know what is forward—and he helps to clear the object, and then, when it is fairly visible, adjudges its value in cartridges. A fair-sized fragment of sculpture may be put down at one shot, a complete basalt slab with figures and inscriptions will rise to seven or eight, and so, whether we are on the work or in the house, we can by listening to Hamoudi's revolver make a very fair guess as to what he has to show us. But the object of the firing is not simply to draw our attention—it is a *baksheesh* to the finder, valued quite as highly as the reward in cash that luck has added to his wage, and at the same time it is, in the eyes of many of the men at least, a form of homage to the stone or to the fortune that put it in their path. The finder will grow quite pathetic over the *chawîsh's* judgment. "Oh, but six shots, *yah chawîsh*, six shots: was it not five for the chariot yonder? And here there are three sons of Adam; by God, they deserve two rounds apiece"; and the men will count up throughout the season how many cartridges have been expended in honour of their finds. I remember one Yasin Hussein coming to me almost in tears and saying that he was leaving the work; I asked him why, and then he burst out, "Effendim, I cannot stand it; my luck is evil: this season so much has been found, there is shooting every day—now it is Hamdôsh, ping-ping-ping, now it is Mustapha Aissa, ping-ping-ping-ping, now another, but for me not one cartridge since work started. I must go, Effendim, or else you must put me where I shall find something. Honestly, I don't want the *baksheesh*—don't give me money for it; it is the honour of the thing—I want to hear the *chawîsh* shooting for me, and to have men saying afterwards, 'That is the stone of Yasin Hussein for which he had eight shots.' "

The whole thing may sound childish, as much on our part for encouraging the practice (for we keep Hamoudi in cartridges) as on the men's for caring so deeply for it; but in fact it is such things that make the work go well, and when digging at Jerablus ceases to be a great game and becomes, as in Egypt, a mere business, it will be a bad thing for the work. But as long as we have people like Haj Wahid and Hamoudi with us life is not likely to be altogether dull.

There is another way in which the high spirits of our workmen can be turned to good account. The whole gang is divided into companies of four, consisting of a pick-man, a shoveller, and two basket-men who carry the loose earth from the diggings to the light railway, which transports it clear of the work and dumps it in the river. All these are paid alike, but there is great emulation for the post of pick-man, for he has on the whole the easiest job, and also has far the best chance of finding antiquities and thereby earning *baksheesh* and honour. The pick-men therefore are carefully selected from the best workers in the whole gang, the spade-men are in the second grade, and the basket-carriers are, for the most part, the recruits and the boys. Most of the small objects are found by the wielder of the pick, who therefore earns most; but should a thing escape him and fall to the spade-worker the reward for it is slightly raised as an encouragement to careful work; should the basket-carrier find a thing which had been overlooked by both his seniors and was therefore in danger of being lost altogether, then the reward is more generous still. Thus all eyes are on the alert, and from the time the earth is first loosened till the moment when it is chucked down the dumpside some one is always searching it for "finds." In the case of big stones the bulk of the reward goes to the pick-man who unearths it, and the remainder is divided in proportion between the other three members of his gang. All this leads to a good-humoured rivalry between the different tools, and the nature of the soil at any moment may bring this to a head. When there is to be removed a mass of soft surface soil where "finds" are unlikely, the pick-man has an easy time; he cuts down a heap of loose earth that will keep his two baskets busy for twenty minutes, maybe, and then sits down to a cigarette and the enjoyment of seeing others work; the spade-man too has a light job filling baskets, while the carriers are run nearly off their feet. On the other hand, when the ground is hard and stony the pick cannot make progress fast enough; the carriers come up and sit on their baskets waiting for a load and the spade-man has nothing to give them. In either case Hamoudi sees his chance, and, standing on a mound with his head-rope on one side and his hands in his pockets, he will pour scorn on one side or the other. If the earth is soft and plentiful, he begs the picks to kill the basket-carriers, sons of sloth and eaters of unearned bread; if the picks are wrestling with stones and hard-set earth, he will exhort the basket-men to make the pick-fellows, greedy seekers after *baksheesh*, cry *"pardûn."*

At once the fun begins. Both sides fall to work with a frenzy, the pick-men taunt the baskets and the basket-carriers threaten the picks; the latter, if the ground is hard, will soon be pouring with sweat and writhing under the opprobrium of the waiting basket-men, while these, if soil is soft, will be racing at full speed from trench to truck, pick- and spade-men shouting to them to hurry up: it is "Baskets, baskets, ho! baskets!" from the one side, and "Earth, earth, give us earth!" from the other; the excitement grows, and the noise gets louder and louder, while Hamoudi from his perch with wild gesticulations cheers on both sides alike; the men grow exhausted, and the winning side yells all the louder, demanding that the others say *"pardûn."* "Never!" will cry the pick-men, if they be the challenged side, "we will die, but we will not say *pardûn*," and they will attack the wall of earth and stone as if their lives really depended on the effort. But the baskets work too fast for them and the spade-men can find no loose soil to scrape up: then the empty baskets are hurled into the air with screams of triumph, or flung at the heads of the pick-men as they sink breathless and fagged out to the ground. Hamoudi, as umpire, raises his hand and grants them ten minutes' rest wherein the weary gang can refresh itself with cigarettes and

*T. E. Lawrence (left) and Leonard Woolley pose at Carchemish with a Hittite
carving of a three-person war chariot trampling on a dead enemy.*

laughter—and a good hour's work has been done in twenty minutes! Of course
this is only allowed when barren soil is to be cleared, but then, when there are
no "finds" to keep up the men's interest, to let them go *fantêh*, as we call it, is
the quickest way of getting through a dull job and acts like a tonic on the men.
You can only do it once or twice a day, for the fury of the work—or game—is
too exhausting, but it is a fine system, and one of the most amusing things to
watch.

But though there are times when the work can be speeded up in this way,
when it does not matter that the baskets are flying through the air, the men
blind with sweat, and the Décauville cars swinging nearly off the rails as they
race each other to and from the dump-heaps, yet, on the other hand, when finds
are probable, there are no more careful diggers than these Arabs. Even the
Egyptian, skilful as he is with his *touriya*, is not more delicate of touch than a
pick-man after two seasons' practice. As soon as his sense of touch tells him that

*A small army of workers clears the ruins of the ancient Hittite city, hauling away
tons of surplus masonry to gain access to building foundations.*

a stone which he has reached with his point below the soil but has not yet seen
is a large block or one bedded in a wall, he sets to work as gingerly as though
he were unearthing buried glass; then if things look promising the pick-axe is
exchanged for the knife, and with Hamoudi hovering about like an anxious hen,
or sometimes ousting the workman to do the job himself, the object is cleared
without the possibility of damage. Again, to find and follow a mud-brick wall
buried deep in soil which is itself composed of mud bricks, loose or fallen in
masses, is no easy task, especially as the wall-face is usually plastered with mud,
and this plastering must remain, so far as may be, intact. The digger will cut
along, trying to keep the side of his trench an inch or so away from the wall-
face; then as the earth dries he will retrace his steps, and with the blunt end of
his pick or with a knife dislodge the film of soil that adheres loosely to the
brickwork and so expose the true surface. The men soon learn to take a pride
in their skill in following the line as closely as can be without cutting into the
wall itself and then in baring the undamaged face. The wall and the brick debris
surrounding it are sometimes so hard to distinguish that the work has to stand
over for a few days until the weathering of the bricks shows which is really wall
and which but fallen wall-material, and great is the workman's joy then if he
prove to have been right where I was undecided.

One of the curses of the digger in Egypt is the wandering antiquity-dealer,
who will hang about in the neighbourhood and buy from your workmen anything that they may steal from the excavations. Only once has one of these
gentry turned up at Jerablus, and then the men were so furious at the insult to
their loyalty that they were all literally out for his blood, and the tempter had

to lie hidden until he could take the train back to Aleppo. They are not less keen to prevent any outsider from taking photographs, and if I do give permission to a visitor to snapshot one or two points of general interest, either Lawrence or myself must always go with him or there will surely be trouble; indeed on one occasion, when I was delayed on the way down and reached the field a little behind my guest, I found him looking very bewildered and not a little alarmed, with Hamoudi holding his camera and half-a-dozen workmen with revolvers blocking the view of his proposed "subject." On another occasion it was only a timely disappearance that saved a Turkish major-general from being thrown into the Euphrates because one of his staff had tried to photograph a bas-relief against the orders of the Arab on guard; luckily the men were at work some way off on the cemetery site, and by the time the alarm had been given and they were streaming pell-mell across the intervening fields the general had effected a strategic retirement from the Kala'at.

The wilder the country in which you work the more important is it that you be on good terms with your men; the truth of that was borne in on me by the only serious accident that happened on the work. We had been clearing some Hittite remains which lay ten or twelve feet down under light mixed soil, and the vertical face of our cutting came close up to a huge block of Roman stone that lay upon the surface. Until the stone had been shifted it was unsafe to dig any farther, and as I was not sure that any advance would be necessary I moved the whole gang to another spot and announced through Hamoudi that the cutting was dangerous and nobody was allowed to go into it. Two days later there was a violent wind and a sandstorm and conditions on the dig were most unpleasant, the men almost blinded by the driving dust, and one of them slipped away for a rest and a cigarette. The forbidden cutting offered a shelter from the wind and a hiding-place from the eyes of the foreman, so there he went; and as he smoked in peace down came the huge stone and tore away the whole front of his body. We dug him out from the fallen earth and carried him on a door up to the house, where by chance I was entertaining a guest, old Dr. Altounyan, the finest surgeon in the Middle East; after a mere glance he told me that the case was hopeless. Naturally I was much upset, but at the same time I had the unpleasant knowledge that a death on the dig meant, by Arab law, a blood-feud between his relatives and us; the whole of our work was in jeopardy. The man was not quite dead and, more to show sympathy than anything else, I poured a little brandy between his lips, and his eyes opened and he saw about him the bearers who had carried him up, and to them he gasped out his last words: "I bear witness to God that the fault was mine. I broke orders. The English are not guilty of my blood." I called his kinsfolk together and asked if they had any claim against me, and they said none; the dead man had absolved me in front of witnesses. When therefore I gave a sum of money to the young widow (for he had married not long before) it was accounted to me for righteousness. Incidentally, her family took over the money in trust, fearing that if she had the free handling of it she might be the prey of some gold-digging suitor, since she was now an heiress; the only complaint that I ever heard was from one of the work-men, who said, grinning, "*W'Allah*, it is a pity that you have done this; now all our wives will wish us dead!"

Such are our Arab workmen: loyal and good-tempered, honest, hard-working—provided that you humour them and do not press unduly or out of season, for they are not your slaves but your fellow-workers—and careful when care is needed.

Tutankhamun's Wife

MARY CHUBB

When the New Kingdom pharaoh Akhenaten moved his royal capital from Memphis to el-Amarna in Upper Egypt in about 1350 B.C., he founded a new city from scratch. Akhenaten himself lived in the North City, in a fortified palace complex, complete with its own warehouses and granaries. There the pharaoh dwelt in splendid isolation, emerging on ceremonial occasions to drive down a processional way, which led to the Great Palace and Temple of Aten in the central city. Akhenaten considered himself a living god, the intermediary between the sun-god Aten and the people of Egypt. His bold experiment in religious innovation did not survive his death in 1335 B.C. Within a generation, Amarna was abandoned—its palaces, temples, and residential quarters reverting to desert.

Amarna has proved a gold mine for archaeologists, offering a unique chance to study a large Egyptian city occupied for only a short period of time. The British Egyptologist Flinders Petrie was the first to excavate Akhenaten's capital in 1892. It was he who unearthed the celebrated Amarna tablets, a record of diplomatic correspondence between the royal court and foreign rulers throughout the Near East. Early in his career, Petrie worked on behalf of the Egypt Exploration Fund, founded in 1882 by Amelia Edwards and others interested in preserving ancient Egypt. The fund has continued work at Amarna at intervals ever since, focusing its recent attention on houses and the residential quarters of the city. Archaeologist John Pendlebury worked at Amarna in the early 1930s, expanding on the work of Petrie and other early excavators. A young woman named Mary Chubb (b. 1903) gave up a desk job at the fund in London to join his excavations. She labored at various tasks, especially the recording of artifacts as they streamed in from the dig. But she also worked in the trenches, where she was fortunate enough to unearth a statue of Ankhesenpaaten, the wife of Tutankhamun.

Her account of this important find is memorable for its immediacy and freshness, although she wrote it in 1954, a quarter century later. This selection from Nefertiti Lived Here *is a charming vignette of 1930s archaeology.*

The afternoon wore on and the heap had been reduced to a foot or so above ground level, when my brush moved over something curved and hard; perhaps a big stone. I blew away the sand, and saw a grey-white ridged surface, with flecks of black paint; certainly not a stone. Hilda leaned over and looked.

"Try getting the stuff away from the front," she said. "We ought to get a look at it from another angle, before it's moved." I came round and began brushing and blowing at the vertical side of the heap. Down trickled the sand between the harder bits of mud brick, like tiny yellow waterfalls, and nearer and nearer I came to the side of the buried object. A final gentle stroke with a brush tip, and the whispering sand slid away from the surface—and we could see more of the grey and white ridges, and beneath it a smooth curve of reddish-brown paint. The sand had poured away below it and left a cavity. "Can you see inside the hollow?" Hilda asked. I lay down flat and got one eye as close as I could to the rubble.

And then I suddenly saw what the brownish paint was—part of a small face. I could just see the curved chin and the corner of a darker painted mouth. Hilda knelt up and beckoned to John, who was not far away.

"It's the head of a statue, I think," she said quietly as he joined us. He took a long look, and then sat back on his heels. His face was very compressed and tense.

"I'll wait while you get it out," was all he said.

Infinitely slowly we cut back the caked rubble in which it was embedded. The hardest thing on earth is to go slow when you are excited. But we had to— we could never tell how strong or how fragile a find was until it was finally detached from its hiding-place. For all we knew there might be a crack right across the unseen face, so that the whole thing might crumble into powder at a clumsy movement.

We widened the cavity just beneath it, so that John could get his fingers into it in case the head dropped suddenly. He held them here unmoving for at least five minutes, while we worked round the top. "It's coming," he said suddenly.

Hilda blew once more at the surface, and the head sank on to John's hand. He drew it slowly away from the debris. Then very gently he turned the head over on his palm.

Framed by a dark ceremonial wig, the face of a young girl gazed up at us with long, beautifully modelled eyes beneath winging dark eyebrows. The corners of the sweet, full mouth drooped a little. The childish fullness of the brown cheeks contrasted oddly with the tiny determined pointed chin. Somehow the sculptor had caught the pathetic dignity of youth burdened with royalty. The little head was another exquisite example of the genius of the sculptors of Akhenaten's day for perceiving more than the surface truth, and expressing to perfection what they had seen.

I looked up from the head to John's face. In those few moments it had completely lost its gaunt grey look of the past few weeks. He knelt there in the dust, brown and radiant, looking down at the beautiful thing on his hand.

*Mary Chubb attending to a sick
child at the informal clinic run
by the excavators at Amarna.
Chubb's main job was to catalog
artifacts and to ensure that they
were properly documented.*

"Now," he said slowly, "our season has been crowned." It was only now that
I knew the true exhilaration that comes from literally unearthing a treasure
which in one flash eliminates time; when the ancient artist speaks direct through
his creation to all those coming after, who understand his language.

I thought . . . of the Central School, and of my own tentative dabbing at
clay and chipping at stone. I knew well the difference between average talent
and the work of a master when I saw it. I felt very humble. Yet I think my own
struggles in the same craft gave me a special insight into the skill of that long
dead artist. I'd tried so hard myself to express in clay and stone the living bone
formation beneath the softness of flesh and muscle. I knew from my own experience how much observation, how much sensitivity, how much skill must be there
to carve a head which convinces that bones really lie beneath the surface, the
unseen strength and framework of the whole. It's easy enough to produce a
superficial mask, a slick portrait with nothing behind it. And I knew, too, that
even when a craftsman had gained that degree of excellence, the creative work
of a true artist might still be beyond him. That ultimate gift—the mysterious

gift of expressing the metaphysical in inanimate clay or stone—lies somewhere in the depths of the artist himself, and can neither be imparted nor learned. But here in my hand lay the flowering of both skills—and looking down at the small head, I, a student-apprentice, saluted my unknown artist-craftsman, dead these three thousand years and more.

The wonder of touching something that had lain buried and unmoving for so long came over me again, just as I'd felt when I was new to all this, four months ago. But I'd found that to say: "This was made three thousand years ago" now hardly stirred my sense of time at all. But I thought of it this way: the little head, wedged in that rubble, up against a ruined wall in this silent, sunny place in Egypt, had been lying there, face downwards, while Troy was burning; while Sennacherib was ransacking the cities beyond his borders; on through the slow centuries, while the greatness of Athens came and went, and while Christ lived out his days on earth. It was still lying there when the Romans first marched on London, when Harold fell at Hastings, and the last Plantagenet at Bosworth Field. On and on through the years, until this hot afternoon when the brush and knife came nearer and nearer to it through the yielding rubble, until it stirred, dropped, and lay once again in a warm human hand.

The Battle of Maiden Castle

R. E. MORTIMER WHEELER

Sir R. E. Mortimer Wheeler (1890–1976) was one of the great archaeologists of the twentieth century. Forceful, opinionated, and a gifted excavator and writer, he exercised an enormous influence over the development of archaeological excavation before and immediately after World War II. Wheeler trained at the University of London, became an artillery officer in World War I, and discovered that he had a gift for soldiering. While director of the National Museum of Wales, he began applying General Pitt-Rivers's long-ignored archaeological methods to Roman sites with brilliant success. He and his first wife, Tessa, improved on Pitt-Rivers's work, stressing careful observation of stratigraphic layers and techniques of open-area excavation, which could be used to expose entire street plans or fortifications. The Wheelers refined their methods at a series of Roman sites, especially the Roman town of Verulameum (modern St. Albans in eastern England), and at Maiden Castle, a large Iron Age hill fort near Dorchester, about eight kilometers inland from the English Channel.

Maiden Castle is famous for its elaborate earthworks, which rise in steep, serried rows from rolling hillsides. The Iron Age Celts fortified the hilltop in depth, as a defense against arrows, slingshots, and other longer-distance weapons. But their ramparts were no match against a formidable Roman force—Vespasian's Second Legion, which attacked and captured the fort in A.D. 43. Wheeler's excavations, which began in 1934, dissected the complex history of Maiden Castle and traced its history back to a small herding camp long before any ramparts adorned the hilltop. The site was so complex that the Wheelers developed a gridlike form of horizontal trenching to expose the northern entrance, with brilliant success. This part of the excavation unfolded in 1937, in the hands of both paid laborers and volunteers, many of whom later became prominent archaeologists themselves. And from it came Wheeler's inspired reconstruction of the Roman assault on the fort, which appears here.

Maiden Castle, Dorset, Wheeler's monograph on the excavations, is dedicated to the memory of Tessa, who died when the excavations were still under way. On the whole, it has stood the test of the years well, and recent excavations have confirmed many of Wheeler's conclusions. But it is only fair to say that they have cast some doubt on his interpretation of the assault. For example, some of the wounds on the skeletons

417

in the so-called war cemetery show signs of healing and may be from earlier engagements long before the individuals concerned died of natural causes. But such reinterpretations do not detract from a classic example of archaeological writing.

Mortimer Wheeler's play-by-play account of the Roman attack, which first appeared in Maiden Castle, *is as efficiently constructed as a forensic report of the scene of a crime. Equally elegant is his use of historical data to interpret the significance of the events he describes in a larger political context. This is, quite simply, an archaeological classic.*

And so we reach the Roman invasion of A.D. 43. That part of the army of conquest wherewith we are concerned in Dorset had as its nucleus the Second Augustan Legion, whose commander, at any rate in the earlier campaigns, was the future Emperor Vespasian. Precisely how soon the invaders reached Maiden Castle can only be guessed, but by A.D. 47 the Roman arms had reached the Severn, and Dorset must already have been overrun. Suetonius affirms that Vespasian reduced "two very formidable tribes and over twenty towns *(oppida)*, together with the Isle of Wight," and it cannot be doubted that, whether or no the Durotriges (as is likely enough) were one of the tribes in question, the conquest of the Wessex hill-fort system is implied in the general statement. Nor is it improbable that, with the hints provided by the mention of the Isle of Wight and by the archaeological evidence for the subsequent presence of the Second Legion near Seaton in eastern Devon, a main line of advance lay through Dorset roughly along the route subsequently followed by the Roman road to Exeter. From that road today the traveller regards the terraced ramparts of the western entrance of Maiden Castle; and it requires no great effort of the imagination to conjure up the ghost of Vespasian himself, here confronted with the greatest of his "twenty towns." Indeed, something less than imagination is now required to reconstruct the main sequence of events at the storming of Maiden Castle, for the excavation of the eastern entrance has yielded tangible evidence of it. With only a little amplification it may be reconstructed as follows.

Approaching from the direction of the Isle of Wight, Vespasian's legion may be supposed to have crossed the River Frome at the only easy crossing hereabouts—where Roman and modern Dorchester were subsequently to come into being. Before the advancing troops, some 2 miles away, the sevenfold ramparts of the western gates of Dunium towered above the cornfields which probably swept, like their modern successors, up to the fringe of the defenses. Whether any sort of assault was attempted upon these gates we do not at present know; their excessive strength makes it more likely that, leaving a guard upon them, Vespasian moved his main attack to the somewhat less formidable eastern end. What happened there is plain to read. First, the regiment of artillery, which normally accompanied a legion on campaign, was ordered into action, and put down a barrage of iron-shod ballista-arrows over the eastern part of the site. Following this barrage, the infantry advanced up the slope, cutting its way from rampart to rampart, tower to tower. In the innermost bay of the entrance, close outside the actual gates, a number of huts had recently been built; these were now set alight, and under the rising clouds of smoke the gates were stormed and the position carried. But resistance had been obstinate and the fury of the attackers was roused. For a space, confusion and massacre dominated the scene. Men and women, young and old, were savagely cut down, before the legionaries were called to heel and the work of systematic destruction began. That work included the uprooting of some at least of the timbers which revetted the fighting-platform on the summit of the main rampart; but above all it consisted of the demolition of the gates and the overthrow of the high stone walls which flanked the two portals. The walls were now reduced to the lowly and ruinous state in which they were discovered by the excavator nearly nineteen centuries later.

That night, when the fires of the legion shone out (we may imagine) in orderly lines across the valley, the survivors crept forth from their broken stronghold and, in the darkness, buried their dead as nearly as might be outside their tumbled gates, in that place where the ashes of their burned huts lay warm and thick upon the ground. The task was carried out anxiously and hastily and without order, but, even so, from few graves were omitted those tributes of food and drink which were the proper and traditional perquisites of the dead. At daylight on the morrow, the legion moved westward to fresh conquest, doubtless taking with it the usual levy of hostages from the vanquished.

Thereafter, salving what they could of their crops and herds, the disarmed townsfolk made shift to put their house in order. Forbidden to refortify their gates, they built new roadways across the sprawling ruins, between gateless ramparts that were already fast assuming the blunted profiles that are theirs today. And so, for some two decades, a demilitarized Maiden Castle retained its inhabitants, or at least a nucleus of them. Just so long did it take the Roman authorities to adjust the old order to the new, to prepare new towns for old. And then finally, on some day toward the close of the sixties of the century, the town was ceremoniously abandoned, its remaining walls were formally "slighted," and Maiden Castle lapsed into the landscape among the farm-lands of Roman Dorchester.

So much for the story; now for its basis. First, scattered over the eastern end of Maiden Castle, mostly in and about the eastern entrance and always at the same Romano-Belgic level, were found upward of a dozen iron arrowheads of two types: a type with a pyramidal point, and the simple flat-bladed type with turn-over socket. Arrowheads occurred at no other Iron Age level, but both types are common on Roman military sites where *ballistae* but not hand-bows are to be inferred. There, then, in the relatively small area uncovered, are the vestiges of the bombardment.

Secondly, the half-moon bay which represents the Iron Age B adaptation of the Iron Age A barbican, close outside the portals of the eastern entrance, was covered with a thick layer of ash associated with the post-holes of three or more circular or roundish huts. In and immediately below this ash were quantities of late Belgic or "Belgicizing" pottery. In the surface of the ash was similar pottery with scraps of pre-Flavian Samian. There are the burned Belgic huts, covered by the trodden vestiges of the continued post-conquest occupation for which more tangible evidence will be offered shortly.

Thirdly, into this ash a series of graves had been roughly cut, with no regularity either of outline or of orientation, and into them had been thrown, in all manner of attitudes—crouched, extended, on the back, on the side, on the face, even sitting up—thirty-eight skeletons of men and women, young and old; sometimes two persons were huddled together in the same grave. In ten cases extensive cuts were present on the skull, some on the top, some on the front, some on the back. In another case, one of the arrowheads already described was found actually embedded in the vertebra, having entered the body from the front below the heart. The victim had been finished off with a cut on the head. Yet another skull had been pierced by an implement of square section, probably a ballistabolt. The last two and some of the sword-cuts were doubtless battle-wounds; but one skull, which had received no less than nine savage cuts, suggests the fury of massacre rather than the tumult of battle—a man does not stay to kill his enemy eight or nine times in the melee; and the neck of another skeleton had been dislocated, probably by hanging. Nevertheless, the dead had been buried by their friends, for most of them were accompanied by bowls or, in one case, a mug for the traditional food and drink. More notable, in two cases the dead held joints of lamb in their hands—joints chosen carefully as young and succulent. Many of the dead still wore their gear: armlets of iron or shale, an iron finger-ring, and in three cases bronze toe-rings, representing a custom not previously, it seems, observed in prehistoric Britain but reminiscent of the Moslem habit of wearing toe-rings as ornaments or as preventives or cures of disease. One man lay in a double grave with an iron battle-axe, a knife, and, strangely, a bronze ear-pick across his chest. The whole war cemetery as it lay exposed before us was eloquent of mingled piety and distraction; of weariness, of dread, of darkness, but yet not of complete forgetfulness. Surely no poor relic in the soil of Britain was ever more eloquent of high tragedy, more worthy of brooding comment from the presiding Spirits of Hardy's own *Dynasts*.

The date of the cemetery was indicated by a variety of evidence. Most obvious is the Roman arrowhead embedded in the vertebra, but other associated relics point to the same conclusion. The seventeen pots put into the graves at the time of burial are all of that Wessex "Romano-Belgic overlap" class which has long been recognized at Jordan Hill, Weymouth, and elsewhere. The gear with one of the skeletons included, as has been remarked, a Roman "ear-scoop," the use of which may or may not have been understood more clearly by its Belgic possessor than by the modern antiquary; at least it implies Roman contacts which, in Wessex, appear not long to have anticipated the Roman Conquest. One grave, moreover, contained a late British coin, and though it was impossible to say safely whether the coin was inserted at the interment or was incorporated in the loose ash into which the grave was cut, at least it was dropped within a very short time of the event. And finally, the materials included in the strata which "bracket" the cemetery are themselves, as noted, sufficient to indicate a date at the end of the pre-Conquest period.

There, then, is the climax of the more human side of the story of conquest. But on the structural side the evidence for that event and for its sequel is no less vivid. On the topmost Belgic road-metal, in both portals of the eastern entrance but particularly in the southern, excavation revealed the tumbled stones from the massive walls that had formerly flanked the entrances. Here and there the fallen stones lay overlapping, like a collapsed pack of cards, in the sequence in which they had formerly stood as a vertical wall. With them was no cascade of rampart-earth such as might have implied a fall through subsidence, even could one presuppose the coincidence of the simultaneous fall of every part of the structure; the walls had been deliberately pulled down and no attempt had been made to replace them. But that was not all. Over the debris in each portal a new road had been built, metalled like the Belgic roads now buried beneath them. The new roads partially covered the surviving bases of the flanking walls, showing that the condition of these today is identical with their condition at the time of the road-building and confirming the permanence of the structural ruin. No provision of any kind was made in the new scheme for a gate; not a single post-hole was associated with the new road, and indeed the mutilated rampart-ends would have provided a poor setting for a fixed barrier. The implications of all this are evident. The entrance had been systematically "slighted" and its military value reduced permanently to a minimum; but traffic through it did not cease, no interval occurred in the continuity of the occupation.

That this dramatic episode should be ascribed to the Roman invader is proved by a liberal supply of associated evidence. The road-surface underlying the tumbled sidewalls in each portal is the last of a series of three or more which are all interleaved with British coins of the late "south-western" type, and with the coins were Belgic or cross-bred "BC" sherds, and fragments of Roman amphorae. Samian pottery was not found in these levels. On the other hand, in and on and beside the new road-surface which was laid down *over* the fallen walls, Samian sherds began to occur with some freedom. Where identifiable, these sherds are mainly of pre-Flavian type or fabric, and, in the whole of the eastern entrance, only *two* Samian sherds (both of them from the surface-soil) are later than the Flavian period. A detailed analysis, by Dr. T. Davies Pryce and Mr. J. A. Stanfield, . . . may here be summarized . . . :

Samian sherds from the eastern entrance
Datable fragments are assignable as follows:

To the pre-Flavian period	45
To the Nero-Vespasian period	9
To the Flavian period	4
To the Antonine period	2

Many small fragments, which do not admit of approximate dating, appear to be pre-Flavian.

Dr. Pryce concludes that the Samian from the entrance "indicates a definite occupation in the pre-Flavian period. The evidence for its continuation into the Flavian period is slight." It should be emphasized that seventeen of these Samian

Tourists view the excavations at Maiden Castle, England, in the late 1930s.

sherds, all ascribed by Dr. Pryce to the time of Claudius and Nero, were found embedded either in the road-metal of the new road in the southern portal (where the structural evidence was clearest) or in the layer of trodden mud upon its surface. On the other hand, the two Antonine sherds were both, as already remarked, in mixed topsoil.

Two conclusions emerge from this structural and ceramic evidence. First, the destruction of the sidewalls of the entrance occurs exactly between the Belgic and the Claudian occupation of the site: i.e., at the moment of the Roman invasion. Secondly, the occupation of the site continued, in spite of this interruption, to the beginning of the Flavian period, i.e., to c. A.D. 70, whereafter a break supervened. Other evidence amplifies this result.

A test-section cut through the rampart between the portals of the entrance revealed one of the large post-holes of the Belgic palisade or revetment. The post, like its equivalents on site E, had been about a foot in diameter, and its socket was 4 feet deep. At a depth of 2 feet in the filling of the socket (and 4 feet from the present surface) occurred a Samian sherd of distinctively early fabric, and in the same filling were two bronze scales of a Roman cuirass. These objects indicate that the socket was empty in early Roman times, and the complete uniformity of the filling indicates rather the uprooting of the post than its gradual decay. There is at least a strong probability that the slighting of the entrance was accompanied by a removal of the stockade along the rampart.

. . . The sherds . . . from the main occupation may be considered in summary here. . . . On this site, the thick layer of Belgic occupation passed, without structural division, into the early Roman, and its topmost portion contained Samian pottery. This has been examined by Dr. Pryce, who reports that every sherd is Flavian or pre-Flavian, with a strong predominance of the latter: the evidence for occupation actually within the Flavian period is "very meagre." In other words, the evidence here—and, it may be added, elsewhere in Maiden Castle—tallies exactly with that of the eastern entrance.

The picture is now complete in outline. Disarmed at the Roman Conquest, Maiden Castle remained in use for about a quarter of a century after the invasion, a pre-Roman city still in all essentials, partaking only a little of the cultural equipment of its conquerors. The picture is a reasonable and convincing one. The first generation of Roman rule was preoccupied with the subjugation of the difficult hill-countries of the north and west, with the development of mining areas, the planning of arterial roads, the founding or development of those few towns which had an immediate military or commercial function. Dorset offered, it is true, iron ore on a modest scale; but between Sussex and the Mendips there was little mineral wealth to attract the Roman prospector in the first flush of conquest. Wessex could wait. There was no urgent need to upset the traditional economic basis of the urbanized peasantry which crowded the downlands. To do so would have been to court added political difficulties at a time when difficulties were already manifold. It was better that, under surveillance, the Wessex farmers should for a time (and doubtless in return for the periodical payment of just or unjust dues) be allowed to maintain themselves in the fashion which they knew. The removal or, alternatively, the ennoblement of their rulers would rob them of independent leadership. A few police-patrols would do the rest.

Here, too, the evidence fits comfortably into place. The famous little Roman fort set in a corner of the Iron Age town on Hod Hill near Blandford—some 20 miles from Maiden Castle—has not been scientifically excavated, but pottery and other objects have been recovered at various times from it or its immediate vicinity. This material includes many Roman weapons and some Samian pottery dating from the time of Claudius and Nero. The occupation, in other words, was something more than transitory, and would appear to have lasted approximately from the time of the Roman invasion to c. A.D. 60 or a little later. With this supposition the comparatively elaborate plan of the Roman earthwork agrees: it is not that of a mere "marching camp," but rather that of a "semi-permanent" work possessing some of the attributes of a permanent fort. At its strategic point above the valley of the Stour, this little Roman hill-fort was a fitting center for the policing of a part of the native hill-town region during the interval between conquest and romanization.

The period of guarded *status quo* came to an end, it seems, in the reign of the actual conqueror of Maiden Castle. Under Vespasian and Domitian, notably in the governorship of Agricola, the systematic development of the civil life of

Roman Britain was at last undertaken throughout the lowland region. Hitherto such development had been in a large measure opportunist; it now became an avowed part of the official policy for the final and complete subjugation of the provincials. Towns were rebuilt in the comfortable Roman fashion or were newly founded; and among the new foundations—if the available evidence is representative—would appear to have been Dorchester, Durnonovaria or Durnovaria of the Itinerary. Of seventy-five Samian sherds from Dorchester, examined by Dr. Pryce in the Dorchester Museum, four or less are likely to be earlier than Vespasian. The proportions of early and late sherds, on a comparison of the groups from Dorchester with those from the main occupation of Maiden Castle, are thus approximately reversed; and, on the evidence, it may be affirmed provisionally that the occupation of the two sites is complementary. Dorchester begins where Maiden Castle ceases, i.e., c. A.D. 70. The sequence is doubtless significant. In Gaul under Augustus the process of romanization had entailed the removal of the more inaccessible hill-populations to new Roman cities founded under official auspices in the valleys. In Britain it is reasonable to suppose that, in the equivalent regime of the Flavians, a similar procedure was followed: that Flavian Caerwent, for example, became the Roman focus for the little native towns of Llanmelin and Sudbrook, that Uriconium was (then if not earlier) the heir of the *oppidum* on the Wrekin, and similarly that Roman Dorchester inherited something of the population and prestige of Maiden Castle. Certain it is, at least, that after the beginning of the Flavian period the eastern entrance of Maiden Castle fell into disuse. A layer of humus 7–9 inches deep was found to overlie the early Roman road-surfaces, implying that the site was, at the end of the first century A.D., as overgrown as in modern times. When we come to examine the final phase of Maiden Castle, it will be seen that this layer of barren mold intervenes between the first- and the fourth-century levels, so that its context is not open to doubt. In the second and third centuries A.D. Maiden Castle had reverted to downland or to tillage.

Of the actual moment of the official abandonment of the site, a vestige may indeed be recognized with some probability at the fruitful eastern entrance. Reference has been made in a preceding section to the stone-faced platform or bastion on the western flank of the southern causeway cut through the original barbican in phase IV (c. end of first century B.C. or beginning of first century A.D.). As excavated in 1936, this revetment was preserved to a maximum height of five courses; but the remainder of the wall still lay piled up alongside, upon the metalling of the roadway. The evidence compelled certain inferences:

1. The wall had been *deliberately* pulled away from the bank which it revetted, for the bank itself stood firm and had not fallen forward with the masonry, as would have been the case if the latter had been thrust outward by pressure from the bank.

2. The wall had not been demolished for the reuse of its stonework, since the fallen stones lay untouched where they had fallen.

3. The fallen stones lay on, and in contact with, the actual metalling of the road: i.e., they had fallen when the road was still in use and unencumbered with the covering of wind-blown earth which (as experience shows) accumulates within a month on exposed surfaces at Maiden Castle.

4. Both the road and the adjacent city went out of use immediately after the fall, since the debris blocked a good half of the roadway and—an important point on a stoneless site where stone is proportionately valuable—had not been appreciably plundered for its useful building-material.

It is fair to infer that this important and striking structural feature of the entrance had been "slighted" deliberately at the precise moment when the population was finally moved down from the ancient city to the new Roman town which must now have been prepared in the valley below. It is not difficult to imagine something of the pomp and circumstance with which this revolutionary incident in the history of the region was carried out—the solemn procession of civic and religious authorities, perhaps with some rather anxiously important emissary of the provincial government in attendance; and the ultimate ceremonial defacement of a work which had already, a generation previously, received its first and more drastic disarming at the moment of conquest—the earlier slighting carried out, perhaps, at the actual order of Vespasian, commander of the Second Legion, and the later slighting under the remote eye of Vespasian, now emperor of Rome.

Foragers at Koster, Illinois

STUART STRUEVER

Popular writing about archaeological discoveries rarely dwells on the remarkable ways in which modern science can conjure up minor details of the past from apparently inconspicuous finds. This is a new form of archaeological discovery, made famous by excavations at the Koster site in the American Midwest in the 1970s.

The Koster site lies amid fertile farmland in the bottom of the Illinois River Valley near the small village of Kampsville, Illinois. Located by the discovery of surface-artifact scatters on a farmer's plowed fields, the massive Koster excavation involved the collaboration of three archaeologists and six specialists from such other disciplines as zoology and botany, as well as intensive use of computer technology to record strata and artifacts and to analyze all manner of finds. Archaeologists James Brown and Stuart Struever (b. 1931) faced a formidable challenge. Koster was unusual in that the location was visited again and again over thousands of years. No fewer than thirteen occupation layers were isolated one from another by sterile zones of soil, providing the excavators with a unique opportunity to study changing lifeways and settlements buried over a vertical distance of 9 meters. The first visitors were Paleo-Indian foragers before 7500 B.C. Seasonal camps covered 0.3 hectare a thousand years later. An extended family group of about 25 people returned to the site again and again, perhaps to exploit rich fall nut harvests. Between 5600 and 5000 B.C., several permanent settlements flourished at Koster, each double the size of earlier camps. By this time, the Koster people were practicing highly intensive foraging: hunting deer and other game; harvesting enormous quantities of pecans, hickories, and other nuts each fall; and fishing. By 3500 B.C., the Koster settlement covered about 2 hectares and housed between 100 and 150 people. Game and nut harvests were still important, but now bottom fish from nearby shallow lakes, edible grasses, and waterfowl were vital to the diet, as populations rose and there were occasional food shortages. These were the conditions under which many midwestern groups began experimenting with the deliberate cultivation of native grasses like goosefoot and sumpweed to supplement the wild-food supply. This simple form of agriculture preceded maize farming in the area by at least two thousand years.

Koster's occupation levels contained tens of thousands of seeds, nuts, and other food remains. Struever used a new technique called flotation to recover these tiny finds,

*floating large samples of the occupation layers through water, so the fine seeds floated to
the surface. Flotation allowed Struever to write very complete portraits of ancient life,
a classic example of how archaeological discoveries come as much from the laboratory as
from the spade.*

In this selection, from his popular book, Koster, *Stuart Struever describes the life
of Koster foragers in their heyday.*

Much of the work we are doing with archaeological remains is still in the
experimental stage. We are trying to reconstruct on paper an extremely complicated ecosystem. What kinds of changes have taken place in Lowilva in the last
ten thousand years—in the rivers, creeks, lakes, swamps, floodplains, bluffs, hillside slopes, and upland prairies? What was the climate like during that period?
We must try to determine how hot or cold it was, how much rain fell, what
kinds of winds prevailed during all that time. In addition, we want to know what
kinds of plants grew there, and what kinds of animals were able to thrive.

The NAP [Northwestern Archaeological Program] botany laboratory is
housed in a small white house on a side street in Kampsville, across from St.
Anselm's Church parish hall. The director of the botany laboratory is Nancy
Asch, a paleoethnobotanist (a botanist who studies ancient cultures). Her husband, David, an archaeologist and NAP's statistician, works with her, analyzing
plant remains.

In one corner of the laboratory sits a vase filled with dried cattail stalks. On
Nancy's desk, face down, lies a copy of *Earth Basketry* by Osma Gallinger Tod.
Nancy plans to try her hand at weaving baskets with material gathered from the
fields near Koster, just as Amerindian women did thousands of years ago.

Nancy is trying to get a picture of what Lowilva looked like when the first
Euro-Americans arrived to settle there in about 1820. It is difficult to project
back from what one sees today in Lowilva. The land surface has been radically
altered by human activities; the floodplains have been drained for agriculture,
and there are levees built along the Illinois River to prevent flooding.

Nancy consults records of the U.S. Government Land Survey to get a picture of Lowilva before the first Euro-Americans arrived. From 1815 to 1820
surveyors marked off the land in square sections, one mile on a side, and made
observations on vegetation within every quarter section over the entire landscape. They identified "witness" trees and noted whether the land was covered
with forests, prairies, or brush.

The next step is to look at the plant remains from Koster. To aid her in
identifying charred prehistoric plant remains, Nancy spends time in the fields
and forests of Lowilva, hunting modern plants for a reference collection.

She plans to collect, identify, and mount a specimen of every plant and tree
that grows in the 3,200-square-mile area designated by NAP as its research
province. She has marked the area off on a large map, and systematically collects
from different sections. For each specimen, she gathers an entire plant, including
roots, stems, leaves, flowers, and seeds. In the case of trees, she collects leaves,

flowers, fruits, sections of wood from trunk and branches and a piece of root. She goes back to the same stand of plants or trees in different seasons to collect specimens at various stages of growth.

At the botany laboratory Nancy prepares the modern specimens. Each is identified, pressed, dried, and mounted on a large sheet of paper. These are stored in an airtight cabinet with mothballs.

On Nancy's table is a small box filled with sassafras seeds. She takes one, splits it neatly in half with a sharp knife, then glues one half, cut side up, to a glass microscope slide. Next she glues a whole seed to the slide. She is building a collection of seeds and bits of wood from all species of trees and shrubs in the region. The seed collection would enhance any art gallery; the arrangement of the seeds and the colors of the seed coats and their interiors make each slide a small work of art.

Nancy burns some of the modern samples enough to char them, so that they will more closely resemble the archaeological specimens. Ancient plant remains found at a site have survived only in charred form, because they were dropped or fell into the fire and were incompletely burned. The rest of the plant remains have long since decomposed. Nancy drops fresh plant specimens into sand that has been heated in a Dutch oven on the stove, or she may place some in an airtight crucible which she heats over a Bunsen burner. She keeps the specimen in the hot sand or over the burner until it stops smoking. Then she mounts sample bits of the charred fragments on glass slides.

Kathy Freudenrich, one of Nancy's research assistants, sits before a microscope at a worktable. She empties a small pile of archaeological remains onto a petri dish or sorting tray. Using a fine artist's brush, she gently separates them under the microscope. If she can identify a charcoal fragment, Kathy puts it into a small labeled box. If she cannot identify it, she turns to the reference collection of slides containing charred plant specimens and compares the archaeological specimen to them until she can tell exactly which species of plant it is. After the samples have been identified, they are counted, weighed, measured, and stored in gelatin capsules or plastic bags. All the information is then placed on computer coding forms for use in later analysis.

Identifying plant remains takes a sharp eye and a great deal of patience. Between 1970 and 1975 Nancy and her crew had identified more than 100,000 charred bits of nuts, seeds, and wood.

Usually a site holds so much material that it would produce massive quantities of redundant data if all of it were dug up. To avoid this, archaeologists use sampling techniques and dig up only portions of a site. They take samples of material from all areas of a site where human activities are believed to have occurred. It is important that they collect samples of all the human activities which took place, in sufficient quantities to assure an accurate assessment of the data. The degree of efficiency with which a site is dug depends on the accuracy of the sampling technique. David Asch, who is an experienced statistician as well as an archaeologist, uses modern statistical methods to help NAP decide where to take samples on the sites we dig.

We use another sampling technique, called flotation, to collect archaeological remains which are not caught on the screens at a site. Have you ever watched dead leaves floating on the surface of a pond or a puddle? The principle behind that phenomenon, namely that dead plant matter is lighter than water, helped me solve the problem of how to retrieve some very important material from archaeological sites—tiny charred bits of seeds and nutshells, and pieces of animal remains. Many of these are so small that they remain invisible to the naked eye even if you crumble the soil in which they have been embedded for centuries.

Before I developed a method for retrieving this material, along with most other archaeologists, I had been throwing it out, largely unaware that it could be collected. It was an observant botanist who first suggested to me that there might be a way to save these important clues.

In 1959 as we were excavating Kamp Mound Number 9, I noticed that in some of the earth in our trowels there appeared to be small bits of charred materials. I examined these and decided they were fragments of seeds. I was much interested. One of the most important links between a human population and its environment is, of course, the food it eats. I was curious to see what this evidence could tell us about the Hopewellians' diet and their food-gathering habits.

Later, as I looked through the items collected from the screening process at the site, I realized that the bits of charred seeds, falling through the screens, were being tossed out with the dirt.

As we dug, we came across a pit that contained an extremely ashy fill. I examined it and could again see tiny bits of charred seeds. I put aside a fairly good-sized sample until I could figure out a way to remove the seeds from the dirt.

At that time I had a visitor, Dr. Hugh C. Cutler of the Missouri Botanical Garden in St. Louis. Hugh is an expert on early domesticated plants in North America. He is interested in tracing the beginnings of agriculture in the New World and in trying to discover where, how, and when corn, squash, pumpkin, and other plants were first domesticated in what is now the United States. Hugh was especially interested in what we were finding at Mound Number 9, because agriculture is supposed to have begun in the North American Midwest during Hopewell times.

Hugh examined the sample I had saved from the pit at Mound Number 9 and suggested that the burned bits of plant material would float to the surface if the soil was put in water.

So I took a sample of soil from the pit, placed it in a bucket of water, and stirred it. Little black objects began to float to the surface, and as they appeared, I scooped them off with a tea strainer. When I shook out the contents of the tea strainer on some newspaper, I was amazed at the quantity of tiny pieces of charred seeds I had gathered, since many of these had been totally invisible when they were encased in soil.

Over the next couple of years, I kept experimenting with the flotation technique, trying to improve it. The process was not yet refined enough for our purposes. When a sample of dirt from a site is placed in water, flotation yields two sets of products. One, called the light fraction, consists of bits of residue from people's daily meals and includes pieces of animal bones and carbonized plant remains. The heavier fraction contains bits of stone, burnt clay, small pottery fragments, and various other artifacts, such as an occasional bead or tiny stone drills. The technique was not wholly satisfactory because the light fraction contains both carbonized plant remains and bits of animal bones. Each of these types of materials must be sent to a separate laboratory for analysis. They must be separated, and to do this by hand, using a tweezer, as we were doing, takes a great deal of time.

Help came again from an unexpected quarter. Two of my students were Sue Bucklin and Joanne Dombrowski, who were also students of Laurence Nobles, professor of geology at Northwestern University. Sue and Joanne had shared in our frustration when they tried to hand-separate plant and animal remains with a tweezers. Back on campus, they mentioned our experiments in flotation to Nobles. He described a chemical flotation process used in the coal-mining industry employing a zinc chloride solution of a specific gravity which allows the coal to float off and the residue to sink. He suggested we try using a similar solution to float off the carbonized plant remains.

I provided Sue and Joanne with samples of the light fraction, which they took to Evanston. In Nobles' laboratory, they tried the chemical solution and were able to achieve 100 percent separation of plant remains from animal bone remains.

Today NAP runs samples of soil from all the sites it excavates through both water and chemical flotation processes. Each day a crew picks up the half-bushel baskets of flotation samples caught under our table screens at the site and takes them to the Illinois River for the first step in the process.

Passengers using the Kampsville ferry frequently are treated to an impromptu sideshow during the excavation season when the NAP flotation crews take to the river. To float a sample, a worker stands hip-deep in the river holding a galvanized tin washtub. The bottom of the tub has been removed and replaced with one-sixteenth-inch fine mesh screen. The person holding the tub swishes it back and forth in the water, often wiggling his or her hips from side to side in accompaniment. The action sometimes resembles a belly dancer's gyrations. As the tub is gently rotated, the fine-grained silts and sands wash out. Within a few moments only a residue remains. This may include flint chips, animal bone fragments, fish scales, pieces of stone artifacts, and charred seed and nut remains.

Each tub-wielder has a partner, who works with a large hand strainer composed of a metal frame and the exceedingly fine brass screen mesh used in automobile carburetors. We have these made especially for us in a machine shop in nearby Carrollton, Illinois. When the residue from the first tub-shaking settles into the bottom of the tub, the first person dips the tub into and out of the water very quickly, so that the various materials are lifted by the water and then settle again at different rates. The heavier fraction, such as potsherds and pieces of chert, settles fastest. The lighter fraction, which contains animal bones and plant remains, settles more slowly. The person holding the strainer must quickly skim off the lighter fraction before it sinks.

Together the teams of workers dip the tub and strain out the light fraction over and over. The material removed in the strainers is laid on absorbent paper to dry. Although the procedure is simple, each two-person team must learn to work together, co-ordinating tub and strainer action.

After the light fraction has been dried, it is put through the second step of the flotation process in the laboratory. The workers make a bath of zinc chloride solution, and then pour a small amount of the light fraction into the bath. Animal bones go to the bottom; snail shells and carbonized plant remains float to the surface. Fish scales vary: some float, some sink to the bottom.

When we began to excavate Koster in 1969, I expanded the flotation activities. We began to collect more samples of soil for flotation from Koster than we had at any previous sites. And Nancy has told me that the flotation process is producing more than ten times the amount of plant remains and charcoal from Koster and other sites than we had been obtaining by using only the screening method.

These larger quantities of charred plant remains, and the increased number of contexts in which charcoal and plant remains are found, have enabled Nancy to estimate the prehistoric people's plant-food uses with greater accuracy. This is especially important at Koster, because where there are changes in the use of wild plants from one occupation level to another, there appear to be differences in emphasis on certain plant foods rather than complete shifts from one type to another.

Sometimes people ask the Asches how they can make reliable reconstructions of prehistoric environments from charred archaeological samples, given human beings' highly individualistic tastes in foods, and because only certain parts of plants are preserved by chance. As scholars, the Asches use a very conservative approach. They bypass the question of personal choice altogether, and draw implications about a species of plant only if it shows up in the archaeological remains.

We can tell a lot from the presence of a species of plant or tree. If you know the ecological requirements of that species, its presence implies certain environmental limits. For example, the northern distribution of pecans is controlled by the length of the growing season. Remnants of pecan shells have been found in all of the horizons at Koster, and that lets us know that while people lived there, the growing season for plants in Lowilva apparently was not much different from what it is today, since pecan trees are still found in the region.

Cattails grow best in moist places; cacti thrive in the desert. Because different species of plants and trees prefer to grow in specific habitats, the presence of a particular species in the archaeological specimens can tell us what kinds of plant habitats existed in Lowilva in prehistoric times. For example, residents of every village at Koster apparently liked black walnuts, for we find shells from these in

*The excavations at Koster, Illinois, showing the screens used to
recover small artifacts and food remains.*

every level. This lets us know that there must have been moist forests near the
site all during its various occupations. We also found seeds of marsh elder in
the debris from every village and hunting camp, indicating that during all of the
Koster occupations there must have been areas of open, wet, marshy ground in
Lowilva.

Between 5000 and 2000 B.C. (when there were large settlements at Horizons
8 and 6 and a much smaller hunting camp at Horizon 4) the Koster people lived
in a very stable vegetational environment. In all of those settlements, we found
the same wood charcoal, nut, and seed specimens, although in varying amounts.

Apparently the climate in Lowilva had changed very little over the centuries. What change took place was not pronounced enough to cause the disappearance of any one kind of plant in the region and its replacement with another. But the degree of climatic change did affect the size of some plant communities, causing some to expand and others to contract. These changes would have had significant consequences for the Koster people, for they would have affected the availability of various plants for food. We think the bluffs which line the valley on both sides of the Illinois River served as a buffer for the effects of regional climatic changes on the plants and trees within the valley.

When Nancy compared the early U.S. Government Surveyors' records with the Koster data, she noted that the plants, trees, and shrubs which had existed in Lowilva when the first Euro-American settlers arrived were strikingly similar to those which had been there during all of the Koster occupations. Furthermore, the plants and trees which had flourished during the whole time that Koster was occupied are the same as those found in Lowilva today.

Nancy's work with charred plant remains is complemented by the work of NAP palynologists (pollen specialists), who also reconstruct the prehistoric environment, by comparing modern pollen samples to ancient ones retrieved from the site.

Next time you are in the garden, stick a finger into a flower and pick up a few grains of pollen. They may look fragile, and if you blow on them, some will float away, but those tiny pollen grains are among the most durable items nature makes. Thousands of years from now, if archaeologists dig up your garden, some palynologist may be able to tell whether you grew flowers for color or fragrance or whether you helped feed your family by growing vegetables.

Pollen has a unique biochemistry that makes it very resistant to just about everything but oxidation and microbes. If left exposed to air, it can be destroyed by micro-organisms; but it is very resistant to normal soil chemicals, and once it is buried, it will last indefinitely in certain soil conditions. Acidic bog deposits are an ideal source for fossil pollen, but pollen also may be found in silts and clays. At Koster the fossil pollen was preserved in redeposited loess.

Pollen produced by flowering plants is set free to float in the air, and if it happens to drop into the proper soil it will be preserved. Pollen from different species can be identified, and the palynologist can figure out what plant communities grew at a site in prehistoric times by studying the pollen specimens found there. Again, since climate affects vegetation, when the plant (and pollen) pattern in a site or region changes, the palynologist can discern changes in the area's weather.

Dr. James Schoenwetter, a palynologist at Arizona State University, and Rose Duffield, director of the NAP pollen laboratory, are reconstructing the prehistoric plant communities at Koster. If vegetation patterns changed, were these shifts the result of climatic or human agencies? When people settle in a place, they usually change the landscape and, in turn, affect the plant and pollen record. Sometimes they clear land to live on; they cut down forests for wood for houses or fuel. They may plant crops. By comparing the types of pollen which accumulated while the Koster site was occupied with the types of pollen which fell when the site was abandoned, the palynologists can determine what impact, if any, the Koster residents had on their habitat.

Human impact would show up as disturbances of the natural environment, encouraging the growth of weedy herbs and shrubs more characteristic of disturbed or edge situations. This can be seen very readily in the pollen record, because many of the weedy species produce vast amounts of pollen.

Rose's object is to present a picture of the vegetation makeup of Lowilva (similar to that which Nancy is putting together) and of past climatic shifts. As we study the settlement patterns of the people who lived in Lowilva before the Euro-Americans arrived, we need to understand the vegetation makeup of each of the various zones in the region—floodplains, talus slopes (the bottom half of hillsides), bluff crests, and rolling uplands—through time. Because of the sharp physiographic differences in these zones, they supported diverse plant communities and their potential for human beings was varied. We cannot take it for granted that the vegetation in each of these zones was identical during the different prehistoric periods when people lived in Lowilva.

The palynologists collect modern samples of pollen to be used as a reference bank for identifying prehistoric specimens. The collection also serves to document the distribution of modern pollen in the region.

For the reference collection, the palynologists collect two or three plants of a single species, which go into a plastic bag in the field for later identification and pressing. They also collect a number of blossoms, which are immediately sealed in envelopes.

In the field, Rose also collects samples of soil from just below the leaf layer on the ground. And she collects tufts of moss, which are natural pollen traps.

Archaeological pollen samples are collected in soil samples from every three-inch level dug at the site.

The palynologists also have cores of soil taken from deep in the ground. For this, they use a core-drilling machine mounted on the back of a truck. The machine pokes a hollow tube into the ground and collects about a four-foot length of soil, two or more inches in diameter. When the palynologist examines these core samples, he or she also looks for natural carbonized material in the soil which can be used to date the layer from which the pollen is taken. The coring technique provides one of the best ways to avoid possible contamination of the pollen record. So far, we have cores taken to about thirty-five-foot depths from Koster and other sites in Lowilva and from many vegetation zones in the region.

Core-drilling machinery is very expensive, and we cannot afford to purchase any, but several agencies have obtained core samples for us. The Soil Conservation Service of the U.S. Department of Agriculture, the University of Illinois Department of Agronomy, and the Illinois State Geological Survey all have taken cores for us while studying modern vegetation.

To extract fossil pollen from soil, the palynologist literally dissolves the soil from around the ancient pollen grains with strong acids. The pollen grains, being tough, remain. To obtain pollen from fresh flowers, the palynologist grinds the flowers into a fine paste and then treats the paste in several steps with a variety of chemical solutions.

The pollen grains are placed in a glass vial of silicone oil, which will preserve them indefinitely. Reference slides can be made from this solution, which are then identified and counted under a microscope, by being magnified about four hundred times. The palynologist counts each grain of pollen. The percentages of different pollen types in a count reflect a number of things about the environment which affected the plants that produced the pollens. The palynologist takes these percentages into account when trying to reconstruct prehistoric plant communities and past climatic changes.

Jim Schoenwetter's analysis of the pollen record at Koster suggests that when there was a tiny hamlet at Horizon 11 (6500 b.c.), although the site itself was in an open, dry area, it may have been surrounded by forests. These conditions persisted over several thousand years, on through the time when a large village was occupied at Horizon 6 (3900–2800 b.c.). The pollen spectra from the time when Horizon 9 was occupied (about 5800 b.c.) indicates that the area had become more moist. Pollen from cottonwood trees appears, and they prefer a moist habitat. Presumably these grew alongside the Koster creek.

By the time hunters spent time butchering deer at Horizon 4 (2000 b.c)., the dominant element in the region was moist forests.

Overall, the climate changed gradually from relatively dry at about 6500 b.c. to a more moist stage at about 2000 b.c.

Many ancient plant communities have been destroyed not by environmental change but by development of land for agriculture, roads, and houses. Someday we may find a remnant of floodplain prairie that has not been plowed up, from which we can take a pollen sample. A few years back, before I got so involved with Koster, I used to give speeches before the Farmers' Grange or American Farm Bureau groups, and I would always ask: Does anybody know where we might find a bit of floodplain prairie still intact? But no one ever knew of a square foot of pristine, undisturbed floodplain in the entire seventy linear miles of the Lower Illinois River Valley. Now we figure the only way we will get that particular pollen complex is to try to find a place where a floodplain prairie existed, over which early settlers built a levee. If we could find one, we could cut down the levee to find the original ground surface, and take pollen samples.

In another Kampsville laboratory, NAP archaeologist Irwin Rovner, assistant professor of anthropology at North Carolina State University, is trying to reconstruct the prehistoric plant environment using clues so small that they are invisible to the naked eye. And his work is so experimental that we don't have any results yet, but it promises to help us obtain facts about prehistoric people which heretofore have been inaccessible.

Back in 3900 b.c., when people built houses in the Horizon 6 village, we know they used wooden posts for the framework of these structures, because when the posts deteriorated, they left telltale organic staining in the earth. We can still see the imprint of those wooden posts in the ground in the form of round, dark stains going down a few feet below the level of dirt which formed the village floor. But what did they use for roofs? From Irv's work with opal phytoliths, we may be able to determine if they made thatched roofs with grasses.

Opal (a mineral) phytoliths (from the Greek *phyton*, "plants," and *lithos*, "stone") are microscopic structures which have been mineralized in a living plant by progressive silification of cells. Silica and other high-grade minerals are absorbed through a plant's roots. While most minerals are used in the plant's respiratory cycle, silica seems to have no specific function in a plant. It is carried passively through a plant's vascular (water transportation) system and precipitated in or around the cells of root, stem, bark, and leaves. Most frequently, silica is deposited in the wall of a plant's cells. Eventually, because the deposit of silica is continuous, the entire cell may be encased in a cast of silica. When the plant dies and decays, these mineralized casts of cells, which are a bit heavier than pollen and do not float in the air, drop to the soil and remain there where the plant stood. Since the shapes of cells in one plant species differ from those in another species, these casts can be used to identify plant communities as they existed in the past.

Opal phytoliths may prove to be very important in our research, since they preserve better than any other organic fossil and under a wide range of environmental conditions. They also come in large quantities, which is helpful since we need substantial numbers of specimens to reconstruct a prehistoric plant community. Sometimes not enough seeds and pollen have been preserved at a site for adequate analysis.

In addition, in plants such as cereals and fodder grasses, opal phytoliths are more numerous and varied than the pollen. In fact, grasses produce possibly the best identifiable range of opal phytolith types. If Irv can identify grasses in archaeological contexts, this will be an important analytical aid to archaeology for the simple reason that agriculture, worldwide, is based primarily on the domestication of grasses. Corn, wheat, rye, barley, rice, and other grains, as well as sugar cane, are all grasses.

Irv extracts opal phytoliths from soil samples from each horizon of the Koster site by a flotation process similar to that used for plant and animal remains, but employing different chemicals. His work is so new that there are no collections of opal phytolith specimens, no reference texts or sets of reference slides against which his specimens can be compared and identified. His initial task, therefore, is to establish a reference collection of opal phytoliths from known plants in Lowilva, and for this he collects plants from different vegetation zones just as Nancy and Rose do.

Not enough research has been done to make firm conclusions from any of the Koster settlements, but there is one interesting phenomenon. In the soil from sterile levels between the village remains at Koster there is no concentration of opal phytoliths. But in the debris from the different villages and hunting camps opal phytoliths are incredibly abundant, in the tens of thousands per gram of soil. One explanation for this might be that Koster people were using grasses, either wild or cultivated. They may have used them for food, for making thatch for their house roofs, or for baskets or matting.

Eventually Irv may be able to offer proof that the Koster people used grasses in one or more of these ways.

Sometimes, when I watch excavators tossing dirt out of the "big hole," I wonder what other clues to ancient people's behavior we may be tossing out, unknown to us, as opal phytoliths were until recently. I am convinced that as more scientists in other disciplines become aware of what we are trying to do in the new archaeology, they will suggest additional applications of very specialized techniques to increase the amount of knowledge we can derive about the past.

The Underwater Exploration of
the Uluburun Ship

Cemal Pulak and Donald A. Frey

Shipwrecks are priceless archaeological time capsules. Their cargoes are mines of information on ancient trade, trade routes, and daily life, and can usually be dated with considerable precision. Archaeology underwater is just like excavation on land, but the techniques, developed by University of Pennsylvania archaeologists in the 1960s, are modified to assist in recording and recovering artifacts under the water. George Bass (b. 1932) has been a pioneer in underwater archaeology for more than thirty years, but he regards himself as an archaeologist first and a diver second. He is an expert on the Mycenaean civilization of Greece and the Aegean Bronze Age, which made him well qualified to excavate the Uluburun shipwreck off southern Turkey.

The Uluburun ship foundered, perhaps in a sudden squall, in either the late fourteenth or the early thirteenth century B.C. Bass and his colleague Cemal Pulak (b. 1951) believe that the ship was headed from east to west, on a typical coasting voyage. Its cargo was, however, unusually valuable, and may even have been a royal consignment. The hold carried enough copper ingots and tin to make three hundred bronze helmets and breast plates. Six thousand weapons lay aboard, as well as glass ingots, elephant tusks, stacks of finely painted Aegean pottery, and hardwood logs. By using spectrographic analyses and lead isotope tests on the metals, scientists have shown that the copper probably came from nearby Cyprus, a well-known source of the ore in antiquity, while objects from highland Turkey, the Nile Valley, the Levant, and the Aegean also came from the ship. Much of the cargo consisted of incense and spices, almonds, pomegranates, and olives.

Few archaeological discoveries have yielded as much information as the Uluburun ship. The wreck lay at a depth of more than twenty-seven meters, which made the excavation a major technical challenge. The finds have revolutionized our knowledge of the eastern Mediterranean world of 1400 B.C. Here, in an early article on the site, "The Search for a Bronze Age Shipwreck," Cemal Pulak and Donald A. Frey describe the chance discovery of the ship.

The Late Bronze Age shipwreck discovered by Peter Throckmorton in 1959 at Cape Gelidonya, Turkey, is a milestone in the history of underwater archaeology. Excavated by George Bass and Throckmorton, it was the first ancient wreck studied in its entirety on the floor of the Mediterranean. No less important has been the scholarly controversy stirred by the publication of the excavation.

Based on artifacts from the site, Bass—today the archaeological director of the Institute of Nautical Archaeology—concluded that the wreck at Cape Gelidonya was all that remained of a Canaanite (Bronze Age Phoenician) or Cypriote vessel that sank in the thirteenth or very early twelfth century B.C. This agreed with the fact that its cargo of four-handled copper ingots, superficially shaped like dried ox-hides, represented the distinct type usually associated with Syrian traders on fourteenth- and thirteenth-century Egyptian tomb paintings. Restudy of earlier finds in Greece, Cyprus, and the Levant, combined with the evidence from Cape Gelidonya, now suggested that a greater role should be attributed to Semitic seafarers in those centuries than was generally accepted.

These conclusions were subsequently questioned by some scholars. Could the ship not have been Mycenaean Greek, its Syro-Palestinian seal, lamp, weights, scarabs, pottery, and stone mortars simply bric-a-brac taken on board by Mycenaean sailors? Was its cargo not the product of twelfth-century Mycenaean colonists on Cyprus? Was there not, in fact, a Mycenaean monopoly on maritime trade in the eastern Mediterranean?

In an attempt to answer these questions, a number of efforts were made to relocate the other Late Bronze Age wrecks, almost certainly earlier, which yielded "ox-hide" ingots in the opening decades of this century. Peter Throckmorton looked in vain for the wreck off Euboea; he fears it might now be covered by modern harborworks. Donald Frey, using directions given to Throckmorton by an elderly Greek sponger who knew the site, searched unsuccessfully for a wreck not far from Cape Gelidonya, in the Bay of Antalya.

Although scattered copper and tin ingots later were found off the coast of Israel, and although the first mold for casting the same type of "ox-hide" ingot was found in a thirteenth-century Ugaritic palace in Syria, decades passed without the discovery of another ingot-carrying Late Bronze Age shipwreck. If one were to be found at all, it seemed, it would be only by chance. But archaeologists must strive to improve their chances!

First, a method of locating wrecks is needed. We cannot, as do archaeologists seeking wrecks of much later periods, depend on archival work for clues to the whereabouts of specific disasters. Nor are magnetometers, so useful in sensing the iron remains from later ships, helpful in locating such early vessels. Metal detectors are of limited range. Random search by sonar has proven to be possible but extremely inefficient. Visual search, then, remains the best means of spotting exposed cargoes of ancient shipwrecks.

For visual search, a diver is sometimes towed on a wing-like diving plane, but this method is limited by the length of time a diver can stay at depth without risking decompression sickness. To overcome this limitation, we have used a device called a Towvane, a sealed capsule which is towed with a pilot controlling his depth from inside; because the pressure in the capsule remains the same as that at the surface, the pilot may stay down indefinitely. Although the Towvane can be maneuvered up and down by its occupant, it is difficult to steer to the left or right for close inspection of sighted objects. Yet another technique is to tow a television camera instead of a person, but the scope of view is limited, and it is difficult to return exactly to objects that have passed briefly by on the screen.

At present our best "remote-sensing device" remains that used by Peter Throckmorton—the Turkish sponge diver. Every year about 50 of the 150 to 200 registered sponge boats in southern Turkey sail out for sponges. Sponges have been so depleted, and their prices have dipped so low, that about half of these boats supplement or even earn the major part of their income by illegal spear fishing. In spite of the small number of boats that deal only with sponges, the total amount of time their divers spend exploring the seabed is considerable.

Each sponge boat has a minimum crew of about five divers, and usually the captain's son to help out with the daily chores of shipboard life. The captain himself may or may not be a diver. The boats usually set out to sea sometime in late May or early June and do not return until the end of September or early October. The "romantic" and "adventurous" lives of these men are, in reality, unfortunate dramas. They dive at least twice and often three times a day to depths that are not even registered on air-diving tables. Their equipment consists of a shared, well-patched rubber suit (one size for all!), a face mask, fins, and diving weights probably cast from ancient lead anchor stocks recovered from the sea. Their breathing system, known as _narghile_, or _hookah_, utilizes an industrial air compressor "souped up" to deliver greater pressure for the deeper dives through a hose connected to a vintage regulator. Most of the spongers are ignorant of diving facts, and those who seem to understand the mechanism involved in decompression rely on undigested information mingled with old wives' tales. Time seems to have stood still in the sponge industry.

Four months are usually spent at sea in a small, overcrowded, and miserable boat. Port calls are made only if the divers are short of victuals or diesel fuel to run their engines and diving compressors. Occasionally the sponges have to be unloaded to make room on the already cramped boats. They are spread out on a pier and allowed to dry under the sun. The inferior pieces are culled and the remaining collection is sorted according to size, shape, quality, and species. Throughout the procedure, great care is taken not to mix the individual batches of sponges belonging to specific divers—and the inexperienced divers stand out with their modest collections. Once dried, the sponges are stuffed into large sacks to be shipped home for storage until the market season in the fall.

Usually each sponge diver gives half of his share to the captain and owner of the boat in return for his food and the use of the vessel. A seasoned diver on a very lucky day can collect nearly a kilo of sponges, but the average usually does not exceed half a kilo per day. At best, a kilo of sponges sold for about 8,000 T.L. ($27) in 1983. A hardworking diver, then, could expect to earn about

$1,500 to $2,500 for the whole season, half of which would be given to the captain—hardly worth the risk of losing the use of an arm, leg, or entire body, or, for some, even their lives.

Five spongers diving three times a day for half an hour on the seabed totals an incredible seven-and-a-half hours of bottom time per boat per day (not including decompression time). For the full season of four months, or 100 working days, divers on 25 boats would spend 18,750 hours scanning the seabed along the Mediterranean coast. This amounts to over two years spent under water! This lifestyle is an invaluable resource for archaeologists to tap; no amount of remote sensing or any other means could accomplish so much for so little. The only input required by archaeologists is advising the divers as to what to look for under water. Most of the sponge divers do not know what ancient wrecks are, and instead look for modern steel hulls with high scrap values. Therefore, continued marginal efforts on our part—giving slide shows and talks during the dormant winter months, and contacting the sponge boats during summers while all information is still fresh—are well worthwhile. The rewards are certainly high.

During the past thirteen years, the Institute of Nautical Archaeology (INA) has located seventy-three wrecks along the coast of Turkey. Only two were discovered by remote sensing equipment, while the remainder were either shown to us by sponge divers or relocated following their leads. In recent years, a few wrecks have been discovered purely by the efforts of our staff through surveying areas that were dangerous to sailing vessels of antiquity. Even then, we found sponge divers who remembered the same wrecks after we described them. Many other sites, with their exact locations clouded over the years, are imprinted on the minds of this dying breed of weathered old men.

Early INA surveys were somewhat haphazard affairs. If we learned of a wreck from a sponge diver, it was necessary to wait for a full-scale survey project, requiring weeks of outfitting a local trawler as a mobile diving platform, and gathering an adequate team. By that time, it often was impossible to find the sponge diver, who might be at sea.

The purchase of the *Virazon* by the Institute of Nautical Archaeology in 1978 changed the picture radically. Now INA has a sixty-five-foot, steel-hulled vessel, fully outfitted with a double-lock recompression chamber, high- and low-pressure compressors, radar, sonar, a photographic darkroom, living quarters for a dozen diving archaeologists, and an eight-foot drafting table. For the first time we have at our disposal the means to practically, economically, and safely search for shipwrecks along the coast of Turkey. Now we can visit a site within a few days of learning of it, accompanied by the diver who reported it, even during the course of an excavation campaign.

With the acquisition of the *Virazon*, INA President Donald A. Frey instituted a long-range survey program in cooperation with the Bodrum Museum of Underwater Archaeology. Frey travels the coast, meeting dozens of sponge divers. During the off-season he and other Turkish-speaking members of the sur-

*Archaeologist Nicole Hirschfeld
raises a ceramic Canaanite
amphora from the shipwreck
at Uluburun.*

vey team visit the villages where spongers winter, and every autumn he directs
a one- to two-month survey from the *Virazon.*

During the fall of 1982 a diver named Mehmet Çakir told another sponge
diver that he had seen "metal biscuits with ears" on the seabed at Uluburun
near Kaş, at a depth exceeding forty meters. Çakir's friend already knew the
INA survey team, and asked him to draw one of the "biscuits." He immediately
recognized the familiar "ox-hide" ingot shape and advised Çakir to report his
discovery to the Bodrum Museum, where, he was told, a group of underwater
archaeologists were looking for wrecks with ingots of similar shape. A team from
INA and the Bodrum Museum soon dived on the site and raised an ingot for
identification. So began the excitement of a landmark discovery.

In 1983 Pulak received permission from the Turkish Ministry of Culture and
Tourism to direct another INA survey. As part of the survey, we arrived in the
town of Kaş on August 18 to investigate the Bronze Age wreck in preparation
for its full-scale excavation starting in 1984.

We located the wreck area immediately and moored the *Virazon* directly
above it. At the end of a week INA director Jack W. Kelley, a driving force

behind our search for a Bronze Age ship, had made a plan of the site based on photomosaics and direct measurements. We established that the wreck lay between forty-three and fifty-one meters deep, spread over an area ten by eighteen meters. Gigantic limestone blocks which had toppled from the cliffs above the wreck dominated the upslope portion of the site. A large, boulder-like outcrop marked the center of the visible wreckage. Some artifacts lay scattered on the inclined rocky bottom surrounding the boulder, while others were caught in the abounding sand pockets.

The wreck appeared to be far larger than that at Cape Gelidonya. Visible cargo included eighty-four full and half-size "ox-hide" ingots, some still stacked as they once had been stowed on the ship. Surveying with a metal detector revealed additional ingots buried in the sand pockets. Small plano-convex "bun" ingots lay among the "ox-hide" ingots.

Six large storage jars (pithoi) in three sizes were completely covered with sea-growth and originally were mistaken for boulders. The largest, along with two medium-sized pithoi, occupied the central part of the visible wreckage, directly above the boulder, while the others had rolled down the terraced seabed. The sixth and smallest jar still remained upslope where it probably came to rest with the ship. Eight Canaanite amphoras also were seen upslope of the outcrop. The intact pithoi and amphoras contained sediments that can be collected and analyzed, as is now routine on our excavations, providing new knowledge of the perishable export goods of the East.

Two large stone anchors of the type built into temple walls at Byblos and Ugarit on the Syrian coast, and Kition on Cyprus, lay close to the amphoras. The larger, rectangular stone had slid into the base of one of the medium-sized pithoi and caused it to fracture, while the second slab, with a square hole for a hawser, was partially hidden under "ox-hide" ingots. Lying on the latter slab, miraculously intact, was a ladle-shaped, terracotta wall bracket of a type found on Cyprus and at Ugarit in Syria. Similar objects found on land bear smoke-blackened stains suggesting their use as lamps, torch holders, or, most likely, incense burners. Three pilgrim flasks of Canaanite type were also visible, one on the outer edge of the site, while the others were half buried, mouth down, between the two prominent rows of stacked ingots.

Another fully exposed stone anchor estimated at weighing about two hundred kilograms could be observed on the deeper end of the wreck. It is pierced at the narrower end of its slightly tapered body for the securement of a hawser. Bronze Age stone anchors have been recovered in some numbers from the sea in the past, but never before from a datable ship.

The discovery of even the slightest hull remnants, we knew, would immensely increase our almost non-existent knowledge of Bronze Age ship construction in the Mediterranean. Sand from the area thought most likely to yield hull remains was brushed gently away. After a few hand strokes, a well-preserved piece of wood, perhaps an element of the ship's hull, emerged from beneath its protective blanket of sand. A smaller, contorted fragment, most probably part of the ship's dunnage, was recovered for analysis and later identified as pistachio.

A small sample removed from larger lumps of grayish-white, brittle material found in the vicinity of the wood was later shown in a laboratory to be 99.5 percent pure tin. To establish a tentative date for the wreck we also raised one bun ingot, one pilgrim flask, the hanging wall lamp, and one amphora, all of which were transported to the Bodrum Museum of Underwater Archaeology. Preliminary studies showed these to fit most comfortably in the fourteenth century B.C., with the first half of that century providing the closest parallel for the pilgrim flask.

Information gained during the survey was sufficient to plan a full-scale excavation of the shipwreck at Uluburun. INA's first summer campaign, in 1984, was directed by George F. Bass, with Pulak serving as assistant director. The excavation was financed by the Institute, Texas A&M University, and the National Geographic Society.

Finds in 1984 were extraordinary. No other single site—on land or under water—will have provided so much primary evidence for the movement of raw materials in the Late Bronze Age. Both copper and tin ingots of ox-hide shape were in abundance. The first evidence for shipments of raw glass appeared in the form of nearly twenty blue, discoid ingots. About seven inches in diameter, and two inches thick, the ingots were probably used to fashion jewelry and perhaps even drinking vessels. Both elephant and hippopotamus ivory appeared. One Canaanite amphora was filled with glass beads, and others among the three dozen raised contained resin, yellow arsenic, grape seeds, olive pits, and materials still being analyzed. A gold pectoral in the form of a hawk, probably of Canaanite origin, was found near a Mycenaean (probably IIIA:2) *kylix*; nearby were a gold chalice, faience and amber beads, a Syrian pilgrim flask, and a Cypriote White-Slip "milk bowl." Not far distant were other Mycenaean wares and a seemingly Syrian gold medallion. Bronze weapons, at least some Canaanite, abound.

One of the pithoi contained stacks of Cypriote pottery—Bucchero, Base-Ring II, White-Slip II, and White-Shaved wares—along with terracotta lamps of apparent Syro-Palestinian origin. Other finds included weights, silver bracelets, bronze tools, a stone macehead, a stone tray, astragals, and, perhaps most important, a Mycenaean seal. Beneath a row of six anchors running across the ship was found a section of the ship's hull, its fir keel and planks secured with pegged mortise-and-tenon joints similar to those used in the construction of the Kyrenia ship of a millennium later.

Such exciting finds will surely continue as future seasons progress. We estimate it will take four or five summers to complete the job. Although its excavation may not resolve the controversy over early metallurgy and trade in the eastern Mediterranean, the Uluburun shipwreck will certainly provide exciting new data for a better understanding of the Late Bronze Age.

Historical Archaeology: Martin's Hundred, Virginia

IVOR NÖEL HUME

*Ivor Nöel Hume (b. 1927) is a consummate archaeological detective, a brilliant excava-
tor with an uncanny ability to link historical records with archaeological data from the
ground. He has spent much of his career working at Colonial Williamsburg in Virginia,
where he located the buried foundations of a forgotten early-seventeenth-century colonial
settlement named Wolstenholme Towne in the Martin's Hundred plantation along the
James River. A palisaded fort protected the thirty to forty inhabitants from Indian or
Spanish assault, but to no avail. An Indian attack on March 21, 1622, razed the
settlement and outlying farms. The survivors fled, never to rebuild on the same site,
which vanished from history.*

*Nöel Hume excavated Martin's Hundred over a five-year period beginning in 1976.
He uncovered the houses and palisades by plotting the dark stains left by wooden post-
holes in the subsoil. In one instance, he located a discolored rectangle, which turned out
to be the remains of a subsurface dwelling. At first, he was puzzled, until he managed
to track down a contemporary description of subterranean pit houses with roof eaves
resting on the ground built by poor settlers until they could afford to construct more
conventional aboveground dwellings. Nöel Hume found a tiny fragment of twisted gold
thread from a gentleman's coat and a cannonball in the pit-house filling. In a remarkable piece of archaeological sleuthing, he located a 1621 regulation that forbade anyone
in Virginia to wear gold in their clothing except "Council and heads of hundreds."
William Harwood, the administrator of Martin's Hundred, was the only person in the
settlement qualified to wear gold thread. A 1625 census listed Harwood as the only
owner of a "peece of Ordnance," which makes it almost certain the house was his.*

*Few archaeologists rival Ivor Nöel Hume's ability to write engagingly about his
discoveries. In his book* Martin's Hundred, *a popular account of the excavations, he
describes the discovery of a badly decayed iron helmet and the detective story behind its
dating and identification, an excellent example of his meticulous approach to archaeological sleuthing.*

445

What we came to call the "potter's pond" contained a second gun barrel, this one empty and making no pretense at being a ceramicist's tool, any more than did an agricultural bill-hook, which survived in almost mint condition and made us wonder why anyone would have thrown it away. There was also a small, sheet-brass cooking pot that had started life with an iron handle and legs; we wondered why they had been broken off and taken elsewhere when so many other iron objects were lost into the pond. Most of them were in very thin pieces and badly corroded, but thanks to experience gained in raising the helmet from the fort well, salvaging even the most fragile objects had become routine. Recognizing what we were lifting sometimes was more difficult. With depressing ease a crushed iron frying pan could take on the appearance of plate armor. In the space of two days we found both, first the pan and then an armor backplate broken into several pieces before it was thrown away. Only three of them had reached the pond, and again we asked why? Why would anyone discard so basic a piece of armor? Why would they first deliberately break it up, and then not throw all the pieces away together?

As I scraped the silt from around two of the backplate fragments, a lump of clay dropped away to reveal a patch of convex-shaped iron about two inches in diameter. Being busy with the armor, I at first ignored the new find, assuming it to be another pan or, at best, part of a cauldron or flesh pot. Then the backplate fragments reminded me that in the fort well a backplate lay with a helmet, and that the small patch of iron showing through the gap in the clay could as easily be the side of a helmet as of a cooking pot. At least two colleagues were working within six feet of me, but I said nothing, fearing that I would get everyone excited over nothing. The odds against our finding two helmets on one site were astronomically long.

Using a thin spatula and a paintbrush I slowly enlarged the window in the clay wall to reveal more of the convex shape behind it. Inch by inch it got bigger; then the metal took a sixty-degree turn and stopped in a rolled ridge. I knew then that I was looking at part of the crest of another helmet, and it took only a few minutes more to ascertain that it was of the same, face-covering type that we had found in the fort. But unlike the tight confines and constant water problems that beset us in the well, here we could work all around the helmet, using a refined and streamlined version of our original lifting technique—which we now called the "plaster mushroom method."

We continued to reinforce the rusted metal with a 50 percent solution of cellulose glue, just as we had done for the first helmet, and again we exposed only one side, leaving the rest bedded in the clay. I could see that despite some crushing as a result of ground pressure, this helmet was in better condition, and unlike its predecessor, whose recovery had been hampered by its proximity to the backplate, this one's only problem was a small earthenware pot whose projecting handle was stuck up the nose of the visor. With the first coating of glue set, our next step was to cut narrow strips of fiberglass screenwire which, when dunked in the acetone-diluted glue, became supple and sticky. Strip by strip we covered the rusted metal with the wire mesh which, when the glue dried, left the helmet's exposed side wrapped like an Egyptian mummy. Next we cut a trench all around to a depth several inches below the helmet's estimated maximum width, thus leaving it standing on a slightly undercut clay pedestal. We then covered both helmet and pedestal with generous layers of wet paper towels, building up a cushioning surface devoid of any pronounced bumps and lumps. With that done, we coated the whole thing with plaster of Paris, the mixture stiff enough to be smeared and shaped to grip the undercut sides of the clay pedestal.

Plaster sets up at different speeds depending on its ratio to water; too much water and it has no strength, too little and you cannot work it. Like so much in archaeology, getting it right is learned by experience. While setting, plaster becomes very hot, and not until it cools does it acquire sufficient strength for us to take the next step—undercutting the pedestal until it teeters like a mushroom on a damaged stalk. Then slicing the clay stalk right through, we turn the plaster mushroom over, converting it into a bowl filled with the clay in which the artifact lies buried, not to be removed until it reaches the laboratory.

Getting the first helmet out of the well and into the lab had taken two weeks; the second took six hours and a fraction of the labor and equipment. Once there, however, we had no shortcuts. The transition from eggshell-thin rust to a helmet that could be X-rayed, drawn, photographed, and finally exhibited, would still take several weeks.

On the site we were left with some new questions and a lot of old ones, the most persistent being whether or not the juxtaposition of a backplate and a close helmet, first in the well and now in the potter's pond, was telling us something, or whether both were mere coincidences. For my part, I have long argued that it takes three such findings, not two, to turn coincidence into a possibly significant pattern—an extension of the old archaeological adage that any two holes make a straight line, but we need at least three to make a row. Regardless of any yet unrecognized relationship between the discarding into water of identical pieces of armor on two sites, there was no denying that in the Company Compound pond, a potter's garbage and a close helmet made strange pitfellows.

We had been willing to dismiss the first close helmet as an eccentric and unique find into which we should not try to read too much. Finding another quickly made us change our minds and look again at information provided by the Tower of London, whose experts had told us that the fort's helmet, with its one-piece visor, could be considered unrepresentative of the period. The second helmet also had a one-piece visor, though with a larger bill or peak above the eyes to shade and protect them. The Tower of London collections contained no exact parallel for either helmet. Indeed, very little of what we were finding could be precisely matched there. A small, triangular piece of iron from the fort (which I had mistakenly supposed to be part of a couter or elbow cop) was identified by Master of the Tower Armouries A. V. B. Norman as coming from

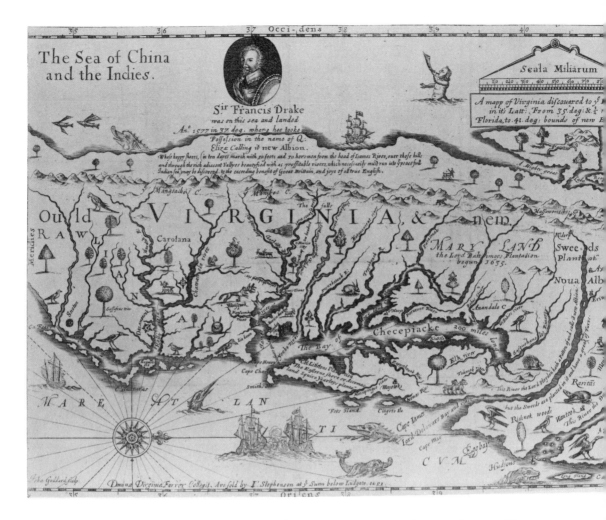

A seventeenth-century map of Virginia and Chesapeake Bay, showing "James Towne" and Martin's Hundred.

the cheekpiece of a burgonet of a fairly common type. Much later, when I asked to borrow a parallel for that helmet for inclusion in a National Geographic Society exhibition, Keeper of Armour Ian D. Eaves confessed that the Tower collection possessed no example that was a sufficiently close match. "If I were to stick my neck out," he wrote, "I would guess that your [helmet] might be Italian."

Our problems of identification were not limited to the armor. No one knew more about early firearms than the Tower of London's Deputy Master, Howard L. Blackmore, and no one was more anxious to help; yet it was discouraging to open the first chapter of his standard work *British Military Firearms 1650–1850* and read in the first sentence that "The middle of the seventeenth century may be taken as a convenient period at which to commence the study of British military firearms, as only a few guns made before then have survived." Alas, the plain and simple versions of anything have rarely excited curators and collectors, and just as we can see Chippendale chairs any day of the week but may wait a lifetime to find a genuine, documented, seventeenth-century kitchen table, so it is the costly and ornate early guns that have survived—not the musketeers' ordinary matchlocks.

Beginning in the second half of the sixteenth century, the musket in one form or another became the battle-winning weapon of every European army, and so it was for the British, as long as the enemy played by the rules. In 1607 a Fleming, Jacob de Gheyn, published a manual of military instruction, illustrating in a series of fine engravings each step in loading and firing a matchlock musket, and for a while it became the drill sergeants' bible. De Gheyn was followed in 1622 by Francis Markham's *The English Military Discipline*, which was easier to read, but still listed nineteen commands for loading and presenting the gun and fourteen more for firing it. In battle, parade-ground orders were cut to three: Make ready. Present. Give fire! Even so, a nimble Indian with a good eye could get off half a dozen well-aimed arrows while a musketeer was getting himself ready to fire one reasonably well-aimed ball a distance of about thirty yards.

A matchlock musket was not only slow to load, it weighed ten or twelve pounds, so that it had to be supported on a U-topped staff—which the musketeer had to carry around with him. If he inadvertently tipped the gun's barrel below the horizontal, the ball was liable to roll out, there being no wads or cartridges to hold it in place. Priming powder was placed in a covered pan which had to be opened by hand before a lever-controlled length of smoldering match was thrust down into it. Several things could go wrong. The pan cover was prone to swing open before you were ready, in which case the priming powder could (1) blow away, or (2) be rained on. Worse still, a little too much saltpeter in the match could make it spark as well as smolder, and an errant spark could fire the gun before you were ready. The manual required that musketeers should stand guard or move in battle array with both ends of a three-foot length of match smoldering. Lack of attention to the "other" end could ignite your own powder supply. While demonstrating in our film how to fire a matchlock, the fuse burned three holes in my shirt and one in my thumb. At night, the glowing match ends provided excellent targets for a waiting enemy—provided you had not spotted his glows first. There were other surprises, too, as a marksman aboard the *Mayflower* discovered off Cape Cod in November 1620. In an effort to irritate a whale "to see whether she would stir or no; he that gave fire first, his Musket flew in peeces, both stocke and barrel, yet thanks be to God, neither he nor any man els was hurt with it."

For all their faults, muskets were among the most important pieces of equipment owned by Martin's Hundred colonists. Although we have no inventory of the supplies brought over in 1619 aboard the *Gift of God*, we do have a copy of a list that John Smith published in 1623 to help would-be settlers pack their bags. Under "Armes for a man" he advised taking the following:

1	Armor compleat, light	17s.
1	long peece five foot and a half, neere Musket bore.	1£. 2s.
1	Sword	5s.
1	Belt	1s.
1	Bandilier	1s. 6d.
20	pound of powder	18s.
60	pound of shot or Lead Pistoll and Goose shot.	5s.
		3£. 9s. 6d.

Smith added that "if halfe your men be armed it is well, so all have swords and peeces." Unclear though this is, we may perhaps assume that at least half of one's servants should be provided with some kind of body armor. Although Smith's list includes everything from augers to waistcoats, no single item approached the value of the musket, an item more costly than a "compleat" suit of armor; as he included no match, he may have been thinking of the more sophisticated snaphaunce rather than a matchlock musket. The list ends with the note that "this is the usuall proportion the *Virginia* Company doe bestow upon their Tenents they send." The same may reasonably be assumed of the Martin's Hundred Society, and if its first group of settlers was at least two-thirds male, that would call for 146 muskets, a lot of guns and a big investment by any contemporary standard.

Smith's pricing of a suit of armor at seventeen shillings suggests that just as nineteenth-century Britons heading for colonial service bought their outfits at the Army and Navy Stores, so in the early seventeenth century Thomas Stevens of Buttolph Lane was the man to see for armor. A surviving invoice shows that in 1620 he supplied Virginia planter Francis(?) Middleton with "23 Armo^rs att 17^sp peece, 2 Armo^rs better then ordinary for Mr. Middleton & his Sone at 25^s p peece." Thus, John Smith may well have obtained his seventeen shillings per suit price from Thomas Stevens. More important is the question of the degree to which such suits differed from the twenty-five-shilling variety. The answer to that came eight years later, from another Thomas Stevens invoice, this one dated March 6, 1628/9, when he sold to the Massachusetts Bay colony "20 armes, viz: coslett, brest, back, culet [a rump protector], gorgett, tases [thigh defenses], & hed peece to ech, varnished all black, wth lethers & buckles, at 17^s ech armour, excepting 4, wch are to bee wth close head peeces, & theis 4 armours at 24, a peece, to bee [delivered] all by the 20th of this monthe; w^r of 1 left noew for a sample." It is a safe bet that the two suits provided for the Middletons at twenty-five shillings apiece had close helmets—which brings us right back to Martin's Hundred and the vexing question of why anyone would throw away two close helmets.

The second, or "potter's pond" helmet proved to be more badly crushed than we had at first supposed, but since all the damage was to the side uppermost in the ground, I could not be sure whether it was caused by earth pressure or by a deliberate effort to render the armor useless. Such helmets certainly were inappropriate headgear for warring in the wilderness with an elusive, unorthodox, and, to the European mind, unsporting enemy. One's head movement was severely restricted, hearing reduced, and vision narrowed. In a Virginia summer, wearing a close helmet would have been akin to sticking your head in a portable oven. Were they, we may wonder, more ceremonial than practical, and as such a potential trophy of sufficient psychological value to the Indians to promote even greater boldness? If so, might not the massacre's survivors have put their officers' helmets out of reach, into water-filled holes, before retreating to Jamestown? The argument is not particularly convincing, for it is evident that the Indians preferred hair to helmets.

Ramesses II's Sons

DOUGLAS PRESTON

The Valley of the Kings, on the west bank of the Nile opposite Thebes, was the burial ground of the New Kingdom pharaohs, rulers of Egypt when it was at its imperial zenith after 1500 B.C. Among the greatest of these pharaohs were Seti I and his son Ramesses II, who ruled for no less than sixty-seven years, from 1279 to 1213 B.C. Ramesses II was an intensely conservative king, who ascended the throne at age twenty-five and spent a lifetime preserving the ancient customs and traditions of Egyptian kingship and religion. His architects built temples the length of his domains, among them the forecourt of the Temple of Amun at Luxor and the cliffside temple at Abu Simbel far above the First Nile Cataract in Nubia. Statues and stelae commemorate his rule from the Delta to the farthest limits of his kingdom. Ramesses outlived twelve of his heirs and died in his early nineties. Like his illustrious predecessors, he was buried in the Valley of the Kings. Egypt went into a slow decline after his death. The last New Kingdom pharaoh, Ramesses XI, was buried in the Valley of the Kings in 1070 B.C. By this time, many of the royal tombs had been ravaged by robbers. The necropolis priests moved several pharaohs' mummies to safety, hiding them in a rock cleft where they remained safe until some modern-day treasure hunters found them in 1881. Ramesses II's body was in the royal cache and now resides in the Cairo Museum after meticulous conservation by French experts.

Two hundred years of archaeological activity have left the Valley of the Kings looking like a battlefield. Today's researcher has to combine historical detective work with archaeological expertise, trying to learn which earlier explorers opened which tombs and engaged in what restoration work. For this reason, much recent work has involved mapping and surveying. For example, the Theban Mapping project has begun to piece together a systematic plan of the maze of tombs, blocked passageways, collapsed chambers, and incompletely excavated sepulchers that makes up the Valley of the Kings and the Theban necropolis. Few of these have been dug with modern techniques, but an estimated four thousand to five thousand tombs still await discovery. Archaeologist Ken Weeks of the American University in Cairo is working on a comprehensive map of the Valley of the Kings. This research involves laborious ground and subterranean survey, the systematic clearance of all kinds of debris from the floor of the valley, much of it generated by Howard Carter in his search for the tomb of Tutankhamun in the early twentieth century. During his work, Weeks uncovered the entrance of tomb KV5, which was known, but was buried under tons of debris from Carter's search for Tutankhamun. After ten days of clearance work, Weeks located the doorway opposite the tomb of Ramesses II. He found himself inside an enormous T-shaped sepulcher, which he soon identified as the burial place for as many as fifty of Ramesses's fifty-two sons. There are at least ninety-two rooms underground, and exploration has hardly begun. So far, Weeks has not found the burial chambers themselves, which may lie at a lower level, conceivably undisturbed. Many seasons' work will be needed to explore this vast burial complex, with tantalizing prospects for truly spectacular archaeological discoveries in the next few years.

Writer Douglas Preston visited Kent and Susan Weeks as they explored the tomb, drawing on the latest scientific methods and the cumulative Egyptological and archaeological expertise of more than a century's research in the area. His account describes not only the slow-moving investigations, the first fully modern excavations in the valley, but also the sensation of being the first person to explore a place undisturbed in more than three thousand years.

On February 2, 1995, at ten in the morning, the archeologist Kent R. Weeks found himself a hundred feet inside a mountain in Egypt's Valley of the Kings, on his belly in the dust of a tomb. He was crawling toward a long-buried doorway that no one had entered for at least 3,100 years. There were two people with him, a graduate student and an Egyptian workman; among them they had one flashlight.

To get through the doorway, Weeks had to remove his hard hat and force his large frame under the lintel with his toes and fingers. He expected to enter a small, plain room marking the end of the tomb. Instead, he found himself in a vast corridor, half full of debris, with doorways lining either side and marching off into the darkness. "When I looked around with the flashlight," Weeks recalled later, "we realized that the corridor was tremendous. I didn't know *what* to think." The air was dead, with a temperature in excess of a hundred degrees and a humidity of 100 percent. Weeks, whose glasses had immediately steamed up, was finding it hard to breathe. With every movement, clouds of powder arose, and turned into mud on the skin.

The three people explored the corridor, stooping, and sometimes crawling over piles of rock that had fallen from the ceiling. Weeks counted twenty doorways lining the hundred-foot hallway, some opening into whole suites of rooms with vaulted ceilings carved out of the solid rock of the mountain. At the corridor's end, the feeble flashlight beam revealed a statue of Osiris, the god of resurrection: he was wearing a crown and holding crossed flails and sceptres; his body was bound like that of a mummy. In front of Osiris, the corridor came to a T, branching into two transverse passageways, each of them eighty feet long and ending in what looked like a descending staircase blocked with debris. Weeks counted thirty-two additional rooms off those two corridors.

The tomb was of an entirely new type, never seen by archaeologists before. "The architecture didn't fit any known pattern," Weeks told me. "And it was so *big*. I just couldn't make sense of it." The largest pharaonic tombs in the valley contain ten or fifteen rooms at most. This one had at least sixty-seven—the total making it not only the biggest tomb in the valley but possibly the biggest in all Egypt. Most tombs in the Valley of the Kings follow a standard architectural plan—a series of consecutive chambers and corridors like a string of boxcars shot at an angle into the bedrock, and ending with the burial vault. This tomb, with its T shape, had a warren of side chambers, suites, and descending passageways. Weeks knew from earlier excavations that the tomb was the resting place for at least four sons of Ramesses II, the pharaoh also known as Ramesses the Great—and, traditionally, as simply Pharaoh in the Book of Exodus. Because of the tomb's size and complexity, Weeks had to consider the possibility that it was a catacomb for as many as fifty of Ramesses' fifty-two sons—the first example of a royal family mausoleum in ancient Egypt.

Weeks had discovered the tomb's entrance eight years earlier, after the Egyptian government announced plans to widen the entrance to the valley to create a bus turnaround at the end of an asphalt road. From reading old maps and reports, he had recalled that the entrance to a lost tomb lay in the area that was to be paved over. Napoleon's expedition to Egypt had noted a tomb there, and a rather feckless Englishman named James Burton had crawled partway inside it in 1825. A few years later, the archeologist Sir John Gardner Wilkinson had given it the designation KV5, for Kings' Valley Tomb No. 5, when he numbered eighteen tombs there. Howard Carter—the archaeologist who discovered King Tutankhamun's tomb in 1922, two hundred feet farther on—dug two feet in, decided that KV5's entrance looked unimportant, and used it as a dumping ground for debris from his other excavations, thus burying it under ten feet of stone and dirt. The location of the tomb's entrance was quickly forgotten.

It took about ten days of channelling through Carter's heaps of debris for Weeks and his men to find the ancient doorway of KV5, and it proved to be directly across the path from the tomb of Ramesses the Great. The entrance lay at the edge of the asphalt road, about ten feet below grade and behind the rickety booths of T-shirt venders and fake-scarab-beetle sellers.

Plans for the bus turnaround were cancelled, and, over a period of seven years, Weeks and his workmen cleared half of the first two chambers and briefly explored a third one. The tomb was packed from floor to ceiling with dirt and rocks that had been washed in by flash floods. He uncovered finely carved reliefs on the walls, which showed Ramesses presenting various sons to the gods, with their names and titles recorded in hieroglyphics. When he reached floor level, he found thousands of objects: pieces of faience jewelry, fragments of furniture, a wooden fist from a coffin, human and animal bones, mummified body parts, chunks of sarcophagi, and fragments of the canopic jars used to hold the mummified organs of the deceased—all detritus left by ancient tomb robbers.

The third chamber was anything but modest. It was about sixty feet square, one of the largest rooms in the valley, and was supported by sixteen massive stone pillars arranged in four rows. Debris filled the room to within about two feet of the ceiling, allowing just enough space for Weeks to wriggle around. At the back of the chamber, in the axis of the tomb, Weeks noticed an almost buried doorway. Still believing that the tomb was like others in the valley, he assumed that the doorway merely led to a small, dead-end annex, so he didn't bother with it for several years—not until last February, when he decided to have a look.

Immediately after the discovery, Weeks went back to a four-dollar-a-night pension he shared with his wife, Susan, in the mud village of Gezira Bairat, showered off the tomb dust, and took a motorboat across the Nile to the small city of Luxor. He faxed a short message to Cairo, three hundred miles downriver. It was directed to his major financial supporter, Bruce Ludwig, who was attending a board meeting at the American University in Cairo, where Weeks is a professor. It read, simply, "Have made wonderful discovery in Valley of the Kings. Await your arrival." Ludwig instantly recognized the significance of the fax and the inside joke it represented: it was a close paraphrase of the telegram that Howard Carter had sent to the Earl of Carnarvon, his financial supporter, when he discovered Tutankhamun's tomb. Ludwig booked a flight to Luxor.

"That night, the enormousness of the discovery began to sink in," Weeks recalled. At about two o'clock in the morning, he turned to his wife and said, "Susan, I think our lives have changed forever."

The discovery was announced jointly by Egypt's Supreme Council of Antiquities, which oversees all archeological work in the country, and the American University in Cairo, under whose aegis Weeks was working. It became the biggest archeological story of the decade, making the front page of the *Times* and the cover of *Time*. Television reporters descended on the site. Weeks had to shut down the tomb to make the talk-show circuit. The London newspapers had a field day: the *Daily Mail* headlined its story "PHARAOH'S 50 SONS IN MUMMY OF ALL TOMBS," and one tabloid informed its readers that texts in the tomb gave a date for the Second Coming and the end of the world, and also revealed cures for AIDS and cancer.

The media also wondered whether the tomb would prove that Ramesses II was indeed the pharaoh referred to in Exodus. The speculation centered on Amun-her-khopshef, Ramesses' firstborn son, whose name is prominent on KV5's walls. According to the Bible, in order to force Egypt to free the Hebrews from bondage, the Lord visited a number of disasters on the land, including the killing of all firstborn Egyptians from the pharaoh's son on down. Some scholars believe that if Amun-her-khopshef's remains are found it may be possible to show at what age and how he died. . . .

———

The Valley of the Kings was the burial ground for the pharaohs of the New Kingdom, the last glorious period of Egyptian history. It began around 1550 B.C., when the Egyptians expelled the foreign Hyksos rulers from Lower Egypt and reestablished a vast empire, stretching across the Middle East to Syria. It lasted half a millennium. Sixty years before Ramesses, the pharaoh Akhenaten overthrew much of the Egyptian religion and decreed that thenceforth Egyptians should worship only one god—Light, whose visible symbol was Aten, the disk of the sun. Akhenaten's revolution came to a halt at his death. Ramesses represented the culmination of the return to tradition. He was an exceedingly conservative man, who saw himself as the guardian of the ancient customs, and he was particularly zealous in erasing the heretic pharaoh's name from his temples and stelae, a task begun by his father, Seti I. Because Ramesses disliked innovation, his monuments were notable not for their architectural brilliance but for their monstrous size. The New Kingdom began a slow decline following his rule, and finally sputtered to an end with Ramesses XI, the last pharaoh buried in the Valley of the Kings.

The discovery of KV5 will eventually open for us a marvellous window on this period. We know almost nothing about the offspring of the New Kingdom pharaohs or what roles they played. After each eldest prince ascended the throne, the younger sons disappeared so abruptly from the record that it was once thought they were routinely executed. The burial chambers' hieroglyphics, if they still survive, may give us an invaluable account of each son's life and accomplishments. There is a remote possibility—it was suggested to me by the secretary-general of the Supreme Council of Antiquities, Professor Abdel-Halim Nur el-Din, who is an authority on women in ancient Egypt—that Ramesses' daughters might be buried in KV5 as well. (Weeks thinks the possibility highly unlikely.) Before Weeks is done, he will probably find sarcophagi, pieces of funerary offerings, identifiable pieces of mummies, and many items with hieroglyphics on them. The tomb will add a new chapter to our understanding of Egyptian funerary traditions. And there is always a possibility of finding an intact chamber packed with treasure.

Ramesses the Great's reign lasted an unprecedented sixty-seven years, from 1279 to 1213 B.C. He covered the Nile Valley from Nubia to the delta with magnificent temples, statuary, and stelae, which are some of the grandest monuments the world has ever seen. Among his projects were the enormous forecourt at Luxor Temple; the Ramesseum; the cliffside temples of Abu Simbel; the great Hall of Columns at Karnak; and the city of Pi-Ramesse. The two "vast and trunkless legs of stone" with a "shattered visage" in Shelley's poem "Ozymandias" were those of Ramesses—fragments of the largest statue in pharaonic history. Ramesses outlived twelve of his heirs, dying in his early nineties. The thirteenth crown prince, Merneptah, became pharaoh only in his sixties.

By the time Ramesses ascended the throne, at twenty-five, he had fathered perhaps ten sons and as many daughters. His father had started him out with a harem while he was still a teenager, and he had two principal wives, Nefertari and Istnofret. He later added several Hittite princesses to his harem, and probably his sister and two daughters. It is still debated whether the incestuous marriages of the pharaohs were merely ceremonial or actually consummated. If identifiable remains of Ramesses' sons are found in KV5, it is conceivable that DNA testing might resolve this vexing question. . . .

The design of royal tombs was so fixed by tradition that they had no architect, at least as we use that term today. The tombs were laid out and chiselled from ceiling to floor, resulting in ceiling dimensions that are precise and floor dimensions that can vary considerably. All the rooms and corridors in a typical royal tomb had names, many of which we still do not fully understand: the First God's Passage, Hall of Hindering, Sanctuaries in Which the Gods Repose. The burial chamber was often called the House of Gold. Some tombs had a Hall of Truth, whose murals showed the pharaoh's heart being weighed in judgment by Osiris, with the loathsome god Ammut squatting nearby, waiting to devour it if it was found wanting. Many of the reliefs were so formulaic that they were probably taken from copybooks. Yet even within this rigid tradition breathtaking flights of creativity and artistic expression can be found.

Most of the tombs in the valley were never finished: they took decades to cut, and the plans usually called for something more elaborate than the pharaoh could achieve during his rule. As a result, the burial of the pharaoh was often a panicky, ad-hoc affair, with various rooms in the tomb being adapted for other purposes, and decorations and texts painted in haste or omitted completely. (Some of the most beautiful inscriptions were those painted swiftly; they have a spontaneity and freshness of line rivalling Japanese calligraphy.)

From the time of Ramesses II on, the tombs were not hidden: their great doorways, which were made of wood, could be opened. It is likely that the front rooms of many tombs were regularly visited by priests to make offerings. This may have been particularly true of KV5, where the many side chambers perhaps served such a purpose. The burial chambers containing treasure, however, were always sealed.

Despite all the monuments and inscriptions that Ramesses left us, it is still difficult to bridge the gap of 3,100 years and see Ramesses as a person. One thing we do know: the standard image of the pharaoh, embodied in Shelley's "frown, and wrinkled lip, and sneer of cold command," is a misconception. One of the finest works from Ramesses' reign is a statue of the young king now in the Museo Egizio, in Turin. The expression on his face is at once compassionate and otherworldly, not unlike that of a Giotto Madonna; his head is slightly bowed, as if to acknowledge his role as both leader and servant. This is not the face of a tyrant-pharaoh who press-ganged his people into building monuments to his greater glory. Rather, it is the portrait of a ruler who had his subjects' interests at heart, and this is precisely what the archeological and historical records suggest about Ramesses. Most of the Egyptians who labored on the pharaoh's monuments did so proudly and were, by and large, well compensated. There is a lovely stela on which Ramesses boasts about how much he has given his workers, "so that they work for me with their full hearts." Dorothea Arnold, the head curator of the Egyptian Department at the Metropolitan Museum, told

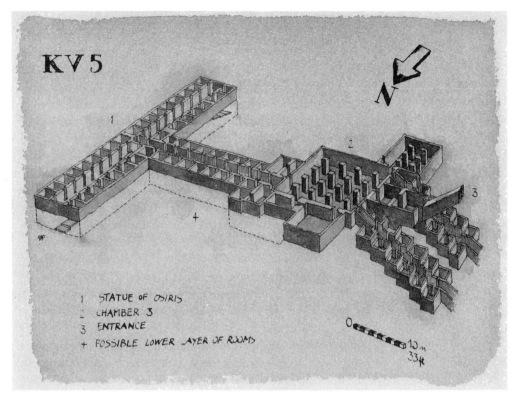

KV 5

1 STATUE OF OSIRIS
2 CHAMBER 3
3 ENTRANCE
4 POSSIBLE LOWER LAYER OF ROOMS

0 _____ 10 m
33 ft

Plan of tomb KV5, Valley of the Kings, Egypt.

me, "The pharaoh was *believed* in. As to whether he was beloved, that is beside the point: he was *necessary*. He was life itself. He represented everything good. Without him there would be nothing."

Final proof of the essential humanity of the pharaonic system is that it survived for more than three thousand years. (When Ramesses ascended the throne, the pyramids at Giza were already thirteen hundred years old.) Egypt produced one of the most stable cultural and religious traditions the world has ever seen.

Very little lives in the Valley of the Kings now. It is a wilderness of stone and light—a silent, roofless sepulchre. Rainfall averages a quarter inch per year, and one of the hottest natural air temperatures on earth was recorded in the surrounding mountains. And yet the valley is a surprisingly intimate place. Most of the tombs lie within a mere forty acres, and the screen of cliffs gives the area a feeling of privacy. Dusty paths and sun-bleached, misspelled signs add a pleasant, ramshackle air.

The valley lies on the outskirts of the ancient city of Thebes, now in ruins. In a six-mile stretch of riverbank around the city, there are as many temples, palaces, and monuments as anywhere else on earth, and the hills are so pock-marked with the yawning pits and doorways of ancient tombs that they resemble a First World War battlefield. . . .

Most of the archeology done in the valley has been indistinguishable from looting. Until the 1960s, those who had concessions to excavate there were allowed to keep a percentage of the spoils as "payment" for their work. In the fever of the treasure hunt, tombs were emptied without anyone bothering to photograph the objects found or to record their positions in situ, or even to note which tomb they came from. Items that had no market value were trashed. Wilkinson, the man who gave the tombs their numbers, burned three-thousand-year-old wooden coffins and artifacts to heat his house. Murals and reliefs were chopped out of walls. At dinner parties, the American lawyer Theodore M. Davis, who financed many digs in the valley, used to tear up necklaces woven of ancient flowers and fabric to show how strong they were after three thousand years in a tomb. Pyramids were blasted open with explosives, and one tomb door was bashed in with a battering ram. Even Carter never published a proper scientific report on Tut's tomb. It is only in the last twenty-five years that real archeology has come to Egypt, and KV5 will be one of the first tombs in the Valley of the Kings to be entirely excavated and documented according to proper archeological techniques. . . .

Work at KV5 in the fall season proceeds from six-thirty in the morning until one-thirty in the afternoon. . . .

On the first day of my visit, I find Kent Weeks sitting in a green canvas tent at the entrance to KV5 and trying to fit together pieces of a human skull. . . .

Relaxing in the tent, Weeks does not cut the dapper, pugnacious figure of a Howard Carter, nor does he resemble the sickly, elegant Lord Carnarvon in waistcoat and watch chain. But because he is the first person to have made a major discovery in the Valley of the Kings since Carter, he is surely in their class. At fifty-four, he is handsome and fit, his ruddy face peering at the world through thick square glasses from underneath a Tilley hat. His once crisp shirt and khakis look like hell after an hour in the tomb's stifling atmosphere, and his Timberland shoes have reached a state of indescribable lividity from tomb dust. . . .

At 9:00 A.M., the workmen laboring in KV5—there are forty-two of them—begin to file out and perch in groups on the hillside, to eat a breakfast of bread, tomatoes, green onions, and a foul cheese called *misht*. Weeks rises from his chair, nods to me, and asks, "Are you ready?"

We descend a new wooden staircase into the mountain and enter Chamber 1, where we exchange our sun hats for hard hats. The room is small and only half cleared. Visible tendrils of humid, dusty air waft in from the dim recesses of the tomb. The first impression I have of the tomb is one of shocking devastation. The ceilings are shot through with cracks, and in places they have caved in, dropping automobile-size pieces of rock. A forest of screw jacks and timbers holds up what is left, and many of the cracks are plastered with "telltales"—small seals that show if any more movement of the rock occurs.

The reliefs in Chamber 1 are barely visible, a mere palimpsest of what were once superbly carved and painted scenes of Ramesses and his sons adoring the gods, and panels of hieroglyphics. Most of the damage here was the result of a leaky sewer pipe that was laid over the tomb about forty years ago from an old rest house in the valley. The leak caused salt crystals to grow and eat away the limestone walls. Here and there, however, one can still see traces of the original paint.

The decorations on the walls of the first two rooms show various sons being presented to the gods by Ramesses, in the classic Egyptian pose: head in profile, shoulders in frontal view, and torso in three-quarters view. There are also reliefs of tables laden with offerings of food for the gods, and hieroglyphic texts spelling out the names and titles of several sons and including the royal cartouche of Ramesses.

A doorway from Chamber 2 opens into Chamber 3—the Pillared Hall. It is filled with dirt and rock almost to the ceiling, giving one a simultaneous impression of grandeur and claustrophobia. Two narrow channels have been cut through the debris to allow for the passage of the workmen. Many of the pillars are split and shattered, and only fragments of decorations remain—a few hieroglyphic characters, an upraised arm, part of a leg. Crazed light from several randomly placed bulbs throws shadows around the room.

I follow Weeks down one of the channels. "This room is in such dangerous condition that we decided not to clear it," he says. "We call this channel the Mubarak trench. It was dug so that President Mubarak could visit the tomb without having to creep around on his hands and knees." He laughs.

When we are halfway across the room, he points out the words "James Burton 1825" smoked on the ceiling with the flame of a candle: it represents the Englishman's farthest point of penetration. Not far away is another graffito—this one in hieratic, the cursive form of hieroglyphic writing. It reads "Year 19"—the nineteenth year of Ramesses' reign. "This date gives us a *terminus ante quem* for the presence of Ramesses' workmen in this chamber," Weeks says.

He stops at one of the massive pillars. "And here's a mystery," he says, "Fifteen of the pillars in this room were cut from the native rock, but this one is a fake. The rock was carefully cut away—you can see chisel marks on the ceiling—and then the pillar was rebuilt out of stone and plastered to look like the others. Why?" He gives the pillar a sly pat. "Was something very large moved in here?"

I follow Weeks to the end of the trench—the site of the doorway that he crawled through in February. The door has been cleared, and we descend a short wooden staircase to the bottom of the great central corridor. It is illuminated by a string of naked light bulbs, which cast a yellow glow through a pall of dust. The many doors lining both sides of the corridor are still blocked with debris, and the stone floor is covered with an inch of dust.

At the far end of the corridor, a hundred feet away, stands the mummiform statue of Osiris. It is carved from the native rock, and only its face is missing. Lit from below, the statue casts a dramatic shadow on the ceiling. I try to take notes, but my glasses have fogged up, and sweat is dripping onto my notebook, making the ink run off the page. I can only stand and blink.

Nothing in twenty years of writing about archeology has prepared me for this great wrecked corridor chiselled out of the living rock, with rows of shattered doorways opening into darkness, and ending in the faceless mummy of Osiris. I feel like a trespasser, a voyeur, gazing into the sacred precincts of the dead. As I stare at the walls, patterns and lines begin to emerge from the shattered stone: ghostly figures and faint hieroglyphics; animal-headed gods performing mysterious rites. Through doorways I catch glimpses of more rooms and more doorways beyond. There is a presence of death in this wrecked tomb that goes beyond those who were buried here; it is the death of a civilization.

With most of the texts on the walls destroyed or still buried under debris, it is not yet possible to determine what function was served by the dozens of side chambers. Weeks feels it likely, however, that they were *not* burial chambers, because the doorways are too narrow to admit a sarcophagus. Instead, he speculates they were chapels where the Theban priests could make offerings to the dead sons. Because the tomb departs so radically from the standard design, it is impossible even to speculate what the mysterious Pillared Hall or many of the other antechambers were for.

Weeks proudly displays some reliefs on the walls, tracing with his hand the figure of Isis and her husband, Osiris, and pointing out the ibis-headed god Thoth. "Ah!" he cries. "And here is a *wonderful* figure of Anubis and Hathor!" Anubis is the jackal-headed god of mummification, and Hathor a goddess associated with the Theban Necropolis. These were scenes to help guide Ramesses' sons through the rituals, spells, and incantations that would insure them a safe journey through the realm of death. The reliefs are exceedingly difficult to see; Susan Weeks told me later that she has sometimes had to stare at a wall for long periods—days, even—before she could pick out the shadow of a design. She is now in the process of copying these fragmentary reliefs on Mylar film, to help experts who will attempt to reconstruct the entire wall sequence and its accompanying text, and so reveal to us the purpose of the room or the corridor. KV5 will only yield up its secrets slowly, and with great effort.

"Here's Ramesses and one of his sons," Weeks says, indicating two figures standing hand in hand. "But, alas, the name is gone. Very disappointing!" He charges off down the corridor, raising a trail of dust, and comes to a halt at the statue of Osiris, poking his glasses back up his sweating nose. "Look at this. Spectacular! A three-dimensional statue of Osiris is very rare. Most tombs depict him painted only. We dug around the base here trying to find the face, but instead we found a lovely offering of nineteen clay figs."

He makes a ninety-degree turn down the left transverse corridor, snaking around a cave-in. The corridor runs level for some distance and then plunges down a double staircase with a ramp in the middle, cut from the bedrock, and ends in a wall of bedrock. Along the sides of this corridor we have passed sixteen more partly blocked doors.

"Now, here is something new," Weeks says. "You're the first outsider to see this. I hoped that this staircase would lead to the burial chambers. This kind of ramp was usually built to slide the sarcophagi down. But look! The corridor just ends in a blank wall. Why in the world would they build a staircase and ramp going nowhere? So I decided to clear the two lowest side chambers. We just finished last week."

He ushers me into one of the rooms. There is no light; the room is large and very hot.

"They were empty," Weeks says.

"Too bad."

"Take a look at this floor."

"Nice." Floors do not particularly excite me.

"It happens to be the finest plastered floor in the Valley of the Kings. They went to enormous trouble with this floor, laying down three coats of plaster at different times, in different colors. Why?" He pauses. "Now stamp on the floor."

I thump the floor. There is a hollow reverberation that shakes not only the floor but the entire room. "Oh, my God, there's something underneath there!" I exclaim.

"*Maybe,*" Weeks says, a large smile gathering on his face. "Who knows? It could be a natural cavity or crack, or it might be a passageway to a lower level."

"You mean there might be sealed burial chambers below?"

Weeks smiles again. "Let's not get ahead of ourselves. Next June, we'll drill some test holes and do it properly."

We scramble back to the Osiris statue.

"Now I'm going to take you to our latest discovery," Weeks says. "This is intriguing. *Very* fascinating."

We make our way through several turns back to the Pillared Hall. Weeks leads me down the other trench, which ends at the southwest corner of the hall. Here, earlier in the month, the workmen discovered a buried doorway that opened onto a steep descending passageway, again packed solid with debris. The workmen have now cleared the passageway down some sixty feet, exposing twelve more side chambers, and are still at work.

We pause at the top of the newly excavated passageway. A dozen screw jacks with timbers hold up its cracked ceiling. The men have finished breakfast and are back at work, one man picking away at the wall of debris at the bottom of the passageway while another scoops the debris into a basket made out of old tires. A line of workmen then passes the basket up the corridor and out of the tomb.

"I've called this passageway 3A," Weeks says. He drops his voice. "The incredible thing is that this corridor is heading toward the tomb of Ramesses himself. If it connects, that will be extraordinary. No two tombs were ever deliberately connected. This tomb just gets curiouser and curiouser."

Ramesses' tomb, lying a hundred feet across the valley, was also wrecked by flooding and is now being excavated by a French team. "I would dearly love to surprise them," Weeks says. "To pop out one day and say *'Bonjour! C'est moi!'* I'd love to beat the French into their own tomb."

I follow him down the newly discovered corridor, slipping and sliding on the pitched floor. "Of course," he shouts over his shoulder, "the sons might also be buried *underneath* their father! We clearly haven't found the burial chambers yet, and it is my profound hope that one way or another this passageway will take us there."

We come to the end, where the workmen are picking away at the massive wall of dirt that blocks the passage. The forty-two men can remove about nine tons of dirt a day.

At the bottom, Weeks introduces me to a tall, handsome Egyptian with a black mustache and wearing a baseball cap on backward. "This is Muhammad Mahmud," Weeks says. "One of the senior workmen."

I shake his hand. "What do you hope to find down here?"

"Something very nice, *inshallah*."

"What's in these side rooms?" I ask Weeks. All the doorways are blocked with dirt.

Weeks shrugs. "We haven't been in those rooms yet."

"Would it be possible . . ." I start to ask.

He grins. "You mean, would you like to be the first human being in three thousand years to enter a chamber in an ancient Egyptian tomb? Maybe Saturday."

As we are leaving the tomb, I am struck by the amount of work still unfinished. Weeks has managed to dig out only three rooms completely and clear eight others partway—leaving more than eighty rooms entirely untouched. What treasures lie under five or ten feet of debris in those rooms is anyone's guess. It will take from six to ten more years to clear and stabilize the tomb, and then many more years to publish the findings from it. As we emerge from the darkness, Weeks says, "I know what I'll be doing for the rest of my life." . . .

Suddenly, Muhammad appears at the mouth of the tomb. "Please, Dr. Kent," he says, and starts telling Weeks in Arabic that the workers have uncovered something for him to see. Weeks motions for me to follow him into the dim interior. We put on our hard hats and duck through the first chambers into Corridor 3A. A beautiful set of carved limestone steps has appeared where I saw only rubble a few days before. Weeks kneels and brushes the dirt away, excited about the fine workmanship.

Muhammad and Weeks go to inspect another area of the tomb, where fragments of painted and carved plaster are being uncovered. I stay to watch the workmen digging in 3A. After a while, they forget I am there and begin singing, handing the baskets up the long corridor, their bare feet white with dust. A dark hole begins to appear between the top of the debris and the ceiling. It looks as if one could crawl inside and perhaps look farther down the corridor.

"May I take a look in there?" I ask.

One of the workmen hoists me up the wall of dirt, and I lie on my stomach and wriggle into the gap. I recall that archeologists sometimes sent small boys into tombs through holes just like this.

Unfortunately, I am not a small boy, and in my eagerness I find myself thoroughly wedged. It is pitch-black, and I wonder why I thought this would be exciting.

"Pull me out!" I yell.

The Egyptians heave on my legs, and I come sliding down with a shower of dirt. After the laughter subsides, a skinny man named Nubie crawls into the hole. In a moment, he is back out, feet first. He cannot see anything; they need to dig more.

The workmen redouble their efforts, laughing, joking, and singing. Working in KV5 is a coveted job in the surrounding villages; Weeks pays his workmen 400 Egyptian pounds a month (about $125), four times what a junior inspector of antiquities makes and perhaps three times the average monthly income of an Egyptian family. Weeks is well liked by his Egyptian workers, and is constantly bombarded with dinner invitations from even his poorest laborers. While I was there, I attended three of these dinners. The flow of food was limitless, and the conversation competed with the bellowing of a water buffalo in an adjacent room or the braying of a donkey tethered at the door.

After the hole has been widened a bit, Nubie goes up again with a light and comes back down. There is great disappointment: it looks as though the passageway might come to an end. Another step is exposed in the staircase, along with a great deal of broken pottery. Weeks returns and examines the hole himself, without comment.

As the week goes by, more of Corridor 3A is cleared, foot by foot. The staircase in 3A levels out to a finely made floor, more evidence that the corridor merely ends in a small chamber. On Wednesday, however, Weeks emerges from the tomb smiling. "Come," he says.

The hole in 3A has now been enlarged to about two feet in diameter. I scramble up the dirt and peer inside with a light, choking on the dust. As before, the chiselled ceiling comes to an abrupt end, but below it lies what looks like a shattered door lintel.

"It's got to be a door," Weeks says, excited. "I'm afraid we're going to have to halt for the season at that doorway. We'll break through next June."

Later, outdoors, I find myself coughing up flecks of mud.

"Tomb cough," Weeks says cheerfully. . . .

Saturday, the workers' taxi picks the Weekses and me up before sunrise and then winds through a number of small villages, collecting workers as it goes along.

The season is drawing to a close, and Susan and Kent Weeks are both subdued. In the last few weeks, the probable number of rooms in the tomb has increased from sixty-seven to ninety-two, with no end in sight. Everyone is frustrated at having to lock up the tomb now, leaving the doorway at the bottom of 3A sealed, the plaster floor unplumbed, the burial chambers still not found, and so many rooms unexcavated. . . .

As we drive alongside sugarcane fields, the sun boils up over the Nile Valley through a screen of palms, burning into the mists lying on the fields. We pass a man driving a donkey cart loaded with tires, and whizz by the Colossi of Memnon, two enormous wrecked statues standing alone in a farmer's field. The taxi begins the climb to a village once famous for tomb robbing, some of whose younger residents now work for Weeks. The houses are completely surrounded by the black pits of tombs. The fragrant smell of dung fires drifts through the rocky streets. . . .

When we arrive in the Valley of the Kings, an inspector unlocks the metal gate in front of the tomb, and the workers file in, with Weeks leading the way. I wait outside to watch the sunrise. The tourists have not yet arrived, and if you screen out some signs you can imagine the valley as it might have appeared when the pharaohs were buried here three thousand years ago. (The venders and rest house were moved last year.) As dawn strikes el-Qurn and invades the upper reaches of the canyon walls, a soft, peach-colored light fills the air. The encircling cliffs lock out the sounds of the world; the black doorways of the tombs are like dead eyes staring out; and one of the guard huts of the ancient priests can still be seen perched at the cliff edge. The whole valley becomes a slowly changing play of light and color, mountain and sky, unfolding in absolute stillness. I am given a brief, shivery insight into the sacredness of this landscape.

At seven, the tourists begin to arrive, and the spell is dispersed. The valley rumbles to life with the grinding of diesel engines, the frantic expostulations of venders, and the shouting of guides leading groups of tourists. KV5 is the first tomb in the valley, and the tourists begin gathering at the rope, pointing and taking pictures, while the guides impart the most preposterous misinformation about the tomb: that Ramesses had four hundred sons by only two wives, that there are eight hundred rooms in the tomb, that the greedy Americans are digging for gold but won't find any. Two thousand tourists a day stand outside the entrance to KV5.

I go inside and find Weeks in 3A, supervising the placement of more screw jacks and timbers. When he has finished, he turns to me. "You ready?" He points to the lowest room in 3A. "This looks like a good one for you to explore."

One of the workmen clears away a hole at the top of the blocked door for me to crawl through, and then Muhammad gives me a leg up. I shove a caged light bulb into the hole ahead of me and wriggle through. I can barely fit.

In a moment, I am inside. I sit up and look around, the light throwing my distorted shadow against the wall. There is three feet of space between the top of the debris and the ceiling, just enough for me to crawl around on my hands and knees. The room is about nine feet square, the walls finely chiselled from the bedrock. Coils of dust drift past the light. The air is just breathable.

I run my fingers along the ancient chisel marks, which are as fresh as if they were made yesterday, and I think of the workmen who carved out this room, three millennia ago. Their only source of light would have been the dim illumination from wicks burning in a bowl of oil salted to reduce smoke. There was no way to tell the passage of time in the tomb: the wicks were cut to last eight hours, and when they guttered it meant that the day's work was done. The tombs were carved from the ceiling downward, the workers whacking off flakes of limestone with flint choppers, and then finishing the walls and ceilings with copper chisels and sandstone abrasive. Crouching in the hot stone chamber, I suddenly get a powerful sense of the enormous religious faith of the Egyptians. Nothing less could have motivated an entire society to pound these tombs out of rock.

Much of the Egyptian religion remains a mystery to us. It is full of contradictions, inexplicable rituals, and impenetrable texts. Amid the complexity, one simple fact stands out: it was a great human bargain with death. Almost everything that ancient Egypt has left us—the pyramids, the tombs, the temples—represents an attempt to overcome that awful mystery at the center of all our lives.

A shout brings me back to my senses.

"Find anything?" Weeks calls out.

"The room's empty," I say. "There's nothing in here but dust."

CREDITS

Allegro, John: From *The Dead Sea Scrolls* by John Allegro. Penguin Books 1956, Second revised edition 1964, pp. 13–32. Copyright © 1956, 1964 by John Allegro. Reprinted by permission of Penguin Books Ltd.

Allesbrook, Mary and Hawes, Harriet Boyd: From *Born to Rebel: The Life of Harriet Boyd Hawes* by Mary Allesbrook. First published in 1992. Reprinted by permission of Oxbow Books (Oxford).

Alva, Walter, and Christopher Donnan: From *Royal Tombs of Sipán* by Walter Alva and Christopher B. Donnan. First published in 1993. Reprinted by permission of the UCLA Fowler Museum of Cultural History.

Andersson, J. Gunnar: From *Children of the Yellow Earth* by J. Gunnar Andersson, translated by E. Classen. First published in 1934. Reprinted by permission of the publisher, Routledge and Kegan Paul.

Bingham, Hiram: From *Lost City of the Incas* by Hiram Bingham. Copyright © 1948 by Hiram Bingham. Renewed copyright © 1976 by Alfred Bingham. Used by permission of Dutton Signet, a division of Penguin Books USA Inc.

Carter, Howard: From *The Tomb of Tut-ankh-Amen* by Howard Carter and A. C. Mace. First published in 3 vols. 1923–1933. Reprinted by permission of Rowman & Littlefield Publishers Inc.

Champollion, Jean François: From a letter by Jean François Champollion, translated by V. M. Conrad in *The World of Archaeology* by C. W. Ceram. Published by Thames & Hudson Ltd. in 1966. U.S. edition published by Alfred A. Knopf, Inc., as *Hands on the Past*. Copyright © 1966 by Thames & Hudson. Reprinted by permission of Thames & Hudson Ltd.

Chubb, Mary: From *Nefertiti Lived Here* by Mary Alford Chubb. Copyright © 1954, © 1955 by Mary Alford Chubb. Copyright renewed 1982, 1983 by Mary Alford Chubb. Reprinted by permission of HarperCollins Publishers, Inc., and the author.

Cotterell, Arthur: From *The First Emperor of China* (pp. 20–40) by Arthur Cotterell. Copyright © 1981 by Arthur Cotterell. Reprinted by permission of Henry Holt and Co., Inc., and Penguin Books Ltd.

Dart, Raymond Arthur: From *Adventures with the Missing Link* by Raymond Dart. Reprinted by permission of The Better Baby Press, The Institutes for the Achievement of Human Potential, 8801 Stenton Ave., Philadelphia, PA 19118.

Daugherty, Richard and Ruth Kirk: From *Hunters of the Whale* by Ruth Kirk. Text copyright © 1974 by Ruth Kirk and Richard D. Daugherty. Reprinted by permission of William Morrow & Company, Inc.

Dekin, Albert: "Tragedy at Utqiagvik, Alaska" by Albert Dekin was specially commissioned for this anthology. Copyright © 1996 by Albert Dekin. All rights reserved.

Evans, John: From the diary of John Evans published in *Time and Chance: The Story of Arthur Evans and His Forebears* by Joan Evans. Published by Longmans, Green & Co. in 1943. Reprinted by permission of Theodore Schuller.

Fagan, Brian: From *Quest for the Past* by Brian M. Fagan. Reprinted from the first edition, 1988, by permission of the publisher, Waveland Press, Inc.

Glob, Peter: From *The Bog People* by P. V. Glob. Reprinted by permission of the publisher, Faber & Faber Ltd.

Green, Charles: From *Sutton Hoo: The Excavations of a Royal Ship Burial* by Charles Green. Copyright © 1963 by Charles Green. Reprinted by permission of Barnes & Noble Books and Merlin Press, London.

Harrington, Spencer: "Bones and Bureaucrats" by Spencer P. M. Harrington first appeared in *Archaeology* 46:2.30–38. Copyright © 1992 by the Archaeological Institute of America. Reprinted by permission of *Archaeology* Magazine.

Higham, Charles: "The Princess of Khoh Phanom Di" by Charles Higham was specially commissioned for this anthology. Copyright © 1966 by Charles Higham. All rights reserved.

Nöel Hume, Ivor: From *Martin's Hundred* by Ivor Nöel Hume. Copyright © 1979, 1981, 1982 by Ivor Nöel Hume. Reprinted by permission of Alfred A. Knopf, Inc., and Curtis Brown Ltd.

Johanson, Donald: From *Lucy, the Beginnings of Humankind* by Donald Johanson and Maitland Edey. Copyright © 1981 by Donald Johanson and Maitland Edey. Reprinted by permission of Simon & Schuster, Inc., and Sterling Lord Literistic, Inc.

Jones, Rhys: From "The Extreme Climatic Place" by Rhys Jones from *Hemisphere*, July/August 1981 issue. Reprinted by permission of the author.

Kenyon, Kathleen: From *Digging Up Jericho: The Results of the Jericho Excavations 1952–1956* by Kathleen Kenyon. Published in 1957 by Frederick A. Praeger, Inc. Reprinted with the permission of Greenwood Publishing Group, Inc., Westport, CT, and Jeremy Ritchie for the Estate of Dame Kathleen Kenyon.

Leakey, Mary: From *Disclosing the Past* by Mary Leakey. Published in the U.S. by Doubleday and in Great Britain by Rainbird, 1984 (pp. 122–129). Copyright © 1984 by Sherma B. V. Reprinted by permission of Doubleday, a division of Bantam Doubleday Dell Publishing Group, Inc., and Penguin Books Ltd.

Matos Moctezuma, Eduardo: From *The Great Temple of the Aztecs: Treasures of Tenochtitlan* by Eduardo Matos Moctezuma. Published by Thames & Hudson Ltd. in 1988. Reprinted by permission of the publisher.

Mauch, Carl: From *The Journals of Carl Mauch*, edited by E. E. Burke. Mauch journals copyright by Linden Museum, Stuttgart. Translation copyright © 1969 by the National Archives of Zimbabwe. Reprinted by permission of the Director of the National Archives of Zimbabwe.

Preston, Douglas: From "All the King's Sons" by Douglas Preston. First appeared in *The New Yorker*, January 22, 1996, issue. Copyright © 1966 by Douglas Preston. Reprinted by permission of the author.

Pulak, Cemal, and Donald A. Frey: "The Search for a Bronze Age Shipwreck" by Cemal Pulak and Donald A. Frey first appeared in *Archaeology* Magazine, Vol. 38, No. 4. Copyright © 1985 by the Archaeological Institute of America.

Rudenko, Sergei: From *The Horsemen of Pazyryk* by Sergei I. Rudenko, translated by M. W. Thompson. Reprinted by permission of the publisher, J. M. Dent & Sons Ltd.

Ruz, Alberto: "An Astonishing Discovery" by Alberto Ruz from *The Illustrated London News*, August 29, 1953. Reprinted by permission of The Illustrated London News Picture Library.

Schrire, Carmel: From *Digging Through Darkness: Chronicles of an Archaeologist* by Carmel Schrire. Published by the University Press of Virginia in 1995. Reprinted by permission of the publisher.

Soren, David and Jamie James: From *Kourion: The Search for a Lost Roman City* by David Soren and Jamie James. Copyright © 1988 by David Soren and Jamie James. Used by permission of Doubleday, a division of Bantam Doubleday Dell Publishing Group, Inc., and the authors.

Spindler, Konrad: From *The Man in the Ice* by Konrad Spindler, translated by Ewald Osers. First published in 1994. Reprinted by permission of the publisher, Weidenfeld & Nicolson.

Struever, Stuart: From *Koster: Americans in Search of Their Prehistoric Past* by Stuart Struever and Felicia Antonelli Holton. Copyright © 1979 by Dr. Stuart Struever and Felicia Antonelli Holton. Used by permission of Doubleday, a division of Bantam Doubleday Dell Publishing Group, Inc.

Wheat, Joe Ben: "The Olsen–Chubbuck Site: A Paleo-Indian Bison Kill" by Joe Ben Wheat first appeared in the *Memoirs of the Society for American Archaeology*, Memoir No. 26, 1972. Reproduced by permission of the Society for American Archaeology and the author.

Wheeler, R. E. Mortimer: From *Maiden Castle, Dorset* by Sir Robert Eric Mortimer Wheeler. First published in 1943. Reprinted by permission of the Society of Antiquaries of London.

Winlock, Herbert Eustice: From *Excavations at Deir el Bahri, 1911–1931* by H. E. Winlock. First published in 1942. Reprinted by permission of William Winlock Lannon, James D. Lannon, and Patricia Janeway Lannon Brown.

Woolley, Leonard: From *Dead Towns and Living Men: Being Pages from an Antiquary's Notebook* by Leonard Woolley. Reprinted by permission of James Clarke & Co., Ltd.

Woolley, Leonard: From *Ur of the Chaldees* by Leonard Woolley. The 1982 edition is published by The Herbert Press ℅ A&C Black. Reprinted by permission of A&C Black (Publishers) Limited.

PICTURE CREDITS

Robert Aberman/Barbara Heller/Art Resource, NY: 254; The Estate of the late John Allegro: 156; Negative #335651, Courtesy Department of Library Services, American Museum of Natural History: 34; Ashmolean Museum, Oxford: 193; Bill Ballenberg, © National Geographic Society: color insert (iv, top); Bettmann: 390; Hiram Bingham Yale Peabody Museum/Courtesy National Geographic Society: 371; Boltin Picture Library: color insert (iii, top); Bridgeman/Art Resource, NY: 84; British Museum: 135, 174, 221, 410; Cape Archives, Photo #M143: 264; D. Baston photo provided courtesy of the Center for American Archeology, Kampsville, Illinois: 432; Mary Chubb: 415; The Cleveland Museum of Natural History: 57; Martha Cooper/Peter Arnold, Inc.: color insert (i); Courtesy, Prof. Albert A. Dekin, Jr.: 319; J. M. Dent & Sons Ltd.: 226, 227; Deutsches Archäologisches Institut Athen: 182; The Dorset Natural History and Archaeological Society: 422; Frey/Institute of Nautical Archaeology: 442, color insert (viii); The Griffith Institute Ashmolean Museum, Oxford: 111; Courtesy, Charles Higham: 284; The Hulton Getty Picture Collection Limited: 102, 194; The Illustrated London News

(continued on page 494)

BIBLIOGRAPHY

Readers who are interested in exploring the world of archaeology in more detail will find the following sources useful.

GENERAL ARCHAEOLOGY

Ceram, C. W. *Gods, Graves, and Scholars: The Story of Archaeology.* New York: Alfred Knopf, 1952.
> A classic account of early archaeological discovery for the general reader.

Fagan, Brian M. *The Adventure of Archaeology*, rev. ed. Washington, DC: National Geographic Society, 1989.
> A lavishly illustrated account of the history of archaeology as a science.

Fagan Brian M., ed. *The Oxford Companion to Archaeology.* New York: Oxford University Press, 1996.
> All you ever wanted to know about archaeology and more. A key reference book.

EARLY HUMAN ORIGINS

Johanson, Donald C. and Maitland Armstrong Edey. *Lucy: The Beginnings of Humankind.* New York: Simon and Schuster, 1981.
> A vivid account of the discovery of Lucy in the Hadar.

Johanson, Donald C., et al. *Ancestors: In Search of Human Origins.* New York: Villard Books, 1994.
> A popular book written to accompany a television series that treats paleoanthropology.

Lewin, Roger. *Bones of Contention: Controversies in the Search for Human Origins.* New York: Simon and Schuster, 1987.
> The best source on the complex history of research into human origins.

Stanley, Steven M. *Children of the Ice Age: How a Global Catastrophe Allowed Humans to Evolve.* New York: Harmony Books, 1996.
> A fascinating book on "punctuation theories" of human evolution. Provocative and closely argued.

STONE AGE ARCHAEOLOGY

Fagan, Brian M. *People of the Earth: An Introduction to World Prehistory*, 8th ed. New York: Longman/Pearson, 1995.
> A widely used college textbook that summarizes major developments in human prehistory.

Gamble, Clive. *Timewalkers: The Prehistory of Global Colonization*. Cambridge, MA: Harvard University Press, 1993.
> Gamble argues for early human migrations throughout prehistory. Idiosyncratic but comprehensive.

Mithen, Steven. *Prehistory of the Mind*. London: Thames and Hudson, 1996.
> Mithen's brilliant synthesis of archaeology and other disciplines results in a stimulating history of the development of our minds, and thus ourselves.

Smith, Bruce D. *The Emergence of Agriculture*. New York: Scientific American Library, 1995.
> An up-to-date essay on the beginnings of farming, which uses sophisticated radiocarbon dating methods to date early cereal and root crops. For the general reader.

Wenke, Robert J. *Patterns in Prehistory: Humankind's First Three Million Years*, 2nd ed. New York: Oxford University Press. 1984.
> Wenke's account of human prehistory has a strong evolutionary background.

THE EARLY CIVILIZATIONS

The Time/Life Books series *Lost Civilizations* offers the best and most up-to-date summaries of the first civilizations. In addition, see the following:

Fagan, Brian M. and Chris Scarre. *Ancient Civilizations*. New York: HarperCollins, 1996.
> A summary account of the world's earliest civilizations up to Greece and Rome, together with some theoretical background. For students and general readers.

Robinson, Andrew. *The Story of Writing*. London: Thames and Hudson, 1995.
> The best and most comprehensive beginner's guide to writing yet compiled. A fascinating introduction to the esoteric world of ancient scripts.

MESOPOTAMIA

Lloyd, Seton. *The Archaeology of Mesopotamia: From the Old Stone Age to the Persian Conquest*, rev. ed. London: Thames and Hudson, 1984.
> A conservative but thorough summary of early Mesopotamian archaeology. Fairly technical.

Maisels, Charles Keith. *The Near East: Archaeology in the "Cradle of Civilization."* London: Routledge, 1992.
> Thoroughly up-to-date and sophisticated summary.

EGYPT

Aldred, Cyril. *The Egyptians*, rev. ed. London: Thames and Hudson, 1984.
> Still the best basic account of Egyptian civilization for the general reader.

Clayton, Peter A. *Chronicle of the Pharaohs: The Reign-by-Reign Record of the Rulers and Dynasties of Ancient Egypt*. London: Thames and Hudson, 1994.
> A reign-by-reign recounting of Egyptian kings. A superb reference book.

Kemp, Barry J. *Ancient Egypt: Anatomy of a Civilization*. London: Routledge, 1989.
> A brilliant analytical summary of Egyptian civilization that stresses kingship, ideology, and bureaucracy. Magnificent drawings.

Reeves, C. N. _The Complete Tutankhamun: The King, the Tomb, the Royal Treasure_. London: Thames and Hudson, 1990.
  Exactly what the title suggests—the ultimate sourcebook on the subject.

LATER MEDITERRANEAN CIVILIZATIONS

An enormous literature, but the following are of general interest:

Harris, Roberta. _The World of the Bible_. New York: Thames and Hudson, 1995.
  An essential summary of biblical archaeology for general readers.

Mazar, Amihay. _Archaeology of the Land of the Bible, 10,000–586 B.C.E._ New York: Doubleday, 1990.
  The best one-volume account of the subject.

Scarre, Chris. _Chronicle of the Roman Emperors: The Reign-by-Reign Record of the Rulers of Imperial Rome_. London: Thames and Hudson, 1995.
  A reign-based guide to Roman civilization. A wonderful starting point.

AFRICA

Connah, Graham. _African Civilizations: Precolonial Cities and States in Tropical Africa: An Archaeological Perspective_. New York: Cambridge University Press, 1987.
  Comprehensive descriptions of early African civilizations from a multidisciplinary perspective. Strongly recommended for interested laypeople.

Oliver, Roland. _The African Experience_. London: Weidenfeld and Nicholson, 1991.
  A survey of African history based on a lifetime of teaching and research. A good starting point for delving into African archaeology.

Phillipson, David W. _African Archaeology_, 2nd ed. New York: Cambridge University Press, 1993.
  Phillipson summarizes the basic cultural history of sub-Saharan Africa. Aimed at more specialist readers.

ASIA

Barnes, Gina Lee. _China, Korea, and Japan: The Rise of Civilization in East Asia_. London: Thames and Hudson, 1993.
  Definitive, if sometimes technical, summary of the rise of civilization in these three areas.

Chang, K-C. _The Archaeology of Ancient China_, 4th ed. New Haven: CT: Yale University Press, 1986.
  Somewhat outdated but a very useful synthesis.

PACIFIC

Bellwood, Peter. _The Polynesians: Prehistory of an Island People_, rev. ed. London: Thames and Hudson, 1987.
  General account of Polynesian archaeology and history.

Finney, Ben, et al. *Voyage of Rediscovery: A Cultural Odyssey Through Polynesia*. Berkeley: University of California Press, 1994.
　　A fascinating account of early Polynesian history and archaeology, which recounts experiments with replicas of Pacific watercraft. Excellent bibliography.

Frankel, David. *Remains to Be Seen*. Melbourne: Longman Cheshire, 1991.
　　An introduction to Australian archaeology; a good starting point.

NORTH AMERICA

Fagan, Brian M. *Ancient North America*, 2nd ed. London: Thames and Hudson, 1995.
　　A comprehensive synthesis of North American archaeology from first settlement to historic times. Lavishly illustrated.

Fiedel, Stuart J. *Prehistory of the Americas*, 2nd ed. New York: Cambridge University Press, 1992.
　　Summarizes the prehistoric archaeology of the entire Americas. Strong on North America.

Jennings, Jesse D. *Prehistory of North America*, 3rd ed. Mountain View, CA: Mayfield, 1989.
　　A textbook with a strong cultural history emphasis. Good on basic chronology and cultural evolution.

MAYA CIVILIZATION

Coe, Michael. *The Maya*, 5th ed. New York: Thames and Hudson, 1993.
　　The most widely read summary of Maya civilization. Authoritative, up-to-date, and constantly revised.

Sabloff, Jeremey A. *The New Archaeology and the Ancient Maya*. New York: Scientific American Library, 1990.
　　Another excellent synthesis of the subject.

Schele, Linda, and David A. Freidel. *A Forest of Kings: The Untold Story of the Ancient Maya*. New York: William Morrow, 1990.

————. *Maya Cosmos: Three Thousand Years on the Shaman's Path*. New York: William Morrow, 1993.
　　Two extraordinary books that bring together archaeology and recently deciphered Maya glyphs in a controversial but thoroughly stimulating synthesis. For both specialist and popular audiences.

ANDEAN CIVILIZATION

Alva, Walter, and Christopher B. Donnan. *Royal Tombs of Sipán*. Los Angeles: Fowler Museum of Cultural History, 1993.
　　A description of the Moche warrior-priests and their sepulchers. Lavish illustrations.

Moseley, Michael E. *The Inca and Their Ancestors: The Archaeology of Peru*. London: Thames and Hudson, 1992.
　　The most widely consulted account of the subject.

Deetz, James. *In Small Things Forgotten: The Archaeology of Early American Life*. New York: Anchor/Doubleday, 1977.

A marvelous account of the basics of historical archaeology by a masterly writer. Ideal for the beginner.

Leone, Mark P., and Neil Asher Silberman. *Invisible America: Unearthing Our Hidden History*. New York: Holt, 1995.

Essays on all aspects of historical archaeology in America. A mine of fascinating information.

Orser, Charles, and Brian M. Fagan. *Historical Archaeology*. New York: HarperCollins, 1995.

A college textbook that surveys the field.

HOW ARCHAEOLOGY WORKS

The best accounts are college textbooks, including the following:

Ashmore, Wendy, and Robert J. Sharer. *Fundamentals of Archaeology*, 2nd ed. Mountain View, CA: Mayfield, 1994.

A comprehensive account of method and theory in archaeology, with considerable Mesoamerican emphasis.

Bahn, Paul, and Colin Renfrew. *Archaeology: Theories, Methods, and Practices*, 2nd ed. London: Thames and Hudson, 1996.

A fundamental source and textbook on archaeology with lavish illustrations. International coverage.

Fagan, Brian. *In the Beginning: An Introduction to Archaeology*, 9th ed. New York: Longman/Pearson, 1997.

A low-end text on archaeology for complete beginners.

INDEX